A
BICENTENNIAL FESTSCHRIFT
FOR
JACOB RADER MARCUS

Alexander Guttmann

A
BICENTENNIAL FESTSCHRIFT
FOR
JACOB RADER MARCUS

Edited by

BERTRAM WALLACE KORN

AMERICAN JEWISH HISTORICAL SOCIETY
WALTHAM, MASS.

KTAV PUBLISHING HOUSE, INC.
NEW YORK, NEW YORK
1976

Library of Congress Cataloging in Publication Data

Main entry under title:

A Bicentennial festschrift for Jacob Rader Marcus.

Includes bibliographical references and index.
1. Jews in the United States — History — Addresses, essays, lectures. 2. Judaism—United States—Addresses, essays, lectures. 3. United States—History—Addresses, essays, lectures. 4. Marcus, Jacob Rader, 1896-   I. Marcus, Jacob Rader, 1896-   II. Korn, Bertram Wallace. III. American Jewish Historical Society.
E184.J5B535   973'.04'924   76-10243
ISBN 0-87068-457-4

MANUFACTURED IN THE UNITED STATES OF AMERICA

TABLE OF CONTENTS

PREFACE

We who are engaged in American Jewish historical and sociological studies are busy enough with our own commitments without having to interrupt ourselves in midstream to contribute to a miscellany. But when we are invited to associate ourselves with a project occasioned by the Bicentennial of the independence of our country, and dedicated to the undisputed master of us all, Jacob Rader Marcus, not only have we been willing to put our own work aside, but we have considered it to be our honor and privilege to participate in this *Festschrift*.

Many essays and books in our field will appear at this time of the Bicentennial celebration, but most of us are aware of our inability to give birth to a definitive history of the American Jewish community. The contributions to this volume give testimony to the need for continuing research at the source level in almost every period, aspect, and theme of the American Jewish experience. Some of us, at least, feel able only now to ask some fundamental questions for the first time. While we are confident that these studies will be valuable additions to our storehouse of insight into many facets of the life of Jews on this continent, we hope that this collection and, indeed, the Bicentennial celebration in general, will encourage many other scholars and students to undertake research in American Jewish history and sociology.

It is especially meaningful that a Jewish Bicentennial *Festschrift* be dedicated to Professor Marcus, because he above all others has mastered the wide-flung materials relating to colonial American Jewry, their life during the American Revolution, and their flowering during the early National period. His achievement has been as monumental as his knowledge is encyclopedic. More data can always be found, of course, especially detailed biographical information about one or another Jew who lived during the colonial, Revolutionary, or federal periods, but it seems assured that nothing fundamental or primary has escaped the wide net of his searching, which stretches now over a period

VII

of forty years. In his two-volume *Early American Jewry* (1951, 1953, reprinted in one volume 1975); his *American Jewry: Documents— Eighteenth Century* (1959); and especially his three-volume master-piece, *Colonial American Jewry* (1970), Marcus has provided the basis for an understanding of the "rise and destiny" of the American Jew. Anyone, in this time of historical interest and perhaps even deeper concern, who seeks some comprehension of our origins need not pursue a thousand clues in a variety of publications and depositories: the de-tailed and synthesized data are in the works which have been pain-stakingly composed in that third-story study so familiar to Marcus's intimates—shelves in room after room bursting with books, filing cabi-nets stuffed to the bulging point, methodological and other outlines affixed to bulletin boards, a couch and a western paperback beckoning when exhaustion or frustration finally overcomes the will to pursue the goals set so high so many, many years ago.

An unintended purpose of this collection of historical papers is to salute its recipient's eightieth birthday. When the officers of the Ameri-can Jewish Historical Society and Bernard Scharfstein of the publishing house of KTAV asked me to undertake this editorship in 1973, none of us realized that Marcus's eightieth birthday would occur in the Bicentennial year. This is an accident of chronology but a fortuitous coincidence which makes us even happier to mark the American Bi-centennial with a fond and respectful and grateful gift of friendship to our teacher.

Marcus was born March 5, 1896 in New Haven (near Connelsville), Pennsylvania, where his immigrant Lithuanian father was a peddler. The family moved to nearby Pittsburgh for a few years, then in 1907–8 to Wheeling, West Virginia, which Marcus remembers best. There this son of an Orthodox East European family was encouraged by Rabbi Harry Levi of the Reform German Jewish community to prepare for a career in the rabbinate. At the age of fifteen the still growing boy entered the Hebrew Union College in Cincinnati, studying Judaic subjects in the afternoon while he attended high school (and afterwards —beginning in 1913—the University of Cincinnati) in the mornings. While he was learning about life and people, culture and civilization, while he was growing in mind and body, he was absorbing the rigorous standards of scientific scholarship which men like Gotthard Deutsch in history and Julian Morgenstern in Bible had derived from their own graduate studies in the German universities. Marcus has reached far beyond the philological and literary concerns of the *Wissenschaft* school of Jewish studies, but he has never surrendered the interest of that school in the fact, the detail, the evidence, the proof, which must provide the ground layer for understanding the truth.

It was typical of young Marcus that he should interrupt his rabbinical studies by volunteering for service in the U.S. Army shortly after the outbreak of World War I, even though as a theological student he was exempt from the draft. After two years in uniform with the AEF in France (which brought him increased understanding of the vast variety of human experience, as well as a growing appreciation of the meaning of America), he returned to Cincinnati, and he was ordained a year later. From 1920 to 1922 he taught Bible, rabbinics, and history at the seminary, but—profoundly aware of his limitations in languages as well as methodology—in 1922 he sought a leave of absence from teaching in order to undertake postgraduate studies in Germany. A year later he was joined in Europe by his friends Nelson Glueck (who would serve as president of HUC from 1947 to 1971), Sheldon Blank (professor of Bible from 1926 to date), and Walter E. Rothman, (librarian of HUC from 1933 to 1944). He accomplished much during his three years in Germany: he was awarded the coveted Ph.D. degree by the University of Berlin; even though Berlin refused to permit him to write a dissertation on a Jewish subject, he mastered the languages and literature of medieval Jewry and gained respect for the systematic, rigorous study of the environment as well as the Jewish entity; he responded to the stimulus of music and fine literature and developed an appreciation of cultured, refined people; in 1925 he married Antoinette Brody, a talented music student whom he met in Europe. After another year of study (and of travel to Israel, then Palestine under the mandate) the Marcus couple returned to Cincinnati, where the professor rejoined the faculty and has worked unremittingly ever since. His wife's early infirmity and death and the tragic loss of his talented and only child, Merle, in a fire might have undermined a weaker man's commitment to a creative and productive life, but Jacob Marcus's inner strength, his ability to grow and learn under all circumstances, his dedication to his work, and his genius for friendship saved him from any possibility of self-pity, despair, or surrender.

As his eightieth birthday approaches, Marcus's frame of mind is not reminiscent but anticipatory. He is older in chronology—but surely not in spirit or mind—than when his students first began to read American Jewish historical documents with him in the 1930s. He knows that he was the first scientifically trained Jewish historian to devote himself to the American Jewish scene; he is aware of the host of students and colleagues to whom he has given discipline, encouragement, knowledge, and specific source materials; he realizes that the American Jewish Archives, which he founded in 1947, is today the largest single depository of manuscript data on American Jewish life, and that its journal, which he has edited year in and year out for nearly three decades, is an important contribution to the published material about American Jewry; he is conscious of the boost he has given toward the increased professionalization of the American Jewish Historical Society. All of this, and more, must surely give him much satisfaction and pleasure—but he would respond by saying that he has so much more to do. His mind teems with lists of articles and books that students and colleagues ought to be working on; at the drop of a question he can come up with descriptions of a dozen reference works which ought to be produced. He continues working—at a pace which would daunt a strong man a quarter-century younger—on a multivolume history of American Jewry which constantly challenges his capacity to synthesize the uncertain and unevaluated. He continues planning the publication of important material in his semi-annual journal. He reads everything important in the field—and much that is unimportant. He answers constant queries from students and scholars throughout the country and the world, and directs their attention to materials in the Archives' files and in his own collection—and indeed in his own memory, for he possesses a seemingly limitless storehouse of inimitable unpublished information about Jewish life in the Midwest and especially about the life and times of Jewish leaders. He maintains a constant involvement in the affairs of Jewish cultural institutions and defense agencies and is frequently called upon to evaluate the potential of new activities in various fields of Jewish scholarship. He is honored as a patriarchal figure by students and colleagues, by rabbis and scholars, by laymen and world-famous leaders alike, yet he sets for himself a schedule which only an aspiring tyro would hope to have the strength to fulfill. At a convention of the Central Conference of American Rabbis (which encompasses more than fifty years' classes of his students), or at an annual meeting of the American Jewish Historical Society (of which he is the senior mentor in terms of service), he is surrounded by fond admirers and grateful beneficiaries of his warmth and friendship and respect; his little black book is filled with appointments for breakfast, lunch, dinner, a late snack, and for many of the hours in between; his telephone rings incessantly with requests for help, interpretation, information, and encouragement.

Marcus is a unique figure in the Reform rabbinate, in American Jewish scholarly circles, and in the Cincinnati Jewish community. There simply is no one like him: a human being who evokes love and appreciation; a scholar who sacrifices no single element of his demanding standards while seeing something of value in even the least scientific piece of work; a teacher who conveys a sense of the drama and tragedy and mystery and zest of history; an American who loves this country and believes in its destiny; a Jew who is committed to the One Lord and loves everything about His people's life and experience, the greatness as well as the pain and pathos; a Reform Jew who still maintains the conviction that a liberal interpretation of his historic heritage will help Western civilization as well as the Jews to survive the dangers of the coming era. May God give him and us many more years of his kindness and wisdom, his friendship and learning.

Bertram Wallace Korn

P.S.—A special word of thanks to Bernard Scharfstein of KTAV for fostering this volume and to Professor Stanley Chyet, Dr. Marcus' devoted student and colleague, for participating in the editorial aspects of its publication.

JACOB RADER MARCUS: AN APPRECIATION

By

ALFRED GOTTSCHALK

President, Hebrew Union College—Jewish Institute of Religion

In one of his last writings, the late Horace M. Kallen declared that "all our living is the struggle to learn; all our learning is the struggle to live." [1] The statement sums up rather well the career of Kallen's younger contemporary, Jacob Rader Marcus, the Nestor of the Hebrew Union College faculty and founder-director of the American Jewish Archives. Jacob R. Marcus, his honors and prestige notwithstanding, understands very well what struggle, personal and intellectual, the life of a scholar involves. His career has been a remarkable identity of life and learning, an identity generating a formidably long list of publications in the field of Jewish history, more than a half-century of teaching at the Hebrew Union College in Cincinnati, and the Archives, which has contributed so substantively to the illumination of the American Jewish experience and to the acceptance in Academe of American Jewish historical research.

Marcus's career, it is worth noting, has not been at all "ivory tower" in character. He has displayed an impressive measure of responsiveness to the changing scene around him and to the intellectual fluctuations of that scene. To cite only one—but a signal—instance, the fact that Marcus devoted two decades to the intensive study of Central European Judaica did not blind him to the potential of American Jewry and to the value of reconstructing the American Jewish past. In the days before World War II there were colleagues who viewed the very notion of American Jewish research with great suspicion, if not outright rejection. What, after all, was there to be studied of the raucous and inchoate community of

1

American Jews? Marcus, however, was undaunted by the prejudice. In 1947, he was able to persuade Dr. Nelson Glueck, the College's new president, to authorize the founding of the American Jewish Archives on the Cincinnati campus. This turned out to be a well-placed trust. The Archives has in the intervening years become a major center for historical research—at the same time that North American Jewry, catapulted out of the subordinate status reserved for it in the years prior to World War II, has moved to center stage in the Jewish life of this century to share the limelight only with the State of Israel.

Interestingly—I might say, even characteristically—enough, it is no apologetic or Carlylean notion of the Great Man of History which has guided Marcus in his inquiry into American Jewish beginnings. It has been, rather, a communal notion. He himself, in explaining the purpose of the Archives, put it this way:

> The study of American Jewish history is primarily the study of the interrelationship and interaction, within the life of the individual Jew and the Jewish community, of the Jewish heritage and the American environment. . . . The American Jew with his composite background, stemming from Slavonic East Europe, or Germanic Central Europe, or Iberian Southwestern Europe, is now in the process of evolving a type of Judaism in this new Anglo-Saxon, Christian environment which will permit him to be all-Jewish and all-American. . . . Whether [American Jewry] has made any special "contribution" to American life is yet to be determined . . . [but] many of us are not particularly interested in studying American Jewish history from this viewpoint. Whether the immigrant Jew came in 1654 to New Amsterdam or in 1924 to New York, we seek to understand how he lived, how he worked, how he established his own cultural-religious community, and how he interacted to this novel environment, creating a new Jewish life and at the same time helping to give birth to a new American world.

He went on to emphasize the need to study American Jewry as a "community," "a fellowship . . . a closely knit ethnic-religious commonalty." [2]

To have opened up and made respectable a whole new academic discipline is in itself a rich achievement. The study of American Jewish history, however, cannot be thought of as merely or purely academic, not at any rate at a school whose primary function is to produce spiritual leaders for the American—ultimately for the world—Jewish community. What Marcus's effort has made possible is the further and extremely important sophistication of the rabbinate. Since American Jewish history had by the mid-1940s become part of the Hebrew Union College curriculum, the school could hope to produce rabbis knowledgeable in the historical and sociological unfolding of the community they were to serve. The school could hope to ordain rabbis whose own sensitivity to the American Jewish communal experience would help them to raise up a generation of American Jews sensitive to the obligations which history had imposed on them. "Know yourself—the unexamined life is not worth living," Socrates had said. Marcus understood and helped his students and colleagues to understand that this was especially crucial for people who would be called upon not only to develop their own community as fully as possible, but to encourage Jewish communal development overseas as well, particularly of course in Israel. Pride and filiopietism have never been absent from his desire to see the American Jewish past explored, but the pragmatic needs (and these include self-awareness) of American Jewry have been given equal priority.

To what degree has Marcus actually succeeded in inculcating his students with the sort of historical consciousness he thinks indispensable for a healthy and thriving Jewish life? This of course remains problematic. It is too soon to say, and as Horace M. Kallen wrote in the same essay to which I alluded before, "no one has yet succeeded in getting the universe to sit for his portrait of it." No teacher can ever fully gauge his effect on his students or be sure that his students find quite meaningful the commitment he is at pains to inspire in them. Even so, there is abundant reason to believe that Marcus's students (and the category includes a very sizeable proportion of the present-day Reform rabbinate) have appreciated his devotion to American Jewish research and have greatly admired the energy with which that devotion has been pursued. They esteem him as an apostle of humanistic learning, a scholar-teacher whose concerns are by no means confined to the dry dust of the past, but attempt some answer to the complexities of contemporary life and seek to evaluate the possibilities of the future.

As a former student of his and a present-day colleague both rabbinically and academically, I take the keenest pleasure in saluting him for his achievements and expressing the heartfelt wish that he be enabled to go on in undiminished charm and vigor *ad meah v'esrim*. For me, "J.R.M." remain initials of admiration and respect—capable of evoking from me a full and unrestrained measure of devotion and love.

NOTES

1. *Toward a Philosophy of the Seas* (Charlottesville, Va. 1973).
2. *American Jewish Archives,* Vol. I, No. 1 (June 1948).

AMERICAN JEWRY AND THAT EXPLOSIVE STATEHOOD QUESTION, 1933–1945

By

SELIG ADLER

State University of New York, Buffalo

On a cold January Monday in 1933, Adolf Hitler was named *Reichskanzler,* ushering in a period of unprecedented agony for European Jewry. On that fateful day, the American Jewish community seemed more united than it had been for five decades. Wholesale immigration from the Old World, which had periodically widened the gap between the acculturated old-timers and the East European masses, had been slowed to a trickle by the 1924 National Origins Act. Moreover, the flush times which accompanied World War I had given many of the newcomers a hoist up the ladder of economic and social success. Few in 1933 could have foreseen the internal tremors which were to rock American Jewry during the bitter Holocaust years; a time when unity was most essential if Washington was to be goaded into significant effort on behalf of the ever-widening list of political refugees.

Yet the calm of those early New Deal years was deceptive, since the vexing question of Jewish nationalism, the major source of division, lay buried beneath the surface of outward harmony. For some years preceding the onset of the Nazi fury the question of statehood had been muted. In 1929 the Jewish Agency had been enlarged by the inclusion of Western non-Zionists; a modus vivendi hammered out by Louis Marshall at Zurich. Here all segments of Jewish opinion save the die-hard anti-nationalists had agreed to accept the Balfour Declaration and to

5

cooperate in non-political spheres under the aegis of the Agency.[1] This rapprochement was made possible because the American Zionists, in the hope of opening additional coffers to their cause, had limited their aims. The Balfour Declaration was now interpreted to mean only the establishment of a spiritual and cultural home, divorced of aspects of Jewish sovereignty. The maximal goal of statehood had all but disappeared from the American Zionist lexicon. Even Felix Frankfurter conceded that the formation of a Jewish state was but a romantic dream.[2] In such scaled-down form the Zionist objective could be reached without the allocation of specific territory and without a direct confrontation with Britons or Arabs.[3] Nor did the Zionists pose a serious threat to the non-Zionist Old Guard, since membership in the ZOA had dropped from 200,000 in 1918 to 8,400 during the nadir of the Depression.[4] With the Arab population of Palestine five times the size of the Jewish population, the very notion of a state appeared chimerical.[5]

Despite the concord of 1933, however, residual tensions remained, and these would mount rapidly once tangible answers to the refugee problem had to be found. The agency itself had lost standing with the passing of Marshall only days after he had brought the Western non-Zionists into the operation. When it became manifest that the Zionists were still in control, many of the anti-nationalists lost interest in the agency or else dropped out.[6] Moreover, the American Zionists found it difficult to work with men who regarded a Jewish Palestine as but another immigrant-aid scheme. The alliance had been an uneasy one from the beginning, and it was not firm enough to bear the new strains and stresses which followed hard upon the Nazi triumph in Germany.

The divisions which were to plague American Jewry during the frightful years ahead can best be explained by analyzing three separate approaches toward the essence and future of the Jewish people. Albeit the Zionist position was not the oldest of these orientations, it seems best to begin with it since it probably mirrored majority opinon.

The roots of American Zionism go back beyond Herzl's clarion call, yet the movement remained a fringe one until the 1917 Balfour Declaration. Owing to a complex set of circumstances prevailing at the close of World War I, Jewish self-determination became the goal of millions.[7] After a setback during the 1920s, when Jews, in the fashion of other Americans, displayed more interest in personal prosperity than public projects, Zionism underwent a great revival as the Jewish people were hammered on the anvil of Fascism. Many complementary factors explain this resurgence. The Zionists knew what they wanted and thus held all the advantages of a pressure group with a fixed objective. With a wide reopening of the traditional American haven a political impossibility, Palestine had, by 1938, absorbed more of Europe's uprooted than any other country.[8] Further, the American Zionists played excellent politics. They forged a working alliance with Henry Monsky, president of B'nai B'rith, who headed an organization of some 200,000 members.[9] From their hard-core base in Orthodox and Conservative circles, the Zionists moved out to make strong inroads into Reform temples and hitherto unaffiliated secular groups. Eventually the vast majority of American Jewish organizations became firm supporters of a Jewish Palestine. Included in this combination were, with but a few noted exceptions, the Yiddish and Anglo-Jewish press.[10] No comparable political-interest group could match the Zionists in fund-raising, dissemination of propaganda, and connections with non-Jewish reporters and grass-roots politicians.[11] During the course of the Holocaust the Zionists secured control over the great majority of Jewish communal federations, which meant in fact jurisdiction over allocations.[12] Rebuffed by Marxist-dominated Jewish labor organizations, the Zionists either penetrated such outfits or else paralleled them with their own labor organizations. Hence to outsiders, Jews and gentiles alike, the Zionists appeared superbly organized, splendidly disciplined, and extremely adept at gaining the ear of the regnant New Deal power structure.[13]

Unfortunately this unity was largely a facade, for the Zionists were seriously weakened by internecine quarrels. Even the various branches of the movement in the United States were infested with the "accumulated poison of years of hate, prejudice and distrust" against one another.[14] While trying to persuade the Washington authorities not to stand by as millions were liquidated, serious rivalry developed between Nahum Goldmann of the Jewish Agency and the American Zionist leadership.[15] In addition there was the long-smoldering rivalry between the two leading American Zionist hierarchs, Abba Hillel Silver and Stephen S. Wise. Each was dedicated, devoted, and willing to labor for the cause beyond the point of exhaustion. But their monumental egos clashed early in 1945, when Wise, after a series of disappointments, still clung to FDR's nebulous promises, while Silver was no longer willing to put his trust in princes. This celebrated quarrel fractured the entire American Zionist structure until it was settled by a reconciliation.

Even more serious was the fact that Zionist ideology, seemingly so stable to the casual observer, was actually in flux. To the right of the mainstream Zionists stood the Revisionists who, in 1935, had seceded from the central organization at the behest of Vladimir Jabotinsky. Uncompromisingly pro-statist, the Revisionists were militant and inclined to give little quarter to the British even in the hour of England's greatest need, when the island kingdom stood up alone to Hitler.

More difficult to assess than the Revisionists was a newly born deviant group formed in 1940 by Peter Bergson, a charismatic young man recently arrived from Palestine. Bergson, an expert in public relations, tried to parallel the American Zionist movement, and he caused the leadership of that organization many anxious hours. Bergson (born Hillel Kook) fashioned himself in the image of Charles De Gaulle and the Free French National Committee. Skilled at loosening the purse strings of sympathetic gentiles and hitherto alienated American Jewish celebrities, Bergson set up a kaleidoscopic series of front organizations, which he boldly publicized through full-page ads in leading newspapers. The Zionists recognized Bergson as an offshoot of the Irgun, an outlawed terrorist fringe group operating in Palestine and prewar Eastern Europe. In the United States, however, Bergson and his confederates showed few traces of their Irgunist past. Unquestionably they drew off considerable money which might have gone into the Zionist treasury. Bergson also struck at the core of Zionist ideology by offering an alternative program. He boldly announced that the "Hebrew nation" did not include Americans but must be confined to Palestinians and stateless Jews. Members of the faith residing in non-totalitarian countries he regarded as "religionists"; a definition that proved congenial to some of his American Jewish supporters. Bergson further embarrassed the Zionists by publically proclaiming his willingness to postpone Jewish claims in Palestine in order to give first priority to the rescue of European Jewry. His brashness was highlighted when, in 1944, he purchased the Iranian embassy in Washington and set up in these luxurious quarters a "Hebrew embassy" with all the trappings of a government-in-exile.[16] It is possible, as Henry L. Feingold has argued, that Bergson played a part in forcing Roosevelt to establish the War Refugee Board, which subsequently saved many lives.[17] But to the beleaguered Zionists, who pressed territorial claims in the Holy Land in order to place their stake on the agenda of Allied war aims, Bergson proved a serious if semicomical nuisance. In frustration they branded the outfit a handful of "pistol-packing" young men who were trying to perpetrate a "cruel hoax" and a "brazen fraud".[18] The

Zionists had serious reservations about the establishment of temporary havens of refuge because all that emanated from the White House about these proposed havens was rhetoric rather than concrete plans. So they continued to insist that the redemption of the Jewish people could be assured only with the legalized mass resettlement in Palestine. Meanwhile, Bergson stated, in ads run in forty city dailies and in countless propaganda pamphlets which his outfit disseminated, that he was willing, at least for the duration of the war, to settle for much less.[19]

Normative Zionism faced still another serious threat from a cadre of Palestinian intellectuals, including the celebrated philosopher of Hassidism, Martin Buber, who declared their willingness to share the Holy Land with its indigenous Arab population on a bi-national basis. Judah L. Magnes, chancellor of the Hebrew University, had long been championing some such scheme to the applause of the American State Department. In 1942 the IHUD (Union) party was formally launched to implement Magnes's proposal. The new party never amounted to more than a marginal group, but it did create a new schism in Zionist ranks, attracting support from the radical Ha-Shomer Ha-Tzair and making deep inroads into Hadassah.[20] Bi-nationalism appealed strongly to the State Department since its platform, if carried out, would allow Washington to appease simultaneously both Jews and Arabs.[21] In fact, IHUD enjoyed greater popularity in the United States than in Palestine, for its tenets were widely publicized by the sympathetic *New York Times*. IHUD's platform attracted a prominent portion of Jews and gentiles dedicated to the proposition that the only hope for future peace lay in defusing all nationalisms so that following victory world organization could really become operative.[22] This sentiment was voiced by the prominent publisher Alfred A. Knopf, who wrote: "Nothing is more likely to destroy the possibility of peace than resurgent nationalism. As a Jew I thing it a great pity that Jews . . . should [be] advocates of still another state." [23] While President Roosevelt characteristically played his cards close to his vest, there is strong reason for believing that he eventually hoped to see a federal union of the territories surrounding Palestine based upon the principles of bi-nationalism. Under Secretary of State Sumner Welles, one of FDR's closest intimates, wrote the President after an interview with Chaim Weizmann: "He believes, as I think you do, that the solution of this problem should, if possible, be found by agreement between the Jews and the Arabs."[24]

All of these dissents from the Zionist norm handicapped the movement from both within and without. In truth, the Zionists were more divided than united; many members joined the organization not because they believed in Herzlian goals but because they thought the situation demanded action of some kind and the Zionists were the most available Jewish group in the country. The divisions that jeopardized effective Zionist action also divided the two groups who opposed them—the unflinching anti-Zionists and the self-named non-Zionists, whose main strength lay within the ranks of the American Jewish Committee.

The polar opposite of the Zionists was the newly created American Council for Judaism. Anti-Zionist feeling in the United States was hardly a novelty since it dated back to the 1897 Basle Conference. While such sentiment was also to be found in certain ultra-Orthodox enclaves and Marxist-oriented Jewish labor groups, it was mainly centered in classical Reform circles. The return to Zion had long since been eliminated from the *Union Prayer Book* and Reform Jewish theology.[25] Much more important is the fact that these old-stock American Jews substituted for the traditional messianic concept a cheery belief in the coming "all-inclusive" brotherhood of mankind. Inasmuch as many of them were on the elderly side and fixed in their opinions, even the gory events of their day were not sufficient to make them switch mental gears. Like the Bourbons of revolutionary France, they had learned and forgotten nothing. Understandably, however, such people opposed the creation of a state which, it was foretold, would erect additional barriers between themselves and the WASPS whose life-styles they so carefully imitated. Moreover, they feared that a Jewish commonwealth would surely bear the image of their East European "co-religionists"; people whom they regarded as "less culturally developed" than themselves.[26] Accustomed to think along prewar lines, they found it absurd to send survivors of the Holocaust to the Mideast after the war when even the Polish Jews would surely want "to go home." [27] The only way, Lessing Rosenwald argued, to prevent misunderstanding on a single-minded allegiance to the United States would be to prevent the creation of a Jewish state.[28] Strange as these thoughts strike us today, they were in high fashion among acculturated American Jews thirty years ago, when the community consisted of far more conspicuously divergent elements.

The last bastion of the anti-Zionists was Reform Judaism and even here they were steadily losing ground. The 1885 Pittsburgh platform of the Central Conference of American Rabbis, with its strident anti-nationalist overtones, was replaced in 1937 by the Columbus Platform, which welcomed the establishment of a Jewish homeland as a center of spiritual life.[29] This shift away from classical Reform was hastened by the advent of World War II, which led to a demand for a Jewish fighting force to halt the Axis advance in the Mideast. When the CCAR endorsed this demand, some ninety dissident rabbis set off the chain reaction which led to the formation of the American Council for Judaism.[30] Dedicated to oppose Zionist "tribal ways of thinking," the fledgling organization was endowed by sympathetic lay donors.[31] While the council had islands of support in the eastern-seaboard cities, its main strength lay among the old German-Jewish families which dotted the southern and western hinterlands.

Between the Council, which despised the very notion of a state, and the Zionist ultraists lay a broad middle ground occupied by the venerable and prestigious American Jewish Committee. But in the fashion of the two groups with polarized positions, these middle-of-the-roaders quarreled among themselves and became, during the unfolding of the European tragedy, increasingly inflexible in their demands. Much of the disunity of that unhappy era can be explained in the shift of the Committee's leadership from the moderates to men whose views approached those of the council.

The Committee had accepted the Balfour Declaration, its delegates present at Versailles had favored the formation of a British mandate over Palestine, and its great leader, Louis Marshall, had been the chief architect of the 1929 enlargement of the Jewish Agency.[32] Following the death of Marshall, the Committee was headed by Cyrus Adler. Deeply influenced in both thought and action by traditional Judaism, Adler was also dogmatic, self-certain, and impervious to argument. He feared during the partition controversy of the late 1930s that the creation of a state would offend the "religious sensibilities" of many Jews, and he thought it foolhardy to press for Jewish sovereignty in a land containing a large Arab majority.[33]

Adler passed from the scene in the early days of World War II. His heirs in the committee's hierarchy, in contrast to the Zionists, wanted no possible embarrassment to Britain as that country stood alone after the fall of France in the path of the Nazi juggernaut.[34] The courtly men of affairs who dominated the Committee were members of a Jewish elite with paranoid fears of diluting their Americanism with possible loyalty to a Zionist state. They wished to follow, moreover, the admonitions of Adler, who had made it manifest before he died that in the struggle against the Axis, Jewish interests must be subordinated to those of humanity. While they were sincerely interested in Palestine, the Committee opted, in the fashion of IHUD, for a land where Jews and Arabs could co-exist as equals.[35] Representing a constituency where Jewish nationalist sentiment was non-existent, the Committee regarded the commonwealth goal not only as unrealistic but also, as the Council was later to argue, as a step backwards towards re-ghettoization.[36] Yet in three ways the Committee came to differ from the Council. Their rhetoric was less caustic, they were more amenable to compromise with the Zionists, and they did demand special privileges for Jews in the Holy Land.[37] They were, however, torn between these moderating influences and a strong belief that nationalism had been outmoded by the pace of history. Therefore, they insisted that Jews did not constitute ethnic minorities in the countries of the remaining free world.

No visible disunity in Jewish ranks existed on the matter of helping the victims of Nazi tyranny by any possible means, including the opening of the doors of Palestine. But discord centered over the political future of the Holy Land as the Zionists, in response to the havoc created by the war, raised their sights and demanded the creation of a Jewish commonwealth in Palestine. It was this explosive issue which severely fragmented American Jewish opinion, just at a time when only unity might possibly have brought forth effective help from the Allied powers in the form of more vigorous rescue work in Europe and/or a firm commitment on a postwar Palestinian settlement. Firm opposition to Jewish nationalism, as we have seen, was no novelty in the United States. But this opposition solidified and grew much more vocal when news of Hitler's genocide sharply escalated Zionist aspirations. By tracing this escalation it is possible to grasp how the controversial issue of statehood rended the American Jewish community asunder during the most critical juncture in Jewish history.

The renaissance of the Herzlian concept of statehood was, of course, triggered by the tragic news from Europe. The movement for statehood was primed by David Ben-Gurion, chairman of the Jewish Agency, while on a wartime visit to the United States. In 1941 the National Conference for Palestine seconded Ben-Gurion's proposal for a commonwealth.[38] The new departure picked up momentum as it became obvious that Britain would not repudiate the 1939 White Paper, which had all but annulled the Balfour Declaration. Hence Chaim Weizmann's moderate program of cooperation with London, at least for the duration, seemed to lose logic since the mandate had become an obstacle to the full utilization of the Palestinian haven.[39] The demand for a commonwealth was augmented by the entry of the United States into the war since this intervention promised an Allied victory. Anticipating the eventual downfall of the Axis, many Zionists reasoned that statehood should be the asking price at the coming peace table. An independent commonwealth, Silver argued, would constitute the only just reward for Jewish suffering which "beggared all human speech".[40]

This maximalist position was buttressed by historical arguments. The eventual creation of a Jewish state, it was argued, was inherent in the terms of Balfour's pledge.[41] Moreover, Jewish sovereignty alone could provide the cure for a millennium of homelessness amidst "recurrent persecutions and sufferings." [42] Thus were Zionist ambitions raised from the ambiguous and novel term of "a national home" to full independence in the ancient homeland.

This switch did not come without dissent even within the Zionist household. Weizmann pointed out that sovereignty was equivalent to the "Shem Ham'forash" and like the ineffable name should not be uttered in vain.[43] But the moderates were engulfed by a tidal wave of pro-commonwealth sentiment at the full-dress Zionist conclave held in New York's Hotel Biltmore in the dreary spring of 1942. Over 600 delegates, including many members of the World Zionist Executive, endorsed the Biltmore Platform, which demanded commonwealth status in Palestine.[44] Subsequently constituent Zionist units in the United States were won over to this goal, and it was endorsed by the Inner Zionist General Council in Jerusalem. Statehood was now the official Zionist solution for the Jewish problem, which had been brought into sharp focus by Adolf Hitler.[45]

The full effects of this démarche were brought home to the American public when, in the summer of 1943, Silver became the dominant force within the American Zionist Emergency Council. With untiring energy the Cleveland rabbi organized a blitz campaign with the twin objectives of forcing England to abrogate the 1939 White Paper and building popular support in the United States for a Jewish commonwealth. Silver breathed new life into his committee, bought huge amounts of radio time for propaganda purposes, and deluged elected officials with incessant pressure.[46] Enlisting stage celebrities, leaders of civic thought, and prominent educators in his struggle, Silver created one of the most forceful pressure blocs operating in wartime America. The rationale behind all of this enterprise was that the Zionists would gain sufficient leverage on the international front only when Jewish bargaining power had been raised to its utmost strength.[47] The intensity of the Silver blitz was certain to create a strong backlash among Jewish groups opposed to statehood. The opposition consisted of people who deplored sledgehammer tactics. They were even more aroused by the diversion of funds raised by the United Jewish Appeal to further Zionist aims. Silver had headed national Jewish fund-raising during the early war years, and this experience helped him in securing allocations for his campaign from UJA and in using UJA machinery to propagandize for statehood.[48] Such methods, no matter how laudable their purpose from the Zionist angle of vision, were bound to create spirited opposition among some opulent contributors to UJA who had given for philanthropic rather than state-making purposes.[49]

As the Zionists exacerbated their aims to meet wartime necessities, their opponents in both the American Council for Judaism and the American Jewish Committee solidified their ranks and became increasingly vehement in their attacks upon Jewish nationalism. The Zionists, charged Rabbi Louis Wolsey of Philadelphia, had created the Council, for "they have conjugated the word 'demand' in all its . . . tenses."[50]

In truth, the Council created dissension within American Jewry hardly commensurate with its tiny membership.[51] The original nucleus of the outfit, mainly unreconstructed Reform rabbis, wished to accent the positive, arguing that by dropping political goals Jews could gain easier entry into Palestine for those victims of the war who chose to settle there.[52] But when the fur began to fly the Council, in the heat of battle, managed to provide an arsenal of arguments for Christian and Arab anti-Zionists. Its representatives lobbied in the halls of Congress when that body, on two separate occasions in 1944, debated the passage of Zionist-inspired pro-commonwealth resolutions. On occasion the Council's spokesmen allied themselves with American Arabs in opposing these declarations.[53] The Zionists fought fire with fire and were, in turn, denounced by the Council as proto-fascists who were waging a campaign of "terror" against rabbis and laymen who refused to conform to the Zionist dictate. President Julian Morgenstern of Hebrew Union College was quoted in the press as comparing the tenets of Jewish nationalism to totalitarian theory. Morgenstern lamented that the very notion of a Jewish state was "sad and tragic."[54] Probably the Council's effusions would have been far less effective had they not been widely disseminated in the *New York Times,* whose editors gave the outfit much space at the expense of covering the 1943 American Jewish Conference, a popularly elected body whose deliberations much more nearly reflected mass opinion.[55]

Brought into being by a reaction against political Zionism, one might expect that the Council would have been free from serious infighting. This, however, did not prove to be the case. Rabbi Elmer Berger, its executive director, undoubtedly went much farther in his anti-Zionist invectives than the Council's founding fathers originally anticipated. This rancor alienated some erstwhile Zionists who had joined the Council in protest against Silver's maximalist aims. This segment and others, offended by Berger's overstatements, resigned in 1944, drawing from the Council's nucleus men who were skeptical of Zionism but nonetheless stout adherents of liberal Judaism who did not wish to travel all that far from the norm of the ages.[56] "You are," one complainant wrote to Berger regarding the Council's *Information Bulletin,* "selling anti-Zionism and not 'information.' " [57] Oddly enough, the Council came into being just at a time when the suffering of European Jewry had markedly increased pro-Zionist sentiment among Christian Americans. Indeed there was almost no organized opposition to Zionism outside of Jewish ranks since the American Friends of the Middle East was not to be formed until well after the war ended. To the many Christian friends of a Jewish Palestine, it must have seemed strange that a cadre of influential Jews were doing their best to thwart this response from gentile America.[58]

A meeting of minds between the Zionists and those prone to the Council's precepts was impossible; unfortunately the caprice of events destroyed any chance of an accommodation between the American Jewish Committee and the proponents of Jewish nationalism. The two groups were near accord when, on June 4, 1942, Maurice Wertheim, president of the Committee, reached a tentative agreement with Ben-Gurion, who spoke for the Jewish Agency. This compromise tentatively bound the Committee to work for unrestricted Jewish immigration to Palestine with the end in view of an autonomous commonwealth *after* a Jewish majority had been achieved. "The establishment of this commonwealth," so the agreement read, "will in no way affect the political or civil status and allegiance of Jews who are citizens of any other country." [59] But news of this accord, supposedly secret, leaked out and its terms enraged the strongly anti-Zionist wing of the Committee. Subsequently Wertheim, on grounds of health, refused to stand for another term, and he was succeeded by Judge Joseph M. Proskauer, who accepted office on the condition that the organization, instead of working for an eventual Jewish commonwealth, press for an international trusteeship over Palestine.[60] Proskauer, born in Mobile, took inordinate pride in the fact that his father had served in the Civil War. Senior partner in a prestigious New York law firm, the judge moved in circles far removed from the American Jewish masses, who were Zionist by inclination. Proskauer's insistence on an international trusteeship for the Holy Land was, of course, directly opposed to the Zionist demand for a commonwealth. Hence, it was apparent from the time that the judge took office that he would shift the Committee's stand in an anti-nationalist direction. Proskauer had, prior to his election as president of the Committee, congratulated Elmer Berger on one of the latter's anti-Zionist discourses, writing that "I find myself in complete sympathy." [61]

Nonetheless, there was a last-ditch effort to prevent a complete break between the Committee and the Zionists. This attempt came before and during the sessions of the American Jewish Conference, an unprecedented assembly of elected delegates representing sixty-five nationwide organizations and said to have been chosen by an electorate of two million constituents.[62] At this colloquy, which gathered during the waning summer of 1943, the Zionists and their allies controlled 80 percent of the delegate voting strength. While the Committee hesitantly sent representatives to the conference, all hope of compromise was lost when the Zionist bloc, steeled by Silver's majestic oratory, refused to sacrifice the Biltmore Platform on the altar of Jewish unity.[63] The Conference, after adjournment, was to be an ongoing affair, with its Interim Committee acting on behalf of the plenary body. But in October, 1943, the American Jewish Committee withdrew its delegates, leading to an impasse. The Zionists claimed, on the basis of having carried the Conference by overwhelming majorities, a popular mandate for statehood. However, even before Proskauer withdrew his delegates from the Interim Committee, the State Department was informed that the Committee, purportedly representing a large segment of non-Zionist opinion, would not accept Jewish nationalism if this concept embraced more than a spiritual or cultural center in ·Palestine.[64] The Committee, Judge Proskauer informed President Roosevelt, refused to "seek the artificial creation of a state identified with a religion." [65] Therefore the Committee recommended that the Holy Land become an international trusteeship where the rights of all the country's inhabitants would be duly safeguarded.

The trusteeship would fall under the jurisdiction of the new world organization to be created following military victory in the war.[66]

In retrospect, there was little chance of a compromise with the Zionists as long as Proskauer dominated the American Jewish Committee. But the judge's actions split his own group, for the Committee lost, in the closing months of 1943, about 10 percent of its membership and a sizable portion of its executive leadership.[67] It is easy to fault Proskauer's intransigence, but we must recall that the Zionists had won a majority of the delegates to the American Jewish Conference only through extraordinary political efforts made during the course of the communal elections. The Committee, an elitist group from its inception, would not and could not compete on a mass popular basis. Hence, Proskauer insisted, and he so told the Washington decision-makers, that the Conference did not truly reflect the large mass of unorganized Jewish opinion on the vital commonwealth issue.[68]

To sum up, the statehood question divided American Jewry into three recognizable factions. These divisions, in turn, were not truly solidified because of internal divergences. Would the end result, which amounted to much rhetoric and little genuine effort on the part of the Roosevelt administration's handling of the Jewish question, have been very different had there been essential unity within American Jewish ranks? The answer is, of course, unknowable, and one can only speculate. It is possible that the exigencies of war and *Machtpolitik* would have led FDR to act as he did regardless of Jewish solidarity.[69] On the other hand, the President at times came close to a definitive promise to the Zionist leaders, and had the White House not been fully aware of Jewish disunity it might have made a significant difference. All that one can say for certain is that both the President and the State Department were fully cognizant of Jewish squabbles, which they readily exploited in order to serve their own purposes.

A few examples of this legerdemain must suffice. After the 1943 American Jewish Conference, both the Zionists and the American Jewish Committee asked Judge Samuel I. Rosenman, the President's close confidant, for an appointment with Roosevelt. Rosenman replied that it would be highly unpolitic to confuse FDR with two utterly contrary views on Palestine.[70] Wallace Murray, the State Department's ranking authority on Middle Eastern affairs, with a long record of hostility to Zionism, insisted repeatedly that the non-Zionists represented the more substantial and responsible portion of American Jewry. Murray had a strong affinity for the American Council for Judaism, but recognizing the controversial nature of that outfit, he preferred to used the Committee's stand for "a rallying-ground for . . . [those] whose allegiance to the United States is undiluted by Jewish nationalism." [71]

Because of the machinations of Murray and other members of the State Department's covey of anti-Zionists, proponents of a Jewish Palestine were forced to divert much of their energy and resources to refute such wild accusations. In addition, Jewish divisions frequently confused sincere Christian friends. Senator Guy M. Gillette of Iowa, long a staunch friend of Jewish causes, told the Zionists that it was tragic to witness incessant Jewish bickering at a time when only unity could bring the desired results in Washington. [72] The noted news columnist George Sokolsky stated that one result of Jewish internal anarchy was that any gentile politico who made a pro-Palestine speech or statement would be "kicked in the pants," not by his fellow Christians but by dissident Jews. [73] When the noted author Jerome Frank, nominally Jewish, called the Zionists "not Americans . . . but . . . only sojourners in America," Rabbi Silver remarked that he had hoped to concentrate his efforts on persuading the non-Jewish world of the merits of the Zionist cause but that circumstances made such a concentration impossible. [74]

Unquestionably the evidence points to measurable harm resulting from the division of American Jewry. This damage to the Jewish cause was all the more unfortunate because the actual creation of an independent Israel has served, since 1948, as a unifying force. Faced with the reality of a state, the American Jewish Committee was quickly won over, as were the *New York Times* and the *Jewish Daily Forward,* while the Council has steadily atrophied. The dreads of thirty years ago proved unfounded, leading to the inescapable conclusion that the heated arguments against the restoration of Jewish sovereignty were superficial in nature. Why then all the excitement of yesteryear? The best answer is that even the impact of the Holocaust could not offset the social, cultural, and economic barriers that then existed within an American Jewry as yet still unhomogenized. It is bitterly ironic to observe that the very existence of Israel, instead of multiplying these historic divisions within the community, has helped to erase them.

NOTES

1. Harry B. Ellis, *Israel and the Middle East* (New York, 1957), p. 97.
2. Frankfurter to Robert Szold, December 1, 1931, Felix Frankfurter Papers, Library of Congress, Box 86, Reel 2.
3. Emanuel Neumann, "Abba Hillel Silver in Historical Perspective," *American Zionist*, LXIV (December 1973), 22–25.
4. Samuel Halperin, *The Political World of American Zionism* (Detroit, 1961), pp. 189, 267.
5. *Ibid.,* p. 193.
6. Nathan Schachner, *The Price of Liberty: A History of the American Jewish Committee* (New York, 1948), pp. 103–4.
7. Louis L. Gerson, *The Hyphenate in Recent American Politics and Diplomacy* (Lawrence, Kans., 1964), p. 86.
8. David S. Wyman, *Paper Walls: America and the Refugee Crisis 1938–1941* (Amherst, Mass., 1968), pp. 33, 209. Wyman calculates that if one includes the entire period, 1933–45, the United States absorbed about 250,000 refugees while Palestine was second with 150,000.
9. Halperin, pp. 145, 147–49; Herbert Parzen, *A Short History of Zionism* (New York, 1962), p. 87.
10. Halperin, pp. 256–57, 300–301.
11. *Ibid.,* p. 189; Richard P. Stevens, *American Zionism and United States Foreign Policy, 1942–1947* (New York, 1962), p. 21.
12. Halperin, pp. 197–201. See also Charles Shulman, "Fund Raiser Par Excellence [Henry Montor]," *National Jewish Monthly* (March 1969), pp. 28–30.
13. Halperin, pp. 173–75.
14. Meyer H. Weisgal to Abba Hillel Silver, April 23, 1942, Abba Hillel Silver Papers, The Temple, Cleveland, Ohio.
15. Unpublished notes, intended as memoirs by Abba Hillel Silver, but never completed before his death in 1963, Silver Papers.
16. For Bergson's views see a release by his "Hebrew Committee of National Liberation," May 18, 1944, which may be found in the Silver Papers. There is much information on Bergson, mostly unfavorable, in the *Washington Post,* October 3, 1944, based upon an investigation of the Bergson outfit by Gloria Lubar and Edward F. Van der Veen.
17. Henry L. Feingold, *The Politics of Rescue* (New Brunswick, N. J., 1970), pp. 174ff.
18. Release of the American Zionist Emergency Council, May 18, 1944, which may be found in the Silver Papers. In recent years surviving Zionists have reappraised Bergson's efforts and have mellowed toward him, believing that Bergson, in the long pull, might have aided their cause: Emanuel Neumann to Selig Adler, March 17, 1967.
19. Feingold, *Politics of Rescue,* p. 264.
20. Jacob C. Hurewitz, *The Struggle for Palestine* (New York, 1950), pp. 162–63.
21. The Consul General at Jerusalem to Wallace Murray, July 26, 1939; memor-

POPULAR GRAPHICS AS DOCUMENTS FOR TEACHING AND STUDYING JEWISH HISTORY

By

JOHN J. APPEL

Michigan State University

"Pictures . . . Pictures . . . Pictures," begins an appeal sent by Jacob R. Marcus in 1973, as director of the American Jewish Archives, to friends of that highly regarded research and study center on the Cincinnati campus of the Hebrew Union College.

We want "pictures of Jewish notables, scenes of synagogues, congregational functions, communal buildings, celebrations, picnics, camp scenes, country club affairs, Jewish homes, cemeteries, and other reflections of the American Jewish experience," the card continued. It ended, perhaps *à la* tongue-in-Clio's-cheek, with the words, "No nudes, please!"

One measure of an historian's stature among his colleagues is the vigor with which they challenge his generalizations. For that reason, I begin this essay in honor of Professor Marcus as historian-emeritus of Jewry's colonial experience with the reminder that in the age of streaking and frontal nudity on stage, in print and film, no conscientious archivist should exclude from his files *any* materials illustrating the full spectrum of Jewish life, including its *au naturel* moments. Yet I stop short of issuing an appeal for studies of Notable Colonial Jewish Nudes. With Dr. Marcus disinclined to produce such a volume to supplement his expertly told story of properly covered early American Jews, no one else could hope to do justice to them in the buff!

I revert to Dr. Marcus' call for pictures, this time to call attention to a not yet fully exploited iconographic adjunct to the study of modern Jewish history: that body of printed and filmed materials (including nudes) disseminated by the popular media since the graphic revolution of the nineteenth century made the speedy creation and cheap reproduction of pictures possible.

Though not always as easy to collect, store, and classify as books, maps, and objects of fine arts (or their reproductions), the disposable, often illustrated artifacts of popular, commercial culture remain underutilized resources for the teaching and study of Jewish history. They include posters, greeting cards, cartoons in humorous and tendentious magazines and newspapers, joke books, almanacs, advertisements for consumer goods and services, sheet music covers and texts, record jackets, message buttons, "underground" and student newspapers, comic strips, and more recently, motion pictures, including animated cartoons.

Crudely made, repetitive in appeal, and limited in range of perception, meant to last but a short time, these objects of popular culture nevertheless often provide reliable indicators of the nuances of popular thought and feeling at a particular time. Even if they fail to give us a complete understanding of the complex nature of a society, they help us to understand some of the shared, common social experiences of many members of it.

For example, jokes and cartoons in popular European and American humor weeklies and on postcards provide a graphic record of how Jews were perceived as businessmen and bourgeois by societies where class and status lines were sharply drawn or hardening. Pictures on sheet music covers and the words of popular songs, in Yiddish as well as in English, are another, little exploited source for tracing the emergence or persistence of Jewish types, stereotypes, and recurring motifs in Jewish-Gentile relationships. The supposed economic and social rise of the newly arrived Jewish immigrant is shown in American trade cards and theater posters from the late nineteenth century. Trademarks and merchandise labels sometimes are useful documents for the resourceful student of Jewish assimilation and adjustment in the pluralistic post-Civil War United States. A young Israeli who studied at Michigan State University some years ago pointed out to me how the decline of the Kibbutznik ideal, which acccompanied the shift of Israeli society from a largely agricultural to an urban, industrial base, could be traced in the changing values reflected in Israeli cigarette advertisements.

And, unfortunately, there are the ubiquitous evidences of anti-Semitism in both the popular and the "fine" arts! For many years Jewish organizations and spokesmen conducted anti-defamation efforts on the assumption that it was best to disregard anti-Semitic attacks in picture and print so as not to give wider publicity to verbal and iconographic calumnies. Partly because of this formerly held belief, partly because of the difficulty and expense invariably connected with the reproduction of pictures, there are thousands of students today who have never seen how the popular as well as the fine arts of the past served to deepen and perpetuate Jew-hatred and Jew-baiting. For them, reproductions of church frescoes depicting Judas as the arch-traitor and of other early and late anti-Semitic themes, including the Nazis' systematic resurrection and up-dating of these ancient slanders, remain under-utilized "visual aids" for a picture-minded generation.

Of course the use of pictures, particularly woodcuts, lithographs, engravings, cartoons, and photos, to illustrate the study and teaching of Jewish history, is not an original notion. Several picture histories of the Jews and many fine plates in books and reference encyclopedias prove what can be done when imaginatively selected pictures supplement well-written texts. Eduard Fuchs' *Die Juden in der Karikatur*, though one-sided in its Marxist interpretation of the Jew's historical experience and badly in need of revision and updating, is still a first-rate source of illustrations culled from European popular media. Alfred Rubens' studies of Jews in English caricature and of Jewish costume and Rudolf Glanz's recent *The Jew in Early American Wit and Graphic Humor* suggest the desirability of producing appropriate teaching aids via slides, films, and filmstrips from the largely untapped resources of archives, libraries, and museums in this country and abroad. Semi-automatic cameras, copiers, and projectors today greatly simplify the reproduction of pictures and bring it within the capabilities of all publishers and educators. Therefore, a call for the greater utilization of images, symbols, and illustrations for the teaching and study of Jewish history bears repetition at this time, when innovative teaching methods and new content are frequently welcomed in established as well as newly created Jewish studies courses from high school through college and adult levels.

Of course popular graphics must be used selectively, like any other teaching device. A course can turn into the educational equivalent of a running roadshow when overloaded with pictures or multi-media gimmickry. Judiciously selected, however, popular graphics provide the inventive teacher with attention-arresting visual devices showing how Jews saw themselves and were perceived by others, from medieval wood-cuts depicting them as allies of the devil to the latest cartoon by Dosh reflecting the self-image of many Israelis.

Under the guidance of a well-prepared, informed teacher, the image on the wall becomes a primary source document for study by a whole group. Given an opportunity to respond to what they see, students can participate in the process of analysis and become genuinely involved with social perceptions. This generalization applies of course to moving pictures or videotapes as well. Their use, in whole or in part, for the study of Jewish history is self-evident, though the production of such teaching films requires funds and expert knowledge not generally commanded by any single teacher, department, or institution. In the remainder of this essay the reader is invited to sample the iconographic approach to the teaching and study of modern Jewish history through illustrations from popular culture. It is hoped that the possibilities for analysis and interpretation suggested by the limited number of pictures and themes represented here will encourage others to undertake similar, perhaps more ambitious forays into the Jewish experience, utilizing pictures to recall and vivify controversial or forgotten issues and episodes of the past. Further, taking a cue from Dr. Marcus' call, quoted at the beginning of this piece, I trust some enterprising librarians, archivists, and private collectors will search for, acquire, classify, and preserve such materials for future researchers, students, and teachers.

The following ten illustrations range from an eighteenth century German anti-Semitic *Schandbild* (Mocking Broadside) to an unidentified late nineteenth century European pro-Zionist drawing. Most are from non-Jewish sources, including the cartoon from the American humor weekly *Puck*. There *was* indeed a shortlived, *Yiddisher Puck*, but *Puck's* founder and chief cartoonist was Joseph Keppler, an Austrian-born Catholic who became, with Thomas Nast, America's best known graphic satirist before his untimely death in the early 1890s.

Fuchs, Die Juden in der Karikatur.

This illustration, reproduced here from Fuchs' *Die Juden in der Karikatur* (Munich, 1921), represents a satiric broadside printed in Frankfurt-am-Main in the early eighteenth century. It combines several enduring European anti-Semitic motifs: the accusation of ritual murder, the Jews' secret fondness for the pig (whose excrement and milk were also regarded as symbols for the Talmud), their generally filthy customs, their familiarity with the devil. Aside from its message, reinforced by descriptive texts in French and German, the picture includes apparel items associated with the Jews' dress in medieval Europe: the Jewish badge, here probably the red-and-white *rouelle,* or wheel, worn in parts of France; the rabbis' distinctive hats and frilled collars or ruffs, and the woman's square veil, a sort of cap with two stiffly starched pointed wings made of linen.

The prominent Jewish nose of later caricature is lacking, but the two rabbis wear spectacles. So does the Jews' devil, apparently also afflicted with eye ailments from reading too much!

The Smithsonian Institution, "America on Stone Collection."

American political caricature came into its own during the age of Jackson, when the introduction of lithography coincided with and in turn facilitated greatly expanded electioneering appeals. Handbills, posters, badges, broadsides, and pictures reproduced by the new, cheap lithographic process allowed the artist to draw directly on the stones from which the finished picture was printed.

This black-and-white lithograph, from the Smithsonian Institution's Peters Collection, was issued by the New York firm of James Fitzsimmons in 1838.

It represents a mare stalled on the racetrack while her rider, Aaron Clark, hands his "Lottery Office" rod, topped by a sheep, to "Dickey" (Richard Ricker), asking him to give his horse a poke. A Jewish passerby, apparently meant to represent Dr. Moses Jacques, leader of a dissident Tammany faction, the Equal Rights Party, leans on his cane and calls out: "Shtop my friendsh I vill shave you shome troublesh. It ish moneysh vat maksh de Mayor [Mare] go!!" The cartoon alludes to the widespread election frauds practiced by the Whigs to secure the victory of Aaron Clark over his Tammany Democrat opponent, Isaac Varian.

The caricature is apparently one of the first to show an American Jew in the role of a political leader. His words are cast in the standardized Jewish stage jargon employed by professional English and American actors as early as the middle of the eighteenth century. The dialect was characterized by the substitution of v for w, t and d for th, the exaggerated sibilant sh for the s-sound, and the use of sh as a kind of dog-latin suffix, as in monish for money. Whether it represented an attempt to imitate or mock the speech of real Jewish persons then living and speaking in New York is not at all clear.

Author's collection.

In the post-Civil War era, three American humor weeklies, *Puck, Judge,* and *Life,* led all the rest. *Life* had the dubious distinction of being the most rabidly anti-Semitic of the three. *Judge,* after some early vicious anti-Jewish caricatures, settled down to being merely periodically offensive in the then not uncommon way of often making cruel and nearly always thoughtless fun of Jews, Catholics, blacks, and foreigners. *Puck,* though it handled ethnic caricature with what one cartoonist described as gloves—boxing gloves!—nearly always lived up to its stated aim of treating Jews no better and no worse than it did any other group which felt the sting of its wit and graphic humor. In this 1885 Puck cartoon by Frederick Opper, representatives of various nationalities wait to gain entry to the office of the *Century Magazine's* editor, who has just paid off ex-President Grant for his Civil War memoirs. Each ethnic-group representative carries a manuscript he hopes to sell for a sum approximating Grant's extremely favorable terms. The Jew, second in line, predictably offers his "Old Clo' Reminiscences of the late War." For those familiar with European Jewish caricature of the same period, this American ethnic line-up reveals one of the essential differences between the treatment of Jews in European and American graphic satire at the time: here the Jew is *one* among several religious (Protestant, Catholic, Mormon) and nationality or ethnic groups (Chinese, Irish, German, black) which felt the sting of racial stereotyping and caricature. In Europe, he was *the* alien in race, religion, and nationality.

Author's collection.

Jews were not only seen by many Americans as one group among many augmenting the Americans already here. In some quarters, they were regarded as certainly more desirable immigrants than the troublesome Irish Catholics. Thomas Nast, in the November 4, 1871, issue of *Harper's Weekly,* pictured Pat, the symbol of the truculent, ill-adjusted Irish, as "The Good-for-Nothing in Miss Columbia's Public School." To Pat's right, just below the desk on which his offenses against good order and the public weal are displayed, may be seen the smiling faces of other well-behaved immigrant children: a Jew, a black, a Chinese, and so on. Dame Britannia confides to her American colleague that "the very same boy has given me so much trouble in my school."

Author's collection.

At the close of the nineteenth century, the type figure of the long-nosed, open-palmed, rapacious Jewish pawnbroker had become so widely accepted that *Judge* could use it to represent the American government as seen by *Judge's* anti-Populist editors and cartoonists. Though *at first* not always and invariably anti-Semitic in intent, the pawnbroker image clearly did, before the end of the century, turn into one of the chief symbols of American anti-Semitic caricature (see also plate # 6).

University of Michigan inter-library loan service.

This venomous anti-Semitic statue cartoon from the September 3, 1896, cover of the Republican-subsidized *Leslie's Weekly* is of interest in respect to the protracted debate among American historians over the relationship of Populism to home-grown anti-Semitism. Were the Populists, some of whom employed anti-Semitic appeals when railing against the international bankers and the "gold bugs," progenitors of the anti-urban, anti-Semitic rhetoric fully developed by later, openly racist anti-Semites, or were they not? The cartoon by itself does not resolve the debate over the extent and nature of Populist responsibility, or lack of responsibility, for begetting anti-Jewish animus. Still, it reveals clearly enough that in September, 1896, some influential New York Republicans enlisted this crudely anti-Semitic appeal to gain votes for McKinley and the Republican ticket.

The Smithsonian Institution, "America on Stone Collection."

On the other hand, Jewish features, including the upturned palm invariably found in anti-Semitic caricatures, could also characterize the Jews' alleged favorable traits: here thrift or savings achieved by smoking the Solomon Isaacs brand of cigars, selling for only five cents. This cigar-box label, from the Warshow Collection of Business Americana of the Smithsonian Institution, was lithographed by L. E. Neuman and Company, New York. Unfortunately, I know nothing further about the label or the product: whether it was as well known as the bread and slogan of today's "You don't have to be Jewish to like Levy's" posters; whether manufacturers or retailers of other products used Jewish types or themes to appeal to prospective customers; whether these were nationally distributed products, or made for local and regional markets or customer groups. In short, we have here a promising subject of research for students of American-Jewish economic and social history!

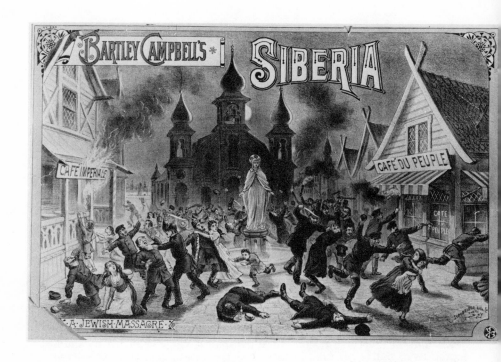

The Smithsonian Institution, "America on Stone Collection."

The firm of Strobridge, Lithographers, of Cincinnati and New York, supplied many gorgeously colored posters for theater, vaudeville, minstrel and circus acts. Few of its giant-size theater posters have been reproduced, partly no doubt because their inspection and use as illustrations present not always easily solved logistical problems for the prospective researcher, as well as for the librarians who (as at the Cincinnati Historical Society) are their custodians. This advance poster for a play dealing sympathetically with the plight of Jews in Czarist Russia, is one of the smaller pieces from Strobridge's surviving sample kits, now at the Smithsonian Institution. The symbolism of its calm Virgin and silent church in the midst of officially sanctioned and assisted murder and mayhem of defenseless Jewish men, women, and children reveals that popular graphics and the stage could also generate sympathy for the Jewish immigrant.

Central Zionist Archives, Jerusalem.

Lastly, the history of Zionism can, and one day surely will, be told as it was seen by cartoonists. Michael Heymann, curator of the Central Zionist Archives, Jerusalem, was kind enough to send me the two Herzl cartoons which are reproduced here. The first, with the lines beginning "Von Sudermann . . . " was published in *Zeitgenossen über Herzl,* compiled by Dr. T. Nussenblatt in 1929 and published in Brünn (Brno) by the Jüdischer Buch-und Kunstverlag. The source given by Nussenblatt reads: "Aus der Damenspende der Journalisten und Schriftstellervereinigung 'Concordia' in Wien, aus dem Jahre 1897. Zeichnung von Theo Zasche, Worte von Julius Bauer."

The source of the second cartoon remained unidentified as of October, 1972, when Dr. Heymann sent off these photos.

ZIPRA NUNES'S STORY

By

RICHARD D. BARNETT

Jewish Historical Society of England

In a recent article[1] I laid bare the background and history of Dr. Diego (afterwards Samuel) Nunes Ribeiro, one of the founding-fathers of American Jewry in the colonial period, and described in some detail the drama of his arrest, trial, and punishment by the Inquisition of Lisbon, culminating in his sentence and appearance in the *auto-da-fé* of September 6, 1705. I also discussed how he passed the next few years, fled to England in 1726, and participated with his family in the settlement of Savannah. It was thanks to Dr. Ribeiro's youngest daughter Zipporah (or Zipra) that we know how he and his family made their successful flight from Lisbon to London. When she died at the age of "nearly 90"—i.e., on November 19, 1799—she had already handed down her extraordinary memories of their escape to her great-grandson, Mordecai Manuel Noah (1785-1851), who forms the subject of one of Jacob R. Marcus's most informative essays.[2]

Either Major Noah or Zipra herself wrote down her story in quiet and carefully chosen words, but it was not published until fifteen years after Mordecai Manuel Noah's death.[3] It is still worth while to review it and test its factual accuracy by such additional evidence as we now possess. It is given in full in an appendix to this article.

The Doctor's Family

Zipra refers to her father's family. It is easiest to grasp their ramifications if set out as a pedigree (fig. 1).

47

We note[4] that her mother, Gracia Caetana da Veiga, when arrested
on August 23, 1703, in consequence of her husband's trial, gave her own
age as twenty-seven; she had at this time only two children, Manoel
(aged three) and Isabel (younger, but age not stated); Zipra was as yet
unborn. But who "Abby de Lyon," mentioned by Zipra, was, is not
quite clear; at least not to me.

Gaspar Vaz m. Monita Nogueira

Andre de Siquera m. Isabel Maria (b. 1653) b. 1646		Maria Soares m. Alvaro Machado	
	(dr. of Andre Soares and Gracia da Veiga)	(tobacco tax farmer)	
Dr Diogo m. Gracia Nunes Caetana da Ribeiro Veiga (b. 1678)	Theresa Eugenia Siquera b. 1680 (Abigail?) m. Isaac Nunes Henriques	Francisca Soares da Veiga b. 1687	Branca Soares
Manoel (Moses) b. 1700	Isabel (Rahel) b. abt. 1702 m. Rodrigo (Jacob) Soares de Bivar	Rodrigo (Daniel) Lopes b. 1710 m. Phila Hays	
		Theresa (Esther) b. abt. 1703 m. Abr. de Leon	
		Maria Caetana (Zipra) b. abt. 1710 m. 1. D. M. Machado 2. Israel Jacobs	

Fig. 1. Family of Dr. Nunes Ribeiro's wife, Gracia Caetana

Gracia's Trial

Gracia Caetana[5] was arrested on the usual charge of judaizing after
she had been denounced by several accusers, many being her relatives;
by Josepha de Vallença, wife of Leandro Cardozo, a goldsmith, orginally
from Oporto, but by then of Lisbon; by Brites Maria de Siquera, wife of
Francisco Ribeiro, a tailor, born in Santarem, but by then of Lisbon;
by her cousin, Leonora Pachequa, daughter of Francisco Lopes, advocate, and Branca Soares da Veiga, of Alvito; by Isabel Garcia, wife of
Joseph Nunes Chaves, of Lisbon (born at London in 1665!), whose

accusations, as I stated elsewhere, started the whole chain of arrests involving Dr. Nunes Ribeiro and his family; and by Maria Soares Pereira, wife of Manoel Franco, from Villa de Fronteira, but by then of Lisbon.

After persistent and courageous denials lasting two years, Gracia Caetana was ordered finally to be put to the rack on July 7, 1705. She then eventually gave way and abjured her Judaism *de vehementi* (a repudiation of grave heresy) and appeared in the *auto-da-fé* of September 6, 1705, to hear her sentence, together with her mother, Isabel Maria (aged fifty-two), two of her sisters, Theresa Eugenia (aged twenty-seven) and Francisca Soares da Veiga (aged eighteen), in company —among many others—of Leonor Nunes, wife of Joaõ da Costa Villareal, who had figured in her husband's trial as one of his denunciators and had been sentenced in the same *auto* of 1704 as he. They were sentenced, relatively lightly, to wearing penitential dress (i.e., the so called *sambenito*) and imprisonment at the will of the Inquisition. Nevertheless, this punishment was not found to be a sufficient deterrent to these brave people. The first three, Gracia Caetana, Isabel Maria, and Theresa Eugenia, were sentenced again in the *auto* of September 17, 1706, for having relapsed. In the same trial their father, Andre de Siqueira, aged sixty, was also sentenced. It was at the doctor's *auto* of 1705 that the archbishop of Cranganor delivered a now well-known sermon of great bitterness attacking Judaism, a sermon which had reverberations as far as London that I have described. To it there appeared replies in both Spanish and Portuguese.[6] They bear the imprint "Villa Franca" 1708 and 1709, and it is generally assumed that "Villa Franca" (free town) means London, and that they were in fact printed only in 1728-29.

Zipra states that her father had a particularly close association with the Grand Inquisitor, whose physician he was. This can hardly now be proved, but is by no means impossible, or even improbable. Already from his trial it becomes clear that he was physician to the monastery of the Dominican Order in Lisbon. It was the Dominicans who organized and staffed the Inquisition; yet four of them appeared as witnesses in his defense at his secret trial. In the aftermath of his trial, other trials inevitably followed, since this was part of the process of lightening punishment by denunciation. These were the trials of his family and the wider circle that formed the little congregation worshipping together in Lisbon in one another's houses (much as described by Zipra, though it was before her time)—which it was clearly the set purpose of the

Inquisition to root out—and which it was evidently unsuccessful in achieving at least at its first attempt.

We do not know in much detail how Dr. Ribeiro and his family survived the succeeding years of inevitable impoverishment by confiscation of his goods and of official disgrace, but the prisons of the Inquisition were probably so full that many of the "safer" prisoners were necessarily allowed out on parole or under supervision, much as Zipra has described. Her account suggests that the doctor was able by his skill and tact to reestablish himself in a position of some affluence and freedom. We know that he was able in 1716 to entertain his nephew, Dr. Antonio Ribeiro Sanches (then young but destined to be afterwards a world-famous scientist), and to open his eyes to the wickedness of the Inquisition.[7] He was also free enough with his tongue to mock it and incur fresh denunciation by Sister Josepha Bernarda de Miranda in the same year.[8] In 1724 there occurred a severe outbreak of plague in Lisbon, in which forty thousand people are said to have died. The doctor's services must have then been very much in demand.

We have now a considerable amount of evidence concerning the large numbers of crypto-Jews escaping from Portugal to join their brethren in London, in the 1720s and 1730s.[9] Many of the refugees were poor or penniless, and the *Mahamad* of Bevis Marks Synagogue paid their fares to the British ship's captains for packets or other vessels who smuggled them out in their ships from the Tagus River at Lisbon direct to England.[10] Others got on board by bribing the captains, as Dr. Nunes Ribeiro clearly did, or as evidently did his chief fellow-sufferer, Joao da Costa Villareal. This person, head of a much persecuted Spanish family of that name (fig. 2), was one of those who had been forced to denounce the doctor, and had thus helped to condemn him. Joao was penanced in the *auto* of October 19, 1704, at Lisbon, being described then as aged fifty-one, a merchant, of Lisbon, but born at Bragança in 1653 and originally from Castile. In the *auto* of September 4, 1705, the Lisbon tribunal[11] punished Joao's wife, Leonor Nunes, age thirty-nine. In that of March 5, 1707, it sentenced Joao's son-in-law, Francisco, son of Alexander Morais Pereira, from Bragança but then of Lisbon, aged twenty-eight. In the *auto* of November 6, 1711, Joao's daughter Luisa was punished.[12] In the *auto* of November 18, 1711, held at Lisbon, Joao's son, Jose da Costa Villareal, appeared, described as a bachelor "without employment," i.e., a gentleman of leisure, while on August 6, 1713, the tribunal of Coimbra similarly[13] punished Joao's son,

Jose's brother, Manoel, described as a merchant of Bragança. Although Joao's wife, Leonor Nunes, was one of those who, as I have mentioned, denounced Gracia, the doctor's wife, it seems possible that they bore no bitterness, or else forgave it; for there is some evidence to suggest that the two families escaped to London together, or at least in close association with each other. In fact one obscure member of the family, Isaac da Costa Villareal, accompanied the doctor to Georgia in 1733.

The refugees from Portugal were now pressing into England by every possible means, chiefly directly by sea, while others, of course, took the land-route to join their brethren in the relative security of Bordeaux or Bayonne in France. I have described in my article how in April, 1726, Dr. Nunes Ribeiro was reported to the Inquisition for having arranged the escape on a British ship of one Manoel Rodrigues de Sarzedas, with the aid of a British merchant named "Pedro Lami," evidently a member of the English factory at Lisbon. The doctor had confessed at his trial in 1704 to having practiced Judaism with Leao Rodrigues de Sarzedas in his mother's house; Manoel was clearly a close relative. Dr. Nunes may even have been one of the chief organizers of this escape route. But I have recently discovered that it was in fact nothing new, since incidents of this kind had formed the subject of strong and repeated diplomatic protests by the Portuguese envoy to the secretary of state in London since 1720. I shall deal more fully with this subject shortly elsewhere.[14]

The English public was not at all unaware of the appalling treatment that the crypto-Jews of Spain and Portugal (regarded as backsliding Catholics) could expect at the hands of the Holy Office and actually suffered. Pamphlets denouncing these evils, such as that of Dr. Michael Geddes,[15] who was chaplain to the British factory at Lisbon, were published in London. A London newspaper, *London Gazette* of August 6th-9th 1726, carried a description in some detail of the punishment by the Portuguese Inquisition at an *auto-da-fé* at Coimbra of numerous crypto-Jews, its information clearly being taken from the printed *lista*, or program, of the ceremony. The British envoys, too, in both Spain and Portugal, often reported such events to the British Secretary of State, with comments.

On August 26, 1726, the *Daily Journal,* another London newspaper, published the following report:

We are informed that Mr. John da Costa Villareal, one of the rich

Jews who, being threatened by the Inquisition, made his escape from
Lisbon with his family, consisting of about 17 persons, and his effects,
during a great conflagration in the city, hath, since his arrival here, given
the sum of £20,000 to be distributed among the poor Jews in the city and
suburbs of London. He was Proveditor to the King of Portugal's armies
and acquitted himself in that and all other stations with good Reputation,
and has brought over with him to the value of £300,000 and upwards.

Dr. Diamond has pointed out[16] that this newspaper report is a trifle
inaccurate, inasmuch as John or Joao da Costa Villareal, though the
head of the family and aged seventy-three,[17] was in fact impoverished.
It was his elder son, Joseph (Jose), who had the money, having already
prudently remitted in advance £15,000 and invested it in Bank of England stock.[18] He did in fact bring with him, or otherwise have at his
disposal, not £30,000 but a total of about £90,000, which was the
equivalent of over a million sterling today, a fortune which he claims
in his will was the result of his own unaided industry and God's blessing,
not got by inheritance or family assistance. He was hardly the gentleman of leisure that the Inquisition had believed him to be in 1711.

Next month (September, 1726) the Amsterdam periodical *Lettres
Historiques* (vol. lxx, Lettre v, p. 308), produced a fuller but no more
accurate version of the story from its London correspondent:

> Quinze juifs qui étoient renfermez avec leurs familles dans les prisons
> de l'*Inquisition* de *Portugal,* ayant trouvé moyen de se sauver avec
> l'Inquisiteur, qui les gardoit, sont arrivez içi depuis peu, et ont aporté
> avec eux, 600 mille livres st. en Lingotes, Moydores, &c.[19] Un de ces Juifs,
> nommé Jean da Costa avoit ete Provediteur-general des armees du Roi
> de Portugal, & a aporté seul plus de 300 mille liv. sterl. Il a donné 2000
> livres st. pour être distribuées aux pauvres Juifs de cette ville.

The story has suffered some subtraction and considerable additions and
embellishments. First, from being merely threatened by the Inquisition,
the party now consisted of escaping prisoners; and while the number
of the fugitives has sunk from "about" to fifteen, all of whom were of
the family of John da Costa Villareal,[20] the party now includes the
"hijacked" guardian "Inquisitor"—an obvious point in common with
Zipra Nunes's story. Finally, from proveditor, John da Costa Villareal
has been promoted to proveditor-general. We note also that the Dutch
report attributes £300,000 to Joao da Costa and as much again to the
rest of the party. This is pure inflation.

But there was some substance in the newspapers' reports of a Villareal's largesse to the poor London Jews, amounting to £2,000. In his will of December 14, 1726, Joseph, (not John!), otherwise Isaac, da Costa Villareal bequeathed £32,500 to the Bevis Marks Synagogue, out of which £2,210 in South Sea Annuities and stock were allocated to founding the Villareal School for twenty poor girls. The will was, alas, revoked, when five months later Joseph married Catherine or Kitty (Rachel) da Costa;[21] but the Villareal School remained and still survives as a trust of the Spanish and Portuguese Synagogue.

The report in *Lettres Historiques* naturally raises the question in our minds whether the doctor, his family, and that of the Villareals, together with their presumably unwilling hostage, the "Inquisitor" (according to Zipra, merely an officer), in fact all made their departure in one and the same ship. Since Isaac de Paiba circumcised Dr. Nunes Ribeiro in London on August 16, 1726, and his son-in-law Rodrigo (Jacob) de Bivar on August 14—their escape must have taken place at least a few days or weeks before. Joseph or José (Isaac) da Costa Villareal followed them into the covenant of Abraham on August 16, his brother Manoel (or Jacob) on August 25, Joao or Abraham, their father, on August 28. On July 28, 1726,[22] Brigadier Dormer, the British minister in Lisbon, wrote to the British Secretary of State, Holles, the duke of Newcastle, that Mendonça, the Portuguese Secretary of State, had complained that a Jew named José (note his name now correctly given!) da Costa Villareal

> has made his escape from hence in the last packet. . . . that person was a debtor to the King [of Portugal]. . . . as the Poor man had been twice in the Inquisition and had now certain information of the Inquisition orders being out against him, it would have been inhumane to have prevented his going which would inevitably have exposed him to a cruel death.

He adds that the fugitive "had left his accounts with the king adjusted and a sufficient sum to cover all demands." In other words, the British envoy argues that he was assisting the escape not of a fugitive bankrupt or civil debtor, but of a religious refugee to reclaim whom the Portuguese could not press so strong a claim. In any event, the Villareal family escaped on "the last packet," i.e., regularly sailing passenger ship carrying mail from Lisbon.[23] The voyage by sea from Lisbon to England would take a week or ten days. From newspapers of the day, reporting the arrival of the packets, it is possible to suggest that the last packet to leave Lisbon prior to July 28 was probably either the *Prince Frederick* (which reached Falmouth that day), or the *Hanover* (which reached Falmouth on the 21st[24], or the *King George* (which reached Deal on August 1), so any of these could have been the brigantine described by Zipra.[25] A brigantine is a two-masted vessel, whose foremast is square-rigged and whose main or aftermast is schooner-rigged. Such ships, managed by a small crew of nine to fifteen, have been described as "maids-of-all-work" ships. They were certainly often used as packets.

Shortly afterwards Brigadier Dormer lost his job at Lisbon, the Portuguese having requested his recall after an unseemly brawl in which they claimed he was involved. He certainly had some enemies: it is possible that his pro-Jewish sympathies procured him more.

Zipra and Her Family

It is not clear when Zipra was born. We are merely told that she was nearly ninety years of age when she died, an event which Dr. Malcolm Stern gives as occurring on November 19, 1799.[26] He, however, puts her birth in 1714, but this is too late, making her only eighty-five at her death; 1710 is more likely since she died "nearly ninety." If born in Portugal, she must be identified with one of the doctor's three known daughters: Izabel (mentioned in his wife's trial), Theresa (mentioned in his own trial and married to Abraham de Leon in 1732 under the name of Esther), or Maria Caetana (mentioned by Diogo Henriques,[27] the doctor's ex-soldier cousin). Zipra must then be identified (by elimination) with Maria Caetana. But she seems to have remained unmarried (though perhaps betrothed) throughout her stay in Savannah.

At last in 1740 she left Savannah with her father for Charleston and New York to escape a threatened attack by the Spaniards. Becoming refugees for the third time, the faithful pair found a final haven in New York; her lot there was to marry the Rev. David Mendes Machado,[28] *hazzan* and *shochet* of the New York community; (he was probably her cousin, since her maternal grandmother was a Machado); her father's lot was to die there. If born, as we have suggested, in 1710, she would have been fully old enough to remember plenty about her family's and her own escape from imprisonment at Lisbon; even if Stern is right about her age, her account must be regarded as substantially based on more or less reliable recollections. That the share of the Villareal family in the adventure is so completely ignored by her may be due to some good reason, now unknown; perhaps once arrived, the two families fell out. In her tale Dr. Nunes Ribeiro planned the whole exploit and takes all the credit. This is probably well justified. He deserved all her and our respect and admiration for all time.

Joao or John (Abraham) da Costa Villareal m. Leonor (Lea) Nunes   Peter (Eliau)
  b. 1653   (2)   de la Faya
  d. 1737   (als. Abraham da Costa da Figueredo)

José or Joseph (Isaac) b. 1688. m. Catherine (Rachel) da d. 1730 Costa	Luiza de Sá (Lisbon) m. Luis Alvarez Nunes (Venice & Genoa)	Mariana (Sarah) m. Alexr. (Moses) de Morais Pereira d. 1742	Manoel (Jacob) d. 1733 m.

Pasquale Alvarez

Sarah (Elizabeth) b. 1728 m. Viscount Galway	Abraham b. 1729	Francisco (Isaac) b. 1679	Samuel b. 1701	Rachel Abraham d. 1756

Note: Mariana de Morais Pereira had a daughter,
      Isabella, by a previous husband.
      Leonor Nunes also had a daughter, Judith
      by a previous husband, Duarte Pereira de Sá

Fig. 2. Family of da Costa Villareal

NOTES

1. "Dr. Samuel Nunes Ribeiro and the Settlement of Georgia," *Migration and Settlement* (Proc. Anglo-Amer. Jew. Hist. Conference, 1970); Jewish History Society, England 1971 [hereinafter referred to as "my article"]. I also take the opportunity to correct some of the more important errors in my article, in many cases due to my carelessness. For several of these corrections I am indebted to Dr. H. P. Salomon.

p. 65, n. 3: In discussing the former custom (especially in the Orient), of adding the letters ס"ט after their names, I wrote that "this is often said to represent the words *Sephardi Tahor,* 'pure Sephardi.' " Add: "in older periods these letters represented originally a benedictory expression. In the modern period they were used to distinguish a Sephardic Jew from Spain or Portugal from Oriental Sephardim."

p. 67, l. 22: for "La Guarda" read "Guarda" and so passim in all subsequent references (pp. 68, 70, 71, 73, 74, 75, etc.).

p. 68, n. 1: for "Francisco de Sa" read "Francisco de Sá."

p. 69, n. 3: for *"Procurador de la casa de los sincos"* read *"Procurador da casa dos sincos."*

p. 73, l. 14: for "(9 September 1705" read "(6 September 1705."

p. 74, l. 14: for "Penamacor" read "Penamacor."

p. 75, end of first par.: delete from "where under the name of Abraham . . . denounce" and delete n. 2. My reading of Dr. Antonio Nunes Sanches's name in the London circumcision register was due to confusion with another person of similar name, but of later date.

p. 77, l. 8: for "I taked" read "I talked."
   l. 12: for [37] read [1].
   n. 1: for "Simao Peres da Solis," read "Simao Pires Solis."

p. 78, f/n 1: for "Daily Journal (no date)" read "Daily Journal, 17th August 1726."

p. 79, l. 22: for "eighteenth century" read "seventeenth century."

p. 81, par. 3, l. 2: for 1786 read 1726.

p. 82, n. 3, l. 2: for "(see note 64)" read "(see note 63)."
Plate titles: For "Order for the arrest of Dr. Nunes Ribero" read "order . . . Ribeiro": for "title page of the first printed edition" read " . . . page of the first Portuguese printed edition."

56

p. 87, l. 10 from bottom: for "pork" read "beef."

p. 100: for "Dr. H. P. Salmon" read "Dr. H. P. Salomon," for "Respueta" read "Respuesta," and for "Ribiero" read "Ribeiro."

p. 84, l. 10: for "died, disappeared, was captured abroad" read "died, disappeared or was captured abroad." Delete rest of par. I withdraw my identification of Zipra with Isabel Nunes.

second par.: after "Shem Noah," delete "possibly a negro; he is never mentioned again after his arrival." Rabbi Dr. Stern, "New Light on the Jewish Settlement in Savannah," *Publications of the American Jewish Historical Society* [*PAJHS*], vol. 52 (1963), p. 175, n. 31, shows that by the time the *List of the Early Settlers of Georgia* was compiled, viz., in 1741, Shem Noah was servant to Abraham Minas (i.e., Minis), while in the same list, "Saml. Noe Costa" is given as servant to "Samuel Nuner" (*sic:* error for Nunes). Rabbi Stern takes Shem Noah and Samuel Noe Costa as being the same person. This is very probable; it may be added that the family name of Noah da Costa, sometimes reduced to Noah, is well attested in the London community. There is thus no reason whatever for assuming Shem Noah to have been a Negro. Dr. Nunes having departed in August 1740, he evidently transferred his services to Abraham Minis.

p. 85, n. 22: Molina: According to the *List*, this person with his wife lived with his sister, Judith Fernando. The minutes of the Mahamad of Bevis Marks call his wife Sarah de Molina *Monanto*.

2. J. R. Marcus, "Mordecai Manuel Noah: Ebullient Politician," *Memoirs of American Jewry 1775–1865*, pp. 117–45.

3. George White, *Historical Collections of Georgia* (1866), pp. 629–30. Story summarized in *Jew. Enc.* s.v. "Nunes (Ribiero) [sic], Samuel." For the text see Appendix.

4. See my article, p. 73.

5. I am much obliged to the director of the Arquivo Nacional, Torre do Tombo, Lisbon, for supplying me with a microfilm of Gracia Caetana's Processo and giving me permission to publish it.

6. A manuscript of the first reply (*Respuesta al Sermon etc.*) exists in the Department of Manuscripts, British Library (formerly British Museum Add. 19263. It has been naturally assumed that this is the original text, possibly in the hand of its as yet not certainly identified author. But when examination of the watermark in the paper was at my request kindly authorized by the Keeper, Mr. Daniel Waley, it was found to be "Baillande 1742," i.e., Leonard Belande of the Périgord-Dordogne region in France. The MS must therefore be a hand copy from the printed book.

7. See my article, p. 75.

8. Ibid., pp. 74–77.

9. See my article, pp. 78–81, and Appendix I, pp. 89–92. Also, A. S. Diamond, "Problems of the London Sephardi Community 1720–1733," *Transactions of the Jewish Historical Society of England* [*TJHSE*], vol. XXI, p. 43.

10. See my article, loc. cit.

11. F. M. Alves, *Os Judeos no distrito de Bragança* (Memorias arqueológico-historicas do distrito de Bragança. Tomo V. 1925, reprinted 1971).

12. Ibid.

13. Ibid.

14. This matter forms the subject of a paper to be read to the Jewish Historical Society of England.

15. "A View of the Inquisition of Portugal" in Michael Geddes, *Miscellaneous Tracts,* vol. 1 (1714).
16. Diamond, op. cit.
17. Not sixty, as given by Diamond.
18. Giuseppi, "Sephardi Jews and the Bank of England," *TJHSE,* vol. xix, p. 61.
19. A Moidore (Portuguese *moeda de oro*) was a Luso-Brazilian gold coin valued in 1720 at 27s. 6d. (C. R. Boxer, *The Portuguese Seaborne Empire 1415–1825,* (1969), p. 165.
20. If my theory is correct that the two families escaped together, the party of Jews combined from the two families will have consisted of the following: John and wife Leonor, Jose & Manoel da Costa Villareal; Alexander and Mariana de Morais Pereira, their sons Francisco and Samuel and daughter Rachel (Christian names not known to me); Dr. Nunes Ribeiro, wife Gracia, sons Manoel, Rodrigo, Andre, and daughters Isabel (and son-in-law Rodrigo), Theresa, and Maria— seventeen persons in all, the number quoted by the *Daily Courant.*
21. M. J. Landa, "Kitty Villareal, the Da Costas and Samson Gideon', *TJHSE,* XIII (1936), pp. 236–291.
22. Public Records Office, Reports of Envoys.
23. *Daily Courant,* August 2, 1726.
24. Ibid., July 21, 1726.
25. Ibid., August 6, 1726.
26. M. Stern, *Americans of Jewish Descent,* p. 170. Marcus (*Early American Jewry,* p. 335) accepts this date, which makes Zipra nineteen years old on her arrival in Savannah.
27. See my article, p. 81. Diogo, however, reported to the Inquisition the doctor as having only two daughters (Izabel and Maria Caetana), omitting all mention of Theresa.
28. I withdraw my suggestion that the name of (Rev.) David Mendez Machado should be seen in that of David Mendoza, who came to Savannah (according to Sheftal) in 1733, and that Zipra married him then and there.

APPENDIX

Zipra Nunes' account of the family's escape. From White (see note 3)

JEWS

On page 101, reference is made to the history of the Jews in this State. Since that part of the work was printed, M. M. Noah, Esquire, of New-York, has kindly favoured us with the following additional items:

Dr. Samuel Nunez, whose name belonged to a distinguished family in Lisbon, was a physician of eminence, and had an extensive practice, even in times when the Jews of that city were under the surveillance of the Inquisition. Jealousy and rivalry, however, caused him to be denounced to that dreadful tribunal, and himself and family were arrested as heretics, and thrown into the dungeons of the Inquisition. At that period the Jews were not permitted openly to follow their religion; they had no synagogues or places of public worship, but assembled for devotional purposes in each others' houses, and their prayer-books were concealed in the seats of chairs, and opened by springs. It had long been observed that the families never ventured abroad on Friday evenings, being the evening of the Sabbath, and suspicions were awakened as to their real faith, although for form sake they all attended mass. The familiars of the Inquisition, who were generally spies, were set to work to discover what their pursuits were on the Sabbath, and detecting them at prayers, seized their Hebrew prayer-books, and threw them all into prison.

Doctor Nunez, who was a most popular and skillful man, was physician to the Grand Inquisitor, who was anxious to save him. He did all in his power to alleviate the sufferings of his family; but one of them, Abby de Lyon, who died in Savannah, carried to her grave the marks of the ropes on her wrists when put to the question. They remained

59

for some time in prison; but as the medical services of Doctor Nunez were very much in demand in Lisbon, the ecclesiastical council, under the advice of the Grand Inquisitor, agreed to set him and family at liberty, on condition that two officials of the Inquisition should reside constantly in the family, to guard against their relapsing again into Judaism. The doctor had a large and elegant mansion on the banks of the Tagus, and being a man of large fortune, he was in the habit of entertaining the principal families of Lisbon. On a pleasant summer day he invited a party to dinner; and among the guests was the Captain of an English brigantine, anchored at some distance in the river. While the company were amusing themselves on the lawn, the captain invited the family and part of the company to accompany him on board the brigantine, and partake of a lunch prepared for the occasion. All the family, together with the spies of the Inquisition, and a portion of the guests, repaired on board the vessel; and while they were below in the cabin, enjoying the hospitality of the captain, the anchor was weighed, the sails unfurled, and the wind being fair, the brigantine shot out of the Tagus, was soon at sea, and carried the whole party to England. It had been previously arranged between the doctor and the captain, who had agreed, for a thousand moidores in gold, to convey the family to England, and who were under the painful necessity of adopting this plan of escape to avoid detection. The ladies had secreted all their diamonds and jewels, which were quilted in their dresses, and the doctor having previously changed all his securities into gold, it was distributed among the gentlemen of the family, and carried around them in leather belts. His house, plate, furniture, servants, equipage, and even the dinner cooked for the occasion, were all left, and were subsequently seized by the Inquisition and confiscated to the State.

On the arrival of Doctor Nunez and family in London, the settlement of Georgia, and the fine climate and soil of that country, were the subjects of much speculation. The celebrated John Wesley, and his brother Charles, had resolved to embrace the occasion of visiting this El Dorado; and when the ship which conveyed Governor Oglethorpe to that new settlement was about sailing, the doctor and his whole family embarked as passengers, not one of whom could speak the English language; and from them the families have descended, already named in the body of this work. After a few years, a number sailed for New York; and Zipra Nunez married the Rev. David Machado, Minister of the Hebrew congregation of that city. Major Noah states that he remembers his great-grandmother, Zipra Nunez, as a very remarkable personage. She died at nearly ninety years of age, and was celebrated for her beauty and accomplishments. She spoke several languages—preserved to the last a beautiful set of teeth, unimpaired, and was observed, whenever the clock struck, to repeat a silent prayer, which had some reference to her imprisonment in the Inquisition. The whole family were rigid in their attachment to the doctrines of their faith. Two of her brothers, who arrived in the same vessel from London, lie buried in the Jewish cemetery in Chatham Square, New York; and from them has sprung a long list of highly respectable descendants in Savannah, Charleston, Philadelphia, and New York, all of them of the Hebrew persuasion at this day.

EZRA STILES AND THE JEWS: A STUDY IN AMBIVALENCE

By

ARTHUR A. CHIEL

Congregation B'nai Jacob, Woodbridge, Conn.

During the thirteen years which Ezra Stiles spent at Yale (1742-55), as student and tutor, he wrestled mightily before he arrived at any theological stance. The Calvinist doctrines of Predestination, Election, and Salvation were serious stumbling blocks to Stiles. "My Deistical Turn," he later recalled, "gave me a very thoro' Disgust against the Authority of Councils and Decretals." [1] But having rejected the bleak dogmas of his Puritan forefathers, Stiles was not satisfied to let the matter rest there. He persisted in his search for some basic religious principles to which he might remain committed as a believing Christian. In that pursuit he read a variety of religious works. Stiles concentrated, in particular, on the Scripture. Was the Bible truly the revealed word of God? That was the question uppermost in his consideration.

Having compared the Bible with other ancient historical sources, Stiles was at last convinced that the Scripture of Israel did contain dependable accounts of historical events. Insofar as the New Testament was concerned, he had had greatest difficulty in accepting the resurrection of Christ. This challenge was finally resolved for him, too, by what he perceived to be the inner consistency of the New Testament. "At first," wrote Stiles about his theological quest," I found myself ready to demand too much. I wanted to have displayed before me Demonstration that every Word, or at least every Sentiment in the Scriptures was inspired by God; and was liable to have my Faith overset, if I found one insuperable Difficulty." But here his exposure, at Yale, to

Newtonian science proved unexpectedly helpful to him in his religious dilemma: "Newton tho't, whether the power by which a stone falls to the Ground might not retain the Moon her Orbit; and then went on and investigated the law of Gravity demonstrably obtaining in the solar system and probably thro'out the stellary Universe." And Stiles had decided to emulate Newton in resolving his religious problems. "In like manner," concluded Stiles, "some *one principle* may be the basis upon which the whole system of Revelation may be firmly supported. *Such* is the fulfillment of Prophecy respecting the Jews. *Such* is the Fact of the Resurrection of Jesus." [2] The credibility of the resurrection, then, together with the fulfillment of biblical prophecy concerning the dispersion of the Jews,[3] constituted for Stiles the bases on which he could accept Scripture and New Testament as divinely inspired. At last, with a reasonably good conscience could he enter the ministry, when he was called to the pulpit of Newport's Second Congregational Church, in 1755.

In Newport, Rhode Island, a flourishing, cosmopolitan seaport town, Ezra Stiles would have the opportunity for an encounter with "Jews of the Dispersion," some twenty families of them, whose origins were in Holland, England, Germany, and Portugal.[4] In a sense, Stiles had in Newport an excellent laboratory in which to observe Jews, to learn at first hand about their customs and traditions, and, eventually to develop into an "Hebrician" with extensive knowledge of the Hebrew Bible, the Commentaries, the Talmud, and the Zohar.[5] His scholarship was further enriched by his long and fruitful dialogues with visiting learned rabbis from Palestine and Poland.[6] And if all this were not enough for Stiles, he became, too, a steady visitant at Newport's *Yeshuat Israel* Synagogue, where he enjoyed Hazzan Touro's "grandeur of utterance, and bold lofty *Sonitus Verborum.*" [7]

Yet, while the Jews and Hebrew lore loomed large in Ezra Stiles's theological and historical scheme, it cannot be said that he was an unequivocal Judeophile. The evidence adduced from his extensive writings reveals an anti-Jewish bias at times, certainly during his early years at Newport, somewhat less so in his later years there, and a growing Jewish sympathy in the post-Revolutionary War period, during his presidency of Yale. Perhaps Stiles's attitude toward the Jews might be best characterized as one of ambivalence. Certainly, Stiles's feelings about Aaron Lopez, Newport's outstanding Jewish figure, could be so described.

Aaron Lopez, a Marrano Jew who had fled his native Portugal, settled at Newport in 1752. Nine years later, in 1761, Lopez, together with Isaac Elizer, petitioned the Superior Court of Rhode Island for naturalization. They had the legal right to do so under an act of Parliament of 1740 which enabled Jews who were domiciled for at least seven years in any of the British colonies to receive their naturalization. Provision had been made, too, that exempted Jewish applicants from swearing "on the true faith of a Christian." But the Superior Court gave Lopez and Elizer no satisfaction for their effort. Whereupon the two petitioners turned to the Rhode Island General Assembly, which body could also grant naturalization to legitimate applicants. In the instance of Lopez and Elizer, however, the General Assembly suddenly decided that naturalization was the legitimate responsibility of the Superior Court! With no alternative available to them, the two hapless applicants once more petitioned the Superior Court for their rightful naturalization. In March 1762, the petitioners of both men were rejected for the second time.[8]

To Ezra Stiles, the Lopez-Elizer case was of the keenest interest, and he recorded fully the court's decision. But stiles was not satisfied with merely fulfilling the chronicler's role. He proceeded to do some strong theologizing.

Begins Stiles:

And on the Eleventh Day of March 1762, Sentence was pronounced upon the Criminals successively bro't to the Bar; first upon Jn°. Sherman a noted Thief & Burglar for Burglary, sentenced to be hanged; secondly upon Fortune an abandoned Negro who set Fire to the Warehouses at End Long Wharf 19th Feb[r]. which did Damage £5,000 ster. & endangered the Conflagration of the Town, sentenced to be hanged; thirdly upon— Lawton for Perjury in swearing to an acco[t]. which he had falsely forged against another, sentenced to the Pillory. . . .[9]

Stiles now reports of the naturalization matter:

And then the Jews were called to hear their almost equally mortifying sentence and Judg[t]. which dismissed their Petition of Naturalization. Whether this was designedly or accidental in proceeding upon the Business of Court I dont learn.[10]

Had Ezra Stiles here ended his entry, it would have left future judgment of his attitude toward the court's decision, indecisive. It might have been interpreted as a somewhat sympathetic reaction on the part of Stiles. He might be decrying the embarrassment brought on Lopez and Elizer by the judges in dealing with their application seriatim with the cases of an unsavory trio of criminals. However, Stiles writes on and makes a telling comment:

> But this I remark, that Providence seems to make every thing to work for the mortification of the Jews, and to prevent their incorporation into any nation; that thus they may continue a distinct people.[11]

Stiles reveals his commitment to the classical Christian stance: For their rejection of Jesus long ago, the Jews suffer divine punishment. They have been and shall continue to be, because of their ancient obdurateness, a people apart, unassimilable. In writing of the court's "mortifying sentence" handed down in the company of three felons— a thief, an arsonist, and a forger, and Stiles's emphasis of "mortification of the Jews," undoubtedly the image in this preacher's mind is that of Jesus cruicified in the motley company of convicted thieves. Here before his very eyes does Stiles see a divine meting out of measure for measure.

And as if theologizing about the Jews' circumstance were not enough, Stiles moves on to editorializing in concluding his very comprehensive report of the Lopez-Elizer case:

> Tho' the Naturalization Act passed by Parliament a few years ago [1753], yet it produced such a natural disgust towards the Hebrews, that the Jews themselves joyned in petition to Parliament to repeal the Act, and it was thereupon repealed for Britain. And tho' it was continued by way of permission in the Plantations upon seven years' residence, yet the tumult in New York in procuring the taking place of their Naturalization there, and the opposition it has met with in Rhode Island, forbodes that the Jews will never become incorporated with the People of America any more than in Europe, Asia, and Africa.[12]

What Stiles may have had to say when Aaron Lopez and Isaac Elizer were soon thereafter granted their naturalization, the first in Massachusetts and the other in New York, is not known. But Stiles was not thereby deterred from further keeping a close eye on Jews and in particular on Aaron Lopez, who was emerging as a very successful sea-merchant in the Atlantic and Caribbean trade. In the decade since his naturalization struggle, he had come up rapidly as a financial equal with his fellow merchant-fleet owners of Newport.

The prospering Newporters, and among them Aaron Lopez, had not been at all enthusiastic about the nonimportation movement which had been underway in the American colonies since the unpopular Townshend Acts of 1767. Newport's sea-merchants had lagged behind those of Boston, New York, and Philadelphia in the measures taken against the importing of British goods. But it was Lopez alone whom Ezra Stiles singled out for condemnation as being the laggard. Stiles criticized Lopez in his *Literary Diary* on August 25, 1772:

> In the late Combinations of the American Merchants against Importation and against the exorbitant Fees of the Customhouses— some Merchants kept themselves from the Combinations. Mr. Aaron Lopez, a Jew Merchant in this Town is one. For this the Collector &c. shew him all Lenity and favor. He has about twenty Sail of Vessels, and his Captains are all exempted from Swearing at the Customhouse, and make their entries &c. without Oath. But the Oath is strictly exacted of all who were concerned with the Non-Importation Agreement. . . . Favor and Partiality!

It was not now "mortification of the Jews" that preoccupied Stiles. It was "Favor and Partiality" being shown to Lopez by the British authorities. With which anti-Tory sentiment of Stiles one might not quarrel, though he himself had arrived at that outlook slowly and with caution.[13] But his singling out of "a Jew Merchant, in this town" is clearly an indication of Stiles's bias. There was, after all, a roster of local sea-merchants and, collectively, they were, all of them, playing the game of the British. *Their* interests lay with importation from abroad rather than with boycott.

That Stiles was focusing rather selectively on Jews at this stage is further evidenced by other of his *Literary Diary* comments, in the early 1770s. In an entry of May 31, 1770, Stiles reports that Newport merchants had held a meeting on May 30th. They had decided, in the face of strong boycott threats against them from Boston and Philadelphia, that they would, henceforth, more vigorously adhere to the nonimportation of British goods. Concerning this most recent development Stiles comments: "An Instance, that five or six Jews & three or 4 Tories may draw down Vengeance upon a Country."

To Stiles, the Jews are obviously a special class of culprits unto themselves. Otherwise he might have placed the blame for Newport's current confrontation with Boston and Philadelphia on nine or ten Tories and left it at that.[14]

Several months later, in August, 1770, Stiles picked up a bit of intelligence that went well beyond the "six Jews and three or 4 Tories" charge. If anything, it presaged an Elders of Zion canard of the future. Stiles derived this sinister information from Captain William A. Peck, who had just arrived from London. Reports Stiles in his *Literary Diary* entry of August 23, 1770:

> . . . he tells me there is a secret *Intelligence office* in London in ——— street where the Jews live. It has subsisted about four years & has thirty clerks: it is supported by the Ministry: & has settled a correspondence in all of America—has four Correspond[ts] in Boston & two in Newport, one of which is Mr. Geo Rome Mercht: to each of whom the Ministry exhibit Stipends.

Now Stiles comes to Peck's major point about this spy operation: "As it appears in London, it is intirely a Jew Affair—a Jewish Compting House, & is unknown in London." How had Captain Peck come upon this extraordinary secret? Stiles reports:

> Capt. Peck sailed to London in a Vessel of the Jews & by this fell into the hands of the Jews there, decried with sundry, and not being strong for American rights, they used to open before him; in company he heard one Mr Clark, I think, speak of their *secret Intelligence office* & upon Peck's questioning, &c. he colored up and diverted the Discourse.

In summary of Peck's report, Stiles notes: "Capt. Peck says, that the office boasted of having Intelligence of every Occurrence of any consequence in America." So there it was. In London there existed a cabal of Jews with international connections, whose attention nothing escaped and to whom "every Occurrence" was known.

For the time being, Ezra Stiles tucked away this nugget of information about Jewish intrigue on behalf of the British government. Two years later he had the opportunity to check it out. Stiles was that kind of diligent researcher in all of his sundry interests, of which he had many. In 1772, Stiles's close friend and parishioner, Henry Marchant, had become the agent in London for the Rhode Island Colony. Stiles now wrote to Marchant to ascertain the veracity of Captain Peck's report. In due course, Stiles received a reply, and he entered Marchant's evaluation of the charge in his *Literary Diary* entry of April 11, 1772:

> I think you must be mistaken about the ministerial Jew-store, 30 Clerks employed &c. if you mean literally so. They [the Government] have Intelligence from secret Quarters undoubtedly, but with such a Staff of Officers, Dependants, and growling Expectants, there can be no great Occasion of a particular Set of Men for that Purpose. . . .

The tale proved to be a product of Captain Peck's fertile imagination.

Stiles made no further mention of a Jewish cabal. But once more he did allude to their presumable collaboration with the British. As in the instance of Captain Peck's story, Stiles again took note of a piece of hearsay. It was in March, 1777, in the midst of the war. Stiles had fled with his family from Newport to temporary refuge in Dighton, Massachusetts. Someone brought him news of Newport's critical situation under the British siege. There was hunger, illness, and general disarray in that formerly pleasant town. Stiles wrote in his *Literary Diary* on March 20, 1777: "It is very sickly both in the Army & among the Inhab. of Newport. Lords dy before last five of the Inhab. were buried."

And he added: "The Jews are very officious at Informing against the Inhabitants—who are one & another frequently taken up & put in Gaol. . . . So that the Inhab. are cautious & fearful of one another. . . . He had again succumbed to rumor even as he had, previously to the Captain Peck report. And what he now had selectively overlooked, consciously or otherwise, was the fact that the majority of Newport's Jewish families had also fled in a variety of directions to avoid the British siege of that strategic town. The few Jewish families who had remained behind might very well be Loyalists, but that they were informers against their long-time neighbors was hardly conceivable. Ezra Stiles had let his bias run away with him one more time.

Stiles must have been disabused of his suspicions as the war years unfolded. For nowhere in his *Literary Diary*, after 1777, is there again to be found any allusion to conspiracy or disloyalty on the part of the Jews. Stiles must have come to know, for little escaped his endlessly, curious mind, that the majority of the Jews in the colonies had identified with the revolution.

In 1778 Stiles assumed the presidency of Yale College. From his earlier years he had known about New Haven's single Jewish family, the Pintos.[15] Now, on his return to New Haven, he found the three Pinto brothers to be ardent Whigs. One of them, Solomon, was in the Connecticut Seventh Line Regiment through all the war, having been taken prisoner, released, and returned to battle. Abraham and William Pinto joined in the resistance to the British invasion of New Haven in 1779. William Pinto, a Yale alumnus, noted for his exquisite penmanship, had transcribed the Declaration of Independence and presented it to Yale. Stiles was certainly aware of the patriotism of the Pinto family. He came also to know of the Jews who had fled to the various towns in southern Connecticut when the British occupied New York. With one of these, Joseph Simson, Stiles made contact. He had learned of that aged Jew's Hebrew erudition. After visiting Simson in his home at Wilton, Connecticut, Stiles described him, on January 18, 1782, as being "a Refugee from N. York." The sight of this patriarchal Jew who had, in his eighties, chosen to leave New York, his home of nearly seventy years, must have moved the Yale president. Simson was widely known as "a very warm Whig" and a good conversationalist.[16] Certainly Simson's political views must have been conveyed to Stiles.

It was 1782, and twenty years had passed since Ezra Stiles had pronounced his judgment on the Lopez-Elizer naturalization case. Ten years had gone by since Stiles had attributed British favoritism to Lopez for the reason that he did not honor the nonimportation agreements. In the years immediately preceding the Revolutionary War and in the war's early years, Stiles had suspected the Jews of possibly conspiring with the British and identified them as Tories. But, as already intimated, a change in his attitude to the Jews would appear to have been in process since his return to New Haven. How far that process had gone may be found in the fact that Stiles, in his capacity as Yale president, was actively negotiating with Aaron Lopez a project which, in Stiles's words, "would be honourable to your Nation [the Jews] as well as ornamental to this University." What Stiles was proposing, in a letter dated May 31, 1781, was his wish to have Lopez present a gift to Yale—a portrait of the late Rabbi Raphael Haim Isaac Carigal.[17]

When Ezra Stiles was still a Congregationalist minister in Newport, he had sought out the several rabbis who had visited there at different times. He was much taken with these men and very especially with Rabbi Carigal, who spent five months, from March through July 1773, as guest of the Newport Jewish community. In the vigorously searching manner characteristic of Stiles, he engaged Rabbi Carigal in a wide-ranging exploration of Jewish sources. Together, they touched on theological issues of the Bible, the Talmud, and the Kaballah. For Ezra Stiles, the many dialogues with the rabbi during that spring and summer were extraordinarily fruitful. For Carigal, it was a wholly new experience, the oportunity to share with a Christian erudite in matters Hebraic. When Rabbi Carigal left Newport for Barbados, Stiles confessed that he "parted with him with great reluctance and should ever retain an affection for him." Stiles continued in correspondence with Carigal until 1777, when, in May of that year, the rabbi died at Bridgetown. How genuine and lasting was the affection in which Stiles held Carigal became further manifest in the 1781 negotiations between Stiles, president of Yale, and Lopez, the philanthropist, now living in Leicester, Massachusetts. Rabbi Carigal and the other rabbis who had come to Newport had their impact on Ezra Stiles. He paid his warm tribute to all of them, in his first major address, at Yale's commencement exercises of 1781.[18] "I have been taught personally at the mouths of the Masters of Wisdom," Stiles proudly declaimed, "at mouths of five Rabbis, Hochams of names & Eminence." Stiles proposed to the Yale faculty and students that the wisdom of Israel conveyed by the Talmud, the Targums, the Zohar, Maimonides, and the Bible commentators was the "kind of Learning worthy to be sought after and transplanted into the Colleges of America." As testimony to the high esteem in which he held the Jewish "Masters of Wisdom," he wanted one of them, if only in the portrait of Rabbi Carigal, to be present at Yale.

Now, in 1782, the news of Aaron Lopez's sudden death reached Stiles and it evoked a profound reaction, perhaps the strongest to be found anywhere in his *Literary Diary*. Not only would Stiles appear to have set aside his earlier biases, but he actually paid tribute to Lopez in a manner uncharacteristic of him. His encomium of Aaron Lopez was grandiloquent! There was only one regret expressed.

In his *Literary Diary* entry for June 8, 1782 Stiles wrote:

On 28th of May died the amiable, benevolent, most hospitable & very respectable Gentleman *Mr. Aaron Lopez* Merchant, who retirg from Newpt Rhd. Island in these Times resided from 1775 to his Death at Leicester in Massachusetts. He was a Jew by Nation, came from Spain or Portugal about 1754 & settled at Rhd. Isld. He was a Merchant of

the first Eminence; from Honor & Extent of Commerce probably surpassed by no Merch^t in America. He did Business with the greatest Ease
& Clearness—always carried about with him a Sweetness of Behav. a
calm Urbanity an agreeable & unaffected Politeness of manners. Without
a single Enemy & the most universally beloved by an extensive Acquaintance of any man I ever knew. His Beneficence to his Fam^y Connexions,
to his Nation & to all of the World is almost without Parallel. He was my
intimate Friend & Acquaintance!

Now there came Stiles's one regret:

Oh! how often I wished that sincere pious & candid mind could have
perceived the Evidences of Xty, perceived the Truth as it is in Jesus
Christ, known that JESUS was the MESSIAH predicted by Moses & the
Prophets!

Stiles held out the hope that Lopez, along with others whom he esteemed, would yet be united in Christian brotherhood:

The amiable & excellent Characters of a *Lopez,* of a *Manasseh Ben Israel,*
of a *Socrates,* & of a Ganganelli,[19] would almost persuade us to hope that
their Excellency was infused by Heaven, and that the virtuous & good
of all Nations & religions, notwithstand^g their Delusions, may be bro't
together in Paradise on the Xtian System finding Grace with the all
benevolent & adorable Emmanuel who with his expiring breath & in his
deepest agonies, prayed for those who knew not what they did.

Stiles remained firm, then, in his hope that the religious "Delusions" of
those whom he considered in error, would be lifted. In the meanwhile,
he was willing to concede that the illustrious Socrates, Manasseh ben
Israel, the Pope, and Aaron Lopez, though religiously misguided, were—
good, virtuous, even excellent.

But Stiles's *Literary Diary,* which he kept until close before his death,
in 1795, reveals no more of the narrow anti-Jewish bias of his earlier
years. If at all, two extensive entries made by Stiles were of an extraordinarily sympathetic nature insofar as Jews were concerned. The
first of these was an open letter by Ben Solomon to Dr. Joseph Priestly.
The second was Voltaire's *Sermon du Rabbin Akib.* That Stiles chose
to copy them into his *Literary Diary* would be a reasonable indication
that their messages had appeal for him, that he was on the side of their
authors vis-à-vis the Jews.

Stiles's entry of January 4, 1788, consists of a lengthy open letter by Ben Solomon to Dr. Joseph Priestley,[20] scientist turned religionist, who "lately addressed the Jews to convert them." Ben Solomon, a champion of his people, ridicules Priestley's efforts to bring over the Jews to Christianity. "The Morality of the New Testament," argues Ben Solomon, "is partly taken from the Old and partly from the doctrine of the Essenes, as you find it described by Josephus." Since Judaism has already offered such good and complete doctrine, including that of Resurrection, what gain could there be for the Jews in converting to Christianity? Stiles had likely read the Ben Solomon polemic in one of the London journals which he read regularly, and the published response to Priestley had apealed to him. He therefore entered it into his *Literary Diary*.

The second entry, a far stronger critique of Christianity from the Jewish vantage point than that of Ben Solomon, was Voltaire's *Sermon du Rabbin Akib*.[21] Stiles translated it from the French and recorded it February 17, 1790. In this sermon, Voltaire puts into the mouth of a Smyrna rabbi a powerful *j'accuse* against the Catholic Church, in reaction to an *auto-da-fé* by the Portuguese Inquisition[22] at Lisbon in 1671. That Stiles was stirred by this work of Voltaire's is attested not merely by the fact of his having included it in his *Literary Diary* in its lengthy entirety, but also by the particular portions which he underlined. These had special meaning for Stiles. The points made in the underlined portions include: the frightful savagery of the Church in murdering human beings for their convictions; the ungratefulness of Christianity and Islam to their mother religion, which gave them the ground of their being; the misreading of the dispersion as divine punishment for the crucifixion of Jesus, which, in fact, had been done by the Romans; the distortion of the Gospels by the Church in their representation of Jesus as God, when Jesus had spoken of himself only as the Son of God, the Son of Man, and no more; that Jesus had not intended the establishment of a Church institution with popes, cardinals, Dominicans, and inquisitors; that Jesus had urged the observance of the Law, and above all, the love of God and neighbor; and was it not therefore *Adonai's* will "that there be no longer on this little Globe, this least of thy Worlds, either Fanatics or Persecutors!" These were the sentiments of Voltaire which seemed to speak to Stiles's heart and mind, if we have judged correctly his underlining of them.

In a self-evaluation which Ezra Stiles did of himself in later life (ca. 1790), he wrote:

> It has been a principle with me for thirty-five years past, to work and live in a decent, civil, and respectful communication with all; although in some of our sentiments in philosophy, religion, and politics, of diametrically opposite opinions. Hence, I can freely live, and converse in civil friendship, with Jews, Romanists, and all the sects of Protestants, and even with Deists.[23]

That there were those who were critical of him for his civility and friendliness, Stiles was well aware, but he was willing to stand his ground.

> I am, all along, blamed by bigots for this liberality, though, I think, none impeach me now of hypocrisy; because I most freely, fully, and plainly, give my sentiments on every thing in science, religion, and politics.[24]

Ezra Stiles kept an open mind through his lifetime, allowing knowledge and ideas to flow freely through it. And although there was undoubtedly an ambivalence in his attitude to the Jews, he had not allowed the scales of judgment to tip over into a fixed, antipathetic stance on his part. His continuing study of the Hebraic sources, which extended throughout his lifetime, his intimate association with Newport Jews and their visiting rabbis, his very profound feelings for Rabbi Carigal in particular,[25] all of these had had their cumulatively positive effect upon him.

As far back as 1749, when he was a young man of twenty-two, Stiles had delivered a valedictory oration at Yale College, in which he apostrophized liberty:

> Tis Liberty, my friends, tis the cause of Liberty we assert—a Freedom from the Bias of vulgar Education, and the Violence of prejudicate Opinions—a Liberty suited to the Pursuit and Enquiries after truth—Natural and Moral.[26]

For a certainty, Ezra Stiles had persisted in his pursuit and inquiry after the truth. His untiring search was well rewarded. He had freed himself substantially from bias and prejudicial notions.

NOTES

1. Autobiographical Fragment, in *Memoirs of the Family of Stiles.* Stiles Papers, Beinecke Library, Yale University.
2. *Review of the Authors I read and admired during the Rise Height and Decline of my Scepticism, Dec. 12, 1768. Stiles Papers,* Beinecke Library, Yale University.
3. In a Stiles *Miscellany* volume (Beinecke Library, Yale University), Stiles indicates that he had arrived at a conviction regarding the return of the Jews to Jerusalem as preliminary to the absolute redemption on the basis: (1) of discussions with Rabbi Moses Malchi, who visited Newport in 1759, from whom he "received great Lights . . . ," and (2) from his (Stiles's) careful study of Justin Martyr's *Dialogue with Tryphon* and Increase Mather's *Mystery of Israel's Salvation.* The dispersion and ultimate ingathering of the Jews were crucial to Stiles's thinking from 1762 and through the rest of his life.
4. Morris A. Gutstein, *The Story of the Jews of Newport: Two and a Half Centuries of Judaism, 1658–1908* (New York: Bloch Publishing Co., 1936).
5. The author's "Ezra Stiles, the Education of an Hebrician," *American Jewish Historical Quarterly* [*AJHQ*], vol. LX, no. 3 (March 1971) 235–41.
6. The author's "The Rabbis and Ezra Stiles," *AJHQ,* vol. LXI, no. 4 (June 1972), 294–312.
7. Franklin B. Dexter, ed., *The Literary Diary of Ezra Stiles,* 3 vols. (New York, 1901), I, 377. (Hereafter referred to as *Literary Diary.*)
8. For full treatments of the Lopez-Elizer case, see: Abram Vossen Goodman, *American Overture, Jewish Rights in Colonial Times* (Philadelphia: Jewish Publication Society, 1947), chap. IV, and Stanley F. Chyet, *Lopez of Newport* (Detroit: Wayne State University Press, 1970), chap. V.
9. Franklin B. Dexter, ed., *Extracts from the Itineraries and other Miscellanies of Ezra Stiles* (New Haven, 1916), 52–53.
10. *Ibid.*
11. *Ibid.*
12. *Ibid.*
13. For Stiles's political views, see Edmund S. Morgan, *The Gentle Puritan: A Life of Ezra Stiles* (New Haven: Yale University Press, 1962), particularly chaps. 15 and 17.
14. That there were Tories among the Jews is a fact. But Jews reflected politically in their communities the split that existed in the communities at large. "Families everywhere were divided," writes Samuel Eliot Morrison. "Almost every leading American—Adams, Otis, Lee, Washington, Franklin, Jefferson, Randolph, and Rutledge—had Loyalist kinsmen" (*The Oxford History of the American People,* 236). See also: Cecil Roth, "Some Jewish Loyalists in the War of American Independence," *Publications of the American Jewish Historical Society,* no. XXXVIII (December 1948), 81–107.

15. *Itineraries,* vol. I, pp. 283–84.

16. "The New York Jew, from the Diary of the Hon. Arthur Lee," *American Jewish Archives,* June 1954, 105–6.

17. For fuller treatment, see the author's "The Mystery of the Rabbi's Lost Portrait," *Judaism,* vol. 22, no. 4 (Fall 1973).

18. *An Oration upon the Hebrew Literature,* Stiles Papers, Beinecke Library, Yale University.

19. Lorenzo Ganganelli, who was Pope Clement XIV and pontiff during the 1770s.

20. Ben Solomon may have been a pseudonym for David Levi, the London Hebraist and polemicist. Dr. Joseph Priestley had published his *Letters to the Jews* in his effort to missionize them. David Levi responded in his *Letters to Dr. Priestley* (1787–89).

21. *Oeuvres Complètes de Voltaire, Mélanges III* (Paris: Garnier Frêres, 1879), vol. 24, 277–87. That Voltaire was hardly a philo-semite is open knowledge. What then had prompted him to write his *Sermon?* His dislike for the Church surpassed even his antipathy to the Jews. In the *Sermon* he was *using* a rabbinic spokesman through whom to lash Christianity. It was a bit of clever Voltairean ventriloquy.

22. Aaron Lopez, Stiles's friend, had fled from the Portuguese Inquisition, as had others who settled in Newport during the years that Stiles had been minister there. Stiles may have found particular poignancy in Voltaire's *Sermon* for this reason, too.

23. Abiel Holmes, *The Life of Ezra Stiles* (Boston, 1798).

24. *Ibid.*

25. Lee M. Friedman, *Rabbi Haim Isaac Carigal* (Boston, 1940) and the author's "The Mystery of the Rabbi's Lost Portrait," *Judaism,* vol. 22, no. 4 (Fall 1973).

26. Valedictory Oration, June 15, 1749, Stiles Papers, Beinecke Library, Yale University.

ISAAC MAYER WISE: PORTRAITS BY DAVID PHILIPSON

STANLEY F. CHYET

Hebrew Union College—Jewish Institute of Religion,
Cincinnati

Skepticism is a great virtue in readers of history. It is not, to be sure, the rarest of virtues, but often enough readers forget the extent to which historians will repeat uncritically the views of their predecessors, thereby perpetuating notions that are at least dubious, or they forget the extent to which most historians seem unwilling to shake tradition. Nowhere, one supposes, is this lack of skepticism more likely to be found than in the realm of biography—which is why biographical revisionism is generally so salutary—and so unsettling.

The biographical accounts of Isaac Mayer Wise are a case in point. The earliest biographical statements—they appeared shortly after Wise's death in 1900—depict him as something of a saint, and the later biographies tend to follow suit.[1] Surely, one would think, Wise's earliest biographer must have been one of his most ardent *hasidim*. The irony is that the creator of this particular tradition—or myth, if one will— would seem to have been consciously rather less than frank in his public appraisals of Wise.

David Philipson was a member of the first rabbinical class to be graduated from the Hebrew Union College and ordained by its founder-president. Philipson spent his first five years as a rabbi in Baltimore and was then in 1888 elected to the pulpit of Cincinnati's Bene Israel Congregation (now Rockdale Temple). He committed to his published writings about Wise a hagiolatrous view and tone very much at variance with the picture of Wise (and of Philipson himself) to emerge from a reading of Philipson's private writings.

Would Wise himself have been surprised? It is difficult to believe that he did not know how much of a hero he really was in Philipson's eyes. In his autobiographical "Meine Buecherei" (1896-97)[2]—whose translation into English, incidentally, unlike the case of his earlier "Reminiscences" (1874-75),[3] was never to suffer Philipson's bowdlerizing hand— Wise recalled the founding of the Central Conference of American Rabbis in 1889. "It is true," he wrote, "that I had written . . . the first draft, but it was presented to the pre-convention group anonymously. Dr. Philipson assumed the chair. . . . My name was not mentioned at all." Wise's colleagues—largely for purposes of public relations, one cannot help thinking—insisted on electing him the first president of the Conference, but Wise understood the situation perfectly well: "I made the job easy for myself: I let the gentlemen of the conference do everything while I learned to be silent in the chair." [4]

Wise went on to say something else equally, or even more, interesting. When in 1893 the Central Conference of American Rabbis asked him to be one of the Jewish representatives to the World's Parliament of Religions in Chicago, he felt himself alone in speaking "on the theology and the ethics of Judaism as a system." Not one of his colleagues attempted anything comparable. "They all spoke as Jewish scholars; none spoke as a Jewish theologian, not because they could not, but because they would not." As Wise put it, "the scholar and the apologete were heard in every lecture, but *positive Judaism* always remained in the background, often almost concealed from the view of the uninitiated." [5] His subsequent discovery that his colleagues were unenthusiastic about his "system" gave him, he said, a certain amount of pleasure. He was "convinced" that he "must have said something which the scholarly gentlemen did not know before . . ." [6]

"Positive Judaism"—not *Wissenschaft*, not apologetics—is what Wise believed he stood for. He doubted that was what his colleagues stood for. Wise, of course, was not minded to censure them; he was seventy-four in 1893 and did not relish the prospect of acting the general without an army. He had no intention of playing Luther to Philipson's Melanchthon. But it is fair to assume that Wise was not unresentful.

Wise's discontent may be why he was unwilling to see Louis Ginzberg appointed to the Hebrew Union College faculty in 1899.[7] Wise left the impression that he opposed Ginzberg's appointment because he failed to see in the young scholar from Heidelberg a man "to whom Judaism stands higher than the learning of the Universities"[8]—that is, he suspected Ginzberg of an addiction to biblical criticism. Such a suspicion may have entered into it, but perhaps what most disenchanted Wise was the fact that David Philipson had offered himself as Ginzberg's sponsor.[9]

The reader will find below two portraits of Wise by Philipson, one (A–D) derived from writings which Philipson published in the years following Wise's death, the other (E) derived from Philipson's hitherto unpublished diary,[10] written in the late 1880s and early 1890s—some ten years before Wise's death. In 1890, Wise was approaching the end of his career; Philipson, twenty-eight years old that year, stood at the beginning of his Cincinnati ministry.

A. From *Selected Writings of Isaac M. Wise, with a Biography by the Editors,* edited by David Philipson and Louis Grossman (Cincinnati: Robert Clarke Co., 1900):[11]

> . . . after a voyage of sixty-three days [Wise] landed in New York on the 23rd day of July, 1846, with his wife and child. He set foot upon this soil animated by high ideals and aspirations. The germs of greatness lay within him, it required only the occasion to develop them; the conditions of Jewish life in the United States offered the opportunity—he rose to it. The man and the opportunity met, and the man has so impressed his personality upon the development of Jewish life during the past half century, that without detracting from the fame rightfully attaching to any of the other great leaders, it may indeed be said that he stands easily first among American Jews for what he has accomplished. *Per aspera ad astra;* the difficulties were many, but he triumphed; he aspired and he achieved . . . [p. 16]

> . . . his career in Cincinnati, the western metropolis, one of whose Jewish congregations called him to its pulpit in the fall of 1853, was the most remarkable of any Jewish leader in the United States, not only for the length of time that it continued, but for the great and lasting good that he wrought for the Jewish cause. Strong and masterful, he was a leader in very truth, toiling unremittingly and unceasingly, so that, looking back over the years that had passed, he could in truth say, "I have achieved." [p. 44]

> He began in the very first volume of the *Israelite* the agitation for the foundation of a college for the pursuit of Hebrew learning and the educa-

tion of rabbis. With his indomitable energy he succeeded in interesting Cincinnatians in his plan and the Zion Collegiate Association was formed. In the fall of 1855 Zion College was opened, the first attempt in this country at the conducting of an institute in the interest of Jewish science. . . .

Isaac M. Wise was now fairly launched upon his life's work. All the great achievements that he carried to a successful issue he had already conceived and brought to the notice of the public. The first practical attempts towards realizing his ideas and ideals all failed, but what of that? he toiled, wrote, agitated and persevered until final success crowned his labors. The earliest efforts at a conference of rabbis, the Beth Din of 1847, failed, but the tireless worker survived to see the successful organization of that representative body of Jewish ministers, the Central Conference of American Rabbis; the first attempt to form a union of congregations in 1849 did not succeed, but he who issued the call for that first convention grew not discouraged; through the years he sounded the same note and his hope was realized in the organization of the Union of American Hebrew congregations [in 1873]; the first college for the education of rabbis lived but a brief span of years, but the idea that called it into existence died not; it found expression in the voice and pen of its originator, and at last came into being with the opening of the Hebrew Union College [in 1875].

In that year—1855—he had the threads of his activity well in hand; those threads he spun into the web of a full, useful, honored life, great in good, rich in achievement. What a faithful commentary is his career of the fine lines of the poet, for truly he was,

> One who never turned his back but marched breast forward,
>   Never doubted clouds would break,
> Never thought, though right were worsted, wrong would
>   triumph.
> Held we fall to rise, are baffled to fight better, sleep to
>   wake. [pp. 56–58]

B. From *Reminiscences by Isaac M. Wise,* translated from the German and edited with an introduction by David Philipson (Cincinnati: Leo Wise and Co., 1901):

In order to give this volume a rounded form, I have added, as a concluding chapter, the short account of the closing scenes of the life of my friend and whilom teacher, which I wrote for the memorial number of the *American Israelite* . . .

We stand perhaps too near to Dr. Wise and his achievements to be able to view them dispassionately and impartially from the purely objective standpoint. The future historian alone will be able to do this. And that historian, whoever he may be, will be compelled to turn to the present volume as one of the most important sources of information, if not the most important, that we have concerning the remarkable leader who, more than any one man, stamped the impress of his powerful personality upon the institutional religious development of Judaism in America. [p. 9]

The Closing Scenes of a Great Life

The week following the death of Dr. Wise, the *Israelite* issued a memorial number. The editor of this volume was requested to write, as a contribution to this number, a description of the closing scenes of the life that had passed to the realm of eternity. This brief essay, written within the shadow of a great grief, is reproduced without change:

"May the Lord bless thee and keep thee! May the Lord let his countenance shine upon thee and be gracious to thee! May the Lord lift up his countenance to thee and grant thee peace!"

The priestly benediction was the subject of the last discourse of the master; each one who had the privilege of being present at that service must consider himself especially blessed, and must feel how singularly appropriate it was that he took leave, though unknowingly, of his people in these soulful words that have sounded through the ages as the blessing of God upon his people. Never had he preached better; although the body had been growing weaker, yet the spirit glowed none the less luminously than in the days of his youthful vigor. It was his swan song; loudly and clearly the ringing voice sounded through the halls of the spacious temple, and the lessons which he drew for his people from that text will abide forever in the hearts and lives of those who listened for the last time to the wise utterances of the prophet who had stood for years upon the watch-tower of Zion and proclaimed the truth of the Lord. After the services were concluded, he was affectionately accosted and surrounded, as had been the case weekly for years, by dear ones and by friends, and for each one he had a genial word; the ever-young patriarch smiled his benediction even as he had spoken it, and so he passed out of the life of his congregation with a blessing upon his lips and with love in his heart, a precious memory, a priceless legacy!

From out the temple halls he wended his way to that other temple, his home, and there his bright cheeriness enlivened the midday meal; no sign was there of the approaching calamity; in response to a wish expressed by one of the company for the possession of the beautiful sermon of the morning, he promised to write it out for publication. With a light, happy word for parting, he left his home to repair to that third sanctuary of his, the college, and his last service on earth was performed in the cause that lay nearest to his heart, the instruction of his disciples. The moments wore on; the hour came to its close; the afternoon service in the college chapel had begun; teachers and pupils had repaired thither. The father of the college had remained below; without warning the blow fell; loving hands helped him to the couch; skilled physicians were summoned, but he was past all human help, although the seriousness of the blow did not appear at first. He was carried to the home whence a few short hours before he had gone forth, and the beginning of the end was to come. The weary hours of the night passed; he grew steadily worse; the dawn brought no comfort; the man of science expressed his fears for the worst. The morning dragged slowly on; the great mind lapsed into semi-consciousness; the dear voice tried to shape a message, but to no avail; the hand skilled in writing refused to obey for the first time the will of the master. The afternoon wore on; the night, too, and brought no change.

The last day, Monday, dawned; consciousness had fled; he knew no pain; thank God for that! From the very first hour that he had been brought back to her, the tender wife sat by him devotedly, patiently, hoping against hope; on that Monday morning she knew that the closing scene in the earthly life of her beloved was drawing toward its consummation. The children watched with her; one by one the colleagues and pupils came to condole with her and them. Below stairs friends made anxious inquiries. In the chamber of death naught but the breathing of the striken man could be heard; the silence was intense; he lay in perfect quiet. As the day advanced his breathing grew softer and lower. The afternoon declined apace; those present felt that they were standing on holy ground. It was a wondrous picture. The westering sun was sinking below the hills; dusk was enshrouding the chamber; the central figure was scarcely breathing; he seemed to be sleeping gently as a little child; there was perfect peace; for hours the faithful wife had knelt by the bedside with her arms thrown around him, peering into the beloved face, but no responsive light came from the eyes that were almost closed in the last long sleep. The weeping children and the few sorrowing friends who had watched the livelong day stood about the bed, a living frame to the picture. The sun had set; the shadows were lengthening; fainter and fainter grew the light of day; softer and softer sounded the breathing; more and more peaceful became the beloved countenance; not a word was spoken, not a sound was heard; a great soul was taking flight; the mystery of mysteries was being enacted; he was at the door of the Infinite; brokenly his oldest colleague spoke: "The Lord has given, the Lord has taken away; may the name of the Lord be blessed!" The end had come. God kissed him, and he slept. [pp. 351–54]

C. From David Philipson, *Centenary Papers and Others* (Cincinnati: Ark Publishing Co., 1919):

My task in this appreciation penned in honor of the centenary of the birth of the great leader is not to produce a biographical sketch. . . . It shall rather be my purpose to attempt to visualize the man and his achievements and thus give a pen picture of the career which stands easily first in the annals of American Jewry.

Isaac M. Wise was both a dreamer and a man of affairs, an idealist and a realizer, a thinker and an achiever, student and an organizer. [His] was the indomitable optimism of the men who dare and who never acknowledge defeat. Obstacle and difficulty but spurred him on to further effort. Discouragement gave way constantly to renewed hope. He fitted thoroughly into the American environment. Freedom was the breath of his nostrils. He came to these shores because of the opportunities here offered for the unhampered development of human powers. As Jew and as man he had chafed under the restrictions of the Hapsburg rule in his native land. Had he remained in Europe he would in all likelihood have cast his lot with the brave spirits who arose against autocracy and tyrannical authority in the revolutionary year 1848; in fact the only time that he ever felt a desire to return to Europe was in that year. But though his was a free spirit he was a devout believer in constituted authority, the authority set up by the people themselves whether now it was in the general sphere of government or in private institutional life. A thorough going individualist he was yet a devoted adherent to the idea of organization. As a reformer he contended for the right of the individual Jew living in the nineteenth century to an interpretation of his faith comfortably with the thought and the needs of the time but he insisted also that such individualism, necessary as it was, must yet be curbed by organization if it was not to degenerate into religious anarchy. Individual freedom and organized effort may therefore be considered the watchwords of his life. His many sided activity as rabbi, as citizen, as editor, as founder of a congregational union, a rabbinical seminary, and a rabbinical conference, was the expression of these watchwords . . . [pp. 19–20] . . . Isaac M. Wise was a prophet and a pioneer. Where others failed, he succeeded. His masterful will, his unquenchable optimism, his unceasing activity and his intrepid spirit rose triumphant over all obstacles; it is not too much to say that his is the most impressive figure in the history of Judaism in the United States. [p. 42]

. . . the college has become the corner stone of the temple of progressive American Judaism. The unconquerable spirit of Isaac M. Wise achieved

this. Through the Hebrew Union College he became the foremost benefactor of American Judaism. Had he done nothing else but found this
institution it would have been enough. But he did much more. And because of all that he dared and achieved, it may be claimed, without
detracting in any way from the merit of others, that his is the first place
among the religious leaders in American Israel. In the Hebrew Union
College he built his own perpetual memorial. . . . Isaac M. Wise built
for the ages. Long as Judaism shall exist in America his name shall stand
among the highest in the record of spiritual achievement. [pp. 48–49]

. . . Dark clouds had appeared frequently on the horizon during his life
time but he never lost heart completely. He continued optimistic and
forward looking to the very end. His elasticity and youthfulness of spirit
never forsook him. Who that was present on the memorable occasion of
the celebration of his eightieth birthday can ever forget that thrilling
moment when at the very close of a prolonged celebration, the hero of
the hour, the ever youthful octogenarian, in response to the call that he
speak a few words before the gathering dispersed, arose in his place and
gave voice to the prophetic utterance: "The teachings of reform Judaism
will be the religion of the twentieth century." Bold words, but announced
with all the intensity of conviction. These words were spoken in the
closing year of the nineteenth century and just one year before the final
curtain was rung down on the stirring drama of the hero's life. . . .

In that faith he lived and in that faith he died. His entire life was a
progression. Obstacles were often thrown in his way, and though he might
be momentarily discouraged, his dauntless spirit conquered and he began
the contest anew. He went from strength to strength. He bore down all
opposition, he triumped [sic] over every difficulty. He was a master in the
sphere of his activity. When the end came life for him was all complete.
The visions of his youth had become realized. Great institutions in American Judaism had arisen as he had planned them. He had grandly conceived, and he had grandly achieved. His soul is marching on. He speaks
today through his disciples from scores of pulpits. On this occasion of
the centenary of his birth, as so frequently before, thousands are arising
and calling him blessed. Blessed was he in his coming into life, blessed
was he in his earthly activity, blessed shall be his name throughout
eternity. [pp. 60–62]

D. From David Philipson, "History of the Hebrew Union College
   1875–1925," *Hebrew Union College Jubilee Volume (1875–1925)*
   (Cincinnati, 1925):

. . . his eightieth birthday was celebrated gloriously on the twenty-ninth of March [1899]. His disciples gathered from far and near. The spiritually youthful octogenarian was the center of the greatest demonstration of admiration and affection ever accorded any man in the history of the American rabbinate. The climax of the celebration was reached when in response to the many expressions of love and appreciation that had been uttered by the speakers at the dinner given in his honor he uttered the striking words, "Twenty-five years hence, or the utmost fifty years hence, the faith of the rational world will be the faith of the rational Jew." The indomitable optimism which was so characteristic of the man and which was in great part the secret of his amazing achievements found expression in this prophecy. Though unfulfilled literally, there can be no doubt that the trend of religious thought is in the direction he indicated. The world is turning towards the vision of Judaism as fashioned by the messages of the prophets and the high spirits in whose company Isaac M. Wise stands. . . .

One year later almost to the day, the mortal end came to this great life of service and achievement on March 26, 1900. He was the last of his generation, the mightiest of them all. He was the great organizer of the religious forces, the constructive builder of the religious institutions. He builded indeed for the ages. His monuments are the works of his own hands, the Union of American Hebrew Congregations, the Hebrew Union College, and the Central Conference of American Rabbis. And best beloved of these children of his spirit was undoubtedly the Hebrew Union College which was "nearer to him than breathing, closer than hands and feet." With it his name and fame are inextricably intertwined, he and his college are one, forever united and inseparable.

. . . The college is the everlasting earthly home of his immortal spirit. Every nook of the institution is eloquent of him and his achievement. Long as the institution shall last, so long shall men say, behold the monument of American Judaism's great spiritual architect and builder! [pp. 37–39]

E. From the manuscript diary of David Philipson, American Jewish Archives (Box 1323):

Baltimore, January 15, 1888:

Dr. [Kaufmann] Kohler's unwarranted attack on Dr. Wise was very uncalled for and very hasty. These errors of the History of the First Commonwealth and the Cleveland Conference have been so often cast up to Dr. W. that it seems as if his opponents had nothing else to take hold of and they seize at any opportunity the rash conclusions of a young man without showing any spirit of pardon for past errors of thought. Surely Dr. W. has advanced and corrected these early opinions and his enemies if fair minded would judge him by his latest and not his earliest expression. The righteous indignation at the fact that Dr. [David] Einhorn is made so little mention of in the so-called History of 50 Years of American Judaism is well assumed by a son-in-law [Kohler] of the eminent reformer but it was ill-advised for Dr. E.'s merits cannot be slighted or passed over by any pamphleteer.[12] His work stands on its own footing, but true it is that he did little of the *work;* he wrote, he studied, he was the scholar, he remained with his books. Dr. W. did the work and more than any other man has stamped his individuality [and ?] spirit [? on ?] a great part of the establishment and development of Judaism in this country particularly in the West and South. . . .

Cincinnati, September 11, 1890:

. . . It is a great comfort to be able to put one's thoughts on paper for outside of my darling Ella, who is a great comfort and aid to me God bless her! and make her well and strong again for she is ailing now, there is no one in whom I can or would confide. . . .

Although I feel that in my work I have improved, although in my home I have been very very happy, although materially I have prospered, yet these two years [in Cincinnati] have contained many a disappointment for me and as I stand at the threshold of the new year it may be well to run these disappointments shortly in review. I have been bitterly, bitterly, disappointed in men whom I had thought my friends. First and foremost in Dr. W. Who would have believed, had he been told two years ago, that Dr. W. would place any obstacle in the way of me, his quondam pupil? Yet so it has been. I have taken scarcely any step that he has not opposed. When I advocated Sunday services in my Temple, when I had succeeded in establishing them (it is unnecessary for me to go into that interesting point in my career (Nov. Dec. 1889) the whole country was agog with it) it was Dr. W. who most violently and bitterly opposed, who aroused fanaticism against the movement, who succeeded in throwing the firebrand of discord into the ranks of my congregation and in temporarily putting an end to the Sunday lectures which however will yet be delivered ere many years have passed not only from my pulpit, but mark me, from the pulpit of [Wise's congregation] B'ne Jeshurun temple, in spite of the present attitude of its rabbi.[13] Then when I was asked by Leo W. to write for the Israelite [the weekly of which Leo's father, Isaac M. Wise, was founder-editor], I replied that I would do so if my name appeared as assistant editor. He seemed perfectly satisfied but Dr. W. objected; he

would have no one associated with him on the paper. Well and good! so
be it. To me it makes no difference, if my writing will only do some good,
my name need not appear at the head of the paper. When, at the Rabbinical Conference held in Cleveland in July last, I offered the resolution
that the term Jew was the proper one to be applied to the adherents of
Judaism Dr. W. the next week came forth with a double-column editorial
protesting against it and in spite of the protest I believe most thinking
people will agree with the statement that we are Hebrews in race and
Israelites in nationality but are *Jews* in religion.[14] And only two weeks
ago Dr. W. had a long and weary editorial in his paper against the lazy
ministers who take vacations in the summer time; whoever could read
between the lines could see that this was directed at me. The editorial
began "we as usual took no vacation."[15] These words, in order that the
whole truth had been told, should have been followed by the parenthesis
(but, as we have been doing for the past thirty years, we went out to our
farm of forty acres in the middle of April and will stay there till the
middle of November, farming, planting, etc. and finding great recreation
in the free pure air).

Dr. W's conduct during all this time that I have been in Cincinnati has
been the source of great sorrow to me. He was my teacher. He was one
of my ideals. He stood on a very high pedestal; I thought him one of the
superior beings but have found him to be only common clay. An ideal
has been shattered. Sad it is, perhaps the saddest experience in my life; I
would have given much not to have lived through it. He is correctly
evaluated in the East; he is a man of great, of vast learning, of mighty
energy but of a very envious and jealous disposition. He can not endure
that anyone shall stand near him, independent in thought and action;
he must rule; the name the Jewish Pope has been well applied to him;
he would gladly excommunicate all whom he cannot subdue, even his
own pupil; but happily we are not in the Church Catholic; I still stand
free and active [?] and will carry on my work as I best know how without
fear and without terror. O! would that my old teacher stood in my estimation where he stood two years ago! but that is past! that can be no more!
Very few men can successfully endure the bright light of scrutiny [?]
to be thrown upon their actions; greatness loses from proximity; how
few great men are great to those with whom they are thrown into daily
contact. When in time the true verdict will have been passed upon Dr.
W. it will read somewhat in this wise: a man who did much for Judaism
but who made everything subserve his own ambition; he would use every
means to crush his opponents; his energy was restless, his mind active,
but his nature jealous of all. He helped to shape or perhaps himself
shaped the form Judaism has taken in the West and South but this will
not last. There is too great an element of time [?] serving, too small an

element of consistency. A man, great in many ways, the center well nigh of Judaism in America for over forty years but very faulty, always at variance with all other leaders. But wherefore write more on this subject? I feel it very keenly and could fill a volume without giving adequate expression to all I feel and know. . . .

Cincinnati, October 29, 1891:

. . . Well, my congregation has done a foolish thing again. . . . it was resolved to have Friday evening lectures. Let them resolve; I will not deliver them; the people do not and will not and can not come on that evening. If Sunday services or lectures are a giving in to the needs of the people, an innovation, Friday evening lectures were none the less so; late services on Friday evening were never known in Judaism until Dr. Wise introduced them.[16] They have not been a success; in his own Temple he never has more than a corporal's guard and yet today in the Israelite he goes into hysterics about Sunday lectures, warns the people not to have anything to do with the innovation, bids them take care of their Friday evening lectures, calls them the salvation of Judaism etc. etc.[17] Not a word of truth in the whole business, but it is quite in the Israelite's usual style, whitewashing, boasting of Cincinnati, B'ne Jeshurun and everything with which the editor of the Israelite has anything to do. No wonder the outside world thinks that Cincinnati is the center of Judaism, that here there is more religious spirit than anywhere else. The boasting tone of the Israelite is the cause thereof but quite the opposite is true. There is less of the true spirit of religion here than in the East. It is remarkable how little influence Dr. W. has had in this community, considering the length of time he has been here. His work here has amounted to very little. He is getting old and in charity I throw a mantle over the many, many things he has done and the many unkind acts he has been guilty of towards me. In spite of all asseverations to the contrary, Friday evening lectures are not the proper thing and I will not deliver them. . . .

Cincinnati, November 1, 1891:

. . . Friday evening lectures were instituted by Dr. W. years ago because his people did not attend on Sabbath. They were an innovation and I firmly believe that to them in great part is due the fact of the non-observance of the Sabbath here. These evening lectures detract from the morning service. Of that there can be no doubt. But of all places here in Cincinnati even they have not been a success. There is as irreligious and at the same time as backward and superstitious a set of Jews here as can be found anywhere. Kaddish Jews, graveyard Jews, club Jews predominate. Of true pure religious feeling there is very little. . . .

NOTES

1. See David Philipson and Louis Grossman, eds., *Selected Writings of Isaac M. Wise, with a Biography by the Editors* (Cincinnati, 1900); David Philipson, article on Wise, *Jewish Encyclopedia* (New York, 1901–6), XII, 541–42; Max B. May, *Isaac Mayer Wise, the Founder of American Judaism: A Biography* (New York, 1916); David Philipson, "Isaac Mayer Wise, 1819–1919," *Centenary Papers and Others* (Cincinnati, 1919); Israel Knox, *Rabbi in America: The Story of Isaac M. Wise* (Boston, 1957); Joseph H. Gumbiner, *Isaac Mayer Wise, Pioneer of American Judaism* (New York, 1959); and James G. Heller, *Isaac M. Wise: His Life, Work, and Thought* (New York, 1965).

   These accounts of Wise's life are obviously all posthumous. An adulatory account of his life appeared while he was still living: see Joseph Krauskopf, "Half a Century of Judaism in the United States," in *The American Jews' Annual for 5648 A[nno]. M[undi]*. (New York, Chicago, and Cincinnati, December 1887), especially pp. 76 ff. Krauskopf was, like Philipson, a member of the Hebrew Union College's first graduating class.

   It is worth noting here that Philipson, in his own autobiography, *My Life as an American Jew* (Cincinnati, 1941), made no mention of Wise that conflicted with the hagiography he had developed in his earlier writings.

2. See Isaac M. Wise, "The World of My Books," translated and annotated by Albert H. Friedlander, in *American Jewish Archives [AJA]*, VI (1954), 107–48. "Meine Buecherei" ("The World of My Books") began appearing in Wise's German-language Cincinnati newspaper, *Die Deborah*, on September 17, 1896.

3. See Wise, *Reminiscences,* translated and edited by David Philipson (Cincinnati, 1901). The German original, "Reminiscenzen," began appearing in *Die Deborah* on July 3, 1894. Philipson declared\ in his introduction to the English version that he had "aimed to conform as far as possible to the original; but my chief object has been to reproduce the spirit of the author" (*Reminiscences,* p. 9).

4. Wise, "World of My Books," *AJA*, VI, 144.

5. *Ibid.,* pp. 145–46 (italics added). See Wise, "The Theology of Judaism," in John H. Barrows, ed., *The World's Parliament of Religions* (Chicago, 1893), I, 290–95.

6. *AJA*, VI, 146.

7. See Harry H. Mayer, "What Price Conservatism? Louis Ginzberg and the Hebrew Union College," *AJA*, X (1958), 145–50.

8. *Ibid.,* p. 149.

9. *Ibid.,* p. 147.

10. The Philipson diary is part of the American Jewish Archives, Cincinnati, Ohio. (Box 1323).

11. See *Selected Writings,* p. iii: "The first part of the [Wise] biography (pp. 1–58) is from the pen of David Philipson . . . "

12. Philipson is referring to Kohler's two-part polemic, "Some Plain and Telling Words Regarding Rabbi J. Krauskopf," in the New York weekly, *American*

Hebrew, December 30, 1887, pp. 131–32, and January 6, 1888, pp. 147–48. Kohler was incensed by the fact that Joseph Krauskopf's "Half a Century of Judaism in the United States," in *The American Jews' Annual for 5648,* issued in December 1887, focused on Wise's "leadership of the Reform Movement in the United States" (p. 76) and scarcely mentioned David Einhorn at all. Kohler snapped: "There is but one I aM Wise, and Dr. Joseph Krauskopf is his prophet." Then Kohler proceeded to excoriate Wise for his readiness to recognize the Talmud as "the legal and obligatory commentary on the Bible" at the Cleveland Conference of 1855 and to shred Wise's *History of the Israelitish Nation, from Abraham to the Present Time,* published at Albany, N. Y., in 1854.

Some years later, it is worth noting, Kohler found it possible to salute Wise as "the master-builder of Progressive American Judaism": See Kohler, "Isaac M. Wise; or, The Heroic Qualities of the God-Chosen Leader," *Hebrew Union College and Other Addresses* (Cincinnati, 1916), p. 51. Kohler had by then succeeded Wise as president of the Hebrew Union College.

13. Wise's opposition to Sunday services is very well documented. See, for example, comments in *American Israelite,* July 15, 1870, p. 8; April 3, 1874, p. 5; May 1, 1874, p. 4; March 21, 1879, p. 4; May 30, 1879, p. 4; August 8, 1879, p. 4; January 2, 1880, p. 4; February 13, 1885, p. 4; August 6, 1886, p. 4; November 23, 1888, p. 7; January 3, 1889, p. 4; December 3, 1891, p. 4. Philipson's remark that, in November-December, 1889, "the whole country was agog with" his introduction of Sunday services is not borne out by a perusal of the *Israelite* during that period (though New York's *American Hebrew,* December 7, 1888, pp. 86, 89—a year earlier, that is—reported with satisfaction how "the effort made in [Philipson's congregation] to institute Sunday lectures . . . failed by so decisive a vote as 50 to 30." A Cincinnati correspondent wrote the *American Hebrew* of young Philipson's "mis-step": "It is a good lesson for those too radically inclined, and let them take note of it!" Wise's *Israelite* gave it only the briefest mention: December 7, 1888, p. 4). Wise did editorialize in the *Israelite,* October 17, 1889, p. 4, that Philipson was expected to "deliver the Friday evening lectures" at Bene Israel, and that: "Wherever the Friday evening services are well attended, Sunday lectures are superfluous and a violation of Jewish custom."

In the *Israelite,* December 12, 1889, p. 6, Wise published a letter by S. M. Winkler, a member of Philipson's Bene Israel board, protesting Sunday lectures at his congregation. (Philipson may have had Winkler's letter in mind when he declared in the *Israelite,* January 2, 1890, p. 4: "Dirty linen should be washed in private, away from the gaze of any looker on.") Even so, the *Israelite* with some regularity—and without critical comment—noted and summarized Philipson's Sunday morning lectures at the Mound Street Temple (Bene Israel): See *Israelite,* November 21, 1889, p. 6; November 28, 1889, p. 6; December 5, 1889, p. 6; December 12, 1889, p. 6; December 19, 1889, p. 6.

Wise did not hesitate to publish the text of Philipson's *Saturday* morning sermon "Ludwig Philippson, a Man of His Time" and quoted in extenso from the *Cincinnati Commercial-Gazette's,* highly complimentary report on the sermon, "a wonderfully clever panegyric, none the less entertaining than instructive": See *Israelite,* January 23, 1890, pp. 4–6.

14. On the July 1890 meeting of the Central Conference of American Rabbis at Cleveland, Ohio, see *Israelite,* July 17, 1890, p. 4; July 24, 1890, p. 7; July 31, 1890, p. 4. Philipson's resolution appears in *ibid.,* July 24, 1890, p. 7, cols. 1–2. Wise's editorial blast against the word *Jew*—"a corruption from the Latin Judaeus"—appears in *ibid.,* July 31, 1890, p. 4, cols. 1–2.

15. See Wise's editorial, "During Vacation," *Israelite*, August 28, 1890, p. 4:
"The writer of these lines, as usual, took also this year no vacation. His colleagues being absent from the city, he preached . . . before the two largest congregations of Cincinnati—the Bene Yeshurun and Bene Israel congregations, worshiping together in the palatial temple of the latter, in which . . . every Sabbath the congregation was very numerous. . . . We think [non-vacationing congregants] deserve the special consideration of their ministers, who should strive to be with them at least every Sabbath. . . . We take notice thereof to inform all earnest preachers that it is not good for congregations to be alone six to eight weeks in succession."

16. See *Israelite*, October 19, 1866, p. 4:
"K. K. Bene Yeshurun, at a general meeting, Oct. 13, gave card-blank to Rev. Dr. Wise, to arrange the time of divine services according to his judgment. Therefore, after due preparation will be made, the service in the Temple will begin on Sabbath morning, at 10 o'clock, and Friday evening at 7 P.M., all year round, the holidays excepted. After arrangements shall be completed, there will be held a regular divine service on Friday evening, with choir and sermon, to last about one hour or thereabout. There is no doubt that this evening service will do a vast deal of good to our cause."
See also *Israelite*, December 31, 1869, p. 8; August 2, 1872, p. 8; July 11, 1873, p. 4; August 8, 1879, p. 4; November 11, 1881, p. 156; April 2, 1886, p. 4; October 29, 1891, p. 4.

17. See *Israelite*, October 29, 1891, p. 4:
"Look out for your Friday evening service and lectures; it is the salvation of Judaism under the circumstances under which we are placed. It is the salvation of the congregation that can not get its members to assemble numerously on Saturday morning. It is the salvation of the rising generation not to be estranged from Judaism and the congregation. It gives satisfaction everywhere, if the preacher is enthusiastic and competent to rouse the dormant sentiments of religion and the attachment to Judaism, also those who are chilled by influences from [a]broad. It is the salvation of the Sabbath in the consciousness and conscience of those whose hearts are still with God and Israel. It redeems men and women out of the bondage of unbecoming habits and the slavery of fashion, the sensual pleasure seeking inebriation which benights and bewilders ever so many. Take care of your Friday evening service and lecture. Be not led astray by the Sunday innovation; it is not for the congregation, it is for outsiders, and will be short-lived everywhere where Judaism is prized higher than style, fashion and whim."

THE RELIGION OF
TOMAS TREVIÑO DE SOBREMONTE

By

MARTIN A. COHEN

*Hebrew Union College—Jewish Institute of Religion,
New York*

Tomás Treviño de Sobremonte was the towering personality among the victims of the Inquisition at the spectacular auto-da-fé held in Mexico City on Sunday, April 11, 1649. He was one of twelve who met death at the stake; fifty-seven others, who had died or fled, were burned in effigy. Treviño had been sentenced for relapsing into the practice of Judaism, for which the Inquisition had first tried and convicted him nearly a quarter-century before. On the same day that Treviño died, thirty-seven first offenders, having repented their Jewish practices, were penanced and given a second chance.[1]

A witness at his trial had characterized Treviño as the most learned and devout of the practitioners of Judaism in his day. With these words in mind the Inquisitors proclaimed at the auto-da-fé "that this Treviño was a great observer of the Law [of Moses] . . . , duly keeping it and duly performing its fasts and ceremonies, to such a degree that his wife called him a saint."[2]

If such claims suggest meticulosity in traditional observance, an examination of the actual content of Treviño's Judaism reveals a bizarre and puzzling pastiche of belief and practice. The sources of our information—the only substantive documentary sources we have on Treviño—are the records of his two trials before the Inquisition. These contain Treviño's own testimony, depositions by witnesses, germane excerpts from the trials of other prisoners, and the Inquisition's charges and summations. Occasional additional mentions of Treviño in other inquisitorial documents are inconsequential for an understanding of his religious life.

These records disclose that Treviño was first arrested, at the age of thirty-one, on November 1, 1644. He was "reconciled" at the auto-da-fé of June 15, 1625, and rearrested on October 11, 1644. Each trial record discloses and emphasizes different aspects of Treviño's religion. The record of the second trial also recapitulates the religious elements mentioned at the first.[3]

According to the record of his first trial, Treviño knew the *Shemá Yisrael* and its liturgical response, and through them expressed his one firmly articulated theological belief, the belief in one God. He recited both before the Inquisitors in a Hebrew preserved in garbled and incomplete form (*Sema, Adonaí . . . Berutó, Ceolan, Banel*). Since similar errors of transcription are found in other inquisitorial records, there is no way of determining whether they originated with the defendant or the inquisitorial scribe. Also garbled is the transliteration of "Holy, Holy, Holy . . . " (Isa. 6:3), which comes out *Coados, meles, que bodo,* and the beginning of another prayer, *Binuam, Adonai, Maciadeno . . . ,* representing the first several words of Psalm 90:17, and used traditionally as a blessing and introduction to prayers like Psalm 91 in the *Keriat Shemá shel ha-Mitá,* prayers before retiring at night.

Treviño, in fact, appears to have used it in this connection. Of the three additional prayers in his repertoire specifically mentioned by the record, one turns out to be Psalm 91. Treviño could recall only a few words of this prayer, but its opening clearly connects it with sleep!

> Beneath the shadow of the Abundant one I fall asleep, *or,* beneath Thy wings shall I be illumined and directed to Thy service. . . I shall not fear the terror of the night . . . the dagger and the shield . . . no harm shall befall thee, nor wound . . . for he says they (the angels) will bear thee upon their hands . . . (?)

The second prayer was to be recited in connection with a ritual washing after a meal and also "in observance of the said Law of Moses": "Blessed be the Almighty Adonai, who in Thy teachings hast taught me to wash my hands, mouth and eyes to laud Thee and serve Thee, in praise and honor of the Lord, and in the Law of Moses."

The third was a pedestrian improvisation:

Unto Thee, great God ineffable,
Unto Thee, essence incomprehensible,
Unto Thee, glory firm and stable,
Unto Thee, Lord infallible,
Unto Thee, I make confession and ask
Pardon, O Lord, and clemency.
If Thou markest that I have offended Thee
With my quibbles and presumptions,
Pardon is not due to me.
Stop regarding me
And my iniquity and corruption,
Great God, and regard Thyself,
And enter not into judgment
With me, who have offended Thee.
More than all others have I sinned—
So has the world managed to deceive me,
So much have I indulged in its pleasures,
That because I remembered it much,
Little did I remember Thee.
      Thou, sovereign and clear light,
Who now taketh me to account,
I find that I was my own enemy
And I see that my faults
Clamor for punishment before Thee.
But if Thou art mindful of me,
Aud trust in my memory
Of how much I am obligated to Thee,
I shall leave with triumph and victory,
From the world, flesh and sin.
      To Thee, infinite sustenance,
To Thee, who alone wert able,
To free the afflicted people,
From the captivity of Egypt,
And open a way for it in the sea . . .

The record also discusses Treviño's observance of the Sabbath and
the Day of Atonement, or, as he and other practitioners of Judaism
called it, the Great Day. The description of Treviño's Sabbath ritual
is confined to the information that he and his family donned good,
clean clothes on the eve of the Sabbath, and rested all day, at least in
principle, though whenever necessary the women kneaded their bread
on the Sabbath to divert the suspicion that they were engaged in Jew-

ish practice. The description of the ritual for the Great Day is somewhat more revealing. Before the Great Day Treviño bathed, in a river
if he was traveling, otherwise in his house in a trough. He then put
on a new shirt and ate fish "because this was mandatory, being a ceremony of the said Law of Moses." The family fasted from sundown to
sunset, and spent all night "discussing matters relating to the said
Law and offering prayers." During these discussions and prayers everyone remained standing, in one place, if possible, otherwise, moving
about "as a required ceremony of the said Law of Moses."

We also learn of a number of other customs and rituals—the ritual
slaughter of "pigeons, chickens and hens"; the avoidance of pork,
in principle, though Treviño and his family were prepared to eat it
to avoid suspicion; and the abstinence from meat and the eating of fish
after the death of a close relative "for the first three days, or nine,
which he believes to be the correct number." [4]

The record of Treviño's second trial does not accuse him of recidivism
in connection with most of the practices recorded in the first. Thus,
not one of the thirty-five witnesses marshaled by the Inquisition dwells
on Treviño's Sabbath observance. And, except for the Great Day, it
mentions no traditional major holiday. It does inform us, for the first
time, of Treviño's observance of the three-day Fast of Esther, common
among the Judaizers in the lands of the Inquisition, but at least one
witness confuses it with the fast of the Great Day. In connection with
the Great Day, it reveals that Treviño and his acquaintances clearly
did not know "the date when it had to be observed, whether a week
earlier or later."

Nor does the record of this trial charge Treviño with continuing the
recitation of the prayers mentioned and alluded to in the first. It gen-
eralizes that Treviño knew many prayers and reveals that he possessed
"a little book" containing a number of prayers. Its novelty consists in
information about the formal aspects of Treviño's prayers: He prayed
three times a day, at eight in the morning, two in the afternoon, and
nightfall, and frequently also between midnight and one o'clock in the
morning. He always preceded his prayers with a ritual washing of his
hands and recited them either kneeling or standing. When he prayed
his head was covered with a cloth cap and a carefully tied kerchief. He
regarded this combination as "a known practice of the Jews, who cover
and tie their heads in order to pray." [5]

The record mentions a number of additional rituals. Treviño had been circumcised by a cellmate in 1624, and he later circumcised his young son. Also, before leaving home on a trip, Treviño would place his hands on his children's heads and recite a blessing, most probably Isaac's blessing of Jacob (Gen. 27:28). Also, Treviño and his circle would confess their sins to God "in the most remote corner of their house, on their knees, with their hands turned toward the floor and their bodies very low so that they nearly touched the ground . . . asking Him for pardon for all they had done, and they remained in this position all or most of the day . . ." Treviño and his circle also practiced ritual slaughter. They would "slaughter the hens, holding them between the legs and with a hand on the head and underneath the beak. They slaughtered them with a sharpened knife, removed the fat from the meat and placed the meat in a tub overnight to drain its blood. Then they put it into the pot." Treviño also blunted the edges of all pocket and household knives, "because he said it was against the Law of Moses for knives in use to have a point."

We also learn that when someone died, all present covered their faces and remained silent for an hour "without spitting or moving, commending the deceased to the Almighty, who revealed the secret of the soul of the departed to his most beloved, as He had frequently done to Treviño."

Also regarded as Jewish was the belief that the crowing of cocks in the first quarter of the night was an ill omen.

The record also indicates that Treviño and his associates were aware of the concept of ritual uncleanness and used the adjectives *trefo* (masculine) and *trefa* (feminine) to refer to someone in this condition.

Of particular interest are two clusters of Treviño's ritual activity stressed at the second trial:

One, revolving around Treviño's wedding feast in 1629, was most fully described by one witness, Margarita de Rivera. Although she was a known enemy of Treviño de Sobremonte, her testimony confirms details mentioned elsewhere and adds several new ones. These are tangential to basic Jewish practice and can hardly be attributed to the inventions of hostility.

Margarita averred:

1. that at the meal, held at noon in the home of his mother-in-law, Treviño de Sobremonte tied "a kerchief from his nostrils to his head," covering it entirely "as a ceremony of the Law of Moses . . . for this is customary among those who observe it";

2. that at the beginning of the meal, again "as a ceremony of the Law of Moses," the guests dipped some cakes, probably pancakes, into bees' honey, "in memory of the honeycomb that the angel had taken out of the storehouse for the young daughter of Potiphar, when she married Joseph";

3. that the hens eaten at the meal had been ritually slaughtered by an unnamed member of Treviño's family or circle, or perhaps the groom himself. The slaughterer held each hen firmly in one hand, and a sharp knife, to minimize their pain, in another. He faced east, plunged the knife through their necks "three times into the ground," and recited three times, "Blessed be He who created you for my sustenance and me for the earth";

4. that after dinner, the guests "washed their hands in the Jewish manner, that is, pouring cold water on each hand three times and rubbing them together." Margarita went on to say that it was also regarded as obligatory to pour three pitchers of cold water over one's entire body when bathing, whether ritually, in connection with fasts, or for simple cleanliness, "in order for them not to be *trefos* or *trefas*";

5. that after his wedding night, Treviño abstained from intercourse with his wife until the seventh day "because in the Law of Moses anyone marrying a virgin was not to repeat intercourse until the seventh day, in order to purify himself from the first blood, so that he would not be *trefo*."

The second cluster comprises the many fasts undertaken by Treviño, his family, and their friends, and all the rituals connected with these fasts. In addition to the Great Day and the Fast of Esther, Treviño and many of the others fasted every Thursday, and ideally, on Mondays as well. Some, however, fasted on Fridays. In addition, they observed special fasts, like the one of three or four days undertaken by Treviño to thank God for having preserved his life when his house collapsed. The record indicates that during a fast a candle, placed on a chair near a door, would burn through the night until it was naturally extinguished. The fast was also accompanied by a confession of sins. At the conclusion of a fast, the participants would dedicate it, "offering it to the Almighty," as one witness put it. They would then wash, light candles again, and feast, but not on meat. The evidence does not reveal whether these practices applied to all fasts, or only the major ones, like the Fast of Esther and the Great Day, or perhaps just the latter alone.

At times they would save the end of the candle, meaning either the part that did not burn out during the fast or the part that remained when they extinguished candles at their feasts.

During the Fast of Esther, the participants would breakfast each night on salad, eggs, and sweets.

In any event the accompanying rituals, however important, merit less attention than the role of fasting itself. The evidence at Treviño's second trial, particularly, makes it clear that fasting dominated Treviño's system of religious rituals and was likewise regarded as paramount by the majority of his associates. Unlike any other ritual or practice, fasting is mentioned in the testimony of almost every witness, and many reveal Treviño's emphasis on the ritual's procedures and his careful explanation of its requirements to others. Fasting is the only ritual consistently mentioned by the witnesses as having been taught by Treviño to others. In addition, the witnesses describe a number of men and women as "a fine leader in carrying out fasts" (*buen oficial [a] en hacer ayunos*). Neither the first nor the second trial record applies any epithet of distinction to any person in connection with another ritual.

The importance of fasting in Treviño's circle is further seen in the statement of Treviño's mother-in-law to the effect that "she had never seen anyone who could perform its rituals as well as he." His mother-in-law believed that "when she performed the fasts, she seemed to be in Paradise, clean and purified."

The sum of all this information about Treviño de Sobremonte's religious life hardly supports the conclusion that he was learned in, or correctly observant of, the Jewish tradition. On the one hand, it discloses serious deviations from normative Jewish customs and law at almost every turn—in the details of his circumcision and that of his son; his mourning customs; his ritual slaughter, including the blessing; his ablutions; his fasting, including his dedications and candlelighting, especially after the fact, as an integral part of the observance; his belief that one had to remain standing all night during a fast and abstain from meat before and after; his manner of confession; and the content, frequency, and hours of his prayers. Nowhere are these deviations more prominent than in two rituals associated with his wedding. There, the dipping of cake into honey "as a ceremony of the Law of Moses" has for its rationale a passage derived from the *Life and Confession of Asenath,* a Greek apocryphon, based on Jewish lore (not law), but hardly Jewish in form, and containing a Christian interpolation. Then, Treviño's abstention from intercourse, while displaying an awareness of rabbinic law, is based on the mistaken notion that his wife's blood made him rather than her unclean.[6]

At his first trial, Treviño claimed that most of the practices he regarded as Jewish had been taught to him by his mother in Spain.[7] If this is correct, it leaves very little that can be attributed to Treviño's own initiative and investigation.

The pervasiveness of error in Treviño's Jewish practice vitiates occasional assumptions that he engaged in additional practices, which somehow escaped the attention of the Inquisition and all its witnesses, and that furthermore these practices accorded with traditional and normative procedures. On the basis of the sources, it is impossible to affirm that Treviño de Sobremonte or anyone close to him had read any halakha, or, for that matter, knew any rabbinic literature, or the full structure of the traditional calendar, or any holidays other than those mentioned. Nor is there any reason to disbelieve Treviño's statement that he first learned of the Feast of Booths, as he called Succot, from the Inquisition's Edict of Faith, read periodically in the churches to alert parishioners to practices suspected of being Jewish, and that he did not know when the holiday fell or the manner of its celebration. Since Treviño could have learned about the Feast of Booths and other basic elements of Judaism from the Bible, his declared ignorance in this area, and the absence of explicit information in the sources about his knowledge of others, cannot fail to leave the impression that Treviño's Jewish learning was elementary and minimal. The evidence specifically mentions that he knew stories of the patriarchs and the prophets, individual accounts like that of Sisera and some from the Apocrypha, but in view of his general lack of biblical knowledge, there is no reason to infer that he acquired these from personal study. Like other Judaizers in Mexico, Treviño appropriated many of these from collections like Alfonso de Villegas' *Flos Sanctorum* (the *Saints' Anthology*).

In view of these facts, it is necessary to call for a revision of statements by a handful of writers, who, for lack of knowledge of Judaism, or lack of investigation of the sources, have assumed that Treviño's was a normative Judaism in content and practice, and in this sense have proceeded to call him a pious Jew. One Jewish writer has even gone so far as to compare Treviño and his circle with modern Orthodox Jews![8]

That Treviño's Judaism cannot be equated with any of the mainstream currents, or, for that manner, any other currents, of Judaism outside the world of the Inquisition, does not mean that he is to be read out of Jewish history or denied the right to be considered, as he considered himself, a Jew. It does mean that his Jewishness is to be sought in his self-definition and his zeal rather than in the correctness of his practice. It was, indeed, these factors that occasioned his arrests and convictions before the Inquisitors. The Inquisitors were not concerned with halakhic propriety; they regarded any practice in the name of Judaism to be authentic. It was on the basis of Treviño's irrepressible devotion to Jewish identity and to what he regarded as authentic Judaism that the Inquisition called him "rabbi," a term it reserved for such people without prior investigation as to whether they possessed any rabbinic or Hebraic knowledge, let alone ordination. It also called Treviño, as it called others, a "false priest" and "a dogmatizer of the Law." [9]

The idea that Treviño could have been a pious Jew in the traditional sense is exploded even more dramatically by the recognition of a series of basic facts, frequently overlooked by Jewish writers bent on promoting his "orthodox" Jewishness.

Although Treviño de Sobremonte considered himself a Jew, he was born into a household that was Catholic, from the point of view of both government policy and canon law. He was baptized and instructed in the rudiments of Catholic doctrine. He was arrested twice by the Inquisition, not because the practice of Judaism by itself was a crime (the Inquisition never knowingly indicted Jews for the practice of Judaism!), but because as a Catholic, the practice of Judaism involved him in the sin and crime of heresy. It should also be noted that in Treviño's day Jews were officially prohibited from living in or coming to New Spain, or, for that matter, any other part of the Hispano-Lusitanian world. There were certainly no "Jewish communities" in New Spain, as one writer claims.[10] If, for whatever reason, occasional authentic Jews from abroad came into any of these territories, they did not publicly proclaim their religious identity or form "Jewish Com munities." Every practitioner of Judaism of Spanish or Portuguese origin in New Spain, as elsewhere under the Inquisition, had to keep his Judaism clandestine, because every one, even if he had avoided baptism, was regarded as a Catholic and under the jurisdiction of the Church.

The fact that Treviño was born and officially bred a Catholic, in an environment hostile to Judaism, helps explain his lack of traditional and even sound biblical learning. It also accounts for the obvious influence of the Catholic environment on his practice—his repeated genuflections, his distinctive confession, his candle ceremonies, his dedication of fasts, and even his emphasis on fasting. It renders understandable his avoidance of confession and communion and of phrases like "In the name of the Father, the Son and the Holy Ghost" after the reading of Psalms or "Praised be the Holy Sacrament" after meals—all as signs of Jewish devotion. After meals Treviño used the Judaizers' typical phrase, "May it [the meal] do you much good."

Thus far, the exposition of Treviño de Sobremonte's attenuated Judaism appears to support a traditional theory regarding the transmission of the faith of the secret Jews. Traditionally it has been believed that, in the main if not in the totality, these New Christian Judaizers, as they are most correctly called, were the recipients of a Judaism that had been transmitted uninterruptedly from generation to generation since the numerous conversions of Jews to Catholicism in Spain at the time of the edict expelling non-converted Jews in 1492 and in Portugal at the time of the forced apostasy of 1497. These climactic events put an end to the free practice of Judaism in the Iberian Peninsula and made all practitioners of Judaism—now officially Catholics—go underground. It has been further believed that the content of this Judaism, particularly in the rabbinic area, gradually eroded under the pressures of secrecy and isolation, the disappearance of irreplaceable sacred books, and the death of teachers who had been instructed in Judaism prior to the last decade of the fifteenth century.

Although this theory would explain a gradual erosion of Jewish knowledge, it fails to account for the precipitate decline which actually took place, often in less than three generations. Nor does it account for the absence among the Judaizers of widespread memorization of sacred writ and doctrine, a survival mechanism particularly suited for times that demanded secrecy and could not guarantee the survival of religious texts. Such memorization, common elsewhere in the Jewish world, where individuals have been known to learn stores of halakhic material, the entire liturgy, the entire Bible, and the entire Talmud by heart, would have made possible the oral transmission among the New Christian Judaizers of a far richer and more authentic Judaism than actually occurred in the world of the Inquisition.

One element in Treviño de Sobremonte's religion explicitly challenges this theory. It is the presence, at times in distortion, of occasional glimmers of traditional recitations and practices which were *not* known to the learned practitioners and leaders of secret Judaism in New Spain in earlier generations. These include Treviño's superficial contact with the traditional calendar, the laws of family purity, the ritual washing of the hands, one or two details in the process of ritual slaughter, possibly the prayer shawl—if that is what the kerchief tied around his head was intended to represent, and certainly the requirement of the head covering, which Treviño appears to have confined to times of prayer, but which even for this purpose was not known in the previous century by the most learned of the Judaizers in New Spain. When we add to this the appearance in contemporary trial records of the substance and even the Hebrew names of prayers like the *Amidá,* holidays like *Tishá be-Ab,* customs like *Avelút,* and ritual objects like the *Tallit,* the puzzlement increases. So, too, the use of the term *trefo* to indicate ritual uncleanness was the one commonly used at this time by New Christian Judaizers in other parts of the world under inquisitorial surveillance.[11]

Patently, there were rabbinic elements within the crypto-Judaism of seventeenth-century New Spain—and elsewhere—which were not transmitted for generations through familial instruction, but derived from other sources instead. These sources are not difficult to locate. By the seventeenth century there were numerous established communities of former crypto-Jews who had openly embraced Judaism outside the jurisdiction of Spain and Portugal and were observing traditional Jewish practice. Occasionally Jews from these areas slipped unobtrusively into territories under inquisitorial surveillance to see relatives or do business. Occasionally, also, crypto-Jews visiting these areas and coming into contact with authentic Judaism, returned to the places of their origin. It is to these seventeenth-century contacts rather than those of the fifteenth that we must assign the increased knowledge of rabbinic Judaism in Treviño's time. Even so, the paucity of these additions is astounding; it reveals not only the limited scope of the contacts between the crypto-Jewish and authentic Jewish worlds, but also the lack of influence, both in breadth and in depth, of authentic Judaism on the crypto-Jews of New Spain.

The recognition that the New Christian Judaizers could have derived significant elements of their knowledge and practice from contemporary rather than inherited sources generates an important question: Might it be that other elements in the religion of the crypto-Jews, usually regarded as traditional because they are found regularly throughout the sixteenth and early seventeenth centuries, were also acquired, at least by some, from outside their familial structures? In other words, instead of

positing an unbroken transmission of crypto-Jewish knowledge for all
or most New Christian Judaizers, is it not possible that the chain indeed
was broken, for at least some and perhaps many, until a point in time
when a family or an individual, for any one of a variety of reasons, found
it desirable to accept Judaism secretly and therefore to seek instruction
from others who had done so previously? The numerous instances of the
occurrence of this phenomenon in the inquisitorial records of Spain,
Portugal, and their possessions support this hypothesis. Implicit in it is
the possibility that the actual number of crypto-Jews among the converts
at the end of the fifteenth century was dwindling, and, furthermore, that
the remaining crypto-Jews, though unsurpassed in zeal, were not as a
group sufficiently learned to maintain the rich intellectual legacy of
Judaism. The fact is that very quickly in the sixteenth century the basic
content of the religion of the crypto-Jews became drastically attenuated,
and its non-biblical elements reduced to a few vaguely remembered and
frequently distorted ancestral practices and customs. The rest of this attenuated religion, it must be recalled, came from the Bible, which was
also the heritage of the Catholic world in whose midst these crypto-
Jews lived. And it was from the "Catholic Bible," the Vulgate, composed
in Latin and including the Apocrypha as canonical, that they derived
their knowledge of biblical Judaism. Even the most learned of the
Judaizers in the history of New Spain, Luis de Carvajal the Younger
(1566–1596), acquired the bulk of his knowledge of Judaism in a
Catholic school where he served as a research assistant and calligrapher
after he had been reconciled at an auto-da-fé.[12]

The possibility of a gap between the voluntary or involuntary acceptance of Christianity by Jewish individuals and families in the fifteenth
century (and in the case of Spain also the late fourteenth) and their
"return" to Jewish identification presents a serious challenge to another
widely held belief, namely, that all the Jewish converts to Catholicism
and their descendants in Spain, Portugal, and their colonies, remained
Jews at heart. The lemma "once a Jew, always a Jew" has frequently
and indiscriminately been applied to all the New Christians almost from
the time of the major conversions. It continues to be espoused today by
strange bedfellows—the doctrinaire defenders of the Inquisition on the
one hand and, on the other, the no less doctrinaire proponents of a racial
conception of the Jews.[13]

The untenability of this proposition for the New Christians has been
recognized by disinterested and responsible thinkers ever since its initial

articulation. It has become dramatically apparent in the last several decades, first, through the revelation of the Jewish ancestry of important Spaniards and Portuguese unlinkable to Jewish identification or practice, but devoted sincerely to Catholicism or non-Jewish dissident movements, and second, with the realization that the number of New Christians accused of Judaizing by the Inquisition represents only a small minority of all the New Christians, and that, indeed, most of those convicted of Judaizing as a first offense were reconciled to the Church and never heard from again.

In recent decades the question has also been raised as to whether some, or even all, the charges of Judaizing brought by the Inquisition might have been false.[14] One writer goes so far as to regard the New Christians as essentially coextensive with the rising bourgeoisie and the Inquisition as a conscious instrument for its destruction in the hands of the Old Guard.[15]

The challenges raised to the traditional concepts regarding the New Christians have produced heated scholarly discussion. If nothing else, these have already succeeded in puncturing the neatly packaged generalizations regarding the New Christians with a rising tide of evidence derived from careful analysis of the sources and methodologically sound inductions. In a limited way, a study from the sources of the religion of a personality as important as Tomás Treviño de Sobremonte may contribute to what must ultimately be a reformulation of the problem of the crypto-Jews.[16]

NOTES

1. On Treviño de Sobremonte, see article by M. A. Cohen in *Encyclopaedia Judaica*, vol. 15, cols. 1379–80; B. Lewin, *Mártires y conquistadores judíos en la América hispana* (Buenos Aires, 1954), pp. 116–76; J. T. Medina, *Historia del tribunal del Santo Oficio de la Inquisición en México*, 2d ed., with notes and additions by Julio Jiménez Rued "Lord"? (Mexico City, 1952), pp. 119, 175, 196 ff., especially 200, 204, and 206; and, for what, despite its limitations, remains the most reliable overview of the seventeenth century in New Spain, A. Wiznitzer, "Crypto-Jews in Mexico during the Seventeenth Century," *American Jewish Historical Quarterly*, vol. 51 (1961–62), pp. 222–68, reprinted in M. A. Cohen, *The Jewish Experience in Latin America* (New York, 1972), pp. 133–77.

2. The quotation is from Treviño's sentence at the end of his second trial. It is based on a statement by Juan de León to Francisco Botello [=Botelho].

3. Treviño's trial records are found in the Archivo General de la Nación, in Mexico City, and are transcribed in the Archivo's *Boletín*, vols. 6–8 (1935–37).

4. See, for most of these details, Treviño's own testimony of November 27 and 28, 1624. A small number of other prayers are found in the trial records of his relatives and associates, as, for example, that of the first trial of his brother-in-law, Francisco López Roldán (1634).

5. See, particularly, the accusation against Treviño, March 14, 1647, and, among the witnesses, the testimony of his son Rafael and of María de Rivera and Gaspar Alfar.

6. See, for example, *Shulhan Arukh, Yore Deah,* sec. 193, par. 1; Maimonides, *Yad ha-Hazakah,* chap. 11, pars. 8, 9, and 10; and the basic discussions in the Talmud, Niddah 64b and 65b.

7. See Treviño's testimony, November 27, 1624.

8. S. Liebman, *The Jews in New Spain* (Coral Gables, Fla., 1970), p. 300.

9. For a fuller discussion of these and other sources of confusion regarding the secret Jews of Mexico, with applicability elsewhere, see M. A. Cohen, "Some Misconceptions about the Crypto-Jews in Colonial Mexico," *American Jewish Historical Quarterly*, vol. 61 (1972), pp. 277–93.

10. Liebman, op. cit., pp. 237, 300, and elsewhere.

11. See, for example, the document from the Inquisition of Toledo reproduced by J. Caro Baroja in *Los judíos en la España moderna y contemporánea*, vol. 1, p. 425, n. 68: . . . "*por deçir quedan t r e p h o s, que es lo mismo que decir que quedan ynmundos. . . .* "

12. On Carvajal's religion, see M. A. Cohen, "The Religion of Luis Rodríguez Carvajal," *American Jewish Archives*, vol. 20 (1968), pp. 33–62, and idem, *The Martyr: The Story of a Secret Jew and the Mexican Inquisition in the Sixteenth Century* (Philadelphia, 1973), pp. 200–204.

13. Thus, for example, I. [F.] Baer, *A History of the Jews in Christian Spain*, vol. 2 (Philadelphia, 1966), pp. 95 ff., and the ideas of I. S. Révah, expressed, for example, in his outlines in the *Annuaire du Collège de France*, inter alia, that of 1971, p. 579.

14. See, for example, the provocative study of Ellis Rivkin, "The Utilization of Non-Jewish Sources for the Reconstruction of Jewish History," *Jewish Quarterly Review*, n.s., vol. 48 (1957–58), pp. 183–203.

15. A. J. Saraiva, *Inquisiçao e Cristãos-Novos* (Porto, 1959). See also his controversy with I. S. Révah in the *Diário de Lisboa*, May 6–September 2, 1971.

16. In a forthcoming study entitled "Toward a New Comprehension of the Marrano Problem," to be published under the auspices of the Catholic University of America by Ediciones Hispam of Barcelona, I go into the reformulation of the problem of the secret Jews in greater detail.

AN UNEASY ALLIANCE: THE FIRST DAYS
OF THE JEWISH AGENCY

By

NAOMI W. COHEN

Hunter College of the City University of New York

The Mandate for Palestine confirmed by the League of Nations in 1922 made provision for a Jewish Agency to be "recognized as a public body for the purpose of advising and cooperating with the Administration of Palestine in such economic, social and other matters as may affect the establishment of the Jewish National Home and the interests of the Jewish population in Palestine." Toward that end the Zionist Organization was charged "to secure the cooperation of all Jews who are willing to assist in the establishment of the Jewish National Home." These articles officially sanctioned what Dr. Chaim Weizmann, president of the Zionist Organization, had long desired—an alliance of non-Zionists with Zionists for the upbuilding of Palestine—and he began negotiations with non-Zionists throughout the world in an effort to secure their participation in a Jewish Agency.[1]

It was a daring scheme which gambled for high stakes. If carried off, the resources of the wealthy Jews, hitherto opposed to the Zionist movement, could be tapped on behalf of Palestine. A union of non-Zionists with Zionists, representative of different economic classes in all modern nations, could also impress the Mandatory Power and the League with the serious determination of world Jewry to realize the promise of the Balfour Declaration. But the risks were equally high. If Zionist ideology were seriously compromised in attempts to ease the antinationalist philanthropists into a partnership, the continued drawing power and vitality of political Zionism would be shattered. Should the scheme fall through, or should a union once established be paralyzed by divisiveness, the world could more easily discount the commitment of the Balfour Declaration and Mandate to a Jewish national home.

While the design of a broad or extended Jewish Agency encompassed all countries with Jewish populations, it was aimed primarily at the United States. The World War had catapulted American Jewry into a dominant position. Around three and a half million strong, it was a thriving community which had responded to the needs of European Jewry through mammoth wartime relief drives. At the same time, American Zionism, under the glamorous leadership of Louis Dembitz Brandeis, had gained added prestige in the eyes of world Jewry. Given the physical devastation wrought by the war and the uncertain future of the Jews in Communist Russia and in the succession states of Eastern Europe, the surest source of wealth and political influence lay in America. It was imperative, therefore, that Weizmann secure the active assistance of the outstanding American non-Zionists.

In 1923 Weizmann entered into negotiations with Louis Marshall and Felix Warburg. Warburg, the banker and philanthropist, was the logical choice for financial angel of the projected agency. Marshall, the prominent attorney and president of the American Jewish Committee, was the recognized voice of American Jewry generally and of the non-Zionists in particular. He and Weizmann were the driving forces behind the exchanges which dragged on for six years, and the agreement they forged testified in no small measure to the abilities of each and to the basic rapport and mutual trust which characterized their relationship.[2]

The Russian-born Zionist and the American-born Reform Jew had more of a common vocabulary than might be expected. Weizmann found Marshall to be a better Zionist than Louis Brandeis. Whereas to Brandeis Zionism was an intellectual challenge or experiment in progressivism, Marshall comprehended its emotional appeal to the Jewish people. Impressed by the teachings of Ahad Ha'am, Marshall, the anti-statist, regarded Palestine as the touchstone for Jewish spiritual survival throughout the world. On the other side, Zionism projected to the non-Zionists in the figure of Weizmann no longer appeared threatening. The Zionist leader himself believed that a Jewish state was "unrealizable" and would not come about "whether we want it or not—unless some fundamental change takes place which I cannot envisage at present. . . . The propaganda . . . for a Jewish State is foolish and harmful, but it cuts no ice, and you could just as well ask for a Jewish State in Manhattan Island." [3]

To allay any scruples American Jews might entertain about associating themselves with Jewish nationalism, Weizmann had launched Keren Hayesod, a fund-raising agency for Palestine but distinct from the Zionist Organization, on a trip to the United States in 1921. Weizmann won the confidence and respect of Marshall's group, and Marshall, by dint of his forceful personality, kept his followers, as well as many European non-Zionists, in line.[4]

Weizmann's views and his style made it easier for non-Zionists to contemplate cooperation with Zionists. So did the Balfour Declaration and the Mandate, which endowed Zionism, or at least the concept of a National Home, with worldwide respectability. No longer could it be discredited as a foolish dream on the one hand or a dangerous political conspiracy on the other. If Palestine in no way impinged on their status as loyal Americans, even Reform Jews could and did turn in all good conscience to the tasks of reconstructing the land.

While Weizmann shelved Jewish statehood for the sake of underwriting practical work in Palestine, forces coalesced to shift American Zionism also to a "Palestinian" rather than "Zionist" orientation.[5] As immigrants who had reached the United States from Eastern Europe before the war became increasingly acculturated and eager to be absorbed into the Jewish establishment, they too shied away from the political and nationalistic elements of Zionist thought. Frightened by the eruption of anti-Semitism caused by the publication of the *Protocols of the Elders of Zion* and by the charges of Henry Ford's *Dearborn Independent,* they strove consciously to prove their rootedness in the United States. The Zionist movement had been weakened by the resignation of the Brandeis group in 1921, and it had produced no leadership that could keep alive an ideological crusade or prevent the drift of the ZOA into what was almost exclusively a philanthropic agency. And, to the extent that Zionists rid themselves of propaganda and cultural campaigns, they became more palatable to the non-Zionists.

It is not unlikely that more than humanitarian interest in Palestine or good will toward their now respectable and chastened Zionist countrymen explained the non-Zionists' tractability. They may have calculated that the projected agency plan afforded them the opportunity to strengthen their control over the American Jewish community at the expense of their Zionist competitors. The two sides had distinct advantages. Men of the Marshall-Warburg group, leaders of the defense and welfare organizations, had money, entrée to government officials even up to the president, and status in the non-Jewish community. The American Zionists had the numbers, or at least the possibility of mobilizing the large East European element of American Jewry. The German Jews, still firmly in control of the Jewish establishment, were sufficiently farsighted to recognize the strength of numbers in a democratic society. If somehow they failed to head off, channelize, or come to terms with the more numerous stratum, they would ultimately lose all power. Worse still, their vision of American Jewry as a community under elitist control, assimilating to the American scene in all but religion, could give way to the reality of a democratic, secularist, and even nationalistic community which might jeopardize the security of all Jews in the United States.

In the past Marshall and those he typified had met the danger of deviationism from the established norm before their power structure was weakened. When a group of wealthy German Jews agreed to revive the Jewish Theological Seminary for forging an American Conservative rabbinate from East Europeans for East Europeans, they designed a school sufficiently traditional to attract the immigrants but one that would simultaneously Americanize the newcomers and wean them from secularist or socialist tendencies.[6] The formation of the American Jewish Committee in 1906 was prompted by the possibility of a more radical organization, calling itself representative of the Jewish community, arising to defend Jewish interests abroad. The Committee gave financial support to the New York Kehillah as a way of keeping a check on the Lower East Side and its potential eruptions. During the war the Committee could not prevent the organization of an American Jewish Congress, so it joined the movement in order to thwart any possible radicalism.[7] Similarly, in the aftermath of the Balfour Declaration Marshall opposed anti-Zionist projects on the part of Jewish irreconcilables which, he warned, would only incite more militant nationalist agitation.[8]

Since a professed goal of the Zionist movement in the United States had always been the democratization of the Jewish community, the American Jewish Committee and the self-appointed Jewish stewards were the consistently favorite targets of Zionist leaders and the Zionist press.[9] Now came the agency plan and with it the possibility of removing the Zionist threat perhaps once and for all. If the establishment showed itself to be pro-Palestine, it could undermine the Zionist appeal to the masses and reduce the support the more restive elements needed for overturning the power structure. By joining the "respectable" elements, Felix Warburg reasoned, the non-Zionists and the moderates could hold the "militant" in check.[10] Perhaps, too, if the non-Zionists became equal partners with Zionists in an agency which formulated overall Zionist policy and assumed the major burden of fund-raising, the very need for a ZOA would be eliminated.

Not all American Zionists accepted Weizmann's scheme without qualms. Some objected to the concomitant watering down of political Zionism or the substitution of philanthropy for ideological commitment. Stephen Wise, who also bemoaned the death of the Zionist democratic mass movement at the hands of a "millionaire-trusteeship," warned that Palestine would be reduced "to a Near East counterpart of the Crimean provinces of the Joint Distribution Committee." [11] No doubt there was resentment, too. They, the Zionists, had set an impossible dream on the road to practical attainment; the non-Zionists now sought to take over the movement and reap the power and the glory. If the agency superseded the Zionist Organization in raising money, the latter would have to carve out new projects in order to insure a meaningful existence. True, the Zionists would be free to return to cultural and propaganda work, but those avenues offered little chance of success, given the weakened state of the organization, its leadership, and the bent of American Jewish sentiment. Nevertheless, the ZOA, under the leadership of Louis Lipsky, a loyal Weizmann lieutenant, officially endorsed the agency plan.[12]

It is doubtful that any Zionists seriously entertained the hope that a partnership might convert the non-Zionists to their cause. The founders of the agency had consciously created a working alliance of ideological opponents. At the meeting in Zurich in August, 1929, at which the agency plan was overwhelmingly adopted, Marshall stated forthrightly: "In spite of our differing ideas and ideals, the result of this union will be a rebuilt Palestine, without anyone being asked to sacrifice his conscience or his principles." [13]

The Zurich meeting was an historic and exciting occasion. Delegations from more than twenty countries brought together east and west, religious and secular, labor and capital, Sephardi and Ashkenazi. The more prominent notables included Albert Einstein, Leon Blum, Sholom Asch, Sir Herbert Samuel, Rabbi Ben Zion Uzziel, and Abraham Cahan. "I do not think that any former occasion, at least for centuries, has seen so many different types of Jewish leaders together, endeavoring to work hand in hand, as on this occasion," Felix Warburg wrote enthusiastically. In a decade reverberating with the echoes of the *Protocols of the Elders of Zion*, contemporaries also hailed the international gathering as proof that

Jews no longer feared that their actions might lend credence to anti-Semitic charges.[14]

Unity on behalf of Palestine was the theme of the sessions, but clearly the ratification of the "Pact of Glory" (as the agency agreement was termed) marked a victory for the Americans and specifically the American non-Zionists. The delegation from the United States was the largest one present, and Marshall shared center stage with Weizmann. Most Americans said that they had come at Marshall's behest, and the American leader's influence permeated the gathering. One commentator noted that Marshall, as chairman of the agency's council sessions, formulated a new procedure by insisting that speeches be kept few and short and by pushing through motions without discussion. Doubtless the veteran Zionist leaders, to whom even technical details had ideological overtones and to whom the *pilpul* over Zionist ideology was as important as the commitment itself, realized that this was a brand new ball game.

The non-Zionists scored another point against the old-line secular Zionists when, at Marshall's insistence, a clause was inserted into the constitution of the agency on the protection of the religious needs of the Palestine settlement. Plans were also broached at the meeting for the creation of a giant corporation for developing agriculture and industry in Palestine—a venture in which both England's Lord Melchett and America's Warburg were ready to invest $500,000 each. While Zionists frankly expected some form of largesse as part of the "membership dues" of their new partners, some worried lest the socialist-labor principles of their movement be swept away by capitalist domination. Marshall insisted publicly that American Jews were not "money bags" but rather Jews who would respond to the needs of Palestine; Warburg asserted that the Americans had joined the agency not "to create a small ruling class" but in order to put the work for Palestine on a sound business basis. Nevertheless, the doubts rankled.[15]

American non-Zionist power was guaranteed by the constitution adopted for the agency. While Zionists and non-Zionists were to be represented equally, forty-four of the 112 council seats allocated to non-Zionists went to the Americans. Since only eighteen seats were earmarked for American Zionists, it was clear that at least with respect to the American scene the Zionist group was the "junior partner." [16]

At the beginning, however, optimism outweighed misgivings. The Jewish press stressed the element of harmony in reporting the Zurich sessions. In the United States some saw a new era of unity for the American Jewish community in particular.[17]

A lot more than enthusiasm was needed to translate the agency design, which attempted to align two distinct, self-motivated, and mutually jealous groups into a working reality. That chance became even more elusive when, in rapid succession, the agency was dealt three blows: the outbreak of Arab riots at the end of August, the death of Louis Marshall at the beginning of September, and the stock market crash in October. Arab resentment against Jewish colonization had been heightened by the fear that a powerful Jewish Agency would succeed in establishing a Jewish Palestine.[18] Even before the agency could prove its strength, it conjured up the image of Jewish power arrayed against the poor and helpless Arabs. Weizmann noted how this view colored the thinking of Lord Passfield, British colonial secretary, whose office had to cope with the highly charged situation after the riots:

> His attitude is that it is his role to protect the poor Arabs against the powerful Jews. . . . In previous years we were always reproached by Governmental circles because Zionists did not represent Jewry as a whole, because the "better" Jews, the wealthier Jews, had nothing to do with us. Since the Agency has been formed, I hear from all sides quite another tune, i.e. that the whole thing has become very dangerous, that here are all the rich and powerful Jews organized, and of course the poor Arabs will get no chance at all.[19]

Tasks of relief and reconstruction necessitated by the riots also distracted the agency from concentrating fully on its projected plans for normal operation. The stock market crash similarly crippled agency activities, for the funds they hoped to raise from the affluent simply did not roll in.

It was Marshall's death, however, which posed the gravest threat to the newborn alliance between Zionists and non-Zionists. The harmony of Zurich quickly dissipated, and during the first months of its existence the agency was rent by bitter acrimony. Felix Warburg, chairman of the agency's administrative committee, succeeded Marshall as leader of the American non-Zionists, but he lacked Marshall's commitment to Palestine, his breadth of understanding, and his ability to lead and to deal with others. Scion of the prominent German banking firm whose marriage to Jacob Schiff's daughter brought him into command of Kuhn, Loeb and Company, Warburg had made his name in American Jewish circles as a person of great charm and aesthetic taste, a bon vivant, and a generous donor to civic and Jewish philanthropies. Under Weizmann's personal influence Felix and Frieda Warburg developed a deep interest in rebuilding Palestine. But Warburg never shared Marshall's religious sentiments or his belief that Palestine was necessary for the sustenance of Judaism. To Warburg, as Weizmann put it, Palestine was just another of his fifty-seven varieties of charity.[20] Nor did he ever attain Marshall's understanding of the problems and currents of the American Jewish community; he certainly did not learn Yiddish, the way Marshall had, to gain a deeper appreciation of his fellow Jews. Where Marshall enjoyed a good fight and the chance to influence others to his point of view, Warburg shrank from the challenges of leadership and preferred to associate with men who did not question his ideas.[21] Despite his forcefulness and self-assurance, Marshall could compromise for the sake of larger principles; Warburg, as the story of the agency reveals, could not.

The problems which arose to divide Warburg and Weizmann had not been taken care of by the agency's constitution. The founders doubtless hoped that difficulties would be ironed out in the course of the agency's operations. Had Marshall lived, he might have experienced the same frustrations which Warburg did, and he might even have shared Warburg's aims. But it is more than likely that he would have handled the situation with greater sagacity and political skill and thereby prevented the dissension which threatened to wreck the agency during the winter of 1929–30.

The Weizmann-Warburg correspondence from September, 1929–February, 1930,[22] discloses a radical change in the personal relations of the two men. The warmth and cordially which marked the period immediately preceding and following Zurich—underscored by generous gifts from the Warburgs to the Weizmanns[23]—gave way to suspicion and recrimination. Warburg, who even threatened to resign from the agency, felt himself the injured party. His complaints put Weizmann on the defensive; the Zionist leader had to soothe, explain, and conciliate. His patience wore thin, too, and not until the administrative committee meeting of March did the atmosphere clear appreciably. The aftermath of the riots, forcing the agency to place top priority on relief work in Palestine and on political negotiations with the Shaw (investigating) Commission, compounded the tensions. But the differences reflected a basic incompatibility. Warburg's jealousy of his authority in the agency, his opposition to Zionist policies and methods, and his desire to obliterate the ZOA testified to the chasm which still separated the non-Zionists from the Zionists. Since the situation was different in London, where "cordial co-operation" between the two groups obtained,[24] the Weizmann-Warburg difficulties support the assumption that the American non-Zionists were using the agency as a means to augment their power over the American Jewish community.

The notion that the non-Zionists' function would be confined strictly to budgetary and financial matters was unrealistic. Marshall had admitted even before Zurich that economic involvement meant political involvement. (It was equally unrealistic for Weizmann to expect that as president of the agency he would be freed from financial concerns and immersed solely in political negotiations.) But even though Weizmann kept Warburg apprised of political developments, the latter wanted more thorough briefings and a larger say in policy-making. On the one hand he promised to be a "good soldier" and follow team policy, yet he became highly incensed when Lord Melchett told him to leave diplomatic concerns to the London group—Weizmann, Reading, Rothschild, and Melchett. Melchett's cable went on to say: "If mandatory were American Government we should not expect to handle it from London. . . . Hope you and your friends will be able to reestablish American stock market which appears to be much more important world proposition." [25]

Had Warburg had his way, the Zionist leaders would have been less critical of the British, more "dove-like" toward the Arabs, and silent, or even backing down, on the nationalist aims for a Jewish Palestine. He believed that peace in the land between the British, Arabs, and Jews was the prerequisite for any constructive work, that the Zionist dream was in fact "utopian," and that the Jews had to show their democratic posture to the world by acknowledging the rights of the more numerous Palestinian Arabs. Ignoring the possibility that such behavior could be interpreted as Jewish capitulation to the Arabs' use of violence, he urged that statements of good will be issued and that clemency be shown to those Arabs found guilty of participating in the riots. For a while he considered the possibility of forming a Jewish-Arab relief committee on behalf of innocent Arab victims of the riots. He was even willing to entertain the scheme broached by Judah Magnes, chancellor of the Hebrew University, which called for a democratic Palestinian parliament representing the Arab majority and Jewish minority and which, in fact, would have meant relinquishing claims to a Jewish state.[26] A careful reading of

Warburg's ideas suggests that he hoped to see the agency behave in accordance with the qualities he expected of *American* Jews: accommodat-
ing and temperate toward the government and toward the majority, and
unswerving in loyalty to the principles of political democracy.

Warburg complained bitterly about the distribution of power within
the agency. He would have liked a centralized structure, where decision-
making rested solely with a small top echelon whose policies in turn
would be executed efficiently and expertly by administrative underlings.
He missed no opportunity to criticize the agency for becoming bogged
down in political harangue and speculation. He especially opposed the
right of the agency's Executive, based in Palestine, to determine policies
independently of New York and London. Weizmann, he insisted, needed
to build up his personal authority:

> I feel that you must, so far as possible, be made into a Mussolini. I don't
> like dictatorships, but Napoleon said a long time ago that one poor general
> is better than three good ones, and it is more true that one good general,
> as you could be if you could have complete authority, is better than
> thousands of chiefs in a thousand cities, from Warsaw to South Africa.

When Weizmann made no move to become the autocrat, Warburg complained that the Zionist leader lacked courage. Warburg even resorted to
using two personal emissaries, Maurice Hexter and Jonah Goldstein, to
report to him directly on the Executive and its work in Palestine.[27]

Warburg may have thought that his own power would increase if he
had merely to cope with one dictator. Ignoring the Zionist commitment
to a democratic organization, he doubtless also hoped that Weizmann in
the less partisan role of president of the agency would take precedence
over Weizmann the president of the Zionist Organization. His preference
for centralization and administrative expertise reflected the bent of his
work in the United States on behalf of the Joint Distribution Committee
and the Federation of Jewish Philanthropies, and ultimately on behalf of
the German-Jewish establishment. When the issue is read in terms of
efficiency versus democracy and administration versus politics, it is reminiscent of the Brandeis-Weizmann rupture of 1921. In the later instance,
however, Weizmann compromised. At the meeting of the administrative
committee in March, 1930, Warburg's suggestion that the Executive in
Jerusalem be freed from political work was turned down. But the committee agreed to place an expert in charge of each department under
the Executive's authority.[28]

A major source of tension between Weizmann and Warburg concerned the role of the Zionist Organization after the creation of the agency. It is clear from the correspondence that Warburg considered the status of the ZOA to have been altered radically. Its new purpose was solely to keep its members informed and interested in Palestinian affairs; it was also to cooperate in communal fund-raising drives in which Palestine was a beneficiary. Questions of politics and diplomacy, however, were outside its jurisdiction. Decisions of policy once adopted by the agency were not to be challenged or contested publicly. "The Zionist Organization is married to the Agency," Warburg wrote, "and has no right to the bachelor habits of the Zionist Organization before the marriage." Warburg's code of behavior for the ZOA left no room for nationalistic agitation and certainly not for any mudslinging against non-Zionists who individually and collectively had been the favorite targets. He expected, too, that if the Zionists deviated from the code, Weizmann would hold them in line. The future of the ZOA was clear; stripped of all its functions and silenced in the marketplace, it would slowly fade away.

When Warburg cemented relations with the Brandeis group on investment plans for Palestine, he aroused the active opposition of the anti-Brandeis administration of the ZOA. Louis Lipsky countered with a recruitment drive, or roll call, for his organization, which, Warburg contended, turned away potential contributors to a joint JDC–Palestine money-raising campaign. In calling upon Weizmann to muzzle his lieutenant, Warburg also charged that Lipsky and his organization were actively obstructing the joint campaign. The ZOA could not be independent or undisciplined, he told Weizmann, and he even called for the suspension of the ZOA organ, the *New Palestine*. "It is a question of who here in America is officially at the head. . . . We have got to know who are the soldiers, who the lieutenants, who the majors, the colonels and the final head."

Weizmann defended Lipsky, the ZOA, and the functions they had to fill in the United States. Although he cabled Lipsky, presumably not to antagonize Warburg unnecessarily, he expatiated at great length and with pride to Warburg on the autonomy of the ZOA, its independence of the Jewish Agency, and on the democratic structure of the Zionist movement. (Ironically, Weizmann described the democratic institution to the American banker as a "European" product.). He, Weizmann, could not "command" the ZOA—a fact which Warburg's predecessor, Marshall, intuitively understood—nor did he even desire to do so.[29]

While Warburg stewed over Zionist noise and over Weizmann's refusal to curb it, his own actions increasingly convinced American Zionists that they had yielded too much to the non-Zionists. "Warburg . . . at this point is the final word in Zionist affairs," Stephen Wise complained bitterly. The Hebrew newspaper in Palestine, *Ha-Aretz,* called the Jewish Agency a "dictatorship" of the non-Zionists. It was Warburg and not Lipsky who led a delegation to Ramsay MacDonald when the British prime minister visited the United States in October. Bad enough that the Zionists had been eclipsed by the agency in the person of Warburg, but worse still were Warburg's public actions, which reeked of antinationalism. He opposed the roll call as well as the idea for an All-Jewish Conference in America; he sought to destroy the *New Palestine*; he organized a joint campaign for Palestine and the JDC, which gave Palestine no more than philanthrophic value; he made no effort to counter anti-Zionist attacks by Jews in the United States. The Zionists further charged that financial contributions from the non-Zionists fell far short of the anticipated mark. They, the Zionists, had compromised and sacrificed, but the debt to be paid by the non-Zionists was still outstanding.[30]

The resumption of control over the ZOA by the Brandeis group in 1930 augured well for more peaceful relations between the contending sides. But the experience of the previous months indicated that harmony could prevail only if the Zionists adhered to a minimal program.[31]

Little more than a year after the establishment of the agency, both Weizmann and Warburg resigned their positions in protest over the Passfield White Paper of 1930.[32] Yet the first months of the agency's existence had proved that only a major crisis could unite the Zionist and non-Zionist factions. In day to day operations each side steered a separate course, following its own self-interest, its own style, its own design for Jewish communal control, and its own interpretation of the meaning of Palestine for the Jews.

NOTES

1. American Jewish Committee, *The Jewish Agency and the Non-Zionists,* mimeographed pamphlet (New York, 1944), pp. 1–5; Chaim Weizmann, *Trial and Error,* 2 vols. (Philadelphia, 1949), II, 304 *et seq.*
2. The best published accounts bearing on the opinions, relations, and negotiations of Marshall and Weizmann are Charles Reznikoff, ed., *Louis Marshall, Champion of Liberty,* 2 vols. (Philadelphia, 1957), II, 731–92, and Weizmann, *Trial and Error,* II, chap. 27. See also Sam J. Chinitz, "The Jewish Agency and the Jewish Community in the United States" (M.A. thesis, Columbia University, 1959).
3. Central Zionist Archives (=CZA), S25/1422: Weizmann to Warburg, January 16, 1930.
4. Frederick H. Kisch, a high-ranking member of the Zionist Executive, commented: "Mr. Marshall's ascendancy over his group is truly astonishing. On even the smallest points concerning matters which have been especially entrusted to Mr. Warburg, Mr. [Bernard] Flexner or Dr. [Lee K.] Frankel, . . . I am unable to get any answer from any of these men unless Mr. Marshall's wishes be first secured. Hardly less remarkable than Mr. Marshall's dictatorial position in regard to his group, is the great deference and devotion which I think every member of the group entertains toward Dr. Weizmann personally, and it is difficult to apprise how much of their undoubted good-will towards our work in Palestine is a reflection of their personal attachment to the President of the Zionist Organization." CZA, 3390-I: Kisch to Weizmann et al., February 27, 1929.
5. Yonathan Shapiro, *Leadership of the American Zionist Organization, 1897–1930* (Urbana, 1971), pp. 188–99; Judd L. Teller, "Zionism, Israel and American Jewry," in *The American Jew: A Reappraisal,* ed. Oscar I. Janowsky (Philadelphia, 1964), pp. 312–15.
6. Nathan Glazer, *American Judaism,* 2d ed. (Chicago, 1972), pp. 73–75.
7. Naomi W. Cohen, *Not Free to Desist* (Philadelphia, 1972), pp. 8–9, 17, 23–24, 91–98.
8. Reznikoff, *Marshall,* II, 721–25.
9. Naomi W. Cohen, "The *Maccabaean's* Message: A Study in American Zionism until World War I," *Jewish Social Studies,* XVIII (July 1956), 166–70.
10. Paraphrased in Shapiro, *Leadership of the American Zionist Organization,* p. 203.
11. *New Palestine,* January 4–11, 1929, pp. 3–5, March 22, 1929, p. 244, July 19, 1929, p. 21; Herbert Solow, "The Era of the Agency Begins," *Menorah Journal,* XVII (November 1929), 117, 122–25; Carl Hermann Voss, ed., *Stephen S. Wise: Servant of the People* (Philadelphia, 1969), pp. 156, 168.
12. Lipsky later voiced the hope that the agency would become an "instrument for the organization of the Jews in this country." *Jewish Daily Bulletin* (=*JDB*), August 10, 1930. If the agency were to capture the masses, non-Zionist control over the community could be effectively challenged.
13. *JDB,* August 13, 1929; Zalman Yoffeh, "Peace in American Zionism," *Menorah Journal,* XIX (October 1930), 52.
14. *New Palestine,* August 23, 1929, p. 69; Solow, "Era of the Agency Begins," pp. 112–14; Warburg Papers, American Jewish Archives (=WP): Warburg to Frieda Warburg, August 13, 1929.

119

15. Solow, "Era of the Agency Begins," pp. 112, 114, 116, 120–22; *JDB*, August 13, 1929.
16. *JDB*, August 7, 8, 1929; Yoffeh, "Peace in American Zionism," p. 52.
17. *JDB*, July 22, August 14, 15, 16, 1929, June 17, 1930.
18. *Encyclopedia of Zionism and Israel*, I, 58; *JDB*, September 3, 1929, on Grand Mufti's statement.
19. CZA, S25/1422: Weizmann to Warburg, November 13, 1929.
20. Frieda Schiff Warburg, *Reminiscences of a Long Life* (New York, 1956), passim; Cyrus Adler, "Felix M. Warburg," *American Jewish Year Book*, XL (1938–39); Weizmann, *Trial and Error*, II, 309–11.
21. CZA, S25/1422: Warburg to Weizmann, February 3, 1930.
22. The written record as pieced together for this article from the files of the CZA and the WP does not appear to be complete. References in the correspondence indicate also that letters were supplemented with phone calls, for which there are no records.
23. WP: Warburg to Weizmann, May 26, 1929; to Frieda Warburg, August 13, 1929; Weizmann to Warburg, June 9, 1929.
24. WP: O. E. d'Avigdor Goldsmid to Warburg, December 12, 1929.
25. Reznikoff, *Marshall*, II, 771; WP: Lord Melchett to Warburg, November 2, 1929; Warburg to Weizmann, November 15, 1929; to Lord Melchett, November 15, 1929; CZA, S25/1422: Weizmann to Warburg, November 13, 1929; Warburg to Weizmann, December 19, 1929, February 3, 1930.
26. WP: Warburg to Weizmann, October 11, November 4, 5, 1929; to J. Goldstein, November 4, 1929; to Judah Magnes, November 12, 1929; to Lord Melchett, November 11, 15, 1929; to Max Warburg, December 24, 1929; to O. E. d'Avigdor Goldsmid, November 22, 1929; to David Brown, October 4, 1929; Lord Melchett to Warburg, November 7, 1929; proposed cable of J. Rosenberg to Weizmann, January 20, 1930; CZA, S25/1422: Weizmann to Warburg, November 13, 22, 1929, January 16, 1930; Warburg to Weizmann, February 3, 1930. Magnes' proposition appeared later in published form under the title *Like All the Nations?* (Jerusalem, 1930). The widespread opposition it evoked in Jewish circles was reported by the *JDB* in numerous articles appearing in November and December, 1929.
27. WP: Warburg to Weizmann, November 4, 15, 1929; to Max Warburg, September 18, 1929; to O. E. d'Avigdor Goldsmid, November 22, 1929; Weizmann to Warburg, November 25, 1929; CZA, S25/1422: Weizmann to Warburg, November 13, 22, 24, December 5, 1929, January 16, 21, 1930; Warburg to Weizmann, December 19, 1929, February 3, 1930; F. Rosenbluth to Palestine Zionist Executive, November 26, 1929. Louis Brandeis agreed privately that the Palestine Executive of the agency should be abolished. WP: memo of conversation with Brandeis, November 3, 1929.
28. *New Palestine*, April 4, 1930, pp. 221, 237.
29. WP: Warburg to Weizmann, November 4, 15, 1929; to H. Fleischhacker, October 24, 1929; to O. E. d'Avigdor Goldsmid, November 22, 1929; O. E. d'Avigdor Goldsmid to Warburg, December 12, 1929; CZA, S25/1422: Weizmann to Warburg, November 13, 22, December 5, 1929, January 16, 1930; Warburg to Weizmann, December 19, 1929. See also *JDB*, November 26, 1929; Shapiro, *Leadership of the American Zionist Organization*, pp. 239–40.
30. Shapiro, *Leadership of the American Zionist Organization*, p. 241; *JDB*, October 1, 1929, August 17, 1930; Yoffeh, "Peace in American Zionism," pp. 52–53, 62.
31. Yoffeh, "Peace in American Zionism," pp. 59–60.
32. *JDB*, October 21, 22, 1930.

THE JEWISHNESS OF THE JEWISH LABOR MOVEMENT IN THE UNITED STATES

By

LUCY S. DAWIDOWICZ

Yeshiva University

According to the findings of the National Jewish Population Study, nearly 90 percent of American Jews in the labor force in 1971 were white-collar workers, whereas less than 10 percent were blue-collar craftsmen and operatives. But half a century ago the proportions were different. Not only did Jewish blue-collar workers preponderate over Jewish white-collar workers, but in centers of Jewish immigrant concentration, Jewish workers were actually a plurality in the total industrial labor force.

Over 1,500,000 Jews were part of the great stream of immigrants that expanded and transformed the industrial and commercial structure of the United States. For the most part they came from the towns and villages of the Russian Pale of Settlement, from the Galician backwaters of the Hapsburg empire, and from the Moldavian heartland of Rumania. In the old country they had been artisans or merchants, but in America most of them became shopworkers, primarily in the clothing industry. (In the 1880s German Jews owned 234 of 241 clothing factories in New York City. The statistic facilitated the influx of the Russian Jews in tailoring.)

From 1881 to 1910 nearly eighteen million immigrants arrived in America. These were the "new" immigrants who came from Southern and Eastern Europe—the Italians, Slovaks, Croats, Poles, Ruthenians, Greeks, Hungarians, and Jews. The "old" immigrants who had come

121

before the Civil War from Northwestern Europe—the English, Scotch, Welsh, Irish, Germans, and Scandinavians—had become assimilated into the native population.

The new immigrants began to replace the old immigrants and the native Americans in the coal fields and in the steel mills. They crowded America's great manufacturing and mining centers—New York, Detroit, Chicago, Pittsburgh, Buffalo, Cleveland, bringing their own ethnic flavor, linguistic variety, religious practices, and political traditions, which still linger, giving each urban community its unique character. Each wave of new immigrants followed their compatriots into the same neighborhoods of the same cities and the same industries, clinging together for comfort and aid in alien urban America. Tensions multiplied between old immigrants and natives, on the one hand, and the new immigrants, on the other. Old-timers resented newcomers, aliens speaking foreign tongues, who displaced them on the job, underbid them in wages, worked longer hours, and were, to boot, full of dangerous ideologies.

The early labor movement incorporated the prejudices of its members, sharing their nativism, xenophobia, and even anti-Semitism. Narrowly construing its interests, the organized labor movement vociferously opposed free immigration. It was not unexpected, then, that the Jewish immigrants from Eastern Europe, long habituated to exclusion from social institutions and to the separatism of their own institutions, should set about forming their own "Jewish" unions. The United Hebrew Trades, organized in 1888, was a natural outgrowth of the inhospitality on the American labor scene to immigrant Jewish workers. Even a quarter of a century later, the formation of the Amalgamated Clothing Workers Union as a split-off from the United Garment Workers reflected the unabating tension between Jewish and non-Jewish workers in the men's clothing industry. Among the hat workers, too, the Jewish and non-Jewish unions had developed in mutual hostility for over thirty years, until 1934 when they finally combined, the conflicts between the "old" and "new" immigrants finally having subsided.

These Jewish unions in the garment trades, born in the struggles of the Jewish immigrant workers to find their place in America's industrial society, eventually helped to shape an enlightened trade unionism in America. In addition, they served as a way station on the road to acculturation. Fortuitously these unions became the vehicle through which the Jewish immigrant workers expressed their values and transmitted their traditions. Blending Russian radicalism with Jewish messianism, these unions sounded an alien note on the American labor scene at the turn of the century. They were too radical for the American Federation of Labor and its head, Samuel Gompers—and English Jew—who feared that the Russian Jewish socialists forever chanting about a better world were jeopardizing the here-and-now of pure-and-simple trade unionism. But the ideological vocabulary of the Russian Jewish radical movement, with its thick overlay of German philosophy, French political slogans, and English economic theories, obscured its emotional impulse and fundamental character.

The Jewish revolutionary passion—whether for socialism, anarchism, and even, finally, Communism—originated in the Jewish situation. Anti-Semitism, pogroms, discrimination had alienated the Jews from Russian society. In the revolutionary movement, the Russian Jews protested against Russia's tyranny, its denial of the common humanity of all men and particularly of Jews, and its refusal to grant the basic political rights already commonplace in most of Western Europe—freedom of speech, press, and assembly, the right to vote and to elect representatives to a legislative assembly, and freedom from arbitrary arrest. The economic goals of the radicals were in fact modest: the right to organize, to work only a twelve-hour day, for a living wage to be paid each week. The Jewish radicals in Russia were not engaged in a class war against a ruthless industrial capitalism, for it did not exist there. They hoped for a revolution that would create a constitutional state and guarantee political equality. These Jewish radicals embraced a liberal-humanitarian utopianism, rational and this-worldly, in contradistinction to the chiliastic utopianism of the *hasidim,* who computed the coming of the messiah by the extent of Jewish suffering.

In America, where they found most of their political utopia already in existence, the Jewish immigrants directed their revolutionary energy toward economic utopia. They talked in class-war terms about redistributing the wealth and taking over the means of production, but in practice they fought on the barricades only for union recognition. That was the American equivalent of the struggle for the dignity of man, the dignity of the worker, and his parity with the boss as a human being. These Russian Jewish immigrants were not really as class-conscious as they sounded and did not perceive their position in the class structure in Marxist terms. Not content to remain proletarians, many "sweated" workers quickly became entrepreneurs—from worker to subcontracter, to contractor, to manufacturer, to jobber, to wholesaler. No group had a more fluid class structure than the immigrant Russian Jews. They soon outranked all other immigrant groups in attaining, in their own generation, a socio-economic status as high as or higher than third-generation Americans.

Not all Jewish immigrants succeeded in escaping from the sweatshop. Those who remained concentrated on educating their children for something better than the shop. They formed a one-generation working class, being "neither the sons nor the fathers of workers." For themselves they sought dignity and community in their unions and the institutions associated with Jewish labor. In Russia the Jewish community had been an organic whole, and most Jews, however alienated, found their place within it, whether as upholders of the tradition or as secularists. In America, however, Jewish communal life was atomized and the immigrant had to recreate a community of his own. The Jewish labor movement and its institutions became the secular substitute for the old community. In many ways, the Jewish immigrant workers looked upon the institutions of the Jewish labor movement—the unions; their fraternal order, the Workman's Circle; their Yiddish daily newspaper, the *Forverts*—as their contribution to Jewish continuity. They brought Yiddish into their unions and sustained a Yiddish labor press for many decades. They were the consumers of a "proletarian" literature in Yiddish (largely revolutionary didacticism tempered with self-pity). They established Yiddish schools with a labor orientation. The labor movement was their vehicle to preserve Jewish values and traditions as they understood them.

François Guizot once wrote that peoples with a long history are influenced by their past and their national traditions at the very moment when they are working to destroy them. In the midst of the most striking transformations, he said, they remain fundamentally what their history has made them, for no revolution, however powerful, can wipe out long-established national traditions. The Jewish revolutionaries who fled Tsarist prisons and Siberian exile were hostile to the Jewish religious tradition, which they rejected as clerical and superstitious. They sought desperately to break out of what to them was its constricting mold. Yet even they had been shaped by that Jewish mold. David Dubinsky, at the convention of the International Ladies Garment Workers' Union (ILGWU) in May, 1962, when he was reelected president, conjured up his youthful dreams, in which Jewish messianism and the perfect society had appeared in a Jewish Labor Bundist guise. "I was sent to Siberia," Dubinsky said, "because I dreamt at that time of a better world. I dreamt of being free, of not being under the domination of a czar and dictatorship." He then recalled that his father, a religious man, used to read to him from the Bible on Saturday afternoons. In reading, his father used to stress that "a good name is better than precious oil." He had heard it so often, Dubinsky confessed, that it became part of him and of the movement with which he was identified: "When we saw the labor movement imperilled because of lack of ethics, I realized a good name is better than all the riches and all the offices to which one could aspire." Like many other Jewish labor leaders, Dubinsky had lived only briefly within the Jewish tradition he wistfully recalled, and had rebelled against it. Yet this Jewish tradition, discarded and unacknowledged, significantly affected the way the Jewish labor movement developed.

In America, shortly after World War I, the Jewish unions pioneered with their social welfare programs: medical care, housing, unemployment insurance, health insurance, vacations (and vacation resorts), and retirement benefits. They were the first to develop educational programs and the first to make philanthropy a union practice. Such activities became accepted in the general labor movement only after the New Deal. That welfare, education, and philanthropy became union concerns in Jewish unions demonstrated the ways through which the Jewish workers transferred the social responsibilities of the East European Jewish community to the labor movement. In the Jewish world of Eastern Europe, the community took care of its sick and its poor, its old and needy, and created the institutions to administer this care. This tradition the unions took over. It was only natural, then, that the ILGWU started the first union health center in 1916 and the Amalgamated started the first *gemilut-hesed* in 1923. The Amalgamated Bank was not the first labor bank; a few labor banks had been established a little earlier, in the hope that banking might yield large profits and make the unions independent. But the Amalgamated Bank was the first to offer union members low-interest loans, without collateral, which they could not get elsewhere. This was the sort of *tsedakah* which Maimonides might have designated as the highest degree.

In 1927 the Amalgamated built the first cooperative houses in New York to provide some of its members with housing that was not only decent but also attractive. Thirty years later other unions followed that example. Probably the most paradoxical episode in union housing occurred in 1957 when the ILGWU lent a corporation headed by Nelson A. Rockefeller $2.6 millions to help finance a workers' housing development in Puerto Rico.

The Russian immigrant passion for learning had been stilled partly by the revolutionary movement, which had been teacher as well as agitator, publishing popular science and philosophy along with political tracts. In America Jews had more educational opportunities. Hutchins Hapgood wrote in 1902 in *The Spirit of the Ghetto* that "the public schools are filled with little Jews; the night schools of the east side are practically used by no other race. City College, New York University, and Columbia University are graduating Russian Jews in numbers rapidly increasing." Despite classes, lectures, and debates at the settlement houses, at the Americanizing agencies like the Educational Alliance, at Cooper Union and the Rand School, the immigrant workers continued to look to the labor movement for learning, so the Amalgamated and the ILGWU gave courses in English and economics, history and philosophy. They were indeed labor colleges. It took a quarter of a century, during Roosevelt's New Deal, for other unions to sponsor labor education.

Philanthropy, too, as the Jewish unions practiced it, demonstrated the pervasiveness of Jewish tradition. For many decades, a small portion of union dues has been set aside for donations—to labor organizations, health and welfare agencies, educational and cultural institutions, civic and political causes, and finally to the ethnic beneficiaries—Jewish organizations, Italian, and later, as a consequence of ethnic succession, Negro and Puerto Rican. During the Nazi period and in the immediate postwar era, the unions distributed colossal sums of money for relief and rescue, mostly for Jews, but also for non-Jewish labor leaders and unionists. Jewish causes—the Jewish Labor Committee and the United Jewish Appeal being the top beneficiaries—enjoyed the support of the ILGWU. The Histadrut and many Israeli labor projects have been the richer for gifts from the Jewish labor movement.

The Jewish influence has perhaps been deepest in the realization of industrial peace in the garment industry, though industrial peace was not particularly a Jewish idea. The National Civic Federation, founded at the turn of the century, had brought together representatives of labor, capital, and the public to head off strikes by mediation and to use conciliation to settle disputes. But the federation had limited success, being accepted, at best, on a temporary basis by some segments of capital and labor, because labor for the most part suspected that cooperation meant sellout, and capital thought conciliation meant surrender. But the situation was different with regard to Jewish labor and capital in the clothing industry.

In 1910 the Protocol of Peace settled the "Great Revolt," an eight-week strike of some 60,000 cloakmakers in New York. The strike involved mostly Jewish workers (with a substantial minority of Italians) and nearly all Jewish manufacturers. The mediators were Jewish community leaders, many associated with the Ethical Culture Society. The most active in the settlement were Louis D. Brandeis, distinguished Jewish lawyer and political liberal; leading Boston merchant and Ethical Culturist A. Lincoln Filene, who was also a member of the National Civic Federation; pioneer Jewish social workers like Meyer Bloomfield in Boston and Henry Moskowitz in New York; and the most prominent of Jewish community leaders, Jacob Schiff and Louis Marshall, of the American Jewish Committee. The manufacturers and the union alike were torn between the militants and the compromisers. Yet a precedent-setting settlement was reached, which, besides increasing wages and decreasing hours, established a preferential union shop, a union-management joint board of sanitary control in the factories, a grievance committee, and a board of arbitration. The arbitration board was to consist of one representative of the union, one of the manufacturers, and one of the public. To be sure, the protocol broke down, was repaired, and broke down again after some years. But most scholars agree that its influence was lasting.

Several months thereafter, a four-month strike of some 8,000 workers at Hart, Schaffner and Marx, the world's largest men's clothing manufacturer, in Chicago, was settled by establishing a three-man arbitration board. As in New York, most of the workers were Jews and nearly all the manufacturers were Jewish. That settlement started a tradition of such harmonious labor-management relations between Hart, Schaffner and Marx and the Amalgamated that, in 1960, the late Meyer Kestnbaum, then president of the company, spoke at the Amalgamated's convention commemorating fifty years of collective bargaining.

Exceptional in this history of cooperation between labor and capital have been its liberal, humanitarian qualities. The unions did not "sell out" their workers nor did they "compromise" their ideals. On the contrary they succeeded in enlisting the employers' support for economic and social programs once considered eccentric and visionary, turning these into commonplace realities.

Was Jewishness the determinant? The existential Jewish situation, Jewish workers and Jewish bosses in a gentile world, must have had an effect, entangling them in one community. They could not extricate themselves, even if they chose, from each other's fate. Nor could they divest themselves of the habits and outlooks of centuries-old traditions. This is not to minimize the specific conditions in the garment industry. Professor Selig Perlman has pointed to its special character—the multitude of small shops in an industry that had not quite reached the factory stage, the cutthroat competition of highly individualistic employers, the industry's seasonal character, in which a strike meant unemployment for the worker and financial calamity for the employer.

But the Jewish differential remains. Jews in a gentile world, despite class differences, workers and bosses felt responsible for one another. The wealthy Jews may have been more sensitive to the Jewish situation, feeling their position and prestige imperiled by the flow of immigration from Eastern Europe. They were ashamed of the appearance, the language, and the manners of the Russian Jews, aghast at their political ideologies, and terrified lest the world crumble by the mad act of a Jewish radical. (The fear was not entirely unfounded: a crazy Polish anarchist had assassinated President McKinley.) Unhappily and involuntarily identified with the immigrant community, the American Jews sought to restrain and tranquilize the revolutionary temper of the immigrant workers with Americanization programs and traditional Jewish education. Afraid to be accused of burdening the public charities with immigrant Jewish paupers, they contributed to Jewish relief societies, welfare and educational institutions. But they knew that employment and labor peace were better guarantees against economic hardship than charity. In the long run, it may have been cheaper to pay higher wages than make bigger donations. Besides, labor unrest was bad for the Jewish name and for the reputation of the Jewish employers. The dignity of man and the dignity of labor were as high in the system of values of the Jewish capitalist as the Jewish worker, for it was Judaism itself which endowed labor with divine attributes ("Israel was charged to do work on the six days, just as they were ordered to rest on the seventh day"). Louis Marshall, who had not much sympathy for radical ideologies, nonetheless had a deep sense of the dignity of labor and the working man. Some months after the Protocol of Peace had been signed, he chided a manufacturer whose workers had struck: "So long as the manufacturer considers his employees as mere serfs and chattels, so long as they are considered as unworthy of being brought into conference or consultation, so long as their feelings and aspirations as human beings are lost sight of, so long will labor troubles be rampant and a feeling of dislike, if not of hatred, will be engendered against the employer in the hearts of the employees."

The practice of Judaism, as well as its principles, helped bridge the gulf between worker and boss. Sholem Asch's Uncle Moses, who brought his whole *shtetl* over to work in his factory, prayed with his workers at the evening services, if only to encourage them to work overtime. Lillian Wald reported an incident about a Jewish union leader who met Jacob Schiff. At first the union man was uncomfortable about his shabby clothing, but this was forgotten when, arguing an issue, both he and Schiff began to quote Bible and Talmud, trying to outdo each other. This kind of familiarity reduced the workers' awe for the boss and made discussion between them not only possible but even likely.

The Jewish situation had made many wealthy American Jews receptive to liberal and humanitarian ideas. They befriended the pioneering social workers of their day and were willing to learn from them about the conditions of the industrial poor. Lillian Wald in New York City taught Jacob Schiff; Judge Julian W. Mack and Jane Addams educated Julius Rosenwald in Chicago. Little wonder, then, that Schiff used to contribute anonymously, through Lillian Wald, for the relief of striking workers and sometimes even to a union treasury. Back in 1897 during a garment workers' strike, he asked Lillian Wald, ". . . is it not possible that representatives of workers, contractors, and manufacturers meet to discuss ways and means in which a better condition of affairs could permanently be brought about?"

The question may have seemed novel or naive in those days of labor's unrest and capital's indifference. Yet in a short period radical Jewish unions, conservative Jewish community leaders, and profit-seeking Jewish manufacturers answered Schiff's question affirmatively. Perhaps the most curious milestone on this path was erected in 1929, when three great Jewish financiers and philanthropists—Julius Rosenwald, Herbert H. Lehman, and Felix Warburg—lent the ILGWU $100,000 to help the union's reconstruction after its locals had been rewon from Communist capture.

The Jewish tradition of arbitration and conciliation had cut a broad swath. Originating in talmudic times, incorporated in the *Shulhan Aruch,* practiced for centuries in all Jewish communities, these principles of compromise, arbitration, and settlement were familiar and venerable to worker and boss alike. The rabbi and *dayanim* decided in the *beth din,* the religious court, but disputants frequently took their case to communal leaders who acted as arbitrators, *borerim.* The procedure must have seemed commonplace to most Jewish workers, not long from the old country and the old culture. As for the manufacturers, they, too, were responsive to the teachings that peaceful compromise was preferable to the humiliation of a court and that Jews should settle their disputes within the Jewish community.

Jewish solidarity and the Jewish tradition, albeit secularized, bred innovations in the institutions of modern American labor. The Jewish situation itself—the Jew poised on the margins of gentile society, in an existential Galut—created the energy and the impetus for those innovations. Whereas lower-class anti-Semitism had separated Jewish workers from the non-Jews, anxiety among upper-class Jews about anti-Semitism had more securely fixed their solidarity with the Jewish workers. The tension of Jews living in a gentile world has accounted for much of Jewish creativity in modern society. The Jewish labor movement, too, shared in that creativity.

A Bibliographical Note

Substantial though the literature on the Jewish labor movement is, much of it suffers from myopic perspective, partisanship, and puffery. The following selected titles represent the best in scholarly writing:

Elias Tcherikower, *The Early Jewish Labor Movement in the United States,* translated and revised from the Yiddish by Aaron Antonovsky (New York: Yivo Institute for Jewish Research, 1961).

Will Herberg, "The Jewish Labor Movement in the United States," *American Jewish Year Book,* vol. 53 (New York, 1952).

Selig Perlman, "Jewish American Unionism, Its Birth Pangs and Contributions to the General American Labor Movement," *Publication of the American Jewish Historical Society,* vol. XLI (June, 1952).

J. B. S. Hardman, "Jewish Workers in the American Labor Movement," *Yivo Annual of Jewish Social Science,* vol. VII (New York, 1952).

Judith Greenfeld, "The Role of Jews in the Development of the Clothing Industry in the United States," *Yivo Annual of Jewish Social Science,* vols. II–III (New York, 1947–48).

Moses Rischin, "The Jewish Labor Movement in America: A Social Interpretation," *Labor History,* vol. 4 (Fall, 1963).

THE AGE OF OPTIMISM IN AMERICAN JUDAISM, 1900-1920

By

EVYATAR FRIESEL

Ben-Gurion University and Hebrew University,
Israel

"What will be the future of Judaism on American soil?" asked the editor of the *American Hebrew,* celebrating in 1905 the two hundred and fiftieth anniversary of the settlement of the Jews in the United States.

> Will there be 'confusion worse confounded' out of the mingling of nationalities and ideas, a gradual renaissance as out of the fusion comes forth strength? There is every reason to anticipate a Judaism loyal to essentials, broad in sympathies, based upon everlasting foundations which shall make for human betterment. Out of the blending of divine elements[,] the crossfertilization of types, views and principles, a Jewish renaissance may be witnessed on American soil, springing from conviction and shaped by our stirring life.[1]

This optimistic vein characterized many of the written expressions of American Jews when, during the first two decades of the twentieth century, they considered their situation or thought about their future in America. It ran parallel to the optimism and the hopes of the general American society during this period, the period of the so-called Progressive movement in American public thought.[2] The purpose of the present essay is to examine the ideological and organizational developments in

American Jewish society during the period mentioned, to discover its own dynamics and its peculiar expressions.

American Jewry Organizes

In a sense, these were the years—from the 1890s till World War I— of the very creation of the American Jewish community as we know it today.[3] It was the time of Jewish mass immigration from Eastern Europe to the United States. Every boat arriving from the Old World disgorged a new legion of Jewish newcomers. Furthermore, it was a time rich in Jewish organizational undertakings. By the beginning of the twentieth century, the Jewish precursors of the real mass immigration, the newcomers of the 1880s and 1890s, had already settled in the new American milieu. Their numbers were still relatively small, but the fact that many of them had reached a degree of stability—and, in not a few cases, even prosperity—had its effect on the general Jewish atmosphere. The immigrants from Eastern Europe brought with them a well-rooted tradition of Jewish communal organization, which throve in the propitious conditions of the New World. During the first decade of the century, we witness the formation of the large *landsmanshaft* federations. The Jewish labor organizations, the United Hebrew Trades and the International Ladies Garment Workers Union, though formed earlier, developed now into powerful bodies. Other organizations were formed by the older, mostly Central European strata of American Jewry, alone or together with the newcomers. We should mention the reorganized Jewish Theological Seminary of America (1902), the American Jewish Committee (1906), the Kehillah of New York (1908), and later, during World War I, the Joint Distribution Committee, the American Jewish Congress, and the Zionist Organization of America.

Furthermore, this was an age which produced a kind of leadership American Jewry had not known before and, one ventures to say, hardly would know again. Men like Jacob H. Schiff and Louis Marshall, Judah L. Magnes, Israel Friedlaender and Solomon Schechter, the young Louis Lipsky, Louis D. Brandeis and Stephen S. Wise, Abe Cahan and Nachman Syrkin—these were personalities which both enriched and bespoke the period.

Two of the organizations formed during these years deserve special consideration due to the breadth of their scope, the amount of Jewish public attention and discussion they generated, and, as we shall see, the way they were representative of the period and its spirit: the Kehillah of New York and the American Jewish Congress.[4] The two organizations were different in their aims. The Kehillah of New York represented a great effort to organize Jewish life and institutions in the largest Jewish center of the modern age—on the eve of World War I already more than 1,000,000 Jews lived in New York. Jewish institutions of every kind and tendency were proliferating in America in general and in New York in particular. A feeling of strength and hope characterized Jewish life— side by side with a sense of disorientation and deep concern due to the proportions of the Jewish organizational problem in America, its disarray, and the questions arising from the process of Jewish immigrant adaptation to the New World. The Kehillah was intended to orient Jewish organizational life and effort in fields like education, religious institutions, and social welfare. It aimed to establish patterns of Jewish communal work geared to American conditions, supported by the whole Jewish community and directed by an accepted leadership. "Nothing Jewish should be foreign to a Jewish Community of New York City," remarked Magnes in 1909.[5]

The American Jewish Congress differed from the Kehillah by being first and foremost a political body. The tasks of the Congress and its composition were fiercely discussed in the Jewish community during the years 1914–16. In its final form, as accepted in 1916 by the different sections of American Jewry, the American Jewish Congress represented a compromise which limited its time of existence and its range of tasks: the Congress was to appear, through its elected representatives, before the Peace Conference to be called after the World War, to act there for Jewish rights in Eastern Europe and in Palestine. After the Peace Conference, the American Jewish Congress was to be disbanded.[6] But this compromise was remote from the designs envisioned by the original sponsors of the Congress idea—the designs we are trying to define and to analyze in this paper. Louis D. Brandeis, certainly the most forceful figure of the first phase of the Congress movement, stressed these aims in a most unequivocal form: "The Congress is not an end in itself. It is an incident of the organization of the Jewish people—an instrument through which their will may be ascertained, and when ascertained, may be carried out. In order that their will may be ascertained truly the Congress must be democratically representative. . . . In order that the support may be adequate, the Congress must also be preceded by such organization of the Jews of America as will ensure their cooperation in carrying out such measures as shall be decided upon. The Congress is not to be an exalted mass-meeting. It is to be the effective instrument of organized Jewry of America."[7] The original concept of the American Jewish Congress had involved a thrust toward the internal unification of American Jewry, a thrust which was lost in the final compromise accepted in the middle of 1916.

Their differences notwithstanding, it is clear that both organizations had important points in common. Both embodied organizational principles quite divergent from the general congregational and centrifugal tendencies in American Jewish life.[8] Both were conceived as bodies aspiring to centralized organizational power, each of course in its own field of activity. Furthermore, from the social point of view, both were able to achieve a meeting and collaboration between the two principal groups in American Jewry in those days. One group was the older stratum, the so-called "Germans"—Jews of Central European origin, many of them settled in the United States since around the middle of the nineteenth century (considerably earlier in some instances), middle-class and in many cases quite prosperous, generally Reform in their religious tendency. The other group was the immigrants from 1881 on, the so-called "Russians"—Jews of East European origin, generally Yiddish-speaking, in many cases religiously orthodox, but in many other cases socialist, mostly proletarians or lower middle-class, most often settling in the large Jewish ghettolike concentrations developing in the principal urban centers of the East Coast.

The meeting of these two groups in the new Jewish organizational initiatives of the first two decades of the century deserves further elaboration.

"Germans" and "Russians" in the American Jewish Community

The meeting—or perhaps we should say, the confrontation—between "Germans" and "Russians" in American Jewish communal life is accepted as one of the central developments in the American Jewish historical experience during the years under consideration. Most Jewish historians, though well aware of the importance to be assigned the meeting between the two groups, have tended to accept it as a natural development, or to explain it in terms of generalities like the growth of a sense of responsibility on the part of the "German" Jewish leadership towards their brethren, the new East European immigrants. To be sure, a sense of responsibility *was* expressed, but it may be asked to what extent it was a "natural" development. Jewish historical experience shows how difficult the settlement of Jewish newcomers was in already existing Jewish communities. The tension between the refugees from Spain and the Jewish communities in whose midst they resettled themselves after their expulsion in 1492, the contempt and separatism which characterize relations between Sephardim and Ashkenazim in seventeenth- and eighteenth-century Amsterdam, or between the German Jews and the "Ost-Juden" in Germany from the end of the nineteenth century on— these examples and others suggest that there was something peculiar about the "German"-"Russian" meeting in America.

Indeed, the relationship between the two groups was highly complex, filled with ambivalent tendencies in which impulses and expressions of mutual repulsion and mutual attraction were interwoven in contradictory patterns. Generally speaking, the "German" leaders active in bringing about a rapprochement with the newer element had a very poor opinion of public life among the East Europeans. When Louis Marshall undertook in 1902 the establishment of a Yiddish newspaper in New York, he explained what he had in mind: "It is understood that the people whom I represent are to have control of the newspaper and are to dictate its policy which is to make the paper everything that the existing Yiddish newspapers are not, namely, clean, wholesome, religious in tone; the advocate of all that makes good citizenship, and so far as politics are concerned, absolutely independent." [9] Furthermore, the "German" leadership had an almost instinctive horror of things like Jewish mass-participation or mass-demonstration, and they were able and ready to cite any number of reasons and arguments to justify their view: improper circumstances, the quest for efficient activity, opposition to demagoguery, un-Americanism, corrupt power politics, and so on.[10] Was it necessary for the American Jewish Committee to "represent the [East European] riff raff and everybody?" exclaimed Adolf Kraus, president of the B'nai B'rith, in 1906. "If this [new American Jewish] Committee represents the representative and high class [German] Jews of America, that is enough." [11] Or, as Marshall put it in 1915: "I repeat what I have said over and over again, that I would consider the holding of [an American Jewish Congress] deplorable, because worse than useless. It might become positively detrimental to all that we hold dear. The agitation [for a congress] is not a general one. It is that of a body of noisy, blatant demagogues, principally nationalists and radical socialists. . . . We shall certainly not consider the calling of a congress, or of any meeting which will result in indiscreet public speeches and inflammatory rhetoric." [12]

Israel Friedlaender's sense of danger and urgency seems understandable, when he wrote, also in 1915: "An enormous amount of explosives had been accumulating between the two sections which if lit by a spark might have wrecked the edifice of American Israel while yet in the process of construction." [13]

The complexity of the relationship between the two parts of the Jewish community expressed itself in the fact that, besides the antagonism, there were forces of mutual attraction acting upon them. After all, Marshall *did* found a Yiddish newspaper in 1902. He had the worst of opinions about the Yiddish press of New York, but he had learned enough Yiddish to understand it and was ready to try to improve that situation. There are further examples. A year before, a group of "German" Jewish notables— Jacob H. Schiff, Felix M. Warburg, Leonard Lewisohn, Mayer Sulzberger, Daniel Guggenheim, Cyrus Adler, and Louis Marshall—most of them Reform in religious affiliation, had decided to reorganize and strengthen an almost moribund rabbinical institution of Orthodox tendency, the Jewish Theological Seminary, and to that end had brought over from England one of the best-known Jewish scholars of the time, Solomon Schechter. Their intention was to transform the seminary into an instrument capable of working towards the Americanization of the future religious leadership of the East European community.[14]

The new attitude of the older part of the Jewish community to the East European immigrants had been slowly developing since the last decade of the nineteenth century. Its growth is clearly shown in the change of attitude of the older Jewish settlers to the immigration question. At the beginning of the Jewish mass immigration to the United States, prominent figures or organizations of the older Jewish settlement had tried either to ignore the newcomers or at least to bring about some selection of the candidates for immigration, or had even attempted to prevent their coming to America. In 1881, for instance, writing to the Alliance Israélite Universelle, the directors of the Russian Emigrant Relief Fund of New York used every conceivable argument against the sending of more East European Jews to the United States, and threatened to return to Europe those considered unfit for American conditions. Any increase in the 3,000 to 5,000 Jews arriving annually "would render the burden upon us absolutely intolerable." [15]

A generation later, however, in 1907, we find Louis Marshall, already by then the most prominent figure in the recently founded American Jewish Committee, trying to enlist the support of Governor Page of Vermont for the Committee's efforts against the Immigration Bill then being discussed by the United States Congress. After explaining the different arguments against limitation of immigration, Marshall added, rather meaningfully: "You would not only place me, but many of my friends who are deeply concerned in the outcome of this legislation, under lasting obligation to you, if you would support us in this endeavor to defeat a measure which, if it becomes a law, will produce incalculable harm . . ." [16]

How explain the fact that in the span of one generation people from the same "German" Jewish group made a complete volte-face on the sensitive issue of Jewish immigration? The significance of the change is even more striking, when we note the discrepancy between Jews and non-Jews regarding attitudes towards immigration. In the 1890s, "America had moved from admission to restriction, while representatives of the Jewish community took the opposite viewpoint." [17]

Several possibilities arise when we try to understand the attitude of the older Jewish settlers. Certain problems had been forecast at the beginning of the 1880s by the older Jewish settlers as a consequence of the mass immigration. Did these problems not, after all, materialize? They certainly did. Even more, we do not overstate the case in saying that the actual troubles caused by the East European Jewish immigrants far surpassed anything that people a generation earlier would have anticipated. Then, perhaps the numerical scope of the Jewish immigration remained low? We know that it did not. The directors of the Russian Emigrant Relief Fund had, in 1881, set a limit of 3,000 to 5,000 immigrants a year. But in 1907, when the Immigration Bill was being considered, Jewish immigration had climbed to some 150,000 a year.

In other words, if the reasoning of the leaders of American Judaism had depended on or reflected only the actual developments in Jewish immigration between 1881 and 1907, their position in 1907 would have been one of absolute opposition to the coming of more immigrants. That would also have been the case if their attitude had reflected, as it did in so many other things, the general American attitude. Instead, the contrary happened. In 1906 the otherwise cautious Jacob Schiff was ready to think and even to plan in terms of a *minimum* immigration of two million Jews over the next five to ten years! [18]

How are we to explain this peculiar development in American Jewry, a development which brought together disparate trends in the Jewish community, different social elements, and created the basis for the rich organizational growth of the age? It is suggested that only an idea, an idea about Israel in America, its characteristics and its future, would have been able to generate the communal forces ready and able to act against accepted and "natural" trends both in American and in Jewish life. Only an idea would have been capable of enlisting a gifted leadership and hundreds of thousands of followers, of building bridges over so many antagonistic motives, of producing communal organizations of a new type, and of bringing about an age in American Jewry which clearly differs from the periods before and after.

The Idea of Optimism

The idea in question regarded a vision of Jewish life in America: that America, being the land of human equality and freedom, held a brilliant future in store here for Jews and for Judaism—even more, that the concretization of these hopes was at hand, that they could be realized by American Jews if the right steps were taken. This optimism reflected similar trends in American public thought during this era, the era of Progressivism. More than a well-defined political theory, Progressivism seems to have been a kind of mentality pervading American public life from the end of the nineteenth century till the outbreak of World War I. As frame of mind it was full of hope, future-directed, believing in human progress, stressing man's positiveness. Its most typical written document, Herbert Croly's *Promise of American Life* (1909), influenced deeply the political thought and action of President Theodore Roosevelt, certainly one of the most representative figures of the Progressive spirit in America.[19]

American Jewry absorbed the spirit and the tendencies of American life through the thick lens of a community of highly developed spiritual and ideological sensitivity, and translated that spirit and those tendencies into terms adapted to its own internal trends. The Jewish community was exceptionally well prepared for the Progressive frame of mind. Jewish immigrants arriving from the Old World came, in a sense, ready for the philosophy of optimism: already in the Jewish villages of Eastern Europe America was seen as the land of hope and opportunity. This kind of preparation may explain the absolute acceptance of the idea of optimism, in its different Jewish formulations, by all the segments of American Jewry at the time. Thus, Solomon Schechter, head of the traditionalist Jewish Theological Seminary of America, spoke of the United States as "the only place on our globe where Israel can dwell in security and look forward to a great future. If there is a spot in the world where Jewish learning, which has so often migrated from land to land, should at last find a resting place and develop freely in accordance with its own laws, it will be America." The same tone is to be found among the leaders of Reform Judaism: "The center of gravity of Jewish life has shifted to America. We are witnessing a new phase of our centuried history in the making," wrote Rabbi David Philipson. "The Jew must become an American in order to gain the proud self consciousness of the free born man," stressed Rabbi Isaac M. Wise. "American Judaism, the soul and spiritual essence of American Jewry, appears to me to be a theme so grand and rich, so bright in outlook, and so suggestive of hope and unlimited potentialities, that the pen quivers and the tongue falters in the endeavor to do it justice," affirmed the Reform theologian Kaufmann Kohler. And he went on:

> Ever since I was privileged to imbibe the invigorating air of this God-blessed land of liberty, American Israel appeared to me as a new type of Joseph, 'the prince among his brethen,' whom Divine Providence entrusted with the mission of not merely preserving the *lives* of the tens of thousands who came to seek bread and shelter under the starry banner, but of reviving the *spirit* of God's chosen people, and of endowing them with new hope and a wider outlook, with a deeper comprehension of their prophetic vision and their world-duty.[20]

The idea about the place and the future of Jews and Judaism in America was so generally accepted and so commonly stressed that it may be asked if we are not dealing merely with some accepted form of speech or with mere lip-service to accepted standards, rather than a factor blessed with a vitality and an impelling force of its own. Several facts seem to militate against such a conclusion. There was in the tendencies of the period too much which ran against accepted criteria and experience. We have already mentioned the immigration question, and the reorganization of the Orthodox-minded Jewish Theological Seminary by "German" leaders of Reform orientation, because they thought it necessary for the future of American Judaism. The same questions also arise regarding the two organizations which have been described as the most typical of the Age of Optimism—the New York Kehillah and the American Jewish Congress. Both were centralistic and non-parochial, therefore different from, even adverse to, established organizational tradition in America.

Furthermore, it should be noted that, in sharp contrast to the far-flung aims both organizations proclaimed, each was able to attain only very modest practical achievements. The American Jewish Congress never realized the great design proclaimed by Brandeis in 1915–16, of being "the effective instrument of organized Jewry in America." As for the achievements of the Kehillah, the field in which it achieved its best results was Jewish education.[21] To be sure, its Bureau of Jewish Education, inspired by the originality and the dynamism of Samson Benderly, made a contribution of primordial importance to Jewish and Hebrew education in the United States. Benderly and his associates laid the foundations of a new kind of Jewish education in America, and from the point of view of our Israel-inspired generation, their ideas were of great pioneering significance. But the whole picture is apt to change if we consider the Bureau of Jewish Education in terms, not of ideological value for the future, but of actual significance and achievement in its own time. How did the educational plans of the Bureau of Education look in the eyes of its own generation—the generation whose children these educational ideas were supposed to reach? How did *they* react, the anti-nationalist Jews uptown, or the Orthodox downtown, or the Jewish socialists—together certainly forming the great majority of New York Jewry? What use had *they* for the kind of Jewish education preached by the Kehillah's Bureau of Education? Even Schechter, who though American-oriented and religious was at least sympathetic to Zionism and certainly interested in Hebrew culture, sharply opposed Benderly's educational theories.[22] In short, could it not be said that both the New York Kehillah and the American Jewish Congress were more organizational visions than actual organizational realizations?

Putting together all these considerations, it seems difficult not to think of and to look for the existence of an ideal trend underlying the thoughts and the acts of American Jewish communal life during the first two decades of the century. The idea suggested—the idea regarding the future of American Judaism—must indeed have been of great internal strength, otherwise it would be hard to explain a historical situation whose internal contradictions and opposing social forces did not result in a social stagnation or even distintegration, but on the contrary brought about an age of social dynamism and communal creativity.

The most elaborate exposition regarding the future of American Judaism was done by the American Zionists during the first decade of the

century. Their most articulate spokesman was certainly Israel Friedlaender, a man of East European birth and West European education,
who had arrived in the United States in 1903.[23] As teacher of Bible and
Jewish philosophy at the Jewish Theological Seminary, he was considered
one of that institution's outstanding figures. Well versed in Jewish history,
Friedlaender analyzed the question of Jewish life in America in the light
of two historical experiences: that of Judaism in Moslem Spain during
the Middle Ages, and that of Western European Jewry in the Modern
Age. Jewish history in the period of the Emancipation,, he said
had indeed displayed characteristics which aroused doubts regarding the
future of Judaism under modern conditions. The Jew had participated in
modern general culture at the expense of his Jewishness. The mistake, as
he saw it, was that Emancipation Jewry had reduced itself, or had allowed itself to be reduced, to the narrow definition of a religious denomination:

> It was the fatal mistake of the period of emancipation, a mistake which
> is the real source of all the consequent disasters in modern Jewish life,
> that, in order to facilitate the fight for political equality, Judaism was
> put forward not as a culture, as the full expression of the inner life of the
> Jewish people, but as a creed, as the summary of a few abstract articles
> of faith, similar in character to the religion of the surrounding nations.[24]

From the narrow point of view afforded by immediate historical experience, then, it would appear that the solution to the dilemma of
Jewish life in modern society would be either a return to the ghetto or
complete absorption into the non-Jewish world—the first solution being,
in Friedlaender's opinion, impossible, and the other unacceptable. But
Friedlaender was sure that it was possible for the Jews "to participate in
the life and the culture around them and yet remain Jewish," for

> the great and glorious Jewish-Arabic period deals a deathblow to the
> dilemma besetting the problem of Judaism, and is in itself an overwhelm-
> ing proof and shining example of the compatibility of an active participa-
> tion of the Jews in the life and culture of the nations around them, with a
> strong, vigorous, genuine development of Judaism.

As Friedlaender understood it, "the amount of freedom enjoyed by the
Jews of the Arabic epoch was in no way inferior to that of our own.
The Jews took an honorable and energetic part in the economic, social

and political development of the Eastern, as well as the Western, Cali-
fate." And he contended that "everything that constitutes the pride of
the Jews found their greatest and most brilliant representatives in that
period, and the profound attachment to Judaism went hand in hand
with a noble enthusiasm for everything noble outside Judaism." [25]

Friedlaender elaborated his theme, linking it to Jewish conditions in the
United States: "If such a Judaism, presenting a harmonious union between the culture of the Jewish people and that of the other nations is
possible in the Dispersion—and that it is possible is convincingly shown
by our history—the only place where it has a full chance of realization
is America." America, as even the Zionists would have to admit,

> is fast becoming the center of the Jewish people in the Diaspora. . . .
> America has every chance of also becoming the center of Judaism, of the
> spiritual life of the Jewish people in the Dispersion. . . . America presents
> a happy combination of so manifold and favorable circumstances as have
> seldom, if ever, been equalled in the history of the Diaspora. It has the
> numbers which are necessary for the creation of a cultural center. It
> possesses the economic prosperity indispensable for a successful spiritual
> development. The freedom enjoyed by the Jews is not the outcome of
> emancipation, purchased at the cost of national suicide, but the natural
> product of American civilization. The idea of liberty as evolved by the
> Anglo-Saxon mind does not merely mean, as it often does in Europe, the
> privilege of selling new clothes instead of old, but signifies liberty of con-
> science, the full, untrammeled development of the soul as well as the
> body. The true American spirit understands and respects the traditions
> and associations of other nationalities, and on its vast area numerous
> races live peaceably together, equally devoted to the interests of the land.[26]

For Friedlaender, these ideas did not constitute some utopian program,
but a reality taking shape before his very eyes and the eyes of his generation: "He who feels the pulse of American-Jewish life can detect,
amidst numerous indications to the contrary, the beginnings of a Jewish
renaissance, the budding forth of a new spirit." The noblest and best
of American Jews displayed "larger Jewish sympathies, a broader outlook
on Jewish life, a deeper understanding of the spiritual interest of Judaism
than most of their brethren of the Mosaic persuasion in the lands of
assimilation and emancipation." American Jews were "fully alive to the
future of their country as a center of Jewish culture." Everywhere Friedlaender perceived "the evidence of a new life. To be sure, we are only at
the beginning. Gigantic and complicated tasks confront us in the future. . . . But we are on the right road." American Jews "would take to

heart the lesson afforded by modern Jewish history in Europe." They would "not bury Judaism in synagogues and temples, nor imprison it in charitable institutions." They would "work and live for a Judaism which will compass all phases of Jewish life and thought . . ." [27]

Friedlaender's vision of the Jewish future in America gives rise to a question: If Judaism should vindicate such great hopes, was it not likely that the civic obligations of the Jew toward the American state and the general American society would suffer? Or, as he put it, "is Judaism, and a Judaism of the kind advocated above, compatible with Americanism?" Friedlaender was sure that the blending of both was possible and desirable.

> Judaism and Americanism will not be intersecting, but concentric circles. In the great palace of American civilization we shall occupy our own corner, which we will decorate and beautify to the best of our taste and ability, and make it not only a center of attraction for the members of our family, but also an object of admiration for all the dwellers of the palace.[28]

Friedlaender expressed these ideas in December 1907, when he had been in America only about four years. It is difficult to believe that he would have been able in such a short time to produce a philosophy of his own regarding Jewish life and the Jewish future in America. It seems much more plausible that his ideas were representative rather than original, and that they reflected a trend of thought current among the American Jewish thinkers and leaders with whom Friedlaender was connected. As a matter of fact, a similar trend is easily recognizable in the writings, speeches, and actions of nearly all the Jewish figures connected with the new Jewish communal initiatives of those days, men like Louis Marshall, Judah L. Magnes, Jacob H. Schiff, and Cyrus Adler, among others.

A further step in the chain of thought we have been exploring is discernible in those days: the idea that Jewish consciousness is the moral duty of the American Jew. Magnes, speaking in 1909, said of the Jew in America, "the more of a Jew he is, the more of a man he is likely to be." Magnes was referring to the danger inherent in the wrong kind of Americanization, one which was apt to induce "dejudaization." [29] The same theme was further elaborated by Louis Lipsky: "If you are Jewish noblemen, American citizens, you are bound to heed the call to defend the interests of Jewish character, of Jewish ideals, of Jewish aspirations." [30]

Some years later, in 1915, Louis D. Brandeis stressed that "we must protect America and ourselves from demoralization, which has to some extent already set in among American Jews." And further: "The sole bulwark against demoralization is to develop in each new generation of Jews in America a sense of *noblesse oblige*. That spirit can be developed in those who regard their people as destined to live and to live with a bright future." [31] It should be mentioned that Magnes, Lipsky, and Brandeis were all Zionists, and that for all of them the moral strength of American Jewry was connected with the development of some form of Zionism among American Jews. But the rationale of each seems well rooted in the general atmosphere of American Judaism of this period, in the sense that their ideas were clearly in harmony with the premises of the Age of Optimism.

The Sponsors of the Idea of Optimism

Three groups in American Jewry may be seen as the principal sponsors of the trend of optimism, in both its ideological and its practical expression: the leadership of the East European community, the Zionists, and the heads of the older "German" Jewish community. Their arrival at a basis of common thought and action should not conceal the fact that each group was driven by a different set of motives.

The standpoint of the large mass of Jewish newcomers, who formed the rank and file of the organizational initiatives of those days, was relatively simple. Despite the amazing internal diversification among the "Russian" immigrants—Jews from different parts of Eastern Europe, religious Jews, socialists of every shade, etc.—they all shared a basic set of beliefs regarding America. Living apart in their own quarters with its language and its atmosphere, they regarded America as the land of hope and opportunity. True, life was hard, but there was always the chance that one would "do well," as so many had before. Economic prosperity, cultural development, organizational expression were among the possibilities or the rights of the "Russian" Jew in America. Their optimism may be seen as a continuation of the expectations they had brought from the Old World, as a reflection of the viewpoint of more settled groups in American Jewish society, and as an expression of the optimism characteristic of America in general before World War I. In spite of the many difficulties immigrants faced in the New World, the Yiddish epithet for the United States—*die goldene medine,* the golden land—remained the most succinct expression of their hopes.[32]

The view of the American Zionists had its own causes. Despite the fact that before World War I organized Zionism was an insignificant factor in American Jewish life, Zionists were most prominent in many of the new communal enterprises of the age. Magnes, the driving personality in the New York Kehillah, had been secretary of the Federation of American Zionists. Friedlaender, another Federation leader, was also active in the Kehillah. Bernard Semel, one of Magnes' important associates in the Kehillah, was a prominent Zionist, as were others among his collaborators. The Kehillah's whole Department of Education was a Zionist preserve, from the head of the department, Samson Benderly, on down.[33] Not only Schechter and Friedlaender, but almost all the other teachers at the Jewish Theological Seminary, were Zionists, and most of the students as well. The American Jewish Congress movement was and remained Zionist-dominated. The communal impact of Zionist activists was a phenomenon which certainly deserves attention.

During the first decade of the century, American Zionists like Friedlaender, Magnes, Friedenwald, Schechter, and others had developed a particular line of Zionist thought. They considered themselves cultural Zionists, spoke with admiration of Ahad Haam, and adopted many of his ideas regarding the development of a spiritual center in Palestine. But it may be said that they were equally close to the viewpoint of the historian Simon Dubnow, who advocated the idea of Diaspora Jewish autonomy. Again, Friedlaender was the leading thinker in the group, and he maintained contact with both Ahad Haam and Dubnow, some of whose writings he had translated from Hebrew and Russian.

The development of the "cultural" trend in American Zionism had its own logic. "Political" Zionism had failed in the United States due, among other things, to the fact that one of its central motives—the "negation of the Diaspora"—had a most restricted appeal and very little possibility of success under American Jewish conditions at the time. It is not surprising that soon after Herzl's death in 1904, American Zionists developed a line of reasoning attuned to the realities of the American Jewish environment and able to overcome the handicaps of classical, European-rooted Zionist thought. This was done by the "cultural" group.

From Ahad Haam the American cultural Zionists adopted their emphasis on the spiritual and revitalizing meaning of Zionism. From Dubnow they adopted a positive attitude toward the Diaspora and were, like him, community-oriented. Since Ahad Haam was both pessimistic about the future of the Diaspora and indifferent to communal matters, it may be said that Dubnow's influence on the thinking of the American cultural Zionists was no less, and perhaps even more, important than the influence of Ahad Haam.[34] The result was something of a contradiction: a Zionist attitude that prepared Zionist leaders for activity outside the Zionist movement and even directed them to communal work. As Magnes said in 1908, when at the eleventh annual convention of the Federation of American Zionists he laid down the office of secretary, shortly before the beginning of the Kehillah movement:

> I feel that I shall be able to do more for our Federation and our movement if I am relieved of the duties which have been mine during the past three years. Our Zionism must mean for us Judaism in all of its phases, Zionism is a complete and harmonized Judaism. Nothing Jewish, whether it be the Jewish land, the Jewish language, the Jewish religion, the Jewish people, can be foreign to a Zionist.[35]

For Zionist activists and the Zionist tradition of militancy to be channeled into general Jewish endeavors was no novelty in Europe.[36] Even so, it seems that only in the United States will we find so extensive a development of Zionist ideology justifying the application of Zionist effort to extra-Zionist Jewish communal causes like the New York Kehillah or the American Jewish Congress. To be sure, many of the "Russian" Zionist activists of New York took part in the work of the Kehillah, but it is almost exclusively among the Zionists of the new cultural trend that we recognize reasons of principle.[37]

The "German" Jewish group, from which the actual leadership of American Jewry came during this period, had quite complex causes underlying its participation in the organizational enterprise of the age. One possible way to understand it is to review some of the aspects of the "German"-"Russian" relationship. For Jews of East European origin, the "Germans" were objects both of interest and of antagonism. The newcomers mocked what they considered their doubtful religion, resented their superior airs, and looked with suspicion on their patronizing charity, mixed with "Americanizing" efforts.[38] On the other hand, the new immigrant, looking around for an example and a model of success in the New World, saw in the prosperous "German" Jew the most obvious case at hand. For the newcomers, the old-stock American, generally Anglo-Saxon in origin and Protestant in religion, was a remote figure, the gentile lord of the land, as it were; his values and manners were nothing a simple *Yid* could have anything to do with. Not so with regard to the "German" Jew: he was a fellow Jew and a former immigrant; he had learned English and become Americanized; he represented a goal which with perspicacity, luck, and hard work could be attained.

The question however is, how "American" had they already become, these Jews of Central European background, whose settlement dated back to the mid-nineteenth century and who were now to undertake the task of teaching the "Russian" newcomers the secrets of the "American way of life"? They certainly were proud of their American citizenship, but they also were proud of their German origin, of their German culture, and of their Jewish-German religion. It has been convincingly shown how much Jewish religion in America during the second part of the nineteenth century was built upon Jewish-German bases.[39] Furthermore, "German" Jews socialized very much with German-American gentile society.[40] And lastly, an analysis of their ideas about citizenship, fatherland, and national loyalty shows that they tended to think in terms that remained quite German, even if applied now to life in the United States.[41]

There were, of course, differences among the "Germans." For instance, the American-born Marshall was clearly more Americanized than the German-born Schiff. As a group, they were certainly much more "American" than the Jewish immigrants from Eastern Europe. But from the point of view of an old-stock American, the "German" Jews looked, we may well suspect, like a group of foreigners, even if quite a distinguished and acceptable one. Therefore, it may be assumed that the American Jews of the older settlement had their own problems of Americanization, their own social goals, aimed logically enough at acceptance by the old Anglo-Saxon American society. But from the 1880s on, and in some cases even earlier, social discrimination began haunting the prosperous Jewish merchants of German origin to a degree previously unknown in the American Jewish experience.[42] The "German" Jew certainly felt the affront of the new limitations much more than the "Russian" newcomer did—after all, few "Russian" Jews of this period would ever have thought about seeking admittance to one of the exclusive centers of Old America.

It has been said that, in comparison to the volatility and mobility of the new immigrant Jewish community, the "Germans" were stable and established. Indeed, established they may have been, but how secure did they feel? It seems that they had their own problem of social and spiritual security. It was a problem different in character from that of the "Russians." It was less visible, more diffused, more sophisticated, less easily defined, but certainly no less deep than the problem which the "Russian" quarter experienced. There is reason to believe that this feeling of social uncertainty contributed to the ambivalent trend which brought the Jews of "German" origin into their complex partnership with the new East European immigrant community. One suspects that if they had felt differently regarding their social position in American society, no partnership of the same significance with the "Russians" would have arisen. After all, it should be remembered, one group in American Jewry *did* remain relatively aloof from the internal developments which went on in the community and brought about what has been called the Age of Optimism. The Sephardic Jews, those Jews who claimed Iberian-Dutch origin and had long been settled in the country, tended to remain aloof. It is significant that the Sephardim constituted a subgroup of American Jewish society not so much in the ethnic as in the social sense. Ethnically, the American Sephardim were a mixed lot, with many ancestors of German or even Polish origin,[43] but they were definitely different in the *social* sense—they were a natural and distinguished part of traditional American society. Well integrated, well accepted in the best circles of Old America, these Sephardim had no "Jewish problem" to deal with and no feeling of uncertainty to push them into a search for solutions. They could afford to remain aloof from the experience and the troubles of the Jewish community at large, even if the consequence was their non-participation as a group in the great communal efflorescence of the time.

To look for a clear turning point in the attitude of the "German" Jewish group to the "Russian" newcomers, then, we should consider the change of attitude, mentioned before, to the question of Jewish immigration. The older Jewish settlers had attempted, in effect, to limit the coming of masses of East European Jews. But the pressures in the Russian empire had kept increasing, and after the expulsion of the Jews from Moscow in 1891, there remained very little hope of diverting, or stopping, or subjecting to selectivity, the ever-rising flow of Jewish immigrants. Gentile America tended to view the Jews as one group. Fine distinctions between the different waves of Jewish immigrants, between "Germans" and "Russians," were generally too subtle for an American society already overflowing with immigrants of every possible origin. The "German" Jews found themselves forced to recognize the realities of a large and ever-swelling Jewish immigrant community: they had to confront the fact that, in the eyes of America, they were considered part of the immigrant community, even if a "better" part. The solution was to welcome the newcomers and to try to "ameliorate" their condition through "Americanizing" them.

This new kind of interest in the immigrants had a formative influence upon the "German" Jews as well and brought about the development among them of an easily recognizable group of communal leaders.[44] They were already recognized by the "Russian" Jewish community, and called *Yahudim*—a term typical of New York Jewry at the beginnings of the century. Headed by Jacob H. Schiff and Louis Marshall, this close-knit group of "German" Jewish notables put its clear imprint on every major Jewish communal initiative of that time.

The reorganization and enlarging of the Educational Alliance of New York by Jacob H. Schiff, in 1893, may be considered one of the first practical steps of the new approach of the older Jewish stratum to the newcomers. As a result of the peculiar dynamics of the American Jewish situation, once the first step had been made, further steps appeared to be indispensable. A momentum was created as every action generated further actions, and in the spiritual atmosphere of the Age of Optimism the whole building of Jewish communal enterprise of this period began to be erected.

We have not attempted to analyze all the positions and motivations of those who participated in the enterprises of the Age of Optimism. There were other tendencies—for instance, those of the Jewish left-wing groups. It is also evident that all the parties did not think alike, but they were all held together by a similar feeling of hope regarding the great future in store for Jewry and Judaism in America. Even if so optimistic a conception may seem to us today rather naive, in its own time it was capable of inspiring enthusiasm and devotion, of diminishing differences and divergences in the Jewish community, of stressing common values, of creating a whole movement in American Jewry expressed in a rich array of organizations.

The End of the Age of Optimism

Parallel to the great developments in Jewish communal life during the first two decades of the century ran a strain of general instability in American Jewry. It is enough to observe the mutations in the ideas and positions of the more prominent Jewish figures during that time to get some measure of the changes that went on in American Jewish life in general.

For instance, Jacob H. Schiff, the proud patrician leader of American Jewry, who in 1907 had sternly upbraided Solomon Schechter for the latter's rather diluted statement of allegiance to a rather diluted Zionist faith, would himself ten years later tap humbly on the doors of the Zionist organization—and be rejected.[45] Louis D. Brandeis, who until 1912 hardly ever remembered that he was a Jew, found himself transformed during World War I into the head of the American Zionist movement, only to retire to the background, first by his own will in 1916 and later, in 1921, by the will of the rank and file of the movement. Judah L. Magnes, who in 1908 was one of the most representative figures in the Jewish community, perhaps the only figure equally accepted by the "uptown" *Yahudim* and the "downtown" *Yidn*, had burned out by 1919 and, in fact, left the United States in 1922. Louis Lipsky, the most interesting figure in American Zionism before 1914, had lost most of his originality by the time he rose to national eminence in the twenties. Louis Marshall, who again and again had opposed what he took to be the demagoguery of the Jewish masses, found himself in 1919 at the head of the delegation of the democratically elected American Jewish Congress to the Peace Conference in Paris and, even more, working hard for Jewish rights in Eastern Europe on a national basis—an idea he had regarded with suspicion for years. Jewish communal life in those days was, then, of a fierce and sometimes burning dynamism, and its prominent participants were apt to undergo changes in public strength and position that apparently were beyond their control and sometimes even beyond their understanding.

Deep changes occurred in the tenor of American public life after World War I, changes that were reflected in the life of the Jewish community as well. The hopes and the atmosphere that had been symbolized by the Progressivist movement in America waned. The twenties in America are remembered as a period of economic prosperity, even of cultural fertility, but of political and public feebleness. The 1920s are not a period of which American historians are proud: "The Tribal Twenties," "Success without Leadership," "American Loses Confidence"—these are the epithets historians have given the 1920s.[46]

The same feebleness observable in general public life seems to have afflicted Jewish life as well: there are many indications that the twenties were a period of communal crisis for American Jewry. The New York Kehillah collapsed around 1922. The Zionist Organization of America, torn apart by the "Brandeis-Weizmann struggle" in 1921, was unable to rally again and remained in a state of demoralization for the next decade.[47] The second American Jewish Congress, called into being in May 1920, immediately after the formal dissolution of the original Congress, limped along, a mere shadow of the former organization.[48] The B'nai B'rith underwent a serious crisis during the second half of the twenties.[49] The Jewish labor movement was torn apart by the struggle between Socialists, Communists, and Independents.[50] The American Jewish Committee, which due to its uniform composition and compact organization was relatively immune to organizational problems, lived through one of its worst periods during the twenties: it was unable to cope with the rising tide of anti-semitism in the United States and lost the battle against immigration restrictions.[51]

All these changes reflected the general atmosphere in American life during the twenties. The question is whether, in addition, there were not in Jewish communal life developments of a specifically internal character, which fed the general disruptive trends of the twenties and thirties. Perhaps in this period American Jewry faced a profounder crisis of acculturation than it had during the first two decades of the century, when immigrants kept pouring in. Now, in the 1920s and 1930s, cleavages began to appear in the basic social structure of the immigrant community, with fathers and sons thrown apart by deep differences in education, mentality, and outlook.

The first two decades of the century—the Age of Optimism in American Jewry—have been presented as the product of a peculiar meeting between two chronologically and culturally different waves of Jewish immigration, the prominent "German" minority within the Jewish community, a minority on the way to acculturating itself in America, and the "Russian" majority of Jewish newcomers, struggling in and with the conditions and promises of the "golden land." In a convergence of characteristics, similarities, and differences, and under the aegis of a positive idea regarding American Judaism and its future, these two groups were able to achieve the degree of collaboration and the organizational impetus that we have described above. But the winds which began blowing during the twenties in the larger American society, and which certainly influenced the Jewish community as well, were essentially unpropitious for trends and movements of an ideal character. Furthermore, the Jewish community, being a community of immigrants, was very unstable. The delicate equilibrium between the ingredients that had produced the Age of Optimism was upset due to modifications in the social and spiritual climate fostering the communal trends of the former period.

Since the Jewish organizations which took shape during the acme of the Age of Optimism were so much the children of the time, almost all of them were to suffer crisis and transformation. For the sake of periodization, we may suggest the collapse of the Zionist Organization of America in 1921 as the dividing line between two periods and the end of the years of optimism in American Jewry. The crisis in the ZOA—the "Brandeis-Weizmann struggle"—symbolized the end of an era, since the organization was split along the lines of "Russian" and "German" elements whose collaboration had been one of the chief features of the former period. As a matter of fact, however, the first signs of the approaching crisis were felt even before 1921. When the American Jewish Congress met in December 1918, it was, as we have said, remote from the concept which the fathers of the idea had envisaged two or three years before. As for the Zionist Organization of America, there were already in 1920 clear signs of an imminent internal collapse—quite apart from the divergences between Brandeis and Weizmann which came to a head in 1921.[52] As far as the Kehillah is concerned, at the time of its greatest apparent strength, in 1917-18, when Benderly and his associates were preparing plans for a far-reaching reorganization of the Kehillah, plans as sensible as they were utopian, the Kehillah was already in decline.[53]

At the end of the second decade of the century, the ideological thrust and the organizational momentum of the former years began fading away. Many of the external signs remained: there were still "German" worthies, there were still "cultural" Zionists, there were still Jews who spoke about the great future in store for Jews and Judaism in the United States. But the inner strength was gone, even if the great words of another era reverberated in the air.

NOTES

The ideas discussed in the present article were explored in courses in American Jewish history taught by me at the University of the Negev (since renamed Ben-Gurion University) and the Hebrew University. Thanks are due to my students, who offered many a comment incorporated in this essay. No less, thanks are due my friend Stanley F. Chyet for his penetrating observations and suggestions in our many talks on the theme and for undertaking the bothersome task of correcting my English.

1. "Glance at the Future," *American Hebrew,* November 24, 1905, p. 742; the same issue, being the 250th anniversary number, also contains articles by K. Kohler, S. Schechter, L. Marshall, A. Leroy-Beaulieu, and others, all dealing with the future of American Jews. See also the article of A. S. Isaacs, "The Jews of the United States," in the first volume of the *American Jewish Year Book [AJYB]* (1899–1900), principally p. 14.
2. See G. E. Mowry, *The Era of Theodore Roosevelt, 1900–1912* (New York and Evanston, 1958); A. S. Link, *Woodrow Wilson and the Progressive Era, 1910–1917,* 2d ed. (New York, 1963).
3. The literature on this period includes C. S. Bernheimer, ed., *The Russian Jew in the United States* (Philadelphia, 1905); M. Rischin, *The Promised City: New York's Jews, 1870–1914* (Cambridge, Mass., 1962); J. L. Teller, *Strangers and Natives* (New York, 1968), chaps. 1–6.
4. On the Kehillah, see Arthur A. Goren's excellent study, *New York Jews and the Quest for Community: The Kehillah Experiment 1908–1922* (New York, 1970). To date, unfortunately, no comprehensive study of the American Jewish Congress has appeared, but much is to be learned about it in Goren's work (see chap. 10) and in Y. Shapiro's *Leadership of the American Zionist Organization, 1897–1930* (Urbana, 1971), chap. 4.
5. "The Jewish Community of New York City," address at the constituent convention of the Kehillah, February 27, 1909 [New York, 1909].
6. See *AJYB* (1917–18), pp. 443–51.
7. "Jewish Rights," address, January 24, 1916, in J. de Haas, *Louis D. Brandeis* (New York, 1929), pp. 226–27.
8. See S. M. Lipset, "The Study of Jewish Communities in a Comparative Context," *Jewish Journal of Sociology,* V (1963), 157–58.
9. Letter to Cyrus L. Sulzberger, June 14, 1902, quoted by L. S. Dawidowicz, "Louis Marshall's Yiddish Newspaper, *The Jewish World*: a Study in Contrasts," *Jewish Social Studies [JSS],* XXV (1963), 126.
10. See Jacob H. Schiff on the American Jewish Congress, in C. Adler, *Jacob Schiff, His Life and Letters* (Garden City, N. Y., 1928), II, 296–99; Oscar S. Straus on the same issue and on the American Jewish Committee, in N. W. Cohen, *A Dual Heritage* (Philadelphia, 1969), pp. 138, 246. On the American Jewish Committee, see also M. Rosenstock, *Louis Marshall, Defender of Jewish Rights* (Detroit, 1968), pp. 21–24.
11. N. Schachner, *The Price of Liberty, a History of the American Jewish Committee* (New York, 1948), 28.
12. Letter to A. Kraus, June 12, 1915, in C. Reznikoff, ed., *Louis Marshall, Champion of Liberty* (Philadelphia, 1957), II, 509.
13. "The Present Crisis in American Jewry," in *Past and Present,* 2d ed. (New York, 1961), p. 219.

14. See N. Bentwich, *Solomon Schechter* (Philadelphia, 1938), chap. VII; Reznikoff, *Marshall,* II, 819, 861–63.

15. See Z. Szajkowski, "The Attitude of American Jews to East European Jewish Immigration (1881–1893)," *Publications of the American Jewish Historical Society [PAJHS],* XL (1950–51), 267. See also I. A. Mandel, "The Attitude of the American Jewish Community toward East European Immigration as Reflected in the Anglo-Jewish Press (1880–1890)," *American Jewish Archives,* III (1950), 11–36.

16. Reznikoff, *Marshall,* I, 114–15.

17. E. L. Panitz, "The Polarity of American Jewish Attitudes towards Immigration (1870–1891)," *American Jewish Historical Quarterly [AJHQ],* LIII (1963–64), 130; idem, "In Defense of the Jewish Immigrant (1891–1924)," *AJHQ,* LV (1965–66), 57–97.

18. Letter to Paul Nathan, August 27, 1906, in Szajkowski, "Paul Nathan, Lucien Wolf, Jacob E. Schiff and the Jewish Revolutionary Movements in Eastern Europe, 1903–1917," *JSS,* XXIX (1967), 24.

19. See Mowry, *Theodore Roosevelt,* pp. 38–58; Link, *Woodrow Wilson,* pp. 13–22.

20. See S. Schechter, "The Assistance of the Public," *Seminary Addresses and Other Papers,* 2d ed. (New York, 1959), p. 233; D. Philipson, "Isaac Mayer Wise," *Centenary Papers and Others* (Cincinnati, 1919), pp. 50–51; idem, "Israel, the International People," *ibid.,* p. 264; K. Kohler, "American Judaism," *Hebrew Union College and Other Addresses* (Cincinnati, 1916), pp. 196–97.

21. See Goren, *New York Jews,* chaps. V–VI. Even Magnes was moved to observe, in 1915, that the main accomplishment of the Kehillah, after six years of work, was the formulation of the Jewish problem in New York City and the search for possible answers to that problem—see his address at the opening session of the sixth annual convention of the Kehillah, April 24, 1915 [New York, 1915].

22. See Schechter to C. Adler, January 8, 1914, in Bentwich, *Schechter,* p. 191; M. M. Kaplan, quoted in N. H. Winter, *Jewish Education in a Pluralist Society: Samson Benderly and Jewish Education in the United States* (New York, 1966), p. 179.

23. On Friedlaender, see his collected essays, *Past and Present;* J. Kohn, "Israel Friedlaender," *AJYB,* XXIII (1922–23), 65–79; E. Friesel, *The Zionist Movement in the United States 1897–1914* (Tel Aviv, 1970), pp. 80–82 [Hebrew]. Unfortunately, no full biography of Friedlaender has appeared yet.

24. "The Problem of Judaism in America" (1907), *Past and Present,* p. 173.

25. *Ibid.,* pp. 169–71.

26. *Ibid.,* pp. 179–80.

27. *Ibid.,* pp. 180–82.

28. *Ibid.,* p. 183.

29. "The Melting Pot," address, October 9, 1909, *Emanu-El Pulpit,* vol. III, no. 1. See also Magnes' address, "A Republic of Nationalities," February 13, 1909, *ibid.,* vol. II, no. 6.

30. "The Duty of American Jews," *Maccabaean,* February 1909, pp. 41–46.

31. "The Jewish Problem and How to Solve It," *Brandeis on Zionism* (Washington, 1942), p. 30.

32. The hopes and problems of the new Jewish settlement, as well as its gradual development, are aptly described by Rischin, *The Promised City.*

33. See Winter, *Jewish Education,* pp. 104, 195 (n. 34).

34. See Friesel, *Zionist Movement,* chap. VII.

35. *Maccabaean,* August 1908, pp. 68–69.

36. A couple of years before, during and after the first Russian Revolution, and also

later, at the Paris Peace Conference of 1919, Zionists were very active on the internal Jewish political scene. See O. I. Janowsky, *The Jews and Minority Rights (1898–1919)* (New York, 1933), pp. 98–118, 309–19.

37. Other ideologically articulate but not "cultural"-oriented American Zionists, people like Richard Gottheil, were not to be found among the Kehillah activists, while a Zionist leader of independent mind like Louis Lipsky was a sharp critic of the Kehillah. See L. Lipsky, "What Ails the New York Kehillah," *Maccabaean,* December 1912, pp. 185–89.

38. See "Germans versus Russians," Rischin, *Promised City,* pp. 93–111; H. Silver, "The Russian Jew Looks at Charity (1890–1900)," *Jewish Social Service Quarterly,* IV (1927–28), 129–44; H. B. Grinstein, "The Efforts of East European Jewry to Organize Its Own Community in the United States," *PAJHS,* XLIX (1959–60), 73–89.

39. See B. K. Korn, *German-Jewish Intellectual Influences on American Jewish Life 1824–1972* (Syracuse, 1972).

40. See R. Glanz, *Jews in Relation to the Cultural Milieu of the Germans in America Up to the Eighteen Eighties* (New York, 1947); H. G. Grinstein, *The Rise of the Jewish Community of New York, 1654–1860* (Philadelphia, 1945), pp. 201–5.

41. See Friesel, *Zionist Movement,* pp. 104–8. The chapter deals with the ideological significance of the dispute between Zionists and Reform Jews in America during the first decade of the twentieth century.

42. See J. Higham, "Social Discrimination against Jews in America, 1830–1930," *PAJHS, XLVII* (1957–58), 11–13; also the interesting chapter, "The Elite and the Marginal Man," in E. Digby Baltzell, *The Protestant Establishment: Aristocracy and Caste in America* (New York, 1964), 62–66.

43. See J. R. Marcus, *Early American Jewry* (Philadelphia, 1955), II, 389–90, 438–39; M. D. Angel, "The Sephardim of the United States: An Exploratory Study," *AJYB,* 74 (1973), 81–82; also Grinstein, *Jewish Community of New York,* pp. 166–70; E. Wolf II and M. Whiteman, *The History of the Jews of Philadelphia from Colonial Times to the Age of Jackson* (Philadelphia, 1957), pp. 375–76.

44. See Z. Szajowski, "The *Yahudi* and the Immigrant: A Reappraisal," *AJHQ,* LXIII (1973), 13–44.

45. See A. Aaronsohn, Washington, to Ch. Weizmann, December 13, 1917 (Weizmann Archives, Rehovot); J. H. Schiff to I. Zangwill, January 15, 1918 (Box 2364, American Jewish Archives, Cincinnati, Ohio).

46. Respectively: J. Higham, *Strangers in the Land: Patterns of American Nativism, 1860–1925* (New Brunswick, N. J., 1955); Baltzell, *Protestant Establishment;* N. W. Cohen, *Not Free to Desist* (Philadelphia, 1972).

47. See Ch. Arlosoroff, *Surveying American Zionism* (New York, 1929).

48. See *Proceedings of Adjourned Session of American Jewish Congress Including Report of Commission to Peace Conference and of Provisional Organization for Formation of American Jewish Congress* (Philadelphia, May 1920) (New York, [1920]).

49. See E. E. Grusd, *B'nai B'rith* (New York, 1966), chap. 14.

50. See W. Herberg, "The Jewish Labor Movement in the United States," *AJYB,* LIII (1952), 35–36; J. S. Hertz, *The Jewish Socialist Movement in the U.S.A.* (New York, 1954), chap. 22 [Yiddish].

51. See Cohen, *Not Free to Desist,* pp. 123–53.

52. Friesel, "The Development of the American Zionist Movement in the Years 1918–1920" [Hebrew] (Master's thesis, Hebrew University, Jerusalem, 1962).

53. Goren, *New York Jews,* pp. 235–37.

TEMPLES OF LIBERTY UNPOLLUTED: AMERICAN JEWS AND PUBLIC SCHOOLS, 1840–1875

By

LLOYD P. GARTNER

Tel Aviv University

I

The moral and social significance of the public school in American democratic thought has probably surpassed that enjoyed by state schools in any Western society. The modern Hebrew poet who called the European Jewish house of study (*bet midrash*) "the potter's shop molding the soul of the nation" could have justly applied that phrase to the American public school as conceived by its founders and philosophers. Free, tax-supported, open equally to all children, it was the place where the child would be imbued with democratic ideals and prepared to assume the responsibilities of citizenship in his maturity. Speaking for the United States Supreme Court in an historic decision which banned religious instruction within public school buildings, Justice Felix Frankfurter called the public school "a symbol of our secular unity . . . the symbol of our democracy, the most pervasive means for promoting our common destiny . . ." [1] We may anticipate our discussion by suggesting that it was appropriate for these memorable words to come from a member of the high bench who was himself an immigrant, educated in New York City's public schools and college, and a Jew.

The idea of public schooling was adumbrated by Thomas Jefferson as early as 1779, but nothing concrete developed in his lifetime. [2] The

157

American public (interchangeably used with common) school rose during the popular democratic agitation of the Jacksonian 1830s. Not only Jacksonian democrats but men of means and conservative social outlook desired public education, as a measure against social disintegration. Their influential leaders considered masses of enfranchised but uneducated citizens dangerous to social order and progress and incompatible with American republicanism. Thus, Governor DeWitt Clinton of New York observed in 1826 that "a general diffusion of knowledge is the precursor and protector of republican institutions, and in it we must confide as the conservative power that will watch over our liberities . . ." [3] The education spoken of continued to be sponsored, at least until the 1840s, mainly by denominational bodies and individual teachers. Edward Everett could appeal to the prudential interests of New England capitalists "to contribute to give security to your own property" by supporting educational institutions in distant Ohio. The religiously indifferent could be urged to support the training of clergy, who would "unite in special benefit to mercantile morality and hence to the safety of business arrangements . . ." [4] The advocacy of education was not usually so crassly self-interested. It has been argued, however, that an underlying interest was to train a working class in the discipline of industry. Thus precision, punctuality, and obedience within bureaucratically organized schools became the supreme virtues in American public education. The argument can be plausible only for public schools in industrial regions. Moreover, precision, punctuality, and obedience as virtues antedate factories in America, and were hardly the virtues only of industry. [5]

Radical Jacksonian democratic thinkers also discussed public education, not in nationalist and conservative terms but within their conceptions of social classes and the distribution of power in society. Charles Stewart Daveis summarized their view: "the distribution of knowledge becomes . . . the distribution of power." [6] Frederick Robinson foresaw that by "the equal mental and physical education of all, at the expense of all . . . our emancipation from the power of aristocracy will be effectual and eternal. . . . When the great mass of the laboring people becoming wise enough to establish institutions for the equal education and maintenance of their children in every neighborhood throughout the country, the reign of equality will then commence." [7] Stephen Simpson complained that when "working men have claimed *public instruction for their children* [they] have been answered by the sneer of derision on the one hand

and the cry of revolution on the other."⁸ This democratic radicalism had the support of distinguished men of letters like James Fenimore Cooper and George Bancroft.⁹ Some Jacksonian democrats, however, opposed govermentally sponsored education, out of suspicion of the motives of conservative advocates and antagonism to the enlargement of state power.¹⁰

The nationalist argument dominated the discussions about public schools. William H. Seward, as Whig Governor of New York, observed that "the most interesting of all our republican institutions is the common school," and privately looked forward to its product, "a homogeneous people, universally educated and imbued with the principles of morality and virtue." ¹¹ He acted on these convictions by playing a central role in establishing the public school system in his state. Indiana's Superintendent of Public Instruction spoke in terms resembling Seward's. "Our policy as a State is to make of all the varieties of population among us, differing as they do in origin, language, habits of thought, modes of action, and social custom, one people, with one common interest." ¹²

Churchmen for their part acknowledged that the historic pattern of education under denominational auspices was antiquated. They supported public schooling for the mass of children whom they could no longer educate, although this meant a sharp limit on denominational influence in American education. In the words of a prominent New England minister, the Reverend Horace Bushnell:

> We can not have Puritan common schools—these are gone already—we can not have Protestant common schools, or those which are distinctly so; but we can have common schools, and these we must agree to maintain, till the last or latest day of our liberties.¹³

Here the liberal, evangelical Bushnell was indirectly posing another question. On all sides, it was agreed that there could be no education without a moral dimension, and that moral education could not be distinct from religious education. Amid the Protestant denominations with their articulate differences, what generally acceptable moral-religious education could be offered in public schools? The existence of public education depended upon an agreed response.

Developments within American Protestantism since the late eighteenth century pointed the way, it seemed, to moral-religious education within public schools. As one ·historian has expressed it, the New England churches, gradually disestablished between the 1780s and the 1820s, found their "tradition, now adjusted and modernized, flourished and spread, surrounding legal separation with the ancient Puritan assumptions, all proclaiming the United States a broadly confessional republic, with 'Moses and Aaron united in counsel . . . the true American union, of which no patriot can ever be ashamed.' " [14] And Daniel Webster, the Solon of New England, declared in 1844:

> Christianity—general tolerant Christianity—Christianity independent of sects and parties—that Christianity to which the sword and fagot are unknown—general, tolerant Christianity is the law of the land! [15]

This "general, tolerant Christianity," shared by all good men, enabled Horace Mann and his fellow-educators to persuade their contemporaries that the basis for moral education could be found in the common, ethical elements of Christianity. [16] Henry S. Randall, New York State Superintendent of Schools, spelled out the consequences:

> [R]eligious education must be banished from the common schools and consigned to the family and the church. . . . Accordingly, the instruction in our schools has been limited . . . to the propagation of those principles of morality [on] which all sects, and good men belonging to no sect, can equally agree. . . . Not only have the Episcopalian, the Baptist and the Methodist met on common and neutral ground in the school room, but with them the Unitarian, the Universalist, the Quaker and even the denier of all creeds. [17]

The omission of Catholics, and of Jews, from Randall's parade of sects was perhaps unconscious. Yet these lapses imply that "general, tolerant Christianity," the moral foundation and political bulwark of the new common schools, meant Protestantism.

The evangelical Robert Baird, surveying American Protestantism during the 1850s, considered moral instruction in the public schools as the means by which "the youth of the nation may be qualified for receiving religious instruction effectively elsewhere, and for the due discharge of their future duty as citizens." Even so, religious teaching might properly be imparted in the public school:

> . . . a pious and judicious teacher, if he will only confine himself to the great doctrines and precepts of the Gospel, in which all who hold the

fundamental truths of the Bible are agreed, can easily give as much religious instruction as he cares.[18]

Neither Baird nor other Protestants placed their entire reliance upon "pious and judicious" public school teachers. Some of them favored parochial schools, but very few were actually opened by native Protestants. Instead, the American Sunday School Union, from its founding in 1830, established Sunday Schools at a vigorous pace in all large cities. The majority of public school children in such cities as Philadelphia, Boston, and Cleveland were enrolled in Sunday Schools by the 1850s.[19] On the other hand, James Ford Rhodes, the historian, recalled that in his native Cleveland, "moral and religious teaching was considered part of the duty of the public school teacher." Some teachers, more pious than judicious, "were ardent Congregationalists and these inculcations were tinctured by puritanical fervor." Besides daily prayers, during the 1857–58 revival meetings were also held in Cleveland High School.[20]

Two historians of American religion sum up this relation between the early public schools and Protestant America. Robert T. Handy has found the "cultural dominance of Protestantism" illustrated by "the transition to a public, tax-supported school system; this transition was palatable to Protestants because the schools were clearly Protestant in orientation, though 'non-sectarian.' "[21] The identification of Protestantism with American culture and nationality has been incisively expressed by Timothy L. Smith:

> . . . it was not secularism but nondenominational Protestantism which won the day. An evangelical consensus of faith and ethics had come so to dominate the national culture that a majority of Protestants were now willing to entrust the state with the task of educating children, confident that education would be "religious" still. The sects identified their common beliefs with those of the nation, their mission with America's mission. . . . [It] was accepted [that] tax-supporting schools were responsible for those parts of learning, whether secular, moral, or religious, thought to be equally necessary for children in all faiths. The family and the church remained responsible for all that related to particular frameworks of belief and value.[22]

Protestants could control the schools in homogeneous local communities, where "the 'public school' inevitably reflected the values and beliefs of the church congregation to which most of the people belonged."[23] This "emerging consensus of evangelical Protestant faith" naturally could not "stretch far enough to include Jews and Roman Catholics. The school systems of cities both large and small were, in fact, instruments of the Protestant establishment . . ." [24] The "evangelical Protestant consensus" stood ready to combat all opposition. Such opposition came shortly, from the large and growing group of excluded Roman Catholics.

II

What Protestants regarded as "general, tolerant Christianity" in the public schools Catholics perceived as Protestantism. Had the Protestant consensus on education existed during the 1820s, when Catholics numbered around 163,500 and Jews no higher than 6,000, it would have been virtually unchallenged. In 1853, however, with the public school movement in full flood, Catholics exceeded 2,000,000. The vast majority were immigrants from Germany and Ireland.[25] Nativism and militant anti-Catholicism were notorious responses to the evident threat to two centuries of Protestant domination in the United States.[26] The controversies which arose from Catholic dissatisfaction with Protestant-tinged public schools were not without connection to these dubious attempts to preserve Protestant America.

Catholic offense at the distinct, if nondenominational, Protestantism in the public schools put New York City through an episode of severe yet ultimately beneficial political stress during the early 1840s.[27] In the booming Hudson River metropolis, public education had been in the hands of the Public School Society. This Protestant body received public funds to maintain its schools, which it insisted were religiously suitable for all children. Catholics saw the matter otherwise and petitioned for funds for Catholic schools. These petitions, which were rejected by the Board of Aldermen, were accompanied by excited scenes at hearings, public demonstrations, and bitter election campaigns. An early, unsuccessful petition for public funds may have come from a Jewish school in 1833; in any event, when the Catholic effort began in 1840, New York City's two Jewish congregations, Shearith Israel and B'nai Jeshurun, joined the Scotch Presbyterian congregation in requesting that if aid went to Catholic schools, their own schools should also receive it.[28]

The struggle in New York City reached fundamental principles. Led by the ardent, dynamic Bishop John Hughes (1797–1864), the city's rapidly increasing Catholic constituency shifted its demand from funds to exposing the unacceptable Protestant bias in Public School Society institutions. Examples of anti-Catholicism in textbooks and classrooms were readily gathered. Bishop Hughes's militancy was met by Governor Seward's political skill. After sharp contests at the polls and in the Legislature, Seward succeeded in neutralizing the religious issue by transferring control of the schools to commissions elected in each of the city's wards. Decentralized control, however, apparently permitted certain excesses in Catholic wards also. Thus, *Popular Lessons,* used in the Ninth Ward, contained such verses as "Punishment of Sin." (One verse: "When the arm of death destroys / All my false and fatal joys / In that hour of deep despair / God will not regard my prayer.") "The Son of God who came from heaven," began another poem, while a reader prepared by the Brothers of the Christian Schools was addressed "To the Blessed Virgin." Most Jewish children attended the Fourth Ward schools, where complaints were presented over prejudicial classroom material.[29]

Ten years later, in 1853, education became completely public with the establishment of the New York City Board of Education, which took over from the Public School Society. Religious tensions were thus compromised and neutralized sufficiently for a public school system to exist. Protestant influence was reasserted, however, when the state superintendent of schools ordered that the Authorized (King James) Version be read from daily in all classes, although without comment by the teacher. Nativism and anti-Catholicism could again flare up at any suggestion that the Protestant definition of public schooling was under attack.

Catholics thus fought with mixed success against the "evangelical consensus of faith and ethics" underlying the public schools. There was little Catholic influence in the public schools to parallel or counteract the Protestant. Neither did Catholics desire education without religion altogether. Years later Bernard J. McQuaid, bishop of Rochester, apologetically summed up the position which the Catholic hierarchy was to adopt:

> To Catholics it became clear that if they meant to transmit the faith of their baptism to their offspring, if they believed that Christ's religion was worth living for, if they held that God should not be driven out of the school-house, and that the virtue, morality, and religion essential to a republican form of government were to be perpetuated, they would have to establish a system of schools for their own children, under their control, and at their own cost . . . [30]

The requirement that every Catholic send his children to a parochial school was not promulgated by the American hierarchy until 1884, and room was left for exceptions. Until then the Catholic faithful were too impoverished to build and support schools unaided, and teaching orders lacked members. A modus vivendi thus developed between Catholics and public schools in many areas as the Protestant tone gradually abated with the enrollment of Catholic children in large numbers. A few leading churchmen, like Archbishop John Ireland and Bishop John L. Spalding, built parochial schools but were less than fervent towards the exclusive parochial school policy. Yet altogether, the ultimate response of American Catholicism to public schools was parochial education.[31]

III

In the new common schools, then, nationalist patriots sought to forge "a homogeneous people"; conservative contemporaries saw a civilizing, restraining influence upon the masses; Jacksonian radicals, the makings of social equality; Protestant America, "general, tolerant Christianity"; Catholics, however, discerned a coercive Protestant enterprise. Reactions from the small but rapidly increasing Jewish community might also be expected. Significant Jewish responses did in fact occur, and the public schools decisively influenced the fate of the Jewish schools, although in a manner different from the Catholic.

There was education under synagogal auspices from early Colonial times, but before the 1830s it was sporadic or haphazard. Among the small tradesmen and craftsmen who constituted most of American Jewry before 1820 approximately, there was a deep, barely articulated feeling that their task was to preserve and transmit Judaism, not alter or adapt it. Most Colonial congregations maintained schoolmasters who gave instruction in the common branches and in Judaism to local Jewish children. Some attended private academies.[32] In striking contrast with contemporary European Jewish controversies over the religious legitimacy of secular studies, these were readily accepted by eighteenth-century American Jews, who were themselves mostly European immigrants. The pious German Jewish immigrants in New York who established the short-lived Hebrah Hinuch Nearim (Society for Educating the Youth) in 1825 out of dissatisfaction with the poor standard in Jewish studies, also did not oppose secular studies.[33]

The first specimen of distinctively American Jewish educational thought comes from the physician Daniel Levi Maduro Peixotto (1799–

1842), active in Jacksonian democracy and in the Jewish community. He proposed in 1830 to found a Jewish school on Pestalozzian principles, especially to train Jewish teachers.[34] Peixotto's frame of reference was still Jewish educational institutions.

During the disputes of the 1840s in New York and elsewhere, no known Jewish discussion took place. The reason may be that before 1843, when Isaac Leeser (1806–1868) began his *Occident,* there was no regular Jewish organ. There may be other reasons. Jews may have avoided a political issue with marked religious overtones. Most of them, as recent immigrants, doubtless retained the centuries-old wariness of Jews intruding themselves into the politics of their countries of residence. Moreover, the common school was unprecedented. In Germany and Bohemia, the acceptability of secular studies was only recently a controversial issue, and the schooling of Jewish children was usually undertaken by the Jewish community. Education was still denominational also in England, the land of origin of a fair proportion of the newcomers.[35]

Against this background German Jewish immigrants began to found schools. One of the sources of friction between native Sefardim and immigrant Germans within Congregation Shearith Israel, New York City's only synagogue before 1825, was the newcomers' discontent with the congregation's provision for Jewish education within its day school. Their Hebrah Hinuch Nearim, mentioned above, was the origin of a new congregation, B'nai Jeshurun, which maintained a school through various changes until 1847. Anshe Chesed's Lomdi Torah school existed in 1830–31, and was reestablished in 1845. Other schools were founded by congregations and also by individuals, notably Rabbi Max Lilienthal (1815–1882), who arrived in 1845. Professor Grinstein estimates seven Jewish schools in New York City in 1854, with thirty-five teachers for 857 pupils. In contrast, the Catholics in that year had seventeen schools and Protestant bodies, six. The Jewish school program included prayer, Bible, religion taught by the new catechistic method, and sundry matters of law and tradition, besides German and the common branches.[36] They advertised in the press the variety and excellence of their secular studies, which were said to include French, German, piano, and embroidery. Only perfunctory mention was given to Jewish studies; although most of the schools were synagogal, were parents enrolling children for the sake of Jewish studies? The decline and disappearance of these institutions was remarkably abrupt. For example, the Hebrew National School of Shaaray Zedek Congregation entered its new schoolhouse in 1853; four years later the school closed down.[37] All Jewish schools were shut by 1860. One may agree with Professor Grinstein that Jewish parents shifted their children straightaway to public schools as soon as those were purged of gross sectarianism.[38] One still wonders, however, at the Jewish schools' minimal powers of attraction and survival. Had they so few financial supporters and spokesmen?

The fate of the Jewish schools in New York was repeated in other cities. In the closer-knit Jewish community of Cincinnati, "most all the children of the members" of B'nai Jeshurun (Isaac M. Wise's congregation from 1954) attended its Talmid Yelodim Institute. In 1854 this was but 150 of that city's 500 Jewish pupils. The day school continued until 1869.[39] The sixty Jews of Detroit opened a Hebrew-English-German Day School in 1850, and terminated it in 1869 "because no such results were achieved as those which the public schools secured." Public school and Sabbath-Sunday religious school were the replacement.[40] Cleveland's Anshe Chesed congregation (now Fairmount Temple) conducted a day school for twenty-five years, closing it in 1867.[41] Several Jewish day schools existed in Chicago, the last of which expired in 1874.[42] In the little Jewish community of Easton, Pennsylvania, a day school was conducted at the synagogue from 1850 to 1853, followed by the transition to public education.[43] There was a movement to close parochial schools in Newark, New Jersey, as a good public school system developed there. That city's B'nai Jeshurun Congregation gave up its day school in 1869, thenceforward teaching religious subjects only in a supplementary school.[44] The school which the Hebrew Education Society of Philadelphia opened in 1851 under Isaac Leeser's inspiration taught both Jewish and general subjects for twenty years or more. Some of the teachers were Christians. However, opposition arose to providing general education, "on account of which we separated ourselves and are looked upon as an exclusive sect," in Rabbi Sabato Morais' regretful words. General studies were given up not long after 1871, and the Hebrew Education Society confined itself to Jewish studies after public school attendance.[45]

The neglected history of German-American education is linked with that of Jewish schools. German-Jewish immigrants shared the German desire to preserve the native culture.[46] Thus, there were many Catholic as well as Protestant parochial schools which were conducted entirely in German. As late as 1890, the passage of the Bennett Law in Wisconsin, mandating English instruction in the common branches in elementary schools, brought disaster on Election Day to the Wisconsin Republicans who had sponsored it.[47] Some Jewish schools also used German as their language of instruction. Isaac Leeser and Isaac Mayer Wise, otherwise opposed, agreed in their demand for English,[48] but other rabbis endorsed German. The Public School Society of New York, seeking to attract German enrollment, established a school in 1839 at Grand and Elm streets, "for the special instruction of German children." With B'nai Jeshurun located on Elm Street and other congregations nearby, this was the center of New York's German Jewry, and Jewish children no doubt attended the Society's school.[49] Extensive Jewish participation in private secular German schools is found in such cities as Chicago, Baltimore, and Milwaukee.[50] Just as desectarianization doomed Jewish schools, however, so did the introduction of German into public school curricula do likewise to German schools.[51] The rise and decline of Jewish schools seems related, therefore, to parental desire for children to receive some German education. Religiously neutral public schools also teaching German perfectly suited the wishes of German-American Jews seeking to transmit their language.

IV

While the final decision on enrollment lay with parents, intermittent discussion took place regarding public or Jewish schooling for Jewish children. It apparently began in 1843, became comparatively extensive during the mid-1850s, and ceased after 1865. The participants in these discussions necessarily expressed opinions of wider scope concerning the status and prospects of American Jews. Both the limited and broader aspects of the debate over Jewish or public schools merit fuller attention.

The Reverend Isaac Leeser of Philadelphia was the first to approach this question. This author, editor, preacher, and educator published an article in his *Occident* in 1843 somewhat ominously entitled, "Jewish Children under Gentile Teachers." It warned parents against sending children to

> a public or private school which is essentially Christian; they hear prayers recited in which the name of a mediator is invoked; they hear a book read as an authority equal if not superior to the received word of God; . . . Besides all this, we are in a great error if we suppose that Christian teachers do not endeavor to influence actively the sentiments of their Jewish pupils; there are some, at least, who take especial pains to warp the mind and to implant the peculiar tenets of Christianity clandestinely . . . [52]

Leeser considered it "would be best to establish Jewish elementary schools" wherever Jews lived in sufficient numbers, and elsewhere to keep a watchful eye on the public schools. To be sure, he was also active in the Hebrew Sunday School of Philadelphia, and *the Occident* published numerous Sunday School reports from various cities.[53] His frequent collaborator, the Reverend Samuel M. Isaacs (1804–1879) of New York, endorsed Leeser's views, adding hortatory remarks.[54] "Philo" of Philadelphia was no less favorable, advocating

> the establishment of Hebrew Public Schools, where our children can be educated in accordance with our faith, without being compelled to listen to the reading and expounding of other religious tenets. Let me not be misunderstood in using the word *compulsion;* there exists so much liberality in the public school system, that no child, contrary to the wishes of its parents, is forced to recite from the New Testament; but you will agree with me, that our children, in particular those of a very tender age, imbibe a considerable portion of the tenets of the Christian faith. Let us, therefore, try and establish schools under our own personal and spiritual guidance . . . [55]

Leeser often returned to the school question. While he spoke of the advantages of a full Jewish education, what he emphasized was the danger in schools where there was a Christian majority.[56] L. M. Ritterband of New York, endorsing Leeser, cited the loss of talented persons to Judaism thanks to the ridicule of their religion in Christian schools.[57] In the outlook of Leeser and these allies, Christianity and public schools were inseparable.

Leeser found additional support from Robert Lyon (d. 1858), the somewhat obscure editor of the New York weekly *Asmonean.* Unlike Leeser, Lyon did not stress the dangers in public schools but the positive benefits of Jewish schools:

> With the State provision for the support of the common schools standing out in bold relief, it appears extraordinary that there should exist a cause for urging the expediency, nay, necessity, of our founding seminaries, yet so it is, with a positive pressure around us we are inactive.[58]

Employing the curious argument that "the sustaining energy of the Catholic religion" derived from its Latin language of prayer, Lyon inquired: ". . . shall we permit our sacred tongue to become unknown to all but the very learned, for so it will be unless active measures are adopted to produce schools and teachers."[59] A few weeks later the *Asmonean* returned to the point:

How, is it, how will it be with your offspring? Will they appreciate, will they feel, or will they know of the faith they are reared in? Is the scanty knowledge of Hebrew gained during the time stolen from their hours of recreation, sufficient to enable them to take up the ordinary ritual? . . . Do you content yourselves with giving them so brief, so contracted an instrument in other languages?[60]

One can only speculate why further discussion is not heard for years to come. Whatever the reason, trenchant opposition to separate Jewish schooling began to be heard after 1851, from Isidor Busch (later Bush; 1822–1898). Not yet thirty years old, Busch had been a Jewish journalist and publisher since his adolescence. Thanks to his father's partnership in the Viennese firm of A. Schmid, whose publications included the Talmud and important writings of Jewish scholarship and the Hebrew Enlightenment, Isidor Busch early became prominent in the circle of young Viennese Jewish scholars and intellectuals. From 1843 through 1847 he edited probably the first Jewish yearbook, the *Volks Kalendar und Jahrbuch für Israeliten,* combining calendrical information with popular scholarly articles.[61] The year 1848 was the climax and transformation in the career of the young journalist, editor, and sometime scholar. He was planning to issue a weekly *Sabbath-Blätter,* but the revolution arrived before the first number appeared. Busch promptly altered his plans and issued instead the weekly *Oesterreichisches Central-Organ für Glaubensfreiheit, Kultur, Geschichte und Literatur der Juden,* which was published throughout 1848. It expressed a fascinating range of opinion on Jewish and general political and social questions in revolutionary Vienna. For all the attention to the revolution, in the *Central-Organ* Busch pressed for emigration to America; in its pages the famous articles "On to America" ("Auf nach Amerika") appeared. The victory of the monarchists in November 1848 ended the revolution in Vienna and with it the *Central-Organ,* and Busch went at once to America, arriving there on January 8, 1849. Soon he began to publish *Israels Herold* to continue the *Central-Organ,* but it lasted merely twelve weeks.[62] Later in 1849 he moved to St. Louis, where he pursued an active business and civic life until his death in 1898.

It was Isidor Busch, with a diversity of experience in Jewish life and contemporary revolutions probably exceeding that of any Jew in America, who raised the school question two years after his arrival, in an article describing the sixfold "Task of the Jews in the United States." One task was to avow that "we are 'Jews' "—meaning, it would seem, that the old term *Jew,* freighted with memories of scorn and mockery, had to be maintained over newfangled names like "Israelite." Second, said Busch, "Give honour to yourselves." Third, "Give to the Bible the full veneration that is due . . ." He also charged Jews to defend Judaism against calumny, and to keep together. Alongside these rather unexceptionable statements, on one point, concerning Jewish and public schools, Busch was highly specific:

> Support as much as you can the public school system, and lend no help whatever to sectarian institutions: *do not send your children,* neither your sons nor your daughters, to such, and don't complain about heavy school taxes;—establish no Jewish school except the only one branch [*sic*] of your religion, history and Hebrew language.[63]

Leeser disagreed in a footnote, but Busch's vigorously stated argument did not evidently draw public notice. Busch himself soon modified his views, at least in practice, and "earnestly tried to promote" the type of school he attacked. "Giving up what might have been my prejudices, I wanted to see it work, either to correct or to strengthen my views by practical experience, and I became fully convinced of the fact, that *common schools for Israelites in the United States cannot and will not prosper, nor will they be efficient.*" [64] His principle confirmed to his satisfaction, Busch returned to the question about three years later with three articles on "Schools for Israelites in the United States." [65] The new meaning of education for Jews in the United States was sized up perceptively:

> Nay, the education of our children is more appreciated now than ever before, and in this country more than anywhere else, for while knowledge was once our solace and support in misfortune and solitude, it is now our pride and ornament in society; while it only strengthened us in our sufferings, it now secures us enjoyment and prosperity . . . [66]

As to the Jewish schools, Busch maintained that "complaints about the ignorance of our children in religious matters, regret about the insufficiency or rather the inefficiency of our schools, the small support they find, the want of support, and the small attendance they meet with" were misplaced.[67] The cause of dissatisfaction lay elsewhere—Jewish schools as such were inevitably inferior:

I.   Because the public schools are better than our schools possibly can be; (particularly in smaller communities).

II. Because public schools are more convenient, near to every family, while our schools (particularly in large cities) must be at inconvenient distances for the majority of the children.

III. Because, as good republicans we *ought* to be in favor of public schools, and opposed to sectarian or church-schools of whatever denomination.

IV. Because direct religious instruction in *any* day school is of very little value.[68]

Busch expatiated upon each reason. The contrast between public "schoolhouses that are models of architecture, built for this purpose with all possible regard for the health and comfort of their children," and "low rooms, narrow, badly ventilated" in a little synagogue was unavoidable. Jewish children lived too widely scattered in large cities to attend a Jewish school, while there were too few Jews in smaller cities. He argued that "in mixing up the teaching of sacred truth, of the holy Bible and the prayers with the hurry, bustle, and often roguish merriment of a day-school, it will miss that solemnity and seriousness with which it should be approached." [69] Yet not all public schools were ample, nor did Jewish schools have to remain mean and physically inaccessible. And was "often roguish merriment" the hallmark of day schools only?

One argument by Busch cut deeper, however:

Should our children be educated as Jews *only* or even as foreigners in language and spirit, or shall they be educated as Americans, as citizens of the same free country, to be with them one harmonious people; or should we ourselves foster that unfortunate prejudice that pressed so many bitter, burning tears from most of us, and from our fathers in the old country? Answer yourselves which system will do the one, and which must result in the other.

Concentrating Jewish residences around a Jewish school might bring on disastrous success, "by the aid of sectarian schools, and by separating ourselves and our children systematically from the rest of society—in getting, as once before in Europe, deprived of the liberty to settle where we choose and restricted to 'Ghettoes,' which we hope will never happen . . ." [70] By fostering separate schooling Jews were hindering their acceptance as Americans. By separating their children and then, inevitably, their residences, they would encourage prejudice against themselves. Busch proposed a system of Sabbath and evening schools, adult classes, and a theological seminary.[71]

Soon thereafter Busch and Leeser debated in the ever-hospitable *Occident*.[72] Leeser again contended that it was necessary "to separate the seed of Abraham that dwell among the Gentiles, that their faith might never lose aught of its purity," and "to make the children susceptible for the sufferings of their religion." He claimed that "the Jewish child soon observes, when mixing with others, that even in America his *religion* is ridiculed and heartily despised by the great majority around him." Replying to Leeser's *galut* pessimism, Busch deplored the "injustice to the pure heart of all children, no matter of what persuasion, to accuse them of hatred, hatred for the sake of religion. They know no such feeling; at least not toward their school-fellows and playmates." What was "religious singularity"? This was "entirely unknown and unintelligible to us; unless it refers to the PECULIARITY of a singing brogue, a slovenly dress, *et id omne genus*"; if so, the sooner discarded the better. Against Leeser's insistence that Jewish schools were needed to extricate Jewish pupils from their plight in the public schools, Busch maintained:

> . . . would this separation be the proper way to cure the evil? Would the descendants of our Christian fellow-citizens be more liberal than their ancestors, or would they not rather be strengthened in their lamentable prejudice?

If Jewish children encountered intolerance,

> . . . let me ask you, which class of our children are in a better condition to meet and overcome the spectre of Intolerance: those whom we have thus excluded from all intercourse with the children of others, who, when they leave the Jewish school are wholly unprepared to meet "the spectre," or those who already learnt to know it, and under our guidance have been taught how to repel such indignity in this country of civil and religious freedom?

Leeser alleged that

when our children attend Gentile schools there are constantly intimations held out, which are at least unpleasant to them, still which they have to submit to, if they wish not to incur the ill-will of their teachers.

Busch firmly replied:

And woe to the teacher of a public school, who would dare to ridicule or sneer at a child, or to show it any ill-will for the sake of its religion.

Moreover, Leeser's usage "Gentile school," granted: "If this denomination is intended for public schools, it is as unjust as the accusation [of inherently prejudiced teachers] itself . . ." Public schools had no religious identification.

Leeser's calm rejoinder closed his debate with Busch, whose "courtesy and dignity" he esteemed.

Mr. Busch overrates the advantages of a public school education, and underrates the difficulties of evening religious schools. The mode of instructing children in the Hebrew, &c., in the extra hours, has been tried and has signally failed; if the success in St. Louis will be more in accordance with the wishes of its advocates, let time show. We are content to let experience justify or condemn the efforts we have made, and caused others to make, in establishing separate Jewish schools.

To Isaac Leeser, the American public school was a fundamentally Christian enterprise. Jewish children could be at best a tolerated minority. They were likely to be morally intimidated into concealing their Judaism or making it as inconspicuous as possible. Busch, to the contrary, insisted that American public schools were, or would become, neutral and unidentified. Hostility or discrimination against Jewish children, or sectarian practices, were to be combatted and eradicated. The future of the Jews in the United States depended upon inducting their children into American society through the public schools. Leeser failed to meet this issue. Restricting himself to the dangers of public schools he did not attempt to reassure Jews that their standing as Americans would be unimpaired by enrolling their children in Jewish schools. He remained cautious and defensive, opposed to Busch's optimistic confidence. American Jews of 1855—indeed, of nearly any age—preferred Busch's combination of optimism and admonition.

V

The ideas which Busch urged so effectively were heard more distinctly in 1855. "Your charitable schools . . . cannot compete with our public school system," declared Samuel L. Moses to the directors of the St. Louis Hebrew school:

> Our public school system has taken too deep a root in the minds of men of all classes and creeds, and has become the grand central idea of the age. . . . As you, my friends, are included who have the rights of citizenship, and claim your portion of that inheritance as a constitutional right, it behooves you as good citizens to sustain that right; and it is very essential for you to have your children associate with the masses, irrespective of creed or religion, in common with these educational pursuits.[73]

In New York City, Emanuel Brandeis, lecturer, musician, and sometime journalist, read Busch's articles with approval. The two men were "not only countrymen, but also from the same city [Prague], both children of the same education, and following the same tendencies and traditions, but now living in vastly different and distant places . . ." Brandeis argued in Busch's terms:

> Hebrew common schools are an unsuccessful and impolitic undertaking. They are superfluous and wrongful, tending to separatism, when we ought to be glad and proud that the public schools of this free country are open alike to all creeds, that no difference is made on account of religion . . . . knowing no diversity between man and man as citizens of this happy country, [we should] foster our religious interests alone between ourselves and our God.[74]

Brandeis also spoke on this before his B'nai B'rith branch.[75]

Thanks largely to Busch, and to Leeser, Moses, and Brandeis, the question of Jewish or public schools became an issue in the American Jewish community. The first conference of American rabbis, held at Cleveland in October 1855, dealt with the "gloomy facts" of Jewish education.[76] "The parents [are] satisfied, if at his Bar-Mitzvah their son can read his Pareshah, say grace after meal, and recite a speech which he was taught six weeks in advance . . ." Rabbi Isidor Kalisch (1816-1886) of Cleveland, where a Jewish school was flourishing, "was decidedly in favor" of public schools with supplementary Jewish schools only. Not only was competition with the public schools futile, but also "it was in the interest of the rising generation, to become thoroughly acquainted with their fellow citizens . . ." The contrary opinion was expressed by Rabbi B. H. Gotthelf of Louisville:

> Willingly and gratefully acknowledging the advantages and excellencies of the public schools, he was afraid of the sectarian and missionary spirit, that governed the teachers and was manifested in the schoolbooks. He considered it therefore almost a religious duty to establish entirely separate schools.[77]

Further discussion, unfortunately unrecorded, ensued. Kalisch and Gotthelf, representing the opposing viewpoints, formed a committee together with Max Lilienthal, to solicit statements from rabbis and teachers concerning this and other educational problems. They would present a full statement to the never-to-be-held synod which was to follow.

Among the participants in the rabbinical conference, Leeser's views were of course well known. Lilienthal, who had just moved to Cincinnati from New York, was beginning his transition from the Orthodox rabbi and private educator he had been in New York, to the moderate reformer and public school stalwart he became in Cincinnati.[78] Isaac Mayer Wise's views were not recorded, but in addition to his congregation's Talmid Yelodim day school he was involved in a Jewish secondary school project, Zion College.[79] Whatever opinions the committee on education received have not been preserved, but Jewish parents' opinion were being expressed by the rapid decline of the Jewish schools.

While all parties considered the dangers to Jewish children in public schools, actual data are scanty. Louis Marshall (1856–1929), the eminent lawyer and leader of American Jewry, recalled in his seventieth year experiences of the public schools in Syracuse:

> When I attended the public schools of Syracuse, and I can assure you that ordinarily the relations between the Jews and non-Jews were most friendly, the Bible was read every morning by the teachers in charge of the various grades. Ordinarily the readings were from the New Testament, and usually I enjoyed them, although there were times when they were not what they should have been. The Catholic boys and girls withdrew when the Bible reading began, and I always honored them and their parents for this action and later regretted that I did not withdraw. On Good Fridays, however, the readings always related to the crucifixion and the teachers seemed to have the habit of intoning their reading, and

especially when the word "Jew" was mentioned in such a manner as to convey the idea not only of contempt, but also of hatred. This was always followed during the recess and for several days after by the most hostile demeanor on the part of the Christian boys and girls of the school, some of whom resorted to physical violence and most of them to the calling of names and the making of scurrilous remarks.[80]

Marshall fought back, as he continued doing throughout an illustrious career. Strange to observe, he was the sole American Jewish leader who favored carefully selected Bible readings in the public schools. Nina Morais (1855–1918), the daughter of Rabbi Sabato Morais, like her fellow-Philadelphian Isaac Leeser, believed that the Jewish child suffered severely in the definitely Christian public school environment. The atmosphere which begat "Jewish Ostracism in America," as Miss Morais entitled her article, began

> in the free schools of America . . . at the public schools the disadvantages of the little disciples of Moses are so great as to cause many a little heart, burning with ambition, to dread the approach of the Mosaic festivals. With the approach of each season, examinations are arbitrarily fixed on the very holiday of the Jew; absence for religious purposes is punished as an offense.

A teacher remarked pityingly to her best pupil, a Jewish child, "I am sorry for you, it is your misfortune, not your fault, that you are a Jew."

> This remark is evidence of the spirit with which secular knowledge is inculcated in the free schools of America. Under the instruction of the unsectarian school mistress, the invention of the press is the result of Christian civilization; the geography of India is the triumph of Christian progress; the science of morals is inseparable from Christian dogma. Hymns to the Trinity, readings from the Testament, resound in the halls of secular learning, and the Jew, perhaps excused by special permission from denying the teachings of his home, is marked with the sign of an invidious separation.

This tone prevailing within the public school would "guide the finger of the street-boy to point at Jewish features with an infant 'Hep, hep',," and it would insure that "the little child in school finds no room for the Jew in the game at recess . . ."[81] Perhaps Nina Morais was reminiscing upon her years as a sensitive schoolchild during the 1860s, the same period as the tougher-fibered Louis Marshall. Their recollections furnish bitter support for the existence of an "evangelical consensus of faith and ethics" which was "clearly Protestant in orientation." [82]

Yet the Jewish day schools closed anyhow. Isaac Mayer Wise's Zion College collapsed by 1858 and, as we have seen, Talmid Yelodim ceased as a day school. In 1870 Wise reported buoyantly to the United States Commissioner of Education:

> It is our settled opinion here that the education of the young is the business of the State, and the religious instruction, to which we add the Hebrew, is the duty of religious bodies. Neither ought to interfere with the other. The secular branches belong to the public schools, religion in the Sabbath schools, respectively.[83]

What Wise called a "settled opinion" became ideology. The second Cleveland conference, which he convened in 1870 to deal principally with liturgical and theological matters, considered two resolutions of civic import introduced by Max Lilienthal. One renewed allegiance to "civil and religious liberty and hence the separation of church and state." The second was orotund:

> We love and revere this country as our home and fatherland for us and our children; and therefore consider it our paramount duty to sustain and support the government; to favor by all means the system of free education, leaving religious instruction to the care of the different denominations.[84]

Both resolutions passed, apparently without serious discussion. Patriotism, obedience to lawful government, and public school education were placed upon the same level.

Did any voice plead for the continuation of the Jewish schools and deplore their demise? Only one appears on record, the moderate Reform Rabbi Bernard Felsenthal (1822–1908) of Chicago. Addressing a B'nai B'rith lodge in 1865, he employed an argument not heard during the debates of the 1850s. Conceding the value of the public school, Felsenthal invoked a higher value, that of Jewish learning, which could not be imparted in the few hours of Sabbath School. In order to teach children Hebrew, Jewish beliefs, Bible, liturgy, rabbinic literature, as well as German, and to provide for the common branches—all of which he desired taught—distinct Jewish schools had to exist. Thus the indispensable

American Jewish learned class might be nurtured. The Chicago reformer's first publication, in 1858, had been *Kol Kore Bamidbar,* "A Voice Crying in the Wilderness," and this title would have fitted *Jüdisches Schulwesen in Amerika,* for the attention which it received.[85]. This forgotten pamphlet, however, looks forward to the rationale of twentieth-century Orthodox day schools.

VI

American Jewish efforts were heavily invested in combatting the "evangelical consensus" and resisting sectarian religious influences. One of the first and most thoroughly argued legal cases of this character concerned Bible reading in the Cincinnati public schools. The case originated in the demand of that city's Catholics for the cessation of King James Bible readings in the public schools as a violation of their children's rights of conscience. The Cincinnati Board of Education, in 1869, ordered the practice discontinued; its two Jewish members' votes were divided. Amid much public excitement, the matter went to the Superior Court of Cincinnati, which upheld the Protestant objections to the Board's decision with a significant dissent by Judge Alphonso Taft. The progenitor of a political dynasty and future U.S. Attorney-General paid attention, in his opinion, to the Jewish position even though no Jew was a party to the suit:

> Another numerous class of heavy tax-payers, the Jews, object [to Bible readings]. . . . But it is claimed . . . that the Jews have met with something like a miraculous conversion, and have become reconciled to the New Testament. . . . There is too much evidence of dissent on their part . . . to permit us to conclude that they have ever intended to waive their rights of conscience and of religious liberty.

Taft sized up the relation between Jews and public schools with shrewd sympathy:

> The truth of the matter undoubtedly is, that the Jews, like many others, have found out that our common schools are munificently endowed, and, in general, well conducted, so that the privilege of attending them is inestimable, and they have wisely concluded to secure for their children the secular education of the common schools, and attend to their religious nurture at home and in their own organizations. A faith which had

survived so much persecution, through so many centuries, they may well have risked in the common schools of Cincinnati, though at some cost in religious feeling.[86]

The judge was clearly implying that the Jews, for prudential reasons, had refrained from pressing the Bible-reading issue, but sympathized with the Catholics when the latter did so. With his close knowledge of Cincinnati life, Taft probably knew whereof he spoke. In 1873 the Supreme Court of Ohio upheld the Cincinnati Board of Education, along the lines of Taft's dissent.

The issue of Bible-reading in the public schools was tied to wider contemporary issues. Protestants of the "evangelical consensus" sought to reassert the conception of Christian America. Catholics, on the other hand, opposed sectarian incursions while asking public funds for their parochial schools. Jews supported half the Protestant and half the Catholic position: no public funds for parochial schools, and no religious incursions into public schools.[87]

The Ohio State Constitutional Convention of 1874 rejected the demand of that state's Catholics for legislation permitting aid to their parochial schools. At the Convention there was a single Jewish delegate, Julius Freiberg (1823–1908), elected in Cincinnati with both parties' endorsement. As a merchant, long-time president of Bene Israel Congregation and later of the Union of American Hebrew Congregations,[88] he was expressing a representative Jewish opinion when he addressed the assemblage in rough and ready fashion:

> Mr. President, I think the Jews had a far better right to ask this [School Fund] division for the reason that if any religion should be taught at all in the public schools, it would be the Christian whether Catholic or Protestant. . . . All we ask is "keep sectarian hands off," and we are the strongest supporters of the free-schools, not only by taxes but by moral support; and there exists a noted fact that while the Jewish population [of Cincinnati] is only one in twenty-three, the pupils who visit the high schools number one-third.

The Jews were "a people who, next to religious liberty, appreciate nothing higher than our excellent free school system . . ." Arguing against sectarianism in the school's he mentioned the experience of "[a] little child of mine, who is only six years old [who] came home one day and asked me, "Papa, what is all that story about Jesus? Our teacher reads so much about a man named Jesus.' (Laughter)" Freiberg was personally untroubled by his daughter's question, but such episodes conflicted with his vision of the American public school:

> Whenever and wherever I see one of these schoolhouses in course of erection, I cannot help exclaiming there is going to be another of those temples of liberty, provided they are not polluted by sectarianism. In them the children of the high and low, rich and poor, Protestants, Catholics and Jews, mingle together, play together, and are taught that we are a free people, striving to elevate mankind, and to respect one another. In them we plant and foster the tree of civil and religious liberty.[89]

The connection between the well-being of American democracy and public school education was as firmly set in the mind of this immigrant German-Jewish merchant as in the mind of Horace Mann or Frederick A. P. Barnard. Possibly Freiberg was influenced by Max Lilienthal, the rabbi of his congregation, a public school activist. Both Freiberg and Rabbi Lilienthal added a particularly Jewish emphasis upon the removal of all distinctive religious manifestations from these "temples of liberty."

One year following the Ohio Constitutional Convention, Joseph Rodrigues Brandon (1828–1916) of San Francisco, unlike Freiberg a minimally affiliated Jew, replied to a local minister's demand that the Lord's Prayer he recited in the public schools. He pleaded for "unsectarian" education:

> The hope of all thinking men is education—education of the highest order—the cultivation of science, the exercise of reason, *unlimited* in its objects; but to this end it must be UNSECTARIAN. . . . Education— unsectarian education is the hope and salvation of the Jew, as of all who have passed through religious persecution . . .
>
> Let all of us, with free thought and free, unsectarian education, seek to lift ourselves and our fellows above the clouds of ignorance, sectarianism and prejudice . . . [90]

Wise's declaration to the U.S. Commissioner of Education; the Cleveland rabbinical resolution of 1870 and the casualness of its passage; the Cincinnati "Bible War" and Taft's realization of the Jewish position; Freiberg's remarks to the Ohio Constitutional Convention; Brandon's inconspicuous pamphlet—all suggest that a Jewish position on public school education was fixed by the 1870s. Twenty years later young Rabbi Edward N. Calisch (1866–1946) of Richmond, Virginia, articulated these convictions in the flush of contemporary eloquence:

> Judaism earnestly upholds the public school system of America, because it believes that the strength and the glory of the country lie therein. The public schools are the corner-stone of the nation, on which and by means of which, she has reared the superstructure of her unparalleled achievements.

European powers have costly armies and navies; "America has her public schools and needs no more." They required, however,

> first, that they shall be essentially and completely under the control of the public and secular authorities, and second, that they shall be upheld and supported by the public, morally and materially.

Public schools had to "remain under influence and authority that are purely secular. They must be kept aloof from every sectarian tendency . . . ." [91] This was a view bound to conflict with rising Catholic demands for religious influences in the schools. [92]

To Rabbi Calisch, "it is in the public schools that the true democracy of our country is displayed . . .," and hence "the first care of the Jewish relief societies that receive the Russian immigrants, is to teach the children and the grown ones the English language, that they may enter the public schools and receive the touch and the influence of American culture and American citizenship." [93] In fact, East European Jews were arriving in huge numbers at the time Calisch wrote. Between them and their Central European Jewish immigrant predecessors two significant differences possessed educational significance. Comparatively few knew Russian or Polish, and they manifested no interest in transmitting either tongue to their children—differing markedly from the German of German Jews. Second, the massing of East European Jews in giant urban colonies insured that their children would not be small minorities in neighborhood public schools; indeed, dozens of New York City schools were 95 percent or more Jewish in enrollment, and other cities also had their "Jewish" public schools.

By all accounts the East European Jewish immigrant child succeeded conspicuously in public school. For them the words of one of their number who attained the highest judicial office rang true: the public school was indeed "the symbol of our democracy, the most pervasive means of promoting our common destiny," and of advancing the fortunes of the coming generation.

The Jewish ideological commitment to religiously neutral American public schools continued for eighty years and more. Rabbinical associations, national Jewish organizations, and local community committees kept watchful eyes on the public schools. Their response to particular situations varied, but Julius Freiberg's words of 1874 could provide a perennial motto: public schools were veritable "temples of liberty" in which American children, "high and low, rich and poor, Protestants, Catholics and Jews," prepared their own future and that of their country. In public schools "we plant and foster the tree of civil and religious liberty . . ." These exalted purposes could be achieved only when the "temples of liberty" were "not polluted by sectarianism." Attending public schools and guarding them from sectarianism was the interest and patriotic obligation of American Jews. Their equality was manifest, and their children's future within American society was assured, by public schooling as defined in these terms.[94] Have not self-confidence as Americans, ethnic assertiveness, and urban troubles lessened this Jewish faith?

NOTES

I wish to express my gratitude to Professors Lawrence A. Cremin, Robert D. Cross, and Timothy L. Smith for their invaluable comments on this study.

Abbreviations used:
Am. Isr. = *American Israelite* (Cincinnati; continuation of *Isr.*)
Isr. = *Israelite* (Cincinnati)
Occ. = *Occident* (Philadelphia)
PAJHS = *Publication of the American Jewish Historical Society*
Grinstein, Rise = Hyman B. Grinstein, *The Rise of the Jewish Community in New York, 1654-1860* (Philadelphia, 1945).
Grinstein, "Studies . . . " = Hyman B. Grinstein, "Studies in the History of Jewish Education in New York City (1728–1860)," *Jewish Review* (New York), II, 1 (April 1944), 41–58; 2–3 (July–October 1944), 187–201.
Gartner, *Documents* = Lloyd P. Gartner, *Jewish Education in the United States: A Documentary History* (New York, 1969).

1. *McCullom* vs. *Board of Education,* 303 U. S. 203 (1948), quoted in R. Freeman Butts, *The American Tradition in Religion and Education* (Boston, 1950), 203–5. On the social and intellectual bearings of American education, see, in general, Merle E. Curti, *The Social Ideas of American Educators, with New Chapters on the Last Twenty-five Years* (Totowa, N. J., 1966), and Lawrence A. Cremin, *The American Common School: An Historic Conception* (New York, 1951).
2. Curti, *op. cit.,* 40–49; Lawrence A. Cremin, *American Education: The Colonial Experience, 1607–1783* (New York, 1970), 436–43, now the standard work, supplemented by Carl Bridenbaugh, *Cities in Revolt: Urban Life in America 1743–1776* (New York, 1955), 172–79, 373–80, and Sidney I. Pomerantz, *New York an American City 1783–1803,* 2d ed. (Port Washington, N. Y., 1965), 421–31.
3. Quoted in Curti, *op. cit.,* 56.
4. Quoted in *Ibid.,* 69.
5. This is the theme of Michael B. Katz's two stimulating books, *The Irony of Early School Reform: Educational Innovation in Mid-Nineteenth Century Massachusetts* (Cambridge, Mass., 1968), esp. 85–93 and 111, and *Class, Bureaucracy, and Schools: The Illusion of Educational Change in America* (New York, 1971), esp. 3–56. The relevance of this indoctrination to Jews is doubtful. It may well be that the previous possession of these virtues partly explains the academic success of Jewish children. Other elements in the Jewish tradition could prepare Jews for a modern economic role.
6. Joseph L. Blau, ed., *Social Theories of Jacksonian Democracy* (New York 1947), 46.
7. *Ibid.,* 337.
8. *Ibid.,* 152.
9. *Ibid.,* 54, 271.

10. Lee Benson, *The Concept of Jacksonian Democracy: New York as a Test Case* (Princeton, 1961), 106 and n.; cf. Edward Pessen, *Most Uncommon Jacksonians: The Radical Ideas of the Early Labor Movement* (Albany, 1967), 183–89, and Curti, *op. cit.*, 90–91.

11. Quoted in Rush Welter, *Popular Education and Democratic Thought in America* (New York, 1962), 85; see, in general, chaps. 6 and 7.

12. *Second Annual Report of the Superintendent of Public Instruction, Indiana, 1853,* quoted in Curti, *op. cit.*, 62.

13. Quoted in Welter, *op. cit.*, 108.

14. James Fulton McClear, "The True American Union of Church and State: The Reconstruction of the Theocratic Tradition," *Church History,* XXVIII, 1 (March 1959), 41.

15. Quoted in *ibid.*, 54–55.

16. Cremin, *Common School* (n. 1 above), 66–70. See also Jonathan Messerli, *Horace Mann* (New York, 1972), 309–15, 332–34, 409–10, 432–34; I did not see Raymond B. Culver, *Horace Mann and Religion in the Massachusetts Public Schools* (New Haven, 1929).

17. [Henry Stephens Randall] *Decision of the State Superintendent of Schools, on the Right to Compel Catholic Children to Attend Prayer, and to Read and Commit Portions of the Bible, as School Exercises* (Albany, 1853), quoted in Butts, *op. cit.*, 136–37.

18. Robert Baird, *Religion in America* (1856), ed. and abr. Henry Warner Bowden (New York, 1970), 138–39.

19. Timothy L. Smith, *Revivalism and Social Reform: American Protestantism on the Eve of the Civil War* (New York, 1957), 40–41.

20. Mark A. DeWolfe Howe, *James Ford Rhodes: American Historian* (New York and London, 1929), 18–19.

21. Robert T. Handy, "The Protestant Quest for a Christian America," *Church History,* XXII, 1 (March 1953), 11. Clifford S. Griffin, *Their Brothers' Keepers: Moral Stewardship in the United States, 1800–1865* (New Brunswick, 1960), 135–39, overstates the case, in my opinion.

22. Timothy L. Smith, "Protestant Schooling and American Nationality, 1800–1850," *Journal of American History,* LIII, 4 (March 1967), 687.

23. Timothy L. Smith, "Parochial Education and American Culture," in Paul Nash, ed., *History and Education: The Educational Uses of the Past* (New York, 1971), 196–97; see also David B. Tyack, "Onward Christian Soldiers: Religious Education in American Public Schools," in *ibid.*, 218–32.

24. Timothy L. Smith, "Parochial Education . . . , " 202.

25. Thomas T. McAvoy, *A History of the Catholic Church in the United States* (Notre Dame, 1969), 114, 127, 133, 166, 173.

26. The standard account is still Ray Allen Billington, *The Protestant Crusade 1800–1860: A Study of the Origins of American Nativism* (New York, 1938; repr. Chicago, 1964 [paperback]).

27. On the New York City episode, see Vincent P. Lannie, *Public Money and Parochial Education: Bishop Hughes, Governor Seward, and the New York School Controversy* (Cleveland, 1968); Billington, *op. cit.*, 142–66, also mentioning cases in other cities; Benson, *op. cit.*, 116–19, 171–73, 187–92; Robert E. Ernst, *Immigrant Life in New York City, 1825–1853* (New York, 1949), 140–45. The treatment in Glyndon G. Van Deusen, *William Henry Seward* (New York, 1967), 67–71, is thin, and not much helped by the same author's "Seward and the School Question Reconsidered," *Journal of American History,* LII, 2 (September 1965), 314–19.

28. Grinstein, "Studies . . . ," 44.
29. New York City, Board of Education, *Document No. 2, January 31, 1843, Report of the Special Committee, To Whom was referred the investigation of certain books with reference to religious sectarianism* . . . (a copy was kindly made available by Teachers College Library); Grinstein, *Rise,* 235–236.
30. Bernard J. McQuaid, "Religion in Schools," *North American Review,* CXXII, (Whole No. CCXCIII) (April 1881), 238.
31. Robert D. Cross, *The Emergence of Liberal Catholicism in America* (Cambridge, Mass., 1958), 130–45; Neil G. McCluskey, *Catholic Education in America: A Documentary History* (New York, 1964), 86–94, 127–74, conveniently presents documents; on John L. Spalding, Curti, *op. cit.,* 348–73. I have not seen Robert D. Cross, "The Origins of the Catholic Parochial Schools in America," *American Benedictine Review,* XVI (June 1965), 194–209, but I did see an earlier draft. John Webb Pratt, *Religion, Politics, and Diversity: The Church-State Theme in New York History,* (Ithaca, 1967), 158–203, is a good review of the subject.
32. Early Jewish education is extensively covered in Jacob R. Marcus, *The Colonial American Jew 1492–1776,* 3 vols. (Detroit, 1970), II, 1059–68 and III, 1195–1211; Edwin Wolf II and Maxwell Whiteman, *The History of the Jews of Philadelphia from Colonial Times to the Age of Jackson* (Philadelphia, 1957), 141–42, 255; Leo Hershkowitz and Isidore S. Meyer, *Letters of the Franks Family (1733–1748)* (Waltham, Mass., 1968), 3, 12–13, 41; Grinstein, *Rise,* 225–30; Grinstein, "Studies . . . ," 41–43.
33. Grinstein, *Rise,* 231; Grinstein, "Studies . . . ," 44.
34. Joseph L. Blau and Salo W. Baron, *The Jews of the United States 1790–1840: A Documentary History,* 3 vols. (New York, 1963), II, 437–39.
35. Of the large literature, see Mordechai Eliav, *Jewish Education in Germany in the Period of Enlightenment and Emancipation* (Hebrew), (Jerusalem, 1960), pt. I; Ernst Simon, "Philanthropinism and Jewish Education" (Hebrew), *Sefer Ha-Yovel liKhevod Mordechai Menahem Kaplan* (New York, 1953), 149–88; A. Kober, "150 Years of Religious Instruction," *Leo Baeck Institute Year Book,* II (1957), 98–119; *Leopold and Adelheid Zunz: An Account in Letters 1815–1885,* ed. Nahum N. Glatzer (London, 1958), xi–xvi, 1–4; Shalom (Salo) Baron, "On the History of Enlightenment and Education in Vienna" (Hebrew), *Sefer Touroff* (Boston, 1938), 167–83, 374–79; Cecil Roth, "Educational Abuses and Reform in Hanoverian England," *Mordecai M. Kaplan Jubilee Volume* (New York, 1953), 469–80 (repr. in his *Essays and Portraits in Anglo-Jewish History* [Philadelphia, 1962]); Jacob Katz: *Tradition and Crisis: Jewish Society at the End of the Middle Ages* (Glencoe, Ill., 1961), 265–67.
36. Grinstein, "Studies . . . ," 53 and passim.
37. Hyman B. Grinstein, "An Early Parochial School," *Jewish Education,* XIII, 1 (April 1941), 23–33.
38. Grinstein, "Studies . . . ," 189–90; Grinstein, *Rise,* 244–46.
39. Isidor Busch in *Isr.,* December 22, 1854, 189; Emily Seasongood in Jacob R. Marcus, *Memoirs of American Jews,* 3 vols. (Philadelphia, 1955–56), II, 60–62 (repr. in Gartner, *Documents,* 80–82); I. J. Benjamin, *Three Years in America, 1859–1862,* trans. C. Reznikoff, 2 vols. (Philadelphia, 1956), I, 310.
40. "A Call to Detroit—1869," trans. A. I. Shinedling, *American Jewish Archives,* XIX, 1 (September 1967), 39; Irving I. Katz, *The Beth El Story with a History of the Jews in Michigan before 1850* (Detroit, 1955), 66, 83.
41. Our forthcoming history of the Jews of Cleveland will discuss this school. A brief comparative view is provided by Ida Cohen Selevan, "The Education of Jewish

Immigrants in Pittsburgh, 1862–1932," *YIVO Annual of Jewish Social Science,* XV (1974), 126–127, 139–140.

42. Morris A. Gutstein, *A Priceless Heritage: The Epic Growth of Nineteenth Century Chicago Jewry* (New York, 1953), 212–25.

43. Joshua Trachtenberg, *Consider the Years: The Story of the Jewish Community of Easton, 1752–1942* (Easton, Pa., 1944), 149, 151, 319 n. 13.

44. Nelson R. Burr, *Education in New Jersey 1630–1871* (Princeton, 1942), 187, 288–89. The traveler I. J. Benjamin (*op. cit.,* I, 229–31) spoke of two Jewish schools in San Francisco, and the absence of further notice suggests that they shared the fate of others of their type.

45. Menahem G. Glenn, "Rabbi Sabato Morais' Report on the Hebrew Education Society of Philadelphia," in *Essays in American Jewish History* (Cincinnati, 1958), 409–11 (Hebrew), 418–19 (English), but the translation here is mine. The HES was actually open to non-Jewish students; *ibid.* A manual training school opened by the HES for Russian immigrant boys also gave up general education; *ibid.* Neighborhood background is provided in Maxwell Whiteman, "Philadelphia's Jewish Neighborhoods", in Allen F. Davis and Mark H. Haller eds., *The Peoples of Philadelphia: A History of Ethnic Groups and Lower Class Life, 1790–1940* (Philadelphia, 1973), 235–236.

46. Rudolf Glanz, *Studies in Judaica Americana* (New York, 1970), 68–75, 229–32. *Cf.* laments by German visitors on the apathy of their immigrant countrymen to education, in Edith Abbott, *Historical Aspects of the Immigration Problem: Select Documents* (Chicago, 1926; repr. New York, 1966), 440, 489, 622.

47. The latest account is Richard Jensen, *The Winning of the Midwest: Social and Political Conflict, 1888–1896* (Chicago, 1971), 122–53.

48. E.g., *Deborah,* XIV (1868–69), 190; XII (1866–67), 82; *Occ.,* July 1856, 200.

49. William Oland Bourne, *History of the Public School Society of the City of New York* (New York, 1870), 176–77; Grinstein, *Rise,* 31–33, 472–73.

50. Isaac M. Fein, *The Making of an American Jewish Community: The History of Baltimore Jewry from 1773 to 1920* (Philadelphia, 1971), 122–27; Louis J. Swichkow and Lloyd P. Gartner, *The History of the Jews of Milwaukee* (Philadelphia, 1963), 52–53; Dieter Cunz, *The Maryland Germans: A History* (Princeton, 1948), 222–32, 336–37; Gutstein, *op. cit.,* 216–22, 237–39.

51. Fein, *op. cit.,* 125–26; Swichkow and Gartner, *op. cit.,* 52; Cunz, *op. cit.,* 334.

52. *Occ.,* I, 9 (December 1843), 411.

53. *Ibid.,* 413; Joseph R. Rosenbloom, "Rebecca Gratz and the Jewish Sunday School Movement in Philadelphia," *PAJHS,* XLVIII, 2 (December 1958), 71–78, esp. n. 29; Maxwell Whiteman, "Isaac Leeser and the Jews of Philadelphia," *PAJHS,* XLVIII, 4 (June 1959), 207–44, esp. nn. 38, 40, 129.

54. *Occ., loc. cit.,* 469–73.

55. *Ibid.,* II, 8 (November 1844), 385–86.

56. E.g., *Ibid.,* IV, 2 (May 1846), 61–62; IV, 3 (June 1846), 109–14.

57. *Ibid.,* IV, 11 (February 1847), 548–50.

58. *Asmonean,* I, 1 (October 25, 1849), 2.

59. *Ibid.*

60. *Ibid.,* I, 6 (November 30, 1849), 45. Lyon later reported on the New York Jewish day schools in favorable detail and requested information on those in other cities; repr. in Gartner, *Documents,* 63–67.

61. Salvatore Sabbadini, "Relazioni epistolari fra I. S. Reggio e Isidore Busch," *Festschrift Armand Kaminka* (Vienna, 1937), 119–24; Salo W. Baron, "The Revolution of 1848 and Jewish Scholarship. Part II: Austria," *Proceedings of the*

American Academy for Jewish Research, XX (1951), 1–33, esp. 19–24; "An Unpublished Letter of Isidor Busch Containing Genealogical Data" sent to Bernard Felsenthal, App. 7 in Guido Kisch, *In Search of Freedom: A History of American Jews from Czechoslovakia* (London, 1949), 230–32; *ibid.,* 123–25.

62. Glanz, *op. cit.,* 25–36; Guido Kisch, "Israels Herold: The First Jewish Weekly in New York," *Historia Judaica,* II, 2 (October 1940), 65–84; James A. Wax, "Isidor Busch: American Patriot and Abolitionist," *loc. cit.,* V, 2 (October 1943), 83–102.

63. *Occ.,* IX, 9 (December 1851), 476–82. Leeser, who characteristically printed this sharp exception to his own program, satisfied himself with a brief dissenting footnote. Busch's article includes a very interesting contrast between Europe and the United States. Recalling the recent revolutions of 1848 and the prominence of Jews among the revolutionists, he attributes this to Jewish love of liberty and independence, which the annual Tisha be-Av fast perpetuated. The article, without Leeser's comments, was reprinted in *American Jewish Archives,* XVIII, 2 (November 1966), 155–59.

64. *Isr.,* I, 22 (December 8, 1854), 174; the first sentence has been repunctuated. The chronology derives from Busch's reference to a "late attempt of establishing such a school in St. Louis," i.e., not long before he wrote in late 1854. For Busch to speak of setting aside his views means that he had already formed the view expressed in the 1851 article.

65. *Isr.,* I, 22 (December 8, 1854), 174; I, 24 (December 22, 1854), 188–89; I, 25 December 29, 1854), 198–208; it will be noted that Busch—or perhaps the editor, Wise—used *Israelite* rather than *Jew,* contrary to Busch's principle of 1851.

66. *Isr.,* I, 22 (December 8, 1854), 174.

67. *Ibid.*

68. *Ibid.*

69. *Ibid.,* I, 24 (December 22, 1854), 189.

70. *Ibid.*

71. *Ibid.,* I, 25 (December 29, 1854), 197–98.

72. Rabbi Abraham J. Karp informs me that Leeser assisted Busch's bookselling business by enclosing copies of his catalogue in mailings of the *Occident.* The exchange is in *Occ.,* XIII, 2 (May 1855), 85–89, repr. in Gartner, *Documents,* 68–75.

73. *Occ., loc. cit.,* 80.

74. *Isr.,* I, 27 (January 12, 1855), 214; Grinstein, *Rise,* 204 and index, s.v. "Brandeis, Emanuel."

75. *Isr., loc. cit.*

76. Historians of the Cleveland conference have surprisingly overlooked this discussion, e.g., Moshe Davis, *The Emergence of Conservative Judaism: The Historical School in 19th Century America* (Philadelphia, 1963), 130–35; James G. Heller, *Isaac M. Wise: His Life, Work and Thought* (New York, 1965), 283–307. The report of the discussion is by "Dr. L[ilienthal]" in *Isr.,* II, 18 (November 9, 1855), 148.

77. On Gotthelf, a Bavarian immigrant of 1840 who served as a hospital chaplain during the Civil War, see Bertram W. Korn, *American Jewry and the Civil War* (Philadelphia, 1957), 82–83; on Kalisch (1816–1886), see Swichkow and Gartner, *op. cit.,* 39, 42–44. In 1857 he attempted to establish a Jewish day school in Milwaukee.

78. Grinstein, *Rise,* 90–91, 233, 239, 243; Grinstein, "Studies . . . " 48–49, 51; on his public school activities, see the panegyric but informative David Philipson,

Max Lilienthal American Rabbi: Life and Writings (New York, 1915), chap. VI. Morton J. Merowitz, "Max Lilienthal (1814–1882)—Jewish Educator in Nineteenth Century America", *YIVO Annual of Jewish Social Science,* XV (1974), 46–65, misses the public school dimension and deals mainly with Lilienthal in New York City.

79. On Wise, see Philipson, *op. cit.,* 122; Heller, *op. cit.,* 275–82, 325, 368, 386, where the point is not made, however, that the institution became an afternoon and Sunday School in 1869.

80. Louis Marshall to William Fox, December 2, 1927, Marshall Papers, American Jewish Archives, Box 1599. I am obliged to Stanley F. Chyet, associate director, and to Mr. James Marshall for permitting the publication of his father's letter. On the background of this letter, see Morton Rosenstock, *Louis Marshall, Defender of Jewish Rights* (Detroit, 1965), 261–62; *cf.* Marshall to Benjamin Stolz, November 21, 1922, in *Louis Marshall Champion of Liberty: Selected Papers and Addresses,* ed. Charles Reznikoff, 2 vols. (Philadelphia, 1956), II, 967–70. In the light of these experiences it is interesting that Marshall favored Bible readings in public schools of passages acceptable to Jews and Christians: "Personally I believe it would not do our Jewish children a bit of harm to become familiar with the Bible even though it be read in the public schools. It will probably be the only way in which many of them would ever gain the slightest familiarity with the Book of Books." *Ibid.,* 968–69.

81. Later Mrs. Emanuel Cohen of Minneapolis; W. Gunther Plaut, *The Jews in Minnesota: The First Seventy-Five Years* (New York, 1959), 147–51. The selections are from her "Jewish Ostracism in America," *North American Review,* CXXXIII (Whole No. CCXCVIII) (September 1881), 268–69.

82. Supra, n. 20, 21.

83. U. S. Commissioner of Education, *Report, 1870* (Washington, 1873), 370, quoted in Gartner, *Documents,* 86.

84. Quoted from Philipson, *op. cit.,* 111.

85. Bernard Felsenthal, *Jüdisches Schulwesen in America* (Chicago, 1866), excerpted in Gartner, *Documents,* 83–84. The bibliographic description in Emma Felsenthal, *Bernard Felsenthal, Teacher in Israel* (London, 1924), is curiously erroneous.

86. Morris U. Schappes, *A Documentary History of the Jews in the United States 1654–1875,* rev. ed. (New York, 1952), 531. On the case, which aroused considerable public feeling in 1869–70, see Harold M. Helfman, "The Cincinnati 'Bible War' 1869–1870," *Ohio State Archaeological and Historical Quarterly,* LX, 4 (October 1951), 369–86. Lilienthal's reports to the *Jewish Times,* December 10 and 17, 1869, repr. in Philipson, *op. cit.,* describe the courtroom proceedings. The basic sources are in Schappes, *op. cit.,* 520–37.

87. Philipson, *op. cit.,* chap. VI, esp. 111–15, 120–24.

88. David Philipson, "Julius Freiberg," *PAJHS,* XIX (1910), 202–5.

89. *Official Report of the Proceedings and Debates of the Third Constitutional Convention of Ohio,* vol. II, pt. 2 (Cleveland, 1874), 2257–58; partly in *Am. Isr.,* XXII, 13 (March 27, 1874), 6. Jewish-Catholic-Protestant relations on this question at the New York State Constitutional Convention of 1894 are discussed in stimulating fashion in Samuel T. McSeveny, *The Politics of Depression: Political Behavior in the Northeast, 1893–1896* (New York, 1972), esp. 72–76.

90. Joseph R. Brandon, *A Reply to the Rev. Mr. Hemphill's Discourse on "Our Public Schools, Shall the Lord's Prayer be Recited in Them?"* (San Francisco, 1875), quoted in Gartner, *Documents,* 92. On Brandon, see *American Jewish Year Book, 1916–1917,* 106, and Neville J. Laski, *Laws and Charities of the*

Spanish and Portuguese Jews Congregation of London (London, 1952), 175.

91. Edward N. Calisch, "Judaism and the Public School System of America," *Central Conference of American Rabbis Yearbook,* III (1892), 125–26. (I owe this reference to my student, Mr. David S. Cohen.)

92. An early instance appears in Bishop McQuaid's article of 1881 (cited *supra,* n. 29): "Between Catholics on one side and evangelicals on the other, infidels, agnostics, secularists, and Jews stepped in and captured the field"—for the secularization of the public schools.

93. Calisch, *op. cit.,* 129. He deplored, as well, Jewish children being sent to any private school.

94. See, for example, the strong support of public schooling by Jews of Burlington, Vermont, in Elim L. Anderson, *We Americans: A Study of Ethnic Cleavage in an American City* (Cambridge, Mass., 1937), 100–106. On the unsympathetic attitude of school officials in New York City to the introduction of Jewish cultural elements, see Superintendent Campbell's observations, and I. S. Chipkin's reply, quoted in Mordecai M. Kaplan, *Judaism as a Civilization* (New York, 1937), 551–53. See also Rezenikoff, *Louis Marshall,* 894–97; Swichkow and Gartner, *op. cit.,* 260; Alter F. Landesman, *Brownsville: The Birth, Development and Passing of a Jewish Community in New York* (New York, 1969), 155–64.

A CONFRONTATION WITH ASSIMILATIONISTS: THE CONCEPT OF A NONSECTARIAN JEWISH COMMUNAL INSTITUTION
(A Memoir)

By

OSCAR I. JANOWSKY

The City College and City University of New York

Assimilation: Meaning and Prevalence

During the nineteenth and early twentieth centuries, the idea of assimilation occasioned controversy and dissension among Jews of the Western world. As legal segregation abated and it appeared possible for Jews to share in the economic, political, cultural, and social life of the peoples among whom they dwelt, some Jews saw in assimilation the means of bringing to a close the era of persecution. They visualized an "open society" beckoning the Jews to abandon the "ghetto" and take their place as free and equal citizens of their countries. Others disdained assimilation as a delusion. The vision of equality they scorned as a mirage, and assimilation was condemned as a siren song which could entrap the unwary to abandon the defenses of Jewish survival.

There was a haze of unreality about this controversy, for it ignored the process of assimilation as a universal factor in historical development and its significant role in the Jewish past as well. Moreover, it failed to come to grips with the precise meaning of the term or the specifics of the process. The result was a clash over catchwords or at best over a vague and ill-defined concept. The contending factions were "assimilationists" and "anti-assimilationists," subsumed as tight groupings, each of one stamp, and each differentiated from the other in purpose, goal, and degree of commitment. In fact, however, there were variations within each faction, and they were not mutually exclusive.

The extreme form of assimilation in Christian lands, its terminus and for some its inevitable goal was baptism; that was a sharply defined step which denoted abandonment of the ancestral group. But many assimilationists did not consciously envision that goal. Some intermarried with or without commitment to raise the children as Christians. Others were indifferent to religion and espoused the prevaling culture, or that vague concept of "cosmopolitan culture." But that stance was not exclusively the hallmark of the assimilationists. Many anti-assimilationists were similarly oriented, at least in indifference to religion and commitment to the dominant culture. Finally, except for pockets of resistance to all compromise or accommodation, anti-assimilationists as well as assimilationists conformed to prevailing norms in language, dress and deportment, cognomens and personal names, and other outer manifestations of culture. Therefore, the issue between assimilationists and anti-assimilationists was not really joined.

The term *assimilation* and its derivitives (*assimilationist, assimilator, assimilable, assimilative*) are imprecise at best. To assimilate is to make or to become alike; to absorb and incorporate or to become absorbed and incorporated; to cause to resemble or to conform to, to take after, to adapt to. The process of achieving or promoting conformity, similarity, or absorption is assimilation.

When identified with the fusion of social and cultural groupings, assimilation involves the redirection of the consciousness of association with one's historical, religious, cultural, and social group to another such group. And the assimilated or merged element loses its original identity in whole or in part.

Historically, assimilation has affected all peoples in contact through war, conquest, trade, immigration, or mere propinquity or neighborliness. Through such contacts, the cultures or ways of life of societies have interpenetrated one another, and intercultural borrowing, or acculturation (the term preferred by anthropologists and sociologists), has had varying results. At times, it has produced a new pattern of culture, a blend of the differing ways of life of the groups affected. On other occasions, the consequence has been the total absorption of one element into the ways of life of another and more dominant society, with the consequent disappearance of the absorbed as a recognizable cultural unit. Still another form of assimilation has been neither the total absorption of one group nor an unconscious blend of the cultures of the interpenetrating societies. It has been a selective process, whereby a people has adopted some elements of a differing culture without marring its own unique character.

We must note further that the process of assimilation, indeed its very definition, embraces two factors, the one that absorbs and the one that is being absorbed. And the promotion and achievement of conformity may be voluntary and unconscious or induced by pressure on the part of the absorber and even by elements among those undergoing absorption. When gradual and imperceptible, a group disintegrates and blends with the dominant or prevailing society with a minimum of vexation. At times, however, uniformity becomes a conscious ideal, and assimilation a desideratum of utmost urgency. Gradual and unforced intermingling is deemed too slow and uncertain to assure the desired effect, and coercion is resorted to—pressure ranging from social approval or legal sanction to extremes of harassment and even violence. Under such circumstances, assimilation is embraced as a *doctrine,* with the consequent presumptions of the "racial," religious, and cultural superiority of the absorbing society and the disparagement of the unassimilated as inferior, bigoted, and untrustworthy. Such compulsion and dispraise have generally encountered resentment and resistance, exacerbating feelings between the dominant and subordinate groups. Within the ranks of the latter, too, assimilation as a doctrine has often occasioned strife, as assimilating elements espoused the dominant cause out of conviction or in justification of their disloyalty to the ancestral group.

The confrontation to be discussed here involved American Jews of the mid-twentieth century, and for Jews, assimilation and its problems were in on wise novel phenomena. A glance at the past will recall to mind the fact that assimilation and its consequences have been recurring if not constant factors in Jewish history. In antiquity, the Hebrews absorbed the culture of their surroundings and, as they penetrated and achieved mastery of Canaan, they reinterpreted and transformed pagan myths in accord with their intense God-consciousness and their extraordinary literary genius. In the main, however, the Hebrews or Jews of that time were assimilators, absorbing religious and ethnic elements within Canaan and, as monotheism was refined and firmly established, extending the faith and culture beyond its borders. Monotheism was the most distinctive feature of Hebrew or Jewish identity, and idolatry, with its vulgarity, cruelty, and licentiousness, was the symbol of the erring or alien.

When dominant, the Jews were not always averse to compulsory assimilation, as is evidenced by the forced conversion of the Idumeans. However, being a small and frequently a subject people, they were often the objects of assimilation. Two instances may be cited at random: the cruel measures during the reign of Manasseh, early in the seventh century before the Christian era, to enforce Assyrian ways of life; and the allurements of Hellenism, as well as the coercive efforts of Antiochus Epiphanes, in the second century before the Christian era, to achieve religious and cultural uniformity. When resident in their homeland, the Jews were able to offer resistance, as they did under Hasmonean leadership, and even to tolerate partial assimilation, that is, the adoption of Hellenistic architectural forms, war implements, and the like, even as they abhorred its religious rites and mores.

The effects of assimilation were most marked when the Jews lived as minorities in foreign lands, and especially so when the Temple and comomnwealth, the "home base," were no more. The "portable homeland," that is, Torah and Tradition, was a powerful cohesive force, but apparently not sufficient to prevent massive defections in the Greco-Roman world, notably at Alexandria, and probably also in Babylonia.

During the Middle Ages and early modern times, the Jews were marked and often segregated minorities in Christian and Moslem lands, a condition hardly conducive to easy intermingling. But rough estimates of world Jewish population reveal a staggering decline in numbers from seven or eight millions during the first century to one-and-a-half or two millions at the close of the seventeenth. Of course, much of the decrease must be attributed to the ravages of war and especially the rebellions against Rome, pestilence, decline of the birthrate attendant upon repeated expulsions, and downright massacre. Yet the forced conversions of the Middle Ages, as well as the allurements of apostasy, cannot be ignored as powerful agents of assimilation.

During the Middle Ages, religious conversion was the hallmark of assimilation, but by the eighteenth century other factors served as its solvents and symbols. The "Court Jews" and "protected Jews," generally exempted from prevailing restrictions, adopted the manner and manners of Gentile society. Far greater was the influence of the Enlightenment of the later eighteenth century, with its emphasis on reason and culture free of "superstition," prejudice, and divisive traditions, and its Jewish counterpart, the Haskalah, which prized secular culture, especially as a precondition for Jewish emancipation. The gradual achievement of citizenship in Western and Central Europe during the nineteenth century and the growth of nationalism encouraged Jews to identify with the prevailing national culture and to purge Judaism of its own national traditions. On the face of it, this assimilation related to language, political allegiance, secular culture, manners, and mores, rather than to theological and ritualistic aspects of religion. But apostasy was not really ruled out, for some 200,000 Jews are said to have been baptized during the nineteenth century.

An important conclusion remains to be noted, namely, that throughout their history, the Jews were not averse to or did not prevail against assimilation; neither as assimilators of other ethnic elements, nor in adapting themselves to certain aspects of alien culture. Proselytizing remained a potent force, despite the opposition of Ezra and Nehemiah to the assimilation of foreign ethnic components during the fifth century before the Christian era. And the Book of Ruth, in tracing the lineage of David, furnishes firm evidence that even mixed marriage was not spurned, provided it did not entail apostasy. "Racism" has not been a Jewish ideal.

Furthermore, in every land where Jews lived, including their own, they adopted languages other than Hebrew, "foreign" names, and the prevailing culture, provided again that the latter did not impinge upon their religion and its social and cultural concomitants. A startling example of assimilation is the abandonment of the ancient Hebrew alphabet and the adoption of the "square script," the "Assyrian" or Aramaic script, even for the Torah scrolls.

The Jews set their faces sternly against idolatry in ancient times and religious apostasy in later periods. And religion embraced far more than faith and ethics. It included the language and literature of Torah, the history of the people of Israel, and the ritual, ceremonial, customs, and mores of the Tradition, all of which constituted a distinctive way of life. To this the Jews clung, even as they partook of the prevailing cultures of the times. These constituted the "Jewish content" of Jewish education and Jewish living.

The Factor of Assimilation Among American Jewry

American Jewry of the mid-twentieth century was heir to the whole gamut of assimilation—history, process, and doctrine. The sparse Jewish population of Colonial times had in large measure been absorbed in Christian society. The immigrants from Central Europe prior to the Civil War reacted to the forces of assimilation much as their brethren in Germany did, except that in the United States there was at that time no need for "willed assimilation." There were few if any rooted Jewish communities with a history of communal cohesion and autonomy to retard centrifugal forces, and an "open society" rendered assimilation outwardly painless. Religious identity was preserved mainly through Reform Judaism, which discarded the "nationalistic" elements of exile and the hope of redemption in a physical Zion. When the Zionist movement arose at the end of the nineteenth century, the large majority of Reform Jews registered strong opposition to that and to every form of Jewish nationalism.

The masses of East European Jews who arrived in the United States between 1880 and the early 1920s constituted a highly visible unassimilated body at least until World War I. They lived mainly in voluntary urban "ghettos" and earned their livelihood in special areas of the economy. They spoke Yiddish, were served by a vigorous Yiddish press and literature, a lively Yiddish theater, and a congeries of institutions reminiscent of the East European Jewish town or city. They constituted a distinct and vibrant subculture.

In one respect, the "ghetto," notably New York's East Side, exhibited a novel form, a type of "inverted assimilation," as it were. Normally, in modern times religious apostasy has been the last phase of assimilation, but there were vocal and aggressive elements in the "ghetto" who flaunted irreligion before they learned English or set foot outside the immigrant quarter. These were extreme radicals who gloried in the anti-religious bias of socialism and railed in Yiddish against Judaism, often in phrases of Karl Marx which hissed a bitter anti-Semitism. These people evidently thought they were preparing the ground for a secular Jewish culture within the framework of a universalist utopia; in effect, they were hacking away at the keystone of Jewish cultural identity.

The "ghetto" appeared to the uninformed a sealed and solid alien body impervious to American influence. In fact, the forces of assimilation were at work, for the new environment eroded traditional ways. For example, the factory system clashed with Jewish religious observance, and those who were obliged to work on the Sabbath became more susceptible to strange ways. At the same time, the public school taught immigrants and especially their children the English language and American history, manners, and customs. Every wave of immigration yielded its component of men and women who found their way into new residential areas and occupations and adopted prevailing cultural and social forms.

By the 1890s, however, spontaneous and gradual assimilation was deemed too slow a process to absorb the foreign masses, who were constantly being reinforced by new arrivals. Moreover, Jews were among the "new immigrants" from Southern and Eastern Europe, who were adjudged by many native Americans as inferior or at least less desirable than their own ancestors who had immigrated earlier. The demand therefore arose for special efforts to accelerate the transformation of the newcomer into an American. Under the name of "Americanization," this movement assumed crusading proportions during World War I and its aftermath. Obviously, this was assimilation espoused as a doctrine, and it was reflected in the Jewish community, as will be noted presently.

So far as the Jews were concerned, developments following World War I showed that willed assimilation, and certainly its willful variety, was quite unnecessary. By the mid-1940s, the urban "ghettos" had been all but emptied of American-born and American-reared Jews, and of many of the immigrants as well. The new generation had acquired an American education, entered new occupations, adopted the language, historical traditions, customs, and mores of the country, and was at home in American government and society. If Americanization means overcoming feelings of strangeness and promoting common fellowship, American Jews had been Americanized. Still, there remained a curious "cultural lag," especially in the field of Jewish community centers, on the question of Americanization and assimilation. By chance, I became involved in this matter, and the involvement resulted in a confrontation with the assimilationists.

The JWB Survey and Report: Assertion of Jewish Purpose for a Jewish Communal Institution

In the fall of 1945, I was invited to direct a survey of the National Jewish Welfare Board (JWB) and its constituency of some three hundred Jewish community centers and kindred associations. My report recommended a strongly affirmative Jewish purpose and program for the Jewish community center: this was epitomized by the principle that "the program of the Jewish center should devote primary attention to Jewish content." A Survey Commission of thirty-five eminent laymen and distinguished scholars, with Professor Salo W. Baron as chairman, approved the recommendations with some modifications. The annual meeting of the JWB National Council at Pittsburgh in May 1947, received the Survey Report with enthusiasm and, after extensive discussion, voted provisional approval of the recommendations (again with some changes), including the affirmation of Jewish purpose for the Jewish community center. The following September, the Jewish Center Division Committee of JWB adopted a tentative Statement of Principles, as recommended by the Survey Report, for the consideration of the affiliated Jewish centers. Included among the principles was the proposed emphasis on Jewish content in the center program.

This strong commitment to Jewish purpose in the Jewish community center encountered vigorous opposition from a small but very influential minority.[1] To understand and appraise the issues in the conflict, it is necessary to review briefly the aims and purpose of the JWB Survey, the procedures employed in the research, the nature of the findings and the recommendations. Then we shall examine the character of the opposition, and their motivations, methods, and relative numerical strength. First, the nature of the JWB Survey and Report.

I was named director of the survey by JWB to work under the aegis of a Survey Commission. A steering committee of eight (with Frank L. Weil, the president of JWB, and Louis Kraft, its executive director, serving *ex officio*) met at intervals and approved every important procedure I recommended. My report and recommendations were submitted to the steering committee in sections as I wrote them. Finally, my twenty-one recommendations, including articles for a Statement of Principles, were approved, as submitted or with modifications, by the Survey Commission in three memorable sessions on March 29–30, 1947. All but three of the recommendations were approved without dissent. One of these three, relating to the Division of Religious Activities, was deferred. Another, on "Social Action," was adopted with two dissenting votes, and a minority report by A. Harold Murray was incorporated in the Survey Report and in the subsequent printed volume.

Aims of the JWB Survey: The aims of the Survey as well as its methodology are described at length in the preface to the JWB Survey Report.[2] The project for a survey was discussed and approved by the JWB Executive Committee on March 17–18, 1945. On that occasion, Frank L. Weil, the president of JWB, declared that there

was a need to determine JWB's responsibilities for the postwar period
and for planning so that the organization might not only render service
to its constituency but also "give guidance and supply leadership . . . to
strike out along appropriate new paths so that we may keep pace with
changing conditions and needs." Maurice Mermey, who introduced
the resolution for a survey, asserted that

> the basic objectives of Jewish Center work as promoted by JWB are not
> sufficiently defined, nor well enough understood by the general public. . . .
> It is also necessary to ascertain whether JWB has a national function and
> a national program over and above the many services that it renders
> directly to its constituent local centers. If there is such a function and
> program, it is desirable to define it and to secure acceptance and recogni-
> tion of this function.

What he had in mind was that JWB had been primarily a service organization rather than the sponsor of a "Center movement." "There
was a definite need," he said, "to go into the community so that it could
be determined just what the Center needed and how far it would go
along with the national organization" toward the fashioning of such a
policy.[3]

The functions of the JWB Survey were discussed at the organizational
meeting of the Survey Commission. When I had outlined the subjects
for inquiry into basic objectives, Maurice Mermey asked: "Will your
survey perhaps indicate objectives that presently are not objectives and
might be? In other words, may you define new objectives?" I replied
that I wished first to ascertain what present objectives were. "But,"
Mermey countered, "assuming that you find that the objectives . . . are
very clearly articulated . . . isn't it possible that you may determine that
those objectives aren't quite sufficient . . . will you then indicate other
objectives?"

This point was pressed on me by other members of the Survey Commission. Frank L. Weil said, "It might conceivably be desirable to
ascertain what ought the objectives be." Professor I. L. Kandel of
Teachers College, Columbia University, said, "The function of the survey is to find out how effective the organization is in carrying things out
and what hasn't been carried out." And Professor Mordecai M. Kaplan
added, "But apart from the effectiveness, it may be that they are effective
within a limited scope; it may be that the scope itself is not adequate."[4]

I was truly appalled by the magnitude of the task. At the time, my knowledge of the field of centers was that of an informed layman. I had lectured extensively in centers throughout the country on Jewish and general subjects and had a superficial acquaintance with their work. But I had no knowledge in depth of either their programs or their objectives. However, I recognized the validity of the point pressed upon me, and I agreed without enthusiasm that it was the function of the survey to suggest new objectives, if found necessary. But I insisted that the proper procedure would be first to analyze the present program and motives of Jewish center work, and then, if they were found inadequate, to formulate new objectives.

The point of all this is that I accepted the mandate without presuppositions, and that neither the JWB, nor the Survey Commission, nor I had the remotest idea of imposing a philosophy or a program on the centers. However, it was equally clear that I was not to conduct a "Gallup Poll," and merely record majority and minority opinions.

Research Procedures of the JWB Survey: I began with a study of the minutes of JWB from its inception in 1917. This was followed by the reading of minutes and reports of every description, memoranda, pamphlets, articles in the professional journals, speeches, correspondence, and the like. I attended sessions of JWB divisional committees, staff gatherings, and regional meetings. Armed with the knowledge thus attained, I conferred with the professional heads of JWB divisions, departments, bureaus, and services, with field workers in every territorial section, and with lay leaders, in order to ascertain strengths and weaknesses, the problems encountered, and the differences over policy in the total operation of the JWB and especially the field of Jewish centers. By March 1946, I had prepared a "Master Questionnaire," or prospectus of subjects to be studied.[5] This served as the basis for the field work: eight varieties of schedules for interviews with executive directors of centers, staff, members of boards of directors of centers and JWB sections, rank-and-file members of centers, rabbis, local Jewish communal leaders, and non-Jewish leaders in general social agencies, that is, YMCA's, YWCA's, community chests, and councils of social agencies.

In addition, I prepared a checklist "Attitude Questionnaire," constructed with an eye to statistical tabulation and an assurance of anonymity, except for the position of the respondent in the JWB, the Jewish center, and/or the local Jewish community. It sought to elicit attitudes on the purposes and functions of the Jewish center, the qualifications of staff, "Jewish content" in the center program, the Jewish center and religion, its relation to controversial public issues, the role of JWB in the Jewish center field, in army and navy and veterans services, the desirability of minimum standards in the Jewish center field, and the desirability and effectiveness of JWB cultural efforts connected with "Book Month" and "Music Week." In constructing this questionnaire I consulted with knowledgeable members of the JWB staff and leading center executives in the New York area.

An attitude questionnaire requires validation. To this end, I tested the draft on the boards of directors, staffs, and local leaders in three communities—Louisville, Kansas City, and St. Paul. Furthermore, I submitted it to a conference on March 26, 1946, of some twelve executive directors of leading Jewish centers in the New York area; and I made certain that the "settlement houses" as well as the Jewish community centers were well represented. Doubtful terms were noted and clarified. Finally, on September 20, 1946, I held a full-day conference with all persons who were doing field work on the survey: survey techniques, including the Attitude Questionnaire, as well as tentative conclusions were discussed.

The field work done from April to the end of November 1946, yielded the following results: A minimum of 3,516 persons were interviewed individually or in groups, among them 1,596 members of center boards of directors, 231 executive directors, 394 members of center staffs, 119 rabbis not directly related to centers, 373 Jewish communal leaders not directly involved in center work, 677 members of Jewish centers, many of whom served on house and youth councils, and 126 leading non-Jews in local non-Jewish social agencies.

Of the Attitude Questionnaires distributed, 2,420 were completed and returned. Since we used less than 10,000 forms, a response of close to 25 percent was secured. Among the 2,420 respondents were 550 members of the professional staffs of centers and JWB (23 percent of total responses); 264 (11 percent) members of JWB national or section boards or committees; 1,022 (42 percent) members of local center boards or committees; 308 (13 percent) rank-and-file center members; 91 (4 percent) rabbis; 135 (5 percent) local communal leaders not directly associated with centers; and 50 (2 percent) unidentified.

The Scope or Range of the JWB Survey: A survey of an organization with so large a constituency could easily get bogged down in detail and in structural or secondary matters. It was, therefore, necessary to concentrate attention on a limited number of major subjects, and this was done. The administrative and financial aspects of JWB and the Jewish centers were outside the scope of the assignment. So was the qualitative evaluation of the great variety of centers.

I did hope to study the problems connected with center membership, but I quickly realized that neither time, nor staff, nor funds would permit a survey of some 350,000 to 400,000 "members." Besides, membership figures were rough estimates in the great majority of centers, and a large number were unable or unwilling to submit even estimates. The reason was that no one knew what constituted membership. There were individual dues-paying memberships and family memberships, health-club members, business and professional members, and contributing members. There were also participants who attended public functions and were often included in membership figures. We did secure figures from 75 percent of the centers to render possible a classification of centers according to size of membership and by regional sections. We also received a small number of Attitude Questionnaires from interested members. But even to secure membership lists for a random sampling would have been a colossal undertaking beyond our means. I therefore recommended that JWB undertake an intensive study of center membership, participation, and attendance. The recommendation was approved but not implemented for lack of funds. Our survey therefore, did not cover membership. It concentrated on *leadership,* the crucial element, especially for the determination of policy and objectives, which the mandate for the survey underscored.

Since the mandate for the survey stressed the need to clarify objectives and formulate policy, I focussed attention on the basic purpose of the Jewish community center. My extensive reading and numerous interviews and conferences convinced me that this was the primary need and major issue in the center field. Two published articles in particular confirmed this conclusion: one was an address, published in 1928, by John Slawson, at the time secretary of the Jewish Welfare Federation of Detroit; the other, by Jesse Bernard, published in 1942. Slawson declared: "Of all the lacks that we now have in the field of Jewish social service . . . the greatest is the absence, on the part of the majority of the army of workers, lay and professional, of a positive philosophy of Jewish adjustment. . . ." He further asserted that "in the light of the chief goal of social work, the preservation and development of personality . . . Jewish education becomes an integral and potent mechanism in the Jewish social work process." [6] Bernard argued that bi-cultural living was a form of schizophrenia; that "belonging to two cultures . . . has its tragic aspects," not unlike the child of quarreling parents.[7] Since this clash of opinion was evident, it was necessary to determine attitudes on the Jewish purpose of the center, especially among the uncommitted. I therefore stressed the matter in the Attitude Questionnaire.

The Sample for the Attitude Questionnaire: I had at first hoped to limit the survey to a sampling of typical centers. But I learned quickly that the affiliated institutions were too varied and diverse to render possible a selection of "typical" centers. I therefore recommended to the Steering Committee of the Survey Commission that we attempt to cover *all* affiiliated centers. This was approved.

We did cover the field. Of the 301 listed affiliates, my staff and I visited 270 (90 percent of the total), and by means of interviews and written records secured the basic factual information regarding programs and facilities and general orientation for the remaining thirty-one centers. We enlisted the aid of field secretaries of JWB and professional or lay directors of the agencies in securing the necessary information, and the latter was supplemented by fugitive sources in JWB files. There was not a single center for which we did not have a minimum of information.

The Attitude Questionnaire, however, still posed a problem of sampling. Here, too, I ruled out a random or "representative" sample because such an instrument would have been of very limited value for the determination of policy and objectives. The constituency we were surveying, even its leadership, made up a mixed bag. Some were active, knowledgeable, and concerned. Others were on leadership councils because of their status in the community, their contributions or potential for contributions, and many of them knew little or nothing about the needs and programs of the centers. To ascertain the range of interests or extent of knowledge of the institutions, a representative sample would have been useful, but not for policy and objectives. It would have diluted considered opinions with pooled ignorance and unconcern.

Again I decided to cover the entire field of center leadership. The Attitude Questionnaire was addressed to all leaders of the centers, and they were urged to come to meetings to complete the questionnaire or to do so privately and transmit it to us. A large number did; others did not. What we secured, therefore, was an "interest-weighted" sample, self-selected because of interest and concern sufficient to give time and thought to the questions at issue. That was precisely what I wanted.

Furthermore, I made it clear in my report, that our tabulation of attitudes represented the "respondents" and no one else.

Findings, Conclusions, and Recommendations: The findings and an analysis of their import and consequences are contained in my report, a volume of close to 500 pages.[8] The descriptive and historical material, carefully evaluated, served as the basis for a history of JWB, an analysis of its services and relationships with its constituency and the community, and a profile of the Jewish community center field, including types of centers, their lay and professional leadership, their programs of activities, and the extent of their Jewish content.

The materials relating to *attitudes* on center purposes, functions, and objectives and on the role of JWB, especially the findings issuing from the Attitude Questionnaire, were in a different category. The views of the persons canvassed were tabulated and included in the report—twenty-seven statistical tables in the text and sixty-nine in an appendix. However, the canvass of opinion was not meant to determine in advance the recommendations on center purposes and objectives or their consequences. In other words, as I have said, the survey was not envisaged as a "Gallup Poll." My job did not end with the neat sorting of tabulated opinions. My mandate was to ascertain and appraise current conceptions of objectives and, if necessary, to propose new objectives.

More than a year of study, observation, and reflection, and numerous interviews and discussions, convinced me that center objectives were neither well defined nor adequately understood. Americanization, a primary aim previously, was no longer relevant as the *raison d'être* of the Jewish center, and the clamor for "social action" as its principal purpose appeared to me unjustifiable. A new conception of purpose was, therefore, obviously necessary.

We shall note presently that the responses to our Attitude Questionnaire revealed a strong majority in favor of an affirmative Jewish purpose for the Jewish community center and emphasis on Jewish content in its program. But our sample was self-selected and interest-weighted, and there was no assurance that the views of its majority represented the prevailing attitudes of the Jewish center field. It was possible to recommend policy in accord with the preferences indicated by the majority on the assumption that our respondents were the active and concerned leaders who would sway the less involved to their views on the basic purpose of the Jewish community center. I made no such recommendation for several reasons.

First, practice in the centers belied the preferences indicated by a majority of our respondents. I had found that nearly 20 percent of the affiliated centers reported not a single project or program or activity of specific Jewish interest or orientation; that over 23 percent reported no Jewish programs for children; nearly 35 percent offered none for adults; and at least 55 percent listed none for youth.[9] And few indeed were the centers in which an atmosphere of intensive Jewish interest or activity prevailed.

Furthermore, the respondents were confused about the consequences of their preferences for Jewish content and purpose. Promotion of the latter would require staff qualified in these areas. But only 66 percent thought a minimum requirement in Jewish education necessary for appointment to the professional staff of the center. When asked to place in order of importance seven listed special qualifications for staff, less than 25 percent included "knowledge of Jewish history" in the first four of the seven categories, and less than 54 percent did so with "familiarity with Jewish religious and organizational life."[10]

Finally, indication of attitudes in response to a questionnaire is the expression of a mood, in this case a predilection for an optimum which might easily prove unattainable. There was no evidence either of conviction that the preferences must become policy or of an awareness of the difficulties such a policy might entail. Therefore, organized opposition might have dispelled quickly the desires noted on a questionnaire.

Still, a very significant number of Jewish center leaders did express a preference for a Jewish purpose of a Jewish institution sponsored by the Jewish community. There was certainly no point in ignoring this fact or in pandering to the minority which scorned Jewish content in programming. The course that appeared to me most reasonable in the light of all the evidence, and in accord with democratic principles as well, was to recommend an affirmative Jewish purpose with emphasis on Jewish content as a provisional or tentative policy for one year, so that the JWB constituency of Jewish centers might consider and discuss the proposals fully and freely. Final action was to be taken after the year of discussion, with such modifications in my proposals as would be deemed necessary.

The Opposition to the JWB Survey Report

The Survey Report, and especially the recommendation of a strongly affirmative Jewish purpose for the Jewish community center, encountered vigorous opposition from a small but very influential minority. Who were they and what motivated their attack?

The proponents of an affirmative Jewish purpose for the center regarded the opposing minority as "assimilationists." But that, as we have seen, is an ambiguous term, and I refrained from using it in the survey and its report. (The terms *assimilationist* and *anti-assimilationist* do not appear in the index to the report.) I felt that to define the issue in terms of assimilation versus anti-assimilation would result in confusion. The proponents of emphasis on Jewish purpose in the center were themselves "assimilationists," in the sense that they approved of English as the prevailing language of American Jews and of American literature, history, ideas, and ideals as their cultural assets; they favored adoption of American manners, customs, mores. But in addition to American culture. American Jews had a history, tradition, and culture, unique to the group. The question was: Should this component be cultivated or spurned and rejected? And central to the issue was whether or not the Jewish community center should emphasize that component in its program of activities. In other words, the issue was not assimilation *per se* but "willed assimilation," assimilation as a doctrine.

The opponents of an affirmative Jewish purpose in the Jewish community center regarded such emphasis as narrow and segregating, as fostering a type of voluntary "ghetto." They favored or gravitated toward a Jewish community center that projected a nonsectarian image either by shunning specifically Jewish programming, or at least by emphasizing nonsectarian activities. This was the issue on which I centered attention in the survey and report: whether the Jewish community center should be a nonsectarian agency in its public image and the emphasis of its program, or whether it should be frankly avowed and unmistakably identified as a sectarian Jewish agency dedicated in its purpose and its activities to the preservation and enrichment of Jewish life.

This sharp definition of the basic issue had the desired effect: the opponents ignored the report as a whole and concentrated their attack on three of its twenty-one recommendations: (1) they opposed primary emphasis on Jewish content in the center program; (2) they rejected the proposal that a statement of principles be adopted incorporating emphasis on Jewish content and requiring JWB affiliates to subscribe to it; and (3) they denounced a recommendation that on controversial public issues, which affect Jews not as a distinctive group but as American citizens, the center should not take any *official* position or sponsor action.

The proponents of a nonsectarian Jewish center—that is, the influential minority which opposed the JWB Survey Report—were not a tightly organized group. At the sessions of the Survey Commission which approved the recommendations as submitted or with some modifications, and at the meeting of the National Council of JWB in Pittsburgh on May 10, 1947, which adopted the recommendations (again with modifications where deemed desirable), the influence of this minority was "relatively unfelt." The Pittsburgh sessions especially must have been a traumatic experience for them. My address, describing the massive work done and the point of view of the report, was greeted with a standing ovation, and the recommendations were approved with enthusiasm. Apparently taken unawares, the opposition appeared discomfited and subdued by the exuberant reception of the new orientation, but as the tentative Statement of Principles was being discussed by the Jewish centers throughout the country, the opposition became more visible and vocal.

The opposition, which desired nonsectarian emphasis in the Jewish center, may be classified broadly into three tendencies. The laymen among them were, as a rule, very influential men and women whose authority as individual leaders was felt in the local centers and in the governing committees of JWB. At their best, they were perhaps represented by Arthur J. Freund, of St. Louis, a member of the Survey Commission and a confirmed "assimilationist."

In the historical section of the report, I had appraised the very significant role played by Judge Irving Lehman in the early JWB. The appraisal, based on the sources and duly documented, indicated his effective leadership, his justification of separate Jewish institutions, and his pride in the Jewish past and culture. But I also adduced evidence that his conception of Jewish leadership was that of "the elders of the Jewish community" rather than its representatives. When the Survey Commission convened to consider and act on my recommendations, Arthur Freund took exception to my appraisal as disrespectful of "a great American and a great Jew." I did not take up the challenge by citing chapter and verse. It would have been a fruitless diversion. Instead, I said that fortunately or unfortunately the work of every leader of the past is inevitably appraised by historians and that Judge Lehman had been similarly treated. There was laughter, in which Freund joined, for he had a sense of humor. Thereafter, he gave us no trouble and voted for the recommendations.

After the sessions of the Survey Commission, he sent me a very cordial letter in reply to a note of mine. In it, he said: . . . "I think you have done a magnificent piece of work even though I believe you would enhance its value . . . [if parts were rewritten]."
Then he came to the point at issue:

> While I can subscribe to your over-all views of cultural-pluralism in the main, . . . more consideration might be given . . . as to whether this is a permanent or temporary phenomenon. My own views are that the emphasis now desired to be placed upon purely sectarian or parochial aspects of Center programs is largely the result of fright hysteria to which we have all been subjected. . . . When UN is functioning perfectly and when man's humanity to man has been achieved most of this will disappear.

Immediately, however, this quixotic messianism was redeemed by a flash of humor: "I hope to see you before this is achieved, however." [11]
To me this letter indicated that a confirmed nonsectarian had been shaken in his view and, being a reasonable man, recognized that a "sectarian" emphasis was necessary, at least "temporarily." Furthermore, as an honorable and manly person, he could commend my work even though he disagreed with my point of view. There were no doubt many others like him in the center field.

Two other tendencies favoring nonsectarian emphasis were evident among the professional staffs of the Jewish centers. The latter were organized in the National Association of Jewish Center Workers (NAJCW), which appeared hostile to a primary emphasis on Jewish content in the Jewish center program, against a statement of principles incorporating such a requirement, and emphatically *for* the involvement of the Jewish community center directly and officially in controversial public questions and social action. In denouncing the position of the JWB Survey Report on these three issues, the deadly solemnity of the staff opponents was unrelieved by a saving sense of humor, or at least by humor I could appreciate. At one of the sessions of the NAJCW, a character brought a toy toilet, ceremoniously tore a sheet of paper, and dropped the fragments into the bowl. When I was told about this, I remarked that in a controversy, those who have minds use them to formulate their arguments; those not so endowed, must make do with what equipment they have.

I did not neglect the NAJCW in the JWB Survey. I read much of the writings of its leaders and members, and I interviewed a considerable number of them. I attended a meeting of at least one of the chapters of NAJCW, and I even read the minutes of one, that of New Jersey. I found that on the issues stressed by the opposition to the JWB Survey Report, NAJCW leadership was by no means of one mind; in fact, two wings were struggling for mastery. One wing was led by Graenum Berger, president of NAJCW during 1946–48, the period of confrontation. I analyzed his position in the Survey Report, and he was satisfied with my representation of his views.

Berger was not fundamentally a nonsectarian who opposed or depreciated Jewish content in the center program. As professional head of a center, he introduced considerable Jewish programming; even at Bronx House he pursued that policy, although it "was never fully realized" because of the institution's "tradition of absolute non-sectarianism." But Berger believed in a Jewish mission of social action for social reform, and that the major function, or at least a primary function, of the Jewish center was to serve as an instrument for human betterment.

Berger's views began to change in 1949, when he became consultant for Jewish centers, camps, and Jewish education at the New York Federation of Jewish Philanthropies. He discovered that "only a few centers were avowedly Jewish, while the majority . . . were largely non-sectarian, despite their high Jewish enrollments." He was also strongly influenced by the rise of Israel.[12] It may well be that the JWB Survey Report, which had indicated what he discovered in 1949, and the favorable action taken by JWB and a majority of its affiliates on the recommendations, had some effect in the change of his position.

The spokesman for the extreme nonsectarian viewpoint in NAJCW was A. Harold Murray, who was a member of the Survey Commission. At the sessions of the latter which acted on my recommendations, he was relatively quiet, but he came to life when social action was under consideration, and he wrote a minority report, which marshaled two votes, including his own.[13]

Murray's minority report and recommendation on social action revealed the major concern of himself and his following. I had recommended that, as an agency of informal education, "the Jewish Center should encourage the *discussion* of every question which is of moment to the community. Nothing human should be alien to the Center." However, on general controversial public issues, "the Center should not take any official position or sponsor action." I was inclined to recommend the same policy even on controversial issues affecting Jews directly in order not to risk disunity and conflict within the centers. But how could one bar a center from passing a resolution on such a matter as anti-Semitism? I therefore recommended that on Jewish issues the center could take an official position or sponsor action, but that such commitments "should be made only by a two-thirds or three-quarters majority of the board of directors, and of the staff and adult membership expressed through a referendum."

In the minority report, Murray argued that a weighted majority of the board and a referendum of staff and adult membership would occasion "delay, tremendous red tape and involved voting procedure, which is unrealistic and unpractical"; that it would paralyze "democratic action"; and his recommendation stated that the Jewish center has the responsibility for concerning itself "with *primary* Jewish issues" (not with Jewish issues primarily), as well as "with *all* matters which affect the individual in the American scene" (italics added); furthermore, that "the Center should take action on all social questions by a majority vote of the membership or the Board of Directors. . . ." How the membership was to be polled, if not by referendum, he did not indicate.

Graenum Berger has informed me that Murray crystallized the "social work—social action" position of NAJCW, which was a substitute and not "an integral part of the Jewish mission idea" which Berger represented. Berger adds: "So I spent the next two years fighting the boys and girls from achieving their all out objective, which would literally have converted the centers into open-membership, non-sectarian agencies, and . . . they would have been prime instruments for the advocacy of left-wing social action positions." I was aware of that in 1947. It meant the familiar tactics of boring from within, capturing agencies, and using them for left-wing agitation. Indeed, I noted at the time a hubbub in certain Jewish centers for aid to Tito's Yugoslavia and similar left-wing causes. In personal interviews with individual professional workers and lay leaders I was also repeatedly told in hushed tones about "communist cells," and accusing fingers were pointed at the brethren and fellow-travelers. I did not pursue this matter in the JWB Survey; the words *communist, Stalinist,* and *fellow-traveler* do not appear in the index to the report. To have done so would only have provided a welcome diversion about "Red-baiting." To feud with presumed Stalinists and fellow-travelers was neither my function nor my inclination. My job was to appraise current objectives of the Jewish center and, if necessary, to propose new objectives. I held fast to that purpose.

It was these elements among the professional workers (and I have in mind here not Murray as an individual but the extreme nonsectarians of NAJCW), and a sprinkling of lay people whose nonsectarian views were otherwise motivated, who attacked the Survey Report with abandon. Excepting the faction of NAJCW led by Berger and lay people of the Freund orientation, the extremists not only favored emphasis on nonsectarian activities in the Jewish center program; they also spurned and ridiculed Jewish content, arguing with vehemence that Jewish programs would be "barren, obsolete and often primitive," that they would be "canned" rather than the outcome of "self-expression"; that they were not "felt needs" because the membership did not want them and did not need them; that they would be "imposed" and, therefore, "undemocratic." A small number of lay leaders in "settlement" centers even questioned whether it was "ethical" to impose Jewish content on children in poor neighborhoods, when they, the leaders, did not believe in the value of "these things" for their own children.

The cliché most frequently heard at the time, especially among center workers, was that they wished the agency to concern itself with "the total personality of the member." This was untrue, for the same people were vigorously opposed to "religious" programs, and religion was certainly a factor in total personality. The argument was also downright silly, and many a lay leader, and professionals too, who favored Jewish content, would quip: "A kid comes to play checkers or basketball, and they affect his total personality." I did not share this appraisal: a child's personality, and an adult's too, could be affected by individual activities if properly motivated and guided. However, if that was what the term signified, why could not a Jewish-content activity similarly affect "total personality"? If basketball and the swimming pool or health club could develop personality, why should Jewish activities—say, the fashioning of a menorah in arts and crafts—be less serviceable than some nondescript object?

One could understand the hostility of the nonsectarians. The professional center workers were no doubt stung by the evidence that their Jewish education was, as a rule, grossly inadequate: over 20 percent of the 550 Jewish center and JWB staff who completed a special questionnaire, had had no formal Jewish education whatsoever, and an additional 40 percent no more than elementary or Sunday school instruction. It was therefore questionable whether the 60 percent who had not attained the secondary level of Jewish education were qualified to perform basic functions of a community center Jewishly motivated.[14]

The lay nonsectarians, as well as the professional center workers, had cause to oppose the JWB Survey Report. It had challenged their basic assumptions in Jewish center work, the merit for the continuity of Jewish life of the fundamental purpose of their efforts, and their warrant to serve as leaders of centers sponsored by the Jewish community. Furthermore, I condemned their scorn for Jewish cultural activities and the resulting exclusion of the latter from the center program as injurious in previous decades and pernicious in the 1940s.

The Survey Report argued that "Americanization," for decades the primary purpose of the Jewish center, was an anachronism in 1947 because American Jews had adopted American ways; that it was slander to imply that Jews needed special institutions to sustain their devotion to their country. They were, of course, furious at the implication that in championing social action, they were not only promoting dissension and hampering the Jewish center in its efforts to serve the entire Jewish community, but were also abetting extreme leftists in using the Jewish center for their agitation.

Most damaging was the challenge that the nonsectarian Jewish center was a contradiction in terms; that it could not be both Jewish and nonsectarian—if Jewish, it must have a Jewish purpose; if nonsectarian, it should be under nonsectarian auspices. They were outraged by my suggestion that a Jewish center had legitimacy only when dedicated to a primary Jewish purpose, but that a center bereft of such purpose constituted a "ghetto." Finally, the Survey Report quoted Louis Marshall, whose memory all revered, in support of my views. He had said in 1908:

> Unless our educational institutions shall create for themselves a Jewish atmosphere . . . they have no reason whatever for exsiting. . . . Unless the Jewish spirit pervades the institution, it might as well be managed . . . by South Sea Islanders.[15]

The Measure of the Opposition to Jewish Emphasis in the Center

It was clear that the lay leaders who favored "nonsectarian" Jewish centers were a minority that exerted great influence. It was difficult, however, to determine the prevalence of nonsectarianism among the professional center workers, and especially the numerical strength of the elements who wished to use the Jewish center to promote "social action."

The tabulated results of the Attitude Questionnaire, which included a total of 2,420 responses, among them 550 from staff persons, held a great surprise. They did corroborate the estimate that the confirmed non-sectarians among the lay center leaders were a minority, and indeed a small minority. The 550 staff responses, however, were startling because they ran counter to the general impression one gained in the Jewish center field. During the period of the survey, the two factions favoring "social action" or leftist agitation or both were well organized, articulate, and very vocal; hence the impression that they spoke for the large majority of the professional center workers on the desirability of Jewish purpose and Jewish content for the center program. The statistical results challenged that assumption. In fact, *on crucial questions involving a Jewish purpose for the Jewish center, the proportion of affirmative responses among the 550 staff persons was generally higher than among total responses!* A few tabulated responses will make this clear.[16]

The most direct question on Jewish content in the center program elicited the following:

4a) Should "Jewish content" be emphasized in the Jewish Center?

	Total of 2,420 100.0	Staff (550) 100.0
Yes	76.4	83.3
No	8.4	5.5
Don't Know	3.0	1.3
No Reply	12.2	10.0

If yes, should Jewish content be emphasized?

	Total of 2,420 100.0	Staff (550) 100.0
In all Center activities (where possible)	26.5	30.9
In most activities	28.2	28.7
In some activities	28.7	30.5
In very few activities	2.2	0.5
No reply	14.3	9.1

4b) Emphasis on "Jewish content" in the Jewish Center program serves

	Total of 2,420 100.0	Staff (550) 100.0
To segregate and isolate Jews from the American environment	5.9	2.9
To integrate Jews into the American environment	71.5	70.5
Other reply	10.1	18.2
No reply	12.5	8.4

4c) Where Jews and non-Jews are members of a Jewish Center, should the program emphasize "Jewish content"?

	Total of 2,420 100.0	Staff (550) 100.0
Yes	58.2	70.1
No	20.9	13.3
Don't Know	7.4	6.7
No Reply	13.1	8.9

5b) Should the laws of Kashruth be observed in the Center?

	Total of 2,420 100.0	Staff (550) 100.0
Yes	59.7	66.5
No	19.8	10.7
Don't Know	13.5	15.8
No reply	6.7	6.9

These tabulations show that of our "interest-weighted" sample, a large majority favored a strongly affirmative Jewish purpose for the Jewish center, and surprisingly *the Staff respondents did too,* and fairly consistently *in larger proportions.* Furthermore, even the high figures of 76.4 percent for total respondents and 83.3 percent for staff (question

4a) do not reveal the full reaction to nonsectarianism or indifference to Jewish content in the Jewish center because of the significant proportions who failed to reply or said they did not know. The truer estimates of opponents of Jewish content are the 8.4 percent of total respondents and 5.5 percent of staff who answered "no" to question 4a above.

Similarly, 54.7 percent of total respondents, *and 59.6 percent of staff* wanted emphasis on Jewish content in all center activities (where possible) or in most activities; and here again it should be noted that only *2.2 percent of total respondents and 0.5 percent of staff* would do so only "in very few activities." Finally, question 4c shows that 58.2 percent of total respondents and *70.1 percent of staff* would emphasize Jewish content, even where non-Jews as well as Jews were members. (The negative replies were 20.9 percent of total and only 13.3 percent of staff.)

Replies to other questions confirmed these attitudes. The responses to 5b above revealed that less than 20 percent of total and *less than 11 percent of staff* would not favor observance of laws of Kashruth in the Jewish center. The reader is referred to the Survey Report for many similar and related questions and tabulated responses.[17] One or two examples may be noted here. Asked to place in order of importance seven stated functions of the Jewish center (question 2a), over 74 percent of total respondents included "to promote Jewish loyalties and identification with the Jewish cultural heritage" in the first four categories; and *82.4 percent of staff respondents did so!* Even when reacting to a similar question on the objectives of the Jewish center as an *agency of personality development* (question 2b), nearly 70 percent (*staff—75.5 percent!*) placed "Jewish loyalties and identification with the Jewish cultural heritage" in the first four of the seven categories.[18]

Conclusion

The conclusion drawn from the above was that among our interest-weighted sample, the opposition to emphasis on Jewish purpose and Jewish content in the Jewish center consisted of a small minority of the lay center leaders and of an *even smaller minority* of the professional staffs of the Jewish centers. My recommendation took this into consideration. It proposed that an emphatic Jewish orientation for the center be approved provisionally for one year for the purpose of discussion. By this means, I sought to confront the constituency with the fundamental issue and compel consideration and action on the nonsectarian conception of the Jewish center. In the course of a widespread public debate, with alternatives clearly envisaged, I believed that the vague desire for Jewish purpose expressed in the responses to the questionnaire could not but be confirmed by commitment.

During the year of discussion—from May 1947, to May 1948—the clamor of the opposition reached bizarre proportions. One group of wealthy and influential nonsectarians mounted a diversionary attack on the intellectual integrity and scholarly validity of the JWB Survey, which I have discussed elsewhere.[19] Among the professional center workers, too, the proponents of "social action" denounced the recommendations as "undemocratic" and "dictatorial." But they were challenged by fellow-professionals at conferences and in print.[20] And it took courage in those days to challenge the well-organized nonsectarians among the center workers.

The result was a compromise. Not all of my proposals were fully accepted, and I did not expect that they would be. However, on the basic issue of nonsectarianism versus Jewish purpose, the opposition was routed. On May 9, 1948, the National Council of JWB, assembled in annual meeting in Chicago, adopted the principle that "Jewish content is fundamental to the program of the Jewish Center."[21]

NOTES

1. The extreme elements among the opposition made an attempt to undermine the affirmative Jewish position by challenging the scholarly competence, methodology, and validity of the JWB Survey Report. This resulted in a confrontation with Louis Wirth, the sociologist, who had been hired to make an "independent study" of my report. An account of that episode appears in O. I. Janowsky, "A Confrontation with Assimilationists: An Oblique Attack on the JWB Survey" (ms. awaiting publication).
2. See O. I. Janowsky, *The JWB Survey* (New York: Dial Press, 1948), pp. xv–xxvii.
3. *Ibid.,* pp. xx–xxi.
4. *Ibid.,* pp. xxi–xxii; Minutes of JWB Survey Commission, November 18, 1945.
5. O. I. Janowsky, "JWB Survey: Master Questionnaire or Prospectus," March 11, 1946, pp. 2 and 36 (unpublished typescript).
6. John Slawson, "Jewish Education as a Jewish Social Work Function," reprint from *Proceedings* for 1928 of the National Conference of Jewish Social Service, pp. 3–4, 6.
7. "Biculturality: A Study in Social Schizophrenia," in I. Graeber and S. H. Britt, eds., *Jews in a Gentile World* (New York, 1942), chap. 10.
8. O. I. Janowsky, *JWB* Survey (see n. 2 above).
9. *Ibid.,* p. 185.
10. See *ibid.,* pp. 387ff., 391. The confusion was even more marked on the questions related to "social action."
11. A. J. Freund to O. I. Janowsky, April 3, 1947.
12. Graenum Berger to O. I. Janowsky, July 19, 1974; O. I. Janowsky, *JWB Survey,* pp. 251–53.
13. The other vote was cast by Norman H. Gill, director of the Citizens' Governmental Research Bureau of Milwaukee. He wrote to B. Rabinowitz of JWB (December 30, 1947), "One of the reactions I got to the Survey . . . is that the Survey was done by a first rate historian using general social service terminology, . . . [whereas] a great many of JWB professional workers are trained in the case work and group work jargon. . . . I find lay persons who are Jewish community leaders, very much in agreement with the recommendations; but most of the professionals with whom I speak take issue vigorously with a number of the recommendations; and I honestly believe that this is more a question of the language used than anything else. Perhaps a semantician should be hired to edit the survey in a special edition of "group-work-ese." I assume that this was naiveté rather than a delaying tactic.
14. See *JWB Survey,* pp. 175–76.
15. See *ibid.,* p. 241.
16. See *ibid.,* pp. 358–63 and tables, pp. 365ff., 380ff., and esp. pp. 392–93, 396.
17. *Ibid.,* pp. 358–417.

18. On "social action," however, staff respondents were far more affirmative than total respondents. To the question: "Should the Center take an official position on questions which affect all citizens (Negro Problem, labor vs. management, etc.)?" 55.3 percent of staff respondents answered yes, whereas only 40.5 percent of total respondents, *including staff*, did so. (See *JWB Survey*, p. 403.) An analysis of the issue of "social action" would require another article.

19. See Note 1 above.

20. See, for example, an excellent article by Fred A. Liff, "The Statement of Principles and the Professional," *Jewish Center Worker*, February, 1948, pp. 10–12. See also, NAJCW, "Report on May 30, 1947 Session on JWB Survey" (typescript).

21. On the significance of this action, see JWB Archives, Annual Meeting, 1948, L. Kraft to F. Weil, May 10, 1948.

HEBREW SOURCES OF
AMERICAN JEWISH HISTORY

By

JACOB KABAKOFF

Lehman College, City University of New York

I

It is almost half a century since Mendel Silber published a volume entitled *America in Hebrew Literature* (New Orleans, 1928), in which he collected Hebrew sources on America and American Jews beginning with the discovery of America down to 1882. The Hebrew literature and press produced in this country contain a considerable amount of material on both American and American Jewish life which should be systematically listed. In addition, the Hebrew periodical press which appeared in Europe and Palestine incorporates a wealth of articles and reports on America and its Jews is of value to the historian.

Various aspects of American Jewish life as reflected in Hebrew sources have already served as material for studies and dissertations.[1] Much more remains to be done in this field. There is need for a bibliography of Hebrew works dealing with the area, as well as for indices of pertinent items in both the American and world Hebrew press.

It shall be the purpose of this preliminary survey to point first to some of the riches which are to be found in American Hebrew works. In addition, some indication will also be offered of the type of material available in American Hebrew periodical literature. Our focus shall be mainly on writings of the nineteenth century and the beginning of the present century, although in some cases a few later works may be mentioned in order to round out the picture of a writer's activity.

Reactions to Reform

In order to illustrate the type of material available in American Hebrew sources, we shall direct our attention to references to the Reform movement. Similar surveys can be made of immigrant problems and other areas. Hebrew literature had a long tradition of polemical writing against Reform, beginning with the days of the Haskalah. This tradition was carried over to the new world by the immigrant writers, many of whom were rabbinic scholars or *maskilim*.

The very first original Hebrew work to appear in America, *Abne Yehoshua* [The stones of Joshua] (New York, 1860) by Joshua Falk, includes as part of its homiletical moralistic comments on the Ethics of the Fathers, to which it is devoted, a number of caustic criticisms of Reform. Rabbi Falk, born in 1789 in Poland, held positions in several communities. He died in Keokuk, Iowa, in 1865 and was buried in New York. While extolling the freedom of America, he took the leaders of Reform to task for shortening the prayers, for permitting mixed choirs and mixed seating, and for using the organ. The volume was printed by the press of the *Jewish Messenger,* whose editor was Rabbi Samuel Meir Isaacs, and it had the support of Rabbi Morris J. Raphall, of the B'nai Jeshurun Synagogue. Rabbis Isaacs and Raphall were both among the ardent critics of Reform.

The second Hebrew item to be printed in America was a pamphlet of twenty-eight pages by Eliahu Holzman, which was given over entirely to an attack on the Reform movement and its leaders. Its title, *Emek Rephaim* [Valley of the shades] (New York, 1865), is obviously a pun on Reform, and it is indicative of the vitriolic tenor of the work. In a biting, albeit halting, style, spiced with undistinguished verse, Holzman attacked the changes introduced by Reform and castigated Isaac Mayer Wise, whose name he rendered as "Laban." Like Falk before him, Holzman received the backing of Rabbis Raphall and Isaacs, as is attested by their endorsements, which follow the English introduction. Holzman's introduction reads as follows:

To the Jewish Public

M. E. HOLZMAN, *Scribe, of Courland, Russia,* begs to inform the Jewish people of the United States that he has now in Press, and will shortly appear, a translation of this work, which has for its object arguments, demonstrating the sinfulness of those who attach themselves to the new system now attempted to supersede the rituals and customs of Israel, established from time immemorial. It is unfortunately too well known that a sect has arisen in Israel who attempt to form a new code for public worship, embracing instrumental and vocal music. Choristers composed of male and female voices. Israelites and non-Israelites, erasing the name of Synagogue and substituting the term Temple. The whole of these charges emanating from men who call themselves Doctors, and who are in fact destroyers of all that is sacred; their lips move in sanctity, and deception is in their hearts. The author, desiring to preserve in fact the prayers compiled by *"the men of the great Assembly,"* has issued this work to prevent further encroachments in our holy ritual, and to prove that the course pursued by these innovators tends to uproot the "Scion of God's planting," and to sow seeds of discord detrimental to the welfare of Israel and opposed to the conservative course which tends to keep Israel distinct and holy.

To this introduction are appended brief endorsements by Raphall and Isaacs, as follows:

I strongly recommend the within meritorious production.
M. J. Raphall, Dr.

I most readily endorse the remarks of the Rev. Dr. Raphall.
S. M. Isaacs.

Another example of an early anti-Reform pamphlet is Nahum Streisand's *Le-Lamed La-To'im Binah* [To teach the straying understanding] (New York, 1872). Streisand, who served as a rabbi in New York and later in San Francisco, proclaimed that he had written his pamphlet "against those who permit the singing of women and the organ in the synagogues during prayer." He directed his remarks against Rabbi Henry G. Vidaver, of B'nai Jeshurun, who had defended these practices in his congregation. He indicated on the frontispiece that the publication costs had been assumed by "a wealthy member of congregation B'nai Jeshurun," who was apparently opposed to the liberal policies of Vidaver, successor to the more conservative Raphall. That Streisand's pamphlet played some role in the controversy surrounding Vidaver is evident from the fact that the latter was obliged to leave B'nai Jeshurun in 1874 and that he was replaced by the more traditional Henry S. Jacobs.

The American Hebrew press, which had its inception at the beginning of the seventies, was largely conservative in spirit. It paid considerable attention to the Reform movement and did not mince words in attacking it. Zvi Hirsh Bernstein, editor of the first American Hebrew weekly, *Ha-Zofeh Ba-Arez Ha-Hadashah,* did not overlook any opportunity to deride the efforts of Reform. In his memoir concerning his publication, which he published in later years,[2] he pointed to the role of his periodical in combatting Reform and quoted the full text of the protest statement by fourteen rabbis which he had published in volume I, number 3 (July 7, 1871) against the rabbinical conference convened by I. M. Wise in Cincinnati in June of that year.

Judah David Eisenstein, who had come here in 1872 at the age of eighteen, wrote extensively on American Jewish life in both the European and the American Hebrew press. Beginning his literary activity at the end of the seventies and devoting himself to it almost exclusively during the eighties, he soon became a leading spokesman of Orthodoxy. In the second part of his autobiographical *Ozar Zikhronotai* [Treasury of my memoirs] (New York, 1929), he reprinted a number of his articles dealing with various phases of American Jewish immigrant life and history. Among these is his article entitled "Yissud Ha-Seminar He-Hadash" [Founding of the new seminary], which first appeared in 1886 in the *New Yorker Yiddishe Tseitung.*[3] Before presenting his views concerning the new rabbinical seminary, which was then under consideration by the Conservative group, Eisenstein saw fit to survey the various religious trends in American Jewry and to offer a strongly worded critique of Reform. He reviewed the platform adopted by the Pittsburgh Conference in 1885 and the beginnings of the Hebrew Union College. All this he deemed necessary in order to caution the founders of the new seminary against halting between two opinions and tilting toward Reform.

In 1887 Moses Weinberger, who served as rabbi of the Beth Hamidrah Anshe Ungarn in New York, published his book *Ha-Yehudim Veha-Yahadut Be-New York* [Jews and Judaism in New York]. His aim was to provide the Hebrew reader in Eastern Europe and his homeland, Hungary, with an overview of the religious and spiritual condition of American Jewry and to caution them against settling here. In describing the status of the New York synagogues, he was led to make the blanket statement that "American Jewry can hope little from the radicals, the Conservatives, and the liberals." He recorded sadly that a number of synagogues had already begun to introduce reforms which could only endanger the future of American Judaism.

At the end of the eighties there appeared also Meir Rabinowitz's volume on Orthodoxy and Reform in America under the title *Ha-Mahanaim* [The two camps] (New York, 1888). Rabinowitz, an Orthodox rabbi and preacher who had arrived in New York in 1871, sought to point to a middle road between the two trends. He was critical of the practices of both Orthodoxy and Reform and posited change, provided, however, that it was based on rabbinic teaching. His practical suggestion to convene a meeting of both camps went unheeded, despite the erudition he exhibited in his book.

During the nineties the struggle against Reform was carried forward in the two Hebrew weeklies that appeared at that time: *Ha-Pisgah,* edited by Wolf Schur, and *Ha-Ibri,* edited by Gershon Rosenzweig. Both periodicals were quick to attack the movement and its proponents and to decry the dangers they saw in it. To the ideological aspect of the debate was now added the immigration factor. Since many of the German Jews who were adherents of Reform opposed the East European Jewish immigration, the editors of these periodicals and their contributors subjected them to bitter criticism. Schur, particularly, sought to obtain the support of leading Reform rabbis in behalf of the cause of East European Jews.

One of Schur's chief aims in his volume *Nezah Yisrael* [The eternality of Israel] (Chicago, 1897) was to combat the inner dangers facing American Jewry from socialism, anarchism, and assimilationist Reform. He dealt with Reform in his chapter entitled "Shall We Remove the Old in Favor of the New?" in which he maintained that only after the establishment of a spiritual and physical center in Zion could the issue be resolved. The question of Reform, he held, would have to be taken up by a Sanhedrin consisting of representatives of world Jewry. Hopefully, the impetus to change would be strengthened by an academy of learning in Palestine whose rabbinical graduates would be acceptable to Jews the world over. Schur remained a staunch adherent of Orthodoxy, maintaining that the Judaism practiced by East European Jews required "refinement rather than reform." [4]

Gerson Rosenzweig, editor of *Ha-Ibri,* was associated with Kasriel Zvi Sarasohn, who, beginning with the seventies, was active as a publisher of Orthodox Yiddish newspapers. The Hebrew weekly reflected therefore the traditional point of view against Reform. As an accomplished satirist, Rosenzweig leveled his critical barbs against the Reform rabbinate in sharply turned epigrams as well as editorial comment. His *Talmud Yankai* [Yankee Talmud] (New York, 1892) contained a special tractate devoted to America (*Ama Reka*), in which he took the

Reform rabbinate to task. In his collection of epigrams, *Hamisha Va-Elef* [A thousand and five] (New York, 1904), he castigated the use of the organ and the actions of the Reform rabbi-doctors.[5]

One of the Orthodox rabbis who resorted to the pages of *Ha-Ibri* to adopt a strong stand against Reform was Abraham Moshe Shershevsky, of Portland, Maine. In volume V of that publication (1895), he set out to refute the arguments for religious reform advanced earlier by Zalman Engleman, a Hebrew *maskil*. The subject became the basis for a continuing polemic in which various Hebrew writers participated. Rabbi Shershevsky left a record of this debate in his volume *Nahal Abraham* [The Brook of Abraham] (New York, 1896), whose third section is given over to a critical evaluation of the spiritual condition of American Jewry. He indicated that the support given his views by such writers as Dov Wasserman and A. I. Rose helped him to prevail in his struggle against religious innovation.

Finally, mention should be made of another volume published during the nineties which took Reform to task. R. B. Raphael, of Pittsburgh, was the author of *She'elat Ha-Yehudim* [The Jewish question] (Newark, 1892), in which he made a strong plea for the nationalist point of view. He penned strong words of criticism against Reform, which he linked with assimilation. He stressed that, despite the emphasis of Reform on equality for the Jew, it was powerless to mitigate the effects of anti-Semitism. In line with his nationalist convictions, he too declared that only a Sanhedrin in the Jewish spiritual center of Zion would be empowered to enact needed reforms.

The American Hebrew literature and press is thus seen to have had as one of its main preoccupations an ongoing quarrel with Reform. The Reform movement and its leaders were a constant butt of criticism. When Hebrew writers did admit the need for change, they adopted a religio-national stance and shifted the problem to a proposed Sanhedrin which would be established in Zion.

The Periodical Press

The American Hebrew periodical press serves as a faithful mirror of the attitudes of the East European Jewish immigrants and as a guide to the issues which agitated them. Mention has already been made of the first American Hebrew weekly, *Ha-Zofeh Ba-Arez Ha-Hadashah,* which remains an invaluable source for the seventies.[6] In addition to reflecting

American Jewish life and recording the happenings in various Jewish communities, the American Hebrew press took note of American life and history. Some interesting items of general Americana dot its pages. We shall present here a sampling of the type of material on American Jewish life and history to be found in some of the representative periodicals of the nineties and the beginning of the century.

The Hebrew weekly *Ha-Pisgah*, edited by Wolf Schur, appeared with several interruptions from 1889 to 1899 in New York, Baltimore, Boston, and Chicago. From October 20, 1899, to November 2, 1900, it was issued under the new name of *Ha-Tehiyah*. Terming his periodical the "organ of the most intelligent class of the Jewish immigrants," Schur devoted its pages to championing the cause of East European Jewry. *Ha-Pisgah* and its successor are an important source for the history of Hibbat Zion and the beginnings of political Zionism in America. They contain much information on the activities of the various Zionist societies during the nineties and at the turn of the century. Because of its services to the cause of Zion, *Ha-Pisgah* virtually achieved the status of a semi-official Zionist organ.

Ha-Ibri appeared in New York from 1892 to 1902, with one major interruption (July 29, 1898, to June 7, 1901). Initially sponsored by the Yiddish publisher Kasriel Zvi Sarasohn, it catered largely to the Orthodox *maskilim*. When Gerson Rosenzweig became editor and later sole publisher, he brought to it his satiric talents, which he exhibited in his weekly editorial comment. *Ha-Ibri* was published in the mold of the European Hebrew press and attracted to its pages a number of the leading immigrant writers. It comes almost as a surprise to find in its dreary pages such items as the translated series of articles on American history in volume II (1892) and the lengthy biographical study of Lincoln by Moses I. Garson, which appeared in thirteen installments in volume VI (1896).

During the cessation in publication of *Ha-Ibri*, Rosenzweig launched his monthly publication *Kadimah* (1899), which was of better literary quality. In the five issues which appeared we find a number of items dealing with the American Jewish past. Akiva Fleishman gave an account of "The First High Holydays in Manhattan" in issues 3 and 4. In issue 4, which marked the eightieth birthday of I. M. Wise, Peter Wiernik devoted an article to "The Life of Haym Salomon." The publication also made an effort to deal with problems of Jewish education and nationalism.

In 1889 M. L. Rodkinson, translator of the Talmud into English, reestablished here his periodical *Ha-Kol,* which he had issued earlier in Europe. In four of the issues of volume VII, note was taken of the centennial of the inauguration of George Washington. Issue 17, for example, published the Hebrew prayer composed for the occasion by Cantor Pinkhos Minkowsky and offered at congregation Adath Jeshurun. The centennial of Washington was also marked in the Hebrew weekly *Ha-Leumi,* which was edited by Ephraim Deinard in the same year. Issue 19 contained a feature on the event which incorporated a translation by Isaac Bernstein of the correspondence between the Jewish congregation and Washington.

Rodkinson made still another effort to publish a Hebrew periodical when he issued *Ha-Sanegor* in 1890, first as a bi-weekly and then as a weekly. He succeeded in attracting such writers as J. D. Eisenstein and Zvi Gershuni (Henry Gersoni). In the first issue of the periodical, Eisenstein published an article on anti-Semitism in America in which he sought to quiet the alarmist views on the subject.[7] Gershuni, who had previously sent correspondence on American Jewish life to *Ha-Heliz* and had gone into English journalism, presented an analysis of the American Jewish scene in issues 2–4.[8] A keen observer, Gershuni reviewed the status of the Russian Jewish immigrants and of Jewish philanthropic endeavor. He took Reform to task for the divisiveness which he perceived in American Jewish life.

With the launching of the monthly *Ner Ha-Maarabi* in January, 1895, by the Society for the Advancement of Hebrew Literature in America, a serious effort was made to channel the efforts of the immigrant Hebrew writers and to give them direction. The aim of the publication was to "cast light on the life of the Jews, Judaism and Jewish literature." The very first point in its eight-point program stressed the need of dealing with contemporary Jewish problems, particularly in America.

The officers of the sponsoring Society for the Advancement of Hebrew Literature in America included K. Z. Sarasohn, president, J. D. Eisenstein, treasurer, and Israel Davidson, secretary. The editorial board was made up of such leading immigrant Hebrew writers as Menahem Mendel Dolitzky, Gerson Rosenzweig, Abraham H. Rosenberg, Moshe Reicherson, and Abraham B. Dobsevage. A new spirit was evinced in the periodical. The leading article by Rosenberg listed among its aims the compiling of a new biblical commentary together with introductions and the preparation of a new translation into English.

Israel Davidson's contribution to the first issue was a brief review of two volumes dealing with American Jewish history: *The Settlement of the Jews in North America* by Charles P. Daley and *The Jews of Philadelphia* by H. S. Morais. The second issue contains Eisenstein's article on "Mordecai Manuel Noah and His Plan for Jewish settlement in America." [9] Eisenstein presented the full text of Judah Jeitteles's satiric account of Noah's project from the Hebrew periodical *Bikkure Ha-Ittim* (Vienna, vol. VII, 1826) and defended Noah against his detractors. In the same issue, the periodical began the publication of a series of articles by M. I. Garson on the Jewish charitable institutions of New York. This was in line with point five in its eight-point program. The first installment dealt with the history and activities of the Montefiore Home for Chronic Invalids. In subsequent articles Garson wrote about the Hebrew Benevolent and Orphan Asylum and the Hebrew Technical Institute.

That the sponsors of *Ner Ha-Maarabi* were especially interested in bringing to their readers articles on American Jewish life and history is evident from the following announcement, which they published in issue 3.

The publishers of *Ner Ha-Maarabi* request of the contributors to write about these matters, which they intend to place before the readers in forthcoming issues:

1. The history of the Beth Midrash Hagadol in New York in particular and the Orthodox congregations in America in general.
2. The history of Temple Emanu-El in New York in particular and the Reform congregations in America in general.
3. Biographies of the leading Orthodox rabbis in America.
4. Biographies of the leading Reform rabbis in America.
5. Biographies of Jewish authors and scholars in America.
6. Biographies of well-known Jews in America.
7. History of the B'nai B'rith organization in particular and of the other organizations in America in general.
8. History of the Jewish periodical press in America.
9. History of the Hebrew Union College.
10. History of the Talmud Torah and of Jewish schools in America.
11. History of the Jewish Publication Society.
12. History of the Jewish colonies in America.
13. History of the Jewish theater in New York.

This program proved to be over-ambitious and beyond the ken of the publishers. Of the various contributors to the periodical, the writer who most closely adhered to this program was Eisenstein. He recounted the history of the first Russian American Jewish congregation, "Beth Hamid-rash Hagadol," in the sixth issue,[10] and traced in detail the history of the Association of American Orthodox Hebrew Congregations in issues 11 and 12.[11] Eisenstein had played an active role in the work of the association and was chairman of the committee that drew up its constitution. Issue 12 was dedicated to Gustav Gottheil, rabbi of Temple Emanu-El, on the occasion of his seventieth birthday, and an appreciation of him was contributed by Adolph M. Radin.

The sponsorship of *Ner Ha-Maarabi* underwent a number of changes. Beginning with volume II, number 1 (July 1897), Samuel Benjamin Schwarzberg is listed as editor and publisher. In his leading editorial he pointed out that, in addition to publishing the writings of leading European Hebrew authors, the magazine would give special emphasis to American Jewish life. He appended the list of suggested subjects that had appeared earlier, stating that only a few had been adequately covered thus far.

In line with his promise, Schwarzberg inaugurated a section called "Jews and Judaism in America," which he hoped would furnish material for future historians of American Jewry. The section featured Eisenstein's series on "The History of the Colonies Which Were Founded by Our Brothers Exiled from Russia to America." [12] The installments appeared in all four issues of volume II, after which the periodical ceased publication. In the concluding section of his study, Eisenstein reported on the Mizpah Colony, in whose founding he played a leading role.

Another writer whose literary development, like that of Eisenstein's, took place in America was Mordecai Zev (Max) Raisin. He, too, wrote extensively on American Jewish life and history and was to produce several works in book form in this area. In volume II, number 2 of *Ner Ha-Maarabi,* Schwarzberg printed Raisin's article on "Washington and His Relations with the Jews of America," which Raisin wrote at the age of sixteen and in which he included his translation of the correspondence between the President and the Jewish congregations. The stirrings of political Zionism are seen in the articles in support of Herzl by Herman Rosenthal in issues 2–4.

In 1899 there appeared a small collective volume, *Sifrat Zion* [Literature of Zion], which was published by the Mefize Zion Society in America. One of the leading spirits of the society was Ephraim Deinard, who contributed a number of articles and was the virtual editor.[13] In addition to general material, the volume contains a number of contributions of Zionist interest by Deinard, Eisenstein, Julius Aronson, and Moshe Weinberger. Of special value is Deinard's statistical survey of the then existing Zionist societies. He also penned an appreciation of Reform Rabbi Bernhard Felsenthal of Chicago on the occasion of his seventy-fifth anniversary. His brief article was in recognition of Felsenthal's ongoing support of Hebraic and Zionist efforts in America. Deinard was a prolific writer and his book *Atidot Yisrael* [The future of Israel] (New York, 1892) and *Misteré New York* [Secrets of New York] (New York, 1909) contain material on Hibbat Zion in America and particularly on the Shavé Zion Society in which he was active. He later published a Hebrew brochure on the *History of the Jewish Settlement at Kearny-Arlington, New Jersey* (St. Louis, 1925), in which he recounted his experiences as one of the early settlers.

The monthly publication *Ha-Modia La-Hadashim,* which was launched in 1900 under the editorship of Herman Rosenthal and Abraham H. Rosenberg, listed among its aims the portrayal of American Jewish life, particularly in the areas of religion, Zionism, and education. We find that Raisin, Eisenstein, and Wiernik provided the main contributions in the area of American Jewish life and literature.

Raisin's survey of "The Jews and Judaism in New York Prior to the 19th Century" appeared in installments in issues 1–3.[14] The longest article, "The Story of the Russian Exiles in America" by Eisenstein,[15] appeared in ten installments beginning with issue 2. In issue 7, we find Eisenstein defending the Russian Jewish immigrants against the arguments raised by Joseph Jacobs in an article critical of Russian Jewry which had appeared in translation in the previous issue.

Among the other contributors to the magazine was Herman Moeller, who discussed "The Position of Russian Jews in Commerce and Industry in New York" in issues 2 and 5. Wiernik turned his attention to "The Economic Development of the Jewish Workers in America" in issue 4, and to "The Life of Michael Heilprin" in issue 10. A survey of the Yiddish theater in America and an evaluation of its contributions and main figures was provided by Akiva Fleishman in five installments, beginning with issue 5. The three issues of volume II which appeared in 1902 were under the sole editorship of A. H. Rosenberg. He devoted an article in the first issue of the volume to the life and work of Bernhard Felsenthal on the occasion of his eightieth birthday.[16]

As a final example of early American Hebrew periodical literature we shall consider *Yalkut Maarabi* (vol. I, 1904), the literary annual issued by the Ohole Shem Association in New York and edited by Herman Rosenthal and Adolph M. Radin. The annual, which was dedicated to the poet Menahem Mendel Dolitzky on the occasion of the twenty-fifth anniversary of his literary work, contains a number of items of American Jewish interest.

Ephraim Deinard recounted "The History of the Communist Settlement known as New Odessa." [17] Deinard had long had an interest in agricultural settlements. In the very first issue of his weekly *Ha-Leumi* (1889), which he dedicated to "agriculture, scholarship and Jewish literature," he appealed for articles on Jewish colonization in America by Russian Jewish settlers. In 1897 he had attempted to establish a Jewish colony in Nevada. In his account of the failure of the New Odessa settlement, which he termed a "tragi-comedy," he described in detail the role of the non-Jewish leader William Frey and his utopian ideas.

An article by Wiernik entitled "On the Hadarim and Melamdim in This Country" dealt with the positive advances made here in the field of Jewish education as compared to overseas. Eisenstein published a responsum by Rabbi Jacob David Ridvaz, then of Chicago, to his query whether a civil marriage required a Jewish divorce by a party who wished to remarry in a Jewish ceremony. Rabbi Ridvaz replied in the negative. This query reflected Eisenstein's interest in American Jewish responsa, which he dealt with in a special study that traced the history of the responsa dealing with American Jewish life.[18] He included several of his own queries, including the one on civil marriage.

Yalkut Maarabi also contains Z. H. Bernstein's Hebrew memoir, "Concerning the Jews and Judaism in New York 34 Years Ago," which was referred to above, and Radin's "Memorial to Rabbi Benjamin Szold." An admirer of Szold, Radin presented a detailed biography and evaluation of the rabbi's communal and scholarly activities. It is to be regretted that the Ohole Shem Society did not continue to publish its literary annual, for in their introduction to volume I the editors stated: "In the volumes which we shall publish in coming years we shall give preference to articles dealing with the history of our brethren in the United States."

At the end of the first decade of the century, new winds began to blow in the American Hebrew literature and press. Considerable development was seen both during and following World War I in the quality of Hebrew writing, and several modern periodicals made their appearance. The years between the two world wars even saw the rise of an indigenous literature which reflected both American and American Jewish life in *belles-lettres*. It is natural, then, that more sophisticated treatment was given to American Jewish life and history. Many items can be culled from both the scholarly and periodical literature which appeared here during the past six decades.

An indication of the wide variety of material on American Jewish life and history which is available in the pages of one current periodical alone, the weekly *Ha-Doar,* can be had from the bibliography of this material which was prepared by Leo Shpall.[19] *Ha-Doar* has the longest record of publication in America, having been established as a daily in 1921 and becoming a weekly after some five months. Covering a little more than the first four decades of the periodical, Shpall's bibliography lists over 1,150 items. Among the rubrics included are: personalities, immigration, education, the Hebrew and Zionist movements, and institutions and organizations.

It is thus abundantly evident that a modest but not insignificant amount of material on American Jewish life and history is available in the Hebrew literature and press produced here. The serious researcher will do well to have recourse to it.

NOTES

1. See, for example: Jacob Kabakoff, *Haluze Ha-Sifrut Ha-Ivrit Ba-Amerikah* (Tel-Aviv, 1966); Aaron Soviv, *Attitudes towards Jewish Life and Education as Reflected in Yiddish and Hebrew Literature in America, 1870–1914* (Dropsie College, 1957) [dissertation available on microfilm]; Harvey A. Richman, *The Image of America in European Hebrew Periodicals of the 19th Century (until 1880)* (University of Texas, 1971) [dissertation available on microfilm]; Jacob R. Marcus, "European Bibliographical Items on Chicago," *The Chicago Pinkas*, ed. Simon Rawidowicz (Chicago, 1952), pp. 177–95; and Joel S. Geffen, "America in the First Hebrew Daily Newspaper: *Ha-Yom* (1886–1888)," *American Jewish Historical Quarterly*, vol. LI, no. 3 (March 1962), pp. 149–67.
2. See his "Al Devar Ha-Yehudim Veha-Yahadut Be-New York Lifné Lamed Dalet Shanim," *Yalkut Maarabi* (New York, 1904), pp. 128–34.
3. An English translation of this article by Robert L. Samuels was published under the title "Between Two Opinions," in *American Jewish Archives*, vol. XII, no. 2 (October, 1960).
4. For a fuller treatment of Schur's views, see my *Haluze Ha-Sifrut*, pp. 143–51; *cf.* my "The Role of Wolf Schur as Hebraist and Zionist," in *Essays in American Jewish History* (Cincinnati, 1958), pp. 425–56.
5. For a fuller discussion of his role as editor and satirist, see my *Haluze Ha-Sifrut*, pp. 213–54.
6. For an analysis of the historical material in this periodical, see Moshe Davis, "*Ha-Zofeh Ba-Arez Ha-Hadashah:* A Source for East-European Jewish Settlement in America," *Beit Yisrael Ba-Amerikah* (Jerusalem, 1970), pp. 31–73. See also my article "The Centenary of the First American Hebrew Periodical" (Hebrew), *Ha-Doar*, vol. L, no. 31 (June 18, 1971), pp. 551–52.
7. Reprinted in his *Ozar Zikhronotai*, pp. 335–36. Eisenstein's interest in American life is evidenced also by his translation of the Constitution and the Declaration of Independence into Hebrew and Yiddish together with explanatory notes in Hebrew (New York, 1901).
8. Reprinted in my *Haluze Ha-Sifrut*, pp. 124–30.
9. Reprinted in *Ozar Zikhronotai*, pp. 242–46.
10. Reprinted in *ibid.*, pp. 245–51. *Cf.* his article on the same subject in *Publications of the American Jewish Historical Society [PAJHS]*, vol. IX (1901), pp. 63–74.
11. Reprinted in *Ozar Zikhronotai*, pp. 252–71.
12. Reprinted in *ibid.*, pp. 271–85.
13. In his *Koheleth America*, a catalogue of Hebrew books printed in America from 1735–1925 (St. Louis, 1925), Deinard indicated that his name as editor was left out by the printer. See p. 55.
14. Reprinted in his *Yisrael Ba-Amerikah* (Jerusalem and Tel-Aviv, 1928). The volume also contains several additional articles on historical themes and personalities, including Haym Salomon, Rebecca Gratz, Mordecai Manuel Noah, and

I. M. Wise. Raisin was also the author of the first Hebrew dissertation presented to the Hebrew Union College. It dealt wtih early American Jewish history and appeared in book form under the title, *Toledot Ha-Yehudim Ba-Amerikah* (Warsaw, 1902). His Hebrew volume, *Mordecai Manuel Noah: Zionist, Author, and Statesman,* appeared in Warsaw in 1905. His *Dappim Mi-Pinkaso Shel Rabbai* (Brooklyn, N. Y., 1941) and *Mi-Sefer Hayyai* (New York, 1956) are valuable for their autobiographical reminiscences, particularly on Jewish cultural life in New York during the nineties and on the early days of the Hebrew Union College.

15. Reprinted in *Ozar Zikhronotai,* pp. 303–16.
16. A short appreciation of Felsenthal by Wiernik also appeared in *Ha-Ibri,* vol. IX, no. 29 (January 17, 1902).
17. The article is signed with the initial "N."
18. Reprinted in his *Ozar Zikhronotai,* pp. 338–58. *Cf.* his "The Development of Jewish Casuistic Literature in America," *PAJHS,* vol. XII (1909), pp. 139–47.
19. "Yahadut Amerikah Be-Shulé Ha-Doar" (from 1921 through 1963), mimeograph (New York, Hadoar Association and National Curriculum Institute), 80 pp.

AMERICAN RABBINIC BOOKS
PUBLISHED IN PALESTINE

By

NATHAN M. KAGANOFF

American Jewish Historical Society

Although the history of the American Jewish community has become the subject of intensive research and investigation, one aspect of American Jewish life has been singularly neglected—namely, the story of Judaism, Jewish religious life, in the United States. No comprehensive or systematic study has as yet appeared describing what is distinctive about Judaism in America, what unique religious practices or institutions it has produced, how traditional Judaism has reacted in a society which, legally at least, maintains a strong separation between church and state, or how voluntarism has affected the religious structure and habits of American Jewry.

This is especially true of American Orthodoxy, a field which has been almost completely untouched. Not only has no study as yet appeared on the major American Orthodox rabbinic figures—except for Bernard Revel—but we do not even possess as yet a basic listing of the outstanding American Orthodox rabbis of the last hundred years. To many non-American Jewish scholars, the United States represents a community which has produced a Jew who is very successful economically and possibly very generous philanthropically, but with no great claim to any significant intellectual achievement or culture. Serious investigation, however, will show that this, too, is one of many popular misconceptions of American Jewry. It is generally accepted among Orthodox circles throughout the world that since the Second World War and the Holocaust, the recognized Orthodox rabbinic authorities and scholars and a major proportion of the more important yeshivot and rabbinic schools are to be found in the United States. Like other historic events, this phenomenon did not appear out of nowhere, and it would be very much worth our while to discover what there was in American Jewish life between the great migrations of the 1880s and the Second World War that paved the way for this flowering of Orthodoxy.

In part our lack of knowledge is due to an almost complete absence of basic tools and information which would provide the scholar with the means upon which to base his research. To date only one bibliography has appeared which lists Hebrew works published in the United States, the *Kohelet America,* published by Ephraim Deinard in 1926.[1]

This paper is a modest attempt to add to our knowledge of American Orthodox intellectual achievements. It is hoped that the data discovered will in addition help dispel another popular myth—that Zionism and the interest and efforts in the rebuilding of Palestine as a Jewish homeland attracted adherents primarily among the American Jewish center, and that just as Reform opposed a Jewish state, Orthodoxy, or at least right-wing Orthodoxy, insisted that the creation of a Jewish homeland must await divine intervention and the appearance of the Messiah.

Deinard's work, noted above, is not only dated, but suffers from personal bias and many lacunae. But even if we did possess a fully comprehensive list of all rabbinica published in America, we could still not proceed with an evaluation of Orthodox rabbinic accomplishments. As is known, there were virtually no prominent native-born American Orthodox rabbis or scholars in America prior to World War II. Almost all had emigrated from Europe and many continued to publish their works outside the United States. While it is perhaps understandable why many continued to do so in Europe, since Europe was still considered the center of Orthodox Jewish life and learning, surprisingly a large number of American rabbis published their work in Palestine. We have located eighty-one such volumes—namely, rabbinic works published by American rabbis in Palestine prior to 1939. Before a fully adequate understanding of American Orthodox achievements can be obtained, a similar compilation of works published in Europe will have to be made.

In *Kohelet America,* Deinard notes 317 rabbinic works published in America. For the same period—that is, until 1926—there were forty-eight rabbinic books by American scholars published in Palestine. This means that the number of such works represents approximately 15 percent of those that appeared in America, or for every seven books printed in the United States, one was published in Palestine. Unfortunately, no bibliography for a later period has appeared. The eighty-one titles discovered are the product of thirty-four American rabbis, and if we add to this the works of four additional Americans who moved to Palestine and subsequently published their works there, Palestine played a role in the publication activities of no less than thirty-eight American Orthodox leaders.

We shall attempt to provide a brief analysis of who these authors were, their status in American life when ascertainable, what they published elsewhere, and why they went to faraway Palestine—at this time no major center of Orthodoxy—to publish their material.

The first work by an American rabbi to be published in Palestine was a volume called מטעי משה , by Moses Aronson, printed at Jerusalem in 1878. Aronson was born in Lithuania in 1805 and achieved prominence as a rabbi and preacher in Europe. He arrived in New York in 1861 and was employed as the rabbi of the Congregation Beth Hamidrash on Allen Street, which had broken away from the famous Beth Hamidrash Hagadol, the first Russian Orthodox synagogue established in New York City. Aronson and Rabbi Abraham Joseph Asch, the rabbi of the original synagoue, did not get along, and Aronson was forced to leave his position to serve as a private rabbi in the community, primarily in matters of divorce and marriage. Because of a conflict that arose between him and other New York rabbis over the *kashrut* of the wine that came from California and also the *shelihim* that came from the Etz Chaim Yeshiva in Jerusalem, Aronson was forced to leave New York, and he traveled throughout the United States. He died at Chicago in 1875. According to Judah David Eisenstein, Aronson had planned to settle with his family in Palestine, a dream that was never realized. His last work was published posthumously by his family in Jerusalem three years after his death. Whether the choice of this place of publication was due to his unfulfilled dream, or because his family felt that after all his suffering at the hands of the New York rabbis, they preferred not to publish in New York City, the only logical place to do so in America, is not known. His final work contains some interesting responsa on problems then agitating the American Jewish community—

whether it is permissible to sell a synagogue building after the people
have moved from the area, whether it is permissible to purchase for
use as a synagogue a building that was formerly a Protestant church,
and whether it is permissible to build a synagogue with the Holy Ark
facing west rather than the traditional east toward Jerusalem.

Following the publication of מטעי משה, seventeen years pass before
we discover a second work published by an American rabbi in Palestine. But with the appearance of שואל כענין by Rabbi Sholom
Elchanan Jaffe in 1895, a pattern of continuous American publication in Palestine begins, and it continues until the outbreak of World
War II. Jaffe was born near Vilna in 1858 and served as a rabbi
in several Jewish communities in Lithuania. He came to the United
States on a family visit in 1889 and returned two years later to become
a rabbi in St. Louis, Missouri, where he served for almost six years
before moving to New York. In 1901 he became the rabbi of the
Beth Hamidrash Hagadol, whose pulpit he occupied until his death
in 1923. Jaffe was one of the founders of the Agudas Harabbonim
(Union of Orthodox Rabbis of the United States and Canada) and
served both as president and honorary president of this group for many
years. Jaffe was also the author of a commentary of the Siddur,
שיחה שלימה , which in 1896, a year following his earlier work, was
also published in Jerusalem. The year 1896 also marks the appearance
of a Haggadah published in Palestine by the printing firm of Zuckerman with an English translation specifically prepared for the Anglo-
American market. There had already apparently developed sufficient
economic contact between Palestine and the United States to make
such a venture economically feasible.

From 1895 until the outbreak of World War I, books by American
authors were published in Palestine on a regular basis although in
modest numbers. Except for 1897, 1899, 1903, and 1907, at least
one book per year appeared, with two titles being published in 1902,
1904, 1909, and 1910, four titles in 1908 and 1913, and no less than
six in 1914. Apparently a trend to publish in Palestine was developing
among American rabbis, and where it would have led we can only
conjecture. The outbreak of World War I stopped almost all contact
between America and the Holy Land and brought an end to these
ventures. The difficulties created by the war in the area of publishing
is very vividly illustrated by the work משנה˙ זכרון , a commentary on

the Bible and the Talmud by Joshua H. Singer, of Buffalo. The book bears a Jerusalem imprint, but the last page of the volume contains the following information: "Because of the war, the printing in Jerusalem was stopped and was completed in the Moinester Printing Company in St. Louis, Missouri, in America."

Continuing our account, we have not been able to locate a single volume published in Palestine by an American author for the period 1915 to 1919. In 1920, this publication begins again with the appearance of מנחת אהרן , a book of responsa by Aaron Gordon, a prominent European scholar known as the Miadler Iluy (he had been born in Miadel, near Vilna, in 1845), who arrived in America in 1890. He served as a rabbi in Rochester, New York, for ten years before moving to New York City, where he served several congregations until his death in 1922. The war no doubt explains the unusual publication of מנחת אהרן . It appeared in four volumes, the first being published in New York in 1918, but the last three printed in Jerusalem in 1920 and 1921. Gordon also published another work, שערי דעת on the Yoreh Deah, in Palestine prior to his death.

The tempo of publication by American rabbis in Palestine in the interwar years increased greatly. Starting with 1921, at least two volumes appeared each year, with the number increasing to three for the years 1930, 1931, 1933, 1937, and 1938, and no less than four titles appearing in 1925 and 1926. In 1932 there were seven volumes published, and the record seems to have been set in 1929, when no less than nine volumes were printed. Strangely enough we have found no book published in 1923; nothing seems to have come out during the years 1934 and 1936, and only one volume in 1935. These were, of course, the most difficult years of the depression in America, and this fact probably accounts for the complete absence of such material.

The role of Palestine in the publications of American rabbis can be appreciated somewhat more when we consider the following. Of the thirty-eight authors represented, the works of three were published posthumously in Palestine by their families. One, Aronson, has already been noted. A second, Joshua Siegel, arrived in New York in 1884. He moved to Palestine in 1908, but was forced to return to America one year later because of illness and died at New York in 1910. Siegel was the author of a famous study, עירוב והוצאה , an extensive halakhic commentary on the problems of the Sabbath in New York and a

collection of his responsa,   שאלות ותשובות אזני יהושע   , was published
by his children in Jerusalem in 1914. The third posthumous publication was also a book of responsa and talmudic commentaries,
עין אליעזר   , by Eliezer Lipman Wolk, who was actually never in
America but lived all of his life in Russia. The work was published
in Palestine by the author's son, Benjamin Jacob Wolk, of New
Haven, Connecticut.

But of those authors who actually published their works in their own
lifetimes, ten published all their writings in Palestine, or at least all the
works they produced after their arrival in America. It is also interesting
to note in some instances where an author published his works both
in Palestine and elsewhere, what proportion of his books were published
where. Gabriel Wolf Margolis was the author of twelve works, of
which eight appeared in Palestine and two in the United States. Simon
Paltrovich, of Buffalo, published three works in Jerusalem and one
in New York, and Moses Simon Sivitz, of Pittsburgh, published no
less than ten works, one of which appeared in Europe, two in America,
and seven in Palestine.

There are, of course, two additional questions to be answered. Who
were these rabbinic authors of books published in Palestine—were they
nonentities or prominent communal leaders and scholars, whose actions would tend to influence the Jewish communities in which they
lived? And why did they choose Palestine as the place to publish their
works? We have already noted that Shalom Elchanan Jaffe, the author
of two works printed in Palestine, was an outstanding rabbi in New
York and a founder of the Agudas Harabbonim. Gabriel Wolf
Margolis, the author of eight books published in Palestine just noted,
was considered one of the outstanding rabbinic scholars and authorities
of his time. Simon Paltrovich, also just noted, was the most prominent
rabbi in Buffalo, New York. Louis Seltzer was the general secretary
of the Agudas Harabbonim for many years. Gedaliah Silverstone, the
author of four works published in Palestine, was the chief rabbi of the
combined Orthodox congregations of Washington, D. C., and Moses
Simon Sivitz, the author of seven books printed in Palestine just noted,
was the most prominent Orthodox rabbi in Pittsburgh, where he
served as a rabbi for forty-seven years. We do not mean to equate
publication in Palestine with importance and prominence in the
American Jewish community. Unfortunately, for many of the thirty-
eight authors, we know nothing more than their names or whatever

other little data may be noted in the volume, and a detailed analysis of the contents of some of the volumes indicates that the absence of prominence is probably well deserved.

Finally, there is another problem—what factors influenced these rabbinic figures to publish in Palestine? In a few instances, there were personal reasons. Chayim Hirschensohn, the author of no less than nine volumes printed in Palestine, was, of course, a native of that country who had emigrated to the United States. The same is true of Biednowitz, Horowitz, and Neches. We have already noted that Siegel had moved to Palestine and was forced to return because of his health and also that Aronson had planned to move to the Holy Land. Another author, Isaacs, also had hoped to live in Palestine, but because of financial reverses had to return to the United States after reaching England. At least three of the authors—Seltzer, Silverstone, and Libowitz—spent extensive periods in Palestine on visits, and in some cases actually published the material while they were there. In at least two instances, Levin and Paltrovich, we are told that the material was presented to the printer by the author's brother who lived in Palestine, and in one case, prior to publication an "approbation" was requested from the rabbis in Jerusalem. Four of the authors were active in Zionist work; of these, Meyer Waxman was the director of the Mizrachi in America, and Zlotnik was the president of the Mizrachi in Montreal. But all this accounts for only sixteen, or somewhat less than one-half of the authors, if we do not include those who had moved to Palestine before the publication of their material.

There is an intriguing explanation which provides a possible solution to this problem, but essentially it is only a conjecture. Perhaps it is only an historic coincidence, but in some way the pattern of American rabbinic publishing in Palestine occurs at the very same time that efforts were made by Americans in Palestine to organize themselves as a community.

For many centuries, the Jews of Palestine subsisted primarily on the *haluka,* a monthly stipend provided by Jewish communities throughout the Diaspora. The Jews in Jerusalem were organized into various *Kollelim,* or communities, based on their city or country of origin. Regular funds were provided by each *Kollel*-member's fellow country-men at home. American Jews in Palestine were too few in number to organize their own *Kollel* and were dependent on a general organi-zation known as the *Vaad ha-Kelali.* In 1878, twenty-eight American

Jewish families emigrated to Palestine, and in the following year an
unsuccessful attempt was made to establish an independent American
Kollel called "Shelom Yerushalayim."

By 1896, American immigrants in Palestine numbered approximately one thousand individuals and were able to establish the Kollel
America Tifereth Jerusalem with offices in New York and Jerusalem.
Among its members were Samuel Zuckerman, who arrived from the
United States with a printing press. Possibly it is only a coincidence,
but it is nonetheless true that the first American rabbinic work printed
in Jerusalem occurred in 1878, the year before the first effort made to
establish an American *Kollel,* and the continuous pattern of publishing
noted above began a year before the establishment of Kollel America.
Whether these contacts were accidental or deliberate, of the eighty-
seven titles located, by far the largest number, nineteen, were printed
by the firm of Zuckerman.

But, perhaps, the explanation for this phenomenon of American
publishing in Palestine is a much simpler one. All of the individuals
involved were observant Orthodox Jews. According to some rabbinic
authorities, settlement in Palestine is one of the positive commandments. But certainly all rabbinic authorities agree that even if not
one of the 613 Mitzvot, there is a special merit in any activity that
helps support and encourages the settlement of Jews in Palestine, regardless of whether one is a Zionist in the more technical sense or
whether one is for or against political Zionism as a movement. This
view is specifically noted in at least two of the volumes that are noted.
In Joseph Elijah Fried's אלומת יוסף , published in Jerusalem in 1909,
the editor adds a postscript to the text: "The author has sent us his
book to edit and to set in type, and we have done as he has directed.
And we are very pleased with his letter that he has written of his own
free will that he will try to find work for the printers in Jerusalem by
speaking to others that they should do the same for the help of the
Jewish settlement in Palestine."

More specific is the following addendum by the printer, Isaac
Nochum Lewy, in the commentary to the haggadah published by
Gittelsohn in 1904:

May he be remembered for glory, Rabbi Benjamin Gittelsohn of
Cleveland. From a distance, the United States, he provided work for
the inhabitants of Jerusalem, so that they might enjoy the labor of their

hands. And praise to the Lord, we have completed the printing with beauty, clear letters, and good paper. And this should be a sign to our brethren that the work of our printing plant is very outstanding. And we hope that all Jews will learn from him and whoever has something to print, will send it to us, and with God's help we will fulfill every request. In addition, they will strengthen the Jewish community in Palestine in a noble and elegant manner.

WORKS BY NORTH AMERICAN SCHOLARS
PUBLISHED IN PALESTINE

1. ARONSON, MOSES[2]
   (Born in Salant, Lithuania, about 1805, Aronson served as a rabbi
   and preacher in several communities in Poland and Lithuania. He
   arrived in New York in 1861 and served at first as the preacher of
   Congregation Beth Hamidrash on Allen Street in New York City
   and then privately as a rabbi. He died in Chicago in 1875. Aronson
   was known at the Baal ha-Pardes, from the title of two books he
   published prior to his arrival in America.)

I.   מטעי משה: הענף הראשון מפרי חכמינו ז"ל ע"פ פרחי ההגיון והחקירה, הסרעף
   השני בתשובות. גם פירוש על שה"ש. ירושלם. בדפוס י.מ. שאלאמאן, שנת
   יתברכו. [1878]   54, 52 l.

2. BACHRACH, DAVID
   (Born and educated in Europe, Bachrach served as a *shohet* in
   Cincinnati in the early part of this century.)

II.   לקוטי דב"ש. והמה שאלות ותשובות בדיני שו"ב. ירושלם, בדפוס של ש.
   צוקערמאן. [1910/11]   14 l.

3. BIEDNOWITZ, ZE'EV[3]
   (A native of Jerusalem, Biednowitz arrived in the United States
   in the early 1920s. Apparently his publishing ventures were his source
   of income. He also published works in Egypt, Hungary, Poland, and
   the United States.)

III. ירושלם,   דברי זאב, כולל חדושים וביאורים והערות בגמ' ופוסקים . . . חלק יב. ירושלם,
   בדפוס "ציון." תרפ"ה. [1925]   12 l.

IV. ," ארץ-ישראל,"   דברי זאב, כולל הרבה ענינים בהלכה. חלק טו. ירושלים, דפוס "ארץ-ישראל,"
   תרפ"ט. [1929]   32 p.

V.   — — — חלק יח. ירושלם, דפוס חיים צוקרמן, תרצ"ב. [1932]   24 p.

תוספות רי"ד מסכת יבמות . . . ע"פ העתקת כת"י . . . נמצא בבית עקד הספרים   .VI
של שכטער . . . בניוארק . . . נערך ונסדר על ידי זאב ביעדנאוויץ. ירושלם,
דפוס חיים י. צוקרמן. [1932?] 32 l.

ל"ו שערים מאת ישראל איסרלין . . . עם הגהות . . . מאת זאב ביעדנאוויץ.   .VII
ירושלם, דפוס חיים י. צוקרמן, תרנ"ן. [1939/40] 28 l.

4. BORUCHOFF, BER[4]

(Born in Vilna in 1872, Boruchoff attended yeshivot in Europe
and was ordained. He arrived in the United States in 1920. He served
as the rabbi of Congregation Beth Israel in Malden, Mass., from 1905
until his death in 1939. An active Zionist, Boruchoff was a member
of the executive board of the Union of Orthodox Rabbis of the
United States and Canada.)

ראשית בכורים . . . א) בחדושי הש"ס . . . ב) הדרנים . . . ירושלים [דפוס ארץ   .VIII
ישראל] [1932] 191 p.

5. FREEMAN, MEYER[5]

(After attending several yeshivot in Europe, Freeman arrived in
New York in 1866. One of the outstanding lay scholars at this time,
he was active in Jewish communal life. He served as president of the
Beth Hamidrash Hagadol and was very active in the negotiations
that brought Rabbi Jacob Joseph to New York as the chief rabbi of
the Orthodox community. Freeman was a businessman but found
time to publish five scholarly rabbinic works, three of which were
published in America. His date of death is unknown, but apparently
he lived to a ripe old age, since his last work appeared in 1928.)

תורת מאיר, מהדורא תנינא, והוא חדושים וביאורים בש"ס בבלי וירושלמי   .IX
ומפרשיהם. ירושלם [1909] 54 l.

יד מאיר, מהדורא תליתאי לספר תורת מאיר קמא ותנינא, והוא חדושים וביאורים   .X
בש"ס בבלי וירושלמי ומפרשיהם. צפת, דפוס "הגליל," תרע"ג.[1913] 137 l.

6. FRIED, JOSEPH ELIJAH[6]

(Born in Lithuania, Fried served as a rabbi in Shukian for sixteen
years before coming to America in 1891. For many years he served
as the rabbi of Congregation Kehal Adath Jeshurun on the East

Side of New York City. He died in 1927. Fried was also the author
of a volume of responsa published in New York in 1903.)

XI. אלומת יוסף. כולל ח"י דרושים. ירושלם, בדפוס של ש. צוקערמאן, תרס"ט.
58 1. [1908/09]

7. GITTELSOHN, BENJAMIN[7]
(Born in Lithuania in 1853, Gittelsohn studied in the yeshiva in
Slabodka under Rabbi Jacob Joseph. He served as a rabbi in two
communities in Lithuania. In 1890 he came to Cleveland, where
he served as a rabbi until his death in 1932. Gittelsohn also published a work in New York in 1898.)

XII. סדר הגדה של פסח עם באור נגיד ונפיק, מאת בנימין גיטעלסאהן. ירושלם, בדפוס
הרי"ן לעווי, תרס"ד. [1903/04] 62 1.

8. GORDON, AARON[8]
(Born in Miadel, near Vilna, in 1845, Gordon attended yeshivot
in Europe and was known as the Miadler Iluy because of his brilliance. After serving as a rabbi in Lithuania, Gordon arrived in the
United States in 1890. After ten years as a rabbi in Rochester, N.Y.,
he moved to New York City, where he served several congregations
until his death in 1922. Gordon was the author of two works published in Europe, and the first part of a third work was published in
New York.)

XIII מנחת אהרן, חלק שני. בו יבואר שאלות ותשובות ... בענין גיטין. ירושלם,
בדפוס ש. צוקערמאן, תר"פ. [1919/20] 59 1.

XIV. מנחת אהרן, חלק שלישי ורביעי, בו יבואר שאלות ותשובות ... בעניני דיני
עגונות ומנקת. ירושלם, בדפוס ש. צוקערמאן, אפר"ת. [1920/21] 53, 12 1.

XV. שערי דעת על שני חלקי יורה דעה ... ירושלם, בדפוס ש. צוקערמאן, תפא"ר.
102 1. [1920/21]

9. GORDON, JACOB[9]
(Born in Danilowitz, Russia, in 1877, Gordon was educated in
yeshivot in Lithuania and ordained. He arrived in Toronto in 1904.
A founder of several Jewish educational institutions and an active
Zionist leader, he served as the rabbi of several congregations in
Toronto until his death in 1934.)

XVI. מנחת יעקב לשבתות השנה, מועדים, חגים וזמנים שונים. צפת, דפוס "הגליל,"
תרע"ד. [1913/14] 12, 104 1.

10. Hirschensohn, Hayyim[10]

(Born in Safed, Palestine, in 1857, Hirschensohn was educated in
Safed and Jerusalem. He arrived in the United States in 1904 and
was appointed rabbi in Hoboken, N. J., where he served until his
death in 1935. Active in Zionism, he was a delegate to the Sixth
Zionist Congress in Basle. Hirschensohn was also the author of a
dozen works published in the United States, Europe, and in Palestine prior to his arrival in America.)

XVII.   ימים מקדם, הוא הכרונולוגיה הביבלית. ירושלם, תרס"ח. [1908]

8, 246, 37 p.

XVIII..חידושי הרח"ה למסכת הוריות בבלי וירושלמי. חלק א. ירושלם, דפוס העברי,
תרע"ד-תרפ"ד. [1924]   104 l.

XIX.   [1926] ——חלק ב. (וחלק ג.) ירושלם, דפוס "העברי," תרפ"ו.

22 p., 42, 43 l.

XX.   אלה דברי הברית, מתבארות בו כל הבריתות בישראל הנזכרות בתנ"כ ותנאיהן כהן
הדתי, המוסרי, ההלכותי, וההיסטורי. חלק א. ירושלם, דפוס "העברי", תרפ"ו.
190 p. [1926]

XXI.   [1928] ——חלק ב. (וחלק ג.) ירושלם, דפוס "העברי", תרפ"ח.

133, 195 p.

XXII. ברורי המדות, מבאר ומברר כללי ופרטי ותנאי המדות אשר התורה נדרשת בהן.
חלק א. ירושלם. בדפוס העברי, תרפ"ט [1928/29]   18 p. , 302

XXIII. [1930/31] ——חלק ב. (וחלק ג. וחלק ד.) ירושלם, דפוס העברי, תרצ"א.

224 , 314 p.

XXIV..מושגי שוא והאמת. מטרתו להראות כחב מושגים רבים. ונלוה אליו חלק הקטעים,
חמשה קטעים בפילוסופיה הדתית. ירושלם, דפוס "העברי", תרצ"ב. [1931/32]
158, 148 p.

XXV. ... סדר למקרא, או מוקדם ומאוחר במאורע ואין מוקדם ומאוחר בתורה
ירושלם, בדפוס העברי, תרצ"ג [1933, i.e. 1935]   290 p.

11. HIRSCHOWITZ, ABRAHAM EBER[11]
(Born in Russia in 1845, Hirschowitz attended yeshiva in Kovno
and was ordained by Rabbi Isaac Elchanan Spector. After serving
as the superintendent of the Poor Jews' Shelter and as a teacher in
London, he accepted a position as a rabbi in Melbourne, Australia.
He arrived in the United States in 1894 and served as a rabbi in
San Francisco, New York, Toledo, and Brooklyn. There is no infor-
mation about his later years, but one account has it that he moved to
Palestine after World War I and died there. Hirschowitz was also the
author of four Hebrew books and one English work published in
New York and London.)

בית מדרש שמואל, דרושים יקרים. ירושלם, בדפוס האחים סאלאמאן.(1905?).XXVI
8, 80, 8, 32 p.

שו"ת בית אברהם: חלק ראשון: אשר השיבו לי גדולי הדור,וחלק שני: דרושים.XXVII
ירושלם,[בדפוס האחים סאלאמאן], תרס"ח.[1907/08] 62, 96 p.

12. HOROWITZ, ISAIAH
(Born in Palestine in 1883, Horowitz was ordained and served as
a rabbi in Safed. In 1922 he emigrated to the United States and soon
afterward became rabbi in Winnipeg. He remained there until 1953,
when he returned to Israel. Horowitz was also the author of a work in
Hebrew published in the United States and a work published in
Israel after his return.)

פרד"ס הארץ . . . שו"ת בהלכה . . . דרושים על פרשיות התורה . . . ירושלם,XXVIII
בדפוס "ציון".[1933–35] 30 p.

13. HUREWITZ, ISAAC S.[12]
(Born in Kovno in 1868, Hurewitz studied in Volozin and Slabodka and was ordained by Rabbi Isaac Elchanan Spector. He arrived in Hartford, Conn., in 1893 and served as the rabbi of several
congregations in that city until his death in 1935. He was also the
editor of a Yiddish periodical, *Yidishe Shtime.*)

ספר המצות להנשר הגדול רבינו משה בן מיימן. . .ונלוה אליו ספר יד הלוי,.XXIX
פירוש . . . חברתיו . . . יצחק שמחה הורוויץ . . . ירושלם, דפוס   ש.
צוקרמן, תרפ"ו. 286 1. [1925/26]

—   —   חלק א. ירושלם, דפוס "הספר", תרצ"א. 282 p. [1930/31] .XXX

14. HURWITZ, SHMARYA LOEB[13]
(Born in Russia in 1878, Hurwitz served as a rabbi in Ekaterino-

slav. He came to the United States in 1906 and served as a rabbi in
several congregations in New York City. He achieved great fame
as a preacher and died in Brooklyn in 1938. Hurwitz was also the
author of sixteen other works in Hebrew and Yiddish which were
published in the United States.)

הלכות דעות, חלק מספר המדע לרבנו משה ב״ר מימן הספרדי ז״ל.עם באור רחב.XXXI
בשם מדות ודעות ... מאת שמריהו ליב הורביץ. תל־אביב, מצפה. [1932]

176 p.

15. Isaacs, Samuel Hillel[14]

(Born in Poland in 1825, Isaacs arrived in New York City in 1847,
where he served as the principal of the local Talmud Torah and later
became a successful wholesale tobacco merchant. In 1913 he moved to
Chicago, where he died in 1917. Isaacs was also the author of a
Hebrew work published in New York. A volume in English was published posthumously in Chicago and appeared in two editions.)

מאמר חדשי השנה ... ירושלם, בדפוס ש. צוקערמאן, תרס״א. [1900/01] .XXXII

12 l.

XXXIII.   פתח עינים, מאמרים שונים. ירושלים, תרס״ב. [1901/02]

תאומי צביה ... באור בחלוקת שלש ארצות הנזכר במשנה ... ירושלם..XXXIV
בדפוס ש. צוקערמאן [1908?]   15 l.

16. Jaffe, Shalom Elhanan[15]

(Born near Vilna in 1858, Jaffe served as the rabbi of several
Lithuanian communities. He first came to the United States on a
family visit in 1889. He returned in 1891 to serve as a rabbi in St.
Louis, where he remained until 1897. He then served as a rabbi
in Brooklyn, and from 1901 until his death in 1923 he was the rabbi
of the Beth Hamidrash Hagodol in New York City. Jaffe was a
founder of the Union of Orthodox Rabbis of the United States and
Canada and served both as president and honorary president of this
group. He was also the author of two works published in Europe prior
to his arrival in America.)

שואל כענין, יכיל בקרבו שאלות ותשובות להלכה למעשה, ... ירושלם, [בדפוס .XXXV
מ. ליליענטהאל], תרנ״ה. [1895]   10, 248, 32 pp.

סדור שיחה שלימה, באור חדש על הושענות סליחות ויוצרות, והוא חלק .XXXVI
שני מסדור שלי הנקרא תפלה שלימה. ירושלם, בדפוס ש. צוקערמאן,
תרנ״ו. [1895/96]   214, 8 l.

17. Klebanov, Moses Mordecai[16]
(Born in Borisov, White Russia, Klebanov arrived in Boston in
1923 and served first as the rabbi of Congregation Anshe Labovitz,
and after 1927 as the chief rabbi of the South End. In 1938 he
moved to Detroit, where he died in 1940.)

XXXVII.   מדרכי משה, חדושים ובאורים בהלכה.   ירושלם, בדפוס ״המדפיס
ליפשיץ״, תרצ״ב. [1931/32]   88 p.

18. Levin, Joshua[17]
(Levin, who changed his name from Krelinstein, was the son of a
well-known rabbinic scholar in Poland and was a prominent preacher
in New York City during the 1920s.)

XXXVIII.   עטרת ישועה, ביאורים על כל אגדות מסכת שבת . . . ירושלים, דפוס יודא
אהרן וייס [192-?].1 p, 7 ,.1 185 ,4

XXXIX.   מעיני הישועה . . . לקוטים נחמדים . . . על כמה פרשיות . . . ירושלם, דפוס
י.א. וייס, תרפ״ד. [1923/24]   p 90 ,7

19. Libowitz, Nehemiah Samuel[18]
(Born in Poland in 1862, Libowitz arrived in the United States in
1881. He was a very successful dealer in precious stones. In 1927 he
emigrated to Palestine, but returned for personal reasons to America,
where he died in 1939. Libowitz was also the author of over a dozen
works published in the United States.)

XL.   בן תמורה, על דבר האגדה שדוד המלך היה בן־תמורה. ירושלים, תרפ״ט.
15 p. [1928/29]

XLI.'   דורש רשומות האגדה, באורי אגדות חז״ל על דרך העיון והבקורת בדברי הימים
וחקירות בעניני דרשות וכוחיות נגד המינים ודברים שונים. הוצאה ג. עם הוספות
ותקונים והערות חכמים וחוקרים. ירושלים, דרום, תרפ״ט. [1928/29]   59 p.

XLII.   פניאל. על דבר המות אבלות ותנחומים וענינים רבים המסתעפים מהם, ונוספו
עליהם שני מאמרים צדקה וכבוד אב ואם. יסדותם בספרה התלמודית ופתגמי
הפילוסופים. הוצאה שלישית בהוספות ותקונים. ירושלים, ״דרום״, תרפ״ט.
139 p. [1928/29]

XLIII.   אגרת בקרת נגד ס׳ זכרונותי מרא״ה וייס והתנצלות בעד רש״ל ראפאפורט.
[הוצאה ג.] ירושלים, ״דרום״, תרפ״ט. [1929]   31 p.

XLIV. ‏ארי נוהם. נגד חכמת הקבלה ולומדיה ומכחיש שרשב"י הוא מחבר הזהר, מאת רבי
‏יהודה אריה מודינא. יצא לאור עפ"י כתבי יד עם הגהות שמשון בלאך הלוי
‏והערות ר"מ שטיינשניידער הנמצאות בכתב ידם והוספה מיוחדת, טענות ומענות
‏המקובלים ותשובות גאונים מתנגדים. מבוא והערות מאת נחמיה שמואל
‏ליבאוויטש. ירושלים, "דרום", תרפ"ט. [1929]   167 p. XXXI,

XLV. ‏פניני הזהר, המשלים והפתגמים. הוצאה חדשה בתקונים והוספות. ירושלים,
‏"דרום", תרצ"א. [1930/31]   153 p.

XLVI. ‏שרידים, מכתבי הפלוסוף והמקובל ר' יוסף חמיץ. עם הספר בליל חמיץ; כולל
‏שירים ושבחים לכבדו בהשלימו את למדו בהאוניברסטי בפאדובה. נדפסו מחדש
‏עם הערות ומבוא מאת נחמיה שמאול ליבאוויטץ. ירושלים, "דרום", תרצ"ז.
58 p. [1937]

20. MARGOLIN, ISAIAH JOSEPH[19]

(Born in Russia in 1878, Margolin achieved fame as a preacher at
the age of seventeen. After a brief stay in Leeds, England, he arrived in the United States in 1909 and served as a preacher to several
synagogues in New York City. After serving as a rabbi in Rochester,
N. Y. from 1912 to 1914, he returned to New York City and was a
rabbi in several synagogues until his death in 1943. Margolin was
also the author of two works published in New York and Rumania
and the editor of a rabbinic journal that appeared in New York.)

XLVII. ‏המעשה והמדרש על חמשה חומשי תורה . . . ירושלים, [בדפוס ארץ ישראל]
‏תרצ"ז. [1936/37]   188, 8 p.

21. MARGOLIS, GABRIEL WOLF[20]

(Born in Vilna in 1848, Margolis served as the rabbi of several
European communities. Arriving in the United States in 1908, he first
served as a rabbi in Boston until 1912, when he was called to be the
rabbi of the United Hebrew Community of New York [Adath
Israel], which he served until his death in 1935. Margolis was considered one of the outstanding rabbinical scholars and authorities
of his time. He was also the author of four other works, two of which
were published in Europe prior to his arrival in America, and two of
which were published in New York.)

XLVIII. ‏חמשה חומשי תורה בראשית . . . ובאור חדש בשם תורת גבריאל . . . ירושלים,
‏דפוס לעווי, עת"ר. [1909/10]   164, 26 l.

XLIX. חמשה חומשי תורה שמות ... ובאור חדש בשם תורת גבריאל ... ירושלם,
דפוס לעווי, עת"ר. ‏[1909/10] ‏1. 25, 215

L. חרוזי מרגליות, כולל דרושים לעתים מזמנים ... ירושלם, בדפוס לעווי, תער"ב.
‏[1911/12] ‏1. 139

LI. חמשה חומשי תורה במדבר ... ובאור חדש בשם תורת גבריאל ... ירושלם,
דפוס לוי, תרפ"ב.‏[1921/22] ‏1. 34, 214

LII. חמשה חומשי תורה דברים ... ובאור חדש בשם תורת גבריאל ... ירושלם,
דפוס ציון, תרפ"ה. ‏[1924/25] ‏1. 44, 210

LIII. גנזי מרגליות, והוא באור חמש מגילות [מגלת איכה] ירושלם, דפוס ציון, תרפ"ה.
‏[1924/25] ‏1. 27

LIV. גנזי מרגליות. והוא באור חמש מגילות [קהלת] ירושלם, דפוס ציון, תרפ"ה.
‏[1924/25] ‏1. 29

LV. חמשה חומשי תורה ויקרא ... ובאור חדש בשם תורת גבריאל ... ירושלם,
דפוס ציון, תרפ"ו.‏[1925/26] ‏1. 22, 158

22. NECHES, SOLOMON MICHAEL[21]

(Born in Jerusalem in 1891, Neches was ordained there. He arrived
in the United States in 1910 and served communities in Pittsburgh
and Columbus. In 1921 he became the rabbi of the Orthodox community in Los Angeles, where he remained until his death in 1957.
Neches was also the founder of Western Jewish Institute. He was
also the author of eight works in Hebrew and several in English
which were published in the United States.)

LVI. תורתו של שם, בו נמצאים כמה מאמרים ובאורים על הרבה פסוקים שבתורה
מסדרים וערוכים לפי הפרשיות לכל שבתות השנה. ירושלם, תר"ץ. ‏[1930]
212 p.

23. PALTROVICH, SIMON[22]

(Born in Poland in 1843, Paltrovich arrived in the United States
in 1872 and served as a rabbi in Chicago, Boston, and Cleveland
prior to his arrival in Buffalo in 1890. He was the rabbi of the Pine
Street Shul from 1890 to 1914 and the most prominent Orthodox
rabbi in the community. He then moved to New York, where he died
in 1926. Paltrovich was also the author of a work published in New
York.)

כתר צבי ... כולל חידושי תורה ... גם דרושים יקרים ועוד מאמרים LVII
ירושלם.[1906]. 32, 52 l.

קול שמחה ... דרושים נחמדים ... ירושלם, דפוס לעווי. [1913] .LVIII 130 l.

שמחת הגיון ... חדושי חמד על פסוקי התורה ... דרושים על כל מועדי השנה .LIX
... ירושלם, דפוס ש. צוקערמאן. [1922] .p 25 .,l 49 ,46 ,58

24. PERLOW, JUDAH LOEB[23]

(Born in Poland in 1878, Perlow was ordained by Rabbi Chaim Soloveichik and known as the Novominsker Rebbie. He arrived in the United States in 1922 and resided in Brooklyn until his death in 1961. Perlow was also the author of a work published in New York.)

לב אריה החדש. חבור כולל מפירושי התורה ועל כמה מאמרים מדברי חז"ל. .LX
ירושלם, בדפוס "ציון", תרצ"ג. [1932/33] (.p 101 ,302 ,vi) .v2

25. PREIL, ELEAZER MEIR[24]

(Born in Lithuania in 1878, Preil achieved prominence as a rabbinic scholar. In 1909 he went to Manchester, England, and in 1911 he arrived in America. He first served as a rabbi in Trenton, N. J., and afterwards in Elizabeth, where he died in 1933. Preil also served on the faculty of Yeshiva University, and was also the author of a book in Yiddish published in New York. The concluding volume of the following work was published posthumously in New York in 1955.)

המאור. חלק א. שאלות ותשובות והארות כהלכה ובחכמת ישראל. [חלק ב. הארות .LXI
דרושים לכל שבתות השנה.] ירושלם, דפוס "ארץ־ישראל", תרפ"ט. [1928/29]
387, 153 p.

26. ROSHGOLIN, ZALMAN DOV[25]

(Born in Lithuania in 1864, Roshgolin attended yeshiva in Europe and served as a rabbi in Lithuania. He arrived in the United States in 1922, and served for almost twenty years as a rabbi on Staten Island, where he died in 1944. Roshgolin was the father of the prominent Hebrew poet Hillel Bavli.)

הגיוני לב. יכלכל סקירות קצרות על ענינים שונים דרושים למועדים ולכמה .LXII
שבתות השנה ... ירושלם, בדפוס ש. צוקרמן, תרפ"ז. [1926/27] .l 103

27. Seltzer, Louis[26]

 (Born in Russia in 1876, Seltzer was ordained in 1900 and arrived in the United States in 1901. He served as a rabbi in Bangor,
Maine, Paterson, N. J., Minneapolis, and Bridgeport, Conn. He also
served as the general secretary of the Union of Orthodox Rabbis of
the United States and Canada for many years. Between 1911 and
1915, Seltzer served as a rabbi in Safed, Palestine, during which
time he published the following work, which appeared in two editions.)

LXIII. משא יהודה, דרשות ומאמרים מצוינים בהגיונם וסגנונם, ברוח הדת ולצורך הדור.
ספר א. ירושלים, בדפוס הרי"ד פרומקין, תרע"ד. [1913/14] 48 l.

LXIV. Another edition published by   דפוס הגליל, צפת, תרע"ד, [1913/14]
61 l.

28. Siegel, Joshua[27]

 (Born in Poland in 1846, Siegel was ordained and served as a
rabbi in Poland. He arrived in New York in 1884. In 1908 he moved
to Palestine, but was forced to return to New York one year later
because of illness and died there in 1910. Siegel was also the author
of an extensive halakhic study on the Sabbath which was published
in New York. The following was published posthumously by his
children.)

LXV. שאלות ותשובות אזני יהושע. חלק א. ירושלם, בדפוס מוריהו (שעהנבוים את
וייס)[תרע"ד] 236 p. [1913/14]

29. Silverstone, Gedalia[28]

 (Born in Lithuania in 1872, Silverstone was ordained in Russia
and served as a rabbi in Belfast, Ireland, from 1891 to 1896. He was
also a delegate to the Sixth Zionist Congress. He arrived in the
United States in 1904 and came to Washington, D.C., in 1906, where
he served as rabbi of individual congregations and also as chief rabbi
of the combined Orthodox congregations. He was also a vice-president of the Union of Orthodox Rabbis of the United States and
Canada. During the 1920s Silverstone made an extended visit to
Palestine and moved there permanently in 1936. He died in 1944.
Silverstone was the author of over thirty other works, which were
published in the United States, London, and Belfast.)

LXVI. מסכת אבות, עם פרוש לב אבות [מאת] גדלי' סילווערסטאן. ירושלם, בדפוס
"המדפיס ליפשיץ." תרצ"ב.[1932] 96 p.

חבת הקדש, דרושים עם הספדים. ירושלים, דפוס ווינגרטן, תרצ"ז [1936/37].LXVII
8, 86 p.

נאה דורש לכל השנה. ירושלים, דפוס העברי, תרצ"ח. [1938]　　97 p.　.LXVIII

קרבן פסח על הגדה של פסח. הוצאה ב. ... . בביאור הוספה על הראשונה בשם .LXIX
חגיגת פסח ... ירושלים, דפוס העברי, תרצ"ט. [1939]　84 p.

30. SINGER, JOSHUA H.[29]
    (Born in Lithuania in 1847, Singer was a cantor in Kreutzberg,
Russia, for almost twenty years. He arrived in Buffalo in the 1890's
and served as a cantor and preacher first in Congregation Beth Jacob
and then Brith Sholem. Singer also operated a Jewish bookstore,
which was a meeting place for Jewish intellectuals. He died in 1925.
Singer was also the author of a Hebrew work that was published in
Vilna.)

משנה זכרון על מקומות מפוזרות בתנ"ך וש"ס,והדרן, ומקור למנהגים ... ועד .LXX
דרשות שונות ... ירושלם, בדפוס שעהנבוים את וויס, תרע"ג. [1912/13]
214 p.

31. SIVITZ, MOSES SIMON[30]
    (Born in Lithuania in 1855, Sivitz attended yeshiva in Europe and
was ordained by Rabbi Isaac Elchanan Spector. He emigrated to
America in 1886 and was a rabbi in Baltimore, Cleveland, and
Toledo. In 1889 he came to Pittsburgh, where he served several congregations. For the last forty-five years of his life, he was the rabbi
of the Gates of Wisdom Synagogue and was the most prominent
Orthodox rabbi in Pittsburgh. He died in 1936. Sivitz was also the
author of a Hebrew book published in St. Louis. The second volume
and the supplements to his commentary on the Jerusalem Talmud
were published in the United States and Europe.)

חקר דעת, דרושים יקרים בכל פרשה ופרשה. חלק א.ספר בראשית. ירושלם,.LXXI
בדפוס האחים סאלאמאן, תרנ"ח. [1898]　181 p.

חלק ב. ספר שמות. ירושלם, בדפוס האחים סאלאמאן, תרס"ב. —— .LXXII
120 p. [1902]

בית פגא, דרושים יקרים ונחמדים לכל עתות השנה ולכל מועדי קדש .LXXIII
... ירושלם, בדפוס האחים סאלאמאן, תרס"ד. [1904]　193 p.

פרי יחזקאל, אשכול אמרים להיות חומר (טהעמא) לדרוש בשבת . . . ירושלם, LXXIV,
בדפוס האחים סאלאמאן, תרס"ח. [1908] .p 6 ,45 ,152

משבי"ח. חלק א. על הירושלמי מסכת ברכות. ירושלם, בדפוס ש. צוקערמאן, LXXV.
תרע"ג.[1913]

מטה אהרן, אשכל אמרים להיות חומר (טהעמא) לדרוש בשבת . . . ירושלם, LXXVI.
בדפוס סאלאמאן, תרע"ד. [1914] .p 272

משבי"ח על תלמוד ירושלמי. [תוצאה שלישית] ירושלם, דפוס י.א. LXXVII.
וייס, [תרפ"ט] [1929] .p 336

32. Waxman, Meyer[31]

(Born in Russia in 1887, Waxman arrived in the United States in
1905. After several rabbinic posts, he served as the director of the
Mizrachi Zionist Organization. From 1924 to 1955 he was on the
faculty of the Hebrew Theological College in Chicago, after which
he moved to New York, where he died in 1969. Waxman was also
the author of a large number of works in Hebrew and English published in the United States and Europe.)

LXXVIII.

משלי ישראל מכיל יותר משׁשת אלפים משלים, פתגמים ומליצות, מלקטים מן
המקרא מן התלמודים והמדרשים, מספרות ימי הבינים ומן הספרות החדשה,
ערוכים ומסדרים על פי נושאיהם ומנקדים ומסברים. ירושלים, "שילה", [1933]
39, 318 p.

33. Wolk, Eliezer Lipman

(Wolk was born and served as a rabbi in Russia. The following
work was published posthumously by his son, Benjamin Jacob Wolk,
of New Haven, Conn.)

עין־אליעזר. חלק ראשון, שו"ת בד' חלקי השו"ע; חלק שני,' חדושים על LXXIX.
הש"ס והרמב"ם דרושים. ירושלם , תרפ"ח. [1927/28] 84 .l 8 ,.p

34. Zlotnik, Jehuda Leib[32]

(Born in Plotzk, Poland, in 1888, Zlotnik was ordained and served
as a rabbi in Gombin, Poland. In 1917 he founded the Mizrachi in
Poland. In 1921 he was president of the Mizrachi in Montreal, and
he served as the rabbi in Vancouver from 1933 to 1938. He then
moved to South Africa and afterwards to Israel, where he died in
1962. Zlotnik was the author of many works in Hebrew, English,
and Yiddish. The following were published in Palestine while he was
a resident of Canada.)

"בראשית" במליצה העברית, פרקים מספר מדרש המליצה העברית. ירושלים, .LXXX
תרצ"ח. [1938] .p 54

מדרש המליצה העברית, אמרי חכמה ואמרי אנשי. אות א. ירושלים,"דרום",.LXXXI
תרצ"ח. [1938] .p 78

BOOKS BY AMERICAN RABBIS
PUBLISHED AFTER SETTLEMENT
IN PALESTINE

35. ABRAMSON, SAMUEL AVIGDOR[33]
(Born in Russia in 1866, Abramson attended yeshiva in Europe
and was ordained by Rabbi Isaac Elchanan Spector. After a short
period as a rabbi in Latvia, he arrived in the United States in 1904
and served as a rabbi in Lowell and then Lynn, Mass. In 1910 he
arrived in New York, where he remained until 1929 and then
settled in Jerusalem. Abramson was also the author of a work published in New York.)

עם נקדות הכסף, יכלל בתוכו תשובות כהלכה שאסור לשלח שליח לחלוץ .LXXXII
... ירושלם, דפוס ח. צוקרמן. [1929/30] .p 78

נעשה לך, הוא שו"ת אשר השבתי לכל שואל ... ירושלם, דפוס ח. .LXXXIII
צוקרמן, תר"ץ. [1929/30] .p 18

36. DSIMITROWSKY, JOSEF
(Born in Lithuania, Dsimitrowsky served as a rabbi in Lawrence,
Mass., toward the end of the nineteenth century, before moving to
Palestine.)

דרישת ציון לחברת ישוב ארץ ישראל, מאת צבי הירש קאלישער LXXXIV
המו"ל יעקב יוסף דזימיטראוווסקי. ירושלם, בדפוס ש. צוקערמאן, תרע"ט.
69 l. [1919]

37. KOTLER, SOLOMON NATHAN[34]
(After serving as a rabbi in several communities in Lithuania,
Kotler arrived in America. In 1910 he was on the faculty of the
newly established Yeshiva Rabbi Isaac Elchanan in New York City.

After living in Detroit for many years, he moved to Jerusalem in 1935. Kotler was also the author of a work published in St. Louis in 1927.)

LXXXV.   כרם שלמה, שאלות ותשובות על או"ח. ירושלם, בדפוס ח. צוקרמן,
תרצ"ו. [1935/36] 140 1.

38. Shohet, Moses[35]

(Born in Lithuania in 1875, Shohet emigrated to America and became the rabbi in Bangor, Maine. He succeeded his father as the rabbi of Portland, Maine, in 1921 and remained in that pulpit until 1929. After serving as the rabbi of Quincy, Mass., Shohet moved to Jerusalem in 1933. Shohet was also the author of a work published in New York.)

LXXXVI.   שו"ת אהל משה. ירושלם, בדפוס "ציון", תרצ"ג. [1933] 117 p.

NOTES

1. Ephraim Deinard, *Kohelet America* (St. Louis: Moinester, 1926).
2. *Encyclopedia Judaica* (German), vol. III, p. 395; *Otsar Yisrael,* vol. I, p. 167.
3. Benzion Eisenstadt, *Dorot ha-Aharonim* (Brooklyn: Moinester, 1937), vol. II, p. 27.
4. *Jewish Advocate* (Boston), April 7, 1939; Eisenstadt, *op. cit.,* vol. I, p. 50; *American Jewish Year Book,* XLI, 419.
5. *Publications of the American Jewish Historical Soicety,* IX, 71; XLIV, 136–92; Judah David Eisenstin, *Otsar Zikhronotai* (New York, 1930).
6. Benzion Eisenstadt, *Hakhme Yisrael be-America* (New York, 1903), pp. 79–80; *Sefer ha-yovel shel Agudat ha-Rabbanim* (New York, 1927–28).
7. *Der Tog,* January 4, 1932; Eisenstadt, *Hakhme Yisrael,* p. 28; *American Jewish Year Book,* vol. 58.
8. *Der Tog,* July 31, 1922; *Sefer ha-yovel,* p. 138; Eisenstadt, *Hakhme Yisrael,* p. 27.
9. Eli Gottesman, *Who's Who in Canadian Jewry* (Montreal, 1965), p. 115.
10. *Encyclopedia Judaica; American Jewish Year Book,* VI, 217.
11. *American Jewish Year Book,* V, 63–64, VI, 217; Benzion Eisenstadt, *Anshe ha-shem be-Artsot ha-Berit* (St. Louis, 1933), pp. 60–61; Eisenstadt, *Dorot ha-Aharhonim,* vol. I, p. 118.
12. Morris Silverman, *Hartford Jews 1659–1970* (Hartford: Connecticut Historical Society, 1970), pp. 190–91.
13. *American Jewish Year Book,* XL, 386; Eisenstadt, *Dorot ha-Aharonim,* vol. II, p. 59.
14. *Encyclopedia Judaica* (German); Eisenstadt, *Hakhme Yisrael,* p. 11.
15. *Der Tog,* November 16, 1923; Eisenstadt, *Hakhme Yisrael,* pp. 60–61; *Sefer ha-yovel,* p. 147.
16. *Jewish Advocate* (Boston), December 13, 1940.
17. Eisenstadt, *Dorot ha-Aharonim,* vol. II, p. 237.
18. *Encyclopedia Judaica.*
19. *Der Tog,* February 15, 1943; *American Jewish Year Book,* XLV, 390; Eisenstadt, *Dorot ha-Aharonim,* vol. I, p. 244.
20. *Der Tog,* September 9, 1935; *American Jewish Year Book,* XXXVIII, 432; Eisenstadt, *Dorot ha-Aharonim,* vol. II, pp. 240–41.
21. *Universal Jewish Encyclopedia;* Max Vorspan and Lloyd P. Gartner, *History of the Jews of Los Angeles* (San Marino: Huntington Library, 1970), p. 211.
22. Selig Adler and Thomas E. Connolly, *From Ararat to Suburbia* (Philadelphia: Jewish Publication Society, 1960), pp. 190, 434; Eisenstadt, *Dorot ha-Aharonim,* vol. I, pp. 274–75.
23. Interview with Jacob Perlow of New York, July 5, 1972.
24. Eisenstadt, *Dorot ha-Aharonim,* vol. II, pp. 202–3; *American Jewish Year Book,* XXXVI, 285.

25. *American Jewish Year Book*, XLVII, 531.
26. *Who's Who in American Jewry*, 1938–39, pp. 963–64; Eisenstadt, *Hakhme Yisrael*, p. 51; *Sefer ha-yovel*, p. 174.
27. Eisenstadt, *Hakhme Yisrael*, p. 74.
28. *Biographical Dictionary of American Jews*, 1935, pp. 508–9; *National Jewish Ledger*, August 4, 1944; *American Jewish Year Book*, XLVII, 542.
29. Adler, op. cit., pp. 190–91; Eisenstadt, *Hakhme Yisrael*, p. 75; *American Jewish Year Book*, V, 100.
30. *American Jewish Year Book*, V, 100, XXXIX, 597; Eisenstadt, *Hakhme Yisrael*, pp. 45–46; *Jewish Criterion*, July 31, 1936; *Who's Who In American Jewry*, 1928.
31. *Encyclopedia Judaica*.
32. *Universal Jewish Encyclopedia; Encyclopedia Judaica; Minhah Lihudah* (Jerusalem, 1950).
33. Eisenstadt, *Dorot ha-Aharonim*, vol. I, p. 12.
34. Gilbert Klaperman, *The Story of Yeshiva University* (London: Macmillan, 1969), p. 80.
35. Benjamin Band, *Portland Jewry* (Portland: Jewish Historical Society, 1955), pp. 45, 48.

AN EAST EUROPEAN CONGREGATION ON AMERICAN SOIL: BETH ISRAEL, ROCHESTER, NEW YORK, 1874–1886

By

ABRAHAM J. KARP

University of Rochester

On Sunday, June 28, 1874, seven representatives each of *Hevra* Sheves Ahim and *Hevra* B'nai Shalom met as a joint committee for the purpose of consolidation. David Solomon Kaminsky of Sheves Ahim was elected president, and Joseph Minsky of B'nai Shalom, vice-president. A secretary, treasurer, and four trustees completed the roster of officers. A *gabbai* for the cemetery was also elected.

Kalman Bardin, a *shohet,* suggested that the new *hevra* be called Beth Israel, and "all happily agreed."

Committees were appointed to prepare a constitution and by-laws, to set the books in order, and to go to a lawyer to make over all documents and deeds to Beth Israel. It was decided that the whole membership of both *hevrot* meet on Wednesday, July 1, to bring the Scroll of the Torah and the other ritual objects into the Sheves Ahim Synagogue. An expenditure of up to $5 was authorized for the move.[1]

Thus is recorded the birth of the Beth Israel Congregation of Rochester, New York—for forty years the leading Orthodox congregation of that city.

The first Jewish settlers arrived in Rochester before 1840.[2] They came mainly from Germany. A news item in the *Occident* reports: "The congregation consists of Germans, Englishmen and Poles, who all are acting in harmony. Some, indeed, would have liked to have a mode of worship similar to the Emanuel Temple at New York; but they will not desire to introduce any reform which might lead to disunion."[3]

The congregation, B'rith Kodesh, thus served West and East European Jews. The latter were few in number and of traditional bent. So long as the congregation did not turn Reform and East European Jews were few in number, one congregation served all Rochester Jewry.

In the 1860s B'rith Kodesh began veering toward Reform, and a small but steady influx of Jews from Eastern Europe began. The records of the Mt. Hope Cemetery Association, August 4, 1870, disclose that Sheves Ahim purchased a lot to use as its burial ground. A year later another *hevra,* B'nai Shalom, was ready to purchase its cemetery. Three years later, Beth Israel was founded.

The first forty years of Beth Israel provide a case study of the evolution of an East European *hevra* into an American congregation. This period may be divided into three eras.

1. 1874–1886, an East European *hevra.*
2. 1886–1906, from *hevra* to congregation.
3. 1906–1914, an American congregation.[4]

We shall deal with the first period, outlining the organization, personnel, interests, and problems which marked the life of an East European congregation in America.

It is to be expected that an immigrant community will transplant the institutions which served its needs in the "old country." The challenges which are presented by the new environment come later, with acculturation, integration, and the rise of a native-born generation. In the first dozen years of its existence, Beth Israel was an Old World institution transplanted on new soil.

The *hevra,* an independent association joined together for religious, educational, charitable, or occupational needs, existed in all European communities. Professor Baron, in his study of the Jewish community, attests: "Among religious associations, those maintaining synagogues and constituting separate congregations were to be found in practically all communities . . ."[5]

Each synagogue or congregation had its own character. In the south Polish city of Biala, for example, there were four major congregations and fourteen hassidic *shtiblah.* Each synagogue could and did have a number of *minyanim.* Thus, while there was official civic unity in the European Jewish community, there was also congregational diversity. This diversity continued on the American scene, without the formal communal unity.

The East European congregation chose to call itself *hevra,* rather than *kehillah k'dosha* or *bet k'nesseth,* names adopted by West European

American congregations. They eschewed the former name, for they were not a community as they knew it in Europe, and the latter because they were more than a synagogue. *Hevra* was most correctly descriptive, for they were an association of individuals, joined together not only to maintain a synagogue, but to serve other religious needs as well.

A perusal of American East European congregational constitutions discloses that a house of worship is only one of the *hevra*'s interests and activities. Orthodoxy is life-centered, unlike nineteenth-century Reform, which was temple-centered. Religious life is in the home and neighborhood, incumbent upon all, participated in by all, unlike Reform religious practice, which became institutionalized and professionalized.

The constitution and by-laws of America's first East European congregation, Beth-Hamedrash Hagadol of New York, list under "Benefits": sick and death benefits, such as visitations, funeral expenses, funeral arrangements, house of mourning services visit, death benefits to heirs.[6] Life-situation needs were served by fellow congregants. The functionaries whose duties are listed are: *hazzan*, sexton, assistant sexton, and janitor,[7] whose duties are to make it possible for the member to participate in religious life, to fulfill religious obligations.

The constitution of the Oheb Shalom Congregation of Baltimore lists, under duties and rights of members, the right to hold a pew or seat in the synagogue. The functionaries listed are rabbi and reader, whose duties are to serve the congregants' religious needs.[8]

The activities of the European *hevra* also reflected the specific immediate needs of a new immigrant population. Thus the By-Laws of Congregation Beth Hackneses Hachodosh (*sic*) of Rochester provide a wide variety of sickness and death benefits.[9] The *hevra* became the immigrant's family, visiting him in sickness, providing a proper and honorable burial in death, and giving spiritual and monetary aid to the survivors.

The functionaries were of the congregation, members chosen for their particular skills and recompensed for same. It was, in a word, a fraternal fellowship joined together for the purpose of establishing and maintaining a house of worship, but also addressing itself to the requirements of religious duties and usage, and the needs imposed by the exigencies of immigrant life.

BEGINNINGS

The dozen-year history of Beth Israel from 1874 to 1886 was marked by congregational growth and division, by the acquisition of improved

synagogal facilities, and by the professionalization of religious functionaries.

The first home of the *hevra* was the *shul* of Sheves Ahim. The enlarged congregation needed expanded facilities, and the first order of business, after amalgamation, was the appointment of a committee "to seek
a hall to serve as a synagogue." [10] A hall was rented for $250 per annum,
and a committee was appointed to "fix the hall . . . as needed." [11] On
August 17, 1874, the congregation moved into its quarters and began
preparations for the High Holy Days.

Agreement was not considered a virtue "devoutly to be wished," and
disagreements which marked the early life of the congregation began at
its very birth. Two members were charged with rearranging the synagogue from the way it had been set up by the committee and trustees,
placing the Ark and *bimah* where they felt they should stand.

The beginning of differences between "traditionalists" and "progressives" can be found in the vote on where the *hazzan* should stand. A motion was made that the *hazzan* always stand on the bimah. An amendment was offered that during the year he officiate from the *bimah,* but on
the High Holy Days from in front of the Ark. The amendment was defeated. The "traditionalists" gained another victory in voting that a
curtain be hung between the synagogue and the *ezrat nashim* (women's
section). [12]

Preparations for the first High Holy Day services were now made. Kalman Bardin, a *shohet,* and a leader in the congregation, was elected as
shliah zibbur, as first cantor. Thus the European usage of *shohet-hazzan*
was carried on by the *hevra*. The minutes of August 16, 1874, report that
one S. "sent in a petition . . . that he would *daven shaharit* [conduct
morning worship] on Rosh Hashanah and Yom Kippur for $25." One L.
sent in a petition that he would do it free of charge. A secret ballot ("a
vote with tickets") was taken, and by a sixteen to twelve majority it was
decided to engage S. and pay him the requested $25.

Fees for seats for the services for non-members were adopted. Those
nearer to the East-North wall would be $3, and no seat could be sold for
less than $2 to the head of a family. Seats for unmarried men were to
begin at $1 and go higher as the trustees would decide. It was also passed
that: "The brother-in-law of Cohen the tailor should not receive a seat
for less than $3." Also, a policeman was to be "hired for Rosh Hashanah
and Yom Kippur to stand on the steps and not permit the boys to run

around, and to keep out of the synagogue anyone who does not have a ticket, and not to permit anyone in with a small child" [13]

The preparations did not go smoothly. The arguments, recriminations, and fines which marked and marred so much of the early life of the congregation, broke out in all fury even in this season of the year, when Israel is to do penance and lift itself spiritually through forgiveness and conciliation.

A special meeting was called on September 6 by members who wanted to have a say in who would be their fellow worshippers during the Days of Awe. It was decided by a large majority "that no seat should be sold to Cohen the tailor at no price, because many members have heard him abuse the *hevra* with disgraceful talk . . ." A day later the president called a special meeting "because he was abused with disgraceful talk in the synagogue by Mr. M. . . . and Mr. L. . . ." It was voted that each be fined $2, and that they ask forgiveness of the president. It was the season of *slihot* and all were, after all, brothers in the fraternity of Jews joined in service of their God and their holy faith—so both asked forgiveness, and it was granted. Truth to tell, the minutes disclose that fines were rescinded almost as often as fines were imposed. America was the frontier of European Jewry, and these frontiersmen were men of bold, adventurous spirit, strong in character and volatile in personality. But they were, above all, Jews, fellow Jews, sons of Abraham, "advocates of compassion," and disciples of Aaron, "pursuers of peace." As men of the frontier they were of short temper, quick of tongue, ready for strife. As Jews they were ever ready and anxious to forget and forgive.

A Synagogue of One's Own

What is a congregation without a synagogue?

Twice in less than a decade the men of Beth Israel fashioned synagogues.

On February 7, 1878, it was reported that the house at 54 Chatham Street was for sale for $1,650. It was moved that the congregation make plans to buy the house and renovate it into a synagogue. Desire needs to be matched by ability, so a committee of seven was appointed to determine how the purchase money might be raised. A month later the house was bought with a down payment of $700 and a mortgage of $950. The following plans of the committee of seven were unanimously adopted by the congregation:

1. The congregation would elect a standing committee of seven to make plans for a synagogue and *mikveh*.
2. The committee was to elect its own secretary and treasurer.
3. Each member would be taxed $10, to be paid in six months.
4. These monies were to be held by the treasurer for a synagogue and *mikveh*; they were not be used for any other purpose.
5. The committee was to have the power to appoint a committee to solicit and collect contributions for the building fund.
6. A special committee would be appointed to approach non-members for contributions.
7. The committee would order tin boxes to be marked "Women's Contribution" (*nidvat nashim*). These boxes were to be placed in homes. Monthly collections would be made and a record kept with name and amount.[14]

Later the $10 assessment was hotly debated, sustained, and then rescinded, but the planning and work went on.

Harris Levi announced that he planned to build a *mikveh* and that he would charge no more than 50 cents. A committee was appointed to negotiate a contract with Levi.[15] On July 7, an agreement was signed with Levi, and it was ordered that it be announced in the synagogue on the Sabbath that Levi's *mikveh* was "*kosher k'din uk'dos,*" in full accordance with the ritual law. Five months later Levi complained that the members had encouraged him to build a *mikveh* and he had spent a great deal of money to do so. Now their wives were using the *mikveh* of "the goy." He asked for justice.[16] In response to Levi's complaint, he was asked to list the wives of members who used the "goy's *mikveh*" and was promised the *hevra* would then take action.[17]

The minutes indicate internal dissension on many matters, heightened by a disagreement on whether to renovate the house or build a new synagogue. Matters were held in abeyance until February, 1879, when a committee was appointed to see a cabinet maker to get estimates of the cost of renovating the house into a synagogue. After two months of study the committee recommended that a new synagogue be built.[18]

Only a week of further study, however, convinced them that this was beyond the congregation's ability. It therefore withdrew its earlier recommendation and offered plans for renovation of the house at the cost of $700. Each member was to contribute $5 at once. Work proceeded apace, as did the collection of funds as well. Nathan Goldwater, David Caminski, and P. Unterberg were appointed a committee to solicit contributions from the "German Jews." Greenstein, Posner, and Slomianski were to do the same from the "Polish Jews." [19]

On July 13 a committee was appointed to remove, fix, equalize, and arrange benches in the new synagogue. A month later a special meeting of the congregation was convoked to arrange for the move into the new synagogue. A committee was appointed to arrange for gas fixtures, carpeting for the *bimah,* and a reader's table. Another committee was authorized to engage a band of music to accompany the Torah procession at the cost of $10. The dedication celebration was arranged. A guest cantor was invited from Buffalo to officiate on the Sabbath.

The day of dedication was a day of joyous celebration for the Rochester East European Jewish community. Three years earlier their wealthy German brethren had built a temple; now, after years in a rented hall, they were to have their own synagogue. The entire Jewish community was invited to the celebration. Dr. Max Landsberg, rabbi of B'rith Kodesh, a radical Reformer, but a neighbor and head of the congregation of wealth and prestige, gave the dedicatory address in English. A band of music played. Leaders of the congregation marched in the Torah procession (for which honor they had paid at auction prices ranging from $2 to 87 cents). At long last the immigrants from White Russia and Lithuania (mainly from Suvalk and Brajene) were at home in the New World. Beth Israel had a spiritual home, a synagogue it could call its own.

New facilities demanded new laws and activities. Amendments to the By-Laws were adopted:

Article 8, Section 1:
Each member must purchase a pew.
> *Section 2:*
Seats are to be sold to members at auction to highest bidder. The seat is then the property of the purchaser so long as he pays the annual seat tax.
> *Section 3:*
The seats at the East Wall begin at $30; the others at $20. Payments are to be: 20% down; the balance will carry a 7% interest rate so long as the mortgage remains.[20]

Fifty seats were sold at auction at prices ranging from $20 to $91 for a total of $1,596.50.[21]

Arrangements for increased spiritual activity were undertaken as well. The chief religious functionary was the *hazzan.* The congregation, with an eye to the future, decided to undertake an educational program as well. As early as July 4, 1875, it was reported at a meeting that: "Many members stated that they want a *melamed*." A committee of three was appointed to take the names of those who wanted one, how many children they would send, and how much they were willing to pay.[22] But nothing came of this early attempt.

Now, with a new building and a growing congregation, the attempt would be made again. On August 3, 1879, it was moved and passed that the *hevra* would engage a *hazzan*-reader-teacher at the salary of $500. An advertisement was to be placed in the New York Yiddish newspapers. To make this possible the annual dues were set at a minimum of $12.[23] The *hazzan* would have to carry on services in accordance with the *minhag polin v'lita,* the Polish-Lithuanian synagogal style.[24]

On October 26, 1879, Moshe White was elected *hazzan*-reader-teacher. His salary would be $400 if he furnished the *heder;* $350, if the congregation did so. Tuition was set at $3 per year, and a board of education of eight members was appointed. A day later, a joint meeting was held of the board of trustees and the board of education to make the necessary arrangements.[25]

The Expanding Congregation

A building built, a school established, and a cantor-teacher engaged, the congregation now turned to amend its constitution to conform with the new facilities and activities.

At the quarterly membership meeting of March 14, 1880, the following amendments to the constitution and by-laws were enacted:

CONSTITUTION:
Section 2:
   To maintain a synagogue and a cantor-teacher.
Section 5:
   Dues are to be not less than 75¢ a month.
Section 7:
   Only three trustees.
Section 11:
   Each one who is accepted as a member must purchase a seat.
BY-LAWS:
   ARTICLE I:
      Section 1:
      Time of Services on Sabbath and Holidays:

Nisan to Tishri, 7:30 A.M.
Tishri to Nisan, 8:00 A.M.
Section 6:
Aharon Hazak is not to be sold.
Section 8:
Each member and seat-holder is to pay the annual seat tax before
Rosh Hashanah, as well as the payment on the principal as stipu-
lated in his seat agreement. The price of a seat to a member is
a minimum of $30, 25% to be paid immediately, the balance in
annual payments with interest for a period of five years.
Section 11:
A member does not have to pay for a seat for a child under
thirteen. He is responsible for the behavior of the child. If the
child misbehaves, the father is liable for a fine.
Section 18:
The price of $5 for a wedding, is now to be $6 to include $1 for
the *shamash*.
ARTICLE II:
Section 8:
If a member or his wife die, the *hevra* is to supply two carriages
for the officers of the congregation, at the congregation's expense.
Section 9:
A widow of a member, so long as she does not remarry, is entitled
to a grave, as is a child under the age of fourteen.
ARTICLE IV:
Section 6:
When one is suspended for not having paid his dues, and a year
has passed, he cannot become a member until he has paid all he
owes for *aliyot* or *shnoder* [free will offering pledged at the reading of the Torah]. He has to pay half the initiation money before
his application can be accepted.

The congregation was expanding. At a special meeting on March 29,
seven new seat-holders paid between $30 and $54 for seats. At the same
meeting a congregational *hevra kadisha* was organized with an initial
membership of twenty. The board of education notified the assembled
members that no child above the age of thirteen would be admitted to
the school.

While all was going well for the congregation, its *hazzan*-teacher was
having his problems. White petitioned to be reelected for the same salary
for another year. By a vote of twenty-six to fifteen, his tenure was extended for only six months.[26]

A few months later the *hazzan* received notice that he would not be reengaged, and it was decided to advertise for a new cantor-reader at the salary of $600–$700. Many candidates applied for the position. White applied, offering to accept a salary of $350. He was turned down, and one Ticktin was elected *hazzan*-reader-teacher at the salary of $600. A new tuition schedule of 50 cents a month was announced.[27]

But the congregation seemed to be losing interest in the school. A motion to have the school meet on the second floor of the synagogue building was defeated.[28] On July 3, the board of education was discharged and a special committee of six was ordered to investigate whether the *hazzan* was attending to his teaching duties properly. The committee was also to tell the *hazzan*-teacher that he should teach only *Ivri* (Hebrew) reading, and not *Humash* (the Pentateuch).

The new *hazzan* was having even greater problems than his predecessor. Accusations were brought against him. At first the congregation attempted to protect him, adopting a motion that anyone slandering the *hazzan* could be fined by the president up to $2.[29] A month later, formal charges were brought against him at a special meeting. He was called before the meeting, where he was accused of misbehavior. He admitted his guilt and asked for mercy. He was found guilty, his contract was terminated, and he was invited to leave the city, being promised $25 extra when he did so.[30]

With his departure the school came to an end. In electing his successor, *Hazzan* Harris Lewis, the congregation had the choice of electing him *hazzan*-reader-teacher for $500, or *hazzan*-reader for $400. By a vote of twenty-nine to nine, it chose the latter.

The election of officers for the year 5642 brought into the open a serious cleavage that had developed in the congregation. Elections were often heated affairs, but once the ballots had been cast and counted, peace would be restored. Not so in this election. A tie vote was recorded for the two contestants, Kalman Bardin and Aaron Nusbaum, each receiving nineteen votes. An argument ensued. After levying many fines and finding he could not restore order, the president adjourned the meeting. On the next day, October 11, 1881, the congregation met again, Bardin now receiving twenty-three votes to Nusbaum's twenty. Though the congregation remained intact, the breach was never healed, and factionalism continued evident in congregational decisions.

The congregation continued to grow. Immigration from Eastern Europe was on the increase with the promise of further growth. The synagogue now seemed inadequate. Early in 1882 a committee of seven was appointed to make plans for the building of a new synagogue.[31] But internal problems continued to plague the congregation. Aaron Nusbaum, who had been defeated a year earlier, was now elected president by a large majority. His authority was constantly questioned, and the congregation did not always uphold him.

When he brought charges against the *hazzan* that he did not obey the president, the congregation voted to send a notice of warning to the *hazzan*. When, however, his authority was challenged by a member, the congregation equivocated.

Harris Newyorker was ordered by the president not to chant the *Hallel* service from the pulpit. He did not obey the order, and a disturbance ensued. Newyorker then sued the president for $1,000 damages. At a special meeting it was voted that the president have Newyorker arrested for having caused a disturbance. He was authorized to carry on litigation at the congregation's expense.[32] Ten days later, when the president convened a special meeting to bar Newyorker from the synagogue, the president was defeated, sixteen to fifteen.

The issue seized upon by the factions was the building of a fence for the congregational cemetery. Nusbaum, who seems to have been much interested in cemetery matters, was determined to build the fence and would brook no opposition. His opponents, to whom a new synagogue building was top priority, attempted to direct the congregation's interest and resources toward that end. When the president arranged to have the fence built, the vice-president convened a special meeting. He stated he did so in response to a signed petition of thirteen members. By a vote of twenty to zero, with five abstentions, it was voted to order the contractor *not* to begin building the fence for six months.[33]

The opposition faction was in a majority. It voted an amendment to the constitution that a president could not succeed himself in office. It also curtailed the power of the president by voting that a president could not fine a member for being out of order unless he had previously called him to order. The maximum fine for being out of order was set at 25 cents.

The issue of cemetery fence vs. synagogue building was eventually resolved. Both were needed, so a special meeting of the members, on April 27, 1884, ordered payments for the fence, and appointed a committee of seven to ascertain how much a new synagogue would cost. After two weeks, the committee reported that the contractor they spoke to quoted a price of $8,500. It was requested to get more bids.[34]

It is difficult to know whether the factionalism which now rent the congregation was due mainly to personality clashes or to substantive issues. As is usually the case, both were factors. The rancor continued. A fight in the synagogue itself caused considerable damage to the *bimah*.[35]

Outnumbered and outvoted, Aaron Nusbaum resigned from the congregation. His two brothers joined him. Together with some friends, they organized a new congregation, B'nai Aviezer (after their father),[36] commonly called the Nusbaum Minyan. That this new congregation constituted a threat to Beth Israel is attested by an amendment adopted on July 10, 1884:

> *Amendment to Article I, Section 17:*
>
> It is forbidden for a member to attend the Nusbaum Minyan. If a member attends either weekdays or Sabbaths, he is to be fined 50 cents for the first violation and $1 for the second. A third offense brings expulsion.[37]

It may very well be that this controversy was an aspect of the basic difference between the "traditionalists" and the "progressives," which had existed in the congregation from its inception. Traditionalism led to emphasis on the cemetery, which was symbolic of reverence for the past and answered the needs of the present. Commitment to progress led to interest and labors for a school and a new synagogue to serve the requirements of the present but also to prepare for the future.

Another aspect of this division can be glimpsed from a controversy about the printing of the constitution and by-laws. After agreement had been reached that they ought to be printed both in English and Yiddish, it was found that it would be too expensive to do so in both languages. The trustees, sensing the passions that this issue would arouse, voted not to print at all.[38] On October 18, 1883, it was voted to print the by-laws in Yiddish only. This provoked such an argument that the president could not bring the meeting to order and had to adjourn it. Five days later the matter was again debated and voted. By a twenty-one to nineteen vote Yiddish won.[39] But they were not printed.

A Rabbi Comes to Town

Moshe Weinberger, reporting on the religious situation in New York in 1886, wrote:

Established rabbis, capable of giving rabbinic decision on Jewish law in this city of 100,000 Jews and 130 Orthodox congregations, number not more than three or four. Even these were not called to their rabbinic posts with honor but came here like other immigrants in search of a livelihood. After much hardship and labor they found a post. The congregations do not support them adequately, really so inadequately that it is shameful to report it in a book. They support themselves from meagre congregational and from individual contributions which do not provide even minimal necessities.[40]

Small wonder then that Rochester did not boast an Orthodox rabbi till 1883. In the American West European congregation, the rabbi was central. In the East European *hevra,* he was at best peripheral. The immigrant from Western Europe knew a congregation where preaching was central and a rabbi-preacher a necessity. For the East European, however, the synagogue was a place for prayer, which could be led by a layman, and if by a professional, a cantor. The *rov* of Eastern Europe was a communal rather than congregational functionary. The first East European rabbi invited to America, Rabbi Jacob Joseph, was brought here by an organization of congregations which looked on itself as a communal body.[41] Other *rabbanim* came to America and sought out their rabbinic positions.

Rabbi Abba Hayim ben Yitzhak Levinson sent a petition to the Beth Israel Congregation in June, 1883, informing it that he would like to serve as its rabbi. At the June 17 meeting the matter was discussed, and by a one-vote majority, seventeen to sixteen, it was voted that a rabbi be engaged. A committee of five was appointed to determine where funds might be obtained to pay the rabbi.

A month later, July 22, 1883, the matter was brought before the congregation. It was moved that the rabbi be paid $100 per annum. An amendment was proposed that the salary be $600. An amendment to the amendment suggested $150. The latter sum was voted. The petition of Rabbi Levinson was then read, a secret-ballot vote taken, and he was elected rabbi for a year by a vote of seventeen to thirteen. The duties of the rabbi were not spelled out, but we may assume that they were nominal. Those who suggested a salary of $600 perhaps thought that he should serve as a congregational rabbi, giving full time to Beth Israel. The great majority of the membership apparently viewed him as a communal functionary, to be supported, among others, by the Beth Israel Congregation. The *shamash*-collector, for his part-time labors, was receiving a salary of $150, equal to that of the rabbi. The cantor's salary that year was $400.

A decade later, J. Rosenbloom, president of the congregation, expounded in the public press, the congregation's view of the status and functions of a rabbi.

> A rabbi is not a minister. He does not belong to one congregation, but to the city. His duties, only to a very small extent, resemble the duties of a Christian minister. He is an interpreter of the divine law, not a spiritual adviser. His duty is chiefly to interpret the law as it is written and apply it to particular cases as they are brought to him for decision. Moreover the feeling which animates all Orthodox Jews, of obligation to preserve the knowledge of the law and to support students of the law simply as students, is their principal motive in keeping a rabbi.[42]

The first extra salary income for the rabbi was from the congregation itself. He offered to chant the *shaharit* (morning) services of the High Holy Days at a price set by the congregation. It was voted to grant his request, add the sounding of the *shofar* and *neilah* (close or Atonement Day) to his duties, and pay him $40.[43]

Supervision of *kashrut* in the community was among the chief rabbinic duties. In fulfillment of these, the rabbi ordered the *shohatim* of the community to come before him for examination. Kalman Bardin and Jacob Lipski came before him, were examined, and were declared fit. Abraham Rosenthal came three days late, did not pass muster, and was ordered to return for a reexamination. This he refused to do. The rabbi's authority was thus challenged. A special meeting was called to deal with the matter. The matter was placed before the congregation, and it voted to stand behind the rabbi in his supervision of *kashrut*.[44]

Controversy must have arisen in the city, for action had to be taken at the trustees' meeting a week later to protect the rabbi. It was voted that any non-member who abused the rabbi not be permitted into the synagogue, and no outside preachers be permitted to speak. That the rabbi's position was not fully secure can be seen in that both of the above motions were passed only through the president's tie-breaking vote.[45]

The rabbi remained vulnerable to criticism and slander. On July 7, 1884, a special trustees' meeting addressed itself to the report that "Mr. Eliezer Levin spoke disgraceful words against the rabbi of the congregation." A *beth din* was convened, presided over by Rabbi Reb Binyamin.

Levin was called, examined, and asked to substantiate his charges. It was found that "whatever was asked him, he was unable to answer." The *beth din* then issued the verdict that Levin's *mikveh* be put under ban (*herem*) and that no woman should use it until Levin fulfilled the penance imposed on him by the *beth din*. The *herem* was to be announced in the synagogue immediately and again at the morning service.[46]

Three days later the rabbi was reelected unanimously at the same salary. A committee was appointed to place an advertisement in the Yiddish newspapers announcing Rabbi Levinson's reelection. It was also voted, however, that the rabbi could not give decisions on ritual matters to non-members.[47]

When the renewal of the contract came up the following year, a request was made that a vote be taken whether the congregation needed a rabbi. The president refused to permit a vote on this matter. The rabbi's opponents then pointed out that the rabbi had not sent in a petition as the law required. "A great debate ensued." The president then decided that the petition was needed. The *shamash* was sent to the rabbi and returned with the required document. By a vote of nineteen to six, Rabbi Levinson was reelected at the same salary of $150.[48] A month later Cantor Mirsky was given a two-year contract at the annual salary of $500.[49]

The Leopold Street Shul

Moshe Weinberger, in the above-mentioned description of Jewish religious life in New York City, wrote:

> The purpose of most of the Orthodox congregations is to assemble twice daily, or on Sabbaths, for worship, to visit the sick and help them, to bury the dead and pay them last respects, and to help a fellow member in time of need.
>
> But the highest purpose is to build a synagogue—grand and beautiful. The congregation that succeeds in doing so—there is no measure to its joy, and the members feel that thereby they have fulfilled their obligations to the Faith of Moses and Judaism.[50]

In this matter Beth Israel was not to be outdone. A goodly number of the first wave of immigrants, generated by the Czarist May Laws, came to Rochester attracted by the men's clothing manufacturing industry, which was almost wholly in Jewish hands. Strengthened by those who came and emboldened by the promise of more to come, the congregation began to talk of building a synagogue. Only three years after moving into the house which it had renovated into a synagogue, the congregation voted to appoint a committee of seven to make plans for the building of a new synagogue.[51]

Internal difficulties, resulting from a factionalism that eventually caused the defection of a number of members, intervened, postponing plans and even discussion. Two years later, by a three to two vote of the trustees, a committee was appointed to begin planning the erection of a synagogue.[52] When the matter was brought before a congregational meeting three weeks later, such an argument ensued that the president was forced to adjourn the meeting.[53] The faction whose primary interest was the cemetery was able to thwart the action of those who desired a new synagogue. The former were insistent that the congregation's top priority was a fence for the cemetery, and nothing should be done until that was accomplished. An agreement was apparently reached, for a special meeting was convoked on April 27, 1884, to take action on both the fence and the synagogue. Payments were authorized for the fence, and a committee was appointed to make plans for a synagogue. Two weeks later the committee reported that it had drawn up plans for the new building, and had placed them before a contractor, who gave a bid of $8,500. The committee was instructed to take other bids but not to begin building before the following spring.[54] The vote was close, twenty-six to twenty-one. Opposition continued. A fight in the synagogue which caused damage to the *bimah* was apparently touched off by this issue.[55]

The way was cleared for the building of the synagogue by the resignation of a number of members led by Aaron Nusbaum, who had apparently headed the opposition. But now another obstacle appeared. There seemed to be an economic recession in the spring of 1885, for the secretary reported on March 22 that many members claimed that they were unable to make payments on their seats. Payments were postponed until after Passover. And this was not all. The Nusbaum group founded their own congregation. The growing number of new immigrants led to the formation of new congregations which offered competition to Beth Israel. The congregation retaliated. On April 19, 1885, one Finkelstein was fined 50 cents for attending the Nusbaum Minyan. On June 14, an amendment was adopted unanimously forbidding any member to attend the services of *Hevra Tehillim* on Rosh Hashonah or Yom Kippur.

These were accepted as challenges and perhaps even gave added determination to the leaders and membership. On February 6, 1886, the trustees asked the chairman of the Building Committee to ascertain:

1. The possibility of building without cash, through a mortgage only.
2. How much a mortgage would cost and what security would be necessary.
3. How much the desired building would cost.

A month later a congregational meeting considered: "Shall the committee be ordered to bring in plans and specifications?" The president then challenged the members present to declare their intentions to contribute for the proposed new building. Those present were called by name, and eighteen pledged to give. The president, secretary, and treasurer were constituted as a committee to see the other members of the congregation.[56]

New impetus was given to the project in early spring. A sister congregation, B'nai Israel, sent in a written request to join Beth Israel and had appointed a committee to enter negotiations. The rolls of Beth Israel were now swelled by nineteen new members from the former B'nai Israel. At the special meeting where the amalgamation was completed, it was also decided to appoint a committee to consider the purchase of a lot on Leopold Street as the site for the new building. The trustees were authorized to sell the old building for a house or a synagogue. If to be used as a house, the asking price was $2,000; if for a synagogue, $3,000.[57] They apparently sensed that the Nusbaum group might want to purchase the synagogue. Old hurts still rankled, and they were not about to be of help to a dissident faction that had abandoned them.

Things now moved apace. The aim was to have a new synagogue for the High Holy Days.

April 11, 1886: A committee is appointed to bring in plans for a new synagogue on the Leopold Street site. The committee is instructed to bring in the report as soon as possible. The synagogue is to be 75 x 45 feet.

May 16 1886: The low bid reported is $10,717 for building and furnishings. The members are to sign the mortgage.

May 22, 1886: The old synagogue is sold to Nathan Goldwater for $1,920. A bid of $2,200 by Aaron Nusbaum is rejected.

On June 27, the cornerstone was laid with all pomp and ceremony. The *Rochester Democrat and Chronicle* reported:

With Trowel and Mortar

Laying the Cornerstone of the New Beth Israel Temple

Work of Three Presidents

This First Ceremony of the Kind in 25 Years Performed in the Presence of A Large Assemblage with Addresses by Rev. Landsberg and Others.

Yesterday will be a memorable one in the Hebrew history of Rochester and is especially entered in the records of the Congregation Beth Israel. . . .

The Congregation Beth Israel was organized June 27, 1874, in the Jardin block on East Main Street. Its membership was then thirty-five. February 17, 1878 the people purchased a lot in Chatham Street, and a synagogue was erected. In March of the present year commenced the movement which terminated in the purchase of the Leopold Street property and the commencement of the present edifice. . . . [58]

August 8, 1886:

1. Each member must purchase a seat in the new synagogue.
2. The price of the seats should be in accordance with location. Seats 1–80, $175–$125. Seats beyond 80, $100.
3. On the day of purchase, 15% of the purchase price is to be paid.
4. The amounts paid on the seats in the old synagogue will be credited for the new seats.

August 29, 1886: A committee is appointed to make arrangements "to move with a parade." They are empowered to spend what will be necessary.

The "move with a parade" was duly reported in the local press:

In Their New Church

An Important Event for the Beth Israel Congregation

Yesterday was a memorable day to members of the Beth Israel congregation. Shortly after 3 o'clock in the afternoon they moved from their old church on Chatham street, in which they had worshipped for years, into their new synagogue on Leopold street.

The members of the congregation and quite a large number of spectators gathered at the old synagogue at 2 o'clock in the afternoon. The exercises were opened by the pastor, Rabbi Levinson, who in a short address in German congratulated the members of his congregation upon the fact that their numbers had grown so large that a new synagogue was required and that the building had been supplied. When he had finished, the privilege of carrying the scrolls of the law and parchments to the new synagogue was disposed of at auction, book by book and parchment by parchment. This privilege is regarded very highly, and the bidding was quite brisk, much eagerness for the honor being manifested by the ladies as well as the gentlemen. The privileges sold for from 25 cents to $3 and $4. When the books had all been disposed of, the procession formed for its march to the new synagogue, led by the Lincoln Cornet Band, and headed by Rabbi Isaac Yoffe, of St. Louis, Rev. Dr. Rodden, of Elmira, Rabbis Ursky and Levinson, Rev. Erlich, of this city, and J. Lipsky, president of the society, after whom came representative members of the church, bearing the parchments, followed by the congregation. Arriving at the synagogue, the door was unlocked by President Lipsky, and the procession entered. In a very short time the building was completely filled.

The band took seats in the rear gallery and from time to time dispensed very good music. Rev. Ursky sang in German, and short addresses in the same language were delivered by Rabbis Yoffe, Rodden and Erlich. Then came the next feature of the exercises, the selling at auction of the privileges of placing the books and parchments in the Ark of the Holy Scriptures, in the rear of the pulpit. The sales were as lively as those at the old synagogue, and the prices realized were about the same. After these privileges had all been disposed of, the festivities began, cake and wine being passed through the audience. The time until 9 o'clock in the evening was spent in social intercourse.

The new synagogue is a plain but good looking building in size 45 x 85 [sic] feet. The interior is without decoration, but presents a neat appearance. Galleries extend along the sides and across the rear. The synagogue will seat about 800 people. Its erection was begun last June, and when finished, which will be in about two weeks, will cost, together with the site, $15,000. The synagogue has a basement comfortably and neatly fitted up, in which a Hebrew day school will be held. Prayer meetings will also be held there every morning and evening. The first regular services will be held at the synagogue next Saturday.[59]

We can imagine the pride with which the members entered the beautiful new synagogue building. America, which had been haven, now seemed like home as well. Their house of worship now took its place as full and equal partner with the other religious edifices of the city, churches and Temple B'rith Kodesh as well. Their children could feel free and proud in the company of their neighbors.

The leaders of Beth Israel could take justifiable pride in their accomplishment. Only a dozen years earlier they were a small struggling *hevra,* furnishing a rented hall for Sabbath services, holding the daily *minyan* in halls. A mere seven years earlier they had thought that theirs was a heroic achievement in renovating a house to have a synagogue of their own. Now they would be worshipping in a brick building of eight hundred seats. Truly God had been good to them, and they in turn had done valiantly in His service and to His glory.

Role and Function of Hevra-Congregation

Congregation Beth Israel (the term *hevra* was replaced by *congregation* in 1882) was not just a body of like-believers joined for public worship. It was primarily a group of Jews, recent immigrants all, come together to fashion a fellowship-community. The congregation provided not only a place for worship, but also the organizational structure, the experiences of relationship, and the opportunities for status gratification and security assurance which a true community provides.

In answer to the congregants' religious needs, it provided both the place and the requisite personnel for public worship—daily, Sabbath, and holidays. Consecrated ground for burial and the interment preparations and service were available to congregants and their families. And more, in sickness there would be visits by committee in formal obligation and by fellow-congregants in friendship. And when the need for final parting came, the last hours were eased by the knowledge that the bereaved family would be uplifted by visitations and aided by mandated contributions.

Most important of all, the congregation provided the individual immigrant Jew, cut off from home and family, the sense of community—a community large enough to give him the feeling of security, but small enough to provide him with the sense of worth born of being needed. In the immigrant community there was no formal structure or organization. Governmental recognition and status, which were the rule in Europe, did not obtain in the New World, where separation of church and state was a cardinal principle of democracy. Institutions fashioned by needs and vehicles of relationships forged by usage are the products of history. This was a new gathering of people, which, in response to the basic human need for community, planted upon the new soil the old institution, the *hevra,* through it to fashion a community. The *hevra*-congregation provided opportunities for togetherness at services of worship, at meetings, and at congregational celebrations. It enabled the experiencing of a wide gamut of interpersonal relationships touching on power, negotiation, confrontation. Hostility and conciliation, conflict and resolution all come into

play. A structured system of status was provided by the inherited synagogue usage of leadership and honors at services. Role-playing found expression at meetings and celebrations.

Officers

The congregation was run by four officers—president, vice-president,
secretary, and treasurer; and four trustees.

The president presided at all meetings and at services. To strengthen
his authority he was authorized to levy fines against those causing disturbances at services and being out of order at meetings. This presidential
power is reaffirmed periodically. On January 7, 1879, he was empowered
to fine anyone causing a disturbance during the service. A member could
be fined from $1 to $15; a stranger would be shown the door. It was soon
found that a fine could be a double-edged weapon, its indiscriminate
use causing more problems than it alleviated. Only four months after the
granting of the power, a motion was adopted to reduce the fines leveled
against a number of members from 50 cents to 25 cents "so that peace
would be restored." [60] The minutes reflect a struggle for power between
president and trustees and congregants, not unlike that between monarch,
nobility, and parliament in earlier days, but with a difference. Trustees
and congregation could limit and curtail, and this was done time and
time again, especially in the matter of fines. In 1883 a special amendment
was adopted that the president could not succeed himself in office and
that he could not fine a member for being out of order unless he had
previously called him to order, the maximum fine for being out of order
was set at 25 cents.[61] The only prerequisite for presidential office was as
enacted by a congregational meeting, October 5, 1876: no one might be
nominated for the presidency who could not sign his name.

The powers of the vice-president were the usual, to act in the president's stead in case of his absence. The treasurer was bonded, and apparently was recompensed for his labors by not being prohibited from
personal use of congregational funds while in his keeping. The compensation of the secretary was a more formal salary, beginning at an annual
$25 in 1874, but growing as the congregation grew. His duties were to
record the minutes, keep the books, carry on the correspondence of the
congregation, and inform members, trustees, and committees of meetings.
The trustees represented the congregation and were empowered to carry
on its business between the quarterly congregational meetings, as well as

to aid the president and officers in maintaining order and decorum at the services.

Functionaries

The officers were the elected leaders of the congregation experienced to run its affairs. The functionaries were employees of the congregation charged with specified and supervised services to the congregation.

The first functionary of the *hevra* was Aaron Nusbaum, elected as *shamash*-collector on October 18, 1874, at an annual salary of $75. As *shamash* he was responsible for the physical maintenance of congregational facilities and ritual objects, for making these open and available for worship, for arranging and aiding in burials at the congregational cemetery, and for directing (though not leading) the services. As collector, he had the duty of collecting dues and publicly announced donations, of giving receipts for same, and of keeping records of same. He was expected to do so each Sunday, for an early special meeting heard the complaint that the *shamash*-collector "does not go out to collect each Sunday." The president was authorized to order the *shamash* to do so, and to fine him if there were further complaints.[62] The salary of this functionary fluctuated. Reduced to $50 in 1878, it rose to $90 plus expenses in 1880, and $150 in 1884.

The first *hazzan* was Kalman Bardin, a *shohet,* and in the early years, the leader and scholarly authority. The stipulated duties were: to chant the service each Sabbath, read the Torah, and on the High Holy Days, chant the *musaf, kol nidre,* and *neilah* services and sound the *shofar.* A salary $150 was provided (a motion for $200 being defeated). There was apparently a growing opposition to Bardin as *hazzan.* At a strife-filled meeting on December 29, 1878, he was reelected by one vote at the reduced salary of $100. One member stated that he would not vote, since he opposed Bardin in the position at any salary. The incumbent took umbrage and withdrew his application, but agreed to continue on an interim basis. One gets the impression that the cause of opposition was twofold. Bardin was not, after all, a professional *hazzan.* He apparently had competence but lacked talent. Since it was expected that listening to the rendition of the service by the *hazzan* be an aesthetic as well as a spiritual experience, a prerequisite was a musical voice and artistry. For a growing congregation, the leading Orthodox congregation of the community, some felt that a more gifted professional was required.

Bardin was also an influential lay leader, and this prevented his subservience as a functionary. It would be better to get someone, not of the community, to serve the congregation and be entirely dependent upon it for livelihood. Thus the absolute power of leaders over functionaries could be maintained. Only a half-year after Bardin was offered $100 a year (and this by one vote), the congregation empowered the officers to advertise in the New York newspapers for a *hazzan,* teacher, and reader, at a salary of $500.[64] We should note that the congregation sought a functionary who could also serve as teacher of its young. On October 26, Moshe Weiss was elected to the position. His salary was to be $400 per annum if he furnished the *heder* (the room in which classes would be conducted), $350 if it was provided by the congregation. Fifteen dollars was granted the new *hazzan* to enable him to bring his family from New York, and his status was reflected in an amendment to the by-laws, in Section 2, to read that "the purpose of the congregation is to maintain a synagogue, a cantor, and teacher." [65]

The power of the congregation over functionaries and their precarious position is demonstrated by what took place at the October 3, 1880, meeting. The cantor, Moshe Weiss, petitioned to be reelected, requesting the same salary. The laws of the congregation stipulated that a functionary not be invited to serve but that he petition requesting to do so. In response to Weiss's request, it was voted that his term be extended for only six months. On December 5, of the same year, he received notice and read with heavy heart the advertisement that Beth Israel was seeking a cantor, when they were ready to pay up to $700 per annum. Cantor Weiss was in town and wanted to remain. He again petitioned the congregation, offering to serve for $350. At the April 3, 1881 meeting, his request was denied, Moshe Ticktin being elected with a salary of $600.

Soon the congregation was plagued with a problem endemic to congregational life of the time. There was no control over, and little knowledge about, the character of those professing to be religious functionaries. Rabbis needed ordination, and papers attesting to same would be required. But what control and knowledge were available where *hazzanim* were concerned? The majority were, to be sure, men of probity and piety, but the profession attracted a goodly number who were not. At a special meeting convened for the purpose on July 17, 1881, a charge was brought against the *hazzan* that "he didn't behave right and so abused and shamed the *hevra.*" Formally accused at the meeting, he admitted his guilt, and begged for mercy. The nature of his transgression is not recorded, but it was apparently serious enough to forestall mercy, and to make his departure so desirable that his contract was terminated and he was offered $25 to leave the city.

His replacement was Harris Lewis, who served for four years. These were filled with problems. A special meeting was convened on April 15, 1883, to hear charges that the *hazzan* "doesn't obey the president" as stipulated in the contract. Official notice was given to the *hazzan* that unless he obeyed, his contract would be terminated. The source of problems and pressure for the *hazzan* was not always the congregation; it could be a fellow functionary as well. *Hazzan* Lewis apparently served as *shohet* as well as cantor. A new rabbi came to the community and was accepted by the congregation. Rabbi Levinson refused to "give *Kabbalah*" to Harris Lewis—that is, to certify him as a *shohet*. The cantor had to leave his post and the community, taking with him unhappy memories and a letter from the congregation attesting his good character. Itinerant *hazzanim*, of which there were many, would come for a Sabbath, until Cantor Mirsky was elected *hazzan*-reader on July 18, 1885, at the salary of $500 and given a two-year contract.

Rabbi

The rabbi who caused the departure of Cantor Lewis was Abba Hayim ben Yitzhak Levinson. He apparently came to town and then petitioned the congregation to elect him rabbi. This they did by one vote. At the same meeting it was voted twenty-six to three to reelect the aforementioned *Hazzan* Lewis. The congregation never had a clear conception of what ought to be the role and duties of the rabbi. Indeed, the question was raised time and again whether the congregation needed a rabbi. East European Jewry knew a communal rabbi, and there clearly was no precedent in the religious experiences of the congregants of Beth Israel as to what might or ought to be the role and function of a rabbi engaged by a congregation. The West European and American Reform usage of congregational rabbis had little to say to them, for it differed so vastly from their own concept of the place and function of a congregation in the life of its members. Ritual, judicial, and educational rabbinic powers and responsibilities were in the interest of, and therefore the responsibility of, the community, not of an individual congregation. So the question persisted, making insecure the position of the rabbi, and serving as a cause of ongoing friction in the congregation.

As mentioned earlier, the dichotomy of those favoring a salary of $600 and those voting for $100 was no doubt due to a difference in the concept of what a rabbi's duties and responsibilities ought to be, the former viewing them as congregational, the latter as communal. There was no question that his ordination vested him with the power to render decisions and exert control in matters of ritual, particularly *kashrut,* which was a matter communal and personal, not congregational. So he was unanimously supported in his certification of *shohatim,* and kashrut supervision.[66] The same meeting which proclaimed that any stranger (i.e., nonmember) who abused the rabbi should not be permitted in the synagogue, refused to enact a resolution stating that no itinerant preacher be permitted to preach from the pulpit. The matter was so sensitive and potentially so explosive that the president refused to cast his vote to break a tie.[67] In effect the members decreed that no outsider could speak ill of their rabbi, but at the same time their respect for him and his office did not stand in the way of their "enjoying" what they would have wanted to enjoy in Europe, a *maggid*—an itinerant preacher.

The vacillation continued. On July 10, 1884, the rabbi was reelected and a committee was appointed to place an ad in the Yiddish newspaper, announcing his reelection. A year later,[68] at the meeting to consider reelection, the question was raised whether "we want a rabbi." The president refused to permit a vote, but the opponents had power enough to humble the rabbi by demanding that he petition the congregation for reelection. He did so, and was elected. But while the newly elected cantor was granted a salary of $500, and permission to augment it, the rabbi's salary remained at $150.

The ambivalence of the congregation and the uncertain status of its rabbi was not untypical of the situation in East European congregational life in America. The first two leading East European rabbis of note, Rabbi Joseph Asch and Rabbi Moses Aronson, served larger congregations in New York City. Their problems were of similar nature, though the former was rabbi of the congregation proud to call itself first of its kind in the New World, and the latter brought with him a reputation fashioned by two highly praised scholarly books. Ambivalence and uncertainty derived from the confrontation of European usage and American reality, which was not to be resolved for another two generations.

Finances

The sources for financing the congregation were membership dues, donations announced on receiving an honor at services, the sale of seats, and the renting of seats for the High Holy Days. The dues were collected and recorded by the *shamash*-collector, as were the Sabbath donations. On holidays the honors were sold at auctions conducted during the service. This not only was a source of revenue for the congregation, but also enabled a member to establish status by size of bid, and even more by then offering the bought prize as a gift to a relative or friend. The auction itself provided no small source of exciting "entertainment" for the congregants, and served as a topic of titillating conversations long after.

Seats were sold as a source of financing the building of facilities. Forty-two seats were sold in the first permanent synagogue, on August 31, 1879, for a total of $1,596.50. The prices ranged from $91 to $20. At the same time the cost of seats to strangers worshipping there on the High Holy Days was set at from $2 to $5, quite a respectable sum at the time. When the congregation moved into its permanent home, the synagogue it built on Leopold Street, it had no problem selling eighty seats at goodly prices ranging up to $350.

The financial well-being fluctuated with the financial condition of its members. In 1884 seats of resigned members brought prices three times those paid five years earlier. A year later the secretary reported that many members claimed an inability to keep up payments for their seats, and the obligations were postponed "till after Pesah."[69] The depressed financial situation is reflected in the report that the vice-president declared that he was in arrears, and asked the congregation to lend him the money to enable him to meet his obligations, offering his seat as security. "Times are hard," he explained. Discretion came to his aid. It was voted not to consider him in arrears and to permit him to retain his office, for it would be disgraceful for the congregation if its vice-president were missing from his accustomed place on the pulpit.

To bolster the finances of the congregation, a raffle for a watch was undertaken. Three hundred and seventy tickets were sold, bringing in $71.50. The committee reported that since not all the tickets were sold, it was decided to place the unsold tickets in the ballot box in the name of the congregation and God smiled upon "His house," for the congregation won the raffle! The watch was thereupon auctioned and brought

$22. After such success, it was voted to award a medal costing no more than $5 to Peretz Unterberg for having sold the most tickets.[70] He clearly deserved the medal, not so much for enterprise as for heroism. It would take heroic courage to face his "customers" in a raffle won by the sponsoring organization.

Cemetery

The first communal institution was generally a cemetery. Consecrated ground for burial had high priority for the immigrant Jew. The Jews of Rochester were no different from others. Jewish burial ground in the city cemetery of Mt. Hope is as old as the Jewish community. The *hevrot* which preceded Beth Israel had cemetery land, for at the organizational meeting a *gabbai* for the cemetery was elected. At a regular trustees' meeting on November 15, 1874, it was voted to give burial plots in Mt. Hope for two children—one to a non-member, Azriel Michaels, because he was "very poor" and asked for a plot, and the other to Judah Posner, a member. The minute books indicate a very high rate of mortality among infants and children. The congregation through its cemetery was in position to be of great service to grief-stricken bereaved parents. Thus the full minutes of the special trustees meeting of October 24, 1880, read:

> Meeting called to order by the president. The purpose: A stranger applied for a grave for a still-born child. All officers were present. It was moved and seconded that he should pay $5. The meeting is adjourned.

Free burial was provided in instances of tragedy. Thus an immigrant boy of seventeen, killed in an accident, was accorded free burial in a congregational plot.

A special prestigious committee of the congregation, the *hevra kadisha* (holy society) was charged with the responsibility of caring for the cemetery, arranging the body for interment and presiding at the funeral. The society had a quasi-independent status, having an annual dinner sponsored by the congregation and being permitted to utilize the income from donations announced on a specific Sabbath designated for this purpose.[71] Another source of income was the charity money collected at the cemetery during a funeral. This source was at first denied by the congregation. The president reported at the January 30, 1881, meeting that he had requested of the *gabbai* of the *hevra kadisha* that he come for the body of the deceased. This he refused to do unless he received $1 and all the charity money for the *hevra kadisha*. The president refused to accede to the demand, asked for volunteers to prepare the body, and named his vice-president acting *gabbai* of the cemetery. That the head of the *hevra kadisha*, which was a committee of the congregation, could made demands upon and challenge the president is evidence of the power of this "holy society," derived no doubt from the high importance of its work in the life-cycle of the immigrant Jew.

An even more dramatic incident attesting to the high importance placed on burial in consecrated ground is an event in the early life of the congregation. On October 17, 1875, the president reported to a regular meeting of trustees the following.

On Yom Kippur day, a Jew died (apparently the victim of an accident). He was a Jew from Poland, and there was found on him a letter instructing that he be buried in a "Polish cemetery," i.e., a cemetery consecrated by East European Orthodox Jews. A committee was appointed to look into the matter, and it reported that the "Temple Congregation" (i.e., Congregation B'rith Kodesh, the Reform Jewish congregation of Rochester) would bury him in its cemetery. On the day after Yom Kippur, the president of the temple came to the president of Beth Israel and informed him that members of Beth Israel had claimed the body, and now the temple refused to bury him "for any money." So the president had no alternative but to instruct the *hevra*'s committee to bury him. A special meeting called for the purpose approved his burial "in the cemetery line."

On October 17, a special general meeting voted to extend thanks to Zelig Rosenbloom and Isaac Lipsky for attending to the burial of the deceased. A special committee of five was appointed to ascertain who of the congregation claimed the body. No further mention is made of the incident. The burial on its own consecrated ground followed the written desire of the deceased; and the action of those who "saved" him from burial in a Reform cemetery of German Jews no doubt won the approval of Orthodox Jews. The committee to investigate was a gesture of conciliation to the temple. To provide a decent burial for a Jew was always considered a high religious obligation, and both congregations vied for it. It would seem that all were pleased by the final outcome. The president of B'rith Kodesh and his congregation had made the right and generous offer, but seemed too eager to seize a way out of burying a Polish Jew in their cemetery. The members of Beth Israel felt the satisfaction of high virtue of having performed a *mitzvah* and in the process having bested the older, "aristocratic" congregation, which accepted them as fellow Jews but not as social equals.

Relationship with Other Congregations

The above incident is the only recorded relationship with the B'rith Kodesh congregation in the early history of Beth Israel. Contract with the German Jewish community was a bit wider. On June 2, 1879, a committee was appointed to solicit contributions from the "German Jews" for the building fund. After three weeks, two of the members declined to serve further, their resignation being accepted "with thanks." It is not clear whether the resignation was due to frustration or to the successful completion of the mission. At the dedication of the building, the rabbi of B'rith Kodesh, Dr. Max Landsberg, gave the dedication address. A divided community thus joined in the celebration of the dedication of a house of worship. Where social, economic, and cultural considerations divided, religion united.

But religious practice and interpretation could divide where ethno-cultural sharing united. The Nusbaum family and its followers who left Beth Israel to form a congregation of their own did so in large measure because Beth Israel was becoming too "progressive" religiously. A "Polish *minyan*" was in competition with Beth Israel, because of differences in liturgical rite and usage. The "mother congregation" responded to the competition of its daughter *minyanim* with a degree of vindictive jealousy.

Abraham Shencup was unsuccessful in his effort to be engaged to chant the *shaharit* service on the High Holy Days of 1875. He thereupon accepted to do so for "the *minyan*." Charges were brought against him for his disloyalty.[72] Special legislation was enacted against the "Nusbaum Minyan." A member of Beth Israel attending a weekday or Sabbath service would be fined 50 cents for the first "transgression," $1 for the second. A third would bring expulsion.[73] Indeed Finkelstein was fined 50 cents for doing so. A similar enactment was directed against a new congregation, *Hevra* Tehillim. This prohibition extended to the High Holy Days only, indicating that the reason was financial rather than the suppression of competition.[74]

The community was growing. Large-scale immigration from Eastern

Europe was bringing to Rochester groups of Jews differing from one another in place of origin and in liturgical rites and usages. The differences found expression in the proliferation of synagogues. These were *landsmanschaft* congregations determined by place of origin, or rite congregations, which differed one from the other in what might seem to an outsider minute liturgical variations, but apparently were of sufficient caliber to make separation legitimate. The East European Jews of Rochester felt themselves to be one community, a united community. At the same time they accepted as right and legitimate a diversity of liturgical religious expression and the separation into rite congregations. There existed a basic unity which permitted religious diversity. In this sense the East European Jewish community of Rochester was a microcosm of America.

Education

To the observer of the contemporary Jewish scene, in which Jewish education is an overriding interest and program of the congregation, the exertion on behalf of education by the early Beth Israel congregation seems minimal indeed. An educational program was forced upon the leadership of the congregation by demanding parents.

On October 26, 1879, a board of education of eight members was appointed. At the same time the newly elected cantor, Moshe Weiss, was to be *hazzan,* leader, and teacher! A day later the board was empowered to rent and furnish a *heder* at congregational expense. But the motivation seems to have been narrow and parochial. Only a half-year later, the board was instructed not to accept a pupil above the age of thirteen.[75] To prepare a boy for Bar Mitzvah, a synagogue ritual, was deemed a legitimate interest and activity of a congregation, but nothing beyond that. Instruction of this nature went on. The board of education, apparently interested in broader education, aroused the opposition of the congregational leadership. On July 3, 1881, the board was discharged. A committee of six was appointed to probe into what the *hazzan*-teacher was doing. It was instructed to order him to limit himself to the instruction of rote reading of Hebrew, and not teach Bible. Again, the congregation felt it was its duty to prepare children for participation in the synagogue service, and no more.

This was not due to lack of interest in Bible study or broader Jewish education. In the European community education was a private or communal concern, not a province of congregational responsibility. Parents engaged a teacher for their son, or sent him to a private *heder*. The community maintained the school. The American environment and usage made religious education a congregational responsibility. The Beth Israel in its early years was a transplanted European institution. Its conception of role and responsibility did not include a school. If education there was to be, then parents or community needed to make provision. To have any educational program at all was already one accommodation to the "American way," an accommodation they were ready to make only if it was clearly in service of their institutional interests: Bar Mitzvah, rote reading.

Strife, Control, Assistance

The most interesting aspect of the *hevra*-congregation was its function as an arena for the acting out of interpersonal relationships. The minutes record disturbances at services and at meetings; strife and conflict in matters congregational and beyond; control and sanctions employed; exercise of judicial functions; and assistance in time of need.

Charges were brought against Harris Fisher, for "making a disturbance in *shul* at the Sabbath *Minha* service," at the regular trustees meeting of November 15, 1874. Twelve signatories requested a special meeting to deal with the charges. A week later the meeting was held. David Kaminsky, supported by Wolf Meyers and Kalman Bardin, accused Fisher of coming to services in an inebriated condition, causing a general disturbance, and cursing members. Fisher denied being drunk, and claimed that he became highly excited when he was called a nickname. A secret vote was taken and Fisher was found guilty and fined $3, to be paid immediately. At a general congregational meeting the minutes of the special meeting were read and approved. It was voted, however, that the minutes record only that charges were brought and a fine was levied. Justice done, compassion came into play. They were dealing with a friend and neighbor, and one who remained a member for many years to come.

The minutes are replete with accusations made, committees of inquiry established, and punishment meted out. Thus on January 20, 1877, a committee was appointed to investigate charges that Aaron Nusbaum had "slandered" Abraham Shencup by declaring that he lacked the piety which one who chants the service should have. On December 1, 1878, a special meeting was called to consider an accusation of slander by Kalman Bardin against Peretz Unterberg and Hayim Avner. Both were declared guilty. The punishment of Mr. Unterberg was that he might never hold an office, while Avner was fined $10. More often than not, punishment was not carried out and fines were rescinded.

At times congregational disputes were carried beyond the walls of the synagogue. A special trustees' meeting was called "to take action against the members who advertised in the papers and abused the *hevra*." At another meeting, convened the next day, charges were drawn up against Barnet Levine, Aaron Nusbaum, and Abraham Shencup (now joined in alliance and enterprise), but the matter was dropped when it could not be proved that these were the "culprits."

Strife at services was not uncommon. After all, there were honors, prerogatives, and power constantly contested. From time to time contention erupted into fighting. On June 5, 1881, however, the fighting was of such a nature as to be brought before a meeting. A charge was brought against Barnet Levine and the *shamash*, Jacob Cohen, for fighting at the end of the service, "and it was a disgrace before the Gentiles who came running to the windows." The fact that the fines leveled were only 50 cents against each seems to indicate that fighting was not considered a heinous transgression. It is of interest to note that the *shamash* was also ordered to apologize, which he did. He was, after all, an employee, and his adversary a dues-paying member.

Elections were always hotly contested. Symbols of status were few in the immigrant society, so the presidency was eagerly coveted. Generally the victor acted magnanimously and the loser accepted defeat in good grace. But not always. At the election held October 10, 1881, Aaron Nusbaum and Kalman Bardin each received nineteen votes. They were respective leaders of the two factions which existed until the Nusbaum family withdrew to form its own congregation. At this meeting neither faction was ready to give in. Arguments ensued. Many fines were levied, which led to even greater arguments, and the president was forced to adjourn the meeting. It was reconvened the next day. Bardin emerged victorious, and the congregational life returned to its normal flow. No matter how violent an argument, neighbors remained friends. An immigrant community felt beset by all manner of foes, so had to retain an inner solidarity which a settled community could afford to strain. The meeting to consider whether the by-laws should be printed in English as well as Yiddish had to be adjourned, because order could not be maintained,[76] but four days later the matter was settled by a vote, and the life of the congregation continued. One gets the impression that the meetings served a function beyond the obvious. Necessary business was enacted, but they also provided an opportunity for the "powerful" to exert power, for the orators to orate, for elected officials to rule, and for all to rid themselves of the pent-up hostilities and frustrations which immigrant life provided in full measure.

Meetings were held at every opportunity. In the twelve years under study, more than 300 meetings are recorded: 133 regular trustees' meetings, 47 special trustees' meetings, 47 quarterly congregational meetings, and 136 special congregational meetings, or 150 regular and 183 special meetings. Whatever complaint was recorded about the frequency of meetings was not that they were too many, but too few.

The "fraternal lodge" aspect of the congregation was expressed in the pomp and ceremony which took place at the installation of officers, and in the votes on new members. This was by secret ballot. Five blackballs would keep a prospect out of the congregation. When this happened, and it did, it was generally changed at a subsequent meeting. The point made, it was deemed wise to strengthen the congregation by another dues-payer.

The immigrant congregants were not a docile or genteel lot. The meek do not venture forth into a new world. It is an enterprise for the venturesome and hardy. When a *siyum* celebration (at the conclusion of a course of study) was planned, the *hevra* voted to assume responsibility for any damage caused to the house in which the celebration would take place. A committee of seven was appointed to guard against damage.

Judicial

In the European Jewish community a court system existed, and all matters of dispute were adjudicated internally. In the absence of an organized Jewish communal structure in America, the East European immigrants turned to their *hevra*-congregation for this communal function.

On June 20, 1875 a special meeting was held for just such a purpose. Two members of the congregation, Joseph Minsky and Hillel Pashimanski, came before the assembled *hevra*, said that they had differences between themselves, and asked that a court be established to examine their claims, render its decision, and make a settlement between them. It was "moved, seconded and passed" that the *hevra* accept their request. The meeting was then organized as a "court of justice." The litigants were examined, their claims investigated, and a decision rendered. The minutes report that a settlement was reached between the two to the satisfaction of both parties. Again and again members turned to the *hevra* for mediation. Thus, for example, the minutes of March 25, 1883, report that litigation between the *hazzan* and a member was settled out of court, apparently by congregational mediation.

The minutes also preserve a full account of judicial proceedings before a special meeting of the trustees called for that purpose. Joseph Minsky attended the Polish *minyan* on Simhat Torah and was fined 50 cents for violating a congregational rule. He was also charged with slandering the president, the trustees, and the *hevra,* and was ordered to stand trial for his accusation.

November 7, 1875, Special Trustees Meeting.
Joseph Minsky was at the meeting as defendant to the charges. Max Rosenbloom and Simon Levy were present as witnesses against him. The investigation of charges began. Isaac Lipsky was appointed as attorney for prosecution. Joseph Minsky was asked whether he wanted to act on his own behalf or to have counsel chosen for him. He chose to act as his own counsel.

The first witness called was David Kaminsky.

Q. What do you know in regard to Joseph Minsky's abusing the congregation, the president, the *hazzan* and *shohet* (i.e., Kalman Bardin)?

A. I went to the home of Simon Levy on the evening of Simhat Torah and heard Minsky say: "I attended that minyan." He futher stated he doesn't care about anybody. That he will slap Bardin and the president and do so in the synagogue, and will drive Bardin out of town. "One should not eat of the *shehita* of Bardin because he eats *trefa* food. He eats herring by Gentiles."

Cross-examination:

Q. What day was this?

A. Simhat Torah, October 22, Friday.

Q. What kind of day is Simhat Torah?

A. To eat and to drink whatever one has and wants.

Q. Was I drunk or sober?

A. You walked about the house and talked.

Q. Was Max Rosenbloom also there?

A. Yes, he was lying on the couch and kept quiet. He was dozing.

End of cross-examination. Max Rosenbloom called to the stand.

Q. What do you know concerning Minsky's slandering the congregation, the president, and the *hazzan?*

A. On Simhat Torah, during the day, I was in Simon Levy's house. Present were Simon Levy, David Kaminsky, Joseph Minsky, and

many others. This was between three and four o'clock. Minsky said:
"I was at that *minyan* and pledged one dollar. I received the honor
of *aharon* [the last one called to the reading of the Torah]. I paid
the dollar immediately. Before I will give our synagogue one cent, I
would rather give *them* dollars. I'll show them—that everyone can
grab an office in our congregation! I have more sense in the sole of
my foot than Mosely [the president] and Bardin [the *hazzan*] have
in their whole body." He spoke much more against the congregation.
In the evening, I was again at Simon Levy's. Minsky came again
and spoke against the president and Bardin. That Bardin eats *trefa*,
that his house is *tref,* and that no one should eat of his *shehita*. "You
will see. I will slap both Bardin and the president. I'll make them
pay a fine of ten dollars and I'll make Bardin leave the city. I am
Minsky! I will drag the president and Bardin out of the synagogue
by their teeth. Even if I have to pay a fine of ten dollars. But they
will also have to pay it. . . . I will destroy the congregation, in every
way I am able."

Q. Was Minsky drunk or sober at that time?
A. He was quite sober.
Q. Was there anything to drink there?
A. No. He walked about and smoked a pipe.
Q. Did you start up with him, so you could bring charges?
A. No.

Cross-examination:

Q. When was the first time you heard such talk?
A. It was between three and four in the afternoon.
Q. Were you in my house that day?
A. No.
Q. Did you say in my house that the president will drive me out of the
congregation?
A. No. I can swear that I was not in your house, and said no such
thing.
Q. When did you go to Simon Levy's?
A. When you were already there, talking and abusing.
Q. Where do you live?
A. At Simon Levy's, upstairs.
Q. How did I say I will destroy the congregation?
A. You said you will destroy it in any way you can. You said it all cost
you enough money.
Q. How long did you hear me, talking this way?
A. About ten minutes. Then I left you there and went away. What you
said after that, I do not know.
Q. When was the other time that you heard me slandering the president?

A. Between six and seven in the evening.

Q. Who else was there?

A. Simon Levy, David Kaminsky, and a boarder also boards with me.

Q. Didn't you hear me say that the president has no sense, But Kalman Bardin . . .

A. No. I can swear, *no!*

Q. When did you see me again since that time?

A. Saturday, *Parashat Noah.*

Q. What did I say there?

A. The same and more. You said you will organize a new congregation in four weeks. "I will buy cemetery land. Then I will show them that anybody can grab an office in this *hevra!* I was president when B'nai Shalom joined. I can take it away . . ."

Q. Did you pay a fifty cents fine because of me?

A. I paid a fifty cents fine, but not because of you.

Q. Did you ask me to pay the fifty cents for you?

A. Yes.

Q. When you heard me talking that way, did you call over Bardin that I should slap him?

A. No. I can swear, *no!*

Q. Was Bardin present then?

A. No.

Simon Levy was called as a witness.

Q. Mr. Levy, did you hear Minsky say all these things in your house?

A. Yes.

Q. You heard all the slandering, as the first witness stated? Did you give Minsky something to drink when he was in your house?

A. No.

Q. Was he drunk?

A. No. According to my understanding, no.

Q. How many times did Minsky speak that way in your house?

A. Two times.

The taking of evidence was concluded by the attorney for the prosecution. Joseph Minsky, the defendant, was asked whether he denied the charges. The answer is: "No."

"Are you guilty?"

"No!"

The defendant was notified to appear at a special congregational meeting to be held 3:00 P.M. the same day. The trustees debated the evidence presented and voted unanimously that the defendant was guilty. The special congregational meeting voted eighteen to one that Joseph

Minsky was guilty as charged. The punishment: suspended from all rights for eleven months and twenty-nine days; fined $10 to be paid in thirty days; if not paid, "he removes himself from the congregation."

Joseph Minsky's anger was the outgrowth of contention for power between the leaders of the two *hevrot* which joined to form Beth Israel. Minsky was the leader of B'nai Shalom, Bardin of Sheves Ahim. The first slate of officers included David Kaminsky of Sheves Ahim as president and Joseph Minsky of B'nai Shalom as vice-president. Bardin did not seek office, preferring instead the paid position of *hazzan*. But at the next election he put forth David Mosely and had him elected president. Minsky was kept off the slate. Mosely, an English Jew, was a lawyer, whose piety and "Jewishness" were suspected among some members. It was apparently accepted that Bardin was the "gray eminence" behind Mosely. Minsky bridled at being eliminated from power, and lashed out in his frustration. Thus the trial and verdict, the playing out of power and politics in this small community, as in larger corporate bodies.

Despite all, there was desire for peace and conciliation. Time and again the attempt was made to attribute Minsky's "slander" to inebriation, and on the Simhat Torah festival to be in one's cups bordered on virtue. All would have been forgiven if Minsky had bent a little. He would not relent and they could not absolve. The underlying causes, the trial, and its verdict were matters touching more upon the dynamics of communal living than upon purely congregational activities. Beth Israel was a congregation in structure, but a community in essence.

Aid and Assistance

As a community, the *hevra* extended care and a helping hand to its members. Visitation in sickness, burial at death, and assistance to the bereaved family were guaranteed by the laws of the *hevra*. But help went beyond that, to aid those in need.

On November 22, 1875, a special meeting was called by a petition of twelve members. Peretz Unterberg was in financial need and he had applied for assistance. It was voted to lend him $25, with individual members assuming personal obligations of $1 to $5 if the loan should not be repaid to the congregation. On February 5, 1882, it was reported that Harris Fisher was ill and needed help. Twenty-five members signed for him, accepting responsibility for a $20 grant from the congregation, until such time as the congregation would be able to vote on it, which it did at its next meeting.[77] Free cemetery land for the indigent, postponement of monetary obligations where indicated, and direct aid when requested were common. This was a community of friends and neighbors—rubbing against one another as friends are wont to do, and on occasion irritating one another as neighbors sometimes do, but at all times concerned about one another and helping one another.

The sense of security and status which a community provides was granted to its members by the Beth Israel congregation. It was in concept a congregation but in function a mini-community. As such it was a European institution transplanted in American soil. In its first dozen years of existence, America made hardly an impress upon it. As a matter of fact, it may very well have been insulated against American influences, so that it remained unchanged, the *hevra* the immigrant knew in his hometown. America presented so many challenges because of the differences encountered that the *hevra*, unchanged, provided the needed secure soil of the known and the habitual. Or to use another metaphor, it was the secure, sound harbor to which one could return, for services or meetings with cronies, after being tossed about on the uncharted waters of peddling in the countryside or laboring in a not-too-friendly city. In a real sense Beth Israel was the most comfortable and secure haven which the immigrant Jew in Rochester had in the first decades of mass immigration.

NOTES

1. The Minute Book of the Beth Israel Congregation, in the custody of the author. The minute book consists of three volumes. Contemporary paginated ledger books were used. Since the minutes are in Yiddish, and the pagination is from right to left, while the ledger numbers are from left to right, the pagination is in reverse order: vol. 1, pp. 256–2, June 28, 1874–September 10, 1882; vol. 2, pp. 384–7, October 1, 1882–October 20, 1894; vol. 3, pp. 498–15, October 24, 1894–September 30, 1912 (hereafter referred to as MBBI).
2. The author has a card welcoming Jacob Katz, signed by Samuel Loewi, dated Henrietta (*sic*—a town bordering on Rochester), November 15, 1840.
3. *Occident*, vol. XIII, no. 9 (December 1855), p. 467.
4. In 1915 ten members of Beth Israel left to form the Conservative congregation, Beth El. Beth Israel still exists, worshipping in the building erected in 1886.
5. Salo W. Baron, *The Jewish Community* (Philadelphia, 1945), vol. I, p. 350.
6. *Beth Hamedrash Hagadol Constitution and By-Laws* (New York, 1887), pp. 22–24.
7. *Ibid.*, pp. 14–17.
8. *Articles of Incorporation and Constitution of the Oheb Sholem Congregation of Baltimore, Maryland* (Baltimore, 1882).
9. By-laws in minute book. In possession of Abba Nusbaum.
10. MBBI, July 4, 1874. [Notes 11–35 all refer to MBBI]
11. July 26, 1874.
12. August 30, 1874.
13. August 23, 1874.
14. March 10, 1878.
15. May 5, 1878.
16. November 24, 1878.
17. December 1, 1878.
18. April 10, 1879.
19. June 2, 1879.
20. August 17, 1879.
21. August 31, 1879.
22. July 4, 1875.
23. August 3, 1879.
24. August 23, 1879.
25. October 27, 1879.
26. October 3, 1880.
27. April 24, 1881.
28. May 8, 1881
29. June 5, 1881.
30. July 17, 1881.
31. February 5, 1882.
32. June 7, 1883.
33. August 20, 1883.

34. May 11, 1884.
35. June 1, 1884.
36. Its name was later changed to Beth Hakeneset Hehadash. It is better known as the Nusbaum Shul.
37. It seems most likely that the issue which caused the split in the congregation was cemetery vs. synagogue. In a preface to the minute book of the Beth Haknesses Hachodosh, Meir Nusbaum is lauded for his efforts:

   Mr. Meir Nusbaum worked hard for the *hevra* that everything should be in order, that there should be a cemetery. In the second year Mr. Meir Nusbaum bought land for a cemetery, on the third year he had a fence built.
38. MBBI, Special Trustees Meeting, September 23, 1883.
39. *Ibid.,* October 21, 1883.
40. Moshe Weinberger, *Hayehudim V'hayahadut B'New York* (New York, 1887), p. 4.
41. See Abraham J. Karp, "New York Chooses a Chief Rabbi," *Publications of the American Jewish Historical Society,* vol. XLIV, no. 3 (March, 1955), pp. 129ff.
42. *Rochester Union-Advertiser,* April 5, 1895, p. 10.
43. MBBI, September 3, 1883. [Notes 44–49 refer to MBBI]
44. No. 25, 1883.
45. December 1883.
46. July 7, 1884.
47. July 10, 1884.
48. June 14, 1885.
49. July 19, 1885.
50. Weinberger, op. cit., p. 2.
51. MBBI, February 5, 1882. [Notes 52–58 refer to MBBI]
52. March 10, 1884.
53. March 30, 1884.
54. May 11, 1884.
55. June 1, 1884.
56. March 7, 1886.
57. March 28, 1886.
58. June 28, 1886, p. 6, cols. 6 and 7.
59. *Rochester Democrat and Chronicle,* September 20, 1886.
60. MBBI, April 16, 1879 [Notes 61–77 refer to MBBI]
61. September 3, 1883.
62. June 6, 1875.
63. December 20; December 26, 1874.
64. August 3, 1879.
65. March 14, 1880.
66. November 25, 1883.
67. December 2, 1883.
68. June 14, 1885.
69. March 22, 1885.
70. October 6, 1884.
71. October 12, 1884.
72. September 19, 1875.
73. July 10, 1884.
74. April 19, 1885.
75. March 29, 1880.
76. October 18, 1883.
77. March 26, 1882.

BARBADIAN JEWISH WILLS, 1676–1740

By

BERTRAM WALLACE KORN

Reform Congregation Keneseth Israel, Elkins Park, Pa.

By no means the least meaningful and enduring of Jacob R. Marcus's distinguished academic achievements is his creation in the American Jewish Archives of a treasure-trove of invaluable source materials on a vast variety of American Jewish themes. These manuscripts, some originals, some copies in photostat or microfilm or other means of reproduction, single sheets, volumes, letters, autobiographies, business correspondence, minute books, congregational records, and dozens of other forms, have been secured through gift or loan or purchase, by correspondence, research, or on extensive scholarly expeditions. During one of those academic pilgrimages in 1952, Marcus and some of his students visited various Caribbean sites, including Barbados, where typewritten copies were ordered of wills selected according to the names of the testators from indices in the Barbadian Department of Archives. It seems altogether appropriate to this grateful student to submit to this volume, which honors Marcus, a paper which utilizes some of these documents which have been assembled by the honoree himself.[1]

I

The appendices to "A Review of the Jewish Colonists in Barbados in the Year 1680" by Wilfred S. Samuel, prepared for the Jewish Historical Society of England in 1924 and finally printed in Volume XIII of that Society's *Transactions* in 1936 (hereafter referred to as *WSS*), include excerpts from and digests of forty-three wills of Jewish Barbadians (exclusive of Roland or Rowland Gideon, listed, but lacking any specific data). Samuel ranks them by parish of residence, but for our purposes it seems preferable to combine his three lists into one, in chronological order of original composition, with the date of registration in parentheses:

Gomes, Abraham, mid-May, 1676

Pacheco, Jacob, September 28, 1682

Hamis (Gago), Moseh, March 26, 1684 (December 2, 1684/5)

de Acosta, David, February, 1684/5 (April 13, 1685)

Navarro, Aaron, July 4, 1685 (October 29, 1685)

de Mercado, David Raphael, July 21, 1685 (August 28, 1685)

Israel, David, May 24, 1689 (August 12, 1689)

Louzada, Aron Baruh, May 9, 1693 (October 3, 1695)

Dias, Sarah Israel, May 8, 1695 (February 8, 1703/4)

Dias, Luis, April 15, May 24, 1698 (January 16, 1698/9)

Letob, Ishak Gabay, August 24, 1698 (June 20, 1711)

Mendes, Joseph, February 17, 18, 1700; July 17, 1707 (July 7, 1712)

Meza, Jacob Defonseca, January 21, 1700/1 (February 3, 1701/2)

Henriques, Abraham Baruch, February 6, 1700/1 (March 4, 1700/1)

Louzada, Rachell Baruh, October 29, 1703 (November 22, 1703)

Levy, Emmanuel, December 19, 1709 (January 10, 1709/10)

Castello, David, January 9, 1711 (February 5, 1711)

Levy, Rachel, February 24, 1712 (March 30, 1712/13)

Delyon, Benjamin, April 17, 1713 (August 16, 1714)

Mellado, Isaac Henriques, October 28, 1713 (December 20, 1715)

Namias, Manuel, November 30, 1713 (April 26, 1714)

de Azevedo, Moses, October 6, 1715 (October 25, 1715)

Mendez, Manasseh, July 3, 1716 (February 10, 1718/19)

de Peza, Abraham, August 11, 1716 (October 13, 1736)

Pachecho, Esther, July 9, 1717 (August 12, 1718)

Mendez, Moses de Solomon, November 23, 1717 (December 6, 1717)

Brandon, Moses, April 10, 1718 (April 30, 1718)

Carvallo, Raquel Nunez, June 4, 1718 (July 4, 1718)

de Campos, Samuel, January 7, 1720 (January 20, 1720)

Dias, Jael, March 30, 1720 (November 19, 1724)

Valverde, Eleazer, August 1, 1722 (May 14, 1725)

Dellyon, Mathias, April 10, 1724 (September 25, 1724)

de Medina, Jacob, June 24, 1724 (June 26, 1724)

Franco, Jacob, October 20, 1724; March 16, 1724/5 (November 1, 1726)

de Silva, Joseph, April 17, 1725 (November 18, 1725)
Valverde, Jacob, April 19, 1725 (July 10, 1729)
Marquez, Jacob, August 2, 1725 (August 21, 1725)
d'Fonseca, Jacob (Sr.), July 17, 1728 (August 22, 1728)
Franco, Moses, April 16, 1730 (April 27, 1730)
Lopes, Moses Henriquez, October 18, 1731 (October 26, 1732)
Nunez, Abraham, December 29, 1735 (October 27, 1736)
Burgos, Morducay, March 30, 1736 (November 11, 1736)
Valverde, Elias, July 3, 1739 (November 29, 1739)

II

The Archives possesses copies of ten additional wills for the period up
to and including 1740 which are not included in *WSS*. These now
follow, in chronological order of composition, digested in the same
fashion as *WSS*, with additional references (noted *EMS*) to E. M.
Shilstone's *Monumental Inscriptions in the Burial Ground of the Jewish
Synagogue at Bridgetown, Barbados* (London, 1956).

DANIEL ULLOA[2] "of the Town of Speights . . . Merchant & one
of the Hebrew nation," November 23, 1713. "I recommend my soul
into the hands of Almighty God that gave it me and my body to decent
interment according to the usual customs of our Nation here in this
Island." After just debts and funeral charges are paid, £50 to eldest
son David; "I also give unto my said son David Ulloa the five books of
Moses . . . with all its appurtenances thereto belonging . . . "[3] He gives
£30 to his son Isaac; "I also give devise and bequeath unto my said son
Isaac Ulloa all that third part I have in the Synagogue in Speightstown . . . " His wife, Esther Ulloa, is to receive everything else "for and
during the term of her natural life . . . " After her death, all property is
to be equally divided "share and share alike" among his children David,
Isaac, Abraham, Jacob, Moses, Aaron, Solomon, Deborah, and Lee-
bannah. All of the children shall have "such usual maintenance & education as formerly out of the profits and improvements of my estate until
they shall respectively attain to the age of twenty & one years or day of
marriage (which shall first happen) . . ." Wife is to be executrix. Advice
of "My well beloved friends the Honourable Thomas Maycock Esqr. [&]
Wm. Burnett" is solicited.

Witnesses—two non-Jews, who also witness codicil the same day pro-

viding that his daughter Sarah Ulloa "formerly intermarried with one
Daniel Decrofts [de Costa, de Crasto or de Castro?]"[4] shall receive "the
negro woman now in their possession by name Hagar and her two children by name Violet and Phillis . . ."If Sarah has no children, the slaves
are to revert after her death to Sarah's siblings and their heirs and assigns.
One of the witnesses swears to the signature January 14, 1713/14.

(Recorded at Barbados 37/249)

BENJAMIN GABAY LETOB,[5] whom a witness certifies to be "one
of the Hebrew nation," July 19, 1717, "begs of God Almighty forgiveness of my sins and that he may receive my soul under his Glory in a good
place." Appoints wife, Leah Gabay Letob, as executrix and heiress of
entire estate during her lifetime. She is also to be guardian "of ye Bodies
& Estates of my said children" during their minority and also of four
slaves ("Bristoll Simon & William Boyes and Experance a negro Woman") currently in the possession of Rebecca Gabay Letob, widow of
Jacob Gabay Letob.[6] The five children are "Isaac, Rebecca, Rachole,
Sarah,[7] Yeasank [?][8] . . ."
Witnessed by two non-Jews, one of whom swears to the signature on
September 23, 1720.

(Recorded at Barbados 6/134)

JOYCE DE MEDINA "of the Town of Saint Michael in the Island
of Barbados widow[9] . . ." May 30, 1726. All debts to be paid. "I do
hereby manumit & set free from all manner of slavery and servitude my
two negroes by name Warwick & Violet & I do give to each of them the
sum of forty shilling a piece . . ." Gives her sister, "Luna Delapenta"[10]
a chest of drawers. Everything else is to go to her brother-in-law, Aaron
Peiera [Pereira],[11] and Reyna, his wife. Pereira is to be the executor.
Joyce signs with a mark.
Witnesses: a non-Jew and Abram Domotis and Mordacay Nancy—
both seem to be copyists' misreadings. The non-Jew swore to the signature, February 3, 1732.

(Recorded at Barbados 35/108)

MOZES CASTELLO[12] "of the Hebrew nation . . . I recommend my
soul to my maker and Creator, my body to be buried in the Jews burying
place . . ." April 16, 1729. Appoints wife, Judia [= Judith] Castello and
brother Ephraim Castello[13] to be executors. The wife is to receive the

home and "the third part of the house that Aron Mozeno [Moreno?] now lives in." Daughter Rebecca to receive "one Mallatta Woo by name jubah with her son Ventur"; son David[14] "one Negro boy by name Cuffy"; daughter Sarah "one Negroe Woman by name Mally." Remainder of estate to be divided equally among wife and three children.

Witnesses: Simeon Massiah; Benjamin Nunez.[15] Nunez swears to signature on June 16, 1729.

(Recorded at Barbados 16/398)

MIRIAM AROBAS[16] of St. Michael, widow, "being sick and weak in body, but of sound and disposing mind and memory," May 13, 1733. Gives her sons Jacob and Solomon five shillings each. Bequeaths slaves to her other children: to Hezekiah, "two negro boys, called Robin and Johnny"; to Esther, "two negro slaves by name Esperansa & Peggy, women"; to Rachel, "a negro woman called Ruth"; to Hannah, "a negro woman called Franky"; to Rebecca, "two negro slaves by name Phillis, a woman, and little Esperansa a girl." Should Hezekiah, Esther, Rachel, Hannah, or Rebecca die before reaching the age of twenty-one and without issue, the slaves bequeathed to that child are to be divided equally among the other children named, and their heirs and assigns. Hezekiah is to receive all sums of money and outstanding debts that are due to Miriam in Nevis. The remainder of the estate, after the payment of debts and funeral expenses, is bequeathed in equal shares to Esther, Rachel, Hannah, and Rebecca. Hezekiah and Esther are to serve as executors and as guardians to Rachel, Hannah, and Rebecca. "And I desire my loving friends David and Elias Valverde, Jacob Dias Carvallo and Moses Nunes to be aiding and assisting to my said executors in the performance of this my will." Miriam signs with a mark.

Witnesses: a non-Jew and David Aboab and Abm Valverde, Junr. Sworn by first witness July 31, 1733.

(Recorded at Barbados 24/95)

MOSES VALVERDA,[18] St. Michael, March 19, 1738, "desiring my Executors hereunder mentioned to have me decently buried among my bretherin the Jews." A finger ring of five or six pounds value is willed to his brother Isaac Valverde. A finger ring of similar value to each of the following: "my niece Esther the daughter of my said Brother Isaac and unto my niece Deborah the daughter of my brother Abraham Nunes and unto my niece Abigaill the daughter of my brother Moses Nunes &

unto my niece Lunah the daughter of my brother Abraham Valverde . . ."
Five pounds to Mrs. Sarah DaCosta.[19] "I give and bequeath to the
Synagogue of Bridgetown the sum of Six pounds current money." All
the rest is to be shared by brothers David Valverde Junior and Aaron
Valverde, who are also to serve as executors.

Witnesses: David Valverde and Abraham Gomes.[20]
Signature attested by Abraham Gomes, June 26, 1740.

(Recorded at Barbados 32/259)

SOLOMON ULLOA,[21] St. Michael, January 16, 1739, "finding my
self at present indisposed of body but praised be God of perfect mind
and memory . . . I ask the Almighty God of Israel forgiveness for all my
sins and humbly intreat him to receive my soul into mercy and I desire
my honoured Mother to have me buried among my brethren the Jews
observing such obsequies as is usually performed among our nation."
Appoints his "Honoured Mother Ester Ulloa" his executrix and bequeaths everything to her. "Lastly I give me respects to my Honoured
Mother and taking leave and farewell of all my relations and friends like
a penitent sinner I beg pardon of all the world . . ."

Witnesses: a non-Jew and Moses Mendes.
Entered by Moses Mendes, February 13, 1739.

(Recorded at Barbados 32/194)

DAVID DA COSTA DE ANDRADE[22] of St. Michael, "one of the
Hebrew Nation," November 8, 1738, "my body to be interred In the
Jews Yard . . ." Twenty shillings to his son Joseph Da Costa D'Andrade
"one month after my decease In lieu of all demands that he may or can
have against any of my estate here or elsewhere . . ." Twenty shillings
each to "my sons Abraham Jacob Ephraim Morducay, Samuel & Aron
Da Costa Deandrade . . ."[23] The same amount to each of his daughters
Sarah and Rachael. Everything else to his wife, Angela Da Costa De
Andrade,[24] who is to serve as executrix.

Witnesses: Jacob Massiah, Moses Deporto, Raim [Haim!] Abinum.[25]
Sworn to by Abinum, June 3, 1740.

(Recorded at Barbados 32/245)

DAVID BARUH LOUZADA[26] of St. Michael, October 26, 1739.
"First I bequeath my soul to the mercy of Almighty God, whose pardon
of my sins I humbly implore, beseeching him to grant me the hour of sal-

vation, for my soul, & a joyful resurrection with all true Isrealites [*sic*] . . ."
Debts and funeral expenses are to be paid. Bequest of one hundred and
fifty pounds current money to "Rachael the wife of Elijah Abeab
[Aboab] in Curacoa"; in case of her death, the money to be divided
equally among her children.[27] One hundred pounds to "Jeremiah Baruh
Loizado [Louzada] merchant in this Island son of Solomon Baruh Loi-
zado [Louzada]."[28] Thirty pounds to "Rebecca DeLyon Widow"; fifty
pounds to "her daughter Rachael DeLyon."[29] Fifty pounds to David
Burgos; fifty pounds to "his daughter Rachael Burgos."[30] Fifty pounds
to "Rebecca De Argilla [Aguila?] spinster."[31] Fifty pounds to "Ester
Deny [Dina?] the Granddaughter of Sarah Letob.[31] Thirty pounds to
"Jael DeCrasto the wife of DeCrasto."[31] Ten pounds to "Rachael De-
Molino [de Molina?]."[31] Fifty pounds "to Rachael Vas Taro [Vaz
Farro?] of Surinam."[31] Fifty pounds "to her son Isaac Vas Taro [Vaz
Farro?]."[32] Twenty pounds to Moses Franco.[31] Twenty-five pounds to
"Rachael Trois [Frois] daughter of Jacob Trois [Frois] Merchant."
Twenty-five pounds "to her sister Abigael Trois [Frois]."[33] Ten pounds to
"Sarah Letob the daughter of Leah Letob."[34] "I give & bequeath to the
Synagogue in this Island ten pounds like money." "I do hereby manumitt
& set free my negro woman Muiga for the good services she hath done
me, and I also give to her five pounds like money." "All the rest Residue
& Remainder of my Estate real & personal here in this Island, If any such
remain after my debts & legacies are paid I do order & appoint that the
same be distributed to and amongst such poor persons of the Hebrew
Nation here, as to my said Executors or either of them shall think fit." "I
do hereby ratify & confirm the writings that were made by me & my wife
concerning the Estate in Surinam." "My loving friends Aaron Pereira[35] &
Jacob Trois [Frois] Merchants" to serve as executors, with authority to
sell testator's "dwelling house, and also all such negro slaves as I shall die
seized or possessed of here in this Island . . ." Signed by David B. Louzada
Senior.

Witnessed by three non-Jews, one of whom verifies signature on
March 3, 1740.

(Recorded at Barbados 32/357)

AARON PEREIRA[36] of St. Michael, July 4, 1740. Following customary pious phrases: "To prevent any disputes that may arise after
my decease concerning the same I do settle & Dispose of [that Temporal
Estate which God has been pleased to bestow upon me] in manner fol-

lowing . . ." Reaffirms indenture of March 10, 1735 with the Honourable Henry Peers, Esq[ui]re, which provides that Peers will own the house
in which his wife Renia Pereira[37] lives as well as "certain negro and
mullatto slaves in the said Indenture more particularly mentioned &
set forth for the sole use benefit & behoof of the said Renia Pereira During
her natural life . . ." and also that the £650 in the possession of Peers
"should continue in his hands at interest during the natural life of the
said Renia Pereira, and the interest thereof being the sum of fifty pounds,
should be yearly paid to the said Renia Pereira during her natural life . . ."
All this in lieu of Renia Pereira's "dower of my Estate which she might
be entitled to in case she survived me." "Upon the like condition I give
unto the said Renia Pereira one other annuity of twenty five pounds
current money . . ." "Item I give and bequeath to Mrs. Abigail Henriques the sum of Seven hundred pounds current money of this Island
to be paid her immediately after my decease, and I charge my real, as
well as my personal Estate with the payment thereof. And I give to the
said Abigail & to her heirs for ever two negroes such as she shall choose
out of all the negroes I shall die seized & possessed of, except my cooper
negroes or out of the negroes which my wife Renia Pereira had during
her life after the death of the said Renia. And I give to the said Abigail
the Walnut tree furniture of my chamber, and one third part of my
plate." After all of the above legacies, just debts, and funeral charges
have been paid, the remainder is bequeathed to Rachael and Sarah Henriques, daughters of Abigail Henriques.[38] If Rachael or Sarah dies without issue or unmarried, the survivor of the two or her heirs is to inherit
both shares. But if both Rachael and Sarah die under the age of twenty-
one, and without heirs, "I give & devise All my real Estate of whatever
kind to my good friends Morducay Nunes & Moses Nunes . . ."[39] desiring them to sell the property and to pay over the proceeds to Abigail
Henriques. But Rachael and Sarah are not to receive "any part of my
personal estate, until they respectively attain the age of eighteen years
or be married . . ." or "any part of my real Estate until the youngest of
them attain her age of twenty one years." Abigail Henriques is to serve
as sole executrix and as guardian of the bodies and property of Rachael
and Sarah until each reaches the age of twenty-one "if she so lng continue unmarried." If Abigail does marry "my will is that her Executor-
ship shall cease & that she intermeddle no further in the management of
my real or personal Estate, And in such case I nominate & appoint my
good friends the Reverend Abraham Gaybray Ysideo,[40] David Baruch

Luzado Sen[r] and the said Moses Nunes Executors of this my last Will
& Testament and I commit to their care and custody the Estates and interest, and as far as I have power to do the same, the bodies also of the
said Rachael and Sarah. And I desire that they may be maintained and
educated to the circumstances of their Estate and Interest."
Witnesses: three non-Jews, one of whom swears February 17, 1740/4
(Recorded at Barbados 32/352)

III

Four additional Jewish Barbadian wills have been secured directly
from the Barbados Department of Archives.[41] These are presented in the
same format, as follows.

RAHEL MENDES [also spelled Rachel and Rachell] of Speights,
"widow[42] & one of the Hebrew nation being by Gods assistance suddenly
bound of this Island for the Kingdom of Great Britain & considering the
certainty of death and the uncertainty of the time when . . ." July 11,
1711. Gives her niece, Sarah Massiah,[43] "one certain stone house scituate
in Speights Town, in Jew Street bounding East on a house of Daniel
Ulloa,[44] West on a house belonging to myself, South on the pond and
North on the street . . ." Gives fifty pounds sterling to her niece Rebecca
Vaz [misspelled Vaze] Lopez, in Amsterdam, Holland, towards her dowry,
"but in case she marry before my death then this bequest to be void null
and of none effect . . ." Fifty pounds sterling to her nephew Aaron
Vaz (misspelled Viz) Lopez.[45] One hundred pounds current Barbadian money to Manuel Namias for the dowry of his daughter Lunah
"if he think fit to accept of the same . . ." [46] One hundred pounds
current money to her sister Rebecca Castello for her daughter
Hannah's dowry under the same condition.[47] Twenty-five pounds
sterling to her godson, Jacob Massiah son of Simon Massiah,[48]
"to be left in the hands of my son in law Abraham Mendes[49]
to trade for the use of said Jacob Massiah." The same sum to
Angela Massiah, Simon's daughter," towards her dowry, also to be left
in Abraham's hands for trade. Five hundred pounds sterling to "be kept
in the hands of my sons Abraham and Benjamin Mendes and to be employed in the best way and manner they can for the use and maintenance
of my daughter in law Judith Mendes in case her husband my Son Moses
shall not be kind to her and maintain her according to her degree . . ."[50]

After Judith's death the fund and any accrued interest to be given to any of Judith's children by Moses still then alive. Four-fifths of the estate left by her husband "to be equally divided between my four children Jacob Mendes, Moses Mendes, Sarah Mendes and Lunah Mendes," and the final fifth to be divided equally among grandchildren then living of her two sons and two daughters. After debts have been paid, the rest and residue to her "Grandchildren that shall be then living lawfully begotten of my two Sons Jacob and Moses Mendes and to their heirs and assignes for ever." Son Jacob Mendes and sons-in-law Abraham and Benjamin Mendes to be executors and guardians of the Bodys and Estate of my Several Grandchildren."

Witnesses: three non-Jews.

Entered November 29, 1739, after a petition by Moses Francis[51] and his wife Hannah, formerly Hannah Castello. "Simeon Massiah this day was produced and made oath on the five books of Moses that the foregoing will was by the said Rachel Mendes on her going off this Island left in his hands with directions not to deliver the same to any person without her special order and that the said paper writing continued in his possession until he lately delivered the same to the Deputy Secretary of this Island . . ." A non-Jewish attorney and Daniel Massiah[52] testified to the authenticity of the signatures of "the subscribing witnesses to the said will who are all long since dead . . ."

RACHEL PEIXOTTO[53] of St. Michael, February 21, 1727. "I recommend my soul into the hands of Almighty God hoping to obtain pardon and remission of my sins & a joyfull resurrection with all true Israelites . . ." All property to be distributed equally to "my three children Judith Peixotto Joshua Peixotto & Abraham Peixotto their heirs executrs. admrs. share & share alike . . ." Executors are to be "my loveing Son Morducay Gomes[54] Mercht. in New York my friend Aaron Baruch[55] & Thomas Clarke . . ."

Witnesses: Solomon Baruch,[56] Simeon Massiah junr, Isaac Massiah, junr.[57]

Sworn March 4, 1727, by Simeon Massiah junr.

JACOB NUNEZ MONSANTO, St. Michael, October 8, 1729 [in Portuguese] asks to be interred in the Jewish cemetery, and approves of the payment of all justified claims on his estate. He bequeaths his breech-cloth and a mulatto named Manuel to his grandson Abraham Nunez

Monsanto. The remainder of the estate is to be divided into four equal parts for the designated heirs, his grandsons Ishak Nunez Monsanto and Abraham Nunez Monsanto, and Rachel Monsanto and Rebca [Ribca] Monsanto.[58] Appoints Simkon [Simeon] Massiah,[59] "my friend," as executor; Massiah was apparently also in charge of Monsanto's mother's estate.

Witnesses: David Aboab and Benjamin D. Defonseca[60] (the latter signing with a mark)

Entered by David Aboab "of the Hebrew nation," March 13, 1734.

ISAAC FRANCO,[61] St. Michael, March 21, 1730. His father, Jacob, who died October 22, 1726, at the age of eighty,[62] had bequeathed him the income from £2,300 sterling invested in various securities; Isaac was given the right of disposition of the principal in his own will. "Whereas my said father in and by his said will gave an ample & large sum of money to my . . . son Jacob by means whereof I am the better enabled to provide for [my] . . . son Moses.[63] Therefore I give and bequeath to my son Jacob Franco three hundred pounds sterling money of Great Britain out of this said sum of two thousand three hundred pounds so left me to be disposed of as aforesaid. Item I give and bequeath to my said son Moses Franco his Executors and administrators the remaining sum of two thousand pounds sterling . . ." Moses is to be supported and educated from the proceeds until he reaches the age of twenty-one. Isaac's wife, Esther,[64] is to be executrix of the will, guardian of Moses, and residuary legatee. Isaac hopes that "my friends Elias Valverde & David Gomes merchants[65] to be assisting to my said wife with their advice and council as often as occasion requires."

Witnesses: two non-Jews, one of whom enters the document August 12, 1731.

IV

These wills offer some interesting data about the lives of early Jews in Barbados. One of the most obvious concerns details of the ownership of slaves by the Barbadian Jews. According to Samuel's reading of the census of St. Pete's Parish (Speightstown) in 1679, all fifteen of the listed Jewish households included slaves (to the number of fifty-three);[66] the census of St. Michael's Parish (Bridgetown) in 1680 lists fifty-four Jewish households, of which only five are without slaves, the Jewish-owned slaves totaling 163.[67] Here, however, we find only thirty-two of the fifty-seven testators referring to slaves, twenty-seven of them disposing of 115 individual slaves, five simply mentioning "slaves" in the plural without specific enumeration or names. Of the several testators who instructed their executors to invest funds for the benefit of heirs, only Elias Valverde suggested that funds "be laydout in purchasing Negroes for them or put out at Interest or otherwise Employed for their best advantage . . ."[68] Five of the testators made provision for the manumission of slaves. Moseh Hamis (Gago) specified that It is my last wish that our slave named Consciencia continue serving my said Wife all her life, & if she serves her faithfully, & with love and due respect as if I had been living, I desire & direct that on the death of my said wife she shall become free, without any person or persons heirs of myself or my wife, having the right to keep her captive; this being a reward for her good service to me, as I hope to my wife."[69] Jacob Defonseca Meza freed "a certain Molatto woman Isabella" at the time he made an oral last testament;[70] Joyce de Medina, as noted above, freed two slaves and gave each of them forty shillings; David Baruh Louzada, as reported in this paper, gave her freedom to "my Negro woman Muiga for the good services she hath done me" and granted her five pounds. Aaron Navarro had apparently been engaged in a dispute about the ownership of two slaves for whose freedom he wished to make conditional provision: "I say that Entitta & her daughter Hannah are mine, being the daughter grand-daughter of my slave (negress) Maria Arda; if they wish to free themselves, they can come to an arrangement with my wife, & no one may prevent or contradict them; this is my order & desire."[71] It may well be that other Jewish owners of slaves freed them quite aside from testamentary documents, but such information seems to be unavailable,[72] and these may therefore be the only shreds of evidence we can obtain about the willingness of Jewish slave-owners to break the chains of servitude of the Blacks who worked for them.

Another interesting theme which is revealed by these wills is the extensive geographical distribution of relatives of families dwelling in Barbados. London leads other localities; eleven wills refer to relations there. Amsterdam is a close second: seven testators mention members of families in that Jewish center. Scattered families are elsewhere: three wills mention Curaçao, two Jamaica, two Surinam, and one New York City.

Almost twenty of the wills include a provision relating to the Jewish religion (other than instructions in regard to burial). Six of the decedents gave instructions concerning the recitation of the *Kaddish* memorial prayer after their death; four made bequests to the Jewish poor—and in addition David Baruh Louzada provided that the residue of his estate (if any) be "distributed to and amongst such poor persons of the Hebrew Nation here, as to my said Executors or either of them shall think fit." Five of the subjects bequeathed a Torah scroll (or that part of one which they owned) and its ornaments to relatives. One of them (Daniel Ulloa) left to his son (Isaac) "all that third part I have in the Synagogue in Speightstown;" the owner of another third was Joseph Mendes who bequeathed "my 3rd part which I have in the holy Synagogue called *Snead* [*Semah*] *David* consecrated to the Poor."[73] Abraham Baruch Henriques left to the Congregation Nidhe Israel of Bridgetown a twelve-branched and a six-branched candelabrum on which the name and death-day of the donor were to be inscribed; he had already obtained permission from the trustees of the synagogue for his heirs to supply the candles for the *menorot* if they so desired.[74] One of the testators appointed a *hazan* (minister) as an executor, another named a *hazan* as trustee of the estate, and a third bequeathed sums of money to the *haham* (rabbi), the *hazan*, and the *samas* (sexton). Four left comparatively small sums to the Bridgetown congregation, but Abraham Nunez bequeathed the ultimate residue of his large estate to the trustees of the London Sephardic congregation for "marriage portions of poor female orphans" in case his line failed, in addition to specific sums to that congregation and its fund for Jewish orphans as well as to the congregation in Bridgetown.[75] Altogether these bequests represent significant evidences of loyalty to their faith on the part of these Jewish inhabitants of Barbados whose Bridgetown synagogue had been named "The Scattered of Israel" because they were so conscious of the destiny which had driven their people to this little island so far from the Iberian Peninsula where their families had originated.

NOTES

1. A special word of thanks to Malcolm H. Stern, the distinguished Jewish genealogist, for his diligence and meticulosity in reviewing every name in this paper and for making a host of suggestions which are embodied in the reference notes.
2. *WSS*, 55, 57; witnessed will of Joseph Mendes, 1700, 1707.
3. That Daniel named his first son David suggests that Daniel was the son of Ribca, wife of David Ulloa (d. April 10, 1709), whose epitaph is in *WSS*, 105. *WSS*, 30, identifies David and Rebecca, with an infant son, Isaac, as fugitives from the Inquisition living in Pernambuco in 1647. David is in a census list in Speightstown in 1679, *WSS*, 51.
4. Stern suggests that she was probably the "Sarah Decasta" in the list of Jewish names culled by E. M. Shilstone from *A Census of the Island of Barbados . . . Taken in the months of October and November Anno Domini 1715* (typescript list in American Jewish Archives, copy in Stern's possession) = *1715C* henceforth. The entire census, also without slave data, is in *Barbados Museum and Historical Society Journal IV*, No. 2 (February 1937) through IX, No. 3 (May 1942).
5. Benjamin is mentioned in the will of his father, Ishak, written August 24, 1698, proved June 20, 1711. Benjamin and his brother, Jacob, were their father's heirs, urged to be "good and God-fearing sons . . . observant of His precepts and keep from evil ways . . ." *WSS*, 54. Benjamin's mother was the Ribca Letob who died on May 27, 1703, *WSS*, 105. A census of the Jews in Martinique in the American Jewish Archives refers to Benjamin as nine months old in 1683 in the family of Isaac and Rica Le Tob (reference from Stern).
6. Jacob is mentioned in Ishak's will as then being ill, but also as requiring pardon "for the great trouble he has caused me."
7. Recipient of a £25 bequest in the will of Mathias Dellyon, September 25, 1724, to be given at the time of her marriage, *WSS*, 60.
8. Despite the order of names, which might indicate that this is a girl, Stern thinks that this is probably Jeosuah, whose daughter, Lea, was married in Curaçao in 1754 (Isaac S. and Suzanne A. Emmanuel, *History of the Jews of the Netherlands Antilles* [Cincinnati, 1970], I, 177).
9. Joyce was probably the widow of Jacob de Medina, whose will dated June 24, 1724, was proved two days later, *WSS*, 85. Samuel or his copyist misread her name to be "Simtia," but it is now obvious that it was Simha, which is the Hebrew for "Joy" or "Rejoicing."
10. This is Lunah, the wife of Ishak de la Penha, who died in 1740, *EMS*, 32.
11. Aaron Hisquiau Pereira died January 29, 1741, *EMS*, 66. *WSS*, 83, notes his witnessing a will in 1713. Pereira's own will is below.
12. Son of David Castello, whose will was proved February 5, 1711; the mother's name was Rebecca, *WSS*, 82. Mozes and his sister Hannah were to share the income due on one-third of a house in Amsterdam, as well as that part of the house itself which the father owned in partnership with his sisters. He died the

316

day after he wrote his will, named on his tombstone as Moses Haim Nunes Castello, age thirty-three years and four months; his wife Judith/Jeudith died September 23, 1759, at the age of sixty-four, *EMS*, 42.

13. Ephraim, referred to in David's will, is mentioned as the father of Sarah, who will receive £100 from the estate of Morducay Burgos, *WSS*, 88.

14. Probably the David Nunes Castello who died January 6, 1775, at the age of forty-eight, *EMS*, 110–11. This would mean he was not even three when his father died.

15. Massiah must be the man identified in n. 48 infra, forty-one years old in *1715C*. Nunez may have been the son of Abraham Newnes (who is listed as fourteen years old in *1715C*); an infant child of Benjamin and Ester Nunes died in 1749, *EMS*, 40.

16. In view of the reference to debts in Nevis, Stern offers the suggestion that she may have been the widow of Hananiah Arrobas who died January 25, 1729/30, in Nevis, where the family had been in residence apparently since 1707/8: Stern, "A Successful Caribbean Restoration: The Nevis Story," *American Jewish Historical Quarterly*, LXI (1971), 22, 28, 32. The husband may have been a son or other relation of Moses and Rachel (Pachecho) Arrobus at whose home Jacob Pachecho died in 1682, *WSS*, 71.

17. Elias Valverde (b. 1691) died in New York, 1739, *WSS*, 88–90; David (b. 1685) was Elias's brother, although Elias also had a son, David, probably too young to be meant here—the brother David is referred to in Eleazer's will, *WSS*, 85; Moses Nunes was a son-in-law of Jacob Valverde—see Moses Valverde's will, infra. Jacob Dias Carvallo cannot be identified. As to the witnesses, there were three cousins named Abraham Valverde; see Eleazer Valverde's will, *WSS*, 85. David Aboab is in *1715C*, thirty-eight years old, with wife of thirty-two. He may be the David Aboab Furtado who died June 27, 1742, *EMS*, 41. The wife, Ester, died September 24, 1728, but the data in *EMS*, 41, lists her age as thirty-three.

18. Moses (who d. April 25, 1739, age twenty-two years and four months, *EMS*, 64–65) is mentioned in his father Jacob's will (dated April 19, 1725), *WSS*, 60–61, as the recipient of three slaves, including "the negroe boy call'd Purim." Brothers Isaac, David, Aaron, and Abraham are also mentioned in the father's will, but the marriage of two of Moses' numerous sisters to Abraham and Moses Nunes must have taken place after the father's will was written. Jacob left nothing to grandchildren, so there probably were none at that time.

19. This may be the "charitable Sra. Sarah Da Costa de Andrade" who died November 23, 1752, at the age of fifty-six, *EMS*, 139. Stern thinks she may be the "Sarah Decasta" discussed in n. 4 supra. One wonders if she were some relative of the *Hazan* David Da Costa De Andrade, whose will is *infra*.

20. This must be Moses' uncle, David Valverde the elder, but Abraham Gomes cannot be identified with any certainty.

21. Solomon was the son of Daniel Ulloa (supra, will dated November 23, 1713) and Ester (who d. December 26, 1743, *EMS*, 74, which gives her husband's name as Daniel Haim Villao/Vlloa). *EMS* gives Daniel's date of death as 16 Tebet 5474 (January 3, 1713/14). *WSS*, 55, 57, has Daniel witnessing wills in 1700, 1707. The witness, Moses Mendes, is unidentifiable.

22. *EMS*, 35–36, records him as *Hazan* David Hizekiah Da Costa De Andrade, "Reader to this Congregation of Bridgetown 26 Years," who died April 13, 1740, at the age of sixty-three years and three months. The name is spelled three ways in the same document: De'Andrade, D'Andrade, Deandrade. In *1715C* he is listed as "Mr. David Decasla & wife and daughter & 1 apprentis," respectively aged thirty-nine, eighteen, three, and fifteen.

23. Because of the lack of punctuation, it is difficult to count the sons, for one or more may have had two names. But if not, the *Hazan* had fathered seven sons. Only Abraham is recorded in *EMS,* 163–4, dying on January 2, 1783, at the age of sixty-six. A *Hazan* Daniel Da Costa De Andrade is listed in *EMS,* 173, as dead June 1, 1802, at the age of forty-five. Was this a grandson of David?

24. Called "Angel De Costa wife of David De Costa" in the will of her uncle, Morducay Burgos, *WSS,* 88; she is called on her tombstone "Charitable & Pious Anjelah Da Costa de Andrade late wife of David His Da Costa de Andrade," who died April 18, 1748 (note error in date in *EMS,* 5) at the age of fifty years and six months.

25. Jacob Massiah may also have been a relative. A Jacob Messiah, merchant in London, also appears in the will of Morducay Burgos, *WSS,* 88. Deporto is unknown, but Abinum is undoubtedly the Haim Abinum de Lima of Nevis, whose wills (written June 27, 1765 and December 2, 1765), probated in London, December 12, 1766, refer to Sarah de Elias Burgos and David de Abraham de Piza as Barbadian relatives (Stern, "Some Notes on the Jews of Nevis," *American Jewish Archives* X [1958], 159).

26. Since the testator signs himself "David B. Louzada Senior," this must be to distinguish him from David Baruch Louzada, son of Simon, referred to in the will of Morducay Burgos, 1736, *WSS,* 88. The younger David seems to be the "Merchant and Several Years Reader of Their Synagogue," who died November 25, 1759, age forty-seven years and nine months, *EMS,* 134–35. The elder David must be the son of Aron who died October 10, 1695, *EMS,* 10, whose will is given *WSS,* 76–77, which also includes the birth records of children, including our David (Senior), born January 4, 1676/7. The mother was Rachell Baruh Louzada, who died November 2, 1703, *EMS,* 10–11, and whose will is in *WSS,* 80–81.

27. Stern suggests that he is probably Elisha Aboab Cardozo, a plantation owner in Curaçao in 1731 (Emmanuel, *Netherlands Antilles,* II, 641).

28. Solomon (Selomoh) is referred to in the mother's will, and his birth is listed in his father's record of family events. He must be the Solomon Raphael Baruh Louzado who died November 10, 1743, at the age of sixty-five, *EMS,* 38. Jeremiah is the man "Universally known to be Religious & Honest a loving Husband and a tender Parent [who] departed this Life the . . . 6th of Janry 1793 in the 88 Year of his Age," *EMS,* 144–45.

29. Rebecca and Rachael do not seem to fit into any of the Delyon/Dellyon/De Leon families in *WSS* or *EMS.*

30. Rachel, daughter of David Burgos, is the recipient of £35 of her father's debt to the testator in the will of Abraham Nunez, 1735, *WSS,* 61–63, who also asks his executors not to press Burgos too hard.

31. Unidentifiable. But these new names should be a challenge to genealogists of Sephardi Caribbeana.

32. Stern thinks that this is probably the Ishak, son of Aharon Vas Faro, who was married in Surinam to Jeudith, daughter of Samuel Haim Cohen Nassy on August 28, 1743: P. A. Hilfman, "Notes on the History of the Jews in Surinam," *Publications of the American Jewish Historical Society* 18 (1909), 207.

33. Jacob Frois must be the son of Raquel Nunez Carvallo, mentioned in her will, 1718, *WSS,* 84. Jacob died January 8, 1757, *EMS,* 128. Nothing further is known of the daughters.

34. Widow and daughter of Benjamin Gabay Letob, supra.

35. Pereira's will follows.

36. Aaron Hisquiau Pereira, died January 29, 1740/1, *EMS,* 65–66. Pereira and his brother witnessed the will of Isaac Henriques Mellado, 1713, *WSS,* 83.

37. In the will of Joyce De Medina, supra, the name is given as Reyna.

38. Sarah died February 22, 1774, at the age of thirty-six years and four months. The English inscription on her tombstone calls her Sarah Pereira Henriques; the Hebrew refers to her as the daughter of Aaron Pereira Henriques, *EMS,* 145–46. Abigail Henriques/Henriquez died on June 14, 1760. There seems to be no reference to Rachael.

39. Moses Nunes must be the person referred to in n. 17 supra, the son-in-law of Jacob Valverde. See Moses Valverde's will, supra. Morducay Nunez appears to be the son mentioned so frequently in the will of Abraham Nunez, 1735, *WSS,* 61–63.

40. *Haham* Abraham Gabay Izidro was born in Portugal or Spain about 1680, fled from the Inquisition about 1720/1721, was circumcized in London August 20, 1721, then moved on to Amsterdam where he studied under Isaac Abendana de Brito and David Israel Athias. A sermon which he preached in Amsterdam in 1724 was printed in Spanish. Some time subsequently he went to Surinam where he served as *Haham* and *Ab-Bet-Din.* His will, which was dated July 20, 1736, still describes him as being "of the Jewish nation in Surinam." Our reference of 1740 is the earliest known date placing him in Barbados, but he was probably there some time earlier to become Pereira's "good friend." According to Cardozo de Bethencourt, "Notes on the Spanish and Portuguese Jews . . . during the Seventeenth and Eighteenth Centuries," *Publications of the American Jewish Historical Society* 29 (1925), 13, Izidro was still in Barbados in 1753. He must have left soon afterwards, for he died in London on the day of Rosh Hashanah, or a day later, 1755. Three years later, his widow had printed in Amsterdam a poetical version by Izidro of the 613 precepts according to Maimonides, entitled *Yad Avraham* ("The Hand of Abraham"), the title page of which appears from the description in M. Kayserling, *Biblioteca Española-Portugueza-Judaica* (Strasbourg, 1890), 48, to refer to Izidro as Surinamese. Much new material about Izidro has been provided in *Transactions of the Jewish Historical Society of England,* XXIV (1975), 211–213, "The Remarkable Career of Haham Abraham Gabay Yzidro," by the late Cecil Roth, perhaps that distinguished historian's last published work.

41. These were selected from lists assembled and loaned to me by Mrs. Robert (Florence) Abrahams and Stern, to both of whom I am deeply grateful. Despite their names, John Bueno (will written May 7, 1691, proved October 31, 1701) and Nathaniel Brandon (will written June 8, 1738, proved July 17, 1740), whose names were also culled, were not Jewish.

42. Rahel was the widow of Joseph Mendes (*WSS,* 54–57, written February 17, 1700, codicils February 18, 1700 and July 17, 1707, proved in London July 21, 1712, but according to Rahel's will, Joseph had died more than a year previously).

43. Stern suggests that she was the wife of Simon/Simeon Massiah described in n. 48 infra.

44. Daniel had witnessed Joseph Mendes's will, see n. 2 supra; see also Daniel's own will, proved January 14, 1713/14, supra.

45. Joseph had mentioned the names of the parents in his will, "Isaac and my sister Esther Vaz . . . "

46. Manuel Namias's will, written November 30, 1713, and proved April 20, 1714, is in *WSS,* 93. Lunah, according to the will, was his only child. Namias' parents (David and Luna according to *WSS*) are called David and Luna Nahamias in *EMS,* 7.

47. Rebecca was the widow of David Castello (*WSS,* 82); Hannah was unmarried when David died, another daughter (Judith) being married to Moses Mendez.

But by 1739 Hannah was married to Moses Francis. See infra, n. 51.

48. Simon (or Simeon) Massiah was urged in Joseph's will "to be careful of my business & diligent in getting in my debts & to be aiding & assisting my ex'ers." In the first codicil, Simon was asked "to take care of my Books and Accounts and to assist my Wife in all that he can and that he shall have the same salary going on untill my Wife shall leave of Trade or shall be minded to goe for London." Simon was still the family confidante in 1739, producing the will which he had kept secret until then. This may be the Simon who died January 15, 1747, at the age of seventy-three (*EMS*, 36). It is unfortunate that N. Darnell Davis' "Notes from Wills of the Family of Massiah of Barbados," *Publications of the American Jewish Historical Society* 22 (1914), 178–80, does not go back far enough to give us an idea of this Simon's relationship to other members of the Massiah family.

49. Abraham and the Benjamin mentioned below were Joseph's nephews, sons of his brother Menasseh, married to Joseph and Rahel's daughters Sarah and Lunah respectively (*WSS*, 57). They were, then, both nephews and sons-in-law, but referred to as sons! Menasseh's will (his last name is spelled Mendez), is in *WSS*, 57–58.

50. Judith, wife of Moses Mendez, was the daughter of David and Rebecca Castello (*WSS*, 82). Rebecca, supra, was Rahel's sister. Judith and Moses were another pair of marrying cousins, a frequent practice among Sephardim eager to prevent the dissipation of assets which were their only claim to security and mobility.

51. Francis may be derived from the name Bueno Frances or be an error for one of the many Francia variants.

52. This is the Daniel who is the first entry in the Davis article referred to in n. 48 supra, born in 1677, died August 26, 1742.

53. Stern identifies her for me as the widow of Isaac Rodrigues Marques (d. in New York City, 1707), who subsequently married Moses Cohen Peixotto (Peyxotto on the tombstone of his first wife, Debora Sarah Cahanet, of 1709 [*EMS*, 72]). Marques' will is in Leo Hershkowitz, *Wills of Early New York Jews (1704–1799)* (New York, 1967), 8–10.

54. Stern believes that Mordecai Gomez was the husband of Rachel's daughter by her first marriage, Esther Rodriques Marques.

55. Probably Aaron Baruh Louzada, who died March 24, 1768, almost sixty-five years old (*EMS*, 7–8).

56. Solomon Baruh Louzada died in 1747 (*EMS*, 173).

57. Probably sons of the Daniel Massiah who died in 1742 (David, "Family of Massiah," 178), called "junr." to distinguish them from such older relatives of the same name as the Simon or Simeon referred to in n. 48 supra.

58. Neither *EMS* nor *WSS* includes any references to Jacob, Abraham, Ishak, or Rachel. But a Rebecca Monsanto received a bequest from her brother, Moses Henriques Lopes, in his will, *WSS*, 87, proved October 26, 1732. Rebecca and Rachel are not identified by relationship in this Monsanto will; it may be that they were the wives of Jacob's deceased sons.

59. This must be the Simon/Simeon of n. 48 supra.

60. Aboab is probably the David Aboab Furtado of n. 17 supra. The second witness may be the Benjamin da Fonseca who died in August, 1731, and whose tombstone is partly incomplete, *EMS*, 33.

61. His full name was Isaac Franco Nunes, *WSS*, 85–87, wills of his father, Jacob, dated October 20, 1724, and brother Moses, dated April 16, 1730.

62. *EMS*, 16.

63. Grandfather Jacob left grandson Jacob half of the income from £3,100 and title to four slaves. Grandson Moses is not mentioned in Jacob's will.
64. Probably the Ester Franco Nunes who died February 19, 1759, at the age of seventy-five, *EMS*, 146–47.
65. Elias Valverde died in New York City, 1739; his will is in *WSS*, 88–90. David Gomes cannot be identified.
66. *WSS*, 51.
67. *WSS*, 63–65. Unfortunately, *1715C* does not include data about slave ownership.
68. *WSS*, 89. Moseh Hamis (Gago) did include a provision for the payment of two thousand pounds of Muscovado sugar to one or another member of the Massiah family "to help in the purchase of a young negress" (*WSS*, 72).
69. *WSS*, 72.
70. *WSS*, 80.
71. *WSS*, 73.
72. M. J. Chandler, *A Guide to Records in Barbados* (Oxford, 1965), 34, lists manumission books only for 1830 and 1832–34.
73. *WSS*, 57.
74. *WSS*, 80.
75. *WSS*, 62–63.

JULIUS ECKMAN AND THE
WEEKLY GLEANER: THE JEWISH PRESS
IN THE PIONEER AMERICAN WEST

By

ROBERT E. LEVINSON

San José State University

Julius Eckman arrived in San Francisco July 1, 1854. From that date until his death twenty years later, July 6, 1874, he was one of the most influential leaders of the Jewish community in the American West. Except for brief intervals during which he pursued a rabbinical career in Portland,[1] Eckman was to dominate the field of Jewish education in San Francisco and play a leading role in the development of a well-established Jewish literary community.

Only a little is known about Eckman's background, and still less known are the reasons that attracted him to California. He was born in Rawicz, in the Duchy of Posen, in 1805. He lived in London three years, where he was a merchant, and then went to Berlin, where he studied classics at the University of Berlin and received a Doctor of Philosophy degree there and also rabbinic ordination from Leopold Zunz, one of the founders of the *Wissenschaft des Judentums* and a leading intellectual in the Berlin Jewish community.[2]

According to Jacob Voorsanger, one of Eckman's biographers,

> ... Eckman was urged by his Berlin friends to avail himself of his masterful knowledge of . . . [English] to become one of the leaders of Jewish thought in America. There were, at that time, perhaps but half a dozen Rabbis in the United States who could competently address their congregations in the language of the country. ... he determined to come to the United States. He believed he could do some good. . . .[3]

But Eckman was not well suited for the life of a pulpit rabbi in America. From his arrival in 1849, he served three congregations within a four-year period, in Richmond, Virginia, Charleston, South Carolina, and Mobile, Alabama, and during those years, the positive achievements that he wrought took place outside the synagogue.[4]

When he departed for San Francisco, it was probably with the knowledge that Congregation Emanu-El was actively seeking a spiritual leader.[5] San Francisco, during the years of the gold rush, was the largest city in the West. It grew overnight from village to metropolis as a result of being the port of entry to the mines. Tens of thousands of people, representing many nations, races, and religions, came to California in the belief they would profit from the gold discoveries. Many went into the interior, to be closer to the gold that was so great an attraction, but thousands also settled permanently in San Francisco, built homes, schools, stores, and wharves and established the city by the bay as a major trading and commercial center.

Scores of Jews were also attracted to San Francisco and the region of the great gold discoveries.[6] High Holiday services were conducted in San Francisco from September, 1849, and Jewish relief and benevolent societies were established soon after. By 1854 the two congregations that had blossomed from the High Holiday services of 1849 were both in the process of raising money to build their own synagogues. Eckman could not have timed his arrival in San Francisco any better. Congregation Emanu-El noted his appearance on the scene and invited him to officiate at the ceremony of laying the cornerstone for their synagogue. Eckman did so and soon found himself elected spiritual leader of the congregation and principal of its religious school. Serious friction developed in the congregation soon afterward, however, over his relationship with the congregational committee that passed on the qualifications of ritual slaughterers of meat. Because he believed his authority as rabbi was imperiled, he publicly disagreed with the role assumed by the committee, and his one-year contract as rabbi was not renewed. He thereupon left the congregation, and such was his popularity that the student body of his school followed him to new quarters.[7]

Apparently, the school did not take up all of Eckman's time and energy. Freed from the day-to-day responsibilities of the congregational rabbi, he soon resolved to establish a newspaper, *The Weekly Gleaner*. Although Jewish newspapers were being published in the East at that time,[8] Eckman recognized the need for a medium that would bring together the Jews and Jewish communities he soon found scattered as far asunder as Victoria, B.C., Panama and Fillmore City, Utah Territory,[9] as well as in San Francisco, and provide the Jews therein with another form of religious instruction and a method of communicating with one another.

In his first edition, January 16, 1857, Eckman promised his readers that, in future numbers, they could expect news items in seven areas: Biblical and Jewish Antiquities, Eastern Travels, Illustrations, Education, Juvenile Department, Domestic Economy, and General News Regarding our People and Interests. Eckman informed his readers that education was uppermost in his mind:

> We shall endeavor to render the *Gleaner* a medium for the free interchange of thought from whatever source it may emanate—and its columns will always be open for the temperate discussion of all questions connected either with our own or with the public well being. . . . We shall strive so to blend the useful with the agreeable in our columns, so that no one, whether Jew or Gentile, can rise from the perusal of its pages without feeling that he has been at once amused and instructed. . . .
>
> We thus send forth the *Gleaner* upon what we sincerely trust will prove a useful and blessed mission, and, however little temporary profit or advantage may accrue to us, we shall feel amply rewarded if in the end it shall be found to have advanced, however little, the cause of piety and the best interests of mankind upon earth.[10]

From the beginning, Eckman attempted to live up to all his promises, and week in and week out, he nearly succeeded. Volume 1, number 1 contained articles that described the tombs of the Patriarchs at Hebron, Jewish Negroes, current foreign news of Jewish interest, the first part of a lengthy essay, "Evidence of the Existence of God," suggestions for curing the croup, and local news as well.

Eckman must have planned carefully for his entrance into American Jewish journalism. He had circulated an announcement of his intentions,[11] and volume 1, number 1 (like all future editions, eight pages in length), contained almost one-half page of advertisements. Apparently, his initial work was well received. The following week, he addressed his readers: "To judge from the repeated demand for the *Gleaner* at our office, it appears that not one half the number of those who are desirous of its perusal, have as yet been supplied with copies." [12]

Under a column entitled "Opinions of the Press," Eckman then reprinted what seven other newspapers in San Francisco had said about the *Gleaner*. The opinions ranged from ". . . a beautiful sheet . . . a neat typographical appearance . . . filled with interesting original matter . . ." in the *San Francisco Herald*, to the opinion of the *Phoenix*: "Taking this number as indicative of what may be expected hereafter, we incline to the opinion that this will prove to be the most instructive and interesting religious paper in the State." [13]

First and foremost, however, as the voice of the Jewish religious community, Eckman saw to it that the *weekly* Gleaner became his voice and spoke for the furtherance of Jewish education and the maintenance of rabbinic authority. As early as the first edition, Eckman became involved in a disagreement with his short-lived rival, the *Voice of Israel*, over the issue of divorce. The editor of the *Voice of Israel* wrote that so few Jewish divorces had occurred in California because Jews followed the teaching, "Those whom God has united, let no man put asunder." Eckman pointed out to the *Voice of Israel* that the quotation was not of Jewish, but of Christian origin,[14] and that divorce was, in fact, accepted in the Jewish tradition. Additionally, from the advertisements, both paid and gratis, that appeared in the *Gleaner* from its first edition, Eckman informed his readers in San Francisco and all over the West of the presence of synagogues and relief and benevolent societies, cemeteries, Hebrew schools, book stores, the availability of kosher meat and other foods throughout the year and especially at Passover, and the presence of Jewish religious functionaries.[15]

Moreover, he saw to it that his reading audience was kept well informed of events concerning Jews and Jewish communities all over the world. This was especially important for Jews who lived in remote western America, because all of them were recent immigrants themselves and wanted news from their home communities. Such an offering, for example, was the news column "Jewish Intelligence," which appeared April 22, 1859, and contained items from Dayton, Ohio, Hungary, Florence, London, Cochin, Bavaria, Prussia, Russia, Austria, Kai-Fung-Foo in China, the Ionian Islands, New York, Posen, Vienna, Paris, and Sardinia.[16] In addition, Eckman kept his readers informed of current events, such as attempts by organizations to rebuild the Temple in Jerusalem; the news of the death of a Hasidic rabbi in Kracow; and his opinions of the differences between Orthodox and Reform Judaism, which, he said, were based upon geographical determinism.[17]

Eckman performed best of all in the *Gleaner* when he exposed manifestations of anti-Jewish prejudice all over the world and when he raised funds on behalf of Jews in need, wherever they might be. He sprang into action when he received the news that young Edgar Mortara of Bologna, Italy, had been seized by the police and separated from his family. It seems that when Edgar was an infant, he had fallen ill and been secretly baptized by his family's serving girl. Church authorities eventually learned what she had done and consented to the abduction. The Jewish world reacted swiftly to the Mortara affair. Eckman printed news items and editorials on the subject in at least twenty-four different editions of the *Gleaner* between October 29, 1858, and January 6, 1860[18] which noted other such occurrences that had taken place in Prussia, St. Louis, Missouri, Genoa, and Naples.[19] These events stirred up a great deal of anti-Catholic animosity and added to the prejudice against Catholics that was part of the Know-Nothing phenomenon of the 1850s in American political life. Eckman, too, leaped onto the anti-Catholic bandwagon for a while with articles which traced the history of the Jews of Europe under Catholic rule or described forced baptisms in Catholic hospitals as ". . . sufficient to give such a shock to the nervous system and mental faculties, as to produce burning fever, delirium, insanity, and death." [20]

More effective, however, was Eckman's call for a mass meeting in San Francisco to declare the community's outrage at the abduction. He reported the proceedings of the meeting in the *Gleaner,* and they were subsequently republished.[21] Eckman also noted correspondence on the subject with the United States Department of State, but perhaps the most long-lasting effect of these events came from a suggestion by Eckman and others for ". . . a centralization of all Jewish influence, that Israel may form a Unity, regardless of diversity of opinion about *our* Canon Law, and the practice of ceremonies, whatever they may be. . ."[22]

While the Mortara affair was preeminent in Eckman's columns, he did not neglect Jews elsewhere in the world. The *Gleaner* pointed out how Jews in Persia were being persecuted, where funds raised for the benefit of poor Jews in Jerusalem ought to be sent, and how progress was being made, through quiet efforts, to remove some anti-Jewish disabilities in certain cantons of Switzerland.[23]

Eckman also reported local and national news of Jewish interest to his readers. He could always be counted on to share some pieces of information with his subscribers that made them secure in the knowledge that Jewish life in America was growing stronger all the time. His subject matter ranged from a list of rabbis in the United States to a list of Jewish office-holders to a consideration of the advancements made by Jews in society in the previous century.[24]

Since the *Gleaner* was the West's only Jewish newspaper for much of its existence, it was natural that western Jewish news should predominate in its columns. Eckman paid a great deal of attention to the local scene. Before the days of congregational bulletins and community-supported periodicals, privately owned newspapers like the *Gleaner* were the main source of information for activities in the Jewish community. Much is known about the early days of Jewish life in San Francisco and the West from this single source, because the establishment of a Jewish community or a mining-camp congregation in some remote location was important news to Eckman, and he was lavish in granting space to publicize such events. The sphere of Eckman's influence was thus very great. It was almost as if Eckman was the rabbi in absentia of every newly organized western Jewish community that he greeted. He preferred that Jewish communities be formed on the basis of congregational, rather than philanthropic, activity,[52] and he attempted to serve these microscopic outposts of Jewish life as personally as he could. Occasionally, he travelled to a distant city to minister personally to the Jewish community there,[26] but his main service to them was in publishing their news reports about themselves[27] and encouraging their attempts to remain active members of the Jewish people regardless of how far removed from organized community life they found themselves. He served as a one-man placement bureau and printed advertisements from Jewish communities in search of spiritual leaders together with his own comments on the present state of those communities.[28] He also fulfilled one of the traditional roles of the rabbi by replying in the columns of the *Gleanor* to questions on religious procedure which came from distant communities where no rabbi resided.[29]

First and foremost, Eckman published news of the San Francisco Jewish community, where most of his subscribers lived. In this respect, the *Gleanor* was more than an advance publicity sheet, because Eckman also reported on events after they took place. Local organizations and congregations used the *Gleaner* extensively to publicize their activities, either through advertisements or letters to the editor.

Some occurrences within the Jewish community of San Francisco caused a great deal of controversy that may have been transitory but nevertheless reached the *Gleaner*. In 1858 a temporary congregation for the High Holidays was established by some of the members of a local benevolent society, the Hebrath Bickur Holim Ukdoshah. Beneath the advertisement for these services, the president of the society, L. King, stated, in part:

> . . . I hereby declare the proceedings "illegal", ... There are in this city three Synagogues with ample room (and to spare) for all those wishing to attend, and no doubt the cause of Israel would be benefitted by unanimonsly [sic] supporting them.[30]

The following year, when another temporary congregation conducted its services in Apollo Hall, after advertising the event, apparently on posters around town, an irate subscriber noted that he had seen the advertisement ". . . in political papers . . . bar-rooms and the houses of ill-fame, [and it] is more than I can bear. . . ." [31]

What was most characteristic about Eckman was his unwillingness to back away from a dispute. Whenever there was a difference of opinion over some fine point of Jewish law or ritual procedure, or if the political rights of Jews anywhere were being attacked, Eckman used all the influence he could muster to make his opinions heard. Often the tone of Eckman's editorials, always well written and easy to read and understand, was to the point and intemperate.

The controversy concerning the ritual slaughterers of San Francisco continued into 1857 when R. Jacobson advertised that rabbis in Germany and England had approved his qualifications. Not only, announced Jacobson, was he qualified to function as a *shohet,* but the slaughterer approved by Eckman, a Mr. Goldsmith, was not.[32] Eckman could not resist entering the fray, since his reputation as a rabbi was at stake. His comments were typical of the forthrightness that was part of his personality through the entire life of the *Gleaner.*

> . . . as we wish to close, at once, the Shochtim question, for which in this State, but very, very few care, our advertiser, as a Shochat, ought to have known that certificates, of which the latest given by an authorized rabbi, is dated seven years back, are of no value in any other country, much less in the United States. As for a testimonial of a rabbi in London, dated so far back, the Right Reverend Alexander, Bishop of the Protestant Episcopal church of Jerusalem, has had such from a rabbi in London, less superanuated, and surely, little as is cared here about Shochtim and their Shechitah, the certificate could not even make the bishop of the Protestant Episcopate of Jerusalem Shochet of the indifferent city of San Francisco.[33]

It was evident that Eckman was a man of principle who would not back away from an argument easily and who, moreover, at the helm of the only Jewish newspaper within 2,500 miles, commanded a great deal of respect for his learning and for not equivocating when confronted by an issue. He became involved in many major controversies, both religious and secular, and he never shrank from taking a side. He opposed the teaching of religion in public schools, antedating the arguments heard in our own time:

> . . . books should be used which confine themselves to facts, simple narration, or, at most, a general moral reflection, without permitting the author to convey, in a covert manner, his own peculiar ideas, or those of his sect or political party, in the shape of a school geography, or history, or grammar, or spelling-book.
>
> It is possible to do all this; and, being possible, it should by all means be done. And in accomplishing this much, the republic has done all in its legitimate province for the scientific and moral progress of the entire community. It has nothing to do with their several religious opinions, and the duties which every one for himself considers obligatory; consequently it cannot assume any charge of religious training in any manner or quantity. The Bible even has no proper place in the public school under this aspect; and no prayer, except a mere acknowledgement of a superintending Providence, and an invocation of His name in the most general terms, should be enforced, nor should the scholars be even compelled to listen to any which has its origin in the principles of any sect or class.[34]

He also took a strong stand against any public law that recognized Christianity, such as the Sunday closing law, which was ruled unconstitutional by the Supreme Court of California.[35] During the outpouring of patriotism in the early years of the Civil War, Eckman dared to challenge convention and editorialized against displaying national flags in churches and synagogues.

> In the Union, church and State are separate. The Synagogue, mindful of this separation, maintains that dignified position to the State, which the State maintains towards the Synagogue or church. . . .
>
> Under all these circumstances any demonstration of a continuance of loyalty would be uncalled for, undignified, and would render her suspicious. A faithful, sensible wife will never brook the indignity of bearing the mark "faithful" as a sign on her forehead: if she did, we would question her sense, or her honesty. To hoist any sign of a continuance of

faithfulness of the Synagogue to the State, would be as much as a woman calling from the top of the house, "Look up at me, and behold, I have not divorced my husband."[36]

It was his role as spiritual adviser to the Jewish community of the entire North American West that made Eckman unique in this vast region. Although he was a moderate Reformer, he accepted as valid many forms of traditional Judaism. What Eckman probably preferred was for Jews to obtain as much knowledge of Judaism as possible and then recognize the value of maintaining traditional forms of ritual practice while, at the same time, living and participating in a modern, secular world.

Eckman always stressed the importance of Jewish education, and news items concerning his school appeared regularly in the *Gleaner*. For the adults in the community, the *Gleaner* served as a refresher course in Jewish learning. Every edition was devoted, in one way or another, to Jewish education, whether it was simply a description of Jewish life elsewhere or Eckman's preaching on a return to traditional practices. He had lavish praise for Rabbi David Einhorn of Baltimore, who reported that forty members of his congregation there had resolved to close their businesses on the Sabbath, and he reminded his readers that the Sabbath had a twenty-four hour duration and ought to be observed together by the entire family.[37] He also stated that people have an obligation to affiliate with a congregation because "the body is able to do what individuals cannot do . . ."; and he maintained that the foundation of Jewish life was the family and the home.[38]

Eckman and many of his rabbinic colleagues in the United States had differing opinions over what constituted an acceptable standard of Jewish religious practice. To Eckman, certain reforms were quite valid, because customs and rituals never remained static but had undergone reforms in the past.[39] A knowledge of Hebrew and ceremonies was not all there was to Judaism.[40] Parents deserved to be rebuked for sending their children to Christian schools.[41]

A great part of Eckman's philosophy placed him in the traditional sphere of Judaism. He adamantly refused to change the Sabbath to Sunday,[42] and he printed a letter to the editor which complained of a recent sermon by Rabbi Elkan Cohn of Congregation Emanu-El that deprecated the wearing of phylacteries.[43] In answer to a question, Eckman said he preferred to retain the chant while reading the Torah rather than making a revolutionary change that would upset the peace of the congregation.[44] But he also stated: "If the greater, or even the smaller, number of a Congregation alter their views about certain matters of faith, it is better to change the Liturgy than to express what is not believed." [45]

He also rejected intermarriage,[46] and he called for some sort of ecclesiastical authority to recognize conversions.[47] He likewise favored continuing with the practice of divorces that conformed to rabbinic authority.[48] But he supported a reform in Jewish religious practice. Eckman saw nothing objectionable in certain changes, such as introducing an organ into the service[49] or officiating at a wedding without the traditional canopy over the bride and groom.[50] He also, apparently, had no objections to reforms in mourning customs and regulations, because he reprinted without adverse comment the reformed mourning customs of Dr. S. Deutsch of Congregation Keneseth Israel of Philadelphia.[51] Different points of view over worshipping with the head uncovered were also recognized, but Eckman did not take a side on this issue.[52] And, like many other rabbis of the time, he rejected the concept of perpetual mourning for the destruction of the Temple and Jerusalem:

> . . . how long is Jerusalem to be disgraced by a swarm of "anxious idle mourners" over what? Over the Temple? No, that is no more, and if it still existed, it never would be that built by human hands, it never would be the stone, wood and material that would justify such against the dispensation of God,—revolting protracted moan of eighteen hundred years —and as for its true object, as to the proper sanctuary, as a means of sanctification, what prevents them raising it every where, why mourn constantly over a ruin? why not make efforts to build it up a true temple, instead of cold stone and marble, let them build up one of warmly beating, living human hearts. . . . [53]

Eckman's own religious philosophy, as publicized through the *Gleaner,* was based on reason, not emotion. He wrote:

> What are the Principles of the Mosaic system? we would reply: Pure, rational Deism.—Were we asked: What is its Dogma and what are its mysteries? we would reply: it has neither Dogmas nor Mysteries.—its Moral Code is intelligible, plain common sense; the object of its ceremonies was either to impress the mind of him who performed them, and to operate upon his feelings. . . . [54]

Whatever Eckman's theological views were, however, they would not find an audience unless the *Gleaner* could continue meeting its publication deadlines and remain financially solvent. As was the case with many newspapers and periodicals of the period, the one problem that plagued Eckman more than any, during the life of the *Gleaner,* was that of financing. Whether it was a case of poor management or simply overextending himself, Eckman pleaded repeatedly with his readers to pay for their subscriptions. He rewarded those of his subscribers who paid by publishing their names and locations in the *Gleaner,* and this compilation gives us a good knowledge of how widespread Eckman's readers were, outside of San Francisco. In one particular edition, he acknowledged receipts from San Diego, Humboldt Bay, Olympia, and Michigan City; in another, he announced nine subscriptions received from Placerville, four from Mud Springs, and ten from Sacramento. On occasion, Eckman asked merchants in San Francisco to give him names of prospective subscribers from among their customers, and once he reported he had received good responses from Red Bluff, Eureka, Marysville, Wolseys Flat, Shasta, California, and Deer Creek, Oregon.[55]

Advertising, too, was very important in maintaining the *Gleaner.* The second edition contained almost twice the number of advertisements that the first edition had, and many members of the San Francisco Jewish merchant community purchased advertising space. By the fourteenth number, April 17, 1857, the type of advertisements changed from a preponderance of Jewish merchants to advertising one would expect to see in any newspaper, indicating the widespread popularity of the *Gleaner.* By August 28, 1857, advertisements were appearing from such diverse sources as a piano instructor, a chiropodist, shipping companies, a coal merchant, a paint shop, a distillery, and some banks, in addition to dry goods and the advertisements that typified the Jewish religious community: kosher butchers, circumcisers, and local Jewish benevolent organizations. The two and one-half pages of advertisements in the edition for June 12, 1857, grew to nearly four pages on June 26, and to more than five and one-half pages on October 12, 1860.

But even though the number of advertisements in the *Gleaner* kept increasing, Eckman always claimed he was in great financial difficulty, and he pleaded with his subscribers to keep the money coming in to support the paper. Apparently, the costs of maintaining his school were also greater than the amount of tuition money he was receiving.[56]

When the Fraser River gold discoveries occurred in 1858, Eckman's financial problems multiplied. By June 25, so many people had joined the rush for gold and depleted the population supporting the paper that

Eckman announced his intention of ceasing publication.[57] The next week, Eckman complained that he had not received any money to support the paper since May 4,[58] but he also stated his confidence in the future.

> By what we hear, there seems to be a disposition not to allow the publication to cease for want of support.
> We especially return our thanks to some Christian readers who kindly offer their readiness to assist.[59]

That the *Gleaner* missed the next four publication dates and resumed August 6, in an edition of smaller-sized pages, indicated the serious difficulties that gripped Eckman. But matters began to improve with the publication of a letter from a group that pledged to aid the paper. Within a week, the number of supporters increased from ten to twenty-six, and the *Gleaner* was saved.[60] From that time on, Eckman never lost the opportunity to request continued support and also to use the occasion as a recognition of his martyrdom for operating both his school and the *Gleaner* with very little financial backing. Perhaps Eckman was right to praise himself and his work. Probably no one else in San Francisco at that time labored as hard as he did for the advancement of Jewish education, the recognition of rabbinic authority, and the dissemination of Jewsh news. Taking a cue from the leading Jewish newspapers of the United States, which had praised him for his efforts,[61] he informed his readers of his importance to them:

> On the whole Pacific coast we have only four synagogues, open for *form* of worship once a week; and a fifth, three times a year. All these do not maintain the one ordained teacher who, since three years, honestly and conscientiously [*sic*] labors for them, because he was weighed in the scale of national hatred and prejudice—measured by the line of popular ignorance—and "found wanting"—not in honesty, integrity, or energy, nor in zeal and knowledge—not in self-denial and self sacrifice. No, he was found wanting in PLIANCY, WORLDLY POLICY, and HYPOCRICY [*sic*]—hence in POPULARITY. IF THERE WERE, OR ARE ANY OTHER WANTS, HE INVITES THOSE WHO KNOW OF THEM, (AND HE KEEPS THEM RESPONSIBLE FOR HIS MARTYRDOM, IN TIME AND ETERNITY, BEFORE GOD AND THE WORLD, BEFORE JEW AND GENTILE,) TO STATE THEM FAITHFULLY, AND HE WILL GIVE THEM ANY SPACE DEMANDED IN THIS, HIS ORGAN.[62]

Very little information on Eckman exists outside the pages of the *Gleaner*. Regrettably, this study must necessarily end with January 6,

1865, the date the last known edition of the newspaper was published. Our knowledge of early Jewish history in the West will be enhanced if more editions are discovered. On the other hand, such knowledge of the growth and development of the Jewish community in the West does not diminish, because others in San Francisco soon capitalized on the ground-work laid by Eckman and created their own newspapers.[63]

Eckman continued his many-faceted career after the demise of the *Gleaner*. During the last years of its publication, he served as rabbi of Congregation Beth Israel in Portland (1863–66), and the *Gleaner* bore the masthead of San Francisco and Portland, though it was printed in San Francisco.[64] Upon returning to San Francisco, he assumed the editor-ship of the *Hebrew Observer,* which, like the old *Gleaner,* published news of local importance but also described Jewish communities from Hokitika, New Zealand, to Hamilton, Nevada, and Yale, B.C., to Mazat-lán, Mexico. In 1869–72 he was back in Portland, where he served as the first rabbi of Congregation Ahavai Sholom,[65] and after he returned to San Francisco he continued with the *Hebrew Observer* until he died in 1874.

The full impact of Eckman's twenty years of service to the Jewish com-munity of the West is still not fully known or appreciated. The *Gleaner* enjoyed a wide circulation in the East as well as the West and was quoted in the columns of eastern Jewish newspapers.[66] It told Jews in the East that their coreligionists in the West were living in established Jew-ish communities, whether religious, social, or philanthropic, and that they could immigrate to the West and be assured of finding an organized Jewish life there. The *Gleaner* gave a sense of belonging to Jews who lived in scattered and isolated surroundings all over the West; and it also al-lowed Eckman, still one of the few ordained rabbis in the United States at the time, to offer his own views on the necessity of maintaining the Jewish religious tradition. If there was an ethnic Jewish con-sciousness in the West in the middle of the nineteenth century, especially in the smaller towns and villages, where there was only one, if any, Jewish institution, it was created by Eckman and the *Gleaner*. To a greater degree, the *Gleaner* influenced Jewish life in the metropoli-tan community of San Francisco as well. Without the *Gleaner,* instead of the Jewish congregations, synagogues, relief and benevolent societies, and cemeteries that sprang up all over the West, there would have been a lack of spiritual identity, increased assimilation, and the disappearance of Judaism and of committed Jews in the rural and suburban West. Attached as many of them were to small towns and cities, where they were dependent upon the local dominant economy for their income, Jewish merchant families wherever they were looked forward to receiving the *Gleaner,* kept in touch through it with their Rabbi Eckman in San Francisco, and maintained Jewish continuity with greater ease and confidence.

NOTES

1. Jacob Voorsanger, *The Chronicles of Emanu-El* . . . (San Francisco: George Spaulding and Co., 1900), p. 45; Julius J. Nodel, *The Ties Between: A History of Judaism on America's Last Frontier* (Portland: Temple Beth Israel, 1959), p. 22–23, 181.
2. Voorsanger, *op. cit.*, pp. 141–42.
3. *Ibid.*, p. 143.
4. Herbert T. Ezekiel and Gaston Lichtenstein, *The History of the Jews of Richmond From 1769 to 1917* (Richmond: Herbert T. Ezekiel, 1917), p. 244; Barnett A. Elzas, *The Jews of South Carolina from the Earliest Times to the Present Day* (Philadelphia: J. P. Lippincott Co., 1905), pp. 218–19; Alfred G. Moses, "A History of the Jews of Mobile," *Publications of the American Jewish Historical Society*, 12 (1904), 121. See Ezekiel, *op. cit.*, p. 227, for information on the religious school that Eckman was in charge of, and p. 244 for the public prayers he delivered. See also "The Resolution," *Weekly Gleaner* [*WG*], July 6, 1860, p. 4, for Eckman's report of a prayer he delivered in a Christian church at Charleston in 1850.
5. Voorsanger, *op. cit.*, p. 43.
6. Robert E. Levinson, "The Jews in the California Gold Rush" (Ph.D. diss., University of Oregon, 1968).
7. Voorsanger, *op. cit.*, pp. 45, 47, 49, 146–47.
8. *Occident* (Philadelphia, from 1843); *Asmonean* (New York, 1849); *Israelite* (Cincinnati, 1854); *Deborah* (Cincinnati, 1855); *Sinai* (Baltimore, 1856); *Jewish Messenger* (New York, 1857). See *Jewish Newspapers and Periodicals on Microfilm Available at the American Jewish Periodical Center* (Cincinnati: American Jewish Periodical Center, 1957), pp. 21–22, 28–29, 41, 44.
9. "Complimentary Resolution," *WG*, November 25, 1859, p. 5; "Payments. Panama," *ibid.*, p. 8; "Deaths," *ibid.*, April 16, 1858, p. 8.
10. "Prospectus," *ibid.*, January 16, 1857, p. 3. *WG* was not, however, the first Jewish newspaper on the Pacific Coast. *The Voice of Israel*, established October 10, 1856, was edited by the Reverend Herman M. Bien, who followed Eckman as spiritual leader of Congregation Emanu-El, and Henry J. Labatt. Regrettably, no copies of the *Voice of Israel* are known to exist. Eckman's *WG* proved to be so successful that it absorbed its rival and took the name *The Gleaner. As a Voice to Israel*, beginning April 3, 1857. Nearly all of vols. 1 and 2 (1857–59) of the *WG* are known to exist, as well as forty-four editions of vol. 3, twenty of vol. 4, forty-three of vol. 5, thirteen of vol. 6, and one edition each from 1864 and 1865.
11. "Circular," Congregation Emanu-El Archives, San Francisco.
12. "To Our Readers," *WG*, January 23, 1857, p. 12.
13. "Opinions of the Press," *ibid.*, January 23, 1857, p. 15.
14. Matt. 19:6; Mark 10:9. "Our Divorces," *ibid.*, January 16, 1857, p. 4.

15. See the editions for January 15, April 2, and September 4, 1858.
16. "Jewish Intelligence," *ibid.*, April 22, 1859, p. 2.
17. June 25, 1858, p. 1; "Death of a Rabbi of the Hassidim," *ibid.*, March 12, 1858, p. 5; "Asiatic and European Jews: The Difference Between Orthodox and Reform," *ibid.*, March 19, 1858, p. 4; "European and Asiatic Judaism: Number II," *ibid.*, April 9, 1858, p. 4.
18. "What Happened at Bologna," *ibid.*, October 29, 1858, p. 2; "The Mortara Affair," *ibid.*, January 6, 1860, p. 1.
19. "A Mortara Affair in Prussia," *ibid.*, January 13, 1860, p. 5; "A Mortara Affair at St. Louis," *ibid.*, January 14, 1859, pp. 1–2; "The Double of the Mortara Case," *ibid.*, March 25, 1859, pp. 1–2; "Another Mortara Case," *ibid.*
20. "Communicated," *ibid.*, February 4, 1859, p. 5; "Warning," *ibid.*, January 7, 1859, p. 4.
21. "The Mortara Abduction," *ibid.*, January 14, 1859, p. 8. See also *Proceedings in Relation to the Mortara Abduction* . . . (San Francisco: Towne and Bacon, 1859) and Bertram Wallace Korn, *The American Reaction to the Mortara Case: 1858–1859* (Cincinnati: American Jewish Archives, 1957). Eckman objected to the printing of the proceedings by Towne and Bacon because they reprinted typographical errors directly from *WG*'s version. "Proceedings of the Mortara Meeting . . . ," *WG*, February 11, 1859, p. 5.
22. "Intervention," *ibid.*, February 18, 1859, p. 2; "Suggestion," *ibid.*, January 7, 1859, p. 4. But when such an organization, the Board of Delegates of American Israelites, was formed, Eckman criticized it because ". . . every *contributor*, regardless of his religious or irreligious views, is a voter. . . ." "Central Commttee of Israelites of the United States," *ibid.*, April 8, 1859, p. 4. Emphasis was supplied in the original text.
23. "The Jews of Persia," *ibid.*, May 21, 1858, p. 4; "Notice," *ibid.*, November 27, 1857, p. 361. See also "Contributions towards the Poor in Palestine," *ibid.*, April 2, 1858, p. 4, and Eckman's appeal for funds for the Jews of Africa. "The Cry of the Distressed," *ibid.*, January 20, 1860, p. 4. In regard to the Swiss matter, Eckman wished "that our people were as sensitive in regard to their religious *wants* as they are to their political rights; and would that they would be guided religiously, by true and honest men, as they are by demagogues and other leaders. We would then have less cause to deplore our defection and disabilities." "The Swiss Treaty," *ibid.*, March 5, 1858, p. 5. Emphasis was supplied in the original text.
24. He counted nine rabbis, including himself. "List of Rabbis in the United States," *ibid.*, January 23, 1857, p. 14; "Jewish Statesmen in the United States," *ibid.*, August 9, 1861, p. 4; "Our Progress. What a Change!!!" *ibid.*, August 27, 1858, p. 2.
25. "Rise and Progress of Hebrew Congregations," *ibid.*, January 14 1859, p. 4; "Correspondence," *ibid.*, May 28, 1858, p. 5.
26. He officiated at weddings in San Jose ("Married," *ibid.*, March 6, 1857, p. 61), Stockton ("Married," *ibid.*, November 25, 1859, p. 8), and Georgetown ("Marriage Ceremony at Georgetown," *ibid.*, February 11, 1859, p. 2).
27. See "Consecration of a Synagogue in Sacramento," *ibid.*, June 10, 1859, p. 2; "Appeal to the Hebrew Benevolent Societies of the State of California," *ibid.*, May 8, 1857, p. 133; election report of the "Nevada [City] Hebrew Benevolent Society," *ibid.*, May 28, 1857, p. 161; plans to build a synagogue in Jackson, "Communicated," *ibid.*, July 17, 1857, p. 215; "Communication," regarding the founding of the congregation in San Diego, July 12, 1861, p. 2; "Jewish Census of Victoria, V. I.," *ibid.*, July 6, 1860, p. 5.

28. See such advertisements from Stockton ("Wanted," *ibid.*, August 3, 1860, p. 5),
    Sacramento ("Wanted," *ibid.*, December 23, 1859, p. 5), "Personal," *ibid.*, Victoria, B.C. ("Vacancy at Victoria," *ibid.*, August 2, 1861, p. 2), and Portland
    ("Minister Wanted," *ibid.*, March 22, 1861, p. 7).
29. See, for example, a question from Emanuel Linoberg of Sonora, who asked
    whether the remains of a deceased Jew who had married out of the faith could
    be disinterred from the Christian cemetery and reinterred in the Jewish cemetery
    ("Reply to E. L.," *ibid.*, October 23, 1857, p. 324), and one from Abraham
    Blackman of Victoria, who reported on the difficulty of having new-born boys
    circumcised at the age of eight days ("Communication," *ibid.*, July 15, 1859,
    p. 2).
30. "Notice," *ibid.*, September 4, 1858, p. 8.
31. Letter from "P." to "Israelites," *ibid.*, September 23, 1859, p. 5; "Notice," *ibid.*,
    May 10, 1861, p. 5. The spelling of the name of this organization varies. Directly
    above the notice was an advertisement for a meeting of the group, and the last
    word was spelled "Ukdosha."
32. "To the Israelites of San Francisco," *ibid.*, October 16, 1857, p. 321.
33. October 23, 1857, p. 323.
34. "Religion in Public Schools," *ibid.*, May 27, 1859, p. 2.
35. "The Christian State," *ibid.*, December 23, 1859, pp. 4–5; "Christian Legislation," *ibid.*, January 6, 1860, p. 4; "Obligations of a Christian Sabbath," *ibid.*,
    March 12, 1858, p. 4; "The Sunday Law Decision," *ibid.*, July 2, 1858, p. 4;
    "Sunday Laws Again," *ibid.*, May 31, 1861, p. 5.
36. "No Union Flag from the Synagogue," *ibid.*, June 28, 1861, p. 4.
37. "The Sabbath Must be Re-Conquered," *ibid.*, December 2, 1859, p. 5. See also
    "The Sabbath Movement," *ibid.*, December 23, 1859, p. 8, and "The Recuperation of the Sabbath Eve," *ibid.*, October 19, 1860, p. 4.
38. "Our Wants—Our Duty—And Our Interest," *ibid.*, November 5, 1858, p. 4. See
    also "Why so Severe—Who was the Enemy?" *ibid.*, October 26, 1860, p. 4, and
    "What Congregations Want Most and First," *ibid.*, October 19, 1860, p. 4.
39. "Our Ceremonies," *ibid.*, September 22, 1858, p. 5.
40. "Jewish Intelligence," *ibid.*, December 24, 1858, p. 5.
41. "Another Anomoly" [*sic*], *ibid.*, August 13, 1858, p. 5.
42. "Joyful News. Transference of the Sabbath to the First Day of the Week," *ibid.*,
    March 5, 1858, p. 4.
43. "Communication," *ibid.*, June 28, 1861, pp. 4–5.
44. "Chanting in Reading the Law," *ibid.*, June 25, 1858, p. 1.
45. "Another Liturgy," *ibid.*, April 30, 1858, p. 5.
46. "Hebrew Wives" and "Intermarriages," *ibid.*, September 16, 1859, p. 4.
47. "A Dilemma.—To Whom Shall we Refer?" *ibid.*, August 23, 1861, p. 4.
48. "Refutation. Divorces," *ibid.*, January 20, 1860, p. 4.
49. "The Organ Question," *ibid.*, April 4, 1862, p. 4.
50. "Why no Chuppah?" *ibid.*, October 26, 1860, p. 4.
51. "Mourning Regulations," *ibid.*, September 22, 1858, p. 5.
52. "Covered or Uncovered," *ibid.*, December 2, 1859, p. 5.
53. "Jerusalem," *ibid.*, September 22, 1858, p. 2.
54. "Principles of Judaism," *ibid.*, January 29, 1858, p. 432. See also "Principles of
    Judaism," *ibid.*, April 29, 1859, p. 4.
55. "Receipts," *ibid.*, March 12, 1858, p. 4; "Payments," *ibid.*, December 23, 1859,
    p. 5. *WG* also had local agents in San Francisco, Sacramento, Stockton, San Jose,
    Nevada City, Oroville, Mokelumne Hill, and Columbia (*ibid.*, May 22, 1857,
    p. 149) and in large eastern cities ("For the East," *ibid.*).

56. "Country-Subscribers, please remit!" *ibid.,* April 6, 1860, p. 4. See also "Equitable Request," *ibid.,* July 26, 1861, p. 5.
57. "To our Agents and Subscribers," *ibid.,* June 25, 1858, p. 4.
58. "To our Subscribers," *ibid.,* July 2, 1858, p. 4.
59. "The Future of the *Gleaner,*" *ibid.,* July 2, 1858, p. 4.
60. "Circular," *ibid.,* August 6, 1858, p. 4; "Subscription List," *ibid.,* August 13, 1858, p. 5; "Favors," *ibid.,* August 27, 1858, p. 8.
61. "The Weekly Gleaner," *ibid.,* May 8, 1857, p. 136; "From the East," *ibid.,* June 5, 1857, p. 166.
62. "The Colored Wrappers," *ibid.,* July 24, 1857, p. 224. Emphasis was supplied in the original text.
63. Philo Jacoby's *Hebrew* appeared December 18, 1863, and another newspaper called *Voice of Israel* began publication October 7, 1870. See *Jewish Newspapers and Periodicals on Microfilm* . . . op. cit., p. 16; "Unofficial List of Titles Added to the American Jewish Periodical Center . . . ," (n.d.), p. 2.
64. *WG,* January 6, 1865, p. 4.
65. Voorsanger stated that Eckman received no compensation for serving as rabbi in Portland, but he did not specify which of the two congregations in Portland Eckman served gratis. Voorsanger, *op. cit.,* p. 150.
66. See, for example, Bertram Wallace Korn, *American Jewry and the Civil War* (Philadelphia: Jewish Publication Society, 1957), p. 301, n. 67. I wish to thank Professor Lloyd P. Gartner of Tel Aviv University for reading an early draft of this essay and offering his suggestions to me.

THE HISTORICAL BACKGROUND OF PRE-ZIONISM IN AMERICA AND ITS CONTINUITY

By

RAPHAEL MAHLER

Tel Aviv University

I

By its very nature as a movement for national rehabilitation, Zionism postulates in its historical research the application of the law of evolution and continuity. However, the historiography of modern Jewry, and of American Jews in particular, has dealt with individual forerunners of contemporary Zionism as sporadic occurrences rather than representatives of pre-Zionism as a trend. Since Max J. Kohler's pioneering study in this field at the turn of the century,[1] many monographs have been published on early Zionist projects, particularly those of Mordecai Manuel Noah, as well as on the aid of American Jewry to the "poor of Jerusalem." Still, the episodic treatment of the subject may be illustrated by the fact that such a prominent harbinger of modern Zionism as Isaac Leeser was not evaluated in this respect until just a few years ago.[2] Small wonder, then, that the rise of similar ideas and projects about Palestine in other countries was hardly considered more than a mere coincidence. It is even more amazing that no conclusion has been drawn from the fact that the allegedly isolated "dreamers" of Zion were recognized leaders of their respective Jewish communities. In England Moses Montefiore served almost continuously for forty years (1835–74) as president of the Board of Deputies, not to speak of the high moral authority he enjoyed in the British Jewish community and in Jewry the world over; Abraham

Benisch, besides his highly influential post as editor of the *Jewish Chronicle,* was a leading figure in the intellectual and social life of British Jewry. In America, Isaac Leeser was not only the editor of the *Occident,* the leading Jewish periodical until the middle of the nineteenth century, but the widely recognized spokesman and organizer of Jewry in the entire country. Mordecai Manuel Noah was popular with the Jews as a political figure and an active member of almost all the Jewish institutions in New York, his city of residence.[3] The same goes for the place occupied in that community by Gershom Mendes Seixas, the predecessor of both Noah and Leeser in the modern interpretation of the Restoration idea.[4]

The failure to recognize the nature of pre-Zionism in America and its historic significance lies with the specific geographical orientation which has become a tradition in modern Jewish historiography. As a result of Germany's being the country of the birth and flowering of this as of all other branches of the *Wissenschaft des Judentums,* the historiography of the Jews in modern times evolved out of its scope as West European Continental–centered, and to a large extent even as outrightly Germany-centered.[5] The tradition of Central–West European historiography lay at the root of the prevalent misconceptions about the change in the attitute toward the historical perspective of Restoration to Zion that took place at the dawn of Jewish emancipation. It has been maintained that as a consequence of the legal emancipation, or even earlier, in preparation for it, Jews as a rule, and particularly the enlightened class, turned away from the traditional idea of return to Zion, both emotionally and consciously. The closer the attachment of the Jews to their county of domicile, and the fuller their integration into the cultural and political life of their environment—so went the explanation—the looser the ties that bound them to the Land of Promise in the pre-emancipation era of persecution, discrimination, and social isolation. Similarly, the rise of rationalism has been considered a direct factor in the abandonment of the idea of a Messianic Restoration, since it allegedly was based on a belief in the supernatural, miraculous intervention of Providence in the course of history. Accordingly, it was only the Orthodox camp which staunchly adhered to the idea of Restoration as an article of faith. Now and then—it was admitted—rare, isolated individuals, among Jews and non-Jews alike, came along with plans for the rehabilitation of the Jewish people by rebuilding Palestine, but such projects were historical curiosities diverging from the main road of historical development.

Such a notion about the alleged disengagement of nineteenth-century

Jewry from its historical links with Palestine has been accepted as a rule, although on closer scrutiny it could apply only to some Jewish communities, and even then with considerable qualification. We leave alone the fact that the non-emancipated East European Jewish communities in the middle of the nineteenth century, themselves amounted to three-fourths of world Jewry, and that including the Jewish communities of Asia and Africa, those adhering to the traditional way of life and faithful to the idea of Return to Zion, encompassed more than four-fifths of the total number of Jews in the world.[6] Within the limits of Western civilization itself, England and the United States were not the only countries where, contrary to the accepted pattern, the historical link with Palestine was maintained by the Jewish community as a whole, at any rate as late as the middle of the nineteenth century. In this respect Italian Jewry may be classed with the same category. Except perhaps for a small group of extreme assimilationists like Moses Formigini,[7] Italian Jewry in the era of the first emancipation was animated by the expectation of the near advent of the Messiah. The idea of Restoration continued to find its adequate expression in the Hebrew poetry of Italy until late in the nineteenth century.[6]

The respective views on the idea of Return to Zion were, as a matter of course, a determinant factor in the stand of the Jewish community in each country toward religious reform in general and its relevant tenets in particular. Thus in Italy, as also in neighboring France, the Reform movement did not strike roots at all. Even more characteristic is the example of England, where the Reform movement, which arose in the early forties, left intact, without any omission or modification, the traditional prayers for the Restoration to Zion and the ingathering of the exiles. No less significant is the circumstance that in the United States the early, short-lived Jewish Reform movement, though admittedly highly influenced by the movement in Germany, did not consider the belief in Restoration to Zion as incompatible with its principles. In his *Discourse,* delivered before the Reformed Society in Charleston in 1825, Isaac Harby, its prominent leader, chose rather to leave open the question whether the land referred to in Scripture as the land of Restoration meant Palestine, "old Judea renovated and blessed by the munificence of heaven," or whether it signified a heavenly Jerusalem, "happiness in the world to come." While expressing the happiness of the Jewish community, whose fortune it was "to live in this temporal state in America," he reaffirmed his belief in the ingathering of the exiles of the Jewish people, when "the annunciation of the Messiah shall reunite us into one nation, offering with all mankind . . . on the common altar."[9] Such a declaration of faith in the Restoration and the coming of the Messiah, though qualified, could hardly have been pronounced by a leader of the Reform movement in Continental Europe.

The difference of views regarding the idea of Restoration is reflected even within the camp of Orthodoxy itself. In Germany, reasons of hyper-loyalism prevailed to such an extent that some Orthodox rabbis were eager to interpret the talmudic warning against "rebellion" and "press-ing the end" [10] as enjoining servile obedience to the authorities and ab-solute inactivity even after the arrival of the Messiah.[11] As a contrast to this kind of Orthodoxy in the sphere of Western civilization, we may point to the Orthodoxy of the same era in America. The Orthodox rabbi of Baltimore, Abraham Rice, deemed it necessary in his sermon on the Messiah, given in 1842, to quote the passage of Maimonides' *Mishneh Torah* on the future political rehabilitation of Israel,[12] in order to con-clude that "the Jew as a Jew can and should be an upright member of the community, whilst he can and should hold firmly to the hope of his own nation." [13]

Any analysis of the pertinent historical facts, unbiased by a German-centered geographical orientation, necessarily leads to the conclusion that with regard to the historical perspective of Return to Zion, as to the aim of the preservation of the Jewish nationality in general, two different patterns of Jewish emancipation should be discerned: the West-Central European Continental pattern on the one hand and the Anglo-American on the other. The latter pattern fits the Italian Jewish community as well, though it lagged behind the communities across the sea and across the ocean respectively with regard to both political pro-jects[14] and reconstruction schemes.

The pattern of emancipation characterized by a practical or even principled abandonment of the Restoration in Zion as a historical per-spective reflected both the ruling political system and the circumstances of Jewish cultural life in Continental West-Central Europe. Centralism in the state-organization and in political ideology tended to stamp as separatism every vestige of autonomy preserved by a national or religious minority. What is more, the greater the obstacles to be overcome by the Jews in their striving for civil and political equality, the more eager were their communal leaders in their efforts to demonstrate the complete identity of the Jewish population with the ruling nation maintaining that the Jews' only common bonds were those of a religious denomination. A factor no less decisive in this respect than the political system proved to be the degree of integration of the Jews in the cultural life of their country of domicile. The higher the wall that actually separated the Jews from their neighbors with regard to dress, language, culture, and social intercourse in the era of emancipation, the more extreme became the conscious assimilationist tendencies on the part of the Jewish plutocracy and intelligentsia. It goes without saying that this program of assimilation included as one of its main objectives the eradication of the Land of Israel from the minds and hearts of the people.

It is certainly no mere historical coincidence that among the countries of the opposite, Palestine-positive pattern of Jewish emancipation, there was not one where both factors of the conscious assimilationist tendency existed at the same time. In Italy, state centralism was the dominant political system, but the Jews' cultural integration reached an extent unknown anywhere else in all Europe. Very significant for these conditions is the fact that the Haskalah movement did not find fertile ground in Italy: the main slogans of the Haskalah, such as knowledge of the language of the country, application to secular science, and rapprochement with the non-Jewish neighbors, had been the daily bread of Italian Jewry for centuries and needed no agitation or propaganda. Under these circumstances, there was no necessity for Italian Jews to renounce the historic ties with the Land of Promise in order to prove their interest in the welfare of their country of birth, or their loyalty to the authorities.

As to the integration of the Jews of the Anglo-Saxon countries in the social and cultural life of their neighbors, there was a considerable difference between the small Jewish settlement in North America and the sizable Jewish community in England. In America, already in the colonial era, the participation of Jews in the social and cultural life of their environment went so far as to make possible cases of election of some of them to public office, though their legal equality was not established until the adoption of the Federal constitution by the independent states. After the War of Independence, the process of integration of the Jews in all spheres of life received new impetus. Among British Jewry, social and cultural integration into the environment, originally limited mainly to tycoons of the Sephardic community, embraced ever more, after the beginning of the nineteenth century, the plutocracy of Ashkenazi origin. However, the political system of England, like that of the United States, differed from the European continental ones in that it was not based on state-centralism, the root of intolerance to the existence of a Jewish nationality. In America the Federal system of the Union was coupled with the fact of the multinational composition of the population, which varied with each new wave of immigration. Consequently, in neither of the two Anglo-Saxon countries was it urgent for the Jews to prove their loyalty by abnegating their nationality, or the Restoration idea in particular. Just the contrary was the case.

Many theologians of the Anglican, Presbyterian, and Catholic churches in England and North America, and even to a larger extent adherents of the various sects in both countries, gave prominence to their belief in the Restoration of the Jews to their Land as the event preceding and announcing the second advent of Christ. The preservation of the Jews as a distinct nationality was naturally the prerequisite of their Restoration, and thus even the very fact of Jewish group survival was brought as a proof or evidence of the plans of Providence for reestablishing their Commonwealth.[15]

In America even the theological terminology of the dominant denominations, until the middle of the nineteenth century, centered around Zion in the meaning of the New Land, and later of the Christian Church.[16] Small wonder then that even in controversies about the admission of Jews to political rights in particular states, the belief in the Return to Zion was not employed as an argument against them. Most characteristic of the positive attitude on the part of leading American statesmen to the Restoration of the Jews as a program for action is a letter written in 1819 by former President John Adams to M. M. Noah in acknowledgment of his book *Travels*. He expresses the wish for the reestablishment of the Jews in Judea as "an independent nation" through conquest by a Jewish army.[17]

In contradistinction to North America, some opponents of Jewish emancipation in England did not shrink from pointing to the hope of the Jews for rebuilding Jerusalem as an additional justification of their civil disabilities. However, so widespread was the belief in Restoration that the defender of Jewish enfranchisement had an easy task in refuting the argument about Jewish messianic belief in that same future era.[18] Moreover, the steadfastness of the Jews in their adherence to their historical national aspirations enhanced their prestige in the eyes of some leaders of the dominant church itself. In the debate in the House of Lords in 1833 on the Bill for Removing the Civil Disabilities of the Jews, the archbishop of Canterbury, pleading for granting the Jews all rights, except admission to Parliament and to judicial functions, declared, *inter alia*, "As to their expectations of a return to the promised land, I cannot say how far they may indulge them; but even if they turn their eyes ever so earnestly toward that quarter, who is there that will not think more highly of them on that account? Who will not approve of their conduct in not forgetting the promises originally made to this race, and in still entertaining hopes of recovering those advantages of which they have so long been deprived?"[19]

To sum up, just as Germany represented the extreme case of the West-Central Continental European pattern of Jewish emancipation, so was America the classical specimen of the opposite, Anglo-Saxon–Italian pattern. Here, in North America, practically all the conditions favorable to the faithfulness of the Jews to the Restoration idea were to be found together: a noncentralistic system of government and a multinational structure of the general population; a high degree of Jewish integration into the social and cultural sphere and gradually also into the political field of life in the country; a widespread, more than anywhere else, Christian millennarian belief in the Restoration of Israel.

It is true that whereas England's direct political interest in the Near East arose as early as the end of the eighteenth century,[20] the United States at that time had not aspired to playing any role in Palestine, at any rate not until the middle of the nineteenth century (the expedition to the River Jordan under the command of Lieut. William F. Lynch). However, thanks to their early participation in political life, American Jews were able to take the initiative in conceiving schemes for the reestablishment of the Jewish state, while in England such projects were launched by Christian theologians and men of politics.

II

At the end of the eighteenth century and in the first half of the nineteenth, pre-Zionism in America, as overseas, was still deeply embedded in the traditional religious belief in the Return to Zion as the fulfillment of the scriptural prophecies. In this regard, there was no difference between Gershom Mendes Seixas and Isaac Leeser, the "hazzanim," and Mordecai Manuel Noah, the layman. However, the new phase of development of the Redemption belief was marked not only by the expectation of the Return to Zion as an actual forthcoming event, which "stands behind the wall." The decisive elements, which lent the traditional belief the character of a modern conception of national liberation, were the stress on the political aspect of Restoration on the one hand, and on the other the call to Jews, or to Jews and non-Jews alike, to take an active part in the realization of the dream of all generations in exile.

The stress on the political meaning of the Restoration was characteristic of the expectation of that great event already at the dawn of the modern era. In the Hebrew thanksgiving prayer of the year 1784 for peace composed by Hendle Iochanan van Oettinger on behalf of the New York congregation Shearith Israel, we read the following passage: "As Thou hast granted to these thirteen states of America everlasting freedom, so mayst Thou bring us forth once again from bondage into freedom, and mayst Thou sound the great horn for our freedom as it is said . . ." [21]

The fact that America's recently achieved independence is here set as a model of the prayed-for Redemption of Israel is of double significance for the history of pre-Zionism. The Restoration to be achieved as a work of God is conceived as a Jewish national liberation, after the pattern of the liberty won by the Americans; the great historic event of the victorious American Revolution raised the hope of the Jewish community in the liberated country that the Restoration of Israel was near.

In the same year, 1784, that the above discussed prayer was composed, the Rev. Gershom Mendes Seixas returned from Philadelphia to New York, to his post as hazzan of the local congregation. There was hardly a sermon or "discourse" delivered by Seixas on various occasions during his new term of service, which was to last over thirty years, in which the subject of the Restoration was not brought up. The preacher saw fit to bring home to his listeners the political meaning of that perspective: the supplication "to be again established under our own government as we were formerly," voiced in his "discourse" on Thanksgiving Day 1789, is almost literally repeated in one of his later sermons on Thanksgiving Day, held some time after 1801. [22]

In all the schemes of Mordecai M. Noah for the rehabilitation of the Jewish people in its historical homeland, the restitution of the independent Jewish state is the main objective. Thus in the "discourse" held in 1818 at the consecration of the synagogue Shearith Israel, even while praising the United States as the freest country in the world, he did not fail to set his praise in the perspective of the future Jewish state in Palestine: "Until the Jews can recover their ancient rights and dominions, and take their rank among the governments of the earth, this is their chosen country. . . ." [23] In the same wording Noah announces, in his "Proclama-

tion to the Jews on the Founding of Ararat in 1825," the approach of the
period when they are to be gathered from the four quarters of the globe
to resume their rank and character among the governments of the
earth. [24] In the same proclamation Noah states the purpose of the founding of Ararat not only as preparing an asylum for the Jews in "a Land
of milk and honey," but as a school of civilization, political practice, and
government for the future state in the Land of Israel, "where our people
may so familiarize themselves with the science of government and the
light of learning and civilization, as may qualify them for that great
and final restoration to their ancient heritage which the times so power-
fully indicate." The vision of Jews resuming, by dint of their reborn
state, "their rank among the nations of the earth" is reiterated in the
same wording in his *Discourse on the . . . American Indians,* held in
1837.[25] In his *Discourse on the Restoration,* delivered in 1844 in the
Tabernacle, Noah expressly puts the goal of renewed Jewish political
independence above all other aspects of the Restoration, including even
the ideal of a complete ingathering of the exiles: "Let the people go;
point out the path for them in safety, and they will go, not all, but sufficient to constitute the elements of a powerful government . . ." [26] Noah's
Address on the Restoration, delivered on Thanksgiving Day 1848 at the
Crosby Street Synagogue, was occasioned by the collection of funds for
renewing one of the synagogues in Jerusalem, and consequently the rebuilding of the Temple constituted its formal subject. Nevertheless, here
too the dominant vision is that of "the Holy Land sovereign and independent under its rightful proprietors," and "the standard of Judah once
more unfurled on Mount Zion." [27]

Isaac Leeser's views on the means to be taken for raising the Jewish
settlement in Palestine underwent, during the many decades of his literary
activity, considerable development. However, the establishment of a
Jewish national government in the Land of Israel was for him, as for
Seixas and Noah, the ultimate goal of the Restoration—with one difference only: in his earlier sermons Leeser stressed the point of the Jewish state to be governed by "our own laws," which are the "Divine
laws." [28]

However, as if to stress even more the political meaning of the Restoration, in his later articles reference to "Divine laws" is not made any
more. In those years Leeser stated quite unequivocally the secular point
of view on the purpose of reestablishing the Jewish state. A case of anti-
Jewish discrimination in Baltimore in 1856 served him as a demonstra-

tion of the necessity of restoring the Jewish state "on the score of mere worldly independence." [29]

According to tradition, dating back to Scripture, the Restoration of Israel was to be preceded by great wars and other cataclysms. A derivative of that tradition was an optimistic universalist conception of the historical parallel between the rebirth of Israel and the political renaissance of all mankind.[30] No wonder that the great upheaval of the American and French Revolutions and the Napoleonic Wars raised hopes among Jews on both sides of the ocean that the Redemption of Israel was near its fulfillment. The above quoted prayer of the New York congregation of 1784 gave expression to feelings of joyful expectation in face of the victorious America War of Independence. In his earlier discourses and sermons, Gershom Mendes Seixas rather pointed to the aspect of cataclysmic contemporary world events as a sign of the approaching Restoration.[31] It was only in his Charity Sermon of January 11, 1807, that he pinned his hope for near restoration not on the general state of "moral and political" world-crisis, but on a definite contemporary political event. The convocation of the Sanhedrin in Paris by Napoleon in 1806 misled Seixas, like many others in America,[32] to believe in the emperor's alleged aim of restoring the Jews as a nation to Palestine: "Let us pray . . . that they may find favor in the sight of their Emperor & that he under the influence of divine grace, may be a means to accomplish our establishment if not as a nation in our former territory, let it only be as a particular society with equal rights & privileges of all other religious Societies." [33] However cautiously worded, as only one of many exentualities, the hopes he attached to Napoleon testify to Seixas' views on the way the forthcoming Restoration would be accomplished: not as a miracle, in contrast to the laws of nature, but through the action of a second Cyrus, a great monarch who would serve Providence as a means to carry out the Restoration of the chosen people.

A big step further than Seixas, even in his later views, was made by both Mordecai M. Noah and Isaac Leeser in their realistic interpretation of world events as opening all the wide perspectives for Restoration. While basing their prognosis, in the main, on an analysis of the political and economic interests of the great powers in populating Palestine and reestablishing the Jewish commonwealth there, they did not lose sight of the general political trends of their times. The Restoration of the Jews was envisaged within the framework of the political progress of humanity in general, and in particular as a most adequate manifestation of the trend for the national liberation of oppressed peoples. Thus Noah dwells on the disintegration of the Turkish empire in all his discourses, beginning with 1818 and ending in 1848; yet in his *Discourse* in 1818 he also expresses his great optimism in view of the spread of enlightenment and civilization;[34] in his *Ararat Address* in 1825 he derives encouragement from mankind's progress in the field of "learning and civilization," "industry and morality," as well as from the liberation process of "the nations of the Old and New World—including the Children of Africa"; and among them the victorious Greeks in their fight against Turkish domination.[35] No wonder that the "Springtime of the Nations" in 1848 was to Noah a great source of inspiration, as we learn from his *Address* delivered on Thanksgiving Day 1848: "the thunders begin to roll all over Europe; the cry is everywhere heard in despotic governments; 'to arms'; kings are overthrown; priestcraft and fanaticism are overthrown; the Sun of Liberty begins to rise . . . and the age of reason had revived." [36] It was against the background of world events that Noah attributed historic significance to the small episode of the Turkish authorities giving permission to enlarge the synagogue of the Cabbalist community Beth El in Jerusalem: "taken with other extraordinary signs of the times, it has a most important bearing, it is pregnant with great events," it is, namely, a foreboding of the Restoration.[37]

At this same period of the first half of the nineteenth century, we do not find in Isaac Leeser's sermons or editorials on Palestine and the Restoration any reference to contemporary political events. As he declared in his review of Noah's *Discourse* of 1844, he did not consider the political constellation as propitious for the Restoration. The turning point in this respect, as in Leeser's entire conception of the Restoration, came in 1848 under the impact of the revolution in Europe.[38] In his editorial "The Future," he voices in consideration of the upheaval overseas, the same feelings of national pride and ambition that expressed decades earlier, in 1784 in a prayer by the New York congregation Shearith Israel:

And if ancient Germany again becomes a nation—if Poland throws off successfully the chains of mighty oppressors—if fair Italy takes a rank as one people—why should not the patriotic Hebrew also look proudly forward to the time (even without reference to revelation) when he may again proudly boast of his own country of the beneficent sway of his own laws, of the bravery of Judah's sons, of the virtue of Israel's daughters? . . . [39]

The phrase enclosed by Leeser in parentheses was to stress even more the essentially political meaning of the hoped-for Restoration, as a parallel to European national liberation movements.[40]

In his articles on "Restoration; or, The Future of Palestine," published after 1848 and particularly in the sixties, Leeser also adopts the very views of the late Noah that he had sharply criticized in his review of Noah's *Discourse* of 1848[41]—namely, that it is in the interest of the European powers to support the reestablishment of the Jewish commonwealth in Palestine.[42] On another point of his refutation of Noah's *Discourse*— the question of accepting the cooperation of conversion societies— Lesser, within less than a decade, also went over to the view he had strongly opposed.[43]

Of all the traits that lend the Messianic belief at the dawn of modern times the character of a pre-Zionist trend, the most distinctive one is the call for action. As for Gershom M. Seixas, it is true that he never expressly assigned any task to the Jews themselves in preparing the ground for Restoration, either by colonization, or by political action.[44] It was a pupil of Seixas', Mordecai M. Noah, whose discourses and projects concerning the Restoration all issued in ardent appeals for energetic action. In his *Discourse* of 1818, Noah expresses his firm conviction that at the outbreak of the war of the European powers against Turkey, the Jews will not only be able, but willing, "in view of the ultimate restoration of the nation," to bring together "100,000 disciplined troops" at their own expense.[45] As an immediate task he sees the preservation of the Jewish national character, and he exhorts the "Children of Israel" to improve their system of education, particularly by directing the youth to agriculture and crafts and by cultivating the knowledge of the Hebrew language.[46]

Noah's activist philosophy of life, religion, and history was as clearly and passionately formulated in his *Ararat Address* in 1825:

> We have long been captives in the land of strangers; we have long submitted patiently to oppression; we have long anxiously expected temporal deliverance; but throughout the most terrible periods of calamity we have done nothing for ourselves. We have senses, judgment, powers of self-government, energy, capacity and wealth. If with all these requisites we will "hang our harps upon the willow," we still cover ourselves with sackcloth and ashes, and do not make an effort for independence, how shall we reasonably continue to supplicate God for our restoration, who made man in his own image, and proclaimed him free? . . .[47]

Also, in his *Discourses* of 1837[48] and 1844,[49] while appealing in their own interests to the Christian powers, and particularly to the United States, in the name of its ideals of liberty, to aid the Jews in the work of Restoration, Noah repeatedly urges the Jews themselves to act. However, with all his ardor for immediate action, Noah did not fail to realize that the Restoration, far from being a complete, one-time act, rather consists in a long historical process, as a task for generations.[50]

Like Noah, Leeser persistently emphasized the belief, which already had been formulated by Maimonides as a law,[51] that the Restoration would be accomplished "through the agency of men." [52] However, Noah may be regarded as a precursor of Herzl in projecting the founding of the Jewish state as the preliminary condition for the colonization of Palestine. Leeser instead, though never losing sight of the independent state in Palestine as the goal, still, like his contemporaries in England (Moses Montefiore, Abraham Benisch, and others) and later also on the European Continent (R. Judah Alkalay, R. Zvi Kalischer), rather anticipated the pre-Herzl "Lovers of Zion" movement, which practically limited itself to promoting the development of colonies in Palestine. As a first step toward the colonization by new immigrants, Leeser, like Montefiore and his associates, saw the necessity of spreading agriculture and industry among the existing Jewish community in Palestine. Only then would Palestine gain the power to attract immigrants and become a home for the persecuted and impoverished Jews of Eastern Europe, Africa, and the Near East.

In this scheme for rebuilding Palestine, the communities in the West, including that in America, were not left by Leeser without an assignment of an active role. Even if the scourge of discrimination should entirely disappear, there would remain the unsolved problem of the anomalous Jewish economic structure. Sill, "it might be justly asked,—exclaims Leeser in the fervor of his national Jewish ambition—, is this the proper pursuit for high minded Israelites to keep a clothing store, or deal in baubles and jewelry? Is there nothing nobler, nothing more fitting for the high intellect with which we are endowed than to be shopkeepers of the world?" [53] The solution of the problem of spreading productive labor among Jews in prosperous countries coincides, in Leeser's outlook, with the final goal of Restoration. "But while we are in a state of dispersion . . . we should adopt the advice of the prophet[54] and depend upon labor in the field for our subsistence and thus prepare ourselves gradually to become again a united nation, living in one land."[55]

With the new wave of immigrants from Germany and the spread of the Reform movement on the pattern of their country of origin, a new chapter was opened in the socioeconomic and cultural history of the rapidly growing Jewish settlement in America. This also marked a turning point in the prehistory of Zionism in this country. Instead of the dominant ideology of the Jewish community, it became one of its two rival trends.

NOTES

ABBREVIATIONS

AJHS Archives = Archives of the American Jewish Historical Society
PAJHS = Publications of the American Jewish Historical Society
AJHQ = American Jewish Historical Quarterly
HUCA = Hebrew Union College Annual

1. Max J. Kohler, "Some Early American Zionist Projects," PAJHS, VIII (1900), 75–118.
2. Maxime S. Seller, "Isaac Leeser's Views on the Restoration of a Jewish Palestine," AJHQ, LVIII, no. 1 (September 1968), 118–35.
3. See Hyman B. Grinstein, The Rise of the Jewish Community of New York (Philadelphia, 1945), pp. 48, 103, 146, 156, 169, 182–85, 187, 251, 420, 425; cf. also the list of societies and synagogues represented at Noah's funeral: Isaac Goldberg, Major Noah (Philadelphia, 1944), pp. 277–78.
4. In a letter of 1785, the Board of Trustees of the Congregation Shearit Israel assured Seixas: "We know you to have more influence with the whole of the congregation than any other person . . . " Cf. David de Sola Pool, Portraits Etched in Stone (New York, 1952), p. 358.
5. Peretz Smolenskin sarcastically branded the Germany-centrism of Jewish historiography in his letter to Benjamin Mandelstam (published by Mandelstam in his introduction to Hazon-le-Moed [Vienna, 1877]).
6. The composition of world Jewry in 1825–1925 by continents has been elaborated by Jacob Lestschinsky and published in Yivo-Shriftn far Economic un Statistik, vol. I (Berlin, 1928), table 1, p. 6.
7. Cf. R. Bachi "A New Collection of Documents on Italian Jewry in the Days of Napoleon," Zion, VII, 51–54.
8. See Moshe Schulwas, Roma virushalayim: Toledot ha-yakhas shel Yehudei Italia le-Eretz Israel (Jerusalem, 1944), pp. 170ff.; Hayim Shirman, Mivkhar ha-Shirah ha-ivrit be-Italia (Berlin, 1934), pp. 454–517.
9. Quoted by L. C. Moise, Biography of Isaac Harby (1931), 119–21.
10. Babli, Kethuboth 111a.
11. See Tzeror ha-Hayim by Rabbi Abraham Loewenstamm of Emdem (Amsterdam, 1820), f. 72a; we are told by the author in his preface that "the great rabbis of the generation" approved of the book, which they read in manuscript.
12. Chap. XII, sec. "Laws of Monarchs."
13. Occident, I, 271 ff.
14. A very original plan of Livorno Jews for the acquisition of Jerusalem by a transaction with Russian troops belongs to an earlier period, about 1770. Cf R. Mahler, A History of Modern Jewry (New York, 1971), p. 680.
15. On the ideas of Ezra Stiles about this factor in Jewish Restoration, see W. Willner, "Ezra Stiles," PAJHS, VIII (1900), p. 126.

16. *Cf.* Robert T. Handy, "Zion in American Christian Movements," in *Israel, Its Role in Civilization,* ed. Moshe Davis (New York, 1956), pp. 284–97; *cf.* also Selig Adler, "Background of American Policy toward Zion," *ibid.,* pp. 252–60.

17. The letter was published by Moshe Davis in *Bet Israel be-America* (Jerusalem, 1970), pp. 360–61.

18. *Cf.,* e.g., Barnard van Oven, *An Appeal to the British Nation on Behalf of the Jews* (London, 1829), pp. 11–12.

19. *Debates in the House of Commons . . . and in the House of Lords on the Motion for the Second Reading of the Bill for Removing the Civil Disabilities of the Jews* (London, 1834), p. 56.

20. See James Bicheno, *The Restoration of the Jews and the Crisis of All Nations* (London, 1800); see also the analysis of its contents by R. Mahler, *op. cit.,* pp. 690–91.

21. The Hebrew original has been preserved in the AJHS Archives, Lyon Collection 64; the translation—published in *PAJHS,* XXVII, p. 36.

22. Gershom Seixas, *A Religious Discourse,* (New York, 1789), p. 8; idem, "A Sermon for Thanksgiving" (delivered some time after the epidemic of 1801), AJHS Archives, Lyons Collection no. 61, *PAJHS* XXVII, p. 137.

23. M. M. Noah, *Discourse* (New York, 1818), p. 19.

24. See Lewis F. Allen, "Founding the City of Ararat," *Publications of the Buffalo Historical Society,* vol. I (1879), pp. 317–22.

25. M. M. Noah, *Discourse on the Evidence of the American Indians Being the Descendants of the Lost Tribes of Israel* (New York, 1837), p. 39.

26. M. M. Noah, *Discourse on the Restoration, Delivered at the Tabernacle, Oct. 28 and Dec. 2, 1844* (New York, 1845), p. 50.

27. M. M. Noah, *Address Delivered at the Hebrew Synagogue in Crosby Street, New York, on Thanksgiving Day, to Aid the Erection of the Temple at Jerusalem* (Jamaica, 1849), p. 8;*cf.* also pp. 14, 15, *et passim.*

28. See the sermon of 1831 on the Restoration of Israel, in *Discourses,* vol. I, pp. 156–67; "The Messiah," *ibid.,* vol. II, p. 342; "Consolation of Israel," in *Occident,* vol. I, p. 327; *cf.* also his article, "The Mission of Israel," *Occident,* VII (August 9, 1849), p. 6.

29. *Occident* XIV (June 3, 1856), 145–50.

30. See Midrash Lamentations Rabbati 3:21: "Because Thou renewest us at the morn of empires, we know that Thy faithfulness is great to redeem us."

31. G. M. Seixas, Discourse, 1798 (AJHS Archives, Lyons Collection, vol. 2, p. 19); Thanksgiving Day Sermon December 19, 1799 (Lyons Collection 281A, vol. 1; p. 25).

32. See J. J. Shulim, "Napoleon I as the Jewish Messiah: Some Contemporary Conceptions in Virginia," *Jewish Social Studies,* VII, no. 3 (July 1945), 275–80.

33. G. M. Seixas, *Charity* Sermon, January 11, 1807 (Lyons Collection 281 F; *PAJHS,* XXVII, p. 148).

34. M. M. Noah, *Discourse . . .* (New York, 1818), pp. 11, 27, 32.

35. M. M. Noah, Speech, *PAJHS* XXXI– XXXII, pp. 229–31. While expressing his "sympathy" for the Greek insurrection, Noah enjoins "strict neutrality" in the Greek-Turkish conflict because "we must not jeopardize the safety of millions living under the Mussulman Government" (*ibid.,* p. 248). In the reply to Leeser's review of his *Discourse on the Restoration* of 1844, Noah complains about the "want of nationality," lack of national consciousness of contemporary Jews, who "are a sect not a nation." He points to the Greeks an an example worthy to be followed: "The Greeks remained two thousand years in slavery, and yet they arose and redeemed their country, why should not the Jews do the same?" Indeed

the Greek revolution inspired at the same time the rabbi of Corfu, Judah Bibas, to come out with the idea of restoring an independent Jewish state in Palestine by an armed uprising against the Turks. See Andrew A. Bonar and Robert Murray M'Chyene, *Narrative of a Mission of Inquiry to the Jews in 1839* (Edinburgh, 1842), pp. 505, 523, 702.

36. *Address Delivered at the Hebrew Synagogue in Crosby Street, New York, on Thanksgiving Day to Aid in the Erection of the Temple in Jerusalem* (Jamaica, 1849), p. 5.

37. *Ibid.*, p. 9. In his unreserved enthusiasm Noah spoke of the permission "to build a Temple or a magnificent synagogue," but permission to build a synagogue was not granted by the Sultan until 1855, through the efforts of Moses Montefiore (*Diaries*, vol. II [1890], p. 45).

38. The impact of the 1848 Revolution on Leeser, as a turning point in his views, has justly been stressed by M. S. Seller, *op. cit.*, p. 123.

39. *Occident*, VI, no. 2 (May 1848), p. 71.

40. *Cf.* a similar utterance of Leeser's in 1856 "on the score of merely worldly independence," quoted above, p. 350.

41. *Occident*, II, no. 12 (March 1845), pp. 600–606.

42. *Ibid.*, XXII, no. 1 (1864), pp. 5–15; vol. XXIV (November 1866), pp. 366–71.

43. *Ibid.*, XI (October 1854), editorial on Palestine. It is also worthwhile mentioning that Leeser propagated, probably not remembering their originator, some of the ideas in Noah's *Ararat*. In his introduction to Mendelssohn's *Jerusalem* (Philadelphia, 1852), p. 18, he declares: "This country, let my readers believe it, is emphatically the one, where Israel is to prepare itself for its glorious mission of regenerating mankind. Here is freedom for all, bread for all; nay more, there is ample verge for Israelites to cultivate sciences and arts, which liberty fosters."

44. This circumstance has been recently pointed out by Jacob R. Marcus in his penetrating essay on Seixas, "The Handsome Young Priest in the Black Gown," *HUCA*, XL–XLI (1969–70), p. 462.

45. This number is based on the erroneous calculation of a total of 7,688,000 Jews in the world. See *Discourse* (New York, 1818), p. 45, n. 16, 17.

46. *Ibid.*, pp. 21–22, 31.

47. Noah's Address, *PAJHA*, XXI–XXII, pp. 235–36; *cf.* also Noah's reply to Leeser's review of his *Discourse* of 1848 (*Occident*, III, pp. 35–36), a statement which he almost literally repeated in the Crosby Street Synagogue Address in 1848 (p. 14).

48. *Op. cit.*, p. 38.

49. *Op. cit.*, p. 40.

50. *Occident*, III, p. 35.

51. *Cf.* above, p. 344.

52. *Cf.* I. Leeser, Sermons delivered in 1835, 1836, in *Discourses*, vol. II (Philadelphia, 1841), pp. 311, 337.

53. "Our Consolation," *Occident*, XV, no. 6 (September 1857), p. 265.

54. The reference is to the advice of Jeremiah (chap. 29) to the Jews in the Babylonian captivity: "Build ye houses and dwell in them, and plant gardens and eat the fruit of them . . . "

55. "The Future of Israel," *Occident*, XVII, no. 3 (October 27, 1859), p. 182 (editor's note in connection with the project of Simon Berman for Jewish agricultural colonies in the United States).

THE REFUGEE SCHOLARS PROJECT OF THE HEBREW UNION COLLEGE

By

MICHAEL A. MEYER

Hebrew Union College—Jewish Institute of Religion, Cincinnati

In the years 1935 to 1942, the Hebrew Union College in Cincinnati brought to its campus eleven scholars who had become victims of Nazi persecution. For a few of them, the call to HUC literally saved their lives; for others, already outside the German sphere, it made possible a new start in their careers. The formulation and carrying out of this project in its various stages, the difficulties that had to be overcome, and the individual successes and failures constitute a significant chapter in the history of the college even as they shed light on a specific application of the immigration policies of the United States. On the whole, the episode reflects favorably on the HUC, while providing additional evidence of the State Department's callous indifference to the plight of refugees from fascist oppression.[1]

With Hitler's rise to power in 1933, Jewish academicians who had succeeded in gaining university positions during the liberal Weimar period found themselves summarily discharged and hardpressed to earn a living. Some were able to find new employment in universities outside Germany; others languished in unsuitable occupations. Those whose fields were related to Jewish studies in many instances sought to associate themselves with a specifically Jewish institution either in Germany or abroad. In the fall of 1934, at a joint meeting of faculty and Board of Governors, the Hebrew Union College made its initial commitment to

359

help in solving the problem. It was decided to appropriate $4,000 to bring two German Jewish scholars to the college.[2] This project would be carried out in addition to plans then being formulated to provide full maintenance for five German rabbinical students currently enrolled at the liberal seminary in Berlin.[3] The initial proposal was limited indeed. Two refugee scholars already in the United States, Julius Lewy and Guido Kisch, would be asked to teach at the college for a single semester in the year 1935–36. If funds remained, then Michael Wilensky, currently in Lithuania, would be brought to Cincinnati for a year to catalogue the Hebrew manuscripts.[4] While Kisch, a historian of law, did not join the HUC faculty, becoming instead a visiting faculty member at Stephen Wise's Jewish Institute of Religion, Lewy and Wilensky both came to the college, each to remain in Cincinnati until his death.

Julius Lewy had been professor of Semitic languages and Oriental history at Giessen until he was dismissed in 1933. A temporary teaching position at the Sorbonne in Paris[5] was followed by a call to be visiting professor at Johns Hopkins University in the fall of 1934. But Hopkins offered Lewy no permanent appointment and neither did the Jewish Theological Seminary, where he taught on a grant from the Emergency Committee in Aid of Displaced German Scholars the following spring.[6] For the first semester of the academic year 1935–36, Hopkins was again willing to employ Lewy as a temporary replacement for William Foxwell Albright, but after that his prospects were gloomy indeed. There were few positions in Assyriology in the United States. Columbia did not show an interest in Lewy, and at the Oriental Institute in Chicago Lewy's Judaism and his Zionism both worked to his disadvantage.[7] He needed an additional six months of academic employment in the United States in order to be eligible for a permanent immigration visa. The college initially appointed Lewy for a semester and then, against its original intent, kept on reappointing him, at first on a visiting basis to replace the absent Nelson Glueck, and then permanently. Although as late as 1938, Julian Morgenstern, the HUC president, was still trying to find a place for him in a more suitable institution,[8] Lewy adapted himself to giving courses in Bible as well as Assyriology. His appointment, moreover, laid the foundation for what soon became programs in one of the leading American Semitic studies.

Michael Wilensky had managed to leave Communist Russia for Berlin, along with a group of Jewish intellectuals headed by Hayyim Nahman Bialik, in the year 1921. In Germany he had worked with Bialik in the Dvir

Hebrew Publishing House and produced his critical edition of the medieval grammatical work by Jonah ibn Janah, *Sefer ha-Rikmah*. After the Nazi takeover, Wilensky fled to Lithuania, where he was settled in a small town without work and without citizenship when he received his invitation from the college in 1935. Wilensky had been recommended to Morgenstern by a number of scholars though he had had no experience in cataloguing manuscripts. It was intended that he come for only a single year and return upon completion of his task. But from the beginning Wilensky saw it otherwise. He did not believe there would be a return trip.[9] Once in Cincinnati he proceeded with his task slowly and deliberately, making careful and extensive notes on each manuscript. After a year, he fell ill. The college authorities seriously considered returning him to Lithuania, where his wife, a physician, had remained behind. But Mrs. Wilensky wrote Morgenstern emotionally that not only would her husband have no work in Lithuania, but termination of his position would likely bring on a fatal stroke. Ismar Elbogen also wrote to Morgenstern on her behalf. In the end, Wilensky recovered and the college paid for his wife's travel to join her husband in America. He remained at his cataloguing tasks until his retirement in 1943.[10]

Word that the Hebrew Union College was interested in employing displaced Jewish scholars spread rapidly throughout Europe, bringing one application after another to Morgenstern's desk.[11] Some of the men had experience in teaching Jewish subjects, others claimed they could shift from previous academic interests. But their applications were all refused. The college considered the candidacy of Eric Werner, a musicologist who had managed to enter the United States on a visitor's visa in October, 1938, only because there had been no one to teach Jewish music after the retirement of Abraham Z. Idelsohn in 1934. Werner was engaged for two years on the recommendation of Rabbi Jonah B. Wise of New York and was thus enabled to receive a nonquota immigration visa. In this instance, too, the appointment eventually became regular and permanent.[12]

Until the fall of 1938, no further action was contemplated. At this early stage the college was interested only in helping somewhat to alleviate the employment problem by giving temporary work to men who could be useful to it for a limited period of time.

Yet there was one highly respected European scholar who enjoyed such standing in the entire Jewish academic community that the college undertook to initiate a scheme for his resettlement in America—although it would derive no direct benefits. Ismar Elbogen had taught since 1902 at the *Lehranstalt* (formerly *Hochschule*) *für die Wissenschaft des Judentums,* the liberal seminary and school for advanced Jewish studies in Berlin. He had been the teacher and counsellor to HUC students studying abroad after their ordination; for a semester he had taught in New York at the Jewish Institute of Religion. In 1937 Elbogen made the decision to leave Germany, having found life there "insupportable." On the initiative of William Rosenau, rabbi in Baltimore and a member of the HUC Board of Governors, a unique plan was formulated whereby Elbogen would come to America as "Research Professor in the fields of Jewish and Hebrew Research." He would be supported by equal grants of $1,000 per year from the Hebrew Union College, the Jewish Institute of Religion, the Jewish Theological Seminary of America, and Dropsie College in Philadelphia. In the name of all four institutions, Morgenstern issued the call to Elbogen in May, 1938. The elderly man arrived in New York a few months later. There, as earlier in Berlin, he continued to work for the rescue of fellow scholars and former students.[13]

As the situation in Nazi Germany grew ever more grim, the Board of Governors of the college decided much more needed to be done. At its meeting of October 20, 1938, upon the recommendation of Rabbi Solomon Freehof of Pittsburgh, it appointed a committee to consider what the HUC might do to ameliorate the plight of refugee scholars, possibly providing them with room and board in the college dormitory.[14] In the following weeks, an imaginative project was formulated: the Hebrew Union College would establish a "Jewish College in Exile" on its campus. Apparently modeled on the University in Exile, which was established in 1934 by Alvin Johnson as the graduate faculty of the New School for Social Research in New York,[15] it was initially contemplated to provide for some twenty-five German Jewish scholars of repute during a period of two to three years. They would have the library at their disposal to pursue their studies and be able to perfect their English under the tutelage of the College's students. While at HUC, they would be able to establish contacts and adapt themselves to America.[16]

As a result of what was happening in Europe, Morgenstern envisioned a new role for the College. When added to its existing faculty, these new men would make the HUC one of the great centers of Jewish research and scholarship in the world. With the demise of the institutions of higher Jewish learning in Germany, *Wissenschaft des Judentums* would be transplanted to the soil of Palestine and America. It thus became the task to the Hebrew Union College to help raise up a new generation of Jewish scholars, a responsibility previously left to Europe.[17] Although the appointments were to be temporary, it was intended that the scholars' immigration be permanent. For with the *Kristallnacht* pogrom of November 9–10, 1938, only a few weeks after Freehof's initial proposal, any thought of return was patently absurd. With the outbreak of physical violence, the HUC project took on a new dimension of urgency.

In November, two weeks after *Kristallnacht,* Morgenstern informed Elbogen, now settled in New York, of the project which was planned and asked him to draw up a list of names. Besieged by requests for assistance from abroad, the elder scholar was deeply moved at the news: " מים קרים על נפש עיפה שמועה טובה ," he replied. "It is the first act of speedy and ready help after the last pogrom. . . ." From the names which Elbogen supplied, Morgenstern eventually chose nine: Alexander Guttmann, Franz Landsberger, Albert Lewkowitz, Isaiah Sonne, Eugen Täubler, Max Wiener, Walter Gottschalk, Abraham Heschel, and Franz Rosenthal.[18] Official invitations were sent to each of them on April 6, 1939. Adding the name of Arthur Spanier, who, under special circumstances, had been asked to accept a position somewhat earlier, the College thus made an irreversible commitment to ten men, some with families.

In accordance with the current interpretation of United States immigration law,[19] which provided for the granting of nonquota visas only to scholars who would be paid a minimal salary over a period of at least two years, the initial call was issued to seven men to be research professors at $1,800 per year and two (Heschel and Rosenthal) to be research fellows at $500 per year plus room and board. Along with the official letters, to be presented to the local consul, went a private message which noted that the college would expect the men, if possible, to live in the dormitory, deducting a portion of their salary for maintenance, and that the commitment was for only two or three years until they could make an adjustment to America.[20] As the letters of invitation did not go out until after consultations by mail with the Visa Division of the State Department, the college authorities fully expected that the appointments would qualify. They surely did not anticipate the degree to which they would have to increase their commitment, nor that in some of the cases—despite their best efforts—the rescue attempt would fail.

The problems that the entire project faced with the United States government first became apparent in the case of Arthur Spanier.[21] Along with thousands of other German Jews, the former Hebraica librarian at the Prussian State Library and later teacher at the *Lehranstalt* had been arrested and put into a concentration camp following *Kristallnacht*. He wrote to Elbogen, his former colleague, in New York, that he would be released only on the basis of assured emigration. Elbogen thereupon urged Morgenstern to give him an appointment at the college so that he might be immediately released and admitted outside the quota. Through Elbogen and through Rabbi Jonah B. Wise an arrangement was worked out whereby Spanier's sister in New York would pay the difference between the value of her brother's services to the college and the salary of $2,000 he would be offered. She also agreed to be responsible for his support after two years. Elbogen noted that the agreement "fulfills מצות פדיון שבויים and has no risk." [22] The college's appointment of Spanier as instructor of rabbinics, in December, 1938, apparently influenced his release from the concentration camp; [23] but it did not secure him a visa. Unable to discover the reason for the refusal, Morgenstern finally succeeded [24] in arranging an interview with Avra M. Warren, head of the Visa Division of the State Department, for May 20, 1940, in order to discuss the case.

What Morgenstern learned at that conference astonished him greatly, however typical it later proved to be of State Department policy.[25] The Visa Division had ruled that Spanier was primarily a librarian, not regularly a professor at a legitimate institution of higher learning; hence he was ineligible. Moreover—and incredibly—the Berlin consul had accepted as valid the Nazi government's demotion of the Berlin liberal seminary from the status of *Hochschule* to that of *Lehranstalt* in 1934. On this basis, as well, it claimed that Spanier did not qualify: the *Lehranstalt,* as a mere "institute" not of university rank, was clearly inferior academically to the Hebrew Union College, and the immigration law was understood to exclude the grant of a nonquota visa to a scholar coming from an institution of lesser status abroad to one of higher status in the United States.[26]

The decision in the Spanier case threw the success of the entire College in Exile project into doubt. It was now anticipated that Guttmann, who was also associated with the *Lehranstalt,* would be ineligible, as well as Lewkowitz, who had taught at the Breslau seminary, and Sonne, who had taught at seminaries in Florence, Italy, and on the Isle of Rhodes. The cases of Rosenthal and Heschel looked even bleaker as they were young scholars without established academic status. Max Wiener, Morgenstern was told in Washington, would be regarded as a rabbi rather than a professor since he had exercised both functions. Even the remaining invitations, those to men who had taught at recognized German universities, were invalid since the State Department at this stage was no longer willing to admit scholars merely for purposes of research.[27]

Morgenstern returned to Washington three weeks later for a second conference. This time he was joined by Rabbi David Philipson, of Cincinnati, and Rabbi Solomon Freehof, of Pittsburgh. The three college representatives met with Warren and two of his assistants. Their strategy was apparently to persuade the government officials that the project, as initially formulated, was of benefit not only to the college, but also to America. The preservation of *Wissenschaft des Judentums,* they argued, would "redound greatly to the credit of our nation as a center and the fosterer of objective scientific scholarship."[28] They were also trying to counter the anticipated new interpretation of the law which made only those offered permanent teaching appointments eligible for nonquota visas. As Morgenstern could not know how successful any of these men would be in teaching American Reform rabbinical students, he was necessarily reluctant to commit himself to including all of the invitees as regular instructors, nor was he feeling at ease about making a permanent commitment to men whom he and the faculty did not know personally. Indeed, the regular faculty of the college at the time numbered only about a dozen men. He admitted to Warren that their chief service would be that of scientific research. His honesty had the effect of producing a ruling that the project did not qualify for nonquota visas.

Earlier in 1939, at a conference held between representatives of the departments of State, Labor, and Justice, it had been decided that purely scientific institutions without a student body were not eligible to appoint refugee scholars outside the quota. While the HUC was clearly an instructional institution, the College in Exile was not. Warren concluded, six weeks after the interview, that the Hebrew Union College could bring in professors on a nonquota basis only if they were appointed "as regular members of its faculty, primarily to instruct, or to confer the benefit of their knowledge upon, students thereof, and for positions of a continuing, rather than a temporary or intermittent character; provided, of course, such scholars were able to meet the requirements of the law with respect to their past vocational experience."[29] Such a commitment was far beyond that originally intended. But the project was already publicized and funded. Most importantly, its significance and urgency were daily becoming more apparent.

In order to avoid any further misunderstanding, Morgenstern, joined this time by the Board of Governors chairman, Ralph Mack, arranged for a third conference in Washington. On September 20, 1939, they met first with Assistant Secretary of State George Messersmith [30]—an interview arranged by Rabbi Edward L. Israel, of Baltimore, through Isador Lubin, a Jewish senior official in the Department of Commerce. There followed another session with Warren. This time Morgenstern was given precise instructions under what conditions of appointment the men would be granted nonquota visas.[31] The very next day he issued new official letters of invitation. In each instance the recipient was now asked to become a regular "teaching member of the Faculty" for "an indeterminate period," defined to mean "that it is our intention that this appointment shall be permanent." Once again a private supplementary letter went along as well. It indicated that while the college would make use of the man's services for teaching to the extent that it would be feasible and advantageous to the school, there would not be enough instructional opportunities available to allow a full schedule for each man. The work would still basically be that of research. Morgenstern also sent a letter to the American consul in each man's area of residence. A month later the Board of Governors approved the new terms of appointment.[32]

By the time of the third State Department meeting, one of the scholars on the list had already managed to gain admission to the United States. Franz Landsberger had been professor of the history of art at the University of Breslau before the Nazis removed him in 1933. Thereafter, he had served as director of the Berlin Jewish Museum until it was forced to close. Like Spanier, Landsberger had been placed in the Sachsenhausen concentration camp following *Kristallnacht,* and for him as well Elbogen had made a special appeal to Morgenstern.[33] While in the camp, Landsberger had the good fortune of receiving an invitation from British classicist Gilbert Murray to visit him in Oxford. Though the document was sufficient to effect his release, he could remain in England only for a temporary period. In March, 1939, while still in Berlin, he learned that his name was on Morgenstern's list, and he gladly accepted the initial invitation when it reached him in England two months later. Though

Landsberger encountered the same difficulties as the other invitees when he presented his letter of appointment to the American consul in London, he was fortunate in receiving the assistance of a Mrs. Thomas W. Lamont, who was able to persuade the consul to tell her the conditions under which Landsberger would be admitted. When informed, Morgenstern wrote to the consul on July 10, 1939, referring to the proffered position as involving teaching responsibilities and the expectation of permanency. His letter succeeded in securing a nonquota visa for Landsberger and his wife, enabling them to arrive in America late in August, just a few days before the outbreak of war.[34]

A second scholar on the list, Max Wiener, avoided the necessity of awaiting approval of the college's appointment by accepting an earlier invitation to become the assistant rabbi of a Reform congregation in Syracuse, New York. Although he did not intend to fill this rabbinical post except for the briefest period, he decided to use the nonquota visa he received for it in the summer of 1939. His intention was to make his way from Syracuse to the college as soon as possible. Shortly after the High Holydays that year he did indeed come to Cincinnati. But his stay there was not a happy one. Though a profound scholar of Jewish philosophy and intellectual history, Wiener was already fifty-seven years old when he arrived, had difficulty with spoken English, and was asked to teach Mishnah, Talmud, and liturgy rather than philosophy. After two-and-a-half years, the college secured a pulpit for him in Fairmont, West Virginia, which, unfortunately, proved even less satisfying. Max Wiener was the only one of the refugee scholars whom the college decided not to retain.[35]

With the arrival of Landsberger and Wiener, and with the unconditional refusal of a visa to Walter Gottschalk, a Semiticist who was apparently rejected because he had served as a librarian in the Near East Department of the Berlin Municipal Library rather than as a professor in a recognized teaching institution,[36] the list of those still awaited was reduced to seven. Because of their limited academic backgrounds, it was anticipated that the two youngest men, Franz Rosenthal and Abraham Heschel, might have the most difficulty. In fact, because each of them was able to make his way to England, they received visas quite promptly once their second letters of invitation reached the American consul in London.

Though Franz Rosenthal was only twenty-five years old when the college brought him to Cincinnati, he had already gained an enviable reputation as a Semiticist and won a prestigious international prize for his work. From Germany, he had managed to make his way first to Uppsala, Sweden, and then to London. About a month after the second letter of invitation was issued, the London consul received a message from the Secretary of State's office affirming that Rosenthal's as well as Heschel's appointments came within the purview of the nonquota section of the Immigration Act.[37] In the case of Rosenthal it remained only to determine whether his four semesters of teaching at the *Lehranstalt* were sufficient to satisfy the requirement of having previously carried on the vocation of professor at a ranking educational institution. By the end of November, at the discretion of the American consul, Rosenthal was granted his visa. Elbogen's prediction that, once in the United States, the young scholar would get a fellowship within a very short time [38] proved correct as early as 1943, and in 1948 he resigned his position at the college to succeed Giorgio Levi Della Vida in the chair of Arabic at the University of Pennsylvania.

Abraham Heschel had been registered for a regular immigration visa in Frankfurt since June, 1938, and he expected that his number would come up in March, 1939. But when he was deported as an alien Jew from Germany to Poland in November, 1938, the American consul in Warsaw, who received his documents, refused even to look at them for at least nine months. Morgenstern's first invitation, sent to him in Frankfurt, reached Heschel in Warsaw. He was delighted to accept and indicated his intention (a wise one indeed) to try to obtain the American visa in a friendlier country. During the summer of 1939, Heschel was able to get a transit visa to England and eventually, after receiving the revised invitation, to persuade the London consul that his teaching activity at the *Lehranstalt,* in the adult education program of the *Reichsvertretung* (the national Jewish organization in Germany), and in the Warsaw seminary would qualify him for a nonquota immigration visa to the United States. He received the visa in January, 1940, and began teaching at the college later that year.[39] Already known for his books on biblical prophecy and on Maimonides when he arrived at HUC, he soon became the most widely known of the group, not only as scholar, but as a leading theologian. After four years in Cincinnati, he accepted an appointment to the Jewish Theological Seminary of America.

The most delicate case for the college was that of Isaiah Sonne. An erudite scholar of medieval and Renaissance Jewish creativity, Sonne had originally been brought to Morgenstern's attention by Professor

Jacob Mann of the HUC faculty and by Simon Bernstein, the director of the Palestine Department of the Zionist Organization of America. The latter enabled Sonne to get a tourist entry permit for Palestine, good for several months. The Polish-born Sonne, was thus able to leave Italy shortly before he expected to be expelled, along with other foreign Jews. He was given a nonquota visa in Jerusalem on November 15, 1939, not long after he received the College's second letter of invitation. But in his case difficulties then arose from the side of the college. Certain members of the faculty had expressed opposition to seeing Sonne become one of their number, while Morgenstern had serious doubts about his ability to be an effective teacher of American students. Given the specialized area of Sonne's competence, there was, moreover, little possibility of his finding a position elsewhere. "In all probability," Morgenstern wrote candidly to Ralph Mack, "he would constitute a permanent burden on us." A plan was therefore formulated to pay Sonne a stipend for two years in Palestine in lieu of the salary he was promised in Cincinnati. Even Elbogen concurred that Sonne would doubtless be happier in the environment of Jerusalem. Nelson Glueck of the college faculty, who was about to return to his work in Palestine, was given the task of convincing Sonne. The latter, however, would not be persuaded. Before Morgenstern could write a definite letter to him, Sonne was on his way to the United States, fearing that his visa would expire if he delayed unduly.[40] Once he arrived in March, 1940, however, the college fulfilled its obligation to him fully while he, in turn, contributed richly to its scholarly reputation.

Although the consuls in London and Jerusalem responded affirmatively and quite soon after the second letters of appointment were issued, in Berlin—where the situation was most desperate—the consulate engaged in frustrating, frightening delay. Alexander Guttmann, a Talmud scholar, had remained in Berlin as the only full-time regular member of the *Lehranstalt* faculty. With the outbreak of war, his situation became far more difficult. Yet the consulate would not act until it had rechecked the status of the *Lehranstalt* and it was in no hurry to complete that task. Incredibly, it once again turned to "the German authorities" in its attempt, dictated from Washington, to redetermine the matter. By February, 1940, there was still no response.[41] Guttmann himself thereupon made an effort to furnish the consul with documents attesting to the *"Hochschule* status" of the *Lehranstalt,* while Morgenstern did his best to bring pressure to bear on Berlin directly as well as via Washington.[42]

At length, the *Lehranstalt* was declared an institution of higher learning, and Guttmann received his visa on March 26, 1940, fully six months from the date the second invitations were issued. Once in Cincinnati, he was immediately given a full teaching load since Talmud was the one field in which the college then truly needed instructors. Of the refugee scholars, he is the only one still actively on the faculty in Cincinnati.

The case of Eugen Täubler stands out from the others as the only one in which the recipient of an HUC invitation chose initially to refuse it. A distinguished historian of ancient Rome, Täubler had taught at the universities of Zurich and Heidelberg before the Nazi regime forced him to restrict his scholarly pursuits to the Jewish sphere. Beginning in 1935, he taught at the *Lehranstalt*. In March, 1939, Täubler had written to Solomon Zeitlin at Dropsie College and to Henry Slonimsky at the Jewish Institute of Religion in search of an appointment. Each institution had passed the request on to the HUC, which included him on its list. To the April invitation Täubler replied that he was unsure whether he would be able to accept the call and that he was continuing his correspondence with Slonimsky. Then nothing further was heard from him in Cincinnati for eight months, though, like the others, he received the second, more desirable invitation in September. Finally, the college learned in January, 1941, that he had been refused a nonquota visa. The American consul in Berlin had seen fit to rule that the present faculty of the Hebrew Union College was altogether adequate for the size of its student body and that, in consequence, there was no justification for granting visas to prospective additional personnel.[43] Morgenstern wrote immediately to the Visa Division to investigate the matter, with the result that Täubler was granted a visa for himself and his wife within a month. Once in the United States, he claimed that he had remained behind because he regarded his work there as essential; others thought he had been unable to tear himself away from Germany. Never really desirous of coming to HUC, he was not happy in a rabbinical seminary, though he stayed in Cincinnati until his death in 1953. His wife, Selma Stern-Täubler, a historian in her own right, served for a number of years as archivist of the American Jewish Archives.

Of both Guttmann and Täubler it can be said that the college's invitation clearly saved them from eventual deportation and likely death. In the two cases that remain, Lewkowitz and Spanier, the college failed. Albert Lewkowitz was the sole member of the Breslau Jewish Theological Seminary's faculty to appear on Morgenstern's list.[44] He was a teacher of

Jewish philosophy with considerable standing in the field. Both he and Spanier decided to seek temporary asylum in Amsterdam while awaiting the outcome of their efforts to gain visas. Morgenstern addressed communications on their behalf to the American consul in Rotterdam, who had received their files from Germany. Lewkowitz's chances for a visa looked good once the Breslau seminary was recognized by the United States government as an institution of sufficient rank, along with the *Lehranstalt*. But then the Germans bombed Rotterdam and, as a result, the records of his service in Breslau were lost. A new statement from Germany was required,[45] and apparently it was not forthcoming before the United States closed all its consulates in Germany in July, 1941. Another Morgenstern conference with Warren that month, this time arranged by Senator Lister Hill of Alabama, produced no result.[46] Lewkowitz's only hope was to get to Spain and there apply for a regular quota visa. This he was unable, or unwilling, to do. He remained in Holland and was eventually placed in the Bergen-Belsen concentration camp. Fortunately, he was among those selected for a prisoner exchange in 1944[47] and thereupon he was permitted entry into Palestine. Arthur Spanier was not even so relatively fortunate. The American consul in Rotterdam declared him definitely and finally ineligible because he had been a librarian rather than a professor. Though Morgenstern then did his best to get Spanier out as a nonpreference alien, he achieved no result.[48] Spanier died in Bergen-Belsen.

Once the chances of successfully bringing over Spanier and Lewkowitz had receded, and with the prospect of Wiener's departure, the decision was made to attempt bringing one more refugee scholar to Cincinnati. Difficulties were not expected since Samuel Atlas, a scholar of Talmud and Jewish philosophy, had been teaching in England since 1934. A call was issued to him, in May, 1941, on the same terms as the other refugee scholars. Atlas was eager to come to the United States, not only because he had no permanent position in England, but also because the war had stranded his wife in Montreal. But Atlas' case fell under a new set of restrictions, recently imposed out of an imagined fear that Nazi spies might enter the United States as immigrants.[49] Visas could now be refused to anyone who had relatives in Axis-occupied countries, and Atlas had a brother in Lithuania and a sister in Estonia. Moreover, procedures for gaining visas had become considerably more complex and cumbersome than heretofore. It seemed that Atlas' case would be held up interminably and might eventually be decided in the negative. Morgenstern therefore wrote a letter to Henry Morgenthau, Jr., Secretary of the Treasury, whose parents had been interested in the college. In asking the secetary's intervention for Atlas, the HUC president poured out his dismay at the frustration caused him by the long struggle for the refugee project:

> I regret, however, that I must say that, as a result of negotiations with this [State] Department, and with Mr. Warren personally, extending over a number of years, I have no confidence that my request of Mr. Warren will receive favorable consideration, or that this application for a visa will be granted despite the fact that I know of no reason why it should not be. I have had repeated contacts with the Visa Division during the last two years and a half in connection with the efforts of the Hebrew Union College to bring over a number of Jewish scholars to teaching positions in it. And I am sorry to say I have never been able to accomplish anything whatever with that Department unless it was possible to bring pressure from some person high in the present administration upon the Office of the Visa Division.[50]

Morgenthau, who would later assume an independent role in rescuing Jews,[51] asked Under Secretary of State Sumner Welles to investigate Atlas' case. Within a few days the application was approved. After passing through a gauntlet of U-boats in a convoy of cargo ships, Atlas was able to join the faculty in Cincinnati early in 1942. He was the last of the refugee scholars to arrive.

The entire Hebrew Union College project is perhaps best summed up in a letter which Michael Guttmann, the head of the Budapest seminary and father of Alexander Guttmann, wrote to Morgenstern on April 23, 1939. What the college is doing, he wrote in German, "is a deed which has its unique historical value and will remain memorable for all times. It is a noble rescue, not alone of the Jewish teacher, but also of the Jewish teaching."

NOTES

1. I am grateful to the following individuals who orally and in writing responded to my inquiries and supplied me with documents: Samuel Atlas, Alexander Guttmann, Dora Landsberger, Franz Rosenthal, Margit Sonne, Eric Werner, and Theodore Wiener. All written materials have been deposited in the American Jewish Archives in Cincinnati.
2. Board of Governors Minutes (BGM), October 30, 1934.
3. On this subject, and for the history of the Hebrew Union College–Jewish Institute of Religion in general, see *Hebrew Union College-Jewish Institute of Religion at One Hundred Years,* ed. Samuel Karff (Cincinnati, 1975).
4. BGM, May 24, 1935.
5. Lewy's wife, Hildegarde, likewise an Assyriologist, remained behind to salvage as much of their belongings as possible. To elude the Nazi censors, Lewy's instructions to his wife took the form of alleged citations from Akkadian texts he claimed to have found in the Louvre. Not knowing Akkadian and never suspecting the contents of the quotations, the Nazi censors allowed the messages to pass (*Cincinnati Enquirer,* February 15, 1941).
6. HUC President Julian Morgenstern likewise applied to the Emergency Committee for funds to support Lewy's appointment, but he was turned down as at that time there was no thought of providing a permanent position (Edward R. Murrow to Morgenstern, June 14, 1935, File E, Box 1553, American Jewish Archives [AJA]). In addition to the Jewish Theological Seminary, the Emergency Committee made grants to a number of Jewish institutions, including the Hebrew University, the Jewish Institute of Religion, the College of Jewish Studies, the YIVO, and the American Academy for Jewish Research. But the HUC, which absorbed far more refugee scholars than any other Jewish institution except the Hebrew University, was never able to obtain any assistance. On the work of the Emergency Committee, which was supported almost exclusively by prominent Jewish foundations, see Stephen Duggan and Betty Drury, *The Rescue of Science and Learning* (New York, 1948).
7. Morgenstern to Lewy, January 8, 1935, Lewy to Morgenstern, March 11, 1935, Julius Lewy File, Box 3204, AJA.
8. Morgenstern to John A. Wilson at the Oriental Institute, July 26, 1938, *ibid.*
9. Michael Wilensky File, Box 3204, AJA, especially his letter to Morgenstern of August 13, 1935. See also Ismar Elbogen File, Box 1553, AJA.
10. On Wilensky's life and scholarly work, see N. H. Tur-Sinai's introduction to the second edition of *Sefer-ha-Rikmah* (Jerusalem, 1964) and Samuel Atlas in *Studies in Bibliography and Booklore,* December 1955, pp. 51–52.
11. Among those who applied, or whose names were submitted by organizations, were men of scholarly accomplishment, including Fritz Bamberger (philosophy), David Baumgardt (philosophy), Nahum Glatzer (history), Martin Plessner (Semitics), and Joseph Prijs (bibliography and history). The correspondence is mostly in Box 732, AJA.

12. Eric Werner File, Box 3204, AJA; BGM, November 22, 1938.
13. On the Elbogen project, see Elbogen File; Cyrus Adler File, Box 1550; and the correspondence between Elbogen and Adolph Oko, Box 2328, AJA. To Franz Rosenthal he wrote on April 12, 1939: "Uns könnte es gut gehen, wenn die Sorge um die Heimatlosen nicht wäre."
14. BGM, October 20, 1938. The original proposal to work with the Central Conference of American Rabbis and include congregational rabbis as well as scholars seems to have been early abandoned despite the initial intent (*CCAR Yearbook*, XLIX [1939], 31, 34–35). Only one refugee rabbi, Max Vogelstein, of Coblenz, took up residence in the dormitory.
15. On the University in Exile, see Norman Bentwich, *The Rescue and Achievement of Refugee Scholars* (The Hague, 1953), pp. 48–52; Duggan and Drury, pp. 79–82. In 1960 the HUC-JIR awarded Alvin Johnson an honorary degree.
16. Morgenstern to Elbogen, November 25, 1938, Elbogen File.
17. See Morgenstern's speech to the Thirty-Sixth Council of the Union of American Hebrew Congregations, January 15–19, 1939 (*UAHC Proceedings*, XIII, 766–68).
18. BGM, April 19, 1939.
19. The relevant passage was Section 4(d) of the Immigration Act of 1924, which exempts from quota restrictions: "An immigrant who continuously for at least two years immediately preceding the time of his application for admission to the United States has been, and who seeks to enter the United States solely for the purpose of, carrying on the vocation of minister of any religious denomination, or professor of a college, academy, seminary, or university; and his wife, and his unmarried children under 18 years of age, if accompanying or following to join him."
20. The official letters and the private letters are contained in the files of each of the men in the AJA.
21. Unfortunately, the Spanier file has been lost, and the case must be reconstructed from other sources.
22. Elbogen File.
23. Margaret Spanier to Morgenstern, December 16, 1938, Morgenstern File, Box 1560, AJA.
24. Probably thanks to the unnamed "influential friend of the College in Washington" to whom Morgenstern had written in April, 1939 (BGM, April 19, 1939).
25. A great deal of attention has been devoted to this subject in recent years. The basic works are Arthur D. Morse, *While Six Million Died* (New York, 1968); David S. Wyman, *Paper Walls* (Amherst, Mass., 1968); Henry L. Feingold, *The Politics of Rescue* (New Brunswick, N. J., 1970); and Saul S. Friedman, *No Haven for the Oppressed* (Detroit, 1973).
26. BGM, May 25, 1939.
27. *Ibid.*
28. Morgenstern to Warren, July 2, 1939, summarizing the meeting. This letter and related documents are contained in File 811.111 Colleges, Record Group 59, The National Archives (NA).
29. Warren to Morgenstern, August 11, 1939, on the basis of decisions reached two days earlier. These decisions were in turn based on a report by the legal adviser of the State Department, of August 2, 1939, prompted specifically by the case of Franz Rosenthal. The report referred to a letter by Franklin H. McNutt, of the Ohio Department of Education, attesting to the high standing of the Hebrew Union College and also to the "good impression" made by the college representatives at their Visa Department interview. But it concluded that since, according to the "general instruction" of May 9, 1939, only a scholar whose task

would be "primarily to confer the benefit of his knowledge upon the students rather than to pursue his own studies" could qualify, only those to whom the college gave regular teaching assignments would be eligible (*ibid.*).

30. During his earlier service as United States consul in Berlin, Messersmith had urged a liberal policy on granting visas to Jewish refugees (Zosa Szajkowski, "The Consul and the Immigrant," *Jewish Social Studies,* XXXVI [1974], 10). In 1940 he was replaced by the much less sympathetic Breckinridge Long.

31. BGM, October 2, 1939.

32. *Ibid.,* October 19, 1939.

33. Elbogen to Morgenstern, December 8, 1938, Elbogen File.

34. Franz Landsberger File, Box 3204, AJA.

35. Max Wiener File, Box 3204, William Rosenau Correspondence, Box 2330a, AJA.

36. There is no file on Gottschalk in the American Jewish Archives. He was presumably sent the second, revised letter of appointment to Belgium, where he was then residing. Gottschalk's appointment was originally made conditional upon receiving support payments from his cousin, a wealthy attorney in Brussels (BGM, October 19, 1939, January 17, 1940). I have been unable to determine his ultimate fate.

37. The letter of November 9, 1939 (NA) was originally sent to the American consul in Dublin as, for a time, a moratorium had been declared on the granting of additional visas in London.

38. Elbogen to Morgenstern, December 8, 1938, Elbogen File.

39. Abraham Heschel File, Box 3204, AJA.

40. On Sonne see the Isaiah Sonne File, Box 3204, and the Morgenstern File, Box 1351, AJA; also BGM, February 28 and March 20, 1940.

41. Cyrus B. Follmer, American vice-consul, to Alexander Guttmann, February 8, 1940, Michael and Alexander Guttmann File, Box 3204, AJA. At the request of the consulate, Leo Baeck had presented it a report on the status of the *Lehranstalt* as early as December 1939. However, it was apparently deemed insufficient (Alexander Guttmann to Morgenstern, February 28, 1940, *ibid.*). Guttmann recollects hearing from Max Wiener that a U.S. consular official in Berlin had said to him: "Why do you want to emigrate? In five years the situation will be the same in America."

42. BGM, February 28, 1940.

43. *Ibid.,* January 22, 1941; Hilfsverein Zedakah to Hebrew Union College, January 6, 1941, Eugen Täubler File, Box 3204, AJA. This was in keeping with State Department policy at that time (*cf.* Wyman, pp. 173–79).

44. As in the case of Spanier, there is no file extant for Lewkowitz in the AJA.

45. BGM, November 27, 1940.

46. Morgenstern to Carl Pritz, July 23, 1941, Morgenstern File, Box 1354, AJA.

47. Morgenstern to Lt. S. W. Hubbel, USNR, August 3, 1944, Morgenstern Correspondence, uncat., AJA.

48. Morgenstern tried to send a statement supporting Spanier's application as a regular quota immigrant to the consul in Rotterdam via the Visa Division. Three weeks later Warren returned the statement to Morgenstern because no postage was affixed. The letter was sent again with proper postage, but valuable time was lost (Täubler File).

49. For details see Morse, pp. 300–303; Feingold, pp. 160–61; Wyman, pp. 193–205.

50. Letter of September 26, 1941, Samuel Atlas File, Box 3204, AJA.

51. Morse, p. 93; Feingold, p. 297.

YAVNEH VS. MASADA: CONSCIOUS AND UNCONSCIOUS USES OF HISTORICAL LEGEND IN THE FORMATION OF AMERICAN JEWISH IDENTITY

By

NORMAN B. MIRSKY

Hebrew Union College—Jewish Institute of Religion, Cincinnati

Of all the rallying cries which are shouted in the ears of American Jews, hardly any have become less subject to challenge or more cliché-ridden than the call to give our children a "Jewish identity." Some of the same people adept in the jargon of individual psychology glibly describe this person or that as having an "identity crisis," a term usually applied to what might be called the inability of an individual to find a satisfactory relationship between the various factors which make up his self, while at the same time he finds little rewarding in the roles that his society asks him to play. What strikes anyone making an effort to understand American Jews is the almost astonishing lack of overlap in conceptualization in the very people who speak of Jewish identity as a group concern while describing, in quite sophisticated terms, individuals as falling unfortunate prey to identity crises. This is to say that the word *identity* used in one context is not seen to bear a relationship to the term *identity* used in another context.

The lack of overlap is unfortunate. It is unfortunate because while one group of scientists, the ego psychologists, have gathered extensive data of a case-study variety and, building on psychoanalytic theory, have begun to fill in the missing links between individuals and collectivities, another group of scientists attempts to determine whether a person has or lacks a positive Jewish identity by surveying him to see whether or not he meets preestablished criteria deemed necessary if one may be said to possess a "positive" Jewish identity.

The ego psychologists have developed, for those concerned with identity, theories and case histories which seek to demonstrate the inseparability of psyche, body, and cultural complexes in the process we call identity. What is evident to the ego psychologists, but has apparently been lost on those who measure Jewish identity by commitment to Jewish institutions, is that between the individual and the institutions there are his drives with their needs, his body with its needs, his ego defense system with its needs, his family with its needs, his country, his culture, and so forth, all of which must be somehow integrated before it is possible to speak of a person's identity.[1]

The noted psychoanalyst Dr. Jacob Arlow provides the insights which sparked the idea for my speculations in this essay. Arlow argued, in an unpublished lecture given in the spring of 1969 at a meeting of the Cincinnati Psychoanalytic Society, that if a society is to give meaning to the values it wants its members to acknowledge, it must provide its members with some solutions to their interpsychic conflicts. This it does, if at all, through the process of renunciation and identification, i.e., through the formation of the superego, a process which is never completely successful. Nevertheless, the process is more likely to succeed if a "mythos" is operative, one replete with a hero, identification with whom gives the child, the youth, and the adult a feeling that what he is doing is good for him and for his collectivity.[2]

It is noteworthy that in his lecture Arlow illustrated the dynamics of the search for proper heroes (i.e., proper for the collectivity) by contrasting the figures of Rabbi Yochanan ben Zaccai and the Maccabees. He pointed out, as I will too, that historically when the Jewish situation called for a rather compliant, passive hero to be replaced by more active, more iconoclastic heroes, greater emphasis was laid on the Maccabees than on Rabbi Yochanan.[3]

What follows, then, is an attempt to gain a better understanding of the importance of myth-making in identity formation, particularly for those concerned with Jewish identity. I want to explore in some detail the impact of the Yavneh legend and the recent effort by American Jewish educators to replace it with a Masada myth incorporating the achievements of Yavneh into the seemingly antithetical personalities and events which constituted the Masada episode. In this way, perhaps, some light will be shed on the viability of Jewish life in America and especially on what has been overlooked in other studies of the formation of Jewish identity.[4]

When I was a small boy just beginning Sunday school and weekday Hebrew lessons, my teacher told me a story that went something like this: Shortly before the destruction of the Second Temple, Jerusalem was under a heavy siege. The situation was hopeless. The Jewish nation was doomed. Judaism was going to die out. Suddenly, out of desperation, the wise Rabbi Yochanan ben Zaccai seized upon a plan. He would feign death. He would be put in a coffin and his students would carry him out of Jerusalem. Whereupon he would go straight to the Roman general who was laying siege to the city. Yochanan would ask him a small favor: permission to establish a school in a forgotten village.

The story was exciting. First the coffin had to be carefully weighted to ensure the authentic feel of a dead man. Next, Yochanan had to get into the box and have it sealed. Then came the most suspenseful part: the "Roman" guards had to allow the cortège to pass. "Make them open the coffin," yelled a centurion. "No, it's against our religion," replied the students. "Then let's make sure he's really dead. Pierce the coffin with your spears, men," the tough centurion commanded. "Please," the students pleaded, "it's bad enough that we lost our beloved rabbi. Must we suffer further by having his body mutilated?" For some reason that escaped me then, given the reputed cruelty of the Romans, the soldiers desisted from stabbing the coffin. The cortège was permitted to leave the city. Yochanan then went to the Roman general and greeted him by hailing him as emperor. The general was about to chastise the rabbi for his apparent error, when suddenly a messenger appeared breaking the news that the emperor had died and the general had been named his successor. The general was pleased with Yochanan's prophetic qualities. He decreed that Yochanan was entitled to a favor. "I'm not asking you for much, O Caesar. Simply allow me and my few students to establish a little school in a small town named Yavneh." It seemed to the new ruler to be a reasonably insignificant wish, so he granted the old rabbi's request. Then my Sunday school teacher went on to tell us what a fool the emperor had been, since because of that little school the light of Torah was kept burning. Yavneh became the seat of an illustrious rabbinical academy. "Where is the Roman empire now? Dead!" But the Jews survived. "Why? Because there's more strength in learning than in force. Jews have always known that. That's why we're alive despite all the persecutions we've had to endure!'"

I was impressed with that legend and its clear meaning. I heard it for the first time in 1946 when I was nine. World War II had recently ended. Tales of the Holocaust were beginning to enter the perception of American Jewish youth. Remnants of destroyed Jewish communities were struggling to reassemble in Palestine and elsewhere. American Jews were beginning to return to the synagogue in the wake of the Jewish agony. The story of Yavneh's founding seemed to fit the time I first heard it. It was not difficult to picture Yavneh as an ancient prototype of the Hebrew school I was attending. The classrooms were musty. The teacher was known in my city as a scholar. It was rumored that he had received *s'micha* in some Polish yeshiva now laid waste by the Nazis.

The legend of Yavneh's founding which my teacher told and which was presented as history in the textbooks of my childhood differs in some important details from the version in the Talmud. According to the talmudic account,[5] it is not Yochanan, it is his nephew, who devises the escape plan. But, most significantly, it is not the cruel Romans who seek to spear the casket; it is the rabbi's fellow Jews, the *biryonim* (usually thought to be Zealots), who present the final obstacle to Yochanan's exit from the city. It is they and not the Romans who must be persuaded that it would be a political error to mutilate the corpse of a great rabbi. The talmudic account makes the Jewish Zealots into the true enemies of Torah. Furthermore, the Talmud elaborates on the method of prophecy employed by Yochanan. The rabbi recites biblical proof texts through which he has come to know in advance of the Roman general's grand promotion.

It is easy to explain away the differences between the Sunday school version and its talmudic source. Children would find it difficult to accept the fact that Jewish soldiers were a greater hindrance to the rabbi's plan than the hated Roman enemy. It was thought to be pedagogically unsound to admit that Jewish factionalism was rampant when the survival of the people was at stake. As for the deletion of the rabbi's use of proof texts, pure prophecy is more wondrous to an American child than predictions based on the interpretation of Scripture. The use of proof texts as the heart of Torah study would bear an unwholesome resemblance to the rantings of Christian revivalist preachers. The clever twist of a text is lost on a youth ignorant of its place in Jewish tradition.

Both versions of the story—but especially the Sunday derivative—served an important function. The story operated as a rescue fantasy, offering an alternative to the tales of rescue which predominated in an America at war. Freud and others have written extensively on the importance of rescue fantasies in the development of the human personality.[6] Such fantasies provide children with a safe outlet from the parental oppression which is part of the oedipal struggle. A male child who unconsciously desires to rid himself of father so that he might take father's place at the side of his mother needs release from the anxiety this wish may cause. He finds the release in a story like Jack and the Beanstalk, a story—a fantasy—in which a young boy slays a devouring giant and returns to his mother with a goose that lays golden eggs; the boy and his mother are thus provided with the potential for living together happily ever after. Girls who unconsciously see their mothers as rivals for fatherly love find a release in tales like Cinderella and Snow White fantasies in which "some day her prince may come" and remove her forever from the tyranny of "wicked stepmothers" who keep her sweeping cinders or, worse, try to kill her with poisoned apples. The displacement of murderous thoughts onto a fairy tale enables the child to live within the structure of the family.

But there is another utility to rescue fantasies, for they function not only on a psychological level, but on a sociological level as well. Since we are living at a time when women are exploring and reassessing their traditional roles within the family and society, perhaps it is now easier to see the sociological ramifications of rescue fantasies in such tales as Cinderella and Snow White than to move directly into their role in the shaping of male and group identities. Even without our new awareness of the place of women within our culture, it is relatively easy to grasp the psychological value of the Cinderella, Snow White, Rapunsel, and Sleeping Beauty stories. In each of these stories, the young girl is all but totally at the mercy of a witch or wicked stepmother until at some distant time—up to a hundred years in the case of poor Sleeping Beauty—a handsome prince comes along and rescues the girl from her wicked female captors. Well schooled as we now are in the ways of psychoanalytic interpretation, we do not find it difficult to accept the explanation which suggests that wicked stepmothers or evil witches are replacements for real mothers, thoughts about whose removal are dangerous, treasonous even. We do not find it hard to believe that the prince is a replacement for father be-

cause to admit consciously a desire to marry father would be to acknowledge a wish for an incestuous relationship and this would cause guilt
and/or anxiety above a tolerable level.

However, we have been socialized into overlooking other functions of
these tales, the fact that beyond their psychological uses they also serve
sociological ends. They all portray females as being passive recipients of
male benevolence. The girls cannot help themselves. They must sweep
cinders, be locked in towers, or lie in a comatose state until a male res-
cuer chances by. These are not stories in which a Jack climbs a bean stalk
and rids himself of his oppressor, or a St. George slays a dragon to prevent the devouring of virgins. The woods*man* rescues Red Riding Hood
and her grandmother. Without him, Red Riding Hood would be a wolf's
dessert. In short, these stories serve not only to relieve young girls from
oedipal anxiety but also to reinforce social norms about what roles
women are to have—not controlling their own destinies, not taking matters into their own hands, and not becoming active shapers of their own
futures.[7]

A culture which desires passivity in its women and valor in its men
is likely to provide rescue fantasies appropriate not only to its members'
psychological needs but also to the roles it wishes its members to play in
the larger society. Myths, legends, folktales, and fairy tales are thus agencies of socialization, but it must be remembered that in order for them to
have a social value they must be firmly rooted in the realities of the individual psyche.

It is safe to say that the emphasis in American rescue fantasies has
been, for males, on physical action, and even on violence when "necessary." American folktales tell of men heroically confronting the enemy.
Superman fights crime by beating up the criminals. Batman and Robin,
with some help from technology, punch their way to justice. Enough has
been written on the role of the Western to make my point. In the Horatio
Alger epics, it may have been diligence and clean living that got the hero
his reward—but not until he did something of a heroic physical nature,
like saving the millionaire's daughter from drowning, did he get the
recognition we know he deserved. Military exploits have made men
President of the United States. Where would John F. Kennedy have been
without P.T. 109?

Seen in this light, the story of Yochanan ben Zaccai runs counter to the
American grain. It elucidates what had heretofore been a conflict between
the American and the Jewish identity. For, if we reexamine the Yochanan

ben Zaccai tale as a rescue myth, a group rescue fantasy, we find in it elements which seem odd and strangely foreign to the American mentality. It is a legend which is passive in its activity, for while it is true that its outcome was the founding of a school, the method of achieving this goal depended upon passivity. The rabbi must pretend to be dead. His students must be mourners. His meeting with the general must take into account the fact that he recognizes the Roman as having complete control over his and Jewish destiny. As a result, he must demonstrate that he is submissive to alien authority. In the talmudic account, it is not even the rabbi himself who devises the scheme. When the rabbi makes his prophecy, it is through a method which demonstrates his skill at interpreting Scripture, but the method also betrays a certain helplessness in the face of inevitability. Passivity, etiquette, acknowledgment of authority, and skill in ascertaining an already predetermined event through mental acumen —these are what assure the Jewish future.

To be sure, the method worked. Yavneh went on to become the center of Jewish learning long after the Jewish state was destroyed.[8] And it was precisely Yochanan's success, as recorded in the legend, that allowed Yavneh to become woven into the fabric of Jewish identity from that time until the rebirth of active Jewish nationalism within the last hundred years. This is not to say that, within the vast web of life and legend which is the record of Jewish history, other myths have not gained sway over the identity of the Jew. It is to argue, however, that for a people living *semper et ubique* within the borders of alien and often hostile peoples, the Yavneh story could and did serve as a socializing model for Jewish survival. Furthermore, for a people whose leaders were often the heads of academies and as such skilled at interpreting sacred texts, the legend served as a reinforcement of religious authority as well as a reminder of the power of alien secular authority.

It is possible to find within the legend a paradigm for certain aspects of Jewish identity, for indeed it must be granted that, by identifying with Yochanan and his small band of scholars, a Jewish youth could meet his psychological rescue needs as well as develop a relationship to his people, his religion, and external (i.e., non-Jewish) authority. On a psychological level, the legend provides a child with the fantasy of rescuing Torah and Shekinah (two "feminine" aspects of Judaism) while doing no violence to the male authority figures represented by the rabbi-leader and emperor-leader. And, of course, since the Torah and Israel both came into being by Divine sanction, saving them means one is serving the Ultimate

Father, the One in Heaven. Anyone who labors in Torah pleases God. How much more pleasing is one who rescues as well as studies Torah.

As a socializing myth, too, the story has validity. It teaches that cleverness, learning, and the proper recognition of reality are in the end more fruitful than hopeless, violent revolt. This has been a well-honored Jewish attitude throughout the two millennia since Rabbi Yochanan was allowed to settle at Yavneh.

There have, however, been periods in which Yochanan's solution seems particularly inappropriate. Ours appears to be such a time. There are a number of reasons why this is true. One is that when Jews are given access to the culture of the general society, invariably its values become part of their identity. Thus, when a culture extols as heroes those who are activists rather than passive students, a tension develops between two equally compelling sets of cultural values. American culture, we have already noted, has traditionally chosen as role models men who said "Damn the torpedoes, full speed ahead." Even the scholarly achievements of such founding fathers as Franklin and Jefferson are deemphasized in favor of their inventions and their willingness to challenge and confront what they regarded as illicit authority. Americans place a stress on deed rather than word. It is rather pitiful to read textbooks on American Jewish history whose authors seek almost in vain to discover colonial Jews fitting the American image of fighter and activist.[9]

A second and more compelling reason for the need to replace the Yavneh legend with a different type of rescue fantasy lies in the events of the Second World War. Bruno Bettelheim, Hannah Arendt, and others have examined the remains of the European Jewish communities and found them sadly lacking in the will to gain mastery over their own fates. No matter how much respect is inspired by *kiddush ha-shem* (martyrdom), no matter how valiant the defenders of the Warsaw ghetto were, no matter how we detest the attack on European Jewry's few survivors by their critics, we are forced to suspect a certain glimmer of truth in their conclusions. And when we read of the attempts of certain European Jewish communal leaders and even some rabbis to reach a compromise with brutal and merciless authority, we have to find something lacking in the "Yavneh solution." Sometimes passivity in the face of a villainous authority is of no use. How can we offer Yavneh to those reared in the shadow of the Holocaust?[10]

And then, of course, there is the State of Israel. It is impossible to deny that, were it not for the military stance assumed by the Israelis,

there would be no Jewish state today. No matter how much land was redeemed through money, no matter how the genius of the Jews made the
desert bloom, there is one fact which seems irrefutable. Without armed
might and the willingness to employ it, Israel would not be available today to the Torah students who gather there to study and expound the
holy books.

Where rabbis and soldiers are joined, as in the second-century case of
Rabbi Akiva and Bar Kochba, it appears that Akiva falls prey to the
error of considering himself to be living in the time of the Messiah. Believing that one has found the Messiah is a mistake that activist rabbinic
Jews make frequently enough.[11] So we search our history for legends
seemingly more appropriate to our needs. Rabbinical literature fails us,
for it is mostly the work of the men of Yavneh. The Bible is more helpful, but it has too much to do with God—to a skeptical, secular generation, it presents too many theological problems. Where, then, do we
turn for a new myth? We go to Jewish writings that do not have rabbinical authorship. We find in the apocryphal Books of Maccabees and
the volumes of Flavius Josephus some possible alternative legends.

Perhaps it is not too well known that the association of Hanukkah
with the military victories of the Hasmoneans has not always been central
to the festival's celebration. The Talmud makes little of the Hasmoneans
in general and contains only a brief statement about Hanukkah. The
primary emphasis of the talmudic account is on the miracle of the oil
which burned beyond its natural capacity.[12] To the extent that the later
rabbis made use of the narratives found in the apocryphal Books of
Maccabees, it was to emphasize Mattathias' faithfulness to Jewish law
and to extol the bravery of Hannah and her seven sons, who preferred
to be martyred rather than violate God's commandments.[13] For the
Jews of the pre-modern period, Hanukkah was never more than a rather
minor observance. It became an important festival only for modern Jews.

Living in a secular culture, modern Jews have needed the Maccabees
as culture heroes; they have needed Hanukkah as a rival to Christmas;
they have needed a modern concept like freedom of religious choice to tie
the exploits of the Maccabees and the winter solstice festival together in
a package with which both Jews and non-Jews could live. It is unnecessary to dwell on the emphasis given the Maccabees in our lifetime, though
it is worth noting that, in the actual accounts of the sons of Mattathias,
only Judah was called Maccabee, i.e., the "hammer" or whatever. In
modern versions, those connected with the Hasmonean victory are almost

always called Maccabees. Maccabiads are held in Israel, and the story of how Judah fought for religious liberty is well known to Jewish children—and to non-Jewish children schooled where Jews make up enough of the population to warrant equal time!

While Hanukkah enjoys great popularity, the story of the Maccabees and their descendants, the later Hasmoneans, offers some obstacles to those in search of a heroic myth. The first, and least important, is that the victory of the Maccabees was short-lived and that the Hasmonean dynasts subsequently proved to be tyrannical protégés of Rome.[14] A greater difficulty with the heroism of the Maccabees may be that, in being locked into Hanukkah as it is, military force holds certain cultural conflicts for American Jews. If there is any time of year in America when it is inappropriate to speak of war and rebellion, it is in the season of paying homage to the Prince of Peace. One might call it Jewish *mazel* to need to build a festival around military success while the rest of the culture makes a nearly total effort to forget the world as it really is. The Maccabees and their nationalistic revolt fit well into the mythos of the State of Israel, but are not of equal service to American Jews.

There is another place to turn for a suitable myth—the story of Masada. Though its original version makes it questionable as a rescue fantasy, its modern retelling has that possibility, a possibility that has already been exploited by both Israelis and American Jews. At first glance, the account of the defense and destruction of the fortress of Masada presents special barriers for the weaving of the episode into Jewish legendry and fantasy. One obstacle is, of course, the fact that the story of Masada is contained in the works of Flavius Josephus.[15] Now, though Josephus is a friend to those trying to decipher Jewish history, his own personal behavior is not exemplary to those searching for new heroes.

Flavius Josephus, or Joseph the son of Matthias, the name he bore for the first three decades of his life, is known to us nearly exclusively through his own writings. Through these writings he seems to bear much in common with other fabulous characters of the ancient world. At the age of fourteen, he was able to engage the rabbis in discussion so adequately that they asked his advice—a feat allegedly accomplished by another precocious youth, the adolescent Jesus of Nazareth.[16] At the age of sixteen, "on hearing of one [Essene] named Bannus, who dwelt in the wilderness, wearing only such clothing as trees provided, feeding on such things as grew themselves, and using frequent ablutions of cold water, by day and night, for purity's sake, I became his devoted disciple"—in what we would now call a psychosocial moratorium. With the mythic hero's penchant for the number three, he leaves the Essenes after a three-year stay, only to join the Pharisees, a group not known for its love for the Hasmonean family, from which his mother was descended.[17] Seven or eight years after leaving the Essenes and joining the Pharisees, Joseph is sent on his first *rescue mission*. He goes to Rome for the purpose of saving certain Jewish priests whom the brutal procurator Felix had dispatched to Rome to be tried before Nero for some undetermined offense. In Rome he becomes friends with a Jewish actor, who helps him procure an audience with the Empress Poppaea Sabina. She takes a liking to Josephus, and he returns to Judea after having saved the lives of the priests.[18]

He then undertakes an even more heroic task. He goes to the Galilee as a commanding general to lead a rebellion against Rome. Josephus leaves two contradictory accounts of his military mission in the Galilee. In one he claims to have attempted to lead his people to military victory. In the other, he states that his purpose was to convince the Galileans of the futility of challenging Rome. What *is* clear is that a bloody battle exacts heavy tolls in dead and wounded on both sides. Finally the Jews are vanquished, but Josephus survives. Not only does he survive, but he goes over to the Romans—again, he claims, with a rescue mission. This time it is to try to convince any Jews still contemplating rebellion against Rome of the foolhardiness of such plans.[19]

It would be interesting to speculate on the psychological factors involved in Josephus' radical shift of loyalties. Earlier in his life he had abandoned his upper-class origins for a sect renouncing material goods. Then he became a member of a party antagonistic to his family. Next, he employed his high-born status to *save* his father's priestly colleagues. Then he attempted to rescue the rebels of the Galilee. At the age of thirty, he goes over to the Romans, substituting for his own family's name that of the Roman general under whose onslaught he had nearly lost his life (interestingly enough, the same general to whom Yochanan ben Zaccai fled from Jerusalem—and this is not all Yochanan and Joseph have in common).[20] Yet under his new name and under the protection of his new family, something like his biblical namesake Joseph—indeed, in his precociousness, his narrow escape from death, his ability to charm, his ease in the face of a foreign power, along with his view of himself as a deliverer, he seems to identify himself closely with the biblical Joseph (whether by design or chance, we do not know)—he sets out to redeem his people, first by warning them not to resist Rome, and finally by writing a history of the Jews whose purpose is to redeem their dignity in the eyes of the Greco-Roman world.[21]

Yet for all his heroic qualities, Josephus is not the stuff of which Jewish heroes are made. He stood with the Romans while the Holy Temple was being razed and while his people were being slaughtered in its defense. In fact, his name and his work would have perished forever among the Jews were it not for the—quite marvelous—irony that someone forged into his writings what was for centuries thought to be the only historical reference to Jesus of Nazareth.[22] To the Jews, from the time of the fall of Galilee virtually to the present, Josephus' name, when recalled at all, must evoke a set of reactions reserved by Christians for Judas Iscariot.[23] Still—another irony—modern weavers of Jewish myth, including the non-Jew James Michener in *The Source*, cannot do without Josephus, for without his writings there could be no Masada for a new myth and a new generation of Jews.

The fortress of Masada was built by the Hasmoneans and subsequently enlarged by Herod the Great.[24] Later, at the close of the war with Rome which destroyed the Jewish state and with it the Temple in Jerusalem, Masada enabled about 1,000 men, women, and children to hold off the furious attacks of Flavius Silva, the Roman governor of Judea, and the additional legions which he summoned to crush this last citadel of the Jewish Zealots. Finally, after seven months of incredible valor and privation, it became certain that on the morrow Masada would be taken, the men killed, the women raped and along with the children sold into slavery. Josephus writes that he learned of the last hours of Masada from two women and five children who had somehow escaped the fate of the others.[25] Their report inspired him—in proper Hellenistic historiographical fashion—to compose a speech for Eleazar ben Yair, the leader of the defenders of Masada. The speech went, in part, as follows:

> Our rate at break of day is certain capture, but there is still the free choice of a noble death with those we hold most dear. For our enemies, fervently though they pray to take us alive, can no more prevent this than we can now hope to defeat them in battle. Maybe, indeed, we ought from the very first . . . to have read God's purpose and to have recognized that the Jewish race, once beloved of Him, had been doomed to perdition. . . . For not even the impregnable nature of this fortress has availed to save us; nay, though ample provisions are ours, piles of arms, and a superabundance of every other requisite, yet we have been

deprived, manifestly by God Himself, of all hope of deliverance. For it was not of their own accord that those flames which were driving against the enemy turned back upon the [defense] wall constructed by us; no, all this betokens wrath at the many wrongs which we madly dared to inflict upon our countrymen. The penalty for those crimes let us pay not to our bitterest foes, the Romans, but to God through the act of our own hands. It will be more tolerable than the other. Let our wives thus die undishonoured, our children unacquainted with slavery; and, when they are gone, let us render a generous service to each other, preserving our liberty as a noble winding-sheet. But first let us destroy our chattels and the fortress by fire; for the Romans, well I know, will be grieved to lose at once our persons and the lucre. Our provisions only let us spare; for they will testify, when we are dead, that it was not want which subdued us, but that, in keeping with our initial resolve, we preferred death to slavery.

Since Ben Yair's speech proved less convincing than he had hoped, he spoke again:

. . . let us have pity on ourselves, our children and our wives, while it is still in our power to find pity from ourselves. For we were born for death, we and those whom we have begotten; and this even the fortunate cannot escape. But outrage and servitude and the sight of our wives being led to shame with their children—these are no necessary evils imposed by nature on mankind, but befall, through their own cowardice, those who, having the chance of forestalling them by death, refuse to take it. . . . No, while [our] hands are free and grasp the sword, let them render an honourable service. Unenslaved by the foe let us die, as free men with our children and wives let us quit this life together! This our laws enjoin, this our wives and children implore of us. The need for this is of God's sending, the reverse of this is the Romans' desire, and their fear is lest a single one of us should die before capture. Haste we then to leave them, instead of their hoped-for enjoyment at securing us, amazement at our death and admiration of our fortitude.[26]

Josephus then informs us that Ben Yair's words were heeded. First the men quickly killed their wives and children, then each other, and finally the last man fell on his sword and perished. When the Romans entered the bastion they found a scene which threw them into terror. All were dead, except for Josephus' surviving witnesses. All property had been burned, except some provisions which indicated that none had died but for freedom.[27]

The story is attractive, but it clearly violates certain rules necessary for a rescue myth which might help strengthen Jewish identity in America. First, it was recorded by Josephus, whom Jews have traditionally regarded as a traitor.[28] Next, and more crucial, is the tragic outcome of the story. The American mentality is able to assimilate stories of defeat (after all, Texas remembers the Alamo, and the American South the War between the States)—but hardly capable of dealing with a struggle which is not a fight to the finish and which, worst of all, culminates in the mass suicide of the heroes. "Give me liberty or give me death" might be an American rallying cry, and "Better dead than Red" might have inspired some Americans in the 1950s and early 1960s, but neither of these slogans was ever meant to imply suicide. They were taken to mean that the tyrants would have to kill every last freedom-loving patriot. Thus, the Masada story would seem to fail as a replacement for the Yavneh story given us by the Talmud and rabbinical tradition.

However, the story of the Masada myth is not finished. In an ingenious way it has become part of modern Jewish mythology. This has happened largely as a result of the rebirth of the Jewish state. Jewry's survival after the war which ended with Masada, the Roman empire's failure to survive, and the fact that there are today Jewish "Zealots" willing to die rather than lose their homeland and—these circumstances are not in themselves enough to make Masada the psychological substitute for Yavneh. What has happened is that a conscious effort on the part of American Jewish institutions has made Masada into a myth compatible with American Jewish identity needs and institutional values. This has been accomplished by combining elements of the past, the present, and rabbinic tradition. Not surprisingly, much of the work, we shall see, has been done under the auspices of the Conservative movement in Judaism, a movement which might be called, notwithstanding its ties to tradition, the most American of the Jewish religious movements.[29]

Use has been made of a number of factors, chief among them the linking of Masada to the career of a contemporary Jewish military hero victorious in all his attempts to deliver Israel from its genocidal enemies. The man is Yigael Yadin, a figure particularly adaptable to the building of a myth. He is described by one American Jewish writer as

"one of the heroes of modern Israel. Born in Jerusalem in 1917, he got his first taste of soldiering at the age of 14, when he became a member of the Haganah, the underground resistance army fighting against the

British occupation of Palestine." Then, Yadin "rose to become chief of planning and operations for the Haganah."

General Yadin played a major part in Israel's victory in 1948. In one famous incident, he won a crucial battle by using his knowledge of an ancient, forgotten Roman road across the desert.

This knowledge came from Yigael's first great interest in life—the science of archeology. His father [Sukenik] was a world-famous archeologist, and young Yigael had determined to be an archeologist himself, before necessity turned him into a soldier. After the war was over he went back to his studies. In 1952, General Yadin left the army and joined the Hebrew University in Jerusalem. There he became Professor of Archeology.

Professor Yadin was soon as renowned an archeologist and scholar as he had been a general. He conducted a number of important expeditions to ancient sites in Israel, where he made some historic discoveries. He was awarded prizes for his work and won many honors throughout the world.

In 1963 Yigael Yadin led the Masada Archeological Expedition to the mighty citadel near the Dead Sea which every archeologist in Israel had longed to excavate. The expedition dug at Masada until 1965. Its finds amazed the world.[30]

Thus, in the person of Yadin we have an ideal figure to bridge the gap between the ancient and modern world—a hero. As both general and archaeologist, he embodies military prowess, modern science, and a Jewish scholarly love for Israel, its history and (non-suicidal) tradition. In addition to Yadin's vital connection with Masada, there are other factors which make the excavated fortress a neat answer to the American Jewish quest for a new myth.

A book entitled *The Heroes of Masada* by Geraldine Rosenfield has been issued by the Conservative movement. In the opening chapter, called "Heroes of Today," Mrs. Rosenfield introduces us to Reuven:

Reuven is nineteen years old. He is tall and sunburned, is a hard-kicking soccer expert, and plays a very tricky *halil*. (This is a wooden flute which you may know as a recorder.) . . . If you happened to meet Reuven you might think, "This fellow is great fun. He's a great ball player. He's pretty handy with a *halil* and with a tractor." You would probably never come up with the thought, "He is a hero."

But Reuven turned out to be one hero among many, among two and a quarter million, in fact, during the historic six days, that started on June 5, 1967.

. . . When it came his turn to serve in the Army he was assigned to duty with a tank unit. So Reuven found himself behind the wheel of a tank instead of a tractor.

. . . One day the Company commander announced that all soldiers must put on clean dress uniforms. They had been invited to join a ceremony on the rock fortress of Masada.

. . . On the day Reuven and his fellow students climbed up the steep side of Masada they joined in a graduation exercise for men and women who had just become officers in the Israeli Army. The soldiers stood at attention, in V-shaped formation while the band played cheerily and rousing speeches were made. A huge bonfire was lit in the center and smaller fires glowed in a half-circle. Every new soldier was presented with a Bible to remind him above all of his God, his people and his history. Reuven repeated with his comrades "Masada shall not fall again!"[31]

The author's purpose is patent. She wishes her young readers to identify with the farmer-soldier. She also wishes her readers not to see in Masada the reminder of a terrible defeat but rather the reminder of another time of glory which, like our own, offered an opportunity to save the Jewish people, its Torah and its tradition, from threats to their freedom and survival.

Again, by paying little heed to the historical past and laying much emphasis on the present and future, Masada receives a new place in the Jewish mythos. Yadin-Reuven are not losers. They are winners who excel at everything they undertake. They are not passive schoolmasters; they are warrior-scientist-scholars or soccer-kicking-tractor-driving good fellows, and they—more than the eloquent Eleazar ben Yair or the traitorous Josephus—*belong* at Masada.

Masada has other uses, too, as the focal point of a myth. Consider, for instance: the existence of Masada, unlike that of the Temple or the academy at Yavneh, does not have to be imagined. It is there to visit, and, more, to visit us, as it has done in a traveling exhibit under the auspices of the Conservative-sponsored Jewish Museum of New York.[32] It is hard and real and made palpable to us through a knowledge of the Jewish past, the heroics of daring archaeologists, and the mastery of modern scientific tools and concepts. It is no burning bush for whose existence we must take the word of God and Moses on faith.

And there is one final use that it has served. To those who argue that Jewish physical survival and observance of the Law are incompatible, Masada seems to offer refutation. Masada's ruins contain what have been designated ritual baths, a classroom, sacred scrolls, and a synagogue. One of the myth-making books referred to above puts the matter this way:

> To the Zealots, their religious faith was the most important thing in life. Even while they were besieged on Masada, fighting for existence, they still devoutly observed the laws of their religion.
>
> Some of these laws dealt with ritual bathing. On certain occasions, pious Jews were required to dip themselves in a special bathing pool of pure water. This pool had to be of a certain size and shape. And when one day, digging and probing atop Masada, the archeologists came upon an unusual structure that the Zealots had added to the casemate wall, they realized almost at once that they had found an ancient ritual bathing pool.
>
> After excavating the pool, they discovered that it had been built in exact obedience to the ancient rules. It was divided into separate chambers. One chamber caught rain water and stored it. A pipe led from this chamber to the main part of the pool. Before bathing, the Jews would unplug this pipe and let some of the rain water flow into the main part of the pool. According to the ancient rules, the rain water purified the other water there. The devout Zealots could then enter the pool and bathe.
>
> Later, digging elsewhere within the fortress, the members of the expedition uncovered a second ritual bathing pool. It had been built in exactly the same way as the first one. Both structures can be seen at Masada today. Standing on the dry mountaintop under the scorching Judean sun, they show how strong was the Zealots' faith—how fervently they clung to their religion, even under conditions of the most incredible difficulty. But, we are told, "amid all the hardship and danger of life on Masada, the Zealots also kept up their study of the Bible," for the archaeologists also "uncovered a religious schoolroom in which Zealot children used to sit—when they were not needed for other tasks, such as helping to defend the fortress." And there is more:
>
> The most exciting discovery of all, among the religious structures of the Zealots, was made early in the expedition's stay at Masada. "At the very beginning of our first season of excavations, while digging in the northwestern section of the wall of Masada, we came upon a strange structure," says the expedition leader. "It was unlike any of the buildings we had excavated up to then in the casemate wall. Early in the dig we noticed what looked like benches plastered with clay protruding from the debris inside the building, next to the walls. Gradually, pillars began to appear, made in sections. When we had finished excavating, what appeared before us was a rectangular structure with benches all round the walls, tier upon tier, all plastered with clay."

The benches, the archeologists soon learned, had been built by the Zealots. Some of them were made of pieces of stone columns taken from the remains of Herold's palaces. The strange rectangular structure with its many benches had obviously been used for public meetings. But meetings of what sort? Why had the Zealots gathered together there?

The archeologists continued their digging, and finally they had their answer. The Zealots had gathered there to pray. The building was a synagogue.

The archeologists were not really sure at first. But as they dug the evidence mounted. The building faced in the proper direction for a synagogue—toward Jerusalem—and within it they found things that may have been used in religious ceremonies. The diggers' excitement grew.

"If what we had just unearthed was indeed a synagogue," says the expedition leader, "then this was a discovery of front-rank importance in the field of Jewish archeology and certainly one of the most important finds in Masada. For up to then the very earliest synagogues discovered in Israel belonged to the end of the second or beginning of the third century A.D."

In other words, if this building on Masada turned out to be a synagogue, it would be the oldest one in the world. One last discovery finally convinced the [archeologists] that the mysterious structure was a synagogue. They found that below the floor, in two carefully dug pits, the ealots had buried scrolls.[33]

The construction of the modern Masada myth is now virtually complete. The suggestion that there was a classroom in the fortress and that a certain room was used for a synagogue (although there is no way of verifying the fact) makes that clear. The possibility that there were mikvehs (ritual baths), a school, and a synagogue, and the certainty that Masada contained sacred scrolls are central to the building of the new myth. While the scrolls found there included no complete copy of the most sacred Five Books of Moses—in fact, they included excerpts from the Book of Psalms and the non-canonical Jubilees and Ben Sirah (Ecclesiasticus)[34]—the myth-makers could hail the information that the psalm fragments were identical with the official masoretic text of the Bible used today. Masada thus could be used to validate a traditional belief, i.e., the reliability of the traditional rendition of Hebrew Scripture. The Ben Sirah and Jubilees scrolls (found in Hebrew editions) allowed the claim that the books' original language was Hebrew and not the Greek in which they had been found in all other ancient editions.[35]

What could have been concluded by another set of archaeologists and scholars, our myth-makers chose to ignore—namely, that the Zealots might have followed a religion which deviated in significant and even radical ways from what is now accepted as normative Judaism. It would be as though archaeologists would at some future date discover the ruins of a synagogue of today—only a meeting hall, classrooms, and some fragmented copies of the New Testament (which most synagogues have in their libraries)—and conclude that they had found a Christian church.

But myths are not built on hard data, even though today's myths undoubtedly must contain at least shreds of scientific material in order to be credible to a modern Westerner. The Masada myth has such shreds. It has action. It has physical existence. It has a new happy ending and a new hero in the person of Yadin. And most important to those who seek to place Masada within the fortress of other Jewish myths, it contains the elements of existent American institutional Judaism: a classroom, a synagogue, the sacred writings—i.e., the tradition that Jews are dependent on scholarship no matter what. So all the essentials are now in place. What remains to be seen is whether the element most crucial to a myth is also there, its ability to meet the individual psychic needs of enough members of a group so that it is usable as an effective socializing agent by that group.

From the psychological standpoint, the new Masada myth has both strengths and weaknesses. One strength is that, unlike the Yavneh legend, Masada includes among its defenders whole families, with women and children fighting and dying alongside the men. Masada was a family affair. Josephus tells us that after Eleazar ben Yair delivered his oration, he expected he would have to convince them further to accept his fatal plan—"but was cut short by his hearers, who . . . were all in haste to do the deed." [36] Josephus tells of the devotion of the men not only to their own families but to their comrades so that,

> while they caressed and embraced their wives and took their children in their arms, clinging in tears to those parting kisses, at that same instant, as though served by hands other than their own, they accomplished their purpose, having the thought of the ills they would endure under the enemy's hands to console them for their constraint in killing them. And in the end not one was found a truant in so daring a deed: all carried through their task with their dearest ones. Wretched victims of necessity, to whom to slay with their own hands their own wives and children seemed the lightest of evils! Unable, indeed, any longer to endure their anguish at what they had done, and feeling that they wronged the slain

by surviving them if it were but for a moment, they quickly piled together all the stores and set them on fire; then [they chose] by lot ten of their number to dispatch the rest . . . [37]

Psychologically, this part of the story is potent. External authority is ultimately defied. The Roman loses all control over the faithful Jew, while at the same time the Jew finds in death a full commitment to family and community, and perhaps, above all, he wins through his martyrdom the favor of God the Father. If the tragic episode appears unappealing to children, it can be argued that it may prove to be gratifying as well. The fear of being mutilated by father—so much a part of the oedipal struggle—is indeed enacted, but the fact that father does not survive child and that today, when the story is told, the child is not only alive but physically able and called upon, like Yadin and his confrères, to prevent another Masada (i.e., to rescue fathers, mothers, and other children as well as community)—this might suffice to turn the unhappy defeat of the original Masada into a sort of oedipal triumph. Such a triumph would be similar to the psychological satisfaction the believer gets from dying in Christ, only to share in his resurrection—and join the army of the redeemed, whose mission it is to save others who do not share his standing with God.

Given the modern Masada myth, the story now has all the psychological glory of Yavneh. Now the people of Masada may be seen to have preserved Judaism, not only by keeping the faith, but especially by leaving for us a synagogue, a school, and sacred scrolls which help us contemporary Jews to heighten *our* faith in the continuity of tradition. Torah was saved by Masada. The Shekinah was rescued by the Zealots—but this rescue is only accomplished if we today are willing to study and to fight for God, Israel, and Torah. Masada has these psychological possibilities plus an additional advantage over Yavneh—it does not place the Jewish mythos in conflict with American values. The defenders of Masada, either of old or in the person of Yadin, did not passively trick and cajole their way past the enemy. They did not beg the enemy for a small favor. They fought him, finally overcame him, and took back from him not a wretched, musty little yeshiva but the entire Land of Israel. No American could have done more.

Still, there are several flaws in the efficacy of the Masada myth. The most obvious for a person concerned with the building of Jewish identity in America is true of both Yavneh and Masada. In order for either legend to achieve its goals as a myth, i.e., a story which meets both psychological and group needs, it must be transmitted by believing adults to children who are ready to believe. If the chain of belief is broken, and if the matrix within which the myth has preserved its psychological and social reality has been shattered, then the myth will fail in its function. If the community no longer believes the myth but merely feels that it is good for children, then children know that what they are hearing is at best a good story and at worst a package of foolishness. It is doubtful that Jews bereft of belief in their own myths, a condition common among second- and third-generation Americans, can utilize Masada even though Masada conflicts less than Yavneh with the American ethos. It is significant that Masada, though popular with Jewish youth, is most appealing to leaders and members of the Jewish Defense League, an organization which draws its membership from those generationally closest to Europe, young people who are not well entrenched in the middle classes, retain a strong attachment to Orthodoxy, and see their future not in America but in Israel. For them the slogan "Never again" is equivalent to the Israeli soldiers' oath—"Masada shall not fall again." What is ironic in this is that, consciously or not, the JDL, with all of its open rejection of American society, has come to replicate most closely one American way of life. Given to racism, relying on jingoism, instructed to achieve their aims through violence, they seem, externals aside, to emulate John Wayne more than the sage Hillel.[38]

Herein lies the final paradox in the Yavneh-Masada saga. At a time when more and more American youth, Jews and non-Jews, are coming to distrust institutions, to seek to escape from a society which seems to demand individual submission to national societal causes, which appears to demand aggression and violence in the name of freedom, neither myth is satisfying, and *both* are. At Yavneh, one could turn his back on the world so long as one could place ideology and methodology above self and so long as one was willing never to challenge "proper" authority. At Masada, one could live in community, cherish his ties to family and group, and challenge authority to the end so long as one was willing to accept violence as a code of conduct.

What are called for now are not Yavneh and Masada, but new and better myths which will show themselves able to transform social reality without denying its psychological underpinnings.

NOTES

1. See, in particular, Erik H. Erikson, *Childhood and Society* (New York, 1950); Anna Freud, *The Ego and the Mechanisms of Defence* (New York, 1946); and Heinz Hartmann, *Ego Psychology and the Problem of Adaptation* (New York, 1958; first published in the late 1930s).
2. I am basing this on a letter Dr. Arlow addressed to me on May 16, 1974 (copy in American Jewish Archives). See also Jacob A. Arlow, "Ego Psychology and Mythology," *Journal of the American Psychoanalytic Association*, IX (1961), 388 *et seq.*
3. According to Arlow in his letter to me, Ben Zaccai "represents an ego ideal, a character structure to be emulated because [it] was consonant with the conditions for . . . Jewish survival for many centuries. Such a character, however, could hardly serve as an ideal personality type for militant Zionists at the end of the 19th and the beginning of the 20th century."
4. In this discussion I often use the word *myth* where others might use *history*, and *legend* is often used where others might say *true story*. The reader should take it for granted that *myth* and *legend* are intended neither to affirm nor to deny the historicity of the tales analyzed. For makers of myth there is no such distinction.
5. B. Gittin 56a–b.
6. See, for example, Karl Abraham, "Rescue and Murder of the Father in Neurotic Phantasies," *International Journal of Psychoanalysis*, III (1922), 467–74. As Arlow reads the Sleeping Beauty legend, "the dead father re-emerges as the resurrecting prince . . . the fulfillment of oedipal wishes . . ." ("Unconscious Fantasy and Conscious Experience," *Psychoanalytic Quarterly*, XXXVIII [1969], 20).
7. One can, of course, find alternative tales, though they are rarely stressed. In the Bible, for example, Rebekah (Gen. 27) tricks her husband and gets a blessing for her favorite son. Queen Esther (4:16) is prepared to sacrifice herself to save the Jews. In the Book of Judges, Deborah (5:1–31) saves the men of Israel, while Jael (4:21) slays the enemy general with a tent pin. In the Apocrypha, it is Judith—a latter-day Jael—who saves Israel by beheading the enemy warrior Holophernes (Jth. 13:8).
8. B. Gittin 56a–b; Tosefta Berakot 2:6; Tosefta Hullin 3:10; Rosh Hashanah 29b; Shabbat 11a. See also *Jewish Encyclopedia* (New York, 1901–6), VII, 18; Alexander Guttmann, *Rabbinic Judaism in the Making* (Detroit, 1970), pp. 199–200.
9. As examples, see Lloyd Alexander, *The Flagship Hope: Aaron Lopez* (Philadelphia, 1960), pp. 74 *et seq.*, 115 *et seq.*, 137 *et seq.*; and Lee J. Levinger, *A History of the Jews in the United States* (Cincinnati, 1944), pp. 113–23.
10. See Hannah Arendt, *Eichmann in Jerusalem* (New York, 1963); Bruno Bettelheim, *The Informed Heart* (Glencoe, Ill., 1960); Raoul Hilberg, *The Destruction of the European Jews* (Chicago, 1961); and Isaiah Trunk, *Judenrat* (New York, 1972).

11. See Y. Taanit iv. 68d; *Jewish Encyclopedia,* I, 305; Abba H. Silver, *A History of Messianic Speculation in Israel* (New York, 1927), p. 127; Joseph Klausner, *The Messianic Idea in Israel* (New York, 1955), pp. 398–99.
12. See Shabbat 21b; Meg. Taanit 23. See also Elias Bickerman, *From Ezra to the Last of the Maccabees* (New York, 1962), pp. 119 *et seq.*
13. See *Jewish Encyclopedia,* VIII, 378. On Mattathias, see also 1 Macc. 2:1–70. On Hannah and her sons, see 2 Macc. 7:1–41.
14. See, for example, Josephus, *Jewish War,* I. 126–87. See also Bickerman, pp. 148 *et seq.*
15. See Josephus, *Jewish War,* VII. 280–303.
16. Josephus, *Vita,* 9; Luke 2:46–47.
17. Josephus, *Vita,* 11–12.
18. *Ibid.,* 13–16.
19. *Ibid.,* 17–417; Josephus, *Jewish War,* II. 546–654, III. 135–595.
20. *Ibid.,* III. 400–402, IV. 601–63; Josephus, *Vita,* 414–23; Suetonius, *Lives of the Caesars,* VIII. 5–6. Both Ben Zaccai and Josephus are credited with predicting Vespasian's succession to the throne. It is intriguing, then, that both the Yavneh and the Masada episodes—otherwise diametrically opposed—trace back to one and the same Roman general.
21. See Josephus, *Vita,* 358–67; *Jewish War,* Preface, 3–6; III. 108, V. 362–66; *Jewish Antiquities,* XX. 267–68.
22. See Josephus, *Jewish Antiquities,* XVIII. 63–64.
23. It is worth noting that the famous German Jewish novelist Lion Feuchtwanger diverged sharply from the traditional anti-Josephan views of Jewish writers. In his trilogy—*Josephus* (1932), *The Jew of Rome* (1936), and *Josephus and the Emperor* (1942)—he paints a very sympathetic portrait of Josephus. It is as if Feuchtwanger were preparing the Jews for the Masada myth by reclaiming Josephus' reputation!
24. Josephus, *Jewish War,* VII. 280–303.
25. *Ibid.,* VII. 252, 275–79, 304–15, 402–7. See also VII. 399–401.
26. *Ibid.,* VII. 325–28, 331–36, 381–83, 385–88. The translation is H. St. J. Thackeray's in the Loeb Classical Library edition of *The Jewish War.*
27. Josephus, *Jewish War,* VII. 389–407.
28. See, for example, Yigael Yadin, *The Story of Masada, Retold for Young Readers by Gerald Gottlieb* (New York, 1969), where chap. 3 is entitled "The Traitor Josephus."
29. See, for example, Marshall Sklare, *Conservative Judaism: An American Religious Movement* (New York, 1972), pp. 254 *et seq.;* Moshe Davis, *The Emergence of Conservative Judaism* (New York, 1963), pp. 323–26; Arthur Hertzberg, "The American Jew and His Religion," in O. Janowsky, ed., *The American Jew: A Reappraisal* (Philadelphia, 1964), pp. 118–19. See also Solomon Schechter, as quoted in the *Universal Jewish Encyclopedia* (New York, 1942), VI, 245: Conservative Judaism is not "a new party, but ... an old one, which has always existed in this country ... [i.e.,] the large number of Jews who, thoroughly American in habits of life and mode of thinking, and, in many cases, imbued with the vast culture of the day, have always maintained conservative principles and remained aloof from ... Reform ... " Hertzberg, in *Encyclopaedia Judaica* (Jerusalem, 1971), V, 901, says that "the American development [of the Conservative Movement] was parallel to the one in Europe; . . . but it was an essentially autonomous development."
30. Yadin-Gottlieb, foreword.

31. See Geraldine Rosenfield, *The Heroes of Masada* (New York, 1968), pp. 3–4. The volume was published by the (Conservative) United Synagogue Commission on Jewish Education.
32. See *Masada, Struggle for Freedom, and the Finds from the Bar-Kokhba Caves* (New York, 1967). The volume appeared in connection with the Masada exhibition sponsored by the Jewish Museum of the Jewish Theological Seminary of America. The exhibition was held in the Jewish Museum, New York City, between October 1967 and February 1968. It later traveled to Chicago, Dallas, Detroit, Philadelphia, and San Francisco.
33. See Yadin-Gottlieb, chap. 15 ("The Faith of the Zealots").
34. See *ibid.*, pp. 95–98.
35. *Ibid.*, p. 96.
36. Josephus, *Jewish War*, VII. 389.
37. *Ibid.*, VII. 390–98.
38. On the Jewish Defense League, see Ruth A. Buchbinder, "Jewish Vigilantes," *Congress Bi-Weekly*, May 26, 1969, pp. 4–6; *Jewish Currents*, July–August 1969, pp. 33–34; Michael Pousner, "Never Again!" *New York Daily News*, July 27, 1970; Tannah Hirsch, "The JDL: Heroes or Hooligans?" *Jerusalem Post*, March 4, 1970; American Jewish Committee, *Fact Sheet—Jewish Defense League*, February, 1970 (updated January, 1971); *The Jewish Defense League: Principles and Philosophies* (New York: Jewish Defense League, n.d.). All the above are to be found in the Nearprint file of the American Jewish Archives. See also Meir Kahane, *Never Again! A Program for Survival* (New York, 1972), pp. 212 *et seq.*

A MOMENTOUS MEETING FOR THE ENLARGEMENT OF THE JEWISH AGENCY FOR PALESTINE

By

HERBERT PARZEN

Theodor Herzl Institute, New York

FOREWORD

As early as 1923, Chaim Weizmann and Louis Marshall began to exchange views on the enlargement of the Jewish Agency for Palestine (JA), to include Zionists and non-Zionists, for the purpose of unifying Jewry in the support of the upbuilding of Palestine as the Jewish National Home (JNH). The outlook seemed promising; the initiation of formal negotiations actually resulted in the formulation of a constitution for the JA.

In 1926, however, the negotiations foundered due to a presumed ideological conflict—the status of Palestine as the JNH in Jewish life. The Zionists insisted that the primacy of Palestine was dictated by the destiny of the Jewish people, whereas the non-Zionists disbelieved in this doctrine and regarded the colonization of Jews in the Crimea and Ukraine and other relief activities as vital ventures for the well-being and survival of those Jewish communities. This clash of viewpoints dominated the respective drives for funds—the United Palestine Appeal (UPA), sponsored by the American Zionist organs, and the United Jewish Campaign

401

(UJC) launched by the Joint Distribution Committee (JDC). This strife threatened to create an irreparable rift in the two camps.

In the midst of this crisis Weizmann came to the United States on October 29, 1926, for two purposes: to aid in the 1927 UPA campaign and to revivify the negotiations for the JA with the Marshall group.

In due course an accord was attained. It embodied provisions to set up a constitutional structure for the government of the JA and to send to Palestine a nonpartisan commission with a staff of experts to study the various aspects of the Yishuv's economy, and to recommend plans for its effective and intensive development by the contemplated Agency.

In addition, there was also an understanding that the two leaders should exchange letters, to be made public simultaneously, in order to procure the general acceptance of the compact and, particularly, to placate the purblind partisans of both groups. To this end, Weizmann was to write the initial letter—an apology for the Zionist attack upon the non-Zionists, for insisting on the idea that the colonization of Palestine had priority in Jewish affairs and for destroying the created unity and peace in the work for Palestine and European relief; Marshall was to respond— he lauded Weizmann's letter, accepted "the proffered olive-branch", and assured cooperation.

At this time, the Zionist leaders had chosen Judge Otto Rosalsky as chairman of the 1927 UPA drive in New York City. It was scheduled to open with a public rally at the Mecca Temple on January 17, 1927, at 8 P.M. He accepted the assignment on condition that harmony would be achieved prior to that public meeting and that the exchange of letters and the JA agreement would then be read.

However, the contents of the Weizmann letter unexpectedly precipitated a crisis which foredoomed the organization of the enlarged JA and even endangered Weizmann's leadership of the Zionist movement.[A]

The crisis was averted, two hours before the scheduled opening of the Mecca Temple rally.[B]

A. For details: Parzen, Herbert, "The United Palestine Appeal," *Herzl Year Book,* vol. 7, Herzl Press, New York 1971, pp. 358-369.
B. The most accessible references to the texts of the two letters and the Agency agreement are: *The New Palestine,* January 21, 1927, pp. 62-63, and pp. 66-67, respectively. The proceedings at the Mecca Temple meeting are likewise published in this issue. The letters are likewise published in *Louis Marshall Champion of Liberty: Selected Papers and Addresses,* edited by Charles Reznikoff, Vol. II, pp. 760-762.

Minutes of the Meeting of the Administrative Committee of the Zionist Organization of America, Held on Monday Afternoon, January 17, 1927.[1]

Present: Messrs. Lipsky in the Chair, Dr. Weizmann, Dr. Wise, Dr. Kaliski, Samuel, A. Goldberg, Judge Lewis, Lindheim, Neumann, Fierst, Grabelsky, Liebowitz, Bernstein, Halperin, Israel Goldstein, M. Rothenberg, Abramowitz, Stone, Weisgal, and Miss Liebermann.[2]

Mr. Louis Lipsky (to Dr. Weizmann): All the facts connected with this affair have been told over and over again, first, at the meeting of the U. P. A. Executive Committee, and now again, and it seems to have been the consensus of opinion here that the letter, in the form in which it is written, is unworthy of being signed by you, that it does not represent the spirit of Zionism, that it is a letter which is inconceivable as emanating from you, and that it involves certain statements which would reflect on all those who had to do with the controversy, on the part of the Z.O.A. and gives away altogether too much of those ideals which everybody here knows you hold. The expressions are inept, not such as would come from anyone who has been in the Zionist Movement for even a short time. Of course, we know very well that this letter was not written by you, and under the circumstances, the Committee is discussing now what advice should be given you in the matter. The consensus of opinion here is to advise you not to sign that letter. Everybody is in agreement with regard to the Jewish Agency, but to use an instrument of this sort to accomplish that aim, will bring more danger to the Movement than good. It may placate certain elements in the Relief Campaign, but it is bound to arouse animosity in our own Organization, which, if balanced, one against the other, would be to the detriment of our Movement. It is also the opinion, so far as the Organization is concerned, that you are the responsible leader of the International Organization, and that if you want to take the responsibility of writing that letter, the only thing we could do is to enter a private protest.

Dr. Weizmann: Well gentlemen, I realize the critical situation and I hate this letter. It is not my letter. It was a much worse letter. It has been changed and changed, and, unfortunately, it had to be done under very high pressure. As I should like clearly to outline, I drafted a letter before I left for Washington. This letter was, I think, satisfactory, and I was under the impression that this will be the letter which will go through. I went away to Washington, and I only arrived on Thursday. On Friday, to my amazement, I learned that another letter had been proposed. I read the letter. I did not write it. I discussed it. I called for a meeting of the gentlemen whom I could lay my hands on—Lipsky, Neumann *(here Mr. Neumann interrupted and stated that he did not get any notice of such a meeting, and Miss Lieberman³ replied that she had telephoned Mr. Neumann's office on Friday morning and was told that he was not in. Mr. Neumann replied that he had telephoned to the Commodore on Friday afternoon, but was not told anything about this letter.)*

Dr. Weizmann (continued) : I went over this letter. It was discussed by Halperin, Lipsky, and myself. On Friday night I told Mr. Lipsky that this letter more or less is agreeable. On Saturday I saw Mr. Marshall, and made those changes which we thought ought to be made. I had a draft and I asked Miss Lieberman to show this letter to each gentleman. I could not do anything because I had to leave on Sunday morning. On Sunday morning, at 8 o'clock, I told Judge Rosalsky that these changes would be absolutely essential. He promised he would try his best and see that these changes were made. After that, I left for Albany. I have not signed this letter as yet. I do not like this letter. If this letter is not signed, I dare say all that I have been trying to do with your consent and informing you all the time, will fall through, perhaps. I am facing it quite calmly. It may not be a misfortune,—we may be able to go on, as if nothing happened, and the whole chapter of the Jewish Agency will be nothing.

It is unfortunate that it should be like that, and that I should be forced to sign it. It is still more tragic if I sign it, and sign it against your better advice, which I shall not do. I declare this: if a protest is entered privately or publicly, it does not matter to me, for the following reason: the integrity and the good-will of the Zionist Organization of America are essential in the upbuilding of Palestine. If that is risked—that is the reason I cannot sign it. I am saying all that very calmly. I have not slept for nights. I have been going on working all the time. Perhaps I do not express things as well as I could, otherwise, but whatever I am going to say now, please understand is not a threat, not a desire to exercise any pressure, but it would make my further work impossible. I dare say the matter will blow over, and in three months' time, five months' time, things may clear. I thought that we shall all agree, that we are all facing it

out together. It is not my job particularly, it is not yours, but if that
agreement[4] is impossible, I shall not do it. I will ring up Mr. Marshall,
that the thing is off, and we shall consider the consequences. The immediate consequences, so far as I see—perhaps I am mistaken—I may
view it too harshly—is that it would be impossible for me to go on with
the work here. (*Here Dr. Wise interrupted and asked whether it would
be impossible for Dr. Weizmann to go on with the Agency or with Zionist work*).

(*Dr. Weizmann continuing*) With everything, and I could not face it,
and if I failed I would resign. It is as great as that for me. When I came
I had a talk with you, Dr. Wise, and you remember what you told me
—it was perhaps one of the greatest encouragements to me. You told me
"You are coming here with your hands untied. You can accept our
policy; you can disavow it; you can do whatever you like."[5] I need hardly
tell you, after four years of very intimate cooperation that even this letter
is not a disavowal. It may imply a certain amount of force. My spirit is
unbroken. My relation with American Zionists is as before. It is a vicious
circle in which only I find myself, and it is for the sake of Palestine that
I am going through this hell,—it may be that we shall choose, everybody,
to go to hell in their own little way. I am trying to put this clearly. If
I saw a chance of changing it, I would be the first to change it. I went
to the limit. I put on every pressure. Last night, after a very difficult
journey, and after I dug out of the snow, I called on Mr. Lehman,[6] and
I told him that this wasn't in the spirit of close cooperation. It is a matter
of deep regret that Warburg[7] is not here. Otherwise things might be
remedied. I believe that after a fortnight or three weeks, this thing will
blow over, and we may possibly enter upon calmer waters. If you gentlemen do not believe—and I am the last man to convince you and urge
you—I am honest with you and I am telling you about something which
worried me, too—and what the last fortnight or three weeks have been
to me—if you think otherwise, you are to decide.

I am sorry that I have been dragged into a matter which is internal,
and not a matter which is international. I feel that I am at a disadvantage. It is the anomaly of my situation. I feel that if this falls through, it
makes my further continuation of the work, not in spirit, but in action,
impossible, for this year any way. It may mean much, it may mean little,
I don't know what it may mean. I am not ready to appraise it. I need
hardly say that whatever I have done, I have done in good faith, that
whatever I have to answer for, the answer is for the sake of what I hope

in the future is a step forward towards the improvement of the situation in Palestine. I don't want to plead. It is difficult for me to argue it again. I have argued all this time. I have suffered, in all, as much as anyone of you—and that is my conclusion. If that is your consensus of opinion, after carefully weighing everything, I think you are right.

Mr. Lindheim: If Dr. Weizmann has the impression that there has been any agreement as to this assembly I want to tell him that we have been discussing and have not come to a conclusion. It seems to me—and I am not going to revert to everything which we said, before Dr. Weizmann came—it seems to me that we forget what the real situation is. With the exception of Mr. Lipsky, and possibly Mr. Neumann, yesterday, not a single member of this Committee saw a single item of this correspondence until yesterday. This is not important. What is important is the situation of the Zionist Movement today. . . . Let us swallow this distasteful bit of medicine, this nauseous dose, and let the letter go, because negotiations have gone too far. Dr. Weizmann went over the letter with Louis Marshall, and if Dr. Weizmann notifies Marshall today, it means the end of the endeavor for the Jewish Agency, and the endeavor to bring new men into the Movement. Therefore, this letter, not concerning us, is being sent by Dr. Weizmann, with full plenipotentiary exercise of judgment. As he saw it, he did this in order to bring new men into the Movement, and in order that the Zionist Cause may go forward in this country, and stop this miserable attitude of alibis.

Dr. Weizmann: I repeat, I hate the whole thing, I am sorry to interfere even in this way with anything which is internal. You know I have always cooperated with the Zionist Organization of America. I have spoken, I have given my life's blood. I will not change; I shall not change, but I realize that if you feel hurt—not that I hurt you—but if you feel that your position is through this letter hurt, and it is up to me, afterwards, to draw the conclusions. . . . (*here Dr. Weizmann was interrupted by Dr. Wise*):

Dr. Wise: There is nothing to be said or done. If you say that our disapproval of this letter means that you must withdraw, and withdraw from the Agency,—don't you think, Dr. Weizmann, that, assuming that we acted as *Gaslonim* [robbers] throughout the Campaign—don't you think that you made the *Amende Honorable* for the Zionist Organization of America and the United Palestine Appeal, to the Agency crowd at Boston,[8] where, after all, for three and one-half heated hours you presented the facts to us, and you made a plea in the most conciliatory spirit.

It is not as if you returned yesterday,—as if this is the first pound of flesh exacted from you. This pound of flesh was exacted from you before the meeting in Boston. You paid it in your negotiations in the last two months. I am speaking for the record. You will admit that the Zionist Organization of America has both affirmatively and negatively held up your hands, so far as it could, in every way. I am not speaking for myself alone; I went to the limit and beyond even the limit of self-respect when I spoke as I did in Boston. I said it to you a year ago. I said it two years ago. I said it in Vienna. I said to you I am glad for your sake and for our sake that at least you don't have to bow before David A. Brown.[9] You even hinted to me, "I don't like that man. I have not dealt with him at all". (*Here Dr. Weizmann interrupted and asked, "At what period"?*).

Dr. Wise (*continued and said*): Ten days ago you agreed with me about Marshall and Warburg belonging in a different category. *He* was out of the picture. We were dealing with figures whom American Israel and World Israel respect. I would be glad if Marshall is coming to the Zionist Congress. I have not put anything in your way. I came here with my speech for tonight, in which I am prepared to support you and Marshall to the limit. Now for the hypothetical question: Supposing Goldstein, Rothenberg, or I were asked by Neumann and Lipsky to take the Chairmanship of the New York Campaign—any one of us might have to do it—by what abracadabra does this revolve around the relatively unimportant matter—the Chairmanship of the Campaign by Judge Rosalsky. This letter is foisted upon you. You may have to accept it, sign it on the dotted line. It does not change the fact that the letter was foisted upon you in connection with something which is not of the essence of this Agency work, which, I take it, is done.

Dr. Weizmann: I do not want to argue on premises which are not correct. This is a paradoxical situation. I did not invent Rosalsky. The suggestion came from the United Palestine Appeal. I know him comparatively little. In view of what I was told about him, he impresses me very favorably. He behaved very well in this whole matter. I am not sitting in judgment on Rosalsky. I knew him comparatively slightly. In all the negotiations, Brown did not figure. When this commission[10] was agreed upon, then Brown appeared on the scene—after the commission was agreed upon. Brown's ambition in life is to be invited to the Warburgs. Warburg's ambition in life is not to see Brown. Still, he terrorizes them for a very simple reason—because he is doing the work, and they are not. Here they are engaged in a campaign for $25,000,000,—I don't know how many millions, it is telephone numbers.

It is all very well for Marshall to agree on the Agency, but Brown
talks and travels. He talks with the American Jewish community. The
American Jewish community does not consist of people who think, but
they accept what is told them. It is not my fault, and, therefore, these
people are terrified. They want to satisfy Brown. If I have to do only with
these people whom you named, as gentlemen, any letter would have
gone through,—Mr. Lipsky's, or my shorter letter. I thought that five or
six phrases would be an easier thing to swallow. Since I talked to you and
I could testify to you—I always avoided Brown—it was suggested to me
the next day that I should see him. It was essential that I should see him.
He had written me from Chicago. I could not face Brown until Irving
Lehman, a nice man, a gentleman, had arranged the luncheon between
Brown, myself, and Lehman. I would not want my enemy to go through
this luncheon again. I sat for four hours and listened to this gentleman.
I have a few witnesses who will tell you that I was literally in bed the
whole day after the luncheon. I thought to myself, we had to live two
thousand years, in all our checkered history, to land in this situation,—
but gentlemen, it is not my doing. (*Here Dr. Wise interrupted and asked
Dr. Weizmann: "What did he exact at this meeting?"*)

Dr. Weizmann, (*continuing*): He wanted a statement, then I began
the statement which Lipsky wrote, then the one which I wrote. Brown
did not accept. Then he forced the other people not to accept. This is what
I found when I returned from Washington. Marshall is in the same position as I am, but without the heartaches. These are the facts. They are
facts which are incontrovertible. They either have to be taken, or to be
left. This letter, as it stands, is utterly unsatisfactory, but I am perfectly
sure that if this falls through—and Rosalsky has nothing to do with the
thing—the fight does not center around Rosalsky—if that does not go
through, they will come to Marshall and say: "You may decide on the
Jewish Agency, decide on the Commission, but you won't have any following," and Mr. Marshall will not engage in this particular work, and
you may take it for granted that everything falls through.

Dr. Wise: Warburg abroad and Marshall here will publicly break
with you, Weizmann, the leader of the Zionist Organization—the personality—will break with you because you refused to sign a letter which
has been foisted by Brown and his associates?

Dr. Weizmann: I would be very happy if two gentlemen of this assembly have a talk with Mr. Marshall immediately.

Mr. Morris Rothenberg: Would it not be possible for you to get in touch with Marshall and find out if it is possible to alter certain passages of the letter?

Dr. Weizmann: I have told Lipsky, Kaplan, and Semel, etc., that any letter which you will agree upon, I shall sign. It did not happen.

Mr. Neumann: What did not happen?

Dr. Weizmann: They did not agree.

Mr. Morris Rothenberg: Is it essential that the whole matter be settled tonight?

Dr. Weizmann: Perhaps not. I would suggest that a group of people go to Mr. Marshall and settle our position.

Mr. Rothenberg: If anyone can do it, it is you.

Dr. Weizmann: I cannot do it.

Mr. Lindheim: I happened to see Dr. Kaplan on Thursday night, and he told me about the terrible time he had with Brown, and the unfortunate situation to Jewry if Brown could bulldoze them to do the thing they did.

Dr. Wise: It seems to me there is nothing for us left to do. Someone said the letter "stank." This term is rather inelegant, but it is a letter which no gentleman commander-in-chief might sign. The letter cannot be signed by you, Dr. Weizmann. You may think you are under the stress of signing the letter at this time. No friend of yours would ask you to sign this letter. I can well conceive your enemies asking you to sign this. If I were Jabotinsky,[11] I would ask you to sign this letter, but as one who wants to sit at your side, for as many years as will be given to him, I say, you cannot sign this letter, whatever the difficulties are, and whatever the pressure might be. There is a shell game, and I shall use the expression, "they have shell-gamed you." They have done this thing to you, and we have got to save you from the damage which will be done to your great and deserved reputation as the leader of the Zionist Organization, by signing this letter. By implication you consent to all that they have said about us. You are willing to sign a declaration which no gentleman would sign, in order to give in to Brown. It is not the question of priority of things, but the question of the primacy of Palestine. Rosalsky can sign it, Semel can sign it, Kaplan would not. You cannot sign this letter. You cannot sign it in the light of your convictions, in the light of the damage done to Palestine by the whole Russian Scheme.[12] You know that it is a conspiracy of the king of assimilationists—the Russian Yevsektzia[13]—to submerge Palestine.

You were neutral up to this time. In London, we were hungering and we were thirsting, but we never had a word from you. Now you break your silence, and this first word is come that you virtually exonerated them, giving them an absolutely clean slate, and by implication it is perfectly obvious that we might have been more careful—more millions would have been gotten. With a fight we got more millions. We were not neutral. It was the passion that we put into the thing, because we fought for the integrity of Palestine, its primacy and priority—because of this fighting passion and the blood that we put into it that we won, and had the confidence of the Zionists. We did win the battle, despite the hostility of Brown, and we might have gotten one million more if Brown did not close doors to us.[14] Weizmann, you cannot sign this letter, and I do not assent to the alternative that you offer—either that you sign this, or withdraw. You, as a statesman, as a diplomat, must find a way out by 8 P.M.[15] See Mr. Marshall and say: "This is no letter for me, as a gentleman and the leader of the Zionist Organization, to sign." I am thinking, Weizmann, of our Zionist following. We have not got them in our hands today, but we give them a token of our faith by standing up, which is harder to do. It is a hard thing for poor beggars like myself to stand up, week after week, month after month, and fight against the financial omnipotence of Warburg, the legal mastery of Marshall, and the outrages of Brown, now to be told this unfortunate thing. This is just the letter that Brown ought to write. Marshall is an honorable gentleman, whose zeal and devotion are undoubted, and if Marshall had put out both hands as you do in the gesture of peace, then it would be admissable, but for you—and we are you and you are we (*here Mr. Lipsky interrupted and read the letter.*)[16]

Dr. Wise (*continuing*): Marshall's letter does Marshall honor. Your letter does not do you honor. Marshall's letter is Marshall at his best; yours is not even you at your worst. You must say to Mr. Marshall, "I am perfectly satisfied with the letter from you, but I am not satisfied with my letter." Your letter does you a great injustice. It does not rise to the level of Mr. Marshall's letter, because you did not write it.

Dr. Weizmann: I am going to say only two words: All you said, I have felt. You need not rub it in. I take it in the spirit in which you say it. I understand what you feel, but I thought that this second document wipes this letter out. I cannot risk this second document. I am frightened of it. Perhaps I am wrong, but this second document is, in my opinion, the only step which the Zionist Organization of America can take. It is simply a legal documentation of what we have done. I can only say one thing: I cannot reopen these negotiations with Marshall; I am a bad negotiator.

Dr. Wise: Is that reopening negotiations by saying, "Marshall, that letter of yours is superb, I want to write a letter to match it."?

Dr. Weizmann: In my humble opinon, this is not feasible.

Dr. Wise: Not feasible, but necessary.

Dr. Weizmann: If you select someone to see Marshall, I shall be happy. That is all that we can do. It is essential that this goes through tonight. If this falls through, it is unfortunate.

Dr. Wise: You underestimate your strength. This is a mistake.

Dr. Weizmann: Perhaps I do.

Mr. Goldberg: . . . As to the letter, there can be no doubt that it is a bad letter, but, on the other hand, that remark Dr. Wise made now—for you to go and reopen negotiations—what will it mean? It will mean that he came here. We called him over. We said, "Dr. Weizmann, your first opinion is not the right opinion. Unless you change the letter, then you could have peace." It is very clear that Weizmann wants to have peace, but that his group does not want peace—that this group intimidates him at the last moment. I want to say that there is a difference between Dr. Weizmann in accepting this letter—even this bad letter, and Mr. Marshall. Mr. Marshall is not losing anything, but Dr. Weizmann believes that Palestine will lose the Agency. . . . I say it was a vital mistake to have this letter written by somebody else, and I do believe—whenever Weizmann threatens to resign, I always say, let us come to an agreement with his policy—I do believe if this is not done, you cannot go ahead to negotiate again. You are satisfied with the negotiations, but at the last moment, you say to Mr. Marshall to reopen them—why reopen them?— because we asked Dr. Weizmann today. So it seems to me that this argument is not proper, and that, under the circumstances, to my mind, Dr. Weizmann cannot do it. If Weizmann goes to Marshall now, it will seem as if we intimidated him, and they will say that the Agency will not be a success, because men are always interfering, and it will show that Weizmann has not got his own men with him.

I oppose even the sending of the Committee to Marshall. I think this is not proper. I do not know why Weizmann agrees to this. If Dr. Weizmann does not sign this letter, they will say that we have terrorized him, and if we send a committee of three, it shows that Dr. Weizmann could not put this through. We should never agree to this. We have nothing to do with Marshall. We do not see the man. If a Committee goes to Marshall and if he agrees, it will not be a nice thing for Dr. Weizmann. If he does not agree, then it will not be a nice thing for all of us. I think that this letter should be signed and accepted. While I agree that a terrible mistake has been made, the answer is the document about the Jewish Agency. Everybody who will read this document will realize the great sacrifices made by Weizmann. It is like the case of the two women, one the false mother and the other the real mother, who appeared before Solomon. You could remove Brown, but the good of Palestine is paramount.

Dr. Wise: You have sacrificed a pound of flesh; you go out of your way to clear, exonerate, and extenuate them; you give a clean bill of health to those who have set out to destroy the thing which we were instrumental in saving in your absence—in your enforced and voluntary absence. On the other hand, not one word is said in approval of our stand. We found ourselves under the necessity of dealing with Brown, who had set out to destroy us.

Mr. Goldberg: There is no question in my mind that the man that suffers most is Dr. Weizmann. I would relish it much more if after this explanation, you should stand up and say, "that was my pound of flesh, and I am ready to give this pound of flesh if this Agency is to stand. I am willing to bring a great sacrifice in order to see whether the Agency is going to be a success. If Palestine is going to gain something, I am willing to bring this sacrifice."

Mr. Neumann: This letter will affect all Zionist propaganda for years to come in this country. I think it is a sufficiently important matter, before he exercises any opinion himself, that the President of our Organization, upon whom a large responsibility rests, that he give us an expression of his opinion with regard to the situation. Here we have this situation. It is no use talking about it for hours. It is a question of accepting this letter or not. It is a question of making a decision by which we will have to stand, not only now, but for months later, perhaps years hence, and I would appreciate a word from him.

Mr. Lipsky: I believe that the Zionist Organization has started on a road which leads to combinations with non-Zionists. We have re-affirmed our position time and time again. We have recognized the difficulties in the way and have been prepared to meet these difficulties. I regard this letter as one of the smaller incidents of the whole affair. I have objections to the letter mainly on account of its not being Dr. Weizmann's letter.

We know exactly how and why he signs this letter, but for the world at large it is not compatible, but if it is necessary to sign this letter in order to attain a greater purpose, and a great aim, than I say, "sign it." We have undergone a great many humiliations and personal difficulties. We have suffered a great deal from this new element that comes into the movement, but we have got to be ready to stand for all of that, and if we are not ready, then we must admit that we cannot hold this combine. The Zionist movement is growing larger and larger. The work in Palestine is growing bigger and bigger, and the difficulties are getting greater. We cannot overcome this situation ourselves. We cannot get new forces into the movement unless we get them on terms of their own. If these terms are compatible with the general aim, I don't care about the vulgarity connected with it. We have gone through many vulgarities in getting money. Dr. Wise has humiliated himself in order to get money, but he did it for the sake of the Cause.

I don't care if Brown goes all over the United States and calls me any names. The question is whether the public will understand our moves. The public has understood us and knows we are the only people in the United States sacrificing honor and dignity in order to further our Movement. And in all probability, if Dr. Weizmann signs this letter—and we cannot get out of it in any other way—then we come out of this business much stronger than before. We can say, this is the letter that Dr. Weizmann wrote in order to meet the situation. This is the letter which Dr. Weizmann signed in spite of humiliation, to indicate how far we can go in order to do this. I said to Dr. Weizmann, "You will be absolutely free to do anything you please in order to test out this proposition in which you are interested." Any one of our own *baale-batim* [leaders] interested in this peace, will say, "what is the difference what you sign, in order to get this peace."

Dr. Weizmann: The Palestinians, over our heads, have addressed themselves to these people for the sake of a few hundred thousand pounds. I have gotten copies of these letters from Warburg.

Mr. Lipsky: We know very well the needs of Palestine. We foresaw the situation in July.

Dr. Wise: Nothing can be done tonight. It will do much to remedy the present situation. After all the first step cannot take place in a year.[17]

Dr. Weizmann: You do believe me. I hope you do. I don't want to force confidence. I cannot do anything more than sign this letter or not sign it.

Mr. Lipsky: I know that Semel and Rottenberg,[18] etc., are good Zionists. If we stand in the way of overcoming this obstacle, they will be the first ones to say we are in the wrong.

Dr. Weizmann: As for what has been said by Neumann, that we shall have to suffer for months, that depends entirely upon us.

Mr. Lipsky: What will come out of this? With the Jewish Agency will come closer cooperation among the Jews of this country. The people have become more friendly than before. It is a move on the way of securing more and more forces for our Cause. On the other hand, if we do not do anything tonight, there will be immediate recession on the part of a number of the people upon whom Zeldin[19] depends. This feeling of criticism will break out in a hundred different ways. We have not the Zionists behind us in a fight. We had the Zionists behind us eighteen months ago. We cannot endure a fight at this time, and the only way is to go forward in the directions started five years ago.

Mr. Samuel: Some of the things I was going to say have already been said by Mr. Lipsky and Mr. Goldberg. Naturally my first reaction to the letter was one quite of rage when I saw the contents of it, but this question that is involved here just now is a question of rancour. The present letter is a purely personal business. There is a man called Brown in whom there rankles a feeling of discontent and rage with us, and we have to give him a pound of flesh, but I agree with Mr. Lipsky that we must sign this miserable letter which is intellectually beneath us. In my opinion, this present letter is going to draw Brown's teeth to a large extent. He is a man not fighting for an ideal, and it will make him weaker. Of course it is a miserable letter, but if it is dishonorable to accept a ransom for somebody's life, it is not always dishonorable to pay a ransom, and in this case we are paying a ransom. We ought to voice our opinion to Dr. Weizmann to proceed and support him in any case until the time comes when we can voice our opinions. It is not up to us whether he should sign the letter. If Dr. Weizmann says the letter is so miserable, that he won't sign it, we will stand with his view, and we will stand with his view if Dr. Weizmann says he will sign it. Before another five months are over we shall have an opportunity to meet on the real issues. Then the whole question can be fought out, and we shall be fighting the real thing instead of something which is incidental to American Jewry. In any case I feel that as a private individual it does not transgress my principles to permit the political leader to sign this and talk as an individual, and write as an individual, This is a nasty situation but it does not involve fundamental principles,

and, under the circumstances, I feel that Dr. Weizmann should sign this
letter.

Mr. Morris Rothenberg: Mr. Lipsky expressed my views of the situation. There is no disagreement that this letter is "obnoxious," but I
think that the letter will be overlooked entirely in the coming months by
that other document;[20] that letter will not be noticed in the face of that
other document. That document in my estimation is a historic document.
Nobody will take the trouble to read the letter. The emphasis will be
placed in the press on the document.

Dr. Wise: Where do you think—in the JDC publicity—the emphasis
will be placed?

Mr. Rothenberg: That document is of such surpassing importance that
it is bound to attract attention of the entire press. We have been at work
on the Agency for three or four years. Here is something on which both
parties agree. This document is of great importance. The other thing is
not of great importance. I look upon this in this way. I have been supporting Dr. Weizmann not because I believe this is 100 percent. We will
have burdens more disagreeable than the signing of this letter, but we
must go through with it, because we have adopted the view that this is
the line of progress of the Zionist Organization and we must unite the
forces in Jewry, and we must make a test whether this will bring increased
results. And I assure you, Dr. Wise, that it is a great sacrifice for us to
accept this letter. I don't believe that that letter is a surrender of any
principle. I have listened to that letter carefully. It is obnoxious, but there
is nothing contained in that letter which means the surrender of Zionist
principles, or that it is a disavowal of our principles. I wish he were not
compelled to sign it, but I think if he signs it and it is accepted, it will
open up a new epoch in our work for Palestine.

Mr. Neumann: I think it is a *fait accompli*. There is no choice, at the
eleventh hour—only two hours before the meeting at Mecca Temple—
not much can be done now. In my opinion some of the speakers missed
the entire point of this letter. It is not a question of the personal dignity
of Brown or some one of our Committee. What is involved is something
different. The Zionists of America and the Zionists of the whole world
have for years maintained a certain freedom of action and expression. We
conceived the Zionist movement to be just that—an opportunity for the
Jewish people to express itself in Palestine and out of Palestine. If I understand this letter right, it means just one thing. Last year we took a certain
stand—all of us did—in committees, conventions and conferences—and

Dr. Wise, and everyone concerned in this room—Mr. Lipsky was one of the most outspoken in this controversy—(*here Dr. Wise interrupted and said, "with the complete sanction of Dr. Weizmann."*) (*Mr. Neumann continued*) I won't go into that. We had Sokolow come here. He said he came here for the Executive and the Executive is not for peace but for war. Then Schmarya Levin[21] about whose relation to us or to the Executive nobody need have doubts—Schmarya Levin was the first one who pointed out the dangers about Crimea, and instructed us to speak about it. We took a certain stand here. We expressed ourselves.

Now what has happened? What has happened is that the President of the World Zionist Organization comes to America and addresses a communication to the Jewish public and says all this thing is wrong. These people did things which should not have been done. He apologized on their behalf, saying that if they had not done it, we could have gotten more money for Palestine. That should not be done. I tell you that it has been a great struggle and what has been achieved this year has been at a great personal sacrifice, and we have gotten more money. I would like to know who did that? On the face of it, it is untrue, that we would have gotten more millions. There have been no million dollar appropriations. $1,500,000 was appropriated because we fought them. They have a contingent appropriation on their raising $15,000,000 during the first year; they have actually raised $4,000,000 in cash. I think this is gross, because otherwise they would have set net. Therefore, the amount appropriated actually last year for Palestine may be an item of three or four hundred thousand dollars, and so far as I know not one penny of that has been sent to Palestine. Just to say, "You have been giving millions for Palestine," The Zionists are wrong, affects the whole tenor, the whole morale, the whole spirit of Jewish life in America. It will take us a long time before that is wiped out.

In the meantime, we must consider so-and-so's feelings. We must consider also the feelings of the Zionists. In my opinion, the Zionists are also somebody. The Zionists after all have borne the burden until now whether ill, well or indifferent. I see involved in this thing the question of the whole morale for a long time to come. I cannot say, don't sign it. If you tell us there is nothing else to be done but sign, far be it for me to tell you to wreck the Agency, but I must say if we approve this thing now, we cannot turn around and say it is Dr. Weizmann's act. We are stopped forever afterwards, from raising the point that too much has been conceded. We are stopped from throwing the responsibility upon Dr. Weizmann's act. Dr. Weizmann has come here as the leader of the Organization. He has listened to our opinion, and we are stopped from throwing the blame on Dr. Weizmann unless we take the responsibility for it now. I don't know to what extent it is understood that the leaders of the ZOA and the UPA are bound to observe the spirit of that document—I mean our official publications, our addresses, our utterances, publicly. Does it mean that we are henceforth to keep ourselves to that particular tune? (*Dr. Wise interrupting—you mean re Russia, etc."?*)

(*Mr. Neumann continuing*) Everything. You cannot say at one moment we apologize, and then do something contrary to that. Let us face it. We must swallow and keep mum. It is not a question of indignity or humiliation. We must swallow everything. If Rosalsky wants Brown to speak at Mecca Temple, we must swallow this. Rosalsky told me, as you know, I hope I am going to succeed in getting Brown to speak on the same platform with me in the campaign. This is only as an illustration of how far we can go. I for one don't know how far this is going to go, and I should like for myself the right to reserve freedom of action.

Mr. Liebowitz: I listened carefully to everything. I agree that the letter is obnoxious, to say the least. If we could have prevented that letter from being sent, I would be the first to sanction that it should not be sent, but we must take the facts as they are. We cannot change them at the 11th hour. I have a picture before me of a breach with Brown's group, and I am afraid that if this letter is not signed by Weizmann, we are going to have another split. We must make the best of the situation. If Dr. Weizmann signs this letter, which I personally think he should, that does not lessen our hold upon Jewry. I know that there is great difficulty about personnel. If the development of Palestine is going to proceed, we must have new forces. A great many people, once peace is established, will be perfectly satisfied, and we can make good Zionists out of even non-Zionists and anti-Zionists. We cannot afford to antagonize Mr. Marshall. . . . If Dr. Weizmann is careful with his Jewish Agency question, he can make it an instrument of great good to all of us. I don't see how Dr. Weizmann can recall the letter at the last moment.

Judge Lewis: I suppose from my standpoint I ought to grab at it for the fact that it may get us some money. I personally am very much hurt at the phrasing in this letter. Now, what is the consideration—the Agency. Well, I may be pessimistic about it. I still don't see the value of the document as Mr. Rothenberg sees it. I think it is considerably in the offing. I think it is a long distance away. What will be done if this letter is signed?

Do I understand that Judge Rosalsky, the Chairman of the New York Campaign, will get people interested in the New York campaign in a way that will get people on committees and get more money? I listened to Mr. Marshall's letter, and what hurts is that the word, "Palestine," does not appear in the letter.[22] Mr. Lipsky, the head of our Organization in this country, says it has got to be done. Dr. Weizmann, the head of the International Organization, says it is got to be done. I never was so hurt and humiliated in my life. Brown will meet me and say, "See what you did."

Dr. Wise: In the light of the Marshall letter, would it be impossible to get in touch with him and say, "Let Marshall write the first letter and [let] your letter be a reply to him."

Judge Lewis: I venture to say that if Dr. Weizmann went to Mr. Marshall and had him edit it.

Here Dr. Weizmann interrupted: Marshall had the letter and changed it and this is the result. I think it does not contain any humiliation. It does not contain any reffection. It is mostly a formality and the letter will be forgotten, and the outcome of tonights' meeting will be the Agency, and the whole thing about the Agency revolves about Palestine. The consequences which Neumann enumerated are not there.

Along with that we had some other negotiations. Perhaps Dr. Halperin might tell you what I went through. I went through it. I had to go through it. I have gone through hell every night, but I had to go through with it. Ten years ago I could get into the good graces of the British government. The signing of the White Paper is parallel to the signing of this letter tonight.[23]

Dr. Wise: The only difference is that in connection with the White Paper you were dealing with the British Government and not Brown.

Dr. Weizmann: It is not your fault and not my fault. We did our best that it should not happen. It is no use arguing. I still say that it might be possible at the last moment to change it—not I—I cannot do it—I should not do it.

Judge Lewis: I came over on the train from Philadelphia with Billikopf. Will you allow me to meet with Marshall and Billikopf, and perhaps if you think it is worthwhile my trying, I will see if we cannot eliminate some of the poison out of this letter.

Dr. Weizmann: I will be delighted. I share Goldberg's view—I cannot do it.

Irving Lehman has telegraphed to Marshall that this is not a fair letter.

Dr. Wise: I move, not that we take any step whatever to prevent Judge Rosalsky's being chairman, not that we urge Dr. Weizmann not to send this letter—I move that we express our disapproval of the character of the communication addressed by Dr. Weizmann to Mr. Louis Marshall. (*Seconded*).

Mr. Lipsky: A motion has been made and seconded that we disapprove of the letter.

Mr. Neumann: I wish to amend it: That this Committee expresses its opinion to Dr. Weizmann, that every possible effort be made to obtain a modification of this letter, and that we record our deep regret at the necessity which seems to have arisen to express disapproval of the character of the communication addressed to Mr. Marshall.

Mr. Lipsky: After hearing the proposed letter of Dr. Weizmann addressed to Mr. Marshall read, and after the discussion, which has been held, the Administrative Committee expresses no objection with regard to the sending of the letter.

Dr. Wise: That however much we deplore the character of the communication which in the judgment of Dr. Weizmann it has become necessary to address to Mr. Louis Marshall, the Administrative Committee of the Zionist Organization of America cannot ask that the letter be not forwarded in the light of Dr. Weizmann's statement that the failure to forward this communication would make it impossible for him to proceed with the work of the Jewish Agency.

Mr. Rothenberg: It is the consensus of opinion that we raise no objection to the signing of this letter.

I think that we ought to record that opinion and then draft a resolution.

I will withdraw my resolution, provided it is understood that the proceedings of this afternoon be made part of the proceedings of the ZOA.

Dr. Weizmann: I have one feeling—if we all stand in and go on with the work as if nothing happened, it is all right; if not, it is all wrong.

Mr. Lipsky: It is the consensus of opinion that we raise no objection to the sending of this letter.

. . . .

Dr. Wise (again): I think I have the motion now:

"While we do not feel justified in interrupting at this time the negotiations between Dr. Weizmann and the Marshall group, on behalf of the Jewish Agency, we cannot but deplore the character of the communication which Dr. Weizmann has found it necessary to address to Mr. Marshall."

Dr. Weizmann: For me it is important to know whether we go on with the work or not.

Mr. Rothenberg: While we regard the letter addressed by Dr. Weizmann to Mr. Marshall as unsatisfactory, this Committee raises no objection to the signing of the letter by Dr. Weizmann, whilst we deplore the necessity . . . (*here Mr. Rothenberg was interrupted by Dr. Wise who said, "this letter never should have been written. It does Dr. Weizmann a great wrong. It indicates that Weizmann has a small part in this and Brown a large part. It has done Dr. Weizmann a very great injury."*) The motion (as stated above by Dr. Wise) was then carried. . . .

Dr. Wise: We ought to agree to have a committee reformulate "it" in such way as to bring the greatest possible advantage to the Zionist movement.

(*no objection to reformulation.*)

Dr. Weizmann: I still do think that if Lewis, Kaliski and Liebowitz went to Marshall—the ideal thing would be if Lewis could get Marshall to say that tonight he goes forth with the Agency.

Meeting adjourned at 6 P.M.

Respectfully submitted.

IDA FLATOW

NOTES

1. I am grateful to the director of the Zionist Archives and Library, Mrs. S. Landress, for making this document available to me.
2. Biographical sketches of all these personalities are in the *Encyclopedia of Zionism and Israel* (*EZI*) or the *Universal Jewish Encyclopedia* (*UJE*).
3. She was Dr. Weizmann's secretary.
4. The agreement refers to the accord reached by Marshall and Weizmann, including the exchange of letters, to proceed with the enlargement of the JA.
5. This reference requires an explanation: Wise, together with the Brandeis group, withdrew from the official Zionist movement in 1921 as a result of an irreparable disagreement with regard to the nature and function of the Keren Hayesod. Wise, like other leading Brandeisists, returned to the official organization in 1925 and became chairman of the contemporaneously organized UPA. Weizmann met Wise, in this new capacity, for the first time, on his arrival in 1926. Hence this conference. For the Weizmann-Brandeis rift: Herbert Parzen, "The United Palestine Appeal," in *Herzl Year Book: Vol. 7* (New York: Herzl Press, 1971), pp. 357–69.
6. Judge Irving Lehman.
7. Felix M. Warburg, chairman of JDC and very sympathetic to the upbuilding of Palestine.
8. For the Boston UPA Conference, see *New Palestine* (*NP*), November 26, 1926, pp. 347–65; Weizmann's address, pp. 356–61.
9. Brown was the chairman of the UJC drive and without question wrote the letter in question.
10. The Joint Palestine Survey Commission.
11. V. Jabotinsky was an opponent of Weizmann's policies within the World Zionist Organization. Eventually he founded the Revisionist Party. For details see *EZI*.
12. The colonization of Jews in the Crimea and the Ukraine.
13. The Yevsektzia was the Jewish section of the Communist Party in Russia.
14. These references describe the militancy of the first UPA campaign under Wise's leadership; Wise was unquestionably the initiator of the Zionist attack on the Russian colonization program.
15. The Mecca Temple UPA rally was scheduled to open at this time.
16. This refers to Marshall's reply to Weizmann's letter in debate. Both letters were ready to be read at the Mecca Temple later that evening.
17. The next Zionist Congress did have to ratify the compact.
18. These two men, together with Judge Rosalsky, Dr. M. M. Kaplan, and Liebowitz, were members of the committee that mediated the peace accord. They were interested in bringing new forces, new men, into the work for Palestine.
19. Zeldin, at this time, was the director of the UPA campaign in the New York City area.

20. The Marshall-Weizmann accord.
21. Sokolow and Levin were prominent European Zionist figures. Levin was regarded by numbers of American Zionists as their instructor and inspirer in Zionist ideology. For their biographies consult *EZI*.
21A. JDC planned to raise this amount within three years and announced an appropriation of $1,500,000 to be spent in Palestine: Herbert Parzen, *Ibid.*, p. 365.
22. This is true.
23. This apparently refers to the letter which Weizmann wrote to the Colonial Office accepting the Churchill White Paper in 1922, which limited the *JNH* and in fact amputated it by severing Transjordan from its sphere. Unofficially the ZO was threatened that the Palestine Mandate would not be ratified on the scheduled date—July 24, 1922—if the ZO did not approve the White Paper. Weizmann signed the letter of acceptance. For documentation, see *Book of Documents Submitted to the General Assembly of the United Nations, 1917–1947* (New York: Jewish Agency for Palestine, May 1947), pp. 21–34.

THE AMBIGUITY OF REFORM

By

W. GUNTHER PLAUT

Holy Blossom Temple
Toronto, Ontario

It ought to be stated at the outset that even a few years ago the phrasing of my subject would have been unlikely, if not impossible. Certainly, some fifty years ago when the first Union Haggadah was published, and when Reform Judaism was still in what is generally referred to as the "classical" period, few ambiguities were discernible. To be sure, there were some Reform rabbis who stubbornly insisted on being Zionists, but the vast majority of their colleagues, as well as the lay membership, were convinced that Reform Judaism preached a universalism which excluded Jewish national aspirations. The Pittsburgh Platform is perhaps most remarkable in its sense of certainty. Its fifteen framers knew precisely where they were going, they knew what Judaism, as they conceived of it, demanded of them, what its perimeters were, its origins and its directions. There were flurries of debate on such issues as the nature of revelation, but everything was disposed of in three days, and the draft submitted by Kaufmann Kohler was approved with minor amendments.[1]

Contrast this with the deliberations and the notable lack of a single definitive statement produced so far by the contemporary version of the Platform Committee. Established in 1972, it was expected to formulate a new Reform platform in the fall of 1973, in time for the centenary observance of the Union of American Hebrew Congregations.[2] The present platformers are slowly and painfully coming to the conviction that a plat-

Based on the Tintner Memorial Lecture, New York, 1974.

form in the image of Pittsburgh or even Columbus is no longer a possibility. It is my prediction, therefore, that if we produce anything, it will be a series of essays rather than statements. They will outline the ways in which Reform Judaism is attempting to meet the spiritual, intellectual, and social challenges of our day. There will be in every case—whether they be essays on the existence of God or the nature of the Jewish people, the meaning of Israel or our approach to Halakhah—more than one answer. This is the change which has come over our movement. We have moved from the unequivocal to the equivocal, from the clear to the ambiguous. It is the purpose of this paper to show that ambiguity is in fact closer than its opposite to the real nature of our movement. At its inception Reform was, and now has once more become, an ambiguous movement. Therewith it is likely to attain a new dynamism, for while the unambiguous frequently becomes static, the ambiguous tends toward the dynamic.

I

How did Reform Judaism begin? This simple question is not asked often enough, for if it were, some of the problems which many reformers experience during these days could hardly exist, or at least they would be reduced. *Reform Judaism started as an attempt to reform the Halakhah.* It wanted to do no more and no less. The first decades of the movement were given to scholarly investigations of specific Halakhic problems. They dealt with the nature of the service, the permissibility of a sermon in the tongue of the land (this was the reason for Zunz' monumental work in 1832), with the legitimacy of organ music, and the like. This attempt to reform Halakhah was by definition ambiguous: to maintain the *spirit* of Halakhah while breaching some of its *prescripts* in the name of Halakhah. Ambiguity was therefore built into Reform from its beginning.

The first rabbinic conferences at Brunswick, Breslau, and Frankfurt dealt primarily with Halakhic questions. The first conference, in 1844, concerned itself first with mixed marriage, thereafter with liturgy, and it then turned to a discussion of Shabbat and its laws.[3] At the end of the first conference, the chairman, Joseph Maier (who later on became the first and possibly the only rabbi ever to be ennobled), warned his colleagues not to be impatient in their drive for Reform. "Let us not force from time that which it cannot give us," he said. For "he who forces time, time will force him" (*mi shedohek et hasha'ah, hasha'ah doheket 'oto*). The subsequent synods in Leipzig and Augsburg had the same purpose:

to develop Halakhah in a variety of ways. It is now just a little over one hundred years ago that the latter took place. The year was 1871, and it will be well to look at its final statement.

While fully appreciating and venerating the past, said Article III, Judaism strives, in accord with earnest scientific research, to set aside what is obsolete and antiquated, so that it may unfold itself in the spirit of the new age. Note the word *research*. Clearly, this referred to the development of Halakhah, a process conceived by the conveners as continuous, or, as they called it, "unfolding." The synod paid due respect to the past and reiterated time and again that the purpose of the assembly was above all to preserve traditional Judaism, but maintained that this could be done only when dynamic principles were applied. The final statement is equally revealing: "The task of the synod is not concluded by these preceding declarations or principles." [4]

That was a little over a hundred years ago. One need hardly emphasize that the development of Reform did not follow along the intentions and declarations of Brunswick, Frankfurt, Breslau, Leipzig, and Augsburg. In America especially, Halakhah became less and less an issue for the reformers.[5] Substituted for it was a new approach based not on the ambiguities of process but on the certainty of abandonment. *Reform Judaism no longer reformed the Halakhah but abandoned it.* This had one great advantage, or at least it appeared so: it made it possible to speak with certainty—not out of a process of ambiguity but from the clear and unfettered standpoint of philosophic and theological principle. Now, in hindsight, we can see that even the vaunted certainty which the successors of Augsburg (or in America, of the 1869 Philadelphia Conference) tried to achieve involved them in new ambiguities. What is commonly called the "classical" period of Reform Judaism—that is, the period after 1869 and 1871, which reaches up to the time of the Columbus platform in 1937—*was in fact not classical at all.* It was not a culmination of the ideas of the founders but rather a radical departure. It was radicalism, not classicism. It was the relation of revolutionary excess to the purposes of the revolution itself, the relation of a Robespierre to a Diderot and a Montesquieu—that is, the radicalism of the guillotine to the searching pen of the philosopher. The year 1871 concludes the first period of Reform. In North America, the ambiguities of renewing the Halakhah which were inherent in the founding of Reform were abandoned for the ideological certainties, or presumed certainties, of a new radical vision.

Of course, these new certainties were in themselves debated and not always accepted by all reformers, but there was little question in the minds of most that with proper argument and persuasion one could reach some basic agreement. There were three anchor points:

1. Reform Judaism is Judaism purified.
2. Reform is prophetic Judaism.
3. Reform is in consonance with the spirit of America.

II

1. "Reform is Judaism purified." The banner-bearer of this theme was Samuel Holdheim, to whom Halakhah became ceremonial law and eventually identified with the dead letter of the Talmud. "Reform," he said, "must avoid as much as possible pressing the banner of progress into the rigid hands of the Talmud. The time has to come when one feels strong enough vis-à-vis the Talmud to oppose it in the knowledge of having gone far beyond it." [6] This was a cry of war: Halakhah was to be abandoned and no longer developed. By a strange happenstance, the victorious proponent of this anti-Halakhic point of view was none other than a rabbi who had first come to public attention in the early 1840s with a brilliant responsum in the Tiktin-Geiger controversy. He was David Einhorn. His responsum on when a rabbi can be removed from office was replete with scholarly references based soundly on Talmud and the Rambam. His summation read in part as follows:

A Rabbi can be removed from his post if he rejects a talmudic inter-pretation and if the rejected talmudic interpretation and the disputed traditional law concerning tradition which in the Talmud is described and recognized by everyone as genuine and undoubted. Maimonides in his introduction to the Mishnah enumerated such traditional interpreta-tions.[7]

Yet it was this same Einhorn who more than a decade later, upon his arrival in the United States, could propose that Tisha Be'av should be turned into a day of joy rather than remain a day of mourning. For instead of weeping over the dispersion decreed by God one ought to be glad of it.[8]

That was 1855, the same year that Isaac M. Wise, along with eight other colleagues, issued an appeal to the American public asking them to attend a convention in Cleveland which would discuss the articles of a

Union of American Israel. The result of that Conference was an unequivocal endorsement of the *original* principles of Reform—that is, a movement aiming at a development of Halakhah. *"The Talmud,"* said the
statement, *"contains traditional and legal explanations of the biblical laws
which must be expounded and practised according to the comments of the
Talmud."* [9]
Wise saw himself as a classical reformer, as indeed he was. Einhorn
was now the leader of the new radicals. There was hope for an understanding between Isaac M. Wise and conservative Isaac Leeser.[10] There
was none between Leeser and Einhorn. The latter criticized the Cleveland conference bitterly:

> The said Platform would condemn Judaism to a perpetual stagnation,
> consign its countless treasures available at all times, to the narrow confines
> of an exclusive Jewish nationality, and expose to derision its entire his-
> torical development, as well as the incontestable results of a wholesome
> biblical research. The declared legitimacy of talmudic authority cannot
> heal, but on the contrary, will render permanent, our unhealthy religious
> condition, which consists not in the present conflict of parties, but must
> be sought for in the demoralizing effect of an antagonism between theory
> and practice, and in an opposition between descriptive rules and the
> unyielding nature of religious and social wants.[11]

Wise was a spiritual disciple of the early Geiger, and both were, on
the whole, classicists in the sense that they recognized the ambiguity of
Reform because Reform to them was a development of Halakhah. Einhorn had essentially given up this position and could now be considered a
disciple of Holdheim. Einhorn's views prevailed in subsequent conferences
and even more so in the actual life-style of North American Reform
Jewry. Isaac M. Wise is usually called the father of American Reform.
The historian must conclude, however, that he should be described as the
father of American Reform *institutions*—that is, the Union, the College,
the Central Conference of American Rabbis. The true father of American Reform, in the period which in the past was identified as the core
period of our movement on this side of the ocean, was David Einhorn. He
founded no institutions, but his philosophy gained the day and his *Olat
Tamid* was the foundation of the *Union Prayer Book*—and not Wise's far
more traditional *Minhag Amerika*. He was relatively unambiguous. He
was certain that Reform Judaism as he saw it was Judaism purified. His
chief disciples were Kaufmann Kohler and Emil G. Hirsch, who also

happened to be his sons-in-law. And although Wise gave assent to the Pittsburgh Platform, it was the assent of a man who was theologically defeated—or, we might say, deflected from his original purposes.[12] Radical Reform Judaism was espoused by Einhorn, was anti-Halakhic and largely unambiguous. By implication it espoused a total eclecticism, which became the hallmark of the movement. The trend to oppose or even condemn the strictures of tradition was raised to the level of principle. The radicals abandoned Halakhah and no longer made themselves subject to the vagaries and ambiguities of its development.

2. Another way of phrasing the essence of Reform Judaism became popular during the latter part of the radical period. Reform, it was said, is "prophetic Judaism." That, of course, as Professor Shemaryahu Talmon has pointed out, is at best an idealized version of prophetic teaching, but had very little relationship to the Prophets themselves.[13] The reformers chose to quote selected passages, mostly from Amos and Isaiah, which stressed social and universal concerns. They tended to bypass the Prophets' intense nationalism and were never known to quote Ezekiel at length. Yet, for better or worse, the Bible has preserved more of his writing than those of any other Prophet, and though his book is replete with elaborate references to ritual, it says little about war and peace, or other matters usually referred to as "prophetic." "Reform is prophetic Judaism"—that was but another and temporarily more convenient shorthand for saying: "Reform is un-Halakhic, it is Einhornian and not Wiseian."

The radicals took a similar point of view with their exaltation of Psalms, selecting those they liked, and disregarding the others. It is noteworthy that even in 1974, the new Haggadah published by the Conference[14] failed to reintroduce the verse from Psalms which says, "Pour out Your wrath upon the nations that do not acknowledge You." [15] It was "too narrow" and thus continued to be excluded—a heritage of radical Reform. This omission highlights a continuing process of selectivity which does not as yet exhibit the sturdy developmental principles that were part of the truly "classical" period of the early movement and aimed at the development of Halakhah.

3. Finally, in this critique of the middle period of our movement, one needs to confront that now fortunately obsolete identification of Reform Judaism with Americanism.[16] Despite the protestations of the radical reformers, the vaunted policy of integration did in fact assist the process of assimilation, especially so since Reform Judaism became during this

period the way of life and belief for a particular, upwardly mobile, social class, and in that it became a Jewish form of the Protestant way of life.

Reform is usually approached, reproached, and defended in terms of ideology. The class nature of the movement is rarely discussed. Yet it was a potent force, especially in the radical period. This can be illustrated by the inner development of the Reform congregation in St. Paul, Minnesota.

> Until 1881 the great majority of the 75 families of St. Paul, Minnesota, belonged to the old and established Mt. Zion Hebrew Congregation of that city. The Congregation had exhibited moderate liberal tendencies, and had joined the Union of American Hebrew Congregations, but as late as 1879 a motion to remove hats at worship services was roundly defeated. Then, in 1881, the first large group of Russian emigres began to arrive in the city. The first trainload brought at one time 200 people who were poor, hungry, disoriented and did not speak a word of English. These too were Jews—and in the eyes of the Gentile community no distinctions were made between the newcomers and the older established families whose children were now in high school and some of them at University. While the St. Paul Jewish residents extended charitable help to the newcomers who began to arrive in ever larger numbers, there arose among the former a need to differentiate between themselves, the acculturated members of Mt. Zion, and the "others." This need expressed itself dramatically in the rapid radicalization of pre-existing liberal religious tendencies, and this in turn was highlighted by a renewed motion to remove the head covering at worship. Where formerly the issue was decided in favor of tradition, the motion now won overwhelming approval and Mt. Zion henceforth became a member of the radical Reform wing. The confluence of this development with the arrival of East European Jewry is hardly coincidental.[17]

This is but one illustration of how what today in retrospect we are wont to call "ideology" was in part a function of social pressure and status. The appearance of large numbers of East European Jews in America strengthened the earlier residents in their sense of responsibility and charity, but at the same time fractured their sense of peoplehood in its social and political dimensions and eventually turned most Reform Jews into anti-Zionists.

Reform Judaism was in fact a "Protestant version of Judaism." This judgment was often pronounced upon it by its detractors—and vigorously denied by its adherents—the implication being that "Protestant" meant "Christian." However, once the word *Protestantism* is deprived of its emotional content, and seen it for what it was historically—a particular way of protest against the Roman Catholic Church, a way which then took on its own direction—we see that indeed that there are many parallels between this Christian protest movement and Reform Judaism. To be sure, because Reform Judaism flowered in North America, where the Protestant ethic and way of life held sway, it took on the additional coloration of the environment and was severely subject to its influences. These may be seen, for instance, in the shaping of Reform temples. Gone was the *bimah* in the middle, the worshippers were arranged like Christian audiences, and the preaching pulpit became the focus of the structure itself. Where formerly the house of God was also a *beth keneset* and even served as a night lodging for transients, the elements of sociability were reduced in the modern Reform temple, and rarely did a synagogue building have either a lobby for socializing or an adequate hall for get-togethers. The former was deemed unnecessary—what Protestant church, or what church in general had a gathering lobby?—and the latter was frequently superfluous because the members of the congregation belonged to "Harmony" and "Progressive" or "Phoenix" clubs, or later to country clubs, where they could obtain all necessary social contacts. The service had hymns patterned after Protestant song; responsive prayers—quite unknown in this form to Jewish tradition—silent meditation, the inclination of the head by the devout worshippers, the centrality of the sermon—all these are instances of the protestantization of the Reform service. The abolition of the cantor, the introduction of organs and Christian choirs, made the picture rather complete.

Related to these aspects was what may be termed the "internalization" of Judaism. By internalization I mean the emphasis on faith and attitude rather than on *mizvot,* an emphasis that was pioneered by Christianity, which, with all its cross-streams, continued to stress internalized faith over externalized works. It was a standard Reform phrase of the radical period to say, "I don't have to show my Judaism, as long as I am Jewish at heart." One did not have to eat *mazzah* on Passover or have a *mezuzah* on the door. Consequently, the prophetic attitude which the leaders tried to foster remained all too frequently an attitude only. The ideal place for the internalization of Judaism was, of course, the synagogue, where one studied and prayed. Both were activities of the mind rather than of the hand, of thought rather than of deed. In the past it was the males who had been the primary internalizers of Judaism—which they could safely be, because they combined with it an extensive practice of *mizvot,* and neither they nor the women had any problem externalizing their religion as well. But now, with the advent of Reform, a strange reversal took place: the women moved from the home into the synagogue, and with it moved their Judaism as well. The women were the last practitioners of externalized Judaism, that is, of *mizvot* practiced at home. Now the women, too, abandoned this and in time became the prime movers in the synagogue, where they too now internalized their faith. Men, in turn, having no further province of their own, moved out of the synagogue altogether, and frequently out of Jewish life in any meaningful way.

The identification of Reform with America found its expression in many other ways. I mention only three more. One was Reform's unhesitating approval of the rational or scientific approach to all matters of religion, which meant in time the gradual and complete elimination of the religious mystique, which, in its turn, made way for an expansion of humanism within the movement. The identification with America also meant an incorporation of the "pragmatic" into the religious enterprise. One began to ask of innovations in the synagogue, "Will they work?" If they did, they were deemed worthwhile, for the end was worthwhile. This, in turn, steered the movement onto the shoals of very dangerous reasoning. For instance, it was believed that improved mental health would come to congregants from regular attendance. The premise was, of course, wrong, because religious services may at times impart to the worshippers a profound sense of disquiet, for a meeting with the living God is not necessarily identical with peace of mind. But then, not only was the premise wrong, the conclusion emphasized unwittingly that religious services were important because they produced certain pragmatic results, measurable in medical and psychological terms. Of course, religious services were not subject to such pragmatic evaluation, nor did most people ever respond on that basis. If that had been the case, air conditioning, soft seating, good lighting, and all the rest should have improved attendance at religious services, something that manifestly has not happened, and if it has happened, certainly not for these reasons. But Reform was so caught up in its unequivocal acceptance of the American ethic that rationalism and pragmatism, permeated the movement, which began to lose sight of the need for religion to deal significantly also with the nonrational and with the nonpragmatic so that it would in fact often run counter to much of the culture which American society value so highly.

Finally, Reform in its radical phase gave its unhesitating endorsement to America's optimistic approach to social and political problems. It was an American axiom that, given enough time, money, and willpower, one could achieve almost any end, and this became a Reform axiom as well. The innate limitation of man, which is part of the religious stance, was not popular in America's manifest century. Rather, American semi-messianism foresaw the early achievement of universal brotherhood and so did Reform, despite the new social anti-Semitism which established itself during the 1870's as a part of the American way.

Professor Alvin Reines drew a logical conclusion from this period of radicalism. Reform Judaism, he held, could be many things. In fact, it could be all things, for there never was any "Judaism" as such, only "Judaisms." [18] Everything to which Jews responded was, therefore, in line with the thinking of the radical period, legitimate. This point of view represents the inevitable climax of the radical period, though it was formulated after its conclusion.

III

Since 1935, and increasingly since 1948, Reform Judaism has evinced signs of trying to find its way back to fundamentals, of loosening itself from the assumed certainties of its radical period, and of coming back to the ambiguities of its origin. That is to say, Reform Judaism once again began to concern itself with Halakhah and the need for its reform. The radical period produced some magnificent examples of idealism and ingenuity, especially in its commitment to social and esthetic values. In its third, post-radical phase, Reform Judaism has begun to deal once again with *mizvah*, without posting God as the only *mezavveh* of tradition. It acknowledges the demand, yet does not make it in the name of any one source of authority. This tension is now seen to belong to the ambiguity of the movement.

Reform is thus once again understood to be pledged to the development of Halakhah, to the recapture of its meaning and its practice. Because it deals with the certainties of Halakhah and at the same time with the uncertainties of its reform, it is ambiguous by nature. For the process is filled with the tensions between authority and freedom, the uncertain relation of *mizvah* and *mezavveh*, and thus the very process is in itself ambiguous. This ambiguity is both the inherent difficulty but also the potential strength of Reform. It is a movement which deals with questions rather than answers, with partial answers rather than finalities. As it returns to its original purposes and its beginnings, it is again dynamic rather than static, and therein lies its abiding vitality.

NOTES

1. David Philipson, *The Reform Movement in Judaism*, rev. ed. (New York: Macmillan Co., 1931), pp. 355 ff.; W. Gunther Plaut, *The Growth of Reform Judaism* (New York: World Union for Progressive Judaism, 1965), pp. 31 ff.
2. In contrast to the 1885 Pittsburgh Platform and the 1937 Columbus Platform, both of which were framed exclusively by rabbis, the current committee consists also of nonrabbinical representatives of the Union and the Hebrew Union College–Jewish Institute of Religion. The author has been a member of the committee since its inception.
3. The second conference (Frankfurt, 1845) discussed the essentiality of Hebrew at worship services; the Halakhah concerning the Eighteen Benedictions and the Musaf; sacrifices; the triennial cycle of weekly pericopes; prescriptions for Torah and Haftarah readings; whether a Jew was permitted to play the organ on Shabbat; rules for the construction of a Mikveh. The third conference (Breslau, 1846) dealt with the laws of marriage, the *'erubh* and other Shabbat observances; circumcision, especially *peri'ah* and *mezizah;* Passover, *halizah*, etc. See Plaut, *The Rise of Reform Judaism* (New York: World Union for Progressive Judaism, 1963), pp. 74 ff.
4. Ibid., p. 94.
5. On the reasons for this development, see ibid., pp. xxii ff.
6. Ibid., p. 123.
7. Ibid., pp. 119 ff.
8. Ibid., pp. 220 ff.; see also Kaufmann Kohler, *Studies, Addresses and Personal Papers* (New York: Alumni of Hebrew Union College, 1931), pp. 229 ff.
9. Plaut, *Growth,* p. 20.
10. Leeser had entertained serious misgivings about attending the conference, but in the end felt assured that the forces of "positive historical Judaism," as Zacharias Frankel had put it, would win out (ibid., pp. 221 ff.).
11. *Plaut, Growth,* pp. 23 ff.
12. Wise, like Leeser at Cleveland, was doubtful whether to attend the Pittsburgh Conference altogether; see James G. Heller, *Isaac M. Wise* (New York: Union of American Hebrew Congregations, 1965), pp. 485 ff. In the end, he decided to attend but was determined "to fall as a man rather than to rise as a renegade." Heller's analysis of Wise's attitude is as follows:

> It may be well to pause here and ask a few pertinent questions. Wise had declared that "nothing practical had been done at Pittsburgh, and that there was no truth in the charges, which began to be spread, that the Pittsburgh Conference had abolished the "Sinaic Sabbath and circumcision," or had denied the verity of revelation, or the "divinity of the Bible." And yet, as one reads its declarations, one finds it far from easy to understand why Wise went along with it so completely and so enthusiastically. We shall refer in a moment

to the things he wrote of the Conference in the weeks and months that followed it. But it is strange to note that apparently he took no umbrage at the resolution on a Sunday Sabbath, which did violence to all he had been saying and writing for many years—and with great passion. He did not argue about the second paragraph of the Platform, which could have been the words of a "higher critic," and which in the most cavalier fashion passed over the whole issue of the revelation of Scriptures. Some of the qualities and opinions that made the Platform a point either of rallying or of dispute for almost fifty years presented no difficulty for him, as far as it is possible to judge by what he wrote: the denial of the nationhood of Israel; the discarding of all hope of a return to Palestine, the sacrificial cult, etc. But it cannot have been so pleasant for him to have gone along with the specific language in the earlier paragraphs, with their reading out of consideration of the whole doctrine of the uniqueness of Judaism, and calling the Mosaic law only a "system of training."

Wise's whole course of action—at the Conference itself and in the period that ensued—is far from easy to comprehend. The only explanation that offers any degree of credibility is what he himself said, that he was once again willing to go very far in compromise for the sake of unity, in the hope that, by not insisting overmuch upon his own convictions, by not insisting upon issues, he might pave the way for complete rabbinic cooperation in the country.

13. Lecture before the 1974 (Jerusalem) meeting of the Central Conference of American Rabbis.
14. *A Passover Haggadah* (New York: Grossman Publications, 1974).
15. Ps. 79:6. It might be noted that the phrase occurs also in Jer. 10:25.
16. See Kohler, op. cit., on this identification.
17. See the author's *The Jews in Minnesota* (New York: American Jewish Historical Society, 1959), pp. 181 ff. The controversy can be followed in detail in the minute books of the congregation (microfilms available in American Jewish Archives, Cincinnati, Ohio); see, e.g., vol. II, April 20, 1879 (p. 146), as contrasted with the final victory of the radical Reform party (vol. III, April 7, 1890, p. 1).
18. See, e.g., his article "Halacha and Reform Judaism," *Dimensions,* vol. IV., no. 3 (Spring 1970), pp. 20 ff.

THE EARLY JEWS OF COLUMBUS, OHIO: A STUDY IN ECONOMIC MOBILITY 1850–1880

By

MARC LEE RAPHAEL

Ohio State University

Any student of nineteenth-century American Jewish history is able to list numerous Jewish immigrants whose economic successes rivaled the almost legendary fortunes of non-Jewish Americans. But economic portraits of entire Jewish communities, not merely the most prominent Jews, have been ignored by historians. The prevailing "rags-to-riches" ideology is well known; Calvin Colton noted in 1844 that

> this is a country of self-made men. . . . a man has only to work on, and wait patiently, and with industry and enterprise, he is sure to get both [money and property]. The wheel of American fortune is perpetually and steadily turning, and those at the bottom today, will be moving up tomorrow, and will ere long be at the top.[1]

To what extent was this true of the Jews who arrived and settled in antebellum Columbus, Ohio? An answer is possible, due in large part to the medium size of the community and the availability of a variety of public documents.

Despite the claims of many authors of Jewish communal histories to have discovered the first Jewish arrival, there is, of course, usually a Jew who arrived prior to the "first" Jew or Jewess. Ignoring, however, the question of who came first, we may safely conclude that by the year 1840

435

there were two Jewish families in Columbus, Ohio.[2] By the census year
of 1850, Peter Gundersheimer, a sixty-two year-old laborer from Mittelsin, Bavaria, was surrounded by three married sons (Nathan, thirty-five;
Joseph, thirty; Abraham, twenty-five), one unmarried son (Isaac, twenty-
eight), and one unmarried daughter (Caroline, twenty), all born in
Bavaria.[3] In the same year two married Nusbaums (brothers?) from
Mittelsin, Bavaria, Judah, thirty-six, and Samuel, forty-eight, were residing in Columbus. Samuel and Regina had brought Otto, eight months old
upon his arrival in Columbus, with them from Bavaria, and by the summer of 1850 the family included Otto (eleven), Isadore (seven), Rosetta
(two), and Carolina (born in 1850).[4] The Amburghs, Samuel (thirty-
three) and his wife Regina (twenty-nine), both of Bavaria, lived with
their daughter Terressa, age two, in Columbus in 1850, while Simon and
Anadora Mack, ages twenty-three and twenty-five, resided with their two
sons ages four and one.[5] Within the next year or two these early immigrants, the totality of Columbus Jewry recorded in 1850, were joined by
the Goodman and Lazarus families, both of whom we shall speak of
shortly.[6]

It is commonplace to note that Bavarian Jewish immigrants became
peddlers upon their arrival in America, and, if successful, traded their
packs for a store in a stable community. This was overwhelmingly the
pattern in Columbus.[7] All of Peter Gundersheimer's sons peddled in and
around Columbus in the 1840s, some even continuing to do so after their
brothers had ceased. By 1845 Nathan and Joseph Gundersheimer had
opened a store while Isaac continued peddling; by the mid-1850s Nathan
had established himself as a merchant while Joseph and Abraham became
partners in a retail store; by 1860 Abraham had begun his own business
and Isaac joined Joseph as a partner; and by 1866 all four brothers owned
clothing stores on High Street.[8]

Samuel and Judah Nusbaum peddled in the early 1840s, until Judah
opened a clothing store in the middle of the decade (378 south High
Street) and Samuel, after peddling for about another ten years, opened a
store on south High. Samuel Amburgh, a peddler in the late 1840s,
opened a clothing store in the early 1850s at 143 south High (Amburgh
and Company), while Simon Mack, concomitantly, opened Mack and
Bros. clothing store on south High.[9]

The pattern of the families that arrived in Columbus just after 1850
was hardly different from the earliest residents. Selkan and Kehla Goodman, fifty-five and fifty-seven respectively in 1850, came to Columbus

from Sulzbach, Bavaria, together with their sons Jacob (twenty-four) and Joseph (eighteen). The brothers worked as clerks at the Gundersheimers and Nusbaums, and by the end of the decade owned their own clothing store at 213 south High.[10] Simon Lazarus, age forty in 1850, who left Prussia (or was it Bavaria?) in 1851 with his wife, Amelia (twenty-eight), and their one-year old son, Fred, and arrived in Columbus in the same year, quickly opened a clothing store at 153 south High together with his half-brother, Lazarus Aronson. Within a few years Simon was the sole proprietor.[11]

Although there is no direct evidence available from Columbus, accounts of peddling in nineteenth-century America indicate that little or no capital was necessary to embark upon such a venture. Isaac W. Bernheim was outfitted, at no cost to him, by an agent in Wilkes-Barre, Pennsylvania, in 1847; in exchange for the pack the agent retained seven out of every ten cents Isaac was to earn. Simon and Meyer Guggenheim, Meyer later recalled, were supplied with packs at no cost at all for the first week upon their arrival in Philadelphia in 1847. Most common of all was the immigrant whose initial merchandise was furnished by a friend or relative; Levi Strauss is only the most famous of the dozens who have left records of such familial generosity. While no one could guarantee that the pack would turn into a counter, there is abundant evidence that there was little difficulty in obtaining the pack.[12]

While the pattern of Jews from the German States becoming merchants in American cities is not unique, the extent to which the Jews of antebellum Columbus established clothing stores appears quite unusual. Every Jewish family traceable to pre-1855 Columbus was in the clothing business, and all were located on the main shopping avenue of south High Street. This pattern of concentration was to continue for some time and become even more pronounced, for these Jews were not merely to be a large part of the Columbus retail clothing scene, but were to control and dominate it. By 1872 every retail clothing store in Columbus was owned by a German Jew (see table 1)

This concentration, of course, only describes quantity—what of quality? Were these "petty" proprietors (defined as owning less than a total of $1,000 in real and personal property), or were they proprietors (owning more than a total of $1,000 in real and personal property)?[13] An examination of manuscript federal censuses leaves no doubt. The Gundersheimer brothers were extremely successful. Abraham, at age thirty-five in 1860, claimed $1,200 and $1,000 in real and personal property, while

TABLE 1
COLUMBUS RETAIL CLOTHING STORES, 1872

Address	Proprietor	Address	Proprietor
7 s. High	Henry Harmon	213 s. High	B & W Frankel
39 s. High	Joseph Goodman	227 s. High	Samuel Amburgh
81–83 s. High	Jos. Gundersheimer	243 s. High	Samuel Adler & Bro.
100–102 s. High	Louis Kahn	348 s. High	Judah Nusbaum
101 s. High	H & N Gundersheimer	359 s. High	Raphael Vogel
139 s. High	Simon Lazarus	174 n. High	Isaac Hoffman
159 s. High	Abe Gundersheimer	12 w. Livingston	Leo Straus
183 s. High	Arnold Steinhauser	2 Neil House Block	Adolph Aaron
204 s. High	J & H Margolinsky	172 e. Friend	Elias Lehman

SOURCE: *Bailey's Columbus Directory 1872–73* (Columbus, 1872).

Nathan, forty-five years old in 1860, claimed $3,000 in real and $3,000 in personal property. By 1870 they were major proprietors: Abraham (forty-five) possessed $8,000 and $3,200; Nathan (fifty-five) had $18,000 and $15,000; while Joseph (fifty) owned $60,000 and $28,000 in real and personal property respectively.[14]

Whether for expanding a store, purchasing a home, or making an investment, the Gundersheimers were not hesitant to spend significant sums for property acquisition in Columbus. Franklin County records reveal that Nathan made three acquisitions totaling $8,100 during the 1850s, four purchases in the 1860s totaling $20,800, and two acquisitions in the 1870s of $3,500 and $8,000 each. Joseph Gundersheimer expended $1,600 cash in 1850 and $800 cash in 1853 for property, while he purchased $38,800 in property during the 1860s, including a $12,500 expenditure in 1868, and began the next decade with a $19,950 purchase of property in 1870 and a $15,000 purchase in 1873. Abraham bought little property: an $1,100 purchase from Joseph in 1854 (Joseph paid $800 for the land in 1853) and an $8,000 purchase in 1868 completed his transactions.[15]

Simon Lazarus, although off to a much later start than the Gundersheimers, expanded his original 20 x 30 foot (20 x 50?) men's clothing store by purchasing an adjacent shoe store in 1864 for $2,100 and an adjacent lot in 1876 for $7,800. At the time of his death in 1877, Simon was described as "one of the substantial businessmen of Columbus"; during his son Fred's lifetime, sales in the F & R Lazarus & Co. were to pass $1,000,000 (1914), and in 1962 the greatly expanded downtown store was to enjoy its first million-dollar-day. Simon himself, at age sixty, claimed $2,000 in real estate and $8,000 in personal property, owned two homes, and was able to leave his wife, Amelia, sufficient capital for her to bequeath $15,000 to one daughter, $10,000 to each of three other daughters, and $5,000 to her son David (by a previous marriage) upon her death in 1899.[16]

The Goodman brothers, Jacob and Joseph, prospered in the clothing business as well. Joseph, with only $500 of personal property in 1860, had $5,000 in personal property ten years later, while Jacob, with $2,000 in real estate and $1,500 in personal property in 1860, had $9,000 in real and $6,000 in personal property by 1870. Samuel Amburgh, who claimed no real estate or personal property in 1860, listed $8,000 in real and $2,500 worth of personal property in 1870.[17]

German Jews who came to Columbus after 1855, and owned clothing stores by the early 1870s, were unanimously able to secure proprietor status. For example, Henry Harmon (7 s. High) claimed $15,000 in real estate and $3,000 in personal property; Raphael Vogel (359 s. High) had $10,000 in real and $500 in personal property; Leo Straus (12 w. Livingston) owned $3,600 in real estate and $900 in personal property; while Adolph Aaron (2 Neil House Block) possessed $4,000 in personal property in 1870.[18]

This success in business was by no means limited to retail clothiers: Max Gumble, who as a twenty-eight-year-old saloonkeeper from Bavaria had only $400 in personal property in 1860, was able to claim $12,500 in real and $1,300 in personal property by 1870, while Louis Kleeman, a forty-year-old jeweler, possessed $5,000 in real estate and $3,000 in personal property in 1870.[19]

It would appear that the preceding description concentrates on the most successful Jewish merchants in Columbus and ignores the others. While there were others, to be sure, rare was the family without some real or personal property, or without employment which suggested relative economic security. When we examine the entire Jewish community in 1870 (see table 2), the average real and personal property per family is quite substantial in Wards 3, 4, 5, and 7 (Joseph Gundersheimer's $88,000 in real and personal property distorts Ward 5), and quite low in Ward 6 ($2,833 total per family). But Ward 6 housed Henry Straus, thirty-one, just beginning a clothing store business which was to enjoy some success; I. M. Schlesinger, thirty-six, soon to emerge as a prosperous merchant; Joseph Philipson (whose son David was to become a prominent rabbi), who had just come to Columbus; Solomon Weil, a seventy-year-old retired grocer (and former local "rabbi"), whose eighteen-year-old son Samuel was already an independent businessman; and similar persons. Its residents, like those in other wards, were in secure positions for the coming decade.[20]

TABLE 2
REAL AND PERSONAL PROPERTY OF COLUMBUS JEWISH FAMILIES, 1870

Ward	Total Families	Total Real Property	Real Prop./ Family	Total Pers. Property	Pers. Prop./ Family	Total Prop./ Family
3	5	$17,000	$3,400	$10,800	$2,160	$5,560
4	10	44,000	4,400	15,300	1,530	5,930
5	12	72,900	6,075	38,800	4,233	10,308
6	9	13,500	1,500	1,200	1,333	2,833
7	7	24,500	3,500	31,400	4,485	7,985

SOURCE: *Population Schedules of the Ninth Census of the United States, 1870* (Washington, 1965), microcopy no. M-593, roll 1201 (Ohio).

The 1860s and 1870s were to be decades of considerable growth for Columbus. A city of only 6,000 persons in 1840 and 17,900 persons in 1850, Columbus grew hardly at all in the 1850s (672 persons) as westward migration was large and continuous.[21] But in precisely those years when the early Jews were establishing themselves in the city, it grew rapidly. The population in 1870 was almost 13,000 greater than in 1860, and that of 1880 20,000 greater than the population of 1870 (see table 3).

A commercial development, concomitant with the demographic growth, characterized Ohio's capital in the 1860s and 1870s. By 1861 there were five railroads serving the city: the Columbus and Xenia to-

TABLE 3
COLUMBUS POPULATION GROWTH, 1840–1880

Census Year	Population (1,000s)	Percent Gain in Population over past 10 years	Percent Gain in Population over 1840
1840	6.0	148.3	—
1850	17.9	195.6	298
1860	18.6	3.8	310
1870	31.3	68.5	520
1880	51.6	65.1	860

SOURCE: J. D. B. De Bow, *Statistical View of the United States* (Washington, 1854), p. 192; Joseph C. G. Kennedy, *Population of the United States in 1860* (Washington, 1864), p. 230; Francis A. Walker, *Ninth Census: Statistics of Population of the United States* (Washington, 1872), pp. 318 and 390; Henry L. Hunker, *Industrial Evolution of Columbus, Ohio* (Columbus, 1958), p. 40.

gether with the Little Miami, linking Columbus to Cincinnati; the Columbus and Cleveland Railroad, linking Cleveland with the capital; and the
Central Ohio Railroad, connecting Columbus to Wheeling and providing
easy access to Pittsburgh.[22] During 1863 Columbus's main commercial
artery, High Street, was fitted with double tracks the entire length of its
business district and a car ran every six minutes during this first summer.
Soon thereafter additional tracks were put down and street railroads began to link the residential districts with the merchants of High Street.
This principal business artery was 100-feet-wide, surpassed in width only
by 120-foot-wide Broad Street.[23]

Even more important to the growth of the 1860s was the impetus provided by the Civil War to Columbus manufactories, by the thousands of
soldiers quartered in the city to local retailers, by the city's location on the
National Road, ("a great thoroughfare of travel"), and by the direct
railroad connections with the southeastern Ohio coal fields. In brief, as
one chronicler noted, "improvement [during the war] was in most respects rapid, and large acquisitions in wealth and population were
made." [24]

Simon Lazarus typified many of the Jewish merchants in Columbus
during this period of growth. As a result of the demand for uniforms
during the Civil War, he was able to employ seven salesmen after the war
in contrast to one in 1860; with the growth of the street railroad he was
able to attract customers from previously remote areas; and, with his
success in the 1860s, to initiate, albeit one per day, home delivery service
by wagon.[25]

The occupational distribution of the early Columbus Jewish community
during these two decades provides another method of determining the
"success" of these immigrants. While nineteenth-century occupations, in
and of themselves, may not easily be ranked in terms of the prestige they
commanded a century ago, they nevertheless provide, together with indicators of property acquisition and real and personal property possessions,
a reasonably reliable indicator of economic well-being.[26]

The occupational scheme in Table 4 divides the Jewish community into
eight main groupings (for a complete listing of all occupations included
in each category, see Appendix). The most striking observation is the
concentration of the Jews in petty proprietor, proprietor, and clerical
positions: 92 percent of those employed in 1860, 94 percent in 1870, and
80 percent in 1880! It was, in fact, impossible to find a Jew in an unskilled position in 1860, 1870, or 1880. One might imagine that this was

the pattern in Columbus generally: workers concentrated in clerical and mercantile positions. It was not. More than 25 percent of Columbus workers sampled in all three census years (1860, 1870, 1880), as well as a sizable number of the employed in other nineteenth-century American cities, were unskilled. Columbus's Jews were overwhelmingly, on the other hand, using their heads.[27]

TABLE 4

PERCENTAGE OF COLUMBUS JEWS IN VARIOUS SOCIOECONOMIC
GROUPS, 1860–1880, ACCORDING TO MANUSCRIPT FEDERAL CENSUSES

Socioeconomic status group*	1860 Jews in category	1870 Jews in category	1880 Jews in category
1			
2			10.0%
3	50%	25%	17.5
4		2	5.0
5		15	37.5
6			
7	42	54	25.0
8	8	1	3.75
9		1	1.25
N	(12)	(48)	(79)

* 1=unskilled and menial, 2=semiskilled and service, 3=petty proprietors, managers, and officials, 4=skilled, 5=clerical and sales, 6=semiprofessional, 7=proprietors, managers, and officials, 8=professional, 9=single women and retired men.

Not discernible from Table 4, but of much importance, is the large extent to which the sons of Columbus Jewish merchants continued in their father's businesses; thus the continuous stream of clerks and their entrance into the ranks of petty proprietors or proprietors. In 1870 only Henry (eighteen) and Nathan (sixteen) Gundersheimer (sons of Joseph), Fred (twenty) and Ralph (eighteen) Lazarus (sons of Simon), Otto (thirty) and Isadore (twenty-five) Nusbaum (sons of Samuel), and Marcus (seventeen) Harmon (son of Henry), were among the sons old enough to work, and every one was employed in his father's clothing store.[28]

By 1880 Henry Straus (Moses, fifteen), Joseph Gundersheimer (Herman, twenty, and Samuel, sixteen), Samuel Adler (Marcus, eighteen, and Julius, sixteen), Moses Kleeman (William, twenty, and Joseph, sixteen), Max Gumble (Abraham, twenty), Henry Harmon (Aaron, twenty-seven, Harry, twenty-five, Michael, twenty-four, and William, fifteen), Alex Shonfield (Michael, fifteen), Augustus Basch (Frank, twenty-two),

444 EARLY JEWS OF COLUMBUS

Aaron Margolinsky (Marcus, nineteen), Jennie Gundersheimer (Henry, twenty-four, and Samuel, eighteen), and Jacob Goodman (Albert, twenty) all had sons that were employed in clerical capacities in their stores. Only Benjamin Harmon, eventually to become deputy county auditor and assistant postmaster, demonstrated unusual daring and found employment outside of his father's store.[29]

Yet another indication of the success of the early Jewish families is indicated by the abundance of live-in servants employed by the Jews of Columbus. In 1870 six families had at least one servant; in 1880 Henry Straus, Leo Straus, Saul Herman, Aaron Harmon, Moses Kleeman, Jacob Shonenberg, Amelia Lazarus, Aaron Margolinsky, Rev. B. A. Bonnheim ("rabbi"), and Solomon Loeb each had one servant, while Jacob

TABLE 5
BIRTH YEARS OF COLUMBUS JEWISH CHILDREN, 1850–1880

Parents	Number	Children's Birth Years
Henry and Nettie Harmon	10	1852, '54, '56, '58, '62, '64, '66, '73, '75, '77
Max and Marianne Gumble	9	1860, '62, '63, '66, '67, '69, '71, '73, '78
Lewis and Hanna Shonfield	9	1861, '63, '65, '69, '71, '73, '77, '78, '79
Lewis and Iline Jacobs	9	1866, '68, '70, '72, '74, '75, '76, '77, '80
Alex and Rosa Shonfield	8	1865, '67 (2), '69, '74, '76, '78, '80
Henry and Regina Straus	7	1865, '67, '69, '71, '73, '75, '77
Leo and Sarah Straus	7	1855, '59, '61, '63, '65, '67, '71
Louis and Clara Kleeman	7	1866, '68, '70, '72, '73, '78, '80
Morris and Fannie Mayer	7	1860, '62, '64, '66, '68, '72, '76
William and Bertha Goodman	6	1865, '67, '69, '73, '76, '78
Abraham and Regina Gundersheimer	6	1856, '58, '60, '62 (2), '64
Joseph and Fannie Goodman	6	1869, '71, '73, '75, '77, '79
Simon and Amelia Lazarus	6	1850, '52, '54, '56, '58, '66
Michael and Caroline Steinfeld	6	1865, '67, '69, '70, '72, '74
Samuel and Cecilia Adler	6	1860, '62, '64, '68, '70, '73
Joseph and Esther Gundersheimer	5	1852, '54, '58, '60, '64
Moses and Jennie Kleeman	5	1860, '62, '64, '66, '68
Augustus and Lena Basch	5	1857, '61, '63, '65, '67

SOURCE: Jewish sections of Mt. Cavalry and Greenlawn cemeteries; Seventh, Eighth, Ninth, and Tenth United States Census; Franklin County Probate Court/*Birth Records*/1867–99; I. M. Schlesinger, *Circumcision Record Book,* 1873–1904.

NOTE: These children were not all born in Columbus, but their parents were residing in the city in 1880. An occasional date may be plus or minus one year, for the manuscript federal census provides only the age, not the month or year of birth. Those children born during the summer, when the census taker made his rounds, are particularly difficult to date precisely, for their ages usually increased by either nine or eleven years every "decade." It should also be kept in mind that half of the families listed had additional children after 1880!

Goodman, Joseph Gundersheimer, and Caspar Lowenstein, the latter a lawyer, each had two servants.[30]

The utilization of servants was particularly common in the larger families, and most of the immigrant Jewish families were quite large. The usual pattern, and its consistency is quite remarkable, was for the wife (who never worked unless widowed) to bear a child every other year (see table 5). Indeed, there is much to suggest that only age or exhaustion put an end to childbearing; several Columbus Jewesses died shortly after their last child was born, while others bore children well into their forties.

The manuscript federal census of 1870 enables us to examine the family constellation of the Jewish community against the background of the general community. The Jews lived almost exclusively in five of the nine wards (nos. 3, 4, 5, 6, 7), and constituted slightly more than 1 percent of the total population of the area (table 6). The persons-per-family ratio was not substantially different in the Jewish and general communities according to Table 6, but the size of the typical Jewish family is obscured by focusing on 1870 alone. The majority of the members of the small Jewish community were very recent arrivals, and were just entering their prime childbearing years. By 1880 these exclusively immigrant Jewish families, in contrast to the general community, whose ratios continued at about the 1870 level, would have 35 percent more children than were present in 1870.[31]

Helping to explain and to reinforce the economic success of the early Jewish families in Columbus was their extraordinary residential persist-

TABLE 6

POPULATION, FAMILIES, AND DWELLINGS BY WARDS, 1870

Wards	Population	Families		Dwellings	
		Number	Persons/Family	Number	Persons/Family
3(all)	2,575	397	6.54	322	8.00
3(Jews)	29	5	5.80	5	5.80
4(all)	3,671	670	5.48	595	6.17
4(Jews)	60	10	6.00	10	6.00
5(all)	3,849	801	4.81	703	5.48
5(Jews)	63	12	5.25	12	5.25
6(all)	4,728	1,008	4.69	761	6.21
6(Jews)	40	9	4.44	9	4.44
7(all)	3,026	580	5.22	432	7.00
7(Jews)	25	7	3.57	7	3.57

SOURCE: *Population Schedules of the Ninth Census of the United States, 1870* (Washington, 1965), microcopy no. M-593, roll 1201 (Ohio).

ence (table 7). It was almost literally true that the only circumstance which eliminated a head of household present in Columbus in 1860 from a subsequent directory was death. When Louis and Clara Kleeman moved to Cincinnati in 1878 they became the first Jewish family, traceable in the sources after 1860, to leave the community. It was such an unusual event that it occasioned a proclamation in the local fraternal organization records. Such continuity must have aided the economic development of the community.[32]

TABLE 7

PERCENTAGE OF COLUMBUS JEWISH HOUSEHOLD HEADS PRESENT IN
COLUMBUS AT START OF SELECTED YEARS, 1860–1880 (N=33 in 1860,
16 in 1866, 6 in 1869, 9 in 1872) Percentage of N present in:

Year	1860	1866	1869	1872
1860	100	—	—	
1866	96	100.0	—	
1869	93	93.7	100	
1872	85	93.7	100	100
1875	82	93.7	100	100
1880	61	87.5	100	100

Table 8 indicates that despite the persistence of the Jewish community within the city of Columbus, these immigrants were quite actively moving from one residence to another. Computing mobility ratios for the entire group by total moves/total residence years, the thirty-three families of 1860 averaged two moves every five years, the sixteen families that arrived after 1860 averaged almost one move every two years, and the additional nine families residing in Columbus in 1872 averaged almost one move every three years during the 1870s. This, of course, is an absolute minimum, for the directories could only reveal one move per year. Nevertheless, the Jews of Columbus in the 1860s and 1870s were at least twice, and perhaps even more, as mobile as their descendants a century later.[33]

TABLE 8

MOBILITY RATIOS (TOTAL MOVES ÷ RESIDENCE YEARS) FOR HOUSEHOLD
HEADS, 1860–1880 (N=33/1860, 16/1866, 9/1872)

1860 (through 1869)	1866 (through 1872)	1872 (through 1880)
0.407	0.473	0.300

Standard Deviation	0.200	0.240	0.200

Not one of the early Jews of Columbus has left us a written record of either the factors bringing him to Columbus or those accounting for his economic success. We do possess, however, a memoir by William G. Dunn, a successful dry goods merchant in Columbus in the 1870s and 1880s. Some of his reflections are illuminating for our study:

> . . . I looked for a location further west, and finally decided upon Colum-
> bus, Ohio where I opened business . . . in April, 1869. I chose Columbus
> because it was pleasantly and centrally situated with a good prospect for
> enlargement; also because the dry goods business there did not seem to be
> overdone, and was conducted upon the old time plans, trade being held
> to each store mainly by the influence of the salesman and credit, as it
> still is in many country stores. . . . The retail business was at that time all
> done south of Broad Street, and mostly on High Street.
>
> I opened at the appointed time, and was successful from the start. The
> people seemed pleased with a one price store and good merchandise. Our
> sales the first year amounted to $170,000. My trade has embraced not
> only a large number of Columbus families, but also many from neighbor-
> ing cities.[34]

No doubt the Gundersheimers, Nusbaums, Lazaruses, Goodmans, *et al.* shared Dunn's dream of economic success; there is absolutely no doubt that the drama must have been heightened by the actual success of so many of the early Jews of Columbus. While rarely going from peddling to riches, it is certainly a story of solid entry into the middle class.

APPENDIX

Socioeconomic Classification of Occupations of Columbus Jews,
1860, 1870, 1880

I Unskilled and menial
None

II Semiskilled and service
Bartender, Mail Carrier

III Petty proprietors, managers, and officials
Merchant (clothing), Merchant (tailor), Merchant (dry goods),
Peddler, Butcher, Scrap Metal Dealer, Clothing Dealer, Barber

IV Skilled
Cigar Maker, Tailor

V Clerical and Sales
Clerical, Agent (insurance), Bookkeeper, Umbrella Maker,
Traveling Salesman, Agent (news)

VI Semiprofessional
None

VII Proprietors, Managers, and Officials
(All of the occupations, except Barber, in classification III +)
Jeweler, Saloon Proprietor, Grocer, Loan Office Proprietor, Vinegar Factory Owner

VIII Professional
Optician, Editor, Lawyer, Doctor

IX Single Women and Retired Men

NOTES

1. *Junius Tracts* (New York, 1844), pp. 15 and 6, quoted in Stuart Blumin, "Mobility and Change in Ante-Bellum Philadelphia," in *Nineteenth Century Cities: Essays in the New Urban History,* ed. Stephan Thernstrom and Richard Sennett (New Haven, 1969), p. 165.
2. These were the Nusbaum and Gundersheimer families. On the Nusbaums, see *Ohio State Journal,* April 30, 1891; *Westbote,* April 30, 1891; and *Ohio State Journal,* November 12, 1928 ("Otto, born in Bavaria in 1840, arrived in Columbus with his parents at the age of eight months"). On the Gundersheimers, see *Westbote,* December 21, 1879 ("Nathan Gundersheimer resided in Columbus more than forty years") and *Ohio State Journal,* December 22, 1879. This conclusion, however, is not supported by I. J. Benjamin, a visitor to Columbus in 1862; he noted that the first Jews arrived in Columbus in 1842: see *Three Years in America 1859–1862* (Philadelphia, 1956) vol. II, pp. 280–81.
3. National Archives Microfilm Publication, *Population Schedules of the Seventh Census of the United States, 1850* (Washington, 1965), microcopy no. 432, roll no. 679 (Columbus, Ohio), pp. 622 and 624; *idem, Population Schedules of the Eighth Census of the United States, 1860* (Washington, 1965), microcopy no. 653, roll no. 964 (Columbus, Ohio), pp. 167 and 594; *idem, Population Schedules of the Ninth Census of the United States, 1870* (Washington, 1965), microcopy no. M-593, roll no. 1201 (Columbus, Ohio), pp. 8 (Ward 4), 65 (Ward 7), and 75 (Ward 5).
4. *Population Schedules . . . 1850 . . .,* pp. 387 and 390; *Population Schedules . . . 1860 . . .,* p. 79 (Ward 5). Isadore Nusbaum was the first Jewish child born in Columbus.
5. For the Amburghs, see *Directory of the City of Columbus for the Years 1850–51* (Columbus, Ohio), p. 100, and *Population Schedules . . . 1860 . . .,*p. 227. For the Macks, see *Population Schedules . . . 1850 . . .,* p. 389.
6. For the arrival of the Lazarus family, see *Westbote,* December 24, 1879, and *Occident and American Jewish Advocate* X:1, April 1852. For the Goodmans, see *Columbus Directory for the Year 1852* (Columbus, 1852), p. 152. Aside from the six Jewish families mentioned above, no Jews are listed in the manuscript Federal census, city directories, city and county records, the German newspaper *Westbote,* or State of Ohio records; however, Lewis Shrier, who apparently died on November 29, 1852, during the cholera epidemic in Columbus, is buried in the Jewish section of Mt. Cavalry Cemetery. On Shrier and cholera, see Alfred E. Lee, *History of the City of Columbus, Capital of Ohio* (New York, 1892), vol. II, p. 714, and Jonathan Forman, "Ohio Medical History—Pre–Civil War Period—The First Year of the Second Epidemic of Asiatic Cholera in Columbus, Ohio—1849," *Ohio State Archaeological and Historical Quarterly* (October–December, 1944): 303–12. It is possible, although not likely, that a careful reading of the local English newspapers will turn up additional Jewish families.

7. Columbus's non-Jewish peddlers provide a striking contrast. The 1845–56 *Colum-bus Directory* lists eleven such individuals; not a single one of them was to be found in the city five years later!

8. Joseph, Nathan, Abraham, and Isaac's stores were at 75, 115, 129, and 177 South High Street respectively. The occupational information is derived from the *Columbus Directories* from 1843 through 1867. On peddling, see Richardson Wright, *Hawkers and Walkers in Early America* (Philadelphia, 1927), A. V. Goodman, "A Jewish Peddler's Diary, 1842–43," *American Jewish Archives* (June 1951), Isaac W. Bernheim, *The Story of the Bernheim Family* (Louisville, 1910), Thomas Clark, *Pills, Petticoats and Plows* (New York, 1944), and Lewis Atherton, "Itinerant Merchandising in the Ante-bellum South," *Bulletin of the Business Historical Society* 19:2 (April 1945).

9. On the Nushbaums, see the appropriate *Columbus Directories*. Amburgh and Co. was perhaps partly owned by Hezekiah and Abraham Amburgh, residing in Chillicothe and Harrisburg Pleasant, Ohio, respectively, in 1850. On Hezekiah, see *Population Schedules . . . 1850 . . . (Chillicothe, Ohio)*, p. 20; on Abraham, see *Population Schedules . . . 1850 . . . (Harrisburg Pleasant, Ohio)*, p. 119; and on all the Amburghs, see Lee, *op. cit.*, p. 714. On Simon Mack, see the appropriate *Columbus Directories;* Simon was to move to Cincinnati in 1853 and join his brothers Abraham, Henry, and Herman in Mack and Bros. Clothing and Dry Goods at 211 Main (see the *Cincinnati Directories* for 1853, 1855–59).

10. For the Goodmans, see the appropriate *Columbus Directories, Population Sched-ules . . . 1860 . . .,* pp. 223 and 595, and *Population Schedules . . . 1870 . . .,* pp. 67 (Ward 5) and 51 (Ward 7).

11. For Simon Lazarus's family, see the appropriate *Columbus Directories; Popula-tion Schedules . . . 1870 . . .,* p. 52 (Ward 7); Osman C. Hooper, *History of the City of Columbus [1797–1920]*, (Columbus and Cleveland, 1898), p. 216; William Alexander Taylor, *Centennial History of Columbus and Franklin County, Ohio* (Chicago and Columbus, 1909), vol. I, pp. 574–75; and La Vern J. Ripley, "The Columbus Germans," *The Report: A Journal of German-American History*, 33 (1968): 35. Accounts of Simon Lazarus written in recent years claim that he studied for the rabbinate under Abraham Geiger before his de-parture from Germany; see, for example, Samuel M. Gup, *Consider the Years: An Outline History of the Congregation Temple Israel 1846–1946* (Columbus, Ohio, 1940), p. 9.

12. Isaac W. Bernheim, *op. cit.*, pp. 36–39; Lewis Atherton, *op. cit.*, pp. 53 ff.; Richardson Wright, *op. cit.;* M. Lomask, *Seed Money: The Guggenheim Story* (New York, 1964), p. 15.

13. This figure of $1,000 is far from arbitrary. It is utilized in a slightly different context by Peter Knights in *The Plain People of Boston, 1830–1860* (Oxford, 1971), and was selected as the dividing line after careful study of the 1850, 1860, and 1870 manuscript federal censuses.

14. See the sources cited in n. 3 above.

15. Franklin County Recorder, *Grantee Index to Deeds*, No. 1, 1805–1888, and the appropriate volumes listed in the *Index*.

16. William Diehl, Jr., "Lazarus," *Cincinnati* I:3 (December 1967): 32; Tom Ma-honey, *The Great Merchants* (New York, 1947), pp. 103–5; Franklin County Recorder, *Deeds*, 79:343 and 126:462; *Ohio State Journal*, December 6, 1877; *Population Schedules . . . 1870 . . .,* p. 52 (Ward 7); Franklin County Probate Court, *Wills*, T 367 (1899).

17. For Joseph Goodman, see *Population Schedules . . . 1860 . . .,* p. 223, and

Population Schedules . . . 1870 . . ., p. 51 (Ward 7); for Jacob Goodman, see *Population Schedules . . . 1860 . . .,* p. 595, and *Population Schedules . . . 1870 . . .,* p. 67 (Ward 5). Jacob sold part of his store during 1890–91: one part in 1890 for $25,000 and two parts in 1891 for $12,000 and $11,000 each (see Franklin County Recorder, *Deeds,* 219:331, 223:541, and 223:543). For Samuel Amburgh, see *Population Schedules . . . 1870 . . .,* p. 41 (Ward 3).

18. *Population Schedules . . . 1870 . . .,* p. 3 (Ward 4), p. 21 (Ward 6), p. 86 (Ward 5), p. 86 (Ward 4).

19. *Population Schedules . . . 1860 . . .,* p. 204, and *Population Schedules . . . 1870 . . .,* p. 8 (Ward 4), p. 13 (Ward 3).

20. *Population Schedules . . . 1870 . . .,* passim.

21. Jacob H. Studer, *Columbus, Ohio: Its History, Resources and Progress* (n.p., 1873), p. 70.

22. Walter R. Marvin, "Columbus and the Railroads of Central Ohio Before the Civil War" (Ph. D. dissertation, Ohio State University, 1953), pp. 118a, 167a, 229a.

23. Jacob H. Studer, *op. cit.,* pp. 559–61; Hooper, *op cit.,* p. 230; *Tenth Census of the United States, 1880, Report on the Social Statistics of Cities, Part II, Southern and Western States* (Washington, 1887), p. 391; George W. Hawes, *Ohio State Gazetteer and Business Directory for 1859 and 1860* (Cincinnati, 1859) p. 200.

24. Hooper, *op. cit.,* pp. 53 and 229; Lee, *op. cit.,* vol. I, pp. 320–39 and vol. II, p. 221; Hawes, *loc cit.*

25. Diehl, *op. cit.,* p. 32; Fred Lazarus, "The Development of the Delivery System," *Enthusiast* (November 1915).

26. Twentieth-century images of nineteenth-century occupations are often misleading: Joseph Kahn, a perpetual peddler, had $9,000 in real and $2,000 in personal property by 1870. He was only one of Columbus Jewry's successful "peddlers." On the other hand, Abram Polasky, an optician from Hungary, claimed no real or personal property in 1870.

27. The occupational samples were drawn from, relatively speaking, "immigrant wards": the third (1860), the fifth (1870), and the third (1880). Unskilled workers ranged from 27 to 34 percent of the total employees in each ward. For occupational distribution in other mid-nineteenth-century cities, see the essays in pt. I of *Nineteenth Century Cities,* cited above.

28. *Population Schedules . . . 1870 . . .,* passim., and the appropriate city directories.

29. *Population Schedules . . . 1880 . . .,* passim., and the appropriate city directories. Henry and Nathan Gundersheimer, clerks at their father's store in 1870, owned their own ready-made clothing store in 1880. By the time they left Columbus (for Baltimore) in 1892 they had "accumulated considerable property" and felt they had "reached the limit" in Columbus (see *Ohio State Journal,* April 3, 1892, p. 3). On Ben Harmon, see "Columbus 1812–1912," *The Columbus Sunday Dispatch, Centennial Library Edition,* p. 9.

30. *Population Schedules . . . 1870 . . .,* and *Population Schedules . . . 1880 . . .,* passim.

31. In contrast to the Jewish families, by 1880 there were only 12 percent more children in the non-Jewish families of 1870.

32. B'nai B'rith Zion Lodge No. 62, *Minutes,* September 15, 1878. Although precise comparisons are difficult, these persistence rates are much higher than those of Atlanta, a relatively stable city close in size to Columbus. See Richard J. Hopkins, "Patterns of Persistence and Occupational Mobility in a Southern City: Atlanta,

1870–1920" (Ph. D. dissertation, Emory University, 1972), p. 54.

33. Contrast this with Albert Mayor's conclusion ("no trend towards mobility either inside or outside the Columbus area exists") after discovering that 85 percent of Columbus Jewry sampled in 1968 had no plans to move. *Columbus Jewish Population Study: 1969* (Columbus, 1969), p. 31.

34. Lee, *op. cit.,* vol. I, p. 394.

THE AMERICAN AND AMERICAN-JEWISH EXPERIENCE: A STUDY IN UNIQUENESS*

By

ELLIS RIVKIN

Hebrew Union College—Jewish Institute of Religion, Cincinnati

I

This essay is a reflection on the fusing of two unique historical experiences—the American and the Jewish. The American experience is unique in that the United States is the only society in the history of mankind to have developed into a post-industrial society—a society in which a majority of the gainfully employed population earn their living in the service sectors of the economy.[1] The American-Jewish experience is unique in that American Jewry developed a post-industrial community even more precocious than that of the American people as a whole.[2]

This study will attempt to demonstrate (1) that the American experience was unique because the United States was the only nation to create an economic system which was *developmental,* not cyclical; and that (2) the Jewish experience was unique because the Jews came to this country as an urbanized, peasant-free people, resistant to proletarianization and holding learning in the highest esteem.

II

How is the historian to account for this twofold phenomenon—the emergence of the United States as the world's first post-industrial society,

The reader may find helpful my 'A Decisive Pattern in American Jewish History,' in *Essays in American Jewish History* (Cincinnati 1958), pp. 23-61, for the role of capitalistic development in shaping the American Jewish experience.

and of American Jewry as the first "people" to develop a post-industrial profile virtually free of agricultural-industrial residuals.

I would suggest that the resolution of this problem is to be found in the intersection of what I shall call *developmental capitalism,* on the one hand, and an urbanized, peasant-free "people," on the other. But to make clear the uniqueness of this intersection, it is essential that some consideration be given *prior* economic systems—pre-capitalist or traditional; *contiguous* capitalistic systems—replicating, steady-state, and imperialistic; and *alternative* economic systems—Marxist. It is no less essential to analyze how the Jews interacted with these other systems, and to determine how the Jews became an urbanized, peasant-free people.

Prior to the rise of commercial capitalism in the sixteenth and seventeenth centuries, the predominant economic system throughout Europe was a pre-capitalist, or traditional, economic mode of production and distribution. Although we can discern threads of capitalism in the warp and woof of medieval society, the dominant pattern is pre-capitalist. The profit motive may have been present, even active and stirring, but it was subordinated to an economic system that subserved the interests of political and religious elites—kings, nobles, churchmen. These governing elites did indeed own and control the major sources of wealth production, and they were indeed dependent on these sources for their power and style of life, but they were not themselves, as a rule, motivated or driven by the profit motive. They were interested in wealth, and they were very much concerned when their wealth diminished, but they were not themselves active in creating wealth. This they left to peasants, to burghers, to itinerant merchants, and to administrative agents. These European societies may properly be categorized as pre-capitalist, or traditional.

Recent research has revealed that pre-capitalist societies suffer from a built-in limitation on economic growth. Although such societies have again and again demonstrated considerable capacity for expanding wealth-production, they have invariably come up against certain limits which precluded further growth and provoked economic decline and breakdown. These limits were set by the low state of technology, especially in agriculture, which choked off that further extension of economic growth which was absolutely essential for feeding the rising population, encouraged and made possible by previous economic growth. The major impediment to surmounting these technological barriers has been the lack of incentive, a lack nourished by traditional elites, whose motivations and interests were not economic, but political, military, intellectual, and spiritual. They tended to foster *replicating* rather than *innovating* modes of production and distribution. Indeed *replication* is virtually synonymous with *traditional*. Traditional societies were thus locked into a cyclical pattern characterized by economic growth followed by economic breakdown.[3]

The fate of medieval Jewry was umbilically tied to this inexorable cycle characteristic of the pre-capitalist systems of medieval Europe. These cycles occurred in different parts of Europe and at different times.[4] They were (1) the German, French, and English cycle, (2) the Spanish cycle, and (3) the Polish cycle. There was also a fourth cycle—the Italian— which, though revealing a similar trajectory, is somewhat more complex because of the proto-capitalistic system which had developed in such Italian city-states as Florence, Venice, Genoa, and Pisa. Each of these cycles reveals the following stages: (1) an upward economic trend-line, (2) a peaking-out when the growth barrier cannot be surmounted, (3) a downward trend-line leading to economic breakdown. During the first two phases, Jews are not only allowed but encouraged to settle and prosper. In phase 3, however, Jews are generally the first to experience the impact of the downward trend of the cycle, since as a minority group, holding to dissident religious beliefs, they possess no military power with which to defend their interests. The political and ecclesiastical elites, beginning to feel the pinch of reduced revenues, and the threat of political and social upheaval, seek to mitigate the economic pinch by pauperizing the Jews, and the political and social threat, by seeding and encouraging anti-Jewish feelings. In France, England, and Spain, phase 3 was characterized by pauperization, vilification, pogromming, and expulsion, while in Germany and Poland there was pauperization, vilification, pogromming, but no total expulsion. In Italy, there was pauperization, vilification, and ghettoization.

The fact that in late antiquity the Jews had been transmuted into an urbanized people, by virtue of their wide dispersion, facilitated this umbilical relationship. Since the pre-capitalist elites of Islam and Christendom sought a monopoly of land ownership for themselves, Jews were either forced out of, or barred from, agriculture. They were thus effectively compressed into mercantile, fiscal, and urban roles.

The diaspora character of the Jewish people had another significant consequence. As a minority, Jews were granted communal autonomy on religious, not secular or national, grounds. They had a right to rule themselves in accordance with their religious laws because they could not swear fealty to the teachings of either Christianity or Islam. The Jews, therefore, looked to a scholar class for decisive leadership. The scholar class enjoyed high prestige even when non-scholar elites exercised nominal hegemony, since all Jewish communities were legitimitized and regulated by laws believed to have been revealed by God Himself. Thus no "prince" or "exilarch" could exercise authority over Jews unless he had religious sanction—a sanction that could come only from a scholar class thoroughly versed in the divine law.

The ultimate reward for medieval Jews was "the world to come" (*olam ha-ba*) and the resurrection (*tehiat ha-metim*), and since this reward was dependent on the strict observance of the divine law, and was enhanced by the *knowledge* of the divine law, the value most esteemed by Jews was the mastery of the full corpus of divine law and lore. By the sixteenth century this corpus minimally embraced Bible, Mishnah, Talmud, the commentaries of Rashi and the Tosafists, the codes of Maimonides and Jacob ben Asher, and a vast responsa literature.

By the sixteenth century, also, the Jews had become preeminently a diaspora people and had developed a unique profile characterized by (1) geographical spread among different societies going through different phases of the pre-capitalist cycle, (2) a highly urbanized and peasant-free class structure in all these different societies irrespective of the cyclical phase, (3) scholarly elites who gave legitimacy to the communal structures and enjoyed high prestige whether directly exercising hegemony or not, (4) a belief system focusing on rewards and punishments in "the world to come"—rewards and punishments which the individual would either earn or lose by virtue of *his* actions and not by virtue of priestly-ecclesiastical intermediation.

No other "people" in the sixteenth century was either an urbanized people or a peasant-free people. Nor was there any other "people" that was spread throughout Europe and recognized in every society as a distinct, differentiated grouping, entitled to communal automony. Neither was there a "people" whose rulers were dependent on a scholar class for their legitimacy. However interlocked, church and state within medieval Christendom were not fused, as they were in medieval Jewish societies. Learning may have been appreciated and/or even prized in medieval Christendom, but it was subordinated to the sacramental system, whose efficacy was dependent on the legitimacy of the priest, not on his learning. As for the Protestant churches, the stress on justification by faith encouraged the believer to focus on Christ's grace; a grace that was freely given and not earned either by works or by learning.

III

When we turn to the experience of the Jews with the capitalist systems of Europe, we find an equivalent cyclical pattern and an equivalent "special relationship" to that pattern. The pattern, however, becomes far more complex. A sharp distinction must be made between the cycles which are inherent in capitalistic dynamics and the kind of cycle which traverses a trajectory from vigorous economic growth to economic stagnation and breakdown. For Europe, the long-range economic trend was upward from the sixteenth century until the outbreak of World War I, even though this uptrend was periodically disrupted by major economic depressions. Between World War I and World War II, however, the trend-line of European capitalism began to swing downward and skirted on the edge of complete breakdown with the onset of the world economic depression in 1929.[5]

The Jews of Europe were very much affected by this long-range cycle. This experience was hardly different from what they had undergone in pre-capitalist societies—positive interaction along the upward trendline and negative interaction during the downswing. In the sixteenth, seventeenth, and eighteenth centuries, Jews were permitted to resettle in the great commercial centers of Amsterdam, London, and Bordeaux as commercial capitalism made rapid strides in Holland, England, and France. These economic gains were subsequently translated into a radical alteration of both the legal status and the political status of the Jew.

Similarly, the extension of both commercial and industrial capitalism into Central Europe brought in its wake the Bismarckian settlement which granted the Jews juridical and political rights equivalent to those granted to all non-aristocratic Germans. And with the eastward spread of capitalism at the turn of the century, Jews had good reason to believe that within a reasonable period of time they could hope for liberation in Austria-Hungary, and in Russia.

These expectations were rudely shattered when, following on World War I, German capitalism was first battered by the Versailles treaty, and then, following four brief years of resuscitation, collapsed utterly in 1930–32, when the unemployment rate reached more than 30 percent of the gainfully employed population. The Nazi regime moved in to shore up the collapse of German capitalism by smashing the trade unions, dissolving the political parties of the Weimar Republic, rearming to make a bid for continental hegemony, impoverishing, degrading, and ultimately physically annihilating the Jews. Although such extreme solutions were not used in Holland, Belgium, Czechoslovakia, France, and Britain, the economic breakdown encouraged the spread of fascist and anti-Semitic ideologies throughout Europe.

As far as the non-Communist nations, such as Poland, Roumania, and Bulgaria were concerned, their nominal independence had been from the outset accompanied by stillborn economies.

The reasons for the failure of European capitalism to break out of the cyclical pattern characteristic of pre-capitalist economic systems can be attributed to the fact that the nation-state system of Europe was the barrier that the capitalistic dynamic could not surmount. The sovereign nation-state was a carry-over from the medieval pre-capitalist world into the modern capitalist world. The territorial kingdoms of England, France, Germany, Poland, and Russia had been carved out by pre-capitalist, non-economic political elites. The extent or delimitation of those kingdoms followed on dynastic wars which were more politically than economically inspired and motivated.

When, therefore, capitalistic development in England and France led to the overthrow of the ancient regimes in these countries, the new rulers fell heir to the territorial boundaries over which their sovereigns had held sway. The great capitalist revolutions were successful in securing a political framework favorable to capitalistic enterprise within the boundaries of already existing nation-states. They were not successful, however, in drawing together the entire European continent under the aegis of a single capitalist state. When Napoleon made such an effort, he was thrashed by a coalition of ancient regimes still predominantly pre-capitalist and by Great Britain, which was the most advanced capitalist state and which was leading the capitalist world at the time into the industrial revolution. As a consequence, capitalistic development was consigned to the limits set by the nation-states of Europe—a system which had been bred by pre-capitalistic societies.

The nation-state barrier at first proved to be no formidable obstacle. British and French capitalism displayed an upward trend-line throughout the nineteenth century. So, too, the prodigious economic growth of Germany after the Franco-Prussian War seemed not only to be compatible with the limits of a nation-state, but even seemed to be enhanced thereby.

The moment of truth, however, was not long in coming. The efficiency of German industry and banking, the high productivity of its workers, and the quality of its products and salesmanship soon saturated the home market. And when Germany's bursting surpluses sought an outlet beyond its borders, Germany was blocked by France and Great Britain from expansion in Europe and from expansion in Asia, Africa, and the Middle East. The fact that France and Great Britain were capitalist powers and that Russia was pre-capitalist did not militate against forming a coalition to stop Germany. The Treaty of Versailles was to guarantee that once Germany was stopped, it would never start up again.

The narrow confines of the European nation-state inhibited capitalist development in still another way. The home market was too small to encourage the technology of mass production. This is starkly evident in the failure of any European capitalist country to build an automotive industry geared to a mass market. The European motor industry confined itself to producing cars for a limited luxury market. The result of this failure was a diversion of European capital from expanding the technological base into imperialistic investments geared to primary production.

European capitalism, therefore, represented a hybrid of two conflicting elements: the soverign nation-state—a medieval, pre-capitalist hangover, and capitalism—an economic system whose driving principle, the principle of profit, is transnational and global.

This hybrid proved, however, to be so sturdy that even after World War II the initial goals of Holland, Belgium, France, and Great Britain sought to revert to the principle of nation-state sovereignty and to regain firm control over their prewar imperial turfs. Great Britain was especially determined throughout the postwar years to block a federated Europe, a multilateral defense system, and an economic common market. She held on as tenaciously as her power allowed to the sterling bloc, to imperial preference, to economic hegemony within the Commonwealth, and to the control of all the vital strategic choke-points, to sustain her prewar role of mistress of the seas (Gibraltar, Malta, Cyprus, Suez, Aden, Gulf of Hormuz, Straits of Malacca, etc.)[6] Had the European states at the end of World War II been independent of American influence and pressure, they would have once again opted for the hybrid form of capitalism. Had this eventuated, a resumption of the basic downward trend of the interwar years could not have been reversed. The fate which would have very likely overwhelmed the Jews—and all democratic peoples—under such pressures is not pleasant to contemplate.

IV

Jewish experience within Marxist states has largely been limited to the Soviet version, since there are few, if any, Jews in Communist China or Cuba. This single experience with a *functioning* Marxist system has been consistently negative. The fundamental reason for such negative interaction stems from the fact that the Soviet system is a system which is governed by a political elite whose driving motivation is the exercise of undiluted power. The economic system is ruthlessly subordinated to the political system, even when such subordination courts economic disaster. Lenin, Stalin, and their successors had suffocated the entrepreneurial spirit lest it energize a capitalist class, which, in accordance with Marx's teachings, must sooner or later subordinate the political sector to its own drive for profit. The economic consequences of this tenacious commitment to political power have bordered on the disastrous, especially in the agricultural sector. As late as 1974, although about one-third of the Russian population were still engaged in farming, their productvity was so low that they were unable to raise enough grain to feed their own people. By contrast, the European Common Market was faced with agricultural surpluses. The United States, even during a drought year, was able, with only 4 percent of the American population in farming, to raise enough grains, soybeans, etc., to feed not only the American people but to export huge quantities to the Soviet Union, the Peoples' Republic of China, and many other countries of the world.

The productivity of the Soviet worker in 1974 was also unimpressive. Even conservative estimates put the productivity of the Russian factory worker at no more than 25 percent of that of an American worker—a ratio confirmed by the market, not the official, value of the ruble, which has hovered in Zurich consistently between 20 and 25 cents. Nor is the productivity of Soviet scientists any better. Both Peter Kapista and Andrei D. Sakharov have publicly expressed their dismay at the great productivity gap separating Soviet from Western scientists. And finally, this overall profile of underdevelopment is confirmed by the educational system of the Soviet Union, which provides only minimal schooling for the peasantry while entry into college is limited to less than 10 percent of its young people.[7] Perhaps the most glaring exposure of the economic underdevelopment of the Soviet Union has occurred in recent years when Soviet dependence on American high technology and managerial know-how for the exploitation of her natural resources became a matter of public record.

The Soviet system from its very beginning has thus been a system which has functioned solely in the interests of a ruthless political elite. Economic growth was never an end in itself. Potential entrepreneurs were either blocked or physically liquidated. The peasantry was starved into submission to the regime. The working class was harshly exploited. Intellectuals and scientists were frightened into conformity. Even the party cadres themselves were terrorized, purged, and, in large numbers, exterminated. In retrospect, the Soviet system reveals itself to have been a system of organized underdevelopment, a system with no clear-cut upward trend-line for any class other than the political elite and their bureaucratic instruments.[8]

Jews were from the start largely incompatible with such a system. Since Jews were neither peasants nor proletarians, they had no intrinsic claims within Marxian ideology. As an urbanized grouping, clustered in bourgeois and petty bourgeois occupations, the Jews were highly vulnerable from the very outset—even during the early years when Marxist dreams still effectively obscured the designs of the Bolshevik elite. Their vulnerability was institutionalized when Stalin consolidated his dictatorship and put the Jews strictly at his disposal. This "right" he bequeathed to his successors, who have freely used the Jews as scapegoats for the failures of the regime, especially in the agricultural sector.

V

The experience of the Jews in the United States has been interlinked with a fourth system: *developmental* capitalism. Developmental capitalism differs from hybrid capitalism in that it has thus far surmounted the economic growth barrier by creating the first post-industrial society in the history of civilization.

Developmental capitalism is a unique achievement of the American system. European capitalism had been successful in developing from commercial to industrial capitalism, but it had failed to press on to the technology of mass production, as symbolized by the automotive industry. Further development had been blocked by the European nation-state system, a carry-over from the dynastic systems of pre-capitalistic Europe.

In the United States, however, developmental capitalism met no such nation-state obstructions. This potential barrier was dissolved when the framers of the American Constitution rejected the European model of sovereign nation-states, and opted instead for a federal union with ultimate coercive sovereignty securely lodged in the central government. Among the most persuasive reasons advanced for so daring a solution was that a federal union would encourage the free movement of goods, services, capital, and human talent at the same time that it would dissolve a major source of warfare, economic rivalry.

It is in this broad sense that the American Constitution can be viewed as the political infrastructure which made the subsequent achievements of developmental capitalism possible.[9] The westward expansion was the occasion for widening the federal union, not for launching independent sovereign states. And when a confederation of southern states sought to justify secession by an appeal to their sovereign rights, their bid was militarily crushed. As a consequence, the United States entered the new industrial age without sovereign nation-states blocking the free flow of capital, labor, commodities, and talent over a continent-wide land mass. Whereas France and Germany fought bitterly over the resources of Alsace-Lorraine, the states of West Virginia, Pennsylvania, and Illinois were more tightly drawn together into an economic community by the interdependence of coal, iron, steel, and transportation networks.

This capacity for a single nation-state to encompass new territories, absorb growing populations, embrace countless immigrants, and adjust to complex economic, social, and political changes was encouraged not only by the Constitution but by the principles set forth in the Declaration of Independence. These principles identified natural rights with the inalienable rights of individuals, and not with the inalienable rights of either the state or the nation. It was only because the *natural* rights of the colonists had been violated that they had gained the right to establish a state of their own. Indeed, the Declaration of Independence never uses the term *nation,* since the issue was not nationhood, but statehood; i.e., the need for a state which would protect effectively the natural rights of individuals. Consequently, as the United States expanded to draw in more territory, more peoples, and more diversified economic activities, it was only following through on the principles of the Declaration of Independence which had originally legitimatized the split with Great Britain.

The fact, then, that the United States developed as a single nation-state rather than as a jumble of independent sovereign nation-states allowed capitalism in the United States to break through to a stage of economic development—the technology of mass production—which no other capitalist nation had succeeded in reaching. This breakthrough could occur only because there was a continent-wide market nourished by a growing population, with a rising standard of living. Whereas European capital by the end of the century was flowing into imperialist channels, capital in the United States was building vast industrial enterprises to supply an expanding domestic market. As a consequence, American capitalism demonstrated that the key to profits was the heightened productivity made possible through capital-intensive technology. The worker proved to be far more profitable for the industrialist when his muscles were amplified by machines and organized by industrial engineering than when they were used as crude, brawn labor. The worker, in turn, was able to raise his real income because his productivity was amplified by machines and the principles of industrial engineering.

The only major break in the steadily upward trend-line of American developmental capitalism occurred during the Great Depression. During those years the indicators did indeed signal that the economy had peaked out and was doomed to stagnation and decline. Even the huge American market was not sufficient to sustain further development. American capitalism could expand no further because the European capitalist states were determined to defend their territories with all the economic, diplomatic, and military power they could muster. The failure of the international monetary conference in 1933, followed by the Ottawa Agreements setting up a system of Imperial Preference, effectively excluded the United States from British Commonwealth and colonial markets. The Ottawa Agreements thus seemed to mark the end of the road for American developmental capitalism, even as Hitler's continental triumphs cast an ever more ominous shadow on the shape of the world to come.

For American Jews the depression years were fraught with potential danger. So long as developmental capitalism in the United States had been pressing vigorously upward, Jews had been prime beneficiaries. This had been especially true during the years of exuberant industrial expansion and precocious urbanization, when hundreds of thousands of Jews from Eastern Europe were freely allowed to settle on these shores. As an urbanized, peasant-free, proletarian-resistant people, holding learning in high esteem, the Jews, more than any other immigrant grouping in America, were prefitted for a post-industrial society. From the outset, Jews rejected the farm, spurned the coal mine and steel mill, and only reluctantly acquiesced to employment in the textile and garment industries as a temporary station on the way up and out. The vast majority of the Jews sought out that sector of the bursting economy which were to become the hallmark of post-industrialism: the service sector, and in the service sector, the knowledge "industries."

The Depression, however, by stalling the directional thrust of develop-

mental capitalism, threatened to make the Jews expendable, since the
major problem facing society was a *surplus* of every kind of labor. If the
economic system were to stagnate or break down completely, there would
be a massive retrenchment in all sectors of the economy, especially in the
service sectors. The seed-bed for totalitarianism would thus be ready for
rapid cultivation, and the Jews of the United States would be highly
vulnerable to the traditional solution of the Jewish question when an
economic system stagnates and breaks down: impoverishment, degradation, discrimination, and, as likely as not, expulsion. In 1939, it was still
inconceivable that extermination might be substituted for expulsion.
Fortunately for American Jewry, this hypothesis was not tested. World
War II brought the Depression to an end quickly. Surplus labor gave
way to labor scarcity, every sector of the economy pulsed with vigorous
growth, and American Jewry was again in tandem with the basic thrust
of developmental capitalism. The fact that the enemy of America was
also the arch-enemy of the Jews made for a growing positive image of
the Jewish people.

VI

It was not until after World War II, when nation-state impediments
to global expansion were reduced or eliminated, that American developmental capitalism demonstrated its potential for surmounting the growth
barrier. Prior to World War II, American capitalism had indeed broken
through to mass-production technologies, but it had been blocked by the
division of the capitalist world into competing sovereign nation-states.
After World War II, however, the United States was determined to use
its economic strength and military power to dissolve the nation-state barriers so as to make continued expansion possible. The United States
strongly supported every effort to fuse the European nation-states into a
larger community and did its utmost to create the European Common
Market. By contrast, Great Britain opposed every effort to move beyond a
confederation of independent sovereign nation-states, and she countered
the European economic community with a European trading bloc of her
own. Only after the Common Market had outpaced Britain in economic
growth, did Britain seek entry—and even then only on terms highly
favorable to the sterling bloc and the Commonwealth. Similarly, whereas
the United States favored the dismantling of imperial systems so as to
stimulate economic growth in the underdeveloped world, Great Britain

was eager to sustain the patterns of economic underdevelopment—even after political independence had been granted to her former colonial possessions.[10]

Both the political and economic maps of the world today, as compared with those of 1945, testify to the effectiveness of American policies in building an economic and political infrastructure which is supportive of developmental capitalism on a global scale.[11] The economic growth record of American capitalism since 1946 is impressive. From a gross national product of about two hundred billion dollars in 1946, the United States economy soared to well over a trillion dollars by 1974. In addition, American developmental capitalism provided the seed money for the phenomenal economic growth of Europe and Japan; bailed Great Britain out of her financial difficulties time and again; and came to the aid of the Soviet Union and the People's Republic of China when they were faced with chronic grain shortages. Furthermore, American technological and managerial know-how has played, and is playing a vital role in the industrialization of both the Soviet Union and the People's Republic of China—a fact generally overlooked. Without wheat produced in such abundance by capitalist farmers, the people in the Marxist states would face starvation, and without capitalist technology, they would be unable to extract the vast untapped natural resources which they hold in fief.

Even more significant than this quantitative achievement is the structural transformation that followed in its wake. Heightened productivity in both industry and agriculture went hand-in-hand with a reduction in the percentage of blue-collar workers and farmers. At the same time there was a tremendous expansion of the service sectors. By the end of the sixties it was becoming more and more evident that the most profitable sectors of the American economy were knowledge-based. This is how Peter Drucker states it in his seminal *The Age of Discontinuity:*

> Equally important and equally new is the fact that every one of the new emerging industries is squarely based on knowledge. Not a single one is based on experience. . . .
>
> The new emerging industries therefore embody a new economic reality: *knowledge has become the central* economic resource. The systematic acquisition of knowledge, that is, organized formal education, has replaced experience—acquired traditionally through apprenticeship—as the foundation for productive capacity and performance.[12]

This transition from brawn to brain has given birth to the post-industrial stage of economic development—a stage marked by a shift from the traditional concepts of wealth as quantitative (commodities) to that of wealth as qualitative (intellectual and spiritual).

Carl H. Madden in his *Clash of Culture: Management in an Age of Changing Values* (p. 64) prepared for the National Planning Association, spells out the implications of this radical shift:

A new "public philosophy," consistent with the intellectual revolution, is needed to reflect the change in values that it has created. Society, once mainly agricultural, then later dedicated to surmounting the obstacles to industrial production, now looks forward to the prospect that, within less than a generation, all our food and manufactured goods can be produced by a small fraction of the labor force, perhaps less than 20 percent. Ours is a service economy headed toward taking for granted the agricultural/manufacturing sectors and shifting capital to the service/knowledge sectors. Traditional importance given to wealth-generating mechanisms of property and physical resources are giving way to the wealth-generating power of intellect and its development. . . .

A new philosophy of capitalism must portray a positive vision of a future, offsetting in a credible way the doomsday forecasts of a growing group of our wisest and calmest—and, I believe—our most profound scientists and social thinkers. Such a philosophy is possible, and would be built on the insights of the new intellectual era. Corporations would serve measurable and crucial but restricted social as well as economic purposes. They would be led by men and women who would no longer make denigrating distinctions between human thought and human action; indeed, corporations would be celebrators of the integrity in the civilization of thought linked to action. Corporations, then, would become performance-oriented instruments for achieving social good. This would be achieved by a revolution in corporate marketing strategy, so that corporations would create goods and services consistent with a view of reality as an irreversible process, subject to the Entropy Law. They would also act consistently with a projection to the public of the possible benefits of new wealth forms for mankind. Thus, the appeal of capitalism, already powerful in its provisions for freedom, incentive and reward for attainment, would be reinforced by an appeal to a positive vision of mankind's potential for advance.

This transformation likewise makes possible a global spiral of development. As the more advanced societies, such as the United States, shift to the more profitable innovating technologies, they are able to relinquish to the less developed countries the technologies which have become marginal in the advanced countries. Peter Drucker describes this process clearly:

It should already be clear that the new technologies with the industries based on them are the only means for today's developed countries—above all the United States—to maintain their present standards of living and economic health. The new industries use productively the resources in which developed countries have an advantage, that is, educated people. These industries are, one and all, "knowledge industries," using large numbers of "knowledge workers" and producing goods and services with a high knowledge content. The developing, poor countries can become wealthier and economically strong, however, only by developing the industries that have been the "modern" industries in the developed world for the last fifty years: modern and productive agriculture; the automobile industry, fertilizer and organic chemistry, steel and machinery, and so on. . . .

Similarly the West, as well as Japan, is approaching the time when today's "modern" industries, especially the assembly-line, mass-production industries, are no longer going to be competitive with newcomers. For as a country's investment in knowledge and education goes up, employment in mass-production industries becomes increasingly a misallocation of the human resource.

The cost level of an economy is determined by the cost of the most productive resource. Any resource which therefore produces a good deal less than the most productive one will inevitably be too expensive to be used widely. Or, to put it simply, the developed economies already pay the cost of knowledge and now will have to get the productivity of knowledge to remain competitive. This, in turn, means that they cannot expect to remain competitive for very long in those industries in which the knowledge content is comparatively small, as it is in those "modern industries" that have been carrying the load in the developed economies for the last fifty years.

The United States, which pays the most for knowledge and produces the most educated people, will be less and less capable of maintaining its competitive position in the world and thus its own standard of economic performance and standard of living unless it takes and maintains leadership in the development of the new, the knowledge-based industries.[13]

This breakthrough to post-industrialism is a unique American achievement. It was the outcome of a political system grounded in natural-rights philosophy, transcending the nation-state, and an economic system geared more to innovation than to replication.

The post-industrial profile of American Jewry is no less unique.[14] It is even more post-industrial than that of the non-Jewish population as a whole. Very few Jews are farmers. Not many more are blue-collar workers. The economically underprivileged form only a small minority, almost exclusively confined to the older generation. Consequently, most Jews are concentrated in the service sector, and in the service sector they are becoming more and more prominent in the knowledge industries—the innovating frontier of developmental capitalism. This commitment to the frontier is reflected in the fact that, whereas approximately 45 percent of American college-age youth are in college, more than 80 percent of American Jewish youth are in college. By opting so decisively for higher education, American Jewry has already gambled that the spiral of development has infinite possibilities and that the safest place to be is at the cutting edge of the future—knowledge formation.

Such exposure of American Jewry to the developmental frontier is absolutely unique. It is not fully explained by the fact that American society as a whole has become post-industrial. Were this the explanation, the profile of American Jewry would mirror the American profile. The explanation, therefore, must be sought in exclusively Jewish components.

Before reaching these shores the Jews had already been "pre-fitted" for a post-industrial society. These "pre-fitted" components had all been shaped and honed in Europe, prior to the immigration of the Jews to the United States. Indeed, they even antedated the rise of capitalism in Europe, for they were the outcome of the Jewish experience as a vulnerable minority in medieval societies. As a consequence, the Jews had become an urbanized, peasant-free people who looked upon learning as the surest road to salvation. This pre-capitalist profile effectively diverted the Jews from non-urban occupations in the capitalist age, and made them resistant to proletarianization when industrialism became rampant. When, therefore, the Jews settled in the United States, they were already pre-fitted for a post-industrial society in which the majority are *not* farmers and *not* proletarians, but "knowledge" workers. The pre-American profile of the Jews has become the post-industrial profile of the American people.

On the eve, then, of the two hundredth anniversary of American independence, the uniqueness of the American experience and the uniqueness of the Jewish experience are fusing. This fusion is fraught with tremendous implications for the Jews and for humankind. If the post-industrial society does indeed spin-off a spiral of development and proves that the barriers to continuous economic growth are surmountable, then the

United States will have broken the stranglehold of eternal cycles. Under such circumstances the Jews can anticipate an end to their status as a vulnerable minority. The problem of Jewish survival will no longer be physical but spiritual.

If, however, the spiral of development is a mirage, and the post-industry society is only a prelude to cyclical decline, then the disaster that will befall humankind is stark indeed. Under such circumstances, the Jews would very likely find themselves shifted to quite a different frontier—one all too familiar and all too frightening.

Fortunately, on the eve of the two hundredth anniversary of American independence, there are powerful forces at work making for the Second American Revolution.[15] Since this revolution will be marked by a commitment to the spiral of development, it will pose a haunting dilemma for American Jewry. When fear gives way to free choice, will there be Jewish values worth sustaining and a Jewish identity worth preserving?

NOTES

1. On the post-industrial society, see Daniel Bell, *The Coming of Post-Industrial Society* (New York, 1973); Peter Drucker, *The Age of Discontinuity: Guidelines to Our Changing Society* (New York, 1968, 1969); Carl H. Madden, *Clash of Culture: Management in an Age of Changing Values,* Report No. 133, National Planning Association (Washington, 1972).

2. For a comparison of the American Jewish and the overall American structural profiles, see the table in *Newsweek,* March 1, 1971.

3. Cf. W. W. Rostow, *Politics and the Stages of Growth* (Cambridge, 1971), pp. 26–52; idem. *How It All Began* (N.Y., 1975), pp. 1–32.

4. On the cycles in medieval Jewish history, cf. E. Rivkin, *The Shaping of Jewish History: A Radical New Interpretation* (New York, 1971), pp. 106–39. On the economic data, see I. Schiper, *Yiddishe Geshichte,* 4 vols. (Warsaw, 1930).

5. Fritz Sternberg thoroughly documents the two trend-lines in his *Capitalism and Socialism on Trial* (New York, 1950), pp. 19–393.

6. On Britain's efforts to sustain the nation-state imperialist system after World War II, see George W. Ball, "The Larger Meaning of the N.A.T.O. Crisis," *Vital Speeches,* 32 (June 1, 1966), pp. 492–95; *The Discipline of Power* (Boston, 1968), pp. 69–117; Harold Macmillan, *Tides of Fortune* (New York, 1969), pp. 150–277.

7. On Soviet underdevelopment, see Antony C. Sutton, *Western Technology and Soviet Economic Development,* 3 vols. (1968, 1971, 1973); A. D. Sakharov, *Progress, Coexistence, and Intellectual Freedom,* ed. Harrison E. Salisbury (New York, 1968), pp. 72–73; idem, "The Need for Democratization," *Saturday Review,* June 6, 1970, pp. 26–27; Foy D. Kohler and Dodd L. Harvey, "Administering and Managing the United States and Soviet Space Programs," *Science,* vol. 169 (Sept. 11, 1970), pp. 1049–56; Herbert E. Meyer, "Why the Russians Are Shopping in the U. S.," *Fortune,* February 1973, pp. 46 ff.; Nicholas Wade, "Computer Sales to U.S.S.R.: Critics Look for Quid Pro Quos," *Science,* Feb. 8, 1974, pp. 499–501. William E. Colby, director of the CIA, confirmed that as of the summer of 1974, the USSR was a relatively underdeveloped society: "This [technological] gap is an across-the-board one—from ICBM systems to electric razors—and increasing contacts with the developed West have made it harder to conceal this situation from the Russian people. . . . Communist planners . . . underestimated the pace of Western technology and overestimated their own research-and-development effort. . . . The fact that troubles Soviet leaders, despite good progress, is that the USSR remains far behind the U. S. in a number of key areas . . . labor productivity in Soviet industry is only about half the U. S. level. . . . Of all sectors in the United States and Soviet economies, agriculture offers the greatest contrast in terms of organization and efficiency. For example, the

Russians employ 31 percent of their labor force in agriculture as opposed to 4 percent in the United States. The Soviet output per worker is only 11 percent as much as is achieved in the United States." *U. S. News & World Report*, Sept. 9, 1974, pp. 56–57.

As for the all-important educational index, only about 5.5 percent of Soviet citizens above age ten possess some education beyond secondary school; 4.2 percent have completed their higher education. Only about fifty institutions in the Soviet Union are designated universities by Soviet education officials (Susan Jacoby, "Toward an Educated Elite: the Soviet Universities," *Change,* November 1971, pp. 33–39).

8. Cf. Robert Conquest, *The Great Terror* (New York, 1969).
9. The first ten essays of the *Federalist Papers* represent the classic critique of the European state system, even as they are *the* classic expositions of the "spirit" of developmental capitalism.
10. See above no. 6.
11. The anti-imperialist role of the United States was fully appreciated by British statesmen, however blurred it may have appeared to less sophisticated observers. It is a leitmotif of Harold Macmillan's multi-volumed memoirs. The intensity of British resentment may be gauged by Selwyn Lloyd's outburst against Dean Acheson's West Point speech of December 2, 1962:

> No American statesman who wants to emphasize the decline in Britain's imperial power can honestly deny that his own country has done much to make the process of transformation faster than was wise or safe. . . . Whatever Washington may have intended, there is the knowledge in Britain that in Iran, in Egypt, in the Middle East, in Africa and Asia, and, on some issues, in the United Nations, American influence has on a number of occasions been cast against Britain. . . . no American should denigrate Britain on the score of having lost an empire without accepting some of the responsibility. . . . The United States seems to many to want to have it both ways. It is all right for the United States to take *savage* action against our shipping, to reject the idea of interdependence over weapon production, to try to deny entry into the United States market of our aircraft, to encourage American businessmen in economic imperialism and to have them compete against their allies, not always with complete scrupulousness. . . . On the topic of United States leadership I will be frank. For a long time the United States' role in the world outside was regarded by the Americans as that of the great champion of theoretical liberal principles. The supporters of any subversive or insurrectionary movement anywhere in the world were given freedom of the American press and platform. How the Kremlin must have been delighted to see the United States' friends and allies undermined in this way! (Selwyn Lloyd, "England's Place in the Sun," *Saturday Evening Post*, March 2, 1963, pp. 6–8. Italics mine.)

Cf. also Julian Amery, "East of Suez Up for Grabs," *Atlantic Community Quarterly,* Vol. 5 (Summer 1967), pp. 209–18.

The struggle between nation-state imperialist capitalism, as represented by Great Britain, and developmental capitalism, as represented by the United States, has been, in many respects, even more tenacious than that between developmental capitalism and Marxist systems. Cf. Rivkin, *The Shaping of Jewish History,* pp. 215–48.
12. Drucker, *The Age of Discontinuity*, pp. 39–40.
13. Ibid., pp. 72–73.
14. Cf E. Rivkin, "An Image of a Jewish Tomorrow," *European Judaism* vol. 7

(Winter 1972–73), pp. 16–23; idem, "The Jew in American Society," *CCAR Yearbook,* vol. 77, pp. 200–217.

15. This concept of the Second American Revolution is developed by John D. Rockefeller III in a remarkable little work entitled *The Second American Revolution: Some Personal Observations* (New York, 1973). Rockefeller makes clear his own commitment to "humanistic capitalism" (pp. 78–90) and to the quality of life which this form makes possible. Rockefeller's views are shared by his brother David Rockefeller and a large number of the most influential spokesmen of the business community.

The force most responsible for the radical transmutation of American values associated with the Youth Revolt, the New Left, etc., has been the developmental, innovating sectors of American capitalism. Enno Hobbing quite correctly calls the corporation the genuine left wing of American and international life:

The corporation must realize one thing about itself that may come as some surprise: The corporation represents the genuine left-wing of American and international life. For all its conservative semantics, the modern corporation is the most change-oriented, most change-producing, the most radical institution that exists. Government, churches, schools, and other institutions, with all their vested interests and traditions, are reactionary compared to the corporation.

That being the case, the corporation should help to publish precisely those root-and-branch radical views of politics, economy, sociology, philosophy and other disciplines which now get no hearing in the conventional media, through the conventional publishing houses, or in the conventional, follow-the-intellectual climate of academe. The corporation should publish the voices of reasoned optimism because that is its own radical view of life and history. The corporation should publish articles and books promoting production, because it is only by production that massive unsatisfied human needs will be met, and the corporation is the instrument for meeting them. ("Business Must Explain Itself," *Business and Society Review,* Autumn 1972, p. 86.)

Cf. also John D. Rockefeller III's strong support for the youth revolt in his "In Praise of Young Revolutionaries," *Saturday Review,* vol. 51 (Dec. 14, 1968), pp. 18–20; "Reconciling Youth and the Establishment," ibid., vol. 54 (Jan. 23, 1971), pp. 27–29. See also David L. Rich, "Monitoring American Business' Influence in Planned Social Change" (master's thesis, University of Cincinnati, Graduate Department of Community Planning); and Rivkin, "The Jew in American Society," pp. 207–10.

DEPENDENT CHILDREN IN THE
JEWISH COMMUNITY

By

KENNETH D. ROSEMAN

Institute for Jewish Life

Communal responsibility for the care of dependent children has consistently been accorded very high priority in both Jewish values and practice. Biblical legislation enjoined upon the community a clear mandate to care for the orphan and added to that an equally unequivocal responsibility for the poor. Subsequent *halacha* continued this emphasis throughout the rabbinic period, although the dependent child most frequently specified was the orphan. As early as the tannaitic period, the Jewish community was urged to extend its educational system to all male children, regardless of their parents' ability to pay.[1] As communal structures became more complex in late-medieval Germany and in Eastern Europe, and as economic and social conditions worsened, various obligations were extended explicitly to children who were not orphans but who, because of the destitute circumstances of their parents, had become dependent upon the Jewish community. Schooling and vocational apprenticeships were provided for the sons of the poor, dowries for their daughters. Generally in the literature, the dependent youngster was characterized as a child of God who, through no fault of his own, became the focus of an especially important and meritorious *mitzvah*.

As Jewish communities were established in America, these emphases were continued. Orphanages, schools, and communal agencies came into being during the nineteenth century, particularly as immigration increased, and this trend persisted into the next century. Extensive immigration after 1880 and its attendant problems of child dependency led the Jewish communities of America to respond to the needs with a variety of innovative and farsighted programs. This study focuses on the full-blown system of communal endeavors on behalf of the dependent child which existed in the 1920s and on several major changes in direction which occurred following World War I.

The dependent children to whom we shall be referring were actually of four different types. There were, of course, children who had lost both parents. The proportion of dependent children who were full orphans appears to have declined over the decades to the point where, during the 1920s, they constituted less than half of all dependent children. An equally large group were children with only one parent. The balance, perhaps 10 or 15 percent, was divided between children whose parents simply could not support them adequately and neglected children. This last category included children of "mental defectives," criminals, alcoholics, and others who failed to assume a mature and adult responsibility for their children. All of these were dependent upon the Jewish community for support and care, partially or totally.

Between the Civil War and World War I, considerable changes occurred in the ways Americans treated dependent children. Prior to 1860, a few fortunate children were placed in orphanages, but the majority were either bound out as indentured apprentices without subsequent communal supervision or cast indiscriminately into general, adult almshouses. Concerned philanthropists during the early nineteenth century began to understand the evils of the binding out process and a movement arose emphasizing congregate, institutional care.[2]

After the Civil War, the sizable increase in the number of orphaned and dependent children led to a reconsideration of the nature of institutional arrangements. The almshouse as orphan asylum was replaced in the most progressive states (Ohio, New York, Massachusetts, and Michigan, especially) by separate county homes for children. After January 1, 1884, it became unlawful in Ohio to intermingle dependent children with adult paupers or the infirm. An exception, however, was made with respect to idiots, imbeciles, and insane children, and it was only fifty years later that adequate separate institutional care was provided for these and other special classes of dependent children.[3]

During the late nineteenth century and early twentieth century, Jewish communities established orphanages and other homes for dependent children. There was, however, very little attempt to distinguish among the various kinds of dependent children. This endeavor emerged as a major focus of communal effort during the 1920s. The discovery that many of the institutionalized Jewish children previously classified as "mentally defective" were actually suffering from physical ailments and cultural deprivation led to the establishment of specialized diagnostic clinics. Often associated with Jewish hospitals, these clinics sought to identify various subcategories among dependent Jewish children. Even among the mentally and emotionally ill, attempts were made to distinguish between those who required institutional care and those who could be helped on an outpatient basis. (The number of problem children discovered among Jews during these years should not be underestimated. Kohs, reporting on San Francisco's Jewish population of 30,000 in 1927, indicated that "one is well within the margin of safety in estimating approximately 150 to 200 Jewish problem children in San Francisco: defectives, delinquents, potential delinquents, unstable children, those presenting marked behavior difficulties, etc.") [4]

In Cincinnati, for example, a 1920

> psychological study of Jewish children in the elementary grades of the Cincinnati Public Schools found 72 Jewish children to be definitely feeble-minded, and, according to their ratings on the psychometric tests, eligible for commitment to the State institution for the feeble-minded.

Fifty-five of these children were referred to the neuropsychiatric clinic of the United Jewish Social Agencies (later the Child Guidance Home), where they received both psychological and physical examinations and where a complete social history was taken. (Prior to this, it should be noted, commitment would have been made on the sole basis of I.Q. testing.) Working under the modern theory that feeble-mindedness is not incurable, but that it might be the symptom of a remediable constitutional disturbance or social situation, the Child Guidance Home was able to report in 1928 that all but nine of these fifty-five children had made a reasonable social adjustment and that many were making useful contributions to society, either as employees or as housekeepers. Only four of them were so severely disturbed as to indicate that they should be sent to the state home in Columbus.[5]

During this decade extensive efforts were undertaken to identify the mentally retarded and emotionally disturbed Jewish child. It was widely believed that delinquency among children and criminality among adults were related rather directly to undiagnosed and untreated mental problems, and that a program of treatment aiming to improve both the individual's behavior and his environment would lead to a decrease in antisocial behavior. This pragmatic motivation was reinforced by the expanding popularity of psychiatric and psychological theories and, even more, by an awareness that a large percentage of diagnosed defectives among children could be helped by remedial treatment. Freud's medical career had begun in 1881, barely a generation before the period discussed in this study, but his creative insights had had a lightning-fast impact. The notion of treatment rather than permanent custodial care for the mentally ill and potentially delinquent was particularly influential in the Jewish communities of America and was a major factor leading to the founding of such organizations as Chicago's Institute for Juvenile Research and others.

At the same time, social workers, such as Sadie Saffian of Philadelphia's Jewish Welfare Society, were despairing that educational efforts on behalf of mentally retarded children were woefully inadequate. Commenting in her study of 326 mentally retarded Jewish children in six Philadelphia institutions, she held that

> the children we have studied are bound to a system of education, into which they obviously do not fit, many of them making their own crude adjustments by running away, becoming truants or developing other undesirable traits. While every effort seems to be directed toward compelling them to assimilate academic training beyond the limits of their capacity, very little effort is being made to train this mentally below average group for social usefulness or even self-support.[6]

To assist mentally retarded but educable youngsters to develop as productive citizens to the extent of their capacities, and to provide research information on the care of such children, some diagnostic centers created small, residential treatment facilities. The Home School, founded in Cincinnati on July 26, 1920, under the direction of Dr. Louis A. Lurie, may have been the first of these. After a full examination of many children, about twelve were admitted to the residential program. Connected with the University of Cincinnati's Department of Psychiatry, the Home School program attempted

> to make every encounter of the child with the other children and with the members of the staff a psycho-therapeutic experience. This relation-

ship not only helped the child but at the same time aided those in charge
in understanding the psychopathology and psychodynamics involved in
his behavior. In a residential setting, all facets of daily living . . . assume
meanings that are helpful in understanding the child's behavior. In other
words, this type of facility created a milieu that was both diagnostic and
therapeutic.[7]

Twelve years later, Lurie and his associates were able to report that
only a very small percentage of the children treated had made no social
adjustment. In their words, "Feebleminded children need not necessarily
be thrown on the scrap heap. The majority are potential assets who can
be converted into real assets if the proper therapeutic measures are instituted." [8]

Communities as diverse as Detroit, Brooklyn, Philadelphia, and
Omaha joined in the creation of a network of psychiatric services for
Jewish children. There is reason to believe that these services were not
only far superior to those available in public agencies, but also that they
were unique among ethnic and religious groups. Nonetheless, this frontier
of children's services still had room for expansion. The Boston Jewish
Federation, located in a city where some of the finest children's homes
existed, had no mental hygiene service,[9] nor did San Francisco's Jewish
community have a "program for the development of complete and satisfactory psychiatric social service for the mentally ill." [10] New theories and
techniques were gaining acceptance, but there was an inevitable lag before their application was effected.

New approaches to the treament of emotionally disturbed and mentally
retarded children were paralleled by changes in the care of other dependent children. Two national conferences were held under White House
sponsorship to discuss the care of dependent children. In 1909 and again
in 1919, the conferences affirmed the centrality and value of the natural
family and adopted the principle that family agencies should exert every
effort to preserve the family, disrupting that unit through institutionaliza-
tion only as a last resort. In the light of the nineteenth-century stress on
congregate care, the emphasis on preserving the family acted as a welcome corrective to many and as an alien intrusion to others. In this controversy, Jewish social agencies took an emphatic position of leadership;
as so often in American social welfare history, Jewish communities were
on the forward edge of the pendulum's swing.

During the years following World War I, of course, many forces in

American society made the continuity of traditional family life, especially among immigrant groups, exceedingly problematic. Even during the economically "good" years of the twenties, the physical conditions of family existence among new arrivals were rarely far above subsistence. To the insecurity of survival itself were added the pressures of adjusting to new cultural climates, continuing mobility within the United States, and fundamental xenophobic tensions within American postwar society.

Many of the activities undertaken by Jewish community agencies during the 1920s, valuable as they were in their own right, were invested with additional importance as supports for the family. The popularization of Big Brother and Big Sister services during this decade is clear testimony to their assumed value as an instrumentality for the preservation of the family. The purpose of the Big Brother–Big Sister relationship was often avowedly preventive, especially "with the girls during the most trying period of their development, the adolescent period because the parents do not understand the children. . . ." [11] Big Brother–Big Sister programs endeavored to counter the effects of such social problems as cultural maladjustment, generational conflict, poverty, unemployment, and criminality which threatened to disrupt family unity.

This effort was often undertaken in concert with family case-work agencies. In Cleveland, for example,

> the work of the Big Brother Department is mapped out in accordance with the needs and problems presented by the entire family group as indicated by the family case worker. Obviously, any attempt of the Big Brother Association to work as a separate unit just with the problem boy could bring a successful solution at but infrequent intervals, since the family situation is so important in any treatment. . . . [12]

Coordination among agencies on behalf of dependent or potentially dependent children, another major innovation during the decade, became institutionalized with the creation of children's bureaus. The bureaus were established to coordinate all work in child-care within a city and specifically to counter the widespread tendency to remove children from their homes without adequate exploration of alternatives. Standardized criteria for placement and care were developed, and efforts were made at a periodic review of each child's situation. Both in Baltimore and Philadelphia, an explicit goal of the bureau was "to insure the return of the child to his people at the earliest desirable moment." [13] The bureaus served as the representatives of the total Jewish community, transcending the desires or advantages of any individual agency. Both mirroring and advancing trends toward interagency cooperation throughout the Jewish community, the creation of children's bureaus was a significant forward step in raising and equalizing the qualitative standards of child-care agencies. They served as models both for other areas of the Jewish community and as forms to be emulated in general social welfare organizations.

One additional step was taken to avoid the removal of a child from his home. Many agencies recognized that some family misfortunes were only temporary and that, with a bridging of the passing problem, the family could be preserved. Illness of one parent, childbirth, incarceration, and other short-term crises called forth a new solution—the visiting housekeeper. By placing a visiting housekeeper in the home for a brief period (in twenty Chicago cases, the duration ranged from three days to seven and one-half months),[14] a number of advantages were noted. Kepecs, describing the pioneering program in Chicago, comments that the innovation helped

> to prevent discomfort to the members of the family, if not disintegration caused by separation, dispersion and necessary adjustment to a new and strange environment, and secondly, this saves the organization from wasteful effort and energy involved in temporary placements. Incidentally, other advantages have become apparent, namely, the lessening of the cost to the community, objective lesson to the family in household management and economy, etc.[15]

Despite all these efforts, the care of dependent children who had no families and the removal of children from disintegrating families remained unavoidably necessary. In New York City and Brooklyn, over three thousand children were resident in the three major orphanages. Reports from other cities indicate that there existed a widespread need to provide residential facilities for the Jewish dependent child, especially for orphans. New homes were built in Milwaukee, New Haven, St. Louis, and Cleveland, and others were improved. Experiments with a novel arrangement, the cottage plan, were attempted in New York (Pleasantville) and in Baltimore (Levindale), and efforts were made to provide regional centers serving areas of more diffuse Jewish population. A contemporary survey in Omaha, for example, reported that thirty dependent children had been placed by the Jewish community: two in foster homes in Omaha, three in the Denver National Home for Children, and twenty-five in the Cleveland Orphan Home.[16]

Proponents of congregate care argued emphatically that it presented distinct advantages. The history of placing-out, whether through foster home or adoptive placement, had been filled with stories of abuse, neglect, violation of child-labor statutes, and similar kinds of improper care and exploitation. Social agencies found it difficult to supervise these placements, with the result that the foster parents exercised a nearly unlimited autocracy following the initial trial period. Arguments were raised on behalf of the character-building value of group discipline and on behalf of the more structured educational process in institutional settings.

A report by the executive director of the Marks Nathan Jewish Orphan Home in Chicago held

> that from the standpoint of both the physical development and the adjustment of health problems as such, the claim to superiority of the boarding-out type of care is, to say the least, not justifiable, the advantage being decidedly in favor of institutional care.[17]

Others held that removal from an inadequate home was a preventive measure designed to reduce the incidence of delinquency among "a certain class of children." Writing about the Cedar Knolls School for delinquent girls near New York City, Alice D. Menken held that

> The School has been the means of developing habits of industry and imparting to the children secular and religious education, until, in the judgment of competent authority they can take their places again in society. During the time that the girls are in the School, effort is made to readjust those conditions in their homes which caused or contributed to the failure of the children to comply with the ordinary standards in the community.[18]

Were these institutions, it ought to be asked, all that they claimed to be? Certainly, compared to the contemporary descriptions of public institutions, whose prisonlike degradation reminds the reader of Dickens' accounts in *Oliver Twist*—certainly by comparison these orphanages, shelters, and schools were far superior. As early as 1887, Elbridge T. Gerry, president of the New York Society for the Prevention of Cruelty to Children, wrote about the New York Hebrew Orphan Asylum:

With all my experience in the management of institutions for the benefit of children, I have yet to find any which compare with those in charge of your people. I only wish that the example which your institution has set would be followed by others, because your system demonstrates how easily and how well children may be cared for. . . . [19]

The children's institutions run by Jewish philanthropies during the twenties were marked by a progressive and "scientific" management and a dedication to the creation of an environment which respected individual needs and engendered an affectionate relationship between workers and children. A professional staff replaced the earlier volunteers; where professionals were not available, efforts were made to train them. A commitment emerged to the development and provision of professional services of the highest quality. In 1926, for example, Cincinnati's United Jewish Social Agencies sent prospective professionals to the New York Graduate School for Jewish Social Work and to the University of Cincinnati for specialized training.[20]

Every effort was made to create institutions which closely resembled the normal, happy home. Extensive recreational, religious, social, and educational programs were offered, including vocational education classes. In the most modern homes, particularly those designed according to the cottage plan, efforts were made to select staff who would serve as effective adult models with desirable personality and character traits. The cottage plan itself was an attempt to mitigate the undesirable aspects of institutions by organizing the residents into a number of medium-sized "families." Most orphanages enrolled their charges in public schools as another attempt at normalizing their life-situation, although some orphanages found it more convenient to conduct their own schools, and all provided religious instruction on the premises. A number, especially those in suburban and rural settings, enlarged their populations during the summer months by adding fresh-air camp programs. It was considered valuable for institutionalized youngsters to have this supplementary, intensive contact with "normal" children, for the realistic fear persisted that prolonged segregation might make reentry into society difficult.

Despite the qualitative advances in the congregate care of Jewish dependent children during the twenties, the advocates of maintaining the "normal" or "nuclear" family became increasingly influential. A widespread consensus developed that far too many children were removed from their own homes and, further, that nearly all who had to be placed could be handled by foster-home placement. They cited increasing economic and social stability among immigrant Jewish families, better case work, and efforts to eliminate temporary placements through such techniques as visiting housekeeper services and more careful screening, all making possible the proposed reduction in institutional placements. Jewish family and children's workers held that only a small residual group of problem children should remain in institutions, and these primarily in specialized-care facilities.

Nowhere was the impact of this new philosophy more starkly evident than in Baltimore. In 1922 the Jewish community had built a thoroughly modern, cottage-plan orphanage called Levindale. Only six years later, Levindale had been closed to children except for one small diagnostic cottage, and its facilities were being used as a residence for the Jewish aged. The need for institutional care had decreased by 75 percent; the complete transition from institutional to foster-home care moved very rapidly. Baltimore's leaders reported that all of the foster children were

> living normal lives in good Jewish homes. They have efficient parental guidance and care; they have normal relations with brothers and sisters; they have the stimulation of normal community contacts.
>
> Under the supervision of our workers, they are receiving good medical attention, the best school and play facilities the community possesses, religious instruction and expert advice and guidance in every phase of their development. For the normal child, deprived of its own home and people, either temporarily or permanently, the foster home seems the best substitute that can be found.[21]

Neither commitment to these beliefs nor progress in their implementation was unanimous throughout America's Jewish communities. Tension persisted between the strong advocates of both schools of thought. In Boston, foster-home placement was reserved for "special medical care including cases of behavior problem children." Only toward the end of the decade was there attention to the placing-out of older children as mothers' helpers or with a capable big brother.[22] Cleveland authorities complained that "the Jewish Orphan Home, being directed by a regional organization, finds it difficult to adapt its methods to the local wishes and needs of the Jewish community of Cleveland." [23]

The trend toward foster-home placement was, however, widespread and clearly discernible. Milwaukee reduced the number of its charges placed in the Cleveland home by half and rescinded its policy of placing

Jewish children with non-Jewish foster parents when Jewish families were unavailable. Under pressure from the Orthodox elements of the Milwaukee Jewish community, a pool of qualified Jewish foster parents was trained, and by 1927 the Jewish Social Service Association was supervising twenty dependent children in Jewish foster homes.[24] In the same year, St. Louis began a program of child placement. The executive director of the Jewish Federation reported twenty-two placements in the first year, plus eight children who were returned to their own families.[25] A major shift in child-care philosophy had occurred rather quickly, and its impact was felt in every Jewish agency.

No community, however, became so committed to this new philosophy of child placement as to neglect alternatives. Family and children's agencies continued to judge each child's needs on an individual basis and to decide what care would be best for him as an individual. The widespread agreement that family-centered placement was preferable does not seem to have prevented institutional assignment, although the literature of the period leaves a strong impression that the latter decision required particular justification.

Communal care for dependent children did not cease with discharge from the institution or from the foster home. The minutes of Cincinnati's Convalescent and Foster Home reflect an embryonic followup system to ascertain the condition of discharged youngsters.[26] By 1926 Baltimore had a full After Care Department working "to evaluate the results of institutional training and at the same time . . . to tide over the child at a critical transition period. This care continues until it becomes reasonably assured that the child is vocationally adjusted and that his social adjustment seems more secure." [27] Other communities established residential homes for young working women; Cincinnati's Martha House was probably the first. Jewish settlement houses, community centers, and various other groups provided supervised recreational, educational, and social activities to which former dependent children were enthusiastically directed.

The 1920s began with America's Jewish communities facing extensive problems in caring for dependent children. To the essentially qualitative aspects of the family situations—immigrant acculturation and stabilization and generational conflict—was added the quantitative dimension of greatly increased incidence. During the decade Jewish communal agencies sometimes followed and often led America's child-care workers in the development of new techniques and approaches. Pioneering efforts led to new differentiations among the various types of dependent child and to sophisticated treatment for emotionally disturbed and mentally retarded youngsters. The introduction of psychological and psychiatric criteria for the diagnosis and treatment of children was itself a significant change.

The efforts of the decade were also characterized by shifting attitudes concerning the removal of children from their homes and the kinds of placement which should be encouraged. A major controversy between the advocates of congregate care and the proponents of foster-home placement continued throughout the decade. While a complete resolution never emerged, by 1929 it was clear that the majority of Jewish child-care workers favored family-centered placement and that this would be the trend of the future.

The decade ended as it began, with a crisis of numbers—the Depression and the devastation it brought to immigrant families—but, despite temporary setbacks, the philosophy and techniques which were developed in Jewish communal agencies during the 1920s continued as major building-blocks for all subsequent care of dependent children.

NOTES

1. *Baba Batra* 21a.
2. Robert W. Kelso, *The Science of Public Welfare* (New York: Henry Holt and Co., 1928), p. 345.
3. Aileen E. Kennedy, *The Ohio Poor Law and Its Administration* (Chicago: University of Chicago Press, 1934), pp. 53–54.
4. S. E. Kohs, "Needs and Facilities for Psychiatric Social Service," *Jewish Social Service Quarterly*, III:3 (March, 1927), 57–58 (*Jewish Social Service Quarterly* hereafter referred to as *JSSQ*).
5. Louis A. Lurie, Leah Schlan, and Margaret Freiberg, "A Critical Analysis of the Progress of Fifty-Five Feeble-Minded Children over a Period of Eight Years," *American Journal of Orthopsychiatry*, II:1 (January, 1932), 58.
6. Sadie Saffian, "The Mentally Retarded Children of Jewish Dependents," *JSSQ*, III:3 (March, 1927), 32.
7. Louis A. Lurie, "The Genesis of the Child Guidance Home," *Cincinnati Journal of Medicine*, LI: 4 (April, 1970), 100.
8. Lurie, Schlan, and Freiberg, *op. cit.*, p. 69.
9. Maurice Taylor, "[Mental Hygiene in] Boston," *JSSQ*, III:3 (March, 1927), 61–62.
10. Kohs, *op. cit.*, p. 60.
11. Board of Governors, United Jewish Social Agencies. *Minutes* (Cincinnati, Ohio: March 1, 1922), p. 401.
12. Fred J. Stern, "Jewish Big Brother Work in Cleveland," *JSSQ*, VI:3–4 (March–June, 1930), 154.
13. Sidney Hollander, "Child Welfare Unified: The Baltimore Experience," *JSSQ*, IV:3 (March, 1928), 206.
14. H. L. Lurie, "Jewish Communal Progress: Chicago," *JSSQ*, II:2 (December, 1925), 120–21.
15. Jacob Kepecs, "Housekeeping Service in Chicago," *JSSQ*, VI:3–4 (March–June, 1930), 114–15.
16. Samuel Gerson, "Omaha Takes Stock," *JSSQ*, VI: 3–4 (March–June, 1930), 170.
17. Elias J. Trotzkey, "The Physical Development of Dependent Children under Institutional and Private Home Care," *JSSQ*, VI: 3–4 (March–June, 1930), 129–30.
18. Alice D. Menken, "Delinquent Girls on Parole: A Study of Girls Paroled from Cedar Knolls School, 1909–1925," *JSSQ*, III: 1 (September, 1926), 47.
19. Jacqueline Bernard, *The Children You Gave Us: A History of 150 Years of Service to Children* (New York: Jewish Child Care Association of New York, 1970), p. 22.
20. Board of Governors, United Jewish Social Agencies, *Minutes* (Cincinnati, Ohio: June, 1926), p. 1211.

21. Harry Greenstein, "Reorganization in Baltimore," *JSSQ*, VI: 1–2 (September–December, 1929), 50. On Levindale, see also Hollander, *op. cit.*, and Sidney Solender, "Levindale: An Experiment in Child-Care," *JSSQ*, III:2 (December, 1926), 41–48.
22. Maurice Taylor, "Jewish Communal Progress: Boston," *JSSQ*, II: 2 (March, 1926), 209.
23. John Slawson, "Communal Progress in Cleveland," *JSSQ*, II:4 (June, 1926), 308.
24. Benjamin Glassberg, "Milwaukee—The End of a Quarter Century," *JSSQ*, IV: 2 (December, 1927), 164–65.
25. Ferdinand S. Bach, "Progress in St. Louis," *JSSQ*, IV: 2 (December, 1927), 167–68.
26. Convalescent and Foster Home, *Minutes* (Cincinnati, Ohio: November 9, 1921, and February 7, 1922), n.p.
27. Solender, *op. cit.*, 46.

INTERMARRIAGE AND CONVERSION
IN THE UNITED STATES

By

JOSEPH R. ROSENBLOOM

Temple Emanuel, St. Louis,
Adjunct Professor of Classics
at Washington University

INTRODUCTION

The Jew in the United States finds himself in a dilemma. He lives in a society in which he moves freely. There are no legal restraints on him because of his Jewishness. While there are some socially defined limitations to his activities, he has partaken fully of the generally free atmosphere of America. This, in part, has led to gradual and dramatic increases in the rate of intermarriage, together with a concern for the survival of Jews as a corporate entity.

At the same time, conversion to Judaism, a device for assimilating Gentiles into the Jewish group, has been given relatively little formal attention. Conversionist activities, widespread in Judaism in the biblical and talmudic periods, fell into general disfavor with the strictures placed upon them by Christianity and Islam, under whose authority most Jews lived in later times.

It has been suggested that the Jewish commitment to a free and open society will mean an accelerated rate of intermarriage, and that the integrity of the Jewish group will be maintained only by more self-conscious programs of conversion to Judaism. My essay engages this twofold situation as it has developed in the United States.

INTERMARRIAGE

The survival of the Jewish people and Judaism has been one of the preoccupations of contemporary Jewry. Significant losses were suffered during World War II. Although no accurate or comprehensive statistics are available, it is also believed that a substantial number of Jews are lost to Judaism through intermarriage, which has reached high levels in the past and is once again increasing. The zeal for conversion on the part of many Jews relates directly to this phenomenon. It is hoped that when a Jew marries a non-Jew, the non-Jew will be encouraged to convert to Judaism. However, the practice varies greatly from individual to individual, family to family, and Reform rabbi to Reform rabbi. Virtually no Orthodox or Conservative rabbi will marry a Jew to a non-Jew unless there is conversion. Because the phenomenon of intermarriage is intimately connected with conversion in modern Jewish communities, it must be carefully studied.

Two systems are operative in the process of intermarriage. The first is the contradiction between the Jewish aspiration of being a part of a free and open society, where Jews may live and prosper without many of the discriminations with which they have been historically confronted, and the subsequent mingling of Jew and non-Jew often leading to intermarriage. The second, which also affects the relations of Jew and Gentile, is the "acculturation to assimilation" pattern.

In the case of the first system the contradiction is more apparent. Jews, individually and collectively, have actively sought out and helped develop social situations where opportunities would not be limited by their religious identity. This has brought them to an increasing number of situations where attributed status has been replaced by earned status determined by the value of the individual to the society. The openness of such societies makes for greater freedom in other social situations as well. Mates for marriage are increasingly chosen for romantic reasons rather than because they are of the same religion or ethnic group. Individual Jews as well as Jewish organizations find it increasingly difficult to inhibit the resulting intermarriage when, at the same time, they positively identify with the values of freedom, liberalism, and individualism which promote it.

The "acculturation to assimilation" process leads to similar results in the same societies.[1] This process operates on three levels. First, there is acculturation, the shedding of foreign language, customs, and work and leisure-time habits and the adopting of new cultural traits. This is followed by a decrease in the social distance between the immigrant group and the other component groups of the society. Finally, feelings of belongingness and group identification change. Intermarriage may be viewed as part of the final stage of assimilation in the process which begins with conflict and competition and ends after an intermediate phase of accommodation.

The relatively low rate of intermarriage of Jews (random selection of mates by Jews from the general population would be 97 percent) is the result of resistance to this race-relations cycle. Jews are concentrated geographically, with about half of them residing in the New York City area, and more than another third in the next ten largest metropolitan centers. Furthermore, most Jews live in neighborhoods with sizable percentages of Jews. Of course, this cohesiveness is vitiated somewhat because the majority of young Jews attend college.[2]

Other inhibiting factors which operate against assimilation, the final step in the race-relations cycle, are Jewish education and Jewish self-consciousness, or identification with the Jewish group. Contrary to what might be expected, the decline in cultural differences has not been accompanied by a decline in Jewish self-consciousness. The apparent heightened self-consciousness seems to be the result of the growth of Nazi anti-Semitism and the Nazi definition of Jew along racial and ancestral lines, reinforced by the more recent problems of Jews in Russia and the Middle East.[3] Unsettling, however, are the statistics of intermarriage in Washington, D.C., San Francisco and vicinity, Iowa, and Indiana,[4] which have now been generally substantiated by a national survey based on 7,000 interviews indicating that between 1966 and 1972 31.6 percent of all Jews marrying, married persons who were not originally Jewish.[5] These appear to be indications of a high future overall rate, indicating that the efficacy of the survival formula of neighborhood and education must be seriously doubted.[6] There can be no doubt that the likelihood of intermarriage increases with increased acculturation; the Washington survey indicated that persons born in the United States with an educational achievement beyond high school and with high professional status are the most likely to enter into intermarriage.

Researchers have identified numerous other factors which they have related to the rate of intermarriage. Community size appears to be one of these (see table 1). In Iowa between 1953 and 1959, in towns of 10,000 or more, the rate fluctuated between 36.3 percent and 53.6 percent, averaging 42.4 percent. It was almost twice as high in smaller towns and rural areas.[7] Similarly in Indiana: the intermarriage rate in the five counties with the highest concentration of Jews was 38.6 percent, while in the other eighty-two counties it was 63.5 percent.[8] However, because

TABLE 1

Source	Locale	Period	Rate of Intermarriage per 100 Marriages
Engelman	Germany [a]	1901	14.0
	Germany [a]	1906	17.0
	Germany [a]	1911	22.0
	Germany [a]	1916	42.0
	Germany [a]	1921	25.0
	Germany [b]	1927	35.0
	U.S.S.R. [c]	1926	15.0
	Switzerland [d]	1880	5.7
	Switzerland [d]	1900	7.0
	Switzerland [d]	1920	13.0
Barr & Cahnman	Switzerland [e]	1950	19.4
Davis	Australia [f]	1911	20.5
	Australia [f]	1921	22.9
	Australia [f]	1933	15.5
Rosenberg	Canada [g]	1926–30	2.5
	Canada [g]	1931–35	2.6
	Canada [g]	1936–40	3.2
	Canada [g]	1941–45	5.0
	Canada [g]	1946–50	4.8
	Canada [g]	1951–55	6.2
	Canada [g]	1956–60	7.6
Davis	U.S. [h]	1776–1840	20.5
Glick	U.S. [i]	1957	7.0
Greeley	U.S. [j]	1961–68 (college graduates)	16.0
Lenn	U.S. [k]	1971	11.0
	U.S. [k]	1971 (age 20–24)	33.0
Sklare	New York City [l]	1908–12	1.2
Kennedy	New Haven [m]	1870	0.0
	New Haven [m]	1900	1.18
	New Haven [m]	1930	2.99
	New Haven [m]	1940	5.68
Shanks	New Haven [n]	1958	5.0
Kennedy	Cincinnati [o]	1916–19	3.6
	Stanford, Conn. [o]	1938	7.2
Rosenthal	New London, Conn. [p]	1938	5.2
Goldstein &	Providence [q]	1963 (parents)	4.5
Goldscheider	Providence [r]	1963 (men, 30 & under)	9.0
Rosenthal	Dallas [s]	1939	6.1
	Duluth [s]	1939	15.1
Shanks	Trenton [t]	1937	1.0
	Des Moines [t]	1949	8.0
Sklare	Camden, N. J. [u]	1964	4.0
	Boston [v]	1965 (whole sample)	7.0
	Boston [v]	1965 (30 & under)	20.0
Lazerwitz	N. Illinois [w]	1966–67	11.0
Shanks	Indianapolis [x]	1941	12.0
Rosenthal	Indiana [y]	1960–63	49.0
	Marion County, Ind. [y]	1958	34.5
	San Francisco [z]	1938	6.9
	San Francisco [aa]	1958	17.2
	Marin County, Calif. [aa]	1958	37.0
	Washington, D.C. [bb]	1956	13.0
	Iowa [cc]	1953–59	42.0

a Uriah Z. Engelman, "Intermarriage among Jews in Germany, U.S.S.R., and Switzerland," *Jewish Social Studies,* vol. II (1940), p. 157.

b *Ibid.,* p. 158.

c *Ibid.,* p. 168.

d *Ibid.,* p. 175.

e Jacob Barr and Werner J. Cahnman, "Interfaith Marriages in Switzerland," in *Intermarriage and Jewish Life: A Symposium,* ed. Werner J. Cahnman (New York, 1960), p. 53.

f Moshe Davis, "Mixed Marriage in Western Jewry: Historical Background to the Jewish Response," *CCAR Journal,* vol. X (1962), p. 17.

g Louis Rosenberg, "Intermarriage in Canada," in Cahnman, *Intermarriage and Jewish Life,* p. 62.

h Davis, *op. cit.,* p. 5.

i Paul Glick, "Intermarriage and Fertility Patterns among Persons in Major Religious Groups," *Eugenics Quarterly,* vol. VII (1960), p. 34.

j Andrew Greeley, follow-up of *The Great Aspirations Study* (Report no. 82, National Opinion Research Center, University of Chicago) by James A. Davis and Norman Bradburn (Chicago, 1961). Personal Communication.

k Theodore Lenn and associates, *Rabbi and Synagogue in Reform Judaism* (West Hartford, Conn., 1972), p. 217.

l Marshall Sklare, *America's Jews* (New York, 1971), p. 184.

m Ruby Jo Reeves Kennedy, "Single or Triple Melting Pot? Intermarriage Trends in New Haven, 1870–1940," *American Journal of Sociology,* vol. XLIV (1944), p. 333.

n Herschel Shanks, "Jewish-Gentile Intermarriages: Facts and Trends," *Commentary* vol. 26 (1953), p. 370.

o Ruby Jo Reeves Kennedy, "What Has Social Science to Say about Intermarriage?" in Cahnman, *Intermarriage and Jewish Life,* p. 29.

p Erich Rosenthal, "Some Recent Studies about the Extent of Jewish Outmarriage in the U.S.A.," in Cahnman, *Intermarriage and Jewish Life,* p. 86.

q Sidney Goldstein and Calvin Goldscheider, "Social and Demographic Aspects of Jewish Intermarriage," *Social Problems,* vol. XIII (1966), p. 389.

r *Ibid.,* p. 390.

s Erich Rosenthal, "Acculturation without Assimilation—The Jewish Community of Chicago, Illinois," *American Journal of Sociology* (1960).

t Shanks, *op. cit.*

u Sklare, *op. cit.,* p. 187.

v *Ibid.,* p. 189.

w Bernard Lazerwitz, "Intermarriage and Conversion," *Jewish Journal of Sociology,* vol. XIII (1971), pp. 34f.

x Shanks, *op. cit.*

y Erich Rosenthal, "Jewish Intermarriage in Indiana," *American Jewish Year Book,* vol. 68 (New York, 1967), p. 263.

z Rosenthal, "Some Recent Studies . . ."

aa Rosenthal, "Acculturation without Assimilation," p. 288.

bb Rosenthal, "Studies of Jewish Intermarriage," p. 16.

cc *Ibid.,* p. 51.

many communities have their own unique qualities, narrower generalizations are difficult to make. San Francisco is very cosmopolitan, while Washington, D.C., has a very transient and highly professionalized population, factors which apparently also seem to increase the rate of intermarriage.

A major concern is the fate of the children of intermarried couples. Morris Fishberg, in an early twentieth-century study on New York, reported that 75 percent of all children born to Jews married to Christians were baptized at birth. The remaining 25 percent were reared as Jews.[9] In Washington, D.C., in 1956, 17.5 percent of the children of intermarried Jewish households were identified as Jews.[10] This contrasted with the experience in Providence. There, where the non-Jewish parent converted, all children involved were reared as Jews, while where there was no conversion, eighty-four were reared as Jews and sixty were not, or a 58 percent rate.[11] The disparity between the Washington and Providence rates may be attributed to the former being a community with a transient population while the latter is an old, well-established Jewish community with a strong organizational structure. The recent national study cited above, however, points to far higher rates of Jewish identity of such children.[12] Where the wife was Jewish, 98.4 percent of the children of intermarriages were being raised as Jewish. Where the husband was Jewish and the wife Gentile, the percentage dropped to 63.3 percent.

The study of intermarriage rates also suffers from methodological problems. In Boston the average rate in 1965 was thought to be 7 percent, but this does not reflect the true situation since the rate varies from a low of 3 percent of husbands fifty-one years of age and over to a rate of 20 percent for husbands age thirty and younger. Since this latter group is predominant in new marriage formation, the figure of 20 percent should be approximately the current rate.[13]

TABLE 2

Age	80+	70–79	60–69	50–59	40–49	30–39	20–29
		%	%	%	%	%	%
Religion of Spouse							
Jewish	100	87	93	90	87	89	82
Non-Jewish	0	10	8	10	12	11	18

This conclusion is borne out by two other studies. In a 1971 survey of Reform Jews, the rate of intermarriage generally steadily increased as the age decreases (see table 2).[14] A comparable rate is seen in a survey made of college graduates of 1961 and their martial status as of 1968 (see table 3).[15]

TABLE 3

	Men	Women
in-marry	62%	71%
out-marry	16% 18% of those married	6% 8% of those married
unmarried	19%	18%
no response	3%	5%

That losses to the Jewish group correlate with the rate of intermarriage is most apparent in the religious identity of the children of such unions. But it is exacerbated in other ways as well. Fewer women intermarry, perhaps half, than do men. The result is significant demographically in that as spinsters they typically do not bear children. Furthermore, those who are urban dwellers, are in the professions, hold white-collar positions, and are highly educated tend to have fewer children. Jews are concentrated in each of these categories. They are 96 percent urban. In addition, they are almost seven years older than the average American (their median age is 36.6 years against 29.9 years). The Jewish fertility rate, for all of these reasons, is only 75 percent that of Catholics and Protestants. Even where they share characteristics with other religious groups, their birth rate is lower: 14 percent lower than other urban groups and 5–15 percent lower than others in the professions and white-collar occupations.[16]

Intermarried Jewish couples also have smaller families; a higher percentage are childless and have fewer higher-order births than couples born Jewish. Where the husband and wife were both born Jewish, 9.7 percent were childless, while 26.1 percent of the intermarried couples were childless. The mean number of children where both parents were born Jewish was 2.2, while it was 1.6 where there was intermarriage.[17]

Such figures and trends are perceived as a threat to the survival of Jews in the United States and other nations, with the exception of Israel. Although statistics are not as available outside of the United States, intermarriage rates are known to be high, sharing the same demographic problems as those of the Jews of America. No activity or pronouncement by laity or clergy has been successful in stemming intermarriage. Mordecai M. Noah declared in 1845 that if marriage between Jews and Christians were to be permitted, Judaism and Jews would disappear in two or three generations.[18] In the middle of the nineteenth century, congregations in New York City barred synagogue seats and cemetery rights to those who intermarried.[19] David Einhorn, a leading radical Reform rabbi, viewed each intermarriage as a nail in the coffin of Judaism.[20]

Generally negative attitudes on the part of Jewish parents seem ineffective, although some researchers believe Jewish intermarriage to be quite low, considering the size of the Jewish group and intermarriage rates among other religious groups.[21] A study of a midwestern suburb indicated that virtually no Jews of East European origin in the first, second, and third generations would be happy with intermarriage in their families. Only about one in five would be indifferent to it. There was less concern among those of German and mixed descent. Somewhat more than half of the fourth generation would feel indifferent to or happy about their children's intermarrying. Relatively few oppose intermarriage out of concern for Jewish survival or because of Judaism (14 percent). Their primary concern was that it would lead to marital discord. Romantic love was viewed as more important than Jewishness: 85 percent preferred a loved Gentile to an unloved Jew as a mate for their child. Only 1 percent would reject their child who might intermarry, while 94 percent would accept the marriage and retain a meaningful relationship with their child.[22]

The Jewish experience throughout history has included widespread and varying rates of intermarriage. Current trends in most Jewish communities lead to the conclusion that intermarriage will continue and in all probability increase. Attempts to stem this trend, increased Jewish education for the young and other institutional programs, will certainly not be completely effective. Therefore, it would seem the Jews would turn once again to conversion as an historically tested Jewish survival mechanism. Bernard Lazerwitz states the case succinctly: "The basic threat to Jewish continuity does not stem from intermarriage. Rather, intermarriage (without conversion) is but a symptom of diaspora Jewry's growing dissatisfaction with contemporary Jewish institutions and cultural forms." [23] Similarly, the Levinsons write:

> Whether the rate of intermarriage by Jews rises or falls in the future will depend not on pronouncements for or against intermarriage as such, but on more fundamental social and psychological changes: in secularization

and urbanization of American society, in the bases that can be found for building a distinctive but not insular Jewish identity, in the emotional quality of the Jewish family and the like.[24]

Until these monumental changes in Jewish life come about, and it is doubtful if even they can stem the tide of intermarriage, conversion may help maintain the Jewish body politic.

Furthermore, each instance of intermarriage may also have a multiplier effect. The multiplier effect comes about when intermarriage reaches such frequency that it creates greater approval for itself. It becomes fashionable and acceptable.[25]

Rather than being viewed solely as a threat to Jewish survival, intermarriage may be considered an opportunity to increase the number of Jews. Assuming that an equal number of Jewish men and women intermarry and succeed in maintaining their own Jewishness and inducing their spouses to identify with their group, the Jewish community would be magnified rather than diminished by intermarriage.[26] The problem is to welcome the prospective convert and to provide something worth converting to.

CONVERSION

As an aftermath of the anti-conversionist stance of Judaism as it developed after the establishment of Christianity and Islam, attitudes toward conversion to Judaism developed in a mixed way. Few individuals have been outspoken advocates for conversion and fewer organizations have made it their central cause or even a cause of much importance. Many have been outspoken opponents of proselytizing. For the most part, however, most Jews have been indifferent to it and remain so now.

A leading nineteenth-century Reform rabbi, David Einhorn of Baltimore, included in his prayerbook a service for the acceptance of proselytes.[27] Rabbi Adolph Moses, in a sermon delivered at the Hebrew Union College in Cincinnati in 1894, suggested that the name of Judaism be changed from what he felt was a nationalist term to the universalist "Yahvism" to make it more acceptable to the many he was convinced wanted to convert to Judaism.[28] Two leaders of Reform Judaism, Isaac M. Wise and Kaufmann Kohler, among eight others, indicated that circumcision was not essential for conversion. This was in response to a petition made in 1890 by a non-Jew to Rabbi Henry Berkowitz of Kansas City.[29] Circumcision is still not required by Reform Judaism, although it is by Conservative and Orthodox rabbis except where health reasons allow only a symbolic circumcision.

The Reform Central Conference of American Rabbis, while never hostile to conversion, has taken only minimal steps to encourage active proselytizing. In 1927 it published a manual for instructing converts. An effort to do something more in 1950 led to the creation of a committee to study practical means "of extending the influence and acceptance of the Jewish religion." During the next year a committee on the unaffiliated was appointed. After six years of study and the acceptance of its report, a call was made for the preparation of literature, radio and television programs, and congregational preaching missions. Nothing came of this proposal.[30] Even now little has changed among Reform rabbis. Only 8 percent feel "strongly," and 25 percent agree "somewhat," that more time and energy should be given making an effort to win converts.[31] Presumably, Orthodox and Conservative rabbis would resist efforts to recruit proselytes even more than Reform rabbis.

Acceptance of converts by Jews is often mixed. Startlingly, some converts are identified as Gentiles. This may simply indicate incomplete assimilation into the Jewish group. But it also marks the remarkable influence of ethnicity among Jews, in spite of an extremely high level of acculturation. In some instances, however, such converts to Judaism are characterized "as more Jewish than anyone else." This indicates the feeling that such converts have not only become acculturated to Jewish ways but have also been detached from Gentile clique groups.[32]

The first Jewish missionary society of modern times was organized by an American, David Horowitz, a Swedish-born journalist. Horowitz had an Orthodox Jewish background and was married to a convert. In 1944 he incorporated the United Israel World Union, "an international movement to disseminate the Decalogue Faith both within and beyond the confines of Jewry." He gained little support from either rabbis or Jewish laymen, apparently because of the kind of Judaism he advocated. He called for a reunion of "the two separated houses of Israel whose breach has remained unhealed since the split of the Commonwealth after Solomon's reign." Proselytes of this movement established their own congregations in Wilbur, West Virginia, and West Olive, Michigan.[33]

In 1958, Robert Gordis, a leading American Conservative rabbi, issued a call for a conference of national Jewish religious organizations and rabbis to discuss all aspects of Jewish missionary activities. He specifically suggested the establishment of a pilot missionary effort in Japan, where there seemed to be great interest in Judaism and where the small number of Christians would not complicate interfaith relations. He advocated information centers for the United States. His call for missionary activities was motivated by the need to compensate for those Jews lost during World War II and those being "spiritually asphyxiated under communism," as well as the benefits which Judaism offered Gentiles theologically and in family and personal relations.[34]

In 1959, with promised rabbinical support, Ben Maccabee, a refugee from Nazi Germany and a Chicago engineer, led the effort to organize the Jewish Information Society. He was supported by many prominent Reform and Conservative rabbis and laymen. The society published a monthly journal from 1960 until 1969. It included articles explaining aspects of Judaism and frequent testimonials from converts to Judaism.[35] The society's purpose was clearly conversionist, and it was the most sustained and broadly based effort to win converts to Judaism in modern times, but, once again, it floundered from general lack of interest by Jews. In a personal communication, Maccabee writes that "promises of financial and literary contributions were reneged. . . . I am sorry to report that there are not even ten dedicated persons or foundations willing to make subtsantial contributions to the cause. . . . I nevertheless persisted spending thirteen years and substantial funds until illness stopped me."

In 1949, Leo Baeck, the leading liberal rabbi of Germany before and during World War II, spoke of the mission of Israel.

> Mankind is hungry and thirsts for that which Judaism can say, what Jews full of Judaism can say. Many an example can be remembered. Judaism became, so to speak, attractive to the gentiles and many a one became a proselyte, educated people, high-minded people. Should we not begin anew? Should we not send our missionaries to Asia, to East Asia and to other places to the people there waiting for us? We are in need of expansion for our own sake.[36]

This most eloquent plea brought only a "confused, evasive and unimaginative" response.[37] Allen S. Maller, a Reform rabbi committed to this mission, sees it as the Jewish "obligation to teach all men and to welcome them into the Jewish people. . . . There can be no reason to prefer an assimilated Jew who has no desire to be Jewish to an interested gentile unless one believes in racial theories for either Jews or gentiles." [38]

The absence of a central Jewish secular or religious organization, and generally inadequate statistical records by the numerous national Jewish organizations of all kinds in this area, make an estimate of the number of converts to Judaism most tenuous. David Max Eichhorn, a Reform rabbi who has maintained a zealous interest in this subject for several decades, provides the most detailed data. In 1954, he estimated that Reform rabbis converted between 1,000 and 1,200 per year and Conservative rabbis between 500 and 550. At this time 333 members of the Central Conference of American Rabbis indicated that they had converted 855 men and 3,390 women during their ministries. Another 120 members estimated their conversions at 1,193 men and 4,106 women. By calculating the number of rabbis, 453, with the number of conversions, 9,544, and their years in the rabbinate, 7,744 Eichhorn found that rate of conversion was 1.2 per year per rabbi.[39] Rabbi Leon Fram of Detroit reported twenty-seven conversions during 1952–53, and Rabbi Morris Goldstein of San Francisco specified 125 for the five-year period 1948–53.[40] Eichhorn estimated in 1963 that between 2,000 and 3,000 non-Jews were converting annually.[41]

Maller in 1967 estimated that 7,000 converts came into Judaism annually. He felt that by 1980 there would be more than 100,000 families in which one parent would be a convert. This would be 10 percent of the families formed in a fifteen-year period.[42]

It may be assumed that the rate is much higher now, with the growing number of intermarriages and somewhat matched by rabbinically sponsored conversion classes. In addition, the rate of conversion seems to rise with younger Jews. In a Providence study of 1963, the rate of conversion of wives of Jewish males sixty years and over was 0 percent. The rate of those fifty-nine years and younger varied between 33.3 percent and 100 percent.[43] This is borne out further in a 1971 survey indicating that while one in three Reform Jews of the sample aged twenty to twenty-four intermarry, three out of four of their spouses convert to Judaism.[44] The national Jewish population study indicated that 26.7 percent of the non-Jewish husbands of Jewish wifes converted. Almost 50 percent of non-Jewish wives of Jewish men converted, while only 8.3 percent of the both the non-Jewish wives and husbands identified themselves as Jews.[45]

Throughout Jewish history many converts, perhaps most of them, converted because of marriage to a Jew. Some, including those who strongly favor conversion, estimate that 90 or 95 percent come to Judaism because of marriage.[46] This practice, however, has been generally condemned as resulting in insincere conversions and conversions of convenience rather than from conviction.

Richard Rubenstein strongly disagrees with this view. First of all, he contends, a healthy reason for conversion is to seek to have a religiously unified home. In addition, he maintains that Gentiles often consciously seek to become Jewish, or may even unconsciously want to identify with Jews. Marriage to a Jewish mate provides a socially accepted motive for conversion. He writes: ". . . marriage is the best rather than the worst reason for conversion today. Young people create the first atom of community life by forming a family. They share each other's fate and destiny. It is best that this explicitly be shared within a common religio-ethnic community." [47]

The following is at least a partial profile of the background characteristics of converts and those who marry them.[48] The typical convert is a non-Jewish woman married to a Jewish man. (Conservative rabbis report one male convert to every six female converts, while Reform rabbis, one male to every four females.)[49] Families with Jewish converts are of distinctly higher social status than other Jewish change groups. Spouses of converts report a greater amount of Jewish education than those whose wives do not convert. The spouses of converts are also active in Jewish religious and organizational life. Those who intermarry without conversion are frequently marginal religio-ethnic members marrying similar persons. They have less religious training and education than most of their faith. After marriage such persons frequently reduce or eliminate any involvement in their childhood faith.

The faithfulness of converts has been attested to. In his 1954 survey of 785 Reform and Conservative rabbis, Eichhorn discovered that the majority of the rabbis ranked Jewish-born members and converts of their congregations about equal in their Jewish loyalties and interests, but they also tended to describe converts as more loyal more frequently than they accorded this designation to the Jewish-born.[50] For this reason, Eichhorn views converts as a precious spiritual asset and a challenge to the Jewish-born to be more worthy of their priceless spiritual inheritance.

This accords well with the Lazerwitz and Lenn studies. Lazerwitz found that converts usually blended successfully into their new religio-ethnic community and were often more active than persons born Jewish.[51] Utilizing a religiosity index including belief in God, Jewish identification, ethical living, and other such factors, Lenn found that Reform Jews with two Jewish parents ranked 47 percent on the scale against 77 percent for those with one non-Jewish parent. Reform Jews married to converts are more religious than those married to born Jews, while those married to spouses who have not converted are still more religious. Furthermore, those who intermarry and remain Jewish tend to be more religious ritualistically than those whose spouses are born Jews.[52]

There are records of individual blacks professing Judaism in the antebellum South of the United States. Most of the members of the small urban black Jewish sects that originated after World War I usually attached themselves to a charismatic figure. These sects were frequently syncretistic. The major groups are the B'nei Israel, the Commandment Keepers, Temple of the Gospel of the Kingdom, and Kohel Beth B'nai Yisrael. They may number between 2,000 and 6,000 members. Relations with the white Jewish community are most tenuous. After World War II small numbers converted, attaching themselves to established congregations.[53] In 1970 a small group of Chicago black Jews settled in Dimona, Israel, after a brief period in Liberia. Deteriorating relations between Jews and blacks and growing black ethnicity and racial pride probably preclude any sizable conversion to Judaism.

CONCLUSIONS

The integrity of Jewish communities in the Diaspora, potentially even in Israel, is threatened by diminished relative and absolute numbers. Attrition is brought about by increasing intermarriage, frequently without conversion and therefore losses from Judaism, low fertility rates, strong pressures from acculturation and absorption into the general culture, freely in some countries and forced in others, together with a general malaise about Judaism and Jewish culture and affairs. In Israel many Jews identify more as Israeli nationals than as members of a religious group. There is also the problem of the large numbers of Arabs both in Israel and the occupied territories, people who threaten to overwhelm the Jews because of their very high birth rate.

The process of acculturation is thwarted somewhat where institutional and cultural life is strong. Events and developments such as the Holocaust, Arab threats to Israel, anti-Semitism in one place or another, and the rise of ethnicity especially in America have helped reinforce Jewish identity.

At the same time, many of the special benefits that accrued to Jews because they were Jews are gone. Economic specialization is far less important than it was, since economic systems have become more open, inducing utilization of the best person for a particular economic role regardless of any other characteristic. Additionally, Jews are no longer favored by some ruling elites as buffers between themselves and the dominated classes of their societies.

Theological belief seems to be less important to more and more Jews. The Reconstructionist movement rejects the ideology of a chosen people and a Jewish mission. Jews generally continue to see themselves as a special, separate group, almost a super-tribe, dispersed throughout the world but still bound together by ties of lineage, history, and destiny.

All these factors, together with the general Jewish malaise toward seeking converts, both from among those who marry Jews but especially from others, makes it difficult to see where Jewries will gain the persons they need to maintain their present numbers, let alone grow numerically. Major, well-organized missionary efforts, which could maintain and even increase the number of Jews, seem remote.

NOTES

1. Erich Rosenthal, "Studies of Jewish Intermarriage in the United States," *American Jewish Year Book*, vol. 64, (New York, 1963), p. 8.
2. *Ibid.*, p. 9. Erich Rosenthal, "Acculturation without Assimilation—The Jewish Community of Chicago, Illinois," *American Journal of Sociology*, vol. 66, (1960–61), 11/(1960), pp. 275, 281.
3. *Ibid.*, pp. 275, 286.
4. Unless otherwise noted, statistics of rates of intermarriage are included in Table 1, page
5. George E. Johnson, "Comparing the Inmarried and Intermarried," *Analysis*, no. 32 (January 15, 1973), p. 2.
6. Rosenthal (1960–61), p. 288.
7. Rosenthal (1963), p. 51.
8. Rosenthal, "Jewish Intermarriage in Indiana," *American Jewish Year Book*, vol. 68 (New York, 1967).
9. Morris Fishberg, *The Jews* (New York, 1911), p. 214.
10. Rosenthal (1963), p. 31.
11. Sidney Goldstein and Calvin Goldscheider, "Social and Demographic Aspects of Jewish Intermarriage," *Social Problems*, vol. XIII (1966), p. 398.
12. Johnson, *op. cit.*, pp. 4 f.
13. Marshall Sklare, *America's Jews* (New York, 1971), p. 184.
14. Theodore Lenn and associates, *Rabbi and Synagogue in Reform Judaism* (West Hartford, Conn., 1972), p. 218.
15. Andrew Greeley, follow-up of *The Great Aspirations Study* (Report no. 82, National Opinion Research Center, University of Chicago) by James A. Davis and Norman Bradburn (Chicago, 1961). Personal communication.
16. Paul C. Glick, "Intermarriage and Fertility Patterns among Persons in Major Religious Groups," *Eugenics Quarterly*, vol. VII (1960), pp. 32, 34, 37.
17. Goldstein and Goldscheider, *op. cit.*, pp. 397 f.
18. Moshe Davis, "Mixed Marriage in Western Jewry: Historical Background to the Jewish Response," *CCAR Journal*, vol. X (1962), p. 6.
19. *Ibid.*, pp. 6 f.
20. *Ibid.*, p. 7.
21. Glick, *op. cit.*, p. 35; Ruby Jo Reeves Kennedy, "What Has Social Science to Say about Intermarriage?" in *Intermarriage and Jewish Life: A Symposium*, ed. Werner J. Cahnman (New York, 1960), p. 31; Louis Rosenberg, "Intermarriage in Canada," in *ibid.*, p. 62.
22. Marshall Sklare and Joseph Greenblum, *Jewish Identity on the Suburban Frontier* (New York, 1967), pp. 309, 311, 314, 315.
23. Bernard Lazerwitz, "Intermarriage and Conversion," *Jewish Journal of Sociology*, vol. XIII (1971), p. 60.

24. Maria H. Levinson and Daniel J. Levinson, "Jews Who Intermarry: Socio-Psychological Bases of Ethnic Identity and Change," *Yivo Annual of Jewish Social Science,* vol. 12 (1958–59), p. 130.
25. Sklare, *America's Jews,* p. 183.
26. *Ibid.,* p. 203.
27. Abraham Shusterman, "The Last Two Centuries," in *Conversion to Judaism: A History and Analysis,* ed. David Max Eichhorn (New York, 1965), p. 141.
28. *Ibid.,* p. 143.
29. *Ibid.,* p. 148.
30. *Ibid.,* pp. 148, 165 ff.
31. Lenn, *op. cit.,* pp. 184 f.
32. Sklare and Greenblum, *op. cit.,* pp. 272 f.
33. Shusterman, *op. cit.,* p. 164; *Encyclopedia Judaica,* vol. XIII, p. 1191.
34. Robert Gordis, "Has the Time Arrived for Jewish Missionaries?" *National Jewish Monthly* (March 1958), pp. 6 f., 24 ff.
35. *The Jewish Information Society: Its Background, Purpose and Program* (Chicago, 1959); Shusterman, *op. cit.,* p. 169; *Jewish Information* (Chicago, 1960–69).
36. Leo Baeck, "The Mission of Judaism," *World Union for Progressive Judaism, Report Sixth International Conference* (London, 1949), p. 74.
37. Allen S. Maller, "The Mission of Israel and Reform Theology," *Reconstructionist,* vol. XXXII (1966), p. 16.
38. *Ibid.,* pp. 19, 21.
39. David Max Eichhorn, "Conversion to Judaism by Reform and Conservative Rabbis," *Jewish Social Studies,* vol. XVI (1954), p. 301.
40. *Ibid.,* p. 302.
41. Albert I. Gordon, *The Nature of Conversion* (Boston, 1967), p. 5.
42. Allen S. Maller, "From Gentile into Jew," *Reconstructionist,* vol. XXXIII (June 23, 1967), pp. 25, 27.
43. Goldstein and Goldscheider, *op. cit.,* p. 393.
44. Lenn, *op. cit.,* pp. 217 f.
45. Johnson, *op. cit.,* p. 4.
46. Gordon, *op. cit.,* p. 5.
47. Richard Rubenstein, "Intermarriage and Conversion," *Reconstructionist,* vol. XXVIII (April 29, 1962), p. 20.
48. Lazerwitz, *op. cit.,* pp. 42, 48, 52, 58 f.
49. Erich Rosenthal, "Some Recent Studies about the Extent of Jewish Outmarriage in the U.S.A.," in *Intermarriage and Jewish Life: A Symposium,* ed. Werner J. Cahnman (New York, 1960), p. 88.
50. David Max Eichhorn, "Conversion: Requirements and Results," in *Intermarriage and Jewish Life: A Symposium,* ed. Werner J. Cahnman (New York, 1960), p. 120.
51. Lazerwitz, *op. cit.,* p. 58.
52. Lenn, *op. cit.,* p. 261.
53. *Encyclopedia Judaica,* vol. IV, pp. 1068 ff.; Howard Brotz, *The Black Jews of Harlem* (New York, 1970); Murray Polnar, "Being Black and Jewish," *National Jewish Monthly,* vol. 87 (October 1972), pp. 38–43.

THE ABOLITIONISTS AND THE JEWS:

SOME FURTHER THOUGHTS

By

LOUIS RUCHAMES

University of Massachusetts, Boston

About twenty-five years ago, in a paper presented at the annual meeting of the American Jewish Historical Society,[1] this writer delivered a rather vigorous critique of the views of Isaac Mayer Wise and Bertram Korn—especially of the latter's volume, *American Jewry and the Civil War*[2]—concerning the abolitionists and other antislavery leaders. The paper was essentially polemical in nature. It consisted, for the most part, of a defense of the antislavery movement against the accusations that had been made against it by Wise and Korn, who, in the words of this writer, pictured abolitionists "as power-hungry politicians, heedless of the welfare of minority groups other than Negroes, and guilty of prejudice and discriminatory acts toward foreigners and Jews."[3] It did not pretend to be a complete evaluation of all that had been written by antislavery men and women about foreigners and Jews. It sought rather to provide evidence warranting a different and more sympathetic interpretation of a misunderstood and much maligned group of American reformers. In essence, it argued, "their efforts were concentrated upon helping the free Negro and the slave, for these were the most oppressed elements of the population of their day; but their devotion to equal rights extended also to the Jew, the foreigner and members of other minority groups. Although one sometimes finds in their letters and other writings expressions of racial stereotypes and prejudices, concerning both Negroes and Jews, these are infrequent and atypical, and do not affect their devotion to equal rights for Negroes and Jews."[4]

In the perspective of twenty-five years, a rereading of the essay evokes several thoughts. First, because of its limited theme and polemical nature, the essay presents a negative impression of Korn's volume, one that does not accord with this writer's view of the volume as a whole. For *American Jewry and the Civil War* is an important contribution to our understanding of the history of American Jewry during the Civil War, of the many political and social issues which it faced, and its relations to the broader American community. Whatever Korn's views of abolitionist attitudes toward the Jews, these constitute but a very small portion of the entire work, which is a distinguished contribution to the history of the period.

Second, although the essay mentioned abolitionist "racial stereotypes and prejudices," it emphasized that these were "infrequent and atypical" and did not weaken the abolitionist devotion to equal rights for Jews and Negroes. It may not be amiss, however, to discuss the nature of these stereotypes and prejudices, some of which are to be found in the writings of the most prominent abolitionist, William Lloyd Garrison. There are several references to Jews and Judaism in his letters and editorials, almost always of a religious and derogatory nature. Thus, on September 23, 1836, in a letter to Samuel J. May, a prominent abolitionist and Unitarian clergyman, who was then a minister in South Scituate, Massachusetts, Garrison writes as follows:

> O, the rottenness of Christendom! Judaism and Romanism are the leading features of Protestantism. I am forced to believe, that, as it respects the greater portion of professing Christians in this land, Christ has died in vain. In their traditions, their forms and ceremonies, their vain janglings, their self-righteousness, their will-worship, their sectarian zeal and devotion, their infallibility and exclusiveness, they are Pharisees and Sadducees, they are Papists and Jews.[5]

A year later, in another letter, he exclaims, "What an oath-taking, war-making, man-enslaving religion is that which is preached, professed, and practised in this country! . . . Its main pillars are Judaism and Popery. . . ."[6] Finally, in a reply to a newspaper editor in Boston, who had attacked him for Christian infidelity and for non-attendance at Sunday church services, Garrison writes: "It is one of your legal impostures to represent a building made of bricks and mortar as 'the house of God' There is no such holy locality, or holy building on earth, and if you were not groping in Jewish darkness, you would perceive this truth." [7]

In these excerpts, Garrison expresses his abandonment of the Protestant Christian orthodoxy in which he was raised, and criticizes the emphasis upon ritual, ceremony, and attendance at formal church services as expressions of religion. But in his denunciation of Protestantism and orthodox Protestants of his day, he reveals his religious bias, absorbed in his youth, as a fundamentalist Protestant, taught to regard both Judaism and Catholicism as benighted religions representative of the most harmful religious attitudes and practices. The Judaism which Garrison has in mind is defined by certain New Testament writers, and although his mastery of the Old Testament, especially the prophetic portions, equaled his mastery of the New Testament, these are seen through the eyes of the New Testament writers. Thus, although time and again he attacks the priests and rabbis as representatives of Judaism, he nowhere appears to associate the Hebrew prophets, whom he quotes time and again, with Jews or Judaism. Garrison's view of Judaism, at least during the 1830s and 1840s, does not reveal any acquaintance with Jewish scholarship or Jewish sources concerning Jews and Judaism. Moreover, at no time does he draw a distinction between ancient Judaism and the Jews and Judaism of his own day; of these latter he seems to have no knowledge.

Any evaluation of Garrison's attitude toward Jews should include some reference to his relationships to two prominent Jews of the antebellum period: Ernestine Rose, the woman's rights advocate and abolitionist, and Mordecai Manuel Noah, Democratic leader, playwright, editor, opponent of the antislavery movement, and sometimes regarded as an apologist for slavery.

Garrison, apparently, first met Ernestine Rose in the early 1840s—she seems to have been the first Jew whom he knew personally—and although she was by no means always in agreement with his views on antislavery or woman's rights, he had a deep admiration for her abilities and idealism, referred to her in the most laudatory terms,[8] and often reprinted her speeches in the *Liberator*. Their friendship continued even after 1869, when Ernestine Rose and her husband left the United States to resettle in England. As late as 1877, about two years before Garrison's death, she sent a note of condolence to him on the death of his wife, Helen.[9]

Accounts of her speeches in the *Liberator* sometimes carried references to her Jewishness, and to the fact that her father was a rabbi. Although she herself was an atheist and did not participate in any way in Jewish

communal life or express publicly her views about the religion or culture
of Judaism, she did sometimes write and speak about the oppression and
discrimination which Jews have had to endure throughout history and in
her own day and of the need for freedom and equality for her people.

But it is important to note that, although Garrison knew that Rose
was Jewish and the daughter of a rabbi,[10] he rarely referred to her Jewishness and never intimated that her reformist activities and beliefs cast
any credit upon the Jewish people or Judaism itself. In fact, when re-
printing some of her speeches the *Liberator* identified her as "one born
and educated in Poland," [11] and as "a native of Poland," [12] but made no
mention of her Jewishness.

On the other hand, when referring to Noah and Noah's anti-abolitionist
writings, Garrison did so in the most derogatory and antagonistic terms
and rarely failed to mention Noah's Jewishness or the odium which, in
his opinion, Noah's views and activities cast upon Judaism and the
Jewish people. Thus, on May 20, 1842, Garrison reprinted in the *Liberator* a charge by Noah, who was then a judge in New York City, to the
grand jury of the Court of Sessions of New York. The charge expressed
sentiments hostile to the abolitionists. In commenting on it, Garrison
refers to Noah as "a Jewish unbeliever, the enemy of Christ and Liberty."
Several years later, in the *Liberator*,[13] Garrison reprinted a portion of an
article by Noah from the *New York Sunday Messenger,* Noah's newspaper, and in his comments referred to Noah as "the miscreant Jew." In
September of the same year, in the *Liberator*,[14] he refers to Noah as
"that lineal descendant of the monsters who nailed Jesus to the cross between two thieves," and ends his comment with: "Shylock will have his
'pound of flesh' at whatever cost."

In his later years, i.e., during the 1860s and 1870s, Garrison's attitudes
toward Jews and Judaism seem to have mellowed somewhat, and one
notes signs of perhaps a greater recognition of the contribution of ancient
Judaism to the spirit of antebellum reform. There is an interesting letter,
written by Garrison when in England, dated Huntley Lodge, Edinburgh,
July 15, 1867, to the Reverend S. Alfred Steinthal (1826–1910), a Unitarian minister of Bridgewater, England, active in the temperance movement and a longtime friend of Garrison. The letter expresses Garrison's
regret over a misunderstanding that had occurred in Manchester, England, as a result of certain remarks that he had made in an address at a
banquet in that city. The relevant extract is self-explanatory.

Thanks for your letter of the 10th inst. The reading of it caused equal amusement, surprise, and regret—the regret having reference to the annoyance caused good Dr. Gottheil by the ludicrous perversion of the term I used, "Fourth of Ju-liars," (not Jew-liars) in my remarks at the Manchester [England] banquet, by such of his people as were not present. I am thus admonished that it is a hazardous thing to indulge in punning! As soon as I received your letter, I sent an explanatory note to Dr. G., showing that, so far from having cast any imputation upon Jewish vera-city, I was "an Israelite indeed, in whom there was no guile," in the matter referred to, and that they were those who professed to be Chris-tians to whom my criticism was applied. I have given him liberty to publish my note in any way he may think best.[15]

The "Dr. Gottheil" referred to by Garrison was Gustav Gottheil (1827–1903), rabbi of the Manchester Congregation of British Jews from 1860 to 1873, and thereafter rabbi of Temple Emanu-El in New York for twenty-three years until his retirement as rabbi emeritus at the age of seventy-two. Garrison may have been especially solicitous of his feelings because of Gottheil's antislavery views, expressed in a volume en-titled *Moses versus Slavery* and published in Manchester in 1861.

On his way to England in 1867, Garrison had an encounter aboard ship with three Jewish former slaveholders. He describes the incident in a letter to his wife dated May 15, 1867.[16] "Sitting opposite me at the table," he writes "are three German Jews, Louisiana planters, who have lost all their slaves by the rebellion, and who profess to regret their loss chiefly be-cause their slaves, now that they are free, will be unable to take care of themselves! Of these Israelites it cannot be said that they are without guile; nevertheless, they are unobtrusive in manner and very respectful (as indeed all on board are) to Mr. Thompson and myself."

Most interesting of all, perhaps, is a letter by Garrison to the Reverend Samuel Hunt, a Protestant clergyman of Massachusetts, who assisted Henry Wilson, Republican senator from Massachusetts and vice-president of the United States during Grant's second term in office. Hunt had acted as private secretary to Wilson in 1873–75, assisted Wilson in writing the three-volume *History of the Rise and Fall of the Slave Power in America* (Boston, 1872–77; reprinted by Negro Universities Press, New York, 1969), and completed the work after Wilson's death in 1875. Hunt sent Garrison the page-proofs for chapter XLIX of volume III, entitled "Influence of Christian Churches and Associations." In his letter, dated Roxbury, December 26, 1876, Garrison offers the following criticism:

On page 822 you say, "Antislavery was the child of Christian faith," but why any more so than of the Jewish faith? What can surpass the denunciations against oppressing the poor and needy that can be found in the Old Testament, "Deliver him that is spoiled out of the hand of the oppressor"—"undo the heavy burdens, break every yoke, and let the oppressed go free"—"your hands are full of blood; seek judgment, deliver the oppressed"—"he that stealeth a man, and selleth him, or if he be found in his hand, he shall surely be put to death"—&c., &c. Quotations of this nature, and reiterated "in season and out of season," exerted a powerful influence in discussing the duty and necessity of abolishing slavery.[17]

The one abolitionist who equaled and probably even exceeded Garrison in his tendency to identify the negative characteristics of individual Jews with the entire Jewish people, and even with the principles of the Jewish faith, was Edmund Quincy, of Boston, who often edited the *Liberator* in Garrison's absence and was a prominent abolitionist leader. Quincy was a Boston blue-blood, his father having been a member of Congress, mayor of Boston, and president of Harvard University. A graduate of Harvard University in 1827, he joined the Massachusetts Anti-Slavery Society in 1837 and the American Anti-Slavery Society the following year. During the ensuing years, he was corresponding secretary of the Massachusetts society from 1844 to 1853 and vice-president of the national society in 1853 and 1856–59. He was also an editor of the Massachusetts *Abolitionist* in 1839, the *National Anti-Slavery Standard* in 1844 and subsequent years, and contributed numerous essays to these and other newspapers and journals.

As an example of Quincy's opinions of Jews and Judaism, one may cite an essay in the *Liberator,* August 10, 1848, signed "Q" for Quincy, entitled "A Jew and a Christian." Quincy cites certain of Mordecai M. Noah's opinions of the abolitionists, of blacks, and of slavery, and refers to Noah as "that Judge in Israel, Mordecai Manasseh Noah, the leader of the chosen seed into the land flowing with milk and honey on Grand Island, and the charger of grand juries to indict abolitionists for being mobbed. . . ." Quincy then gives his opinion of Noah: "It would be difficult even for American Christians to match this Jew for meanness and servility. We think none the worse of a man for being a Jew, but we must say, that if this Judge be a fair specimen of the race, it is no wonder they have been an insulted and despised people."

Quincy's opinions of Jews were expressed, too, in a novel that he wrote in 1854, *Wensley, a Story with a Moral* (reprinted in 1885 in *Wensley and Other Stories*). The only Jews in the novel are villains and obnoxious characters. They are Aaron Abrahams; his wife, portrayed as a loud-mouthed shrew; and one son, whose name is also apparently Aaron. Quincy, it seems, did not know that in a traditional Jewish family, a son did not have the same first name as his father. The son, who is de-scribed as "a sort of Jew lawyer," is the real villain. But the father is mentioned as having been a commissary to the American Army in 1777. He is described as follows by another character in the novel: "I guess I had reason to know him. I know he almost starved us; and would quite, had not a lot of our men threatened to burn his house down about his ears for him. They tried to do it, too. Ben Simpkins was hanged for it, poor fellow!" (p. 252). Referring to the Abrahams home during the Revolution, the same character remarks: "It was an awful wrecking-place, and old Abrahams's house was full of cabin furniture and things. Folks said he had got rich by wrecking. He was rich, any way. But I don't believe such riches is any good to people" (p. 252).

Two other abolitionists deserve mention for their attitudes toward Jews Samuel J. May and Nathaniel Peabody Rogers. The former, a native of Boston, was one of the pioneers of the antislavery movement, an early friend of Garrison, and a Unitarian minister highly respected and loved by all who knew him, friends and opponents alike. As a minister, he served churches in Brooklyn, Connecticut (1822–36), South Scituate, Massachusetts (1836–42), and Syracuse, New York (1845–67), where he spent the last years of his life. In a volume entitled *Memoir of Samuel J. May* (Boston, 1873), prepared by George B. Emerson, Samuel May, and Thomas J. Mumford, much of which consists of May's autobi-ography, there appears a sketch by May of his earliest relationships with Jews. The selection is worth quoting in its entirety.[18]

If the children of my day were taught, among other things, to dread, if not despise, Jews, a very different lesson was impressed upon my young heart. There was but one family of the despised children of the house of Israel resident in Boston,—the family of Moses Michael Hays: a man much respected, not only on account of his large wealth, but for his many personal virtues and the high culture and great excellence of his wife, his son Judah, and his daughters,—especially Catherine and Slowey. His house, far down in Hanover Street, then one of the fashionable streets of the town, was the abode of hospitality; and his family moved in what were then the first circles of society. He and his truly good wife were hospitable, not to the rich alone, but also to the poor. Many indigent families were fed pretty regularly from his table. They would come especially after his frequent dinner-parties, and were sure to be made welcome, not to the crumbs only, but to ampler portions of the food that might be left.

Always, on Saturday, he expected a number of friends to dine with him. A full-length table was always spread, and loaded with the luxuries of the season; and he loved to see it surrounded by a few regular visitors and others especially invited. My father was a favorite guest. He was regarded by Mr. Hays and his whole family as a particular friend, their chosen counsellor in times of perplexity, and their comforter in the days of their affliction. My father seldom failed to dine at Mr. Hays's on Saturday, and often took me with him; for he was sure I should meet refined company there.

Both Uncle and Aunt Hays (for so I called them) were fond of children, particularly of me; and I was permitted to stay with them several days, and even weeks, together. And I can never forget, not merely their kind, but their conscientious care of me. I was the child of Christian parents, and they took especial pains that I should lose nothing of religious training so long as I was permitted to abide with them. Every night, I was required, on going to bed, to repeat my Christian hymns and prayers to them, or else to an excellent Christian servant woman who lived with them many years. I witnessed their religious exercises,— their fastings and their prayers,—and was made to feel that they worshipped the Unseen Almighty and All-merciful one. Of course I grew up without any prejudice against Jews,—or any other religionists, because they did not believe as my father and mother believed.

Nathaniel Peabody Rogers (1794–1846) was a well-known abolitionist in his day, a New Hampshire man, a lawyer, and, finally, editor of the *Herald of Freedom,* which he established in Concord, New Hampshire, in 1838. On April 25, 1845, in the *Herald of Freedom,* in an essay entitled "The Jews and Holy Land," he expressed his views of Mordecai Noah's efforts at Jewish restoration in Palestine. These views are especially interesting for what they reveal of the opposition of a radical Christian toward Zionism, an opposition repeated in almost the very same terms by many radicals, Jews and Christians, through the succeeding decades of the nineteenth and twentieth centuries. Rogers is opposed to nationalism as contrary to a universal humanity, he dislikes religious distinctions, he fails to understand the religious and nationalistic attachment of Jews to Palestine, and he regards any American Jewish effort to rebuild a Jewish

Palestine as a weakening of the struggle for justice and equal rights in the United States. Because it appears to be the only extant evaluation of American Zionism by an abolitionist, the major portion of the essay is reproduced here.

Now, I desire most truly, that an end may be put to the religious persecution of the Jews. Christendom has persecuted them as barbarously as ever Jews did Christians. And it ought to stop. But then the rescue of the Jews, is of no more consequence than the rescue of any other people—of Turks, Greeks, Polanders, or American slaves. The intolerance and persecution inflicted on them, ought to cease, not because they are Jews,—nor because they are Old Testament people, but because they are men, women and children. It is not because they were a "chosen people," and had Abraham, Isaac and Jacob among them, and Moses and David. Nor because it was prophesied they would return. But, because they are sufferers under persecution, and it is base and bigoted and barbarous to inflict it upon them. Because persecution is grievous to be borne, and wrong to inflict.

As to the Jews flocking to Palestine, I would say of it, as I do of the slaves running to Canada,—and colored people "returning" to Africa. So long as Jews can't have quarter, any where out of Palestine, I should advise them to run there, and the slave to Canada, that is, if they could have quarter when they get there. But were I Major Noah, I would put in for a better destiny for my countrymen. I would go for their rights where they are. I will join him in an agitation for their liberation here, on the spot, as many of them as are in the country. It is their country, as much as it is anybody's. They need not run to "Holy Land." They have a right to this country. Not as Jews, against Americans, but as men. As all other people have a right here. And I would not go to Jerusalem, or Jordan. New England or New York is as good as Palestine, and a great deal better. And Connecticut River, or the Merrimack, or the Old Hudson, are either of them as good rivers as any Jordan that ever run into a dead or a live sea. And as "Holy," for that matter. The Jews had better stay where they are, every where, for all going to Jerusalem. If they can better their condition, by migrating, I would migrate. I would go East—West—South—any point of compass,—to *better my real condition*. But they better leave off being Jews and turn *mankind*. They will make as good folks as any body. And if these Americans won't tolerate them, or allow them human rights here, I tell Major Noah, the Herald of Freedom shall be at *their service,* for an agitation that shall shake Christendom—till its bigotry is shaken out of it! Not that the Herald can *alone* shake Christendom, unless Major Noah will help us *write for it.*

But, then, if Jews can't have a home, where they happen to be, the Major, and everybody else, ought to go in for a shaking of the Earth about it. And the Major would be better employed in carrying on such an agitation for Jewish Rights, than in summoning Israelites from the four quarters of the globe, to Palestine, Goat Island, or any other island in the Niagara River. . . .

And the idea of keeping up this Jewish distinction, is inhuman and unwise. It is time it was merged, and annihilated. In Humanity, as in "Christ Jesus," as Paul says, "there is neither Jew nor Greek." And there ought to be none. It is high time all these hostile distinctions were annihilated; these obstacles to the harmony and fellowship of mankind, done away. Down with all of them.

Much more may be said on the subject of abolitionist-Jewish relationships and attitudes and much more research is needed. Although the abolitionists and other antislavery men and women were in the forefront of the effort to achieve a more just society, and opposed discrimination in all its forms, they were not without prejudices and some of the religious and racial stereotypes which prevailed in the society of their day. In part, these prejudices existed in the absence of any direct contact with Jews and a sparsity of Jewish inhabitants, especially in Boston. They were often the result of either literary influences, as was probably true of Edmund Quincy, or fundamentalist Protestant indoctrination, as with Garrison. Yet, while deserving condemnation, they must be seen within the context of the consistent devotion of the abolitionists to equal rights for all men in the United States and their opposition to discrimination in this country against any racial, religious, or national group.

NOTES

1. Subsequently printed as "The Abolitionists and the Jews," in *Publications of the American Jewish Historical Society,* XLII (December 1952), 131–55.
2. Philadelphia: Jewish Publication Society, 1951.
3. Ruchames, p. 131.
4. *Ibid.,* p. 132.
5. Louis Ruchames, ed., *The Letters of William Lloyd Garrison,* vol. II, *A House Dividing Against Itself, 1836–1840* (Cambridge, Mass., 1971), p. 178.
6. Letter dated August 14, 1837, to Oliver Johnson, *ibid.,* p. 281.
7. Letter dated October 20, 1839, to the editor of the *Spectator, ibid.,* p. 314.
8. In the *Liberator,* March 23, 1855, Garrison characterized her as "one of the most remarkable women, and one of the ablest and most eloquent public speakers in this country."
9. Yuri Suhl, *Ernestine Rose and the Battle for Human Rights* (New York, 1959), p. 271.
10. See the report in the *Liberator,* October 8, 1852, of the National Woman's Rights Convention at Syracuse, New York, which describes Ernestine Rose's speech, and notes that she was introduced as "a Polish lady" and as having had an early education "in the Jewish faith." It quotes her as saying that "even that downtrodden people, the Jews, were sensible of the wrongs inflicted upon woman."

    On May 16, 1856, the *Liberator* reprinted from the *Excelsior* a short biographical sketch by "L. E. B.," which mentioned that "her father was a very pious and learned rabbi" and referred to her "strict observance of all the religious rites and ceremonies of the Jewish faith," in her youth.
11. June 1, 1855.
12. June 8, 1855.
13. May 18, 1849.
14. September 21, 1849.
15. The original is in the Boston Public Library.
16. The original is in the Boston Public Library.
17. The original of the letter is to be found in the Sophia Smith Collection, Smith College, Northampton, Mass.

    It may be noted that Hunt kept his original formulation. See vol. III, p. 718.
18. Pp. 15–16.

ISAAC MAYER WISE'S
PRONAOS TO HOLY WRIT

By

SAMUEL SANDMEL

Hebrew Union College—Jewish Institute of Religion, Cincinnati

Diverse factors make Isaac Mayer Wise's *Pronaos to Holy Writ* a curious and even interesting book. It was published in 1891. The title page adds to the name the following: "Establishing, on Documentary Evidence, the Authorship, Date, Form and Content of Each of Its Books, and the Authenticity of the Pentateuch." The latter four words are in larger type than the preceding clauses, though not in as large a type as the title itself. Essentially the book is a defense of the Mosaic authorship of the Pentateuch, though its scope is much broader.

The book is curious in at least two ways. It is an assault on the Higher Criticism, as exemplified in the German scholarship of the nineteenth century, yet outside the Pentateuch Wise accepts a generous measure of that scholarship. Second, it scrupulously abstains from citing any scholar, or any scholarly book, by name.

Moreover, on the title page Wise is identified as "President of the Hebrew Union College," not as the rabbi of Congregation B'nai Jeshurun. Also, one wonders about the word *pronaos*. The word means literally "before the temple," and appears in the translation of Schliemann's *Troja* (p. 79) in the sense of a vestibule at the front of a temple. Why this erudite word, which necessarily would send a reader to a dictionary?

A term which Wise uses repeatedly is "Negative Criticism": "The science commonly called Modern Biblical Criticism, actually Negative Criticism, on the strength of unscientific methods, holds that the Pentateuch is not composed of original Mosaic material, no Psalms are Davidian, no Proverbs Solomonic, the historical books are unhistorical, the prophecies were written *post festum* [*sic*], there was no revelation, in-

517

spiration or prophecy, must also maintain that the Bible is a compendium of pious or even impious frauds, willful deceptions, unscrupulous misrepresentations . . ." (p. 4). Again: "The authenticity of the Mosaic records is the foundation of all Bible truth."

The book consists of six chapters, with the chapter on the Mosaic authorship coming last. The chapters are the following:

1. "Main Divisions and Claims of Sacred Scriptures"
2. "The First Canon" [1]
3. "The Former Prophets"
4. "The Later Prophets"
5. "Hagiography"
6. "The Authenticity of the Pentateuch"

In Chapter 2, Wise writes in defense of the Mosaic authorship of Deuteronomy (pp. 30–31) and of Genesis (pp. 31–33), as we shall presently see, but he reserves his full exposition to the last chapter.

The scope of the book is broad. *Pronaos* replaces the terms usual among the "Negative Scholars," *Einleitung* in German, *introduction* in English. It seems reasonable to suppose that Wise chose the word *pronaos* deliberately so as to prevent his book from falling into the same category with the books he deemed distasteful. The breadth of the book may possibly be adequately conveyed by the listing above of its chapters; it may be specified, for fullest clarity, that the book provides the same kind of data that a full introduction normally undertook to do. Accordingly, Wise rather systematically goes through the ordinary preliminary matters of listing the contents of Scripture and the main Jewish exegetical materials (Talmud, Midrash, and Targum). He cites, as is normal, the attestations of Josephus and Jerome, the preface to the translation into Greek of Ben Sirach. The only significant omission is Fourth Ezra. He gives the precise references to the ancient sources.

If, on the one hand, Wise is not to be reckoned as a great scholar in rabbinics, there can be no question, on the other hand, of his personal great familiarity with rabbinic literature.

Moreover, Wise was thoroughly familiar with the Tanach[2]; of this there can be no doubt. Accordingly, as one expects, there is little of significance in the Hebrew text which escapes his notice.[3] He finds in the Pentateuch, on a talmudic basis, evidence for the existence of certain scrolls written by Moses.[4] He states that certain "Mosaic scrolls" should be "noticed particularly": the story and poems of Balaam in Num. 23–24[5] and the "Book of Journeys" (Num. 33) and "The Book of the

Wars of Jehovah [*sic*]" of Num. 21:14. Respecting the latter, Wise writes: "This, critics maintain, must be a book older than the Thorah. We maintain that no war of Jehovah could have existed prior to Moses, and Moses was particularly commanded to write, or rather to start, such a book right after the first war of Jehovah, which was waged against Amalek, as recorded in Exodus XVII.14." A footnote reads: "This is suggested by Abraham Ibn Ezra and Targum Yerushalmi to this verse." Wise concludes the section with these words: "Documentary evidence not merely entitles but compels us to maintain that these manuscript [Mosaic] scrolls, preserved and zealously guarded in the national sanctuary, may have been connected with the Mosaic books of Genesis, Covenant,[6] Leviticus, and Deuteronomy, and shaped in the present form of the Five Books of Moses, if not Moses himself performed this task in the last days of his life . . ." (p. 34). So much in brief for his initial statement in his Chapter 2.

In Chapter 3 Wise cites the material in Baba Batra 14b-15a on the authorship of biblical books.[7] His conclusions about authorship normally accord with that talmudic passage, but not slavishly so. He dares to write about Joshua: "The book as now before us was certainly not compiled or edited by Joshua, nor was the author of the Joshua records different from him who wrote the last chapter of Deuteronomy . . ."

For our purposes, it can be sufficient to set forth certain of Wise's opinions which should enable us to move to a reasonable generalized conclusion. These opinions center on the dates he ascribes to biblical literature, plus comments he makes on the authorship. In virtually no case do his statements agree with the scholarly opinions of his time. His opinions as here summarized are intended to reflect his bent and his occasionally capricious independence.

"Joshua was written by him and his scribes and compiled in its present form by the high priest Phineas 1400 B.C. Judges . . . was written in its present form by the prophet Samuel in 1075 B.C. The appendices[8] were written—author unknown—1025 B.C." (p. 48). "There exists no tenable ground to contradict the tradition that Samuel wrote his book and . . . Judges. 1 Samuel XVII to 2 Samuel v. 3 is from the Book of Gad, different in style and tone from the genuine Samuel. . . . 2 Samuel v. 4 to 1 Kings III.28 is from the Book of Nathan . . . named as the chronographer of both David and Solomon (1 Chronicles XXIX.29 and 2 Chronicles IX.29) . . ." (p. 51). "Kings consists of four sections written at different times" (p. 55).

As to the later prophets, "a regular and uninterrupted current of tradition of prophets is recorded in the sacred books" (p. 60). These include Seth, Enoch, Methusaleh, Noah, Shem, and Eber before the time of Abraham. From Abraham to Moses "the succession was Isaac, Jacob, and their wives, Levi, Kehath, Amram and Moses . . ." (p. 61). The earliest of the minor prophets was Joel; no trace is found in the book "of any time after 880 B.C." (p. 67).

Hosea, Amos, Isaiah, and Michah (*sic*) prophesied simultaneously (p. 67). Their dates, however, are Amos, 816–780; Hosea, 750–730; Isaiah, 735–700 B.C., "with chapter vi from 757 B.C."; Michah, 735–720 B.C. (pp. 68–69).

However, Isaiah 40–66 is "the product of another prophet, or other prophets, that lived . . . 540–510 B.C." (p. 72).[9] Jonah (whose author is unknown (p. 74), is pre-exilic, having been written about 540 B.C. (p. 84). The fifty-second chapter of Jeremiah is an addendum to the book (p. 8).

Ezekiel lived from 640 to 572 B.C. He began his prophetic career about 592 (p. 85). He lived in an obscure colony in Babylon, and his prophecies were therefore not generally known until "the Men of the Great Synod, perhaps after the death of Ezra and Nehemiah, collected and compiled the manuscripts in the present book." The talmudic tradition (Shabbat 13b) that learned men wanted to take Ezekiel out of the canon because "his book contradicts 'words of the Thorah' " can refer only to the third part [chaps 40–48] of Ezekiel. Malachi is a nick-name for Mordechai, as shown "in Meguillah 15" (p. 90).

Chapters 9–13 of Zechariah are not post-exilic, but pre-exilic, the work of "Zechariah, son of Berachiah, mentioned in Isaiah and Chronicles, and were attached to the second Zechariah by mistake[10]" (p. 93).

As to the Hagiographa, Psalms, divided in the Massoretic text into five books, is a series of compilations, with many Psalms anonymous and some, such as Ps. 118, compositions of the Maccabean age[11] (p. 96). Its five books were compiled, respectively, in 900, 800, 550, 450, and 140 B.C. (pp. 101–102).

Proverbs is also a compilation, representing compositions by various hands, both Solomon and others, but by and large it is the work of Solomon, compiled no later than the age of King Hezekiah; "it was evidently the Solomonic age, with its advanced state of culture, peace, and wealth, which produced this book" (p. 108).

Job is "not prophetical, nor yet is it apocalyptic." It was written nearer to the prophetic age than the books of Daniel, Ezra, and Nehemiah, and probably adjacent to the time of Nehemiah, "between 420 and 400 B.C. [*sic*] as the Talmud has it" (p. 119).

As to Ruth, "there is no reason why the authorship . . . should not be given to Samuel and David during the last half of the eleventh century B.C." (p. 121). As to Canticles, Wise is undecided whether it is by Solomon, though compiled by "the men of Hezekiah," or an allegory "written in the time of Ptolemy Euergetes, 221–204 B.C." (p. 127).

Ecclesiastes is basically Solomonic, but in the Greek period "other manuscripts, believed to be by the same author, were added to the older volume, and the present book of Koheleth received its present form" (p. 132). The date of the completion is about 200 B.C.

Jeremiah wrote the first three chapters of Lamentations, and a "contemporary" the last two, between 586 and 560.

Esther describes events that took place in the reign of "Darius Ochus 359–338 B.C. . . . The book of Esther, however . . . was written about 160 B.C." (pp. 138–39).

As to Daniel, the Aramaic portion was written in 540 B.C. and the Hebrew in 170, with Daniel himself "the author of the former, and Jose ben Joezer[12] of the latter" (p. 141).

A compiler assembled the writings of Ezra and Nehemiah between 390 and 360 B.C., with possible later additions (pp. 146–47). "The work of the Chronicles consists of four books: 1) Chronicles proper from 1 Chr. ch. 10 to the end of 2nd Chronicles; 2) 1 Chr. chs. 1–9, written by Ezra; 3) Ezra chs. 1–6; and 4) the notes of Ezra and Nehemiah, compiled about 360. The Men of the Great Synod connected these four books . . . in chronological order" (p. 153).

So much, then, for Wise's opinions.

What seems clear respecting the Prophets and the Hagiographa is that Wise, though partial to the views found in Jewish tradition about the provenience and the authorship, is by no means bound to them, and accords himself some good measure of freedom. I would imagine that he thought himself to be a free, independent researcher. Certainly some of his conclusions are untraditional, and certainly he does not hesitate to speak of errors and of misplacements. Indeed, his tendency to give rather precise dates for the composition or compilation of books is a procedure he borrowed from the "Negative Critics," despite the disparity between his conclusions and theirs.

When, in his last chapter on the Pentateuch, Wise rejects the views of the Higher Critics, he proceeds in manner as if the questions about the Pentateuch are open. I do not find in this chapter, as I do not find in this book, any reflection of a view he expounds elsewhere repeatedly. That view ascribes to Moses a divinely revealed "Constitution," of a perfection and sanctity unique in all history. Indeed, the Talmud in some of his writings emerges as a human distortion of the divine Pentateuch. It is strange that here Wise uses so affirmatively talmudic materials which elsewhere he treats with considerable scorn.

As is known, the four-source hypothesis, a conclusion resulting from about three-quarters of a century of acute (or over-acute) analysis, rested on the supposition that doublet or triplet narrations or laws implied different sources. Jean Astruc (1753) had first suggested that Moses had himself used two sources, differing from each other in the divine names YHWH and Elohim; later scholars affirmed the two sources, but ascribed the use of a person long after Moses. To the two sources, J and E, there was added about 1806 a third, D. Around 1835, the E source became viewed as actually two, an ancient E and a later priestly E; the latter came to be called P. Assuming that there were the four sources, the scholars attempted to fix their sequence and dates, and a variety of opinions were offered. Ultimately K. H. Graf's proposal, that P was the youngest source, gained ascendancy. Since then the general conclusion has been that J comes from about 850, E from 750 (with the two combined by a redactor about 650), D from 621, and P, the creator of the Pentateuch, around 450.[13]

From this source analysis, Julius Wellhausen drew logical conclusions, including the view that the Pentateuch, through growth, accretion, and development, was a post-exilic compilation, which romantically (that is, falsely) read back into the Wilderness period the origin of institutions which emerged only in the post-exilic time. Hence, the pentateuchal view of Hebrew history was completely wrong, and Wellhausen's hypothesis was designed to portray a tenable history to supplant the untenable.

Wise's effort was to supply an alternative to the Wellhausen type of approach he found so uncongenial. Let it be recalled, as stated at the beginning of this essay, that Wise mentions no Higher Critic by name. It is not Wellhausen in particular whom he wishes to refute, but the scholarship typified by the name Wellhausen. Perhaps because he assumes the role of the free, independent researcher, Wise abstains in this book from allusion to Moses' divine "Constitution" which is so prominent elsewhere.

He writes: "The traditions of the Hebrew people and documentary evidence before us preclude the theory of that school of modern criticism which places the Pentateuch at or near the close of the prophetical millennium, as the product of historical development" (p. 153). Again, "the position that [Judges, Joshua, Samuel, Kings], Psalms and Proverbs were written or rewritten with fraudulent intention during the Babylonian exile or thereafter, has been disposed of in the former chapters of this book . . . The origins of the fundamental institutions . . . is [sic] described in the Thorah only; and in all other books of Holy Writ not even a remote intimation of the origin of those institutions . . . can be discovered. This demonstrates at once the existence of the Thorah prior to all other books of the Bible . . ." (p. 159). "There always was a Thorah; a written Thorah, a Thorah of Jehovah, a Thorah of Moses, prior to all other biblical books . . ." (pp. 172–73).

Exodus, Leviticus, and Numbers reflect no editing as late as the period of the monarchy, since they reflect no kingly prerogatives. Moreover, the view that D, Deuteronomy, found in 621,[14] was a forgery, ascribed to Moses but written by Jeremiah, is impossible, for "there would be no reason to forge that book nine centuries after the death of Moses upon his name . . ." (p. 173). Exodus, Leviticus, and Numbers were recast in their present form "from the Mosaic documents, by editors from the period of the Judges" (p. 178) either in the time of Deborah or early in the career of Samuel. Why this theory of recasting? Wise admits that there are anachronisms in the Pentateuch.[15]

But Genesis and Deuteronomy are genuine writings of Moses; the small bit of additional material—the account of the death of Moses was appended—is not significant.

Why does Wise opt for his own view, rather than accept the Wellhausenite? His answer includes the following: We have no legacy of documents such as J and E, but we do possess the "canons" (see above, p. 000). Again, "the whole Thorah is one and the same principle, doctrine, precept and law, which necessarily come from one author, and not possibly from a number of authors." Hence, "the entire fabric of speculation based upon the Jahvistic and Elohistic criteria of authorship is eo ipso false and worthless" (pp. 183–84).

Furthermore, the acute analysis of the critics, yielding plural strata, stems from their Jahvistic-Elohistic premise. If this premise is refuted, then the derived strata analysis "fall[s] with it" (p. 184). The Book of Psalms in its second and third books is partly Elohistic, but the rest is "Jahvistic." Inasmuch as there are attributed to David both Jahvistic psalms (e.g., Pss. 8 and 18) and also Elohist psalms (Pss. 51–63), the different divine names do not denote different authorship. "The few Elohistic pieces in Genesis have been accounted for as old documents partly adopted and partly adapted by the Jahvistic author" (p. 185).

(If the latter part of the preceding paragraph seems to betray contradiction—as it seems to me to do—then Wise seems totally unaware; he seems also unaware that in the last sentence he is in his own way giving a variation of Astruc!)

As to Ezra's authorship of the Pentateuch—Wise abstains from attributing this, as he could have, to Spinoza—Scripture narrates nothing at all to this effect, and the title "Sopher," ascribed to Ezra, means "copyist (and not an author)" (p. 188).

The last sentence in the book reads: "There exists no solid ground on which to base any doubt in the authenticity of any book in Holy Writ."

Wise's "defense" of Scripture unquestionably appeared to him to be based on scholarship, and not on tradition, for his use of traditional, talmudic material, however central it seems, is in his context close to coincidental. He conceived that what he was doing was pursuing objective scholarship; he presents enough deviation from tradition to escape being labeled a mere traditionalist.

It is clear that one who reads all of Wise—I have read all his published books and the chapters in the *American Israelite* of his incomplete *Jesus Himself*[16]—will contend that Wise has come to the *Pronaos* with his mind already made up. He has not really assumed that the questions deserved to be open; rather, he has written in support of antecedent conclusions already repeatedly published in books or in his newspaper columns.

A fair amount of his strictures against the Higher Criticism—for example, the analyses of the Pentateuch into countless strata and substrata—seem to me valid. But I do not believe that he really confronted, absorbed, and mastered the Higher Criticism. He reflects an awareness of it only in general, and exceedingly little in its specifics. He "refutes" on the basis of large blocks of materials, not on the basis of an acute analysis of the component and relevant details. All too often he appears to me to work on the basis of intuition (which can be faulty) or antecedent judgment, not on thorough study. How could a man as busy as he take the time for the requisite study?

The standard "Introductions" of consequence—for example, those by

Eissfeldt and Fohrer—list the introductions known in the public arena. Wise never appears in any sublists. I know of no single instance in which a Bible scholar mentions him or alludes to the *Pronaos*. Since I know a bit about publishers and their mysterious ways, it is they who may be responsible for the total academic unawareness of this book. Wise, as far as I have been able to learn, had no association with professional scholars, as has been the case with later Hebrew Union College faculty, such as Buttenwieser, Morgenstern, Glueck, Blank, Tsevat, Brichto, Orlinsky, or myself. Academically Wise lived quite alone.

I wish he had made a better case against the Higher Criticism. I wish he had had some receptivity to its genuine virtues, rather than the somewhat pitiable sense of outrage at its conclusions. He was brilliant, he was learned, he was independent of mind. But he did not write a good book. Its deficiencies outweigh by far its merits; it is all too often shoddy, inexact and unreliable.

And yet there is a certain quality in it, wrong as I think the book is, that appeals to me. Perhaps it is the architectonic structure of the approach to Scripture, less clearly reflected in the pages of the book than implicit in his mind. He had thought, though perhaps he had not thought through. He had ideas, these in abundance, but some he abstained from developing and some he left quite bereft of that self-challenge and self-criticism which confer tenability to flashes of dangerous brilliance.

Only those who do not read Wise dismiss him, with unbecoming arrogance, as a mere organizer. He was a great deal more than that. He was a man who in scholarship and in theology never realized the potential that existed in him. It is not possible to laud him as a scholar or philosopher. Yet to dismiss him as merely an organizer is a lamentable example of an obscurantist current in present-day Reform Judaism, represented by some spokesmen and writers who seem to think that they alone possess truth and profundity, and who seem to feel that they contribute to the progress of Reform Judaism by defaming their predecessors. Fallible as a scholar and philosopher, Wise was nevertheless, especially in comparison with pygmies, a veritable giant.

NOTES

1. Wise uses the word *canon* ambiguously, as will be seen. Here he means the first segment, namely, the Pentateuch.
2. Wise states (p. 3) that he, the author, "has read all those books [of Holy Writ] and every word thereof in the original for a term of sixty-six years, *i.e.,* from boyhood up to his seventy-second birthday, and has attempted to acquaint himself with all ancient versions and commentaries, and a large portion of the modern translations and commentaries of the Bible. Besides, he expounded Holy Writ these forty-eight years in the synagogues and schoolrooms, and before academical classes in the college these sixteen years."
3. One does not find Wise truly at home in the Septuagint. For example, in his discussion of the Book of Yashar, he mentions Num. 21:17; Josh. 10:12–13; and 2 Sam. 1:17–27 (though in an excusable error he gives the latter as 2 Sam. 2:17–27), but not the LXX to 1 Kings 8:12, where the Book of Shyr ("song") is often regarded as an error for Yshr.
4. The word *written* is mine, not Wise's. He cites part of a passage from the Talmud (Gitin 60a, cited simply as "Guitin 60"), one which states that the Torah was transmitted by God to Moses "scroll by scroll," though another opinion holds that it was transmitted in its entirety. "Scroll by scroll" implies for Wise that as each section was divinely transmitted to Moses, Moses wrote it down, and later joined the sections together. Out of the "scroll by scroll" phrase, Wise infers that Moses recorded sections—Wise calls them "canons" (p. 26)—which constituted the portions of the totality.
5. He cites the Talmud as his authority: "Baba Batra 14 and Yerushalmi Sotah v. 6." He seems to quote Baba Batra 14b from memory, for he errs slightly. He gives the passage as "Moses wrote five books of the Thorah, and then again he wrote the chapter on Balak and Balaam." The Soncino translation runs: "Moses wrote his own book and the portion of Balaam and Job."

    In connection with the authorship of the former prophets, Wise presents "the record of ancient tradition in the Talmud Baba Batra 14b and 15a, which, literally rendered, reads thus . . . " What is presented is not literally rendered; the first sentence is, but what then follows is neither the ensuing talmudic material, nor literal, but a very, very free paraphrase. Not that Wise distorts the content; he only does not give the literal.
6. This "book," according to Wise (p. 27, fn., on the basis of *Mechilta* Ba-Hodesh, no. 3, ran from Gen. 1 through Exod. 24, but R. Jehudah limited it to the commandments given to Adam, Noah's children, Abraham, and "in Egypt, at Marah, and other Commandments," while R. Ishmael adds to the content Lev. 25–26. Wise says: "It appears most likely that originally Exodus XXXIV was the end of the book, to which Moses later on added Leviticus XXV and XXVI."
7. "Joshua wrote his book and the last eight verses of the Torah; or the latter might have been written partly by Eleazar and partly by Phineas. Samuel wrote

his book, Judges, and Ruth, through the prophet Nahum, and God completed it. David wrote Psalms, but incorporated the work of ten older authors. Jeremiah wrote his own book, Kings, and Lamentations. King Hezekiah and his associates wrote Isaiah, Proverbs, Song of Solomon, and Ecclesiastes. The men of the great assembly wrote Ezekiel, the Twelve minor prophets, Daniel, and Esther.

"Ezra wrote his own book, and also Nehemiah and the genealogies in 1 Chron. chaps. 1–9."

Wise adds that "wrote . . . does not always refer to authorship; it refers, also, to the editorship, the parties that collected and compiled the manuscript of any author."

8. Wise means Judg. 17–21.
9. The authority for this is Abraham Ibn Ezra. Moreover, the double tradition in the Talmud of placing Isaiah before Jeremiah, or after Ezekiel, shows that "there were two different books of Isaiah before the compilers of the Canon" (p. 73).
10. Modern analysts speak both of a "second Zechariah" and also a "third," though they ascribe these to the very late post-exilic period.
11. Wise comments that there are two sets of the *hallel*, an older, "great" Hallel, namely Pss. 125 and 126, and the "Egyptian Hallel, Pss. 113–118." The second is an elaboration and amplification of the first and "replaced it in the temple service" (p. 97).
12. He was one of the first "pair" of sages; his "dictum" is recorded in Abot 4:4.
13. Modern scholars, however they have modified and refined the conclusions and the dates and utilized form-criticism and "tradition history," still utilize the four sources. My dissent ("The Haggada Within Scripture," *Journal of Biblical Literature,* vol. LXXX, pt. II, 1961) includes rejection of the J and E "strata" as documents, but retains D and P, though scarcely in the way in which many have viewed them.
14. On the basis of 2 Kings 22–23, which speaks of the discovery of a book of Torah by Moses when, under King Josiah, a refurbishing of the Temple was under way in 621, the view was expressed in 1806 that Deuteronomy was composed about 621. That Jeremiah was the true author of Deuteronomy was sporadically proposed but not treated seriously.
15. Exodus 16:35–36 could have been written only after a different type of measurement—"an omer is a tenth part of an ephah"—arose, and this in Canaan (p. 179). Similarly, the high praises of Moses (Exod. 34:29–33 and Num. 12:3) are of later origin.

In Wise's view, the recasting of Exodus and Leviticus preceded by a generation or two the recasting of Numbers (p. 183).
16. See my essay, "Isaac Mayer Wise's 'Jesus Himself'," in *Essays in American Jewish History* (Cincinnati, 1958).

AFFIRMATION OF THE DIASPORA:
AMERICA AND PALESTINE IN
DUBNOW'S THOUGHT

By

ROBERT M. SELTZER

Hunter College, City University of New York

Of all the ideologists of Jewish nationalism in Czarist Russia, Simon Dubnow was the most appreciative of the Jewish community in the United States, viewing the settlement of European Jews there as normal and thoroughly desirable. His attitude toward America contrasts sharply with his skepticism that the *Yishuv* in Palestine could be the main force for Jewish survival. This paper attempts to explain the constancy of Dubnow's position on the question whither Jewish migration—a constancy which might at first seem paradoxical, since in the meanwhile he turned from vehement opposition to Jewish nationalism to wholehearted support of it.

Dubnow began his literary career at the age of twenty, when his first articles were accepted by the Russian-language Jewish press in St. Petersburg; soon he became a frequent and outstanding contributor to the most important of these journals, Adolph Landau's *Voskhod*.[1] Unlike many Jewish figures of the period, Dubnow's views at that time were not affected by the pogroms of 1881–82, which proved to be a traumatic event in the development of the Russian Jewish intelligentsia. Dubnow in his first essays and reviews remained entirely faithful to the expectation of the sixties and seventies that reason and progress would impel the Russian state to grant equal rights to the Jews, and he also held fast to the conviction, inherited from the late positivist Haskalah, that Jews should prepare for their inevitable emancipation by drastically reforming their traditional way of life. His early remarks on Jewish emigration to Palestine and America resulted from this orientation.

In 1883 Dubnow wrote several long articles criticizing the post-pogrom Jewish nationalist mood among his contemporaries.[2] He considered Leon Pinsker's demand for the political rebirth of the Jewish nation "an ephemeral theory," stimulated by events "the abnormality of which every unprejudiced person acknowledges."[3] The new Hibbat Zion ideal was a step backward:

> The preachers of self-emancipation and especially their most influential wing, the Palestinists ... want to establish something like a law of regression in the development of humanity. .... They have argued that the national principle has triumphed, that the Jews should fit themselves to the new conditions of culture and separate themselves off as a living nation, but this is a superficial attiude toward history. ....[4]

In like manner Dubnow defended the Mendelssohnian Haskalah against Peretz Smolenskin's position that it inevitably led to assimilation. Accusing him of wanting to return to concepts of the fifteenth and sixteenth centuries, Dubnow categorized Smolenskin's view as yet another instance of *ul'trayudofilstvo* ("hyper-Judeophilism"), "the excessive philosophical or historical idealization of Jewry and Judaism with respect to the past and future problems of both."[5] That Smolenskin's spiritual nationalism was quite fashionable in certain circles merely indicated a hasty response on the part of Jews indifferent to religion to "events which bear a character more medieval than contemporary."[6]

Young Dubnow's refusal to view the pogroms and the growing antisemitic movement in Europe as a refutation of Haskalah ideals was a result of his brash and dogmatic cosmopolitan optimism. His conception of history, derived mainly from Auguste Comte and the Russian positivists, led him to dismiss as irrational and unstable any phenomenon contrary to the presumed path to universal human progress. Jewish nationalism was artificial because nationalism was merely a form of egotism, a temporary emotional aberration. The Hibbat Zion writers did not understand, in his opinion, that occurrences like the reemergence of small Balkan nations or the regnant French and German revanchism did not shake "the law, based on the most elaborate induction, that in international as well as interhuman relationships, egotism slowly gives way to altruism."[7] Moreover, no significant class of Jews could follow Pinsker, Smolenskin, and their supporters. The religious would consider the efforts to re-establish a Jewish state by human means "a crime against God." Modernized Jews would refuse to exchange a European culture for a backward Asian one. The former would accuse the nationalists of insufficient faith; the latter of requiring excessive faith. Dubnow acknowledged that there was something to be said for the colonization of Palestine within the limits permitted by current political conditions there, but he remarked that educated Jews would prefer moderate fusion (gradual Russification and a degree of assimilation) to resurgent Jewish separatism.[8] In Dubnow's early articles there is no comparably extensive discussion of the flight of Jews to the United States. However, his recommendation that emigration to America be organized rather than chaotic, and the information (sometimes misinformation) he conveyed to his readers about Jewish life there, showed none of the animus characterizing his remarks on Palestinophilism.[9] Indeed, when he experienced a brief pang of "emigrant psychology" in the mid-1880s, he recalled that were it not for personal circumstances, he would have gone off to America forever.[10]

Instead of going to America or allowing himself to be swayed by the arguments of his beloved brother Wolf, who was a Biluist in Palestine for several years, Dubnow remained in Russia to grapple with the issues facing Jewry there. Inexorably he was forced to shift ground. In the late eighties he underwent a prolonged depression, leading to a reconsideration of his world view. Abandoning the aloof role of "Externus" (one of his pen names), he spoke of "returning home," like many of his generation who strove to re-establish a positive tie to the Jewish masses.[11] (I hope to analyze the factors that effected this metamorphosis of personal and social identity in a separate article.) He found himself confessing that "abstract love for humanity prevented me from experiencing a concrete love for my people [because previously I had been] dissatisfied to work for one people through boundless pretensions to work for all peoples." [12] In his autobiography a revealing passage based on his diary notations for 1887 summarizes this turning point:

> I felt that the fateful tortures of self-definition were coming to an end, and I had to define my calling and choose one of the many projects that pulled me in various directions. The twenty-seventh year of my life was a decisive moment. Until then my thoughts still ran to general literary plans, although actually I only worked in Jewish literature. I had been

unhappy with this narrow sphere of activity and longed for the broader problems which my mentors Mill, Spencer, Renan, and Taine studied. My eye illness, involving the danger of losing normal sight, gave me the impulse for deeper thought. I became convinced that true creativity required the process of self-limitation, that qabbalistic secret of concentration (*sod hatsimtsum*) that the Infinite used to create the world from primordial chaos. I now understood that my path to the universal lay precisely through the field of the national in which I was already working. One could serve humanity only by serving one of its parts, all the more so if that was a nation of the most ancient culture. It became clear that my general knowledge and universal ambitions would give fruitful results in conjunction with the inherited treasures of Jewish knowledge and the yet unformed Jewish national ideals. From this time began my propensity for the great themes of Jewish history.[13]

It was decisive for Dubnow's conversion to Jewish nationalism that he was led in the early nineties to deal with Jewish identity through historical research rather than the analysis of contemporary antisemitism. His first major effort, the investigation of the history of Hasidism, led him to gather primary sources from throughout the Pale, which in turn suggested the idea of a Russian-Jewish historical society.[14] The decision to devote himself to the Jewish past in East Europe was a symptom of his breaking away from the western Jewish experience as the relevant prototype for the Jewish future. At the same time Dubnow set out to evaluate the work of Heinrich Graetz and to continue Graetz's comprehensive treatment of the entirety of Jewish history.[15] Dubnow's introduction to an aborted Russian translation of Graetz's *Popular History of the Jews* (Dubnow's introduction was published in *Voskhod* under the title "What Is Jewish History: An Attempt at a Brief Philosophical Characterization") followed Graetz in conceiving of Jewish history not only as the story of a religion but even more that of *ein lebendiger Volksstamm*.[16] While relying mainly on Graetz's approach, some of Dubnow's ideas prefigure his later distinctive position on the Jewish homeland and diaspora.

Jewish history, Dubnow asserted, was unique with respect both to its qualitative and quantitative dimensions: "an axis crossing the history of mankind from one of its poles to the other." [17] He noted that it was widely accepted that the Jews had created a novel religious world view and moral code during the first half of their history, when they possessed a territory and government. However, in the second half, which was not well enough known, "historical providence" wanted to prove that a people can survive without land and state, the tangible accompaniments of nationality. Far from indicating (in nineteenth-century terminology) that the diaspora Jews were not an historical people, their statelessness showed that they were the *most* historical ("historicissimus"): "If the inner life and the social and intellectual development of a people form the kernel, politics and occasional wars history's husk, then certainly the Jewish diaspora is all kernel." Although the Jews remained "an organic constituent of that portion of mankind which has contributed to the treasury of human thought," their special destiny was to exhibit constant intellectual discipline and periodic martyrdom. In the latter half of its history, therefore, the people was "thinker, stoic, and sufferer," eking out existence under conditions with which no other nation had coped, or could ever do so.[18] Although Dubnow borrowed Graetz's emphasis on the spiritual, his presentation of this factor was far more secular than his German predecessor's. Ignoring Graetz's faith in a transcendent absolute, Dubnow used the spiritual to denote Jewish ideas, memories, and sense of mission, and, above all, that freedom which makes it possible for men to set for themselves goals, withstand adversity, and, if necessary, willingly die for Judaism.[19]

The next stage in the emergence of Dubnow's nationalism dates from 1897, when he began to formulate his own ideological program. Reflecting on the new Zionist and Bundist movements and the quickening of Jewish self-action in Russia, especially after the reappearance of pogroms in 1903, Dubnow published a series of articles on questions of the day, which he collected in 1907 as *Letters on Old and New Judaism.*[20] In these essays Dubnow's first aim was to refute the errors of assimilationism, the Bund, and Zionism. Assimilationists—in his view those who refused forthrightly to use the term *nation* for the Jews—confused citizenship with nationality, not making the correct distinction between the legal obligations of the Jew to the state and his moral duties to the people.[21] The bankruptcy of the ideal of cultural fusion with the surrounding nations required, above all, nationalizing Jewish education. Although Dubnow considered himself a freethinker, he acknowledged that religious Jews instinctively grasped this principle, whereas the secular Jewish intelligentsia and upper classes did not yet clearly perceive that their children must receive universal knowledge in a national form with explicitly Jewish content, for the sake of their psychological health and that of the nation.[22]

The Bund and Zionism were criticized for their divisiveness, since Jewish national interests also required concerted political action in time of crisis. The Bund was accused by Dubnow of putting class politics ahead of defending the Jews against the danger that threatened them all.[23] The Zionists were accused of misleading the people with messianic fantasies. Although the practical activities of the Zionist organization were deemed useful, Dubnow estimated that a century hence there might at most be a half-million Jews in Palestine, not even the Jewish population of the province of Kiev and hardly a comprehensive solution to the Jewish problem.[24] To be sure, the Zionists generated mass enthusiasm, but in the long run they weakened the people's will to organize its life in the diaspora. "Conditional nationalists," they loved their nation only if it would be like other nations, thus emulating an external standard of nationhood, whereas Judaism demanded "Love my soul, my culture, and not just my future territorial qualifications." [25] Not opposed to the colonization of Palestine on principle—"a small ray of light in Zion is desirable"— Dubnow argued that Jewish emigration should be directed wherever Jews could carry on their national-cultural life. Therefore, the new center in America was part of the natural process which continued to insure the survival of the Jewish people.[26]

Dubnow's strictures about political Zionism did not apply fully to the spiritual Zionism of Ahad HaAm, with whom he shared many common views. Both men rebuked Herzl for ignoring the cultural-factor in Jewish identity; both believed that there were distinctive Jewish values and agreed that the diaspora would not disappear. Dubnow and Ahad HaAm had become friends in Odessa during the nineties and remained on good terms despite their polite polemics on whether a geographical center was vital for Jewish survival. Ahad HaAm chided Dubnow for being satisfied with half a cake (the limited Jewish creativity of the diaspora) rather than the whole (the full Hebraic renaissance possible only in the land of Israel).[27] Dubnow continued to reject Zionism's "negation of the diaspora," affirming that it was possible to combine full participation in modern European life with the unique culture of the Jewish nation. Dubnow epitomized his position with the formulas: the Zionists (including Ahad HaAm) faced east while he and his supporters faced west; assimilationism viewed Judaism as a nation in the past, Zionism viewed it as a nation in the future, his ideology alone viewed it as a nation in the present.[28]

Dubnow's ideology was based on a conception of historical evolution which formed the "general theses" of the *Letters on Old and New Judaism*. His arguments, drawn from the Social Darwinism of his time (especially that of Herbert Spencer), buttressed his contention that he could explan Jewish identity scientifically.[29] His *tour de force* was to employ this biological model to transform the apparent abnormality of the Jewish nation into the example which proved the rule: Jewish history illustrated the development of a nation to the point where for the first time the essence of nationhood was fully apparent.

Dubnow's theses derived from the assumption that whereas states were based on the social contract, nations were primordial forces.[30] Individuals were cells of their respective national organisms, which in turn were species within the genus mankind.[31] The nation was an aggregate of generations embodying an elemental vital force, a will-to-live which drove it to adapt to changing conditions or perish.[32] Natural selection weeded out weaker elements within the nation and among them.[33] Even great empires, despite vast military power, ultimately collapsed from unresolved inner tensions, while spiritually cohesive peoples survived territorial conquest by creating new social and cultural forms. Although many nations had endured the temporary loss of political independence, only one had dispersed and continued to thrive for centuries without its original homeland and common language. Such a nation, it could be concluded, was indestructible.[34]

Dubnow used this system of biological analogies to secularize even further the spiritual factor he perceived in Jewish history. As Jewry developed, the spiritual achieved complete dominance. The various historic leadership classes—prophets, priests, and Pharisees—strengthened the national identity to the point that the scattered organism was able to meet virtually unprecedented conditions. The Jewish people compensated for their political limitations in the diaspora "as the blind and deaf compensate for their weaknesses through sharpening other senses." [35] Wherever the vital cultural forces of the Jewish nation were deposited, autonomous communal institutions served as surrogates of a state. The changing forms of Jewish law, literature, and faith were all manifestations of the instinct for national survival.[36] The voluntaristic and subjective nature of this causation became fully apparent in the present: now that the secular Jewish intellectual has dropped his obvious Jewish customs, peculiarities, and religious dogmas, he clearly perceived that his nationality was based on historical memories and ideals, feelings of mutual sympathy, and fundamental intellectual and ethical tendencies.[37] Dubnow concluded: "The nation's consciousness is the main criterion of its existence. 'I think of myself as a nation—therefore I am.' " [38] Far from constituting an historical anomaly, the Jews were the only people which has freed itself from the secondary characteristics of nationhood. Jewry was the supreme example of its category, "the quintessence of a nation," a group held together not by physical circumstances but united solely by inner sentiment.[39]

According to Dubnow, the future of Jewish life required a combination of the autonomous communal institutions of the traditional diaspora with the intellectual freedom of the Haskalah: the *qahal* without its oligarchy, isolation, and religious restrictions; the Haskalah's critical rationalism without denationalization. Dubnow thus considered that he had synthesized the best of medieval and modern Judaism, the success of which was guaranteed by the laws of history.[40] Evolution works toward this beneficent end because "the preservation of strong national individuality is an axiom of sociology." [41] Remaining faithful in his own way to nineteenth-century secular and humanitarian liberalism, Dubnow had constructed an ideology which applied one of the favorite treatises of his youth—John Stuart Mill's defense of personal freedom in his famous essay *On Liberty*—to the collective, in order to justify the national principle to the modernized Jew perplexed about his Jewishness.

It is not our intention here to evaluate Dubnow's theory. Its weaknesses are patent in retrospect, but its strengths should also be noted. Dubnow's ideology enabled him to make his peace with the East European Jewish tradition he had earlier rejected. Unlike many Zionists of the time, he did not repudiate the image of the *galut* Jew: the diaspora was an exemplary achievement, its culture worthy of preservation in a modern form, and Yiddish an important Jewish tie. Nor did Dubnow equate nationalism with opposition to the West, as did many forms of nationalist thought. He refused to leave Europe either physically or spiritually: Jews were one of the most ancient nations there, though they did not inhabit a contiguous territory.[42] The Jewish land was all the discrete places where Jews resided. The new Jewry of America was, therefore, another station established by a diaspora people in response to the demands of history. And, we might add, the subsequent vitality of American Jewry, the forms of Jewish association devised there, even the role it played in aiding the establishment and successes of the state of Israel—all these indicate that Dubnow's assessment of the significance of the migration of Jews to America was more justified than the more negative views of many ideological rivals.[43]

NOTES

1. The following abbreviations are used:
   KZ: Simon Dubnow, *Kniga zhizni* [Book of life: Reminiscences and reflections, material for the history of my time]. Vol. I (to 1903), Riga, 1934. Vol. II (1903–22), Riga, 1935. Vol. III (1922–33), Riga, 1940; republished, New York, 1957.
   Pis'ma: Simon Dubnow, *Pism'a o starom i novom evreistve* [Letters on old and new Judaism] (St. Petersburg, 1907).
   Dubnow's published articles are cited in the notes according to the numbers he assigned them in his "Auto-Bibliography" included at the end of the third volume of *Kniga zhizni* and republished in Aaron Steinberg, ed., *Simon Dubnow: The Man and His Work (A Memorial Volume on the Occasion of the Centenary of his Birth)* (Paris: World Jewish Congress, 1963). For articles extending over two or more issues of a journal, the specific month will be cited in each note.
2. His five major early articles on social and political questions are: #1, "Several Stages in the History of Jewish Thought," *Russkii Evrei*, 1881; #16, "What Kind of Self-Emancipation Do the Jews Need?" *Voskhod*, 1883; #23, "Palestinophilism and Its Main Advocate (Smolenski) [*sic*]," *Voskhod*, 1883; #31, "A Last Word on the Condemned Jewry," *Voskhod*, 1884; #39, "On the Reform of the Jewish School," *Voskhod*, 1885.
3. #16 (July–August), p. 24.
4. *Ibid.*, p. 25.
5. #23, p. 24.
6. *Ibid.*, p. 33.
7. #16 (July–August), p. 26; also #31, p. 104.
8. #23, pp. 32–35.
9. His early attitude can be seen in #3 (1881) on emigration to America, where he asserts that the organization of this movement would aid Jews in helping themselves, and that only the worst elements have gone to Palestine thus far. It is important that only in America was there no division between native and alien. #10, an 1882 editorial on the May Laws, reiterates that emigration should be organized. #8, "An Historical Essay on the Settlement of Jews in America" (*Razsvet*, 1882), indicates that Dubnow felt even then that the settlement of Jews there would be quite large. Among his list of communities established in the eighteenth century by Sephardim is Newport, *Kentucky;* he had not studied his atlas sufficiently.
10. *KZ*, I, p. 210.
11. Not explicitly referring to himself, but implicitly so: #90, p. 25.
12. *KZ*, I, p. 195.
13. *Ibid.*, pp. 206–7.
14. Dubnow's first history of Hasidism was published in *Voskhod* between 1888 and 1893 in a series of articles that ran to over six hundred pages. Much later in life he reworked this material in his famous Hebrew study. Dubnow's essay, entitled "On the Study of the History of Russian Jews and Founding of a Russian Jewish Historical Society" (#98, *Voskhod*, 1891), was reissued soon after as a Hebrew pamphlet and made a great impression on many contemporaries.

15. #105. "Historiographer of Judaism: Heinrich Graetz, his Life and Work," *Voskhod*, 1892.
16. #111, *Voskhod*, 1893. The Graetz translation was ordered confiscated by the church censors and destroyed (*KZ*, I, 276–77).
17. #111 (October), p. 114.
18. *Ibid.*, pp. 117–19.
19. Dubnow's concept of will is reflected in his remark: "The flames issuing from the funeral pile on which martyrs die a heroic death for their ideas is, in its way, as awe-inspiring as the flame from Sinai's height" (#111 [October–November], p. 123).
20. Dubnow began writing his series of *Letters on Old and New Judaism* at the end of 1897. During the summer of 1906 and the spring of 1907 they were in part rewritten and arranged in an orderly sequence for publication. The book is divided into three parts: "General Principles," "Between Social Tendencies," and "Between Inquisition and Emancipation, 1903–1907." Included also is published material not originally labeled "Letters," some of which appears in appendices.
21. *Pis'ma*, pp. 39–42.
22. *Ibid.*, pp. 117–18, 123–25, 127, 269.
23. *Ibid.*, pp. 307–8, 324–26.
24. *Ibid.*, pp. 171, 191–92.
25. *Ibid.*, pp. v, 174, 190.
26. *Ibid.*, pp. 320, 287–88.
27. *Kol kitvei Ahad HaAm*, p. 402. See Ahad HaAm's letter to Dubnow on the question of the future of Jewish life in the diaspora, in *Iggrot Ahad HaAm*, III, 284–89. Also, *KZ*, I, 333, and Simon Rawidowicz, ed., *Sefer Shimon Dubnow* (London: Ararat Publishing Co., 1954), p. 261.
28. *Pis'ma*, pp. 163, 181.
29. *Ibid.*, p. 58.
30. *Ibid.*, p. 10, 31–33.
31. Implied in *ibid.*, p. 14.
32. *Ibid.*, p. 10.
33. *Ibid.*, pp. 7, 3.
34. *Ibid.*, p. 10.
35. *Ibid.*
36. *Ibid.*, p. 7.
37. *Ibid.*, pp. 14, 160.
38. Basing himself on Renan's well-known statement that "a nation's existence is—if you will pardon the metaphor—a daily plebiscite, as the individual's existence is a perpetual affirmation of life" (Ernest Renan, "What Is a Nation," *Poetry of the Celtic Race and Other Essays* [London: Walter Scott Publishing Co., n.d.], p. 80), quoted in the *Pis'ma*, p. 4. See *Pis'ma* p. 26.
39. *Ibid.* p. 14.
40. *Ibid.*, pp. 83–84, 79–80.
41. *Ibid.*, p. 81, 160 (fn.).
42. *Ibid.*, pp. 34–35.
43. In 1904 Dubnow spent the summer at Libau on the Baltic and went to visit the ships leaving there for America. He wrote, "It was painful for me to see in these torments the birth of a new center, but these wanderers, creators of Jewish America, will be blessed later when they more than once save their mother, the European diaspora, from death." *KZ*, II, p. 16.

THE 1820s: AMERICAN JEWRY COMES OF AGE

By

MALCOLM H. STERN

American Jewish Archives

The decade of the 1820s saw the development of a truly American Jewry. Although such present-day terms as *assimilation, outreach,* and *doing your own thing* were unheard of, their effect was present. In 1820, for the first and last time until our own generation, the majority of American Jews were English-speaking, many of them second- and even third-generation (or more) Americans. Some of them had the time and the means to advance themselves culturally and educationally. Their interests extended beyond making a livelihood. In minuscule, they were a generation of American Jews with some resemblances to our own. They were busy exploring ways of adjusting to their environment, concerned with their identity as Jews, and anxious to help their less fortunate Jewish brethren overseas.

Between 1790 and 1820 the general population of the United States grew from 3.9 million to 9.6 million, while the Jewish population—according to a conservative survey—grew only from 1,500 to 2,700.[1] That period coincided in Europe with the French Revolution and Napoleon, with their promises of liberty, equality, and fraternity. The upheaval of war and the promise of civil betterment made emigration from Europe less appealing to the Jews of France and Germany. The flow of Jewish immigrants to America slowed to a bare trickle.[2] The defeat of Napoleon and the subsequent Congress of Vienna brought the return of anti-Jewish legislation in many German states, but the postwar economy on both sides of the Atlantic was not conducive to emigration from Europe. Despite the revival of "Hep! Hep!" riots in South German towns in 1819 and increasingly burdensome restrictions against them, it was not until the 1830s that German Jews emigrated in any appreciable numbers. The Jewish immigrants who began coming in ever larger numbers in the 1820s were chiefly of Dutch and British origin. These had lived long enough in lands of emancipation to have thrown off ghetto traditions and, therefore, blended easily into the American scene.[3]

Meanwhile, in the American communities, the children and grandchildren of the Colonial Jews were growing up as American Jews. The majority of those who resided in the cities where congregations existed were identified with the congregation, even when a mixed marriage occurred.[4] Those in the more isolated communities found it more difficult to retain Jewish identification, but a number succeeded. Girls as well as boys were given classical education in academies or through private tutors. The arts were avidly pursued. One example of these trends is the Moses Myers family of Norfolk. Until he was impoverished by the impossibility of commercial shipping during the War of 1812, Moses Myers had been a prosperous merchant. In the first decade of the nineteenth century, he sent his oldest son, John, on a grand tour of Europe; his second son, Samuel, was the first Jewish matriculate at the College of William and Mary and became a lawyer; all his sons attended the Norfolk Academy; his daughters, tutored at home, could play the spinet and sing. Gilbert Stuart painted portraits of Moses and his wife; Thomas Sully did one of John. Their Federal period home in Norfolk, Virginia, preserved with many of its furnishings, is a model of tastefulness. Their library, with volumes in French as well as English, and the nearly 8,000 letters which have survived, attest to the family's literate interests and abilities.[5]

Perhaps the prototype of the evolving American Jew was Mordecai Manuel Noah, whose father and grandfather served in the Revolution. On his mother's side, he was a fifth-generation American. He grew up in his grandfather's Philadelphia home, taking advantage of Benjamin Franklin's Library Company of Philadelphia, the local theater, and "Poor Richard's" advice on manners and morals for a young man of character, while acquiring a passion for politics, journalism, and playwriting which became his joint career. With mixed success, Noah had already been by 1820 U.S. Consul at Tunis, editor of his uncle's pro-Tammany newspaper, and favorite orator of the New York Jewish community.[6] The same environment which allowed Jews like Noah to feel truly American and to try any endeavor produced a growth of Protestant evangelism and conversionist activity among Jews in Europe and America. Jews invariably overreact to attempts at conversion of Jews, and Noah's reaction was to propose the creation of his proto-Zionist colony on an island in the Niagara River, Ararat. Although, in his lifetime, Noah was to achieve far greater prominence for his journalistic and political activities, it is for Ararat that he is best remembered. The experiment, and his dedication of it, as well as its failure, have been frequently noted and analyzed as idealistic, utopian, ridiculous, impractical, etc. Suffice it to say here that it represents one of the flowerings of American Jewry's "coming of age." The dedicatory ceremony, so flamboyant and dramatic, is an early American public-relations scheme, the product of a fertile mind accustomed to journalism and drama.[7]

Noah's Ararat is only the best known of a number of activities which evolved in the 1820s on the American Jewish scene. Another attempt at colonization and resettlement was carried on by Moses Elias Levy,[8] a native of Morocco, who developed a successful lumber business in St. Thomas before becoming a purchasing agent for the Cuban government in 1816. Attracted by the potentialities of northern Florida, then under Cuban administration, Levy purchased a tract of land which he later traded for a more accessible plot. The latter carried with it the stipulation that at least two hundred colonists had to be settled on it within three years. This sent Levy traveling to Europe and the United States. He arrived in Philadelphia on June 28, 1818,[9] and began to seek out leading Jews in the eastern seaboard communities, proposing the establishment of Jewish agricultural communities and a school for the education of Jewish children. He found enthusiasm for his project among the above-mentioned Moses Myers family of Norfolk, especially with Samuel Myers, the father of two infant sons.[10] Levy carried on a lively correspondence with Samuel Myers, suggesting that the religion in their proposed community be reformed in consonance with the efforts of Israel Jacobson in Prussia.[11] Through the Myers family, Levy obtained an introduction to Rebecca Gratz of Philadelphia, but made an unfortunate impression on that lady by arriving a day late and failing to remember that it was Sukkot![12] The opening of government lands in Illinois led Israel Kursheedt of Richmond and Moses Myers of Norfolk to purchase thirty-four patents, consisting of 5,440 acres, with Levy holding a quarter interest in Kursheedt's twenty-one patents and a one-third share in Myers' thirteen patents. Unfortunately, Moses Myers and Son went into bankruptcy and the land was lost. Undaunted by this and by his own financial reverses, Levy succeeded in interesting Rev. Moses Levy Maduro Peixotto, Mordecai Manuel Noah, and Judah Zuntz, of New York's Congregation Shearith Israel, in joining him in the call to establish at least the boarding school for Jewish children, and a circular to this effect was sent to Moses and John Myers, and their son and brother-in-law, Philip I. Cohen, in Norfolk, dated May 9, 1821.[13] Nothing came of the project, due probably to the inability of those involved to raise funds and to the fact that Levy, the guiding spirit, had left for Florida, whose entrance into the United States had just been ratified. Levy's energies were subsequently devoted to the development of his Florida properties. Like Noah, he was unsuccessful in persuading European Jews to settle on his lands. He did, however, go to Europe for three years, 1825–28, and engaged in active polemics in England against conversionist activities.[14]

These conversionist activities instigated the creation of America's first Jewish periodical, *The Jew; being a Defense of Judaism against all Adversaries and Particularly against the Insidious Attacks of "Israel's Advocate."* In twelve issues, published between March 1823 and February 1825, editor Solomon Henry Jackson[15] denounced and derided the leadership of the American Society for Ameliorating the Conditions of the Jews, founded 1820, and its publication, *Israel's Advocate.* When that society's project of a Christian-Jewish community fell through because of lack of converts, Jackson felt that he had achieved his major purpose and stopped publishing.[16]

To be as openly denunciatory of Christians in print as Jackson was testifies further to the security of the American Jew. So does the freedom with which Jews wrote directly to the President of the United States. On April 17, 1818, Mordecai Noah participated in the dedication of the second Mill Street Synagogue. His discourse, a paean of praise for America and the Jewish religion, urged the Jew to take advantage of the opportunity America afforded for the development of the best in his faith and as a temporary Zion. When the address was printed, Noah sent copies to ex-Presidents Adams, Jefferson, and Madison, and received replies from all three.[17] Noah's example was followed by Dr. Jacob De La Motta when he dedicated Savannah's first synagogue building on July 21, 1820. When his address, extolling the liberty enjoyed by the Jews in America, was printed, De La Motta sent copies to Jefferson and Madison and received complimentary replies.[18] Joseph Marx of Richmond sent

Jefferson a copy of the proceedings of the French Sanhedrin, convened by Napoleon to draft civil law for the Jews of his empire; this too was acknowledged with an expression of compassion for the Jews.[19]

Jews were not hesitant about soliciting federal appointments. When bankruptcy hit in 1818, John Myers of Norfolk sought from Monroe an appointment as Commissioner of Claims, citing his service in the War of 1812 as aide-de-camp to General Winfield Scott.[20] This appointment was not forthcoming, but nine years later, John's father was recommended by John Quincy Adams to the Senate for appointment as Collector of Customs of the Port of Norfolk. The appointment was ratified on January 15, 1828, naming him also Superintendent of Lights and Agent for the Marine Hospital, which Moses held until his resignation on March 28, 1830.[21]

A reflection of the growing liberal spirit in American public life is the battle for ratificaton of the "Jew Bill" in Maryland. As early as 1797, Solomon Etting and his father-in-law, Barnard Gratz, prevailed upon Assemblyman William Pinkney to introduce a bill to abolish Maryland's requirement that anyone dealing with the law was required to declare his belief in the Christian religion. The bill, reintroduced annually, was defeated. In 1818, a Jeffersonian Democrat, Thomas Kennedy, took up the cause, but it was 1826 when a compromise version of the bill finally franchised the Jews of Maryland. Solomon Etting and Jacob I. Cohen were promptly elected members of the Baltimore City Council.[22]

As indicated above in Moses Elias Levy's correspondence with Samuel Myers, the Jews were feeling a need to Americanize their religious practices. At a time when Christians were experimenting with new approaches to religion, Canadian-born Moses Hart, in 1815, published *General Universal Religion* (republished in New York in 1818 as *Modern Religion*), in which he proposed a universal religion with special prayers, rites, theology, commandments, and nature festivals, all derived from the rationalism of the eighteenth-century Deists and the French Revolution.[23] The book ran to a third printing and aroused interest, if not followers, at least as far south as Norfolk, for a copy of the 1818 edition was in the Myers family library.[24]

A more serious attempt to remain within a Jewish traditional framework was the effort of forty-seven Jews of Charleston, South Carolina, to reform the worship in Congregation Beth Elohim. When the Adjunta (Board) rejected their request, the Reformed Society of Israelites was born on January 16, 1825, under the leadership of Isaac Harby. Their

reforms were those which were to dominate Reform Judaism for more
than a century and a quarter: sermons and prayers in the vernacular,
abbreviating the service, the abolition of freewill offerings at worship to
be replaced by dues, the abolition of auctioning *mitzvot,* dignity and
decorum in the conduct of worship. As might be expected, the majority of
this group were English-speaking, with at least thirteen native Charles-
tonians. The group grew to the point of raising funds for a synagogue, but
economic problems in Charleston led to the migration of Harby and other
leaders to New York, and the Panic of 1837 brought the coup-de-grâce to
the Society.[25]

Meanwhile, in 1825 rebellion against synagogue traditions began to
appear in New York. So many members were abandoning the wearing
of the *tallit* (prayer-shawl) in Congregation Shearith Israel that the
Board voted to deny calling to the Torah anyone who failed to wear a
tallit. It is significant that the punishment for infringement was so mild,
an evidence of the breaking down of the authority of the synagogue.[26] In
another instance, Barrow E. Cohen, a comparative newcomer to the
congregation from England, either willfully or from ignorance, failed
to make a charity pledge when called to the Torah. He was called on the
carpet by the Board.[27] Partially as a result of the somewhat high-handed
treatment of Cohen, a group calling itself *Chevra Chinuch Nearim* petitioned the Board for the right to hold services apart from the regular
worship of Shearith Israel. Since the majority of the group were younger,
recent arrivals from Europe, lacking the leisure to attend worship during
working hours, they wanted pre-breakfast services. They also sought
greater democracy in rotation of officers. This was a strictly Orthodox
group; their one reform demand was for a person to preach weekly in
English.[28] Once again vested authority denied the right to change, so a
new congregation was born, Ashkenazic B'nai Jeshurun, New York's second congregation.[29] Such was the influence of America that the twenty-
two-year-old Isaac Leeser, only four years out of Germany, could publish a series of six articles in defense of the Jew in the *Richmond* (Va.)
Whig. These won for him a call, the following year, to serve as minister
of Philadelphia's Congregation Mikveh Israel. A year later—in 1830—
he began regular preaching in English, an innovation which was to earn
him the epithet of "reformer" from his congregants, although to the later
evolving Reform Judaism he was the champion of Orthodoxy.[30]

The 1820s saw the movement of Jews away from the East Coast into
the hinterland. A tiny group of English Jews met for High Holy Day

worship in Cincinnati in 1819, but it was not until January 4, 1824 that they formed Bene Israel Congregation, now Rockdale Temple.[31] Jews, chiefly from Charleston, moved into the South Carolina state capital at Columbia during the 1820s. In 1822 a burial society was organized, subsequently constituted as the Hebrew Benevolent Society. Presumably the Jews met also for worship, and Congregation Tree of Life dates itself from 1822.[32] A pious Jew, Jacob S. Solis, came to New Orleans late in 1827 and was shocked to discover that although the community had at least twenty-five adult Jewish males, no congregation had been formed. Late that year or early in 1828, Solis succeeded in organizing "The Israelite Congregation of Shanarai-Chasset." [33] As in New Orleans, Jews had been living in Baltimore since the last decades of the eighteenth century. The 1820s saw major growth of the Jewish community, but it was not until 1829, with the arrival of Zalma Rehiné from Richmond, that a minyan was formed—it convened in his home. The following year the Baltimore Hebrew Congregation was chartered.[34]

The emergence of the Jew in the Christian communities in Europe and America, combined with the desire to convert him, led to a romanticization of the Jew. The thesis that the American Indian was a descendant of Israel's Ten Lost Tribes had long fascinated Protestants, producing such works as Elias Boudinot's *Star in the West* (Trenton, 1816). William Brown's two-volume *Antiquities of the Jews* (Philadelphia, 1823) paved the way for numerous editions of William Whiston's *The Genuine Works of Flavius Josephus,* which had been printed in America as far back as 1794. But no Jewish figure captured the popular imagination more than Rebecca of Walter Scott's *Ivanhoe,* published in American editions simultaneously in New York and Philadelphia in 1823.[35]

Thus the 1820s can be seen as a productive, creative period for the tiny American Jewish community. Certainly word of Jewish freedom and self-assuredness must have reached abroad, for the following decade saw a new outpouring of immigrants from Europe.

What lasting results did the events of the 1820s have? Noah's dream of Ararat and Levy's colony for Jews in Florida, as well as the latter's Jewish boarding school, were too visionary. However, Levy did bring non-Jewish colonists to Florida at his own expense and developed some areas of that state. His son, from whom he became estranged, changed his name to Yulee and was elected Florida's first U.S. Senator. Levy Lake is named for the father, Levy County and the town of Yulee for the son.[36] As the general and Jewish population of the United States grew, the relationships to the President became more formal, and fewer Jews sought and secured presidential appointments. The Maryland Jew Bill, although not the last civil-rights stumbling block for Jews (it was 1876 before Jews and Catholics could hold office in New Hampshire), was undoubtedly the last in a state which had a sizable Jewish community. Jackson's periodical, the *Jew,* served its purpose and died; it was 1843 before its successor, Leeser's *Occident,* was born. Hart's *Modern Religion* was too radical and visionary to have an effect. The Reformed Society of Israelites was ahead of its time, but its goals penetrated into Beth Elohim, the Charleston congregation which had rejected them, and found fruition in Baltimore's Har Sinai (1843), New York's Emanu-el (1845), and Philadelphia's Keneseth Israel (1847)—although these groups were more influenced by ideas imported from Germany than those planted in Charleston. New York's first Ashkenazic congregation, B'nai Jeshurun, was to spawn a whole series of landsmannschaften. Isaac Leeser, a product of 1820s thinking, became the most influential Jewish religious leader of his generation. The new congregations in Columbia, Cincinnati, New Orleans, and Baltimore were to provide manpower and inspiration for the creation of other congregations in the hinterland. The romantic image of the Jew was dissipated in the nativist Protestant-Catholic struggles of the 1840s and 1850s and in a growing antisemitic sentiment from which America has never been totally free. As for the American Jews of the 1820s in the succeeding decades, they found themselves inundated by German-born, German-speaking immigrant Jews with whom they had little in common. As a consequence, the native-born Jews became more rapidly assimilated, often intermarried, and in many cases disappeared from the Jewish scene. So we see that the 1820s offered little of lasting import for American Jews, but at the time there was a flowering of American Jewry.

NOTES

The following abbreviations are used for sources in these notes:

AJHQ—American Jewish Historical Quarterly.

AOJD—the author's *Americans of Jewish Descent* (Cincinnati, 1960).

B & B—Joseph L. Blau and Salo W. Baron, eds. *The Jews of the United States, 1790–1840: A Documentary History* (New York and London, 1963).

PAJHS—Publications of the American Jewish Historical Society.

1. See Ira R. Rosenswaike, "An Estimate and Analysis of the Jewish Population of the United States in 1790," *PAJHS,* L, no. 1 (September 1960), p. 25; and his "The Jewish Population of the United States as Estimated from the Census of 1820," *AJHQ,* LIII, no. 2 (December 1963), p. 132.

2. An examination of arrival dates in the United States mentioned in *AOJD* between 1805 and 1820 shows a total of ten Jews who came from Europe, viz.,

    1805—Lewis Allen from England

    1812—Abraham Levy from Amsterdam

    Imanuel Gershom Feist (John Maximilian Dyer) from Alzey, near Mainz

    1816—Tobias Tobias from England

    Joseph Jonas from England

    Michael Bomeisler from Bavaria

    1817—Louis Bomeisler from Bavaria

    Levi Moses Kokernot from Holland

    Phineas Israel (Johnson) from England

    1818—David Israel (Johnson) from England

    Unquestionably there were many more, but no great number.

3. B & B, p. 4.

4. The author's "The Function of Genealogy in American Jewish History," *Essays in American Jewish History* (Cincinnati, 1958), pp. 84 ff.

5. Personal observation. The Myers family letters, with the exception of business letters in the American Jewish Archives, are in the possession of the Chrysler Museum, Norfolk, Va., and restricted by the family. The author was privileged to examine and note the contents of a large number.

6. Isaac Goldberg, *Major Noah: American-Jewish Pioneer* (Philadelphia, 1936).

7. Cf. Selig Adler and Thomas E. Connolly, *From Ararat to Suburbia: The History of the Jewish Community of Buffalo* (Philadelphia, 1960), pp. 5–10.

8. I am indebted to Francis James Dallett, archivist of the University of Pennsylvania, for providing me with the following data from U. S. District Court, Philadelphia, *Reports of Aliens Commencing January 5, 1816,* Book B, p. 163: June 8, 1821. Moses Elias Levy, born in the City of Morocco [Mogador] in the States of Barbary 11 June 1781. Migrated from Havanna [*sic!*], arrived Philadelphia 28 June 1818. Intends to settle in Phila. (*signed* M. E. Levy)

9. Leon Huhner, "Moses Elias Levy, an Early Florida Pioneer and the Father of Florida's First Senator," *Florida Historical Quarterly*, XIX, no. 4 (April 1941), pp. 319–45.

10. Letters of Levy to Samuel Myers, from the above-mentioned Myers Collection. Typescript copies made by the author (copies in AJA).

11. Jacob R. Marcus, *Israel Jacobson: The Founder of the Reform Movement in Judaism* (Cincinnati, 1972).

12. Letter of Levy to Samuel Myers, New York, October 18, 1818.

13. Myers family papers. The Levy circular is printed in Bertram W. Korn, *Eventful Years and Experiences: Studies in Nineteenth Century American Jewish History* (Cincinnati, 1954), pp. 199 f.

14. Huhner, op. cit.

15. Solomon Henry Jackson has been the subject of some misinformation. Many sources refer to him as a brother of Mordecai Manuel Noah's wife, née Rebecca Esther Jackson. Thanks to the careful research of Jon Stedman of Denton, Tex., in U. S. Census and New York Marriage records, it can be stated unconditionally that editor Jackson had *children* who were older than Rebecca Jackson Noah. Solomon Jackson was in America by 1787, when Rebecca's father, Daniel Jackson, and her mother, née Mary Phillips, were barely seven years old. There is one genealogical connection between the two Jackson families: Solomon Henry's oldest daughter, Lydia ("Eliza"), married in New York, May 20, 1834, Dr. Thomas Washington Donovan (who was a born Jew, a member of B'nai Jeshurun, and subsequently clerk of Anshe Chesed). After her death, Donovan married in New York, July 15, 1840, Delia, daughter of Haym M. Salomon, whose second daughter, Sarah Louisa, was married to John Daniel Jackson, brother of Rebecca!!

16. S. Joshua Kohn, "Mordecai Manuel Noah's Ararat Project and the Missionaries," *AJHQ*, LV, no. 2, (December 1965), pp. 185 f.

17. Letters described in Goldberg, op. cit., pp. 141 f. The text of Adams's reply appears in B & B, p. 12.

18. The bulk of De La Motta's address appears in Morris U. Schappes, *A Documentary History of the Jews in the United States, 1654–1875* (New York, 1950), pp. 150 ff. The replies of Jefferson and Madison are appended, and also in B & B, pp. 13 f.

19. B & B, p. 13. Other communications with government dignitaries appear in B & B, pp. 311–14.

20. Letters in the Myers collection (Norfolk, Va.).

21. *PAJHS*, vol. 17, pp. 85 f.; the author's "Moses Myers and the Early Jewish Community of Norfolk," *Journal of the Southern Jewish Historical Society*, vol. 1, no. 1 (November 1958), pp. 9 f.

22. Benjamin H. Hartogensis, "Unequal Religious Rights in Maryland since 1776," *PAJHS*, vol. 25, pp. 95 ff.; Schappes, op. cit., pp. 139–41, 160–63; cf. also B & B, pp. 33–54.

23. Jacob R. Marcus, "The *Modern Religion* of Moses Hart," in his *Studies in American Jewish History, Studies and Addresses* (Cincinnati, 1969), pp. 121–53.

24. Personal observation. Regrettably, in the process of preparing the Myers House to become a public museum, this volume disappeared.

25. Barnett A. Elzas, *The Reformed Society of Israelites* (New York, 1916); cf. the author's, Appendix I: "America's First Reform Jews," *AJHQ*, LXIII, no. 2, (December 1973), pp. 118 f.

26. B & B, pp. 533 f.

27. *Ibid.*, pp. 535–39.
28. *Ibid.*, pp. 540–45.
29. Hyman B. Grinstein, *The Rise of the Jewish Community of New York, 1654–1860* (Philadelphia, 1945), pp. 47 f.; *PAJHS,* vol. 27, p. 109 n.
30. Maxwell Whiteman, "Isaac Leeser and the Jews of Philadelphia: A Study in National Jewish Influence," *PAJHS,* XLVIII, no. 4 (June 1959), p. 213, n. 34. Whiteman gives the date of Leeser's first sermon as Sivan 10, 5590, corresponding to June 2, 1830. B & B, pp. 578 ff., date the sermon 1831.
31. Jacob R. Marcus, *Memoirs of American Jews, 1775–1865.* (Philadelphia, 1955), I, pp. 203 ff.
32. Barnett A. Elzas, *The Jews of South Carolina from the Earliest Times to the Present Day* (Philadelphia, 1905), pp. 245 f.; cf. *American Jewish Year Book, 5661* (1900–1901), p. 458.
33. Bertram W. Korn, *The Early Jews of New Orleans* (Waltham, Mass., 1969), pp. 192 ff.
34. Isaac M. Fein, *The Making of an American Jewish Community: The History of Baltimore Jewry from 1773 to 1920* (Philadelphia, 1971), p. 42. Fein spells the founder's name "Rhine," but there is no question that it is correctly "Rehiné." Cf. Richmond City Personal Property and Land Books; Herbert T. Ezekiel and Gaston Lichtenstein, *The History of the Jews of Richmond from 1769 to 1917* (Richmond, 1917), passim.
35. A. S. W. Rosenbach, "An American Jewish Bibliography . . . ", *PAJHS,* vol. 30, nos. 180, 233, 92, 151, 155, 241, 276, 249, 250.
36. Bernard Postal and Lionel Koppman, *A Jewish Tourist's Guide to the U. S.* (Philadelphia, 1954), pp. 120 f., 122.

THE FRANKLIN BROTHERS IN
GOLD RUSH CALIFORNIA

By

NORTON B. STERN

Editor
Western States Jewish Historical Quarterly

Lewis Abraham Franklin and his brother Maurice Abraham Franklin were members of a prominent English Jewish family, several members of which have received attention in historical accounts of British and Canadian Jewry.[1] But the lives of Lewis and Maurice have been virtually unmentioned in historical annals, though both made substantial contributions to early Jewish life on the western frontier, and Lewis was involved with a number of significant "firsts." The earliest known member of the Franklin family was Menachem Mendel Franckel, who was rabbi of Breslau, Poland. His son, Benjamin Wolf Franklin, emigrated to London about 1763. He married Sarah Joseph in London, and two of their children were Abraham and Lewis Franklin.[2]

Abraham Franklin married Miriam Aron and left a large family. Seven of their sons were Jacob, Benjamin, Isaac, Maurice, Lewis, Abraham G., and Ellis. Lewis A. Franklin, who had been born in 1820, in Liverpool, emigrated to the United States in the 1840s, settling in Baltimore. For a short period prior to his going to Baltimore, he worked in Jamaica, assisting his brother Benjamin. The news of the California gold discovery led to his prompt departure, on January 18, 1849, for San Francisco, by means of the schooner *Sovereign*.[3] There he established a retail store in a canvas-covered, wood-framed room, actually little more than a tent, located on Jackson Street near the corner of Kearny.[4]

551

The deep commitment to Judaism of the Franklin brothers in California and their religious activities there can be better understood in the context of their brothers' lives in England and elsewhere. Jacob in 1842, had founded the *Voice of Jacob*, a monthly opposed to the rise of the Reform movement, and he kept it going at considerable expense for five years. Earlier he had been the representative for Manchester on the Board of Deputies of British Jews. He was a founder of the Anglo-Jewish Association, chairman of the Jewish Board of Guardians, and active in the founding of Jews' College. He established the Franklin Fund for the publishing of studies dealing with Jewish religion and history. Isaac, a Manchester surgeon, was the president and the major benefactor of the Jewish schools of his city and served on numerous national Jewish boards. Benjamin founded the Hebrew Benevolent Society at Kingston, Jamaica, in 1851 and was chairman of the Hebrew schools in that Caribbean town. Ellis was vice-president of the Anglo-Jewish Association and of the Jewish Religious Education Board, a member of the Board of Deputies and the Shechita Board, and also a member of the council of Jews' College.[5] With this level of Jewish activity on the part of his brothers, it is not surprising that the first High Holy Day services in western North America were held in quarters provided by Lewis A. Franklin.

A notice was placed in a San Francisco newspaper that Rosh Hashanah and Yom Kippur services were to be held in Franklin's tent-store, and in the fall of 1849 Lewis was host to the first Jewish worshippers in the West. According to one account, about thirty Jews were present. Another account, which may reflect the Yom Kippur observances, noted that "forty or fifty" were in attendance.[6]

In the summer of the following year (1850), a committee leased a portion of the Masonic Hall on Kearny Street in San Francisco for the High Holy Days, and the temporary congregation organized for the occasion called itself the "Kearny Street Hebrew Congregation." The leaders of this group requested that Lewis Franklin deliver the traditional Yom Kippur sermon, and on September 16, 1850, he did so. His efforts met with such appreciation that the officers and trustees of the temporary High Holy Days congregation requested a copy for publication. In the note of request to Franklin was included this sentiment: "We fervently trust that your zeal in the cause of Judaism may meet with happy results, as from our long and intimate acquaintance with you, we are sensible that this is the only reward you desire."[7]

In his letter of assent, which accompanied the copy of his Yom Kippur sermon, Lewis made the usual disclaimers of modesty, noting that he did not enter "the arena of public life to break a lance with more valiant knights; but as one who claims to be a son in Israel, ever ready to stand forth in the defence of his coreligionists. . . ." He further stated that the time he needed to prepare as the reader for the eve of Yom Kippur might explain any errors which would be discovered in his language.[8]

The sermon itself, which was reprinted in full by the *Asmonean* of New York, thus became the first recorded Jewish homiletical effort in western North America. Franklin initiated his sermon by complimenting his fellow worshippers, then followed this up with a question which brought him to the heart of the ethical message which must be the basis of any Day of Atonement sermon.

> I find myself surrounded by those, whose early education has been such, as to satisfy the most skeptical in their fastidious ideas. That your fathers have not been unmindful of their duty, but have instructed you in the paths of righteousness, your gathering here affords abundant evidence.
>
> From many of you I expect to hear, that you have studied the Law. To such I say, ye have done well . . . but is this all? I answer no, emphatically no! What says Rabbi Simeon, the son of Rabbi Gamaliel, one of our learned sages: "The study of the Law is not the principal [duty], but the practice thereof."

From this point on Franklin's sermon can be characterized as insisting on the necessity for living righteously, doing deeds of mercy, loving-kindness, justice, and benevolence. He inveighed against breaking the Sabbath and stressed the need for love and repentance. In his concluding thought he expressed confidence for the future of Judaism in the new West.

> In this new country, ere civilization with its rapid strides has taken foothold, the Jews, persecuted though they be in despotic Europe, will never depart the banner of their creed, but fearlessly unfold it before all eyes, that its peaceful, fraternal and benign influence shall win it adoration.[9]

Lewis Franklin left San Francisco in the summer of 1851 and settled in San Diego, where, with various partners, he operated the Tienda California (California Shop), a general merchandise business. By the

spring of 1852 he was the sole owner of the store.[10] In the fall of the year
he arrived, Lewis repeated his 1849 experience in San Francisco, hosting
in his home the first High Holy Day services ever held in San Diego. He
was joined in these 1851 services, the first Jewish religious rites of which
there is a contemporary record in Southern California, by Mark Israel
Jacobs and Charles A. Fletcher.[11]

A month later San Diego County was visited by an Indian uprising
known as the Garra revolt, and a volunteer force of seventy-nine men
was hurriedly raised in San Diego to protect the town. Franklin took an
active part in the citizens meeting at which the military force was authorized and organized, and he became the quartermaster of the company. After a futile two-week effort by the volunteers to find the Indians,
the company was disbanded, and a detachment of the United States
Army took the field.[12]

In the spring of 1852 Lewis Franklin served as foreman of the San
Diego County Grand Jury, which rendered a lengthy report on the rampant state of vice and crime, the absence of public sanitation, the alco-
holism of the Indians and those responsible for this evil, and the slipshod
way in which both the city jail was kept and the mayor's office was run.
Franklin wrote and signed the report, which deeply impressed the local
editor.

> We will venture to say, that there never was a body of men, convened
> for a similar purpose, in this county, who so ably, faithfully and fear-
> lessly performed their duties, as this present grand jury; and although
> every member of the body deserves, and has received, thanks of both
> the Court and the people, yet we cannot forbear to mention, particularly,
> Mr. Lewis A. Franklin, the foreman, for the zeal with which he entered
> into the great work of correcting the abuses and suppressing crime in
> our midst.[13]

By the end of the year, Franklin was acting as a justice of the peace
and a notary public, in addition to running his store, the Tienda California. The store carried "dry goods, groceries, liquors, crockery, glass-
ware, hardware and ironmongery." [14] In August 1853, Franklin ran for
the office of county judge (court of sessions) and was elected. In one
case which appeared before him, he sentenced some drunk and rowdy
Indians to various degrees of punishment, and in another case he appealed to Benjamin D. Wilson, captain of the Rangers (vigilantes) in

Los Angeles, to see that justice was done for an Indian who had been wronged by some Los Angeles area Californios.[15]

Maurice A. Franklin (1817–1874) joined his brother Lewis in San Diego in 1853. He had been born in Liverpool and arrived in California in 1849, possibly with his cousins on the *St. George,* in October.[16] Maurice's youngest son stated that his father had gone to the gold fields upon his arrival and "devoted several years to mining." [17] Maurice had attended medical school for a brief period in England just before his departure for the Golden West.[18] This background accounts for his establishment of a pharmacy, which he operated with his brother's store in San Diego, as well as the drugstore which he had at a later period in San Bernardino. Maurice bought an interest in Lewis' Tienda California and for several months the firm was operated as a partnership. During this period the local newspaper had this to say about Lewis and Maurice:

> It gives us sincere pleasure to state that the Messrs. Franklin, the only "observing Jews" among a large number in our midst, have signified their willingness to close their place of business, not only on the Jewish Sabbath, which has always been their custom, but also on the Christian Sunday. It is so seldom that we witness such liberality on the part of religionists of any denomination, that it gives us sincere pleasure to record instances of this kind when they do transpire.[19]

Lewis, having been admitted to the California bar at the end of 1853, sold out his interest in the Tienda California to Maurice and prepared to make a trip to the East. He published a broadside in English and Spanish requesting "all persons indebted" to him to settle up on or before January 15, 1854.[20] Lewis Franklin's status as one of the pioneer attorneys of San Diego makes him the first Jewish lawyer in Southern California and also the first Jewish professional in the Southland.

Lewis soon returned to San Diego and resumed his mercantile activities with Maurice and also practiced law.[21] It is to be noted that in the 1850s lawyers in San Diego "were usually occupied in some other business as a necessity for there was little to retain them in the full-time pursuit of their profession." [22]

Maurice became involved in the civic life of San Diego. In the spring of 1854 he was a member of a committee which devised plans to cut a road to Temecula, a significant settlement some sixty miles north of San Diego.[23] Later he was elected one of the directors of the San Diego

and Gila Railroad Company, which was founded to bring rail transportation to San Diego, so as to end the isolation of the town by land.[24]
That his efforts were appreciated is shown by an editorial comment stating that Maurice "has always been popular in this community and as he
is a permanent resident and has solid investments here, he should, and
will receive a large share of our favors." [25]

One of Maurice's advertisements, placed in the local press in the
spring of 1856, reads in part as follows:

> Maurice A. Franklin—Begs most respectfully to inform his friends and
> the public generally, that . . . he hopes by that assiduity and strict at
> tention which has characterized his past success, to merit a continuance
> of public patronage. The present assorted stock, to which attention is
> invited, is of the newest style, selected expressly for this market and will
> receive fresh accession by every steamer from San Francisco. In order to
> meet the exigencies of the times, a bare remunerative percentage on San
> Francisco cost will be charged on all sales made for cash.[26]

Both Maurice and Lewis traveled to San Francisco from time to time
to order goods for their store. On one of those trips Lewis gave a birthday
present to the young daughter of a friend. On May 6, 1856, he presented
a deed for a lot in the Playa section of San Diego to Ellen Cardozo, to
commemorate the first birthday of that young lady. Lewis had apparently
become friendly with Ellen's father, Isaac N. Cardozo, an American-
born Sephardic Jew who had served in the California state legislature in
1852. The lot was located in what is now the Point Loma area of San
Diego. Isaac Cardozo, the uncle of the twentieth-century United States
Supreme Court Justice, Benjamin N. Cardozo, later became an influential figure in the Jewish and civic life of Saint Paul, Minnesota.[27]

In June 1856, Maurice proposed marriage to Victoria Jacobs, who
was just under eighteen years of age at the time. With her mother's permission she agreed to marry Maurice, who then presented her with a
small leather-bound blank diary. This diary was regularly confided to by
Victoria during the latter half of 1856, and it constitutes a valuable
record of the social life and values of a young Jewish girl in the early
West.[28] Victoria's father was Mark Israel Jacobs, a Polish-born San
Diego merchant, who had lived in England (Victoria had been born in
Manchester) prior to emigrating to the United States. Victoria and
Maurice were married on March 31, 1857, with the bride's father officiating. The local press noted the event in this way:

Married.—On Tuesday, March 31, at the residence of and by the bride's father, according to Jewish rites, Maurice A. Franklin, late of London, England, to Victoria, third daughter of Mark and Hannah Jacobs, late of Manchester, England.

In the new relation of husband and wife, may our friends find their cares lessened by sympathy and their joys multiplied by participation. May they be spared to each other to a good old age, and in the evening of life, when hanging with fond affection over the records of the past, may they be able to say, as they take a retrospective view of their lives, "O God, we have endeavored so to serve thee and keep thy commandments, as to entitle us to hope for a place in thy Kingdom, when we shall have ended this earthly pilgrimage."[29]

The first son of Victoria and Maurice, Abraham M., was born on December 23, 1857, in the Franklin House.[30] This structure, which had originally been a one-story adobe located on the Plaza in Old Town, San Diego, had been purchased by Lewis Franklin in July 1855. In the early 1850s it had served as the Exchange Hotel. The Franklin brothers used the building as a store until the fall of 1857, when they agreed verbally to enter into a partnership in the "business of keeping a hotel and vending drugs." Upon making this decision on October 11, they set about adding a second and third story to their adobe. This addition was constructed of wood, and the remodeled building was soon known as the Franklin House, San Diego's most important hotel and the town's first three-story building.[31]

The brothers operated the hotel, which included a saloon, together, and Maurice operated a drugstore in the building. The Maurice Franklins and Lewis also had their living quarters in the Franklin House.[32] The saloon included a billiard table, and the brothers proudly advertised that "a passenger stage is dispatched on the arrival and departure of each steamer, thus affording facilities hitherto unknown in San Diego." [33]

Unfortunately, the brotherly harmony only lasted for six months or less, and their partnership fell apart as a result of what was called by the district court, "their mutual misconduct and . . . a state of wrangling, discord, violence, and an irreconcilable ill will greatly detrimental to, and in the end, proving wholly inconsistent with the safe and profitable transaction of said business as partners." [34] By March 4, 1858 the brothers had come to a complete parting of the ways; Lewis sued Maurice for damages and requested that a receiver be appointed. The receiver, Joseph Reiner, operated the Franklin House for the benefit of the partners from May 5 until late in 1858. All was finally settled in favor of Lewis, with Maurice getting the supply of drugs and a horse and buggy, with which he and his wife and baby departed for San Bernardino in February, 1859.[35]

Lewis remained in San Diego and continued to operate the Franklin House and his law practice. In the spring of 1859 he was named secretary of the county grand jury.[36] In the fall of that year the Jews of San Diego rented quarters in which to conduct High Holy Day services, and Lewis officiated as the reader. A bare minyan of ten men was present for the services on Yom Kippur, October 8, one of whom was Moses Mannasse, who had come to town from his *rancho* fifty miles to the north. Unfortunately, the grand jury was in session and learned that he was in town. They were hearing a case of assault to which Mannasse had been witness, and they sent the sheriff to bring him before them. When the sheriff arrived at the temporary synagogue to get Mannasse to testify, the men of the minyan resisted this diminishment of their essential quorum for religious services, and the sheriff had to depart without Moses. But in spite of the explanation of Lewis Franklin to the sheriff, the grand jury did not understand the reasons for the negating of their subpoena and sent the sheriff back with a posse, and Mannasse was brought before them. But Moses refused to be sworn, stating that it being Yom Kippur, his religious scruples forbade him from testifying. Services were resumed upon his return and in the evening, after sundown, he gave his testimony.

Lewis Franklin wrote a number of letters of protest about this incident, one of which was sent to and reprinted in the *Weekly Gleaner* of San Francisco. Rabbi Julius Eckman, the editor-publisher of the *Gleaner*, was the senior rabbi in the West at that time, and he strongly objected to the abusive language which Franklin used in reference to the judge and grand jury. Eckman felt that Mannasse's action was an unjustified "contempt of court," that Jewish law required "obedience to the laws of the State," even though the situation occurred on Yom Kippur, and concluded that "if more suasion could not have induced the Judge or Jury to respect his religious scruples and to dispense with his attendance on that day, he ought to have repaired to court when the sheriff summoned him the first time." Eckman felt that the incident had been inconsistent with the Jewish emphasis on civic responsibility, referring to "the evil odor in which they [the San Diego Jews] have brought their coreligionists by their transgression of the laws of the land in so serious a matter as that of the administration of justice." [37]

Sometime in 1860 or 1861, Lewis Franklin left San Diego for Baltimore. He apparently leased out his hotel, but he left California owing $2,980 to a fellow Jew, Joseph S. Mannasse, one of the important merchants of San Diego, who had probably been the principal source of supplies for the Franklin House. In 1862 a summons was served on Franklin in Baltimore by J. S. Mannasse & Company, the failure to answer which brought to a foreclosure the hotel property.[38] Shortly thereafter Lewis returned to London, where he married Emily Davis. Three children were born to them. Lewis died on June 16, 1879. Joseph Mannasse used the Franklin House as a store for a time, and ten years later, on April 20, 1872, San Diego's first three-story building was destroyed by a fire which had started in a nearby home, that of Rudolph Schiller.[39]

When Maurice Franklin and his family went to San Bernardino in early 1859, most of his wife's relatives were already living there. In addition to her parents and siblings, Marcus Katz, her brother-in-law, was operating a thriving book and stationery store, he was the Wells Fargo agent for the town, and he was serving as the San Bernardino county treasurer.[40] Maurice opened a drugstore upon his arrival in San Bernardino and also established a photographic studio, which was located on the second floor, over the pharmacy. For a time he was in business with George A. Reich, the firm being called the San Bernardino Drug Store.[41]

The second son of the Maurice Franklins was born on October 19, 1859, and named Selim M. Two years later Victoria died while giving birth to her third child, who was also lost. She was twenty-three years old at the time of her passing on November 12, 1861, and she was interred in Home of Eternity Cemetery, where her monument may be seen today.[42]

In the spring of 1865, when his sons were seven and five years of age, Maurice decided to do something about their Jewish education. His action was termed a "Noble Example," in the heading to the report describing it. It read:

> We learn that Mr. Franklin, of San Bernardino, has opened a Hebrew Free School for the benefit of the Jewish children in that locality. Such a praiseworthy undertaking is deserving of the highest commendation, and we hope that this noble example will be followed by our liberal-minded coreligionists in all sections of the country where such facilities are needed.[43]

A year later, at a festive Purim gathering, Maurice was presented with "a splendid silver pitcher," as a token of the gratitude felt by the Jewish community for his work in instructing the Jewish children "without any compensation" in the "Hebrew language and religion." [44] This award, presented by the San Bernardino Hebrew Benevolent Society, is now in the possession of a great grandson of the recipient. Maurice was active in the benevolent society, serving as its secretary.[45] He was also a member of the San Bernardino Lodge No. 146, Independent Order of Odd Fellows.

Maurice A. Franklin died on September 2, 1874, at age fifty-seven in San Francisco, where he had gone to seek medical care. He was interred next to his wife in San Bernardino's Home of Eternity Cemetery. His obituary noted that he had been in poor health for four years. The resolution adopted by his Odd Fellows lodge referred to his noble virtues, generosity, and unassuming modesty, all of which "inspired every acquaintance with respect, every friend with affection." [46]

Maurice's two orphaned sons had been raised by their aunt, Mrs. Marcus Katz, after their mother's death in 1861. Both became significant figures in Arizona Territory, where their uncles (Victoria's brothers), Lionel and Barron Jacobs, were important pioneer business and civic figures. The older son, Abraham M. Franklin, enjoyed a lengthy career as a rancher, cattle buyer, and real estate developer.[47] The younger son, Selim M. Franklin, became a prominent attorney in Tucson, where his uncles were in business.[48] He was elected to the territorial legislature of Arizona in 1884, and he wrote and "succeeded in getting passed" the measure establishing the territory's institution of higher learning. For this work he was known as the father of the University of Arizona.[49]

The Franklin brothers of gold rush California were typical of the highly committed Jews who came to the Far West in the early days of the American period, and were instrumental in establishing Jewish institutions in the new land. Their devotion to their heritage involved them in a number of significant actions, records of which have been uncovered in our time. Their facility in the English language, along with their Jewish affirmations and background and the natural abilities which they possessed, made them significant leaders in the California Jewish communities in which they resided.

NOTES

1. "Benjamin A. Franklin" and "Jacob Abraham Franklin," *Jewish Encyclopedia,* vol. 5, pp. 496–97; "Franklin" and "Selim Franklin," *Universal Jewish Encyclopedia,* vol. 4, pp. 412–15; Arthur Ellis Franklin, *Records of the Franklin Family and Collaterals* (London, 1915); David Rome, *The First Two Years* (Montreal, 1942), pp. 52–105; "The First Jew in Public Office" and "Lumley Franklin—Mayor of Victoria," *Jewish Western Bulletin,* British Columbia Centenary Edition, 1858–1958 (Vancouver, June 30, 1958), pp. 5, 56.
2. Three of Lewis Franklin's sons, Selim, Lumley, and Edward, who were first cousins of Lewis and Maurice Franklin, the subjects of this study, came to San Francisco from London in 1849. Selim had equipped the *St. George* for the voyage, and it was the first British ship to have made this trip (April–October 1849). Selim and Lumley settled in Victoria, British Columbia, in 1858, having been attracted there by the Fraser River gold rush. Selim Franklin (1814–1883) became the first Jew to sit in a legislature of the Dominion of Canada. Lumley Franklin (1812–1873) was the first Jew to be elected mayor of a Canadian city (Victoria, 1866).
3. C. W. Haskins, *The Argonauts of California* (New York, 1890), p. 491.
4. Seixas Solomons, in *Occident,* October 1854, p. 371.
5. *Jewish Encyclopedia,* loc. cit.; *Universal Jewish Encyclopedia,* loc. cit.; two unidentified newspaper clippings, Manchester and Portsmouth, England, November 30, 1880, on the death of Dr. Isaac A. Franklin, in the possession of Mrs. John H. Carroll, Tucson, Arizona (Mrs. Carroll is a granddaughter of Maurice A. Franklin).
6. *Asmonean,* November 30, 1849, p. 45; *Occident,* November 1849, p. 480.
7. *Asmonean,* November 15, 1850, p. 30.
8. *Ibid.,* p. 31.
9. *Ibid.* For further details on the services in San Francisco in 1849 and 1850, and the events leading up to the founding of the first permanent congregations of the West in 1851, see William M. Kramer and Norton B. Stern, "The Search for the First Synagogue in the Golden West," *Western States Jewish Historical Quarterly,* October 1974, pp. 3 ff.
10. *San Diego Herald,* August 21, 1851, p. 3, November 20, 1851, p. 3; James Mills, "The Franklin House," *San Diego Historical Society Quarterly,* April 1956, p. 24.
11. *San Diego Herald,* October 9, 1851, p. 2.
12. Noel M. Loomis, "The Garra Uprising of 1851," *Brand Book II: The San Diego Corral of the Westerners* (San Diego, 1970), pp. 3–26.
13. *San Diego Herald,* April 17, 1852, pp. 2–3.
14. *Ibid.,* December 4, 1852, p. 2.
15. *Ibid.,* August 13, 1853, p. 3; Lewis A. Franklin, letter to B. D. Wilson, August 5, 1853, Wilson Papers, Huntington Library, San Marino, California.

16. See n. 2; headstone of Maurice A. Franklin, Home of Eternity Cemetery, San Bernardino, California. Maurice and his brother Abraham G. had taken over their father's silversmith business in Liverpool and operated it briefly from about 1846 to 1848. Arthur Ellis Franklin, *op. cit.*, p. 28.
17. *Portrait and Biographical Record of Arizona* (Chicago, 1901), p. 236. This is the biographical account of the Honorable Selim M. Franklin.
18. Mrs. John H. Carroll, Tucson, Arizona, letter to the writer, June 24, 1973.
19. *San Diego Herald*, August 13, 1853, p. 3.
20. San Diego County Law Library, Franklin House Case, No. 11, Box 15025, 1858.
21. *San Diego Herald*, October 25, 1854, p. 2, November 18, 1854, p. 2.
22. Marion H. Bressette, "Notes on the Franklin House Case," May 19, 1973, in the possession of the writer. Mrs. Bressette is a researcher and librarian employed by the San Diego County Law Library, San Diego, California.
23. *San Diego Herald*, April 1, 1854, p. 2.
24. *Ibid.*, October 11, 1856, p. 2; Victoria Jacobs, *Diary of a San Diego Girl—1856,* ed. Sylvia Arden (Santa Monica, 1974), p. 68.
25. *San Diego Herald*, May 17, 1856, p. 2.
26. *Ibid.*
27. San Diego County, Deeds, Book D, p. 218, December 23, 1853, wherein is recorded the purchase of the lot by Franklin from George H. Davis of San Diego; Indenture, May 6, 1856, San Francisco, Lewis A. Franklin to Isaac N. Cardozo, acting as trustee for Ellen N. Cardozo, conveying title to the lot, Minnesota Historical Society, Saint Paul. On I. N. Cardozo's career in Minnesota, see W. Gunther Plaut, *The Jews in Minnesota* (New York, 1959), pp. 35, 46, 58.
28. The diary, which was carefully preserved by the descendants of Maurice and Victoria Franklin, was published in 1974 as *Diary of a San Diego Girl—1856.*
29. *San Diego Herald*, April 4, 1857, p. 2.
30. *Ibid.*, January 9, 1858, p. 2.
31. Bressette, *op. cit.*; Mills, *op. cit.*; Orion Zink, "The Exchange Hotel," *San Diego Historical Society Quarterly*, October 1962, pp. 56 f.
32. San Diego County Law Library, *op. cit.*
33. *San Diego Herald*, February 6, 1858, p. 2.
34. San Diego Judgment Book, pp. 42–86, *L. A. Franklin* vs. *M. A. Franklin*, District Court of the First Judicial District, State of California, December term, 1858, quoted by Bressette, *op. cit.*
35. *Ibid.*; Abraham M. Franklin, "Reminiscences," Arizona Historical Society Library, Tucson, Arizona; *San Diego Herald*, May 8, 1858, p. 2.
36. *Ibid.*, March 6, 1858, p. 2, March 13, 1858, p. 2, April 16, 1859, p. 3.
37. *Weekly Gleaner*, November 4, 1859, p. 4, November 11, 1859, pp. 2, 4.
38. San Diego Judgment Book, p. 86.
39. Arthur Ellis Franklin, op. cit., pp. 28, 47; *San Diego Union*, April 21, 1872, p. 2. Rudolph Schiller, another pioneer Jew of San Diego, was one of that town's first photographers and later engaged in the bookbinding business there.
40. Norton B. Stern, ed., "Memoirs of Marcus Katz," *Western States Jewish Historical Quarterly*, October 1968, pp. 20–21. Katz served from 1857 to 1865 as county treasurer, being elected three times. He was Wells Fargo agent from 1858 to 1874.
41. *San Bernardino Guardian*, November 26, 1870, p. 3; *Pacific Coast Business Directory* (San Francisco, 1870), "San Bernardino."
42. Home of Eternity Cemetery is owned and operated by Congregation Emanu El of San Bernardino, it having been established in May, 1861, through the efforts of Marcus Katz.

43. *The Hebrew* (San Francisco), May 12, 1865, p. 4.
44. *Ibid.,* April 13, 1866, p. 4.
45. *Ibid.* Though the *Hebrew* called it the San Bernardino Hebrew Benevolent Society, its correct name was Chebra Gemeluth Chesed, literally "the organization for the performance of deeds of loving-kindness." *San Bernardino Guardian,* March 14, 1868, p. 2.
46. *Ibid.,* September 19, 1874, p. 2.
47. Abraham M. Franklin, *op. cit.*; Dorothy and Elizabeth Franklin, interview, June 3, 1973. Dorothy and Elizabeth Franklin are daughters of Abraham Franklin, and they reside in Laguna Hills, California.
48. Selim M. Franklin's uncles had sent him to the University of California, from which he was graduated in 1882, and he subsequently was graduated from the law school of the same institution in 1883. After his father died in 1874, Selim had attended Heald's Business College in San Francisco. *Directory of San Francisco 1875,* p. 383.
49. *Portrait and Biographical Record of Arizona*; Mrs. John H. Carroll, interview, June 3, 1973. Mrs. Carroll is a daughter of Selim Franklin.

JEW AND CHRISTIAN IN A NEW SOCIETY: SOME ASPECTS OF JEWISH-CHRISTIAN RELATIONSHIPS IN THE UNITED STATES, 1848–1881

By

ALLAN TARSHISH

Temple Jeremiah, Northfield, Illinois

Explorations toward new patterns of vital significance were woven into the fabric of human and religious life in our country during the period from 1848 to 1881.[1] The genesis of this new development was discernible even before, when there were fewer Jews in the United States. But in this period it had to face the reality of a sizable number of Jews in the country. When the period began, there were about 50,000 Jews in America, and at the end, about 250,000.[2]

Opposing factors of thought and conduct affected the situation. On the one hand, the vast majority of the people of the United States were Christians, many of whom had been taught that the Jews had killed Jesus; that Christianity was the successor to Judaism; that the Jews had been rejected by God and had been scattered over the world to atone for their sins. Moreover, they were influenced by the normal human weaknesses of distrust for someone who was different and of jealousy and suspicion of others who succeeded. In addition, many of them brought from their European past a vast gamut of stereotypes about those who were different, including the Jews.

On the other hand, whatever feelings people had, there was little indigenous history of anti-Jewish activity in the United States. Religious liberty and equality for all groups had been proclaimed by the founding fathers and heroes of early American life and had been imbedded in the Federal Constitution. By law, the United States was not a Christian nation, the first great country so to be founded. So there was a feeling among many that religious prejudice was foreign to the American soil and somewhat "un-American."

Moreover, in the period of the new nationalism, the individual relationship between the state and the citizen was more clearly delineated in America than in European societies, where there were legal relationships between the state and religious groups as such. This pattern of individual relationships tended to minimize some sharp religious differences.

Also, since this country had no national church, and since people of various Christian denominations poured into it, religious sects proliferated. There was no dominant Christian religious group nationally, though some may have been dominant in specific localities. Therefore it was not considered so unusual and strange to be different religiously. The basic theme of the American idea was to be united nationally rather than religiously.

All these factors were, of course, aided by the expanding economy and the healing lure of the great, open western frontier. While economic competition certainly existed and many people failed or suffered economically, there was present the basic hope that people could improve themselves. Thus jealousy toward others was minimized, and there was even the feeling that all who could increase economic wealth were of value to all; that their success did not hurt, but could benefit all others.

Let us now consider, therefore, how these various factors interacted in American society, and how they influenced specific Jewish-Christian relationships in the United States in this perod.

In the Marketplace of Opinion

Certainly, expressions of anti-Jewish feeling often appeared. Even Walt Whitman referred to the "dirty looking German Jews, with a glass box on their shoulders, [who] cry out 'glass to mend' with a stark nasal twang and flat squalling enunciation to which the worst Yankee brogue is sweet music." [3]

On the other hand, if the Jew improved himself and engaged in cultural pursuits by attending the theater, he could be greeted with this comment: "For a few paltry cents he can make himself at home here. . . . This is the place where he finds recognition, where no one can make him feel that he is a Jew. And how the jewelry glitters. . . . Rebecca and

Sarah can lean over the balustrade of the first balcony, showing themselves to all. . . . You will, dear reader, recognize them at a glance by the
way they carry their elbows. But should your eyes not recognize them—
well, then, your nose will let you know in the midst of which species you
find yourself." [4]

A writer in the Cincinnati *Presbyterian Witness* of 1863 listed several
reasons why he thought the Jew was despised: his Semitic and oriental
character made him quicker than the sluggish Japhet. Though it was
true that he had been forced into business life by Christians, still his
character was too commercial. His religion was unworthy and Jews were
foreigners. They were even cursed by their own God, as Jeremiah himself had said (29:9): "I will deliver thee to be a reproach and a taint,
and a curse in all the world." In his response to this article, Isaac Mayer
Wise stated that Jews had superior talents in some fields and Christians
in others. Though many Jews were merchants, so were many Christians,
and as a group neither was more commercial than the other. He denied
that Jews were foreigners and pointed out that many used better English
than the writer of the article. He gloried in the religion of Judaism and
directed attention to its great ideals of universal, ethical monotheism,
justice, and charity. And he concluded that the Jews were more blessed
by God than cursed.[5]

The charge of being aliens came up from time to time. In 1855, when
the question of Sunday laws was on the agenda of the California legislature, one representative claimed that the Jews did not want to remain
permanently in the United States anyway, but they were here only to
make enough money to return to Palestine. The California *Zeitung* responded by listing in detail the amount of land, homes, synagogues, and
other permanent institutions which the Jews had acquired in the state,
and pronounced that Jews were fully determined to dig deep roots in the
United States.[6]

Jews, of course, were occasionally blamed for the crucifixion of Jesus.
In 1872, when a Jewish benevolent association applied to the Texas state
legislature for a charter, one of the legislators expressed his opposition to
incorporating a "Christ killing association." But another member of the
body defended the Jews, yet used a stereotype when he said: "They [the
Jews] are heroes as well as traders . . ." [7]

Jews constantly battled these stereotypes. In 1874, they finally prevailed
upon the Merriam Company to eliminate from the Webster dictionary the
term *to Jew,* which had been defined, "to bargain." [8]

Other latent prejudices were clothed in the guise of compliments. Reporting the dedication of the synagogue in Wilkes-Barre, Pennsylvania, in 1849, one of the local papers was most complimentary about the ceremony, but ended: "One lady with whom I became acquainted appears a truly regenerate person and is so esteemed by some of the best Christian people here. And why should we not expect to find a remnant here and now, as well as Paul in his day? Doubtless a remnant of them will be saved." [9]

When the Reverend S. M. Isaacs preached the dedicatory sermon for K.A.M. Congregation in Chicago in 1851, the *Daily Democrat* commented: "No person that has made up his mind to be prejudiced against the Jew ought to have heard such a sermon preached. . . . We never could have believed that one of those old Jews we have heard denounced so much could have taught so much liberality toward other denominations . . ." [10]

An excellent example of varying random thoughts on Jews can be found in the reaction to Rabbi Morris Raphall's prayer opening the United States House of Representatives in 1860, since he was the first rabbi so invited. Most of the comments were laudatory, but a reporter for the *Philadelphia Press* dourly wrote that beautiful as the prayer was, it was long enough to be a sermon. There were some critical comments from certain church papers. The reporter from the *New York Herald* thought it would be instructive to walk around the galleries and pick up the chance remarks of those attending. These are some of the comments he heard: ". . . the old fellow in his regalia . . . beautiful white embroidered scarf over his shoulder . . . velvet cap on his head. . . . A Jew praying for the American House of Representatives . . . going to pray for ten cents a month . . . the next thing we shall have will be a shaking Quaker doing the reel. . . . Yes, or Brigham Young surrounded by his harem . . . or a pawnshop in the basement . . . but he is a Jew. Yes, the general original Jacobs, the high priest of the tribe of Levi in New York . . . well, after that, I am ready for a black Republican speaker . . ." [11]

Jews were occasionally made the target of some of the jokes of the period. For instance, it was asked, "Why is a Jew like a greenback? Because he doesn't know that his redeemer liveth." [12]

Comments like these were not unusual in Jewish history, but what was different in this period is that Jews had the courage to respond vigorously and boldly.[13] Thus, for instance, when the *New York Herald*, in 1850, hinted that there might be some truth in the charge of ritual murder against the Jews in the Damascus case of 1840, the *Asmonean* responded with a sharp attack against the *Herald,* which in this period often published uncomplimentary statements about the Jews. Isaac Mayer Wise was equally forthright: "we despise them [the *Herald*] too much to discuss this question with them. We do not throw pearls before swine." [14]

In response to criticism, Jews adopted certain techniques of defense. Usually they began by unmasking the lie. Then they pointed to the good qualities of Jews, listing Jewish contributions to the American scene. And then they often concluded by switching to the attack, claiming that Judaism was superior to Christianity and that Jews surpassed Christians in many ways.

They also took certain preventive measures. Some congregational constitutions ruled that no member could bring legal proceedings against another before the case was first tried by the board of trustees of the congregation. [15] One Jewish editor made the supreme sacrifice, announcing that he restrained himself from expressing his low opinion of Jewish clergymen because of his non-Jewish readers! [16]

Community activity was also considered beneficial. When a circular was distributed to Jewish congregations asking them to contribute to the National Lincoln Monument, the Jewish protagonists urged a generous response to strengthen the image of the Jew. [17] When Congregation B'nai Jeshurun of Cincinnati (later the Isaac Mayer Wise Temple) in 1875 tried to persuade the Jewish businessmen of the city to close their establishments on Saturday and attend the synagogue, it averred: "If we respect opinion, we must as Israelites observe the Sabbath." [18] One of the reasons sometimes given for the organization of Jewish hospitals was to win the respect of the Christian community. [19]

It is also of interest that, in order to win the respect of Christians, the Jews of this period often avoided calling themselves Jews for the word *Jew* was often identified in the Christian mind with the Jew of the ghetto, whom many Christians despised or ridiculed. So they often tended to use *Hebrew* or *Israelite,* for these terms were identified with the biblical Jew, whom the Christians respected. Thus: Board of Delegates of American Israelites, the *American Israelite,* the Union of American Hebrew Congregations, the Hebrew Union College, Hebrew Orphan Society, and so on.

In many ways, the Jew himself was his own self-defense. Imperfect as he was, nevertheless his ability, adjustment to American society, ideals, moral family living, pursuit of education and culture, charities for himself and society in general, and other contributions to the environment were often lauded. In 1877, the Illinois *Staatszeitung* published a long article containing many statistics proving that Jews were more generous in philanthropy than others.[20] Jewish home life often elicited admiration. The *Archive Israélite* of France reported that in 1866 a Cincinnati Jew went to court seeking a divorce from his wife on the grounds of her infidelity. The judge denied his plea, stating that such a dereliction was unknown among the Israelites.[21] Whether the *Archive Israélite* reported correctly or the judge's confidence in Jewish family morality was too sweeping, the account does represent the general feeling about the high standards of Jewish morality and family life.

How can we assess the mass feeling about Jews? Certainly there was plenty of latent and not so latent anti-Jewish feeling at this time. It was expressed variously in large cities and in small towns, and mostly among the more fundamentalist Christians, though, as we shall note, it was not absent in the higher echelons of Christian society. Yet, what was different in the new land was that Jews had the courage to stand up and strike back, that they were supported by large sections of the American public, that complimentary assessments of Jews were very frequent, and that the liberal spirit of the country in general and the opportunities for economic improvement were very pervasive. Thus, as the period advances, we shall note a perceptible tide leading to even more acceptance and equality.

Economic Life

How did anti-Jewish feeling affect the very vital factor of economic life and opportunity? At the beginning of our period, most of the bastions of economic privilege, the old established banks and businesses, were almost completely closed to Jews. But with continued economic expansion and the development of the West, Jews were able to find many areas of opportunity, usually in sectors requiring daring, experimentation, and risk. Most Jews started out as peddlers, employees, and small craftsmen, but many rose to establish small businesses of their own, in a period when only a small amount of capital was required. A number pioneered in new patterns of economic activity: the manufacture of wholesale clothing and the department store. Then some went into banking, usually in small towns, for they were willing to take the risks. Some of these Jewish bankers and businessmen moved to the great metropolises and established sizable private banking institutions.[22]

They met some anti-Jewish feeling on every echelon. Peddlers were often fair game and Jewish peddlers even more so. A non-Jewish peddler told of his experience in a small town in the East. He was accosted by an official of the town: "Now, as it happened, I had a ten day growth of stubble on my chin. Noticing it, he next asked if I were a Jew, and when I denied it, seemed reluctant to believe me. Fortunately, I had my passport with me, and was able to convince him. He at once softened up, gave me a sympathetic look and said: 'I see that you're an honest Protestant, I'll let you go, though it's costing me twenty-five dollars. I'm no friend of the Jews, and if you were one . . . you would have been fined fifty dollars or gone to jail, and I would have got half the cash for my pains' . . ." This sort of thing was not uncommon.[23] Glanz even states that in the South, where hatred of the Yankee peddler was apt to be transferred to the Jew, it was not only his property but his very life that was threatened. He recounts that in 1873 a German-Jewish peddler was murdered at Baton Rouge, Louisiana, and three Negroes subsequently lynched for the crime by outraged citizens.[24] However, this really does not seem to be an example of Southern anti-semitism. The Jew was not murdered because he was a Jew, but because he had some money and property. This was simply a case of highway robbery, not infrequent at that time. In fact, the outraged non-Jewish citizens quickly avenged the murder of the Jew, even though it was by lynch law.

In fact, Yankees and Jews were often equated. A German guide for emigrants, published in 1864, for the New England states said this: "The inhabitants are called Yankees in all other parts of the Union. . . . They fraternize closely and are the Jews of the New World. . . . They are dominated by insatiable greediness . . ."[25] Another example, a humorous sketch of a steamboat trip written by a southern writer in 1852, recounted: "As the captain passed the money over . . . the lower jaws of the disappointed sharpers fell about a foot, and almost simultaneously [they] exclaimed: 'Jewed!' 'Yankee'd!' "[26]

In many areas, Jews were accused of sharp dealings, based on the stereotypes of the past. If business malpractices developed, Jews were often accused as a group. This was particularly true of arson in order to collect insurance money. No doubt some Jews were guilty, but so were many others, yet Jews were sometimes singled out as the prime malefactors. Thus, in 1867, a number of large insurance companies banded together and issued secret instructions to their agents not to insure the property of Jews. The secret instructions did not long remain secret and Jews protested vigorously. Large protest meetings were held in Cincinnati, New York, St. Louis, Richmond, Cleveland, and elsewhere.

The New York meeting issued the following statement: "The undersigned suppose that it should need no argument to demonstrate the impropriety and injustice of denouncing a large body of persons for the crimes (if they exist) of individuals, or of regulating commercial intercourse upon the basis of nationality or religion. They had imagined . . . that the bigotry which disgraced other times and other countries . . . can have no place in this enlightened age and favored land . . ." [27]

The Jews promptly agreed to boycott all the participating insurance companies and, as a result, many insurance agents severed their connections with the boycotted companies and the stocks of many of them dropped in value. Moreover, a number of competitive insurance companies were organized by Jewish businessmen, even though the original companies retracted their restrictive orders.[28]

Here, again, it is to be noted that Jews did not hesitate to assert their rights, feeling as they did that they lived in an "enlightened age and a favored land."

Although many Jews in this period did not become rich, and many even failed, it is apparent that whatever minor economic restrictions existed or surfaced, they did not materially affect Jewish economic opportunity. Some Jews became rich. Most bulked largely in the middle class, more than in other societies.

Social Discrimination

Restrictions against Jews manifested themselves more often in social discrimination. Many of the exclusive societies and clubs refused admission to Jews. The older American families tended to ignore the rising, wealthy German Jews, as they did most of the other newly rich. Yet in this period there was less discrimination in the more public institutions than in a a later period. The communal societies, political clubs, artistic circles, and general hotels were in the main open to Jews. It was still a fluid society.

There were, of course, exceptions though they were usually greeted with public outrage. Although Jews participated in the founding of the Arion Choral Society (German *Gesang Verein*) in 1854, twelve years later, in 1866, the society resolved to refuse further admission to Jews. The non-Jew who had proposed the Jew who was denied admission, resigned from the society. The *New Yorker Handelszeitung*, the Illinois

Staatszeitung, and many other newspapers carried editorials against this infringement of the American spirit. Ironically, it was this society which later brought Leopold Damrosch to this country, to become its leader. Also, on the sudden death in New York in 1883 of Eduard Lasker, the Jewish member of the German Reichstag, the Arion Society participated in the funeral—at Temple Emanu-El![29]

Another interesting irony of history occurred in 1879, when a hotel at Coney Island, New York, refused admission to Jews.[30]

The most notable incident touching on social discrimination was the Hilton-Seligman affair of 1877. Henry Hilton, a New York attorney, had become business manager of the A. T. Stewart interests, which, among other things, owned a well-known department store in New York City and a fashionable hotel in Saratoga, New York. When this hotel denied admission to Joseph Seligman, a Jew and one of the most important bankers in the country, much public condemnation developed. The incident was widely discussed not only in the United States but also in Europe. Faced with the furor he had precipitated, Hilton made an attempt to explain that his action did not apply to all Jews, but only to the Seligman-type of Jews, and when he was asked what that meant, he replied "trade Jews," which only served to arouse further antagonism. Leading Jewish businessmen in various towns held protest meetings and issued resolutions threatening to boycott the A. T. Stewart interests. And this was a potent threat.

On examination, the affair was revealed as not primarily one of social discrimination, but as reflecting personal and ideological differences between Hilton and Seligman. One explanation was that Seligman, annoyed because Hilton had charged him an excessively high legal fee, blackballed Hilton's admission into the Union League, of which Seligman was vice-president, and that Hilton had retaliated in kind. The more likely explanation of the blackball was that Seligman, a member of the Committee of Seventy, had been battling the Tweed Ring, of which Hilton was a member, and felt that Hilton did not qualify for the Union League.

In any case, the A. T. Stewart interests lost much business and the hotel in Saratoga never denied admission to a Jew again.[31]

Is the United States a Christian Nation?

How did the Jew fare under the legal system of the country? Article 6 of the Constitution of the United States reads: "No religious test shall ever be required as a qualification to any office or public trust under the

United States"; and the first amendment to the Constitution enjoins Congress from making any "law respecting an establishment of religion, or prohibiting the free exercise thereof."

Many of the early leaders of our country were Deists, deeply devoted to the principle of liberty and equality for all religious groups. Washington's famous letter to the Jews of Newport is well known. In reviewing his life, crowned with many honors, Thomas Jefferson singled out three achievements of which he was most proud and requested that they be inscribed on his tombstone: (1) he was the author of the Declaration of Independence; (2) he was the founder of the University of Virginia; (3) he was the author of the religious liberty clause in the Virginia state constitution.

In that period, also, since there were so many religious sects seeking to be recognized as the state religion, it was considered most wise and practical not to have any state religion at all. Because of both these factors, the United States became the first great nation in the world having no state religion. In law, therefore, the United States is not a Christian nation.

Nevertheless, since most Americans were Christians, many local legal restrictions remained and many local officials discriminated against Jews—as we shall note. Also, there were many Christians who assumed that the United States was a Christian nation, and others who thought it should be. Thus in 1858, President Buchanan, in a dispatch to the queen of England, included the United States in the phrase, "all the Christian nations." When challenged by Jewish leaders, he quickly apologized, affirming that he had made the statement unconsciously and that he firmly believed in complete religious equality for all groups.[32]

However, there were many sporadic attempts to promote the adoption of Christianity as the state religion, but they were always opposed by Jews and liberal Christians and remained ineffective.[33] But a concerted effort toward this end was made in 1863 by a group of Presbyterian ministers meeting in Pittsburgh, who then set out to arouse popular support. By 1865, they were able to persuade Senator Grimes of Iowa to introduce such an amendment into the Senate and have it referred to the Judiciary Committee. Einhorn, Wise, and many other Jewish leaders immediately rose to the attack. The Board of Delegates of American Israelites presented a memorial, written by Isaac Leeser, to the Senate and the House of Representatives. The memorial expressed the confidence of the board in the wisdom of Congress, but considered it necessary to bring the following facts to its attention: the Jews had fought in the American Revolution; they had come to the United States seeking religious freedom; they had contributed to the development of America and challenged any other denomination to a comparison of morality, frugality, honesty, and industry; the framers of the Constitution had been deeply religious, but were great men who wisely and deliberately omitted a state creed and legislated against it; and never had such an omission been harmful to the country. The Judiciary Committee quickly tabled the proposal.[34]

Religious Qualifications for Office

Though the United States Constitution prohibited a religious test for any office in the federal government, a few states retained provisions disqualifying non-Christians from holding state offices. In the 1820s, before our period, such a law had been stricken from the constitution of the state of Maryland, largely through the efforts of a non-Jew, Thomas Kennedy.

When our period began, two states, North Carolina and New Hampshire, still retained such disqualifications. Jews were acutely aware of this discrimination and used every opportunity to denounce these laws, although certainly in North Carolina, the law was practically a dead letter. As far back as 1808, Jacob Henry, a Jew, had been elected to the state legislature and, though challenged on this point by his opponent, remained in office. Nevertheless, the Jews of the state repeatedly pressed for revision of the law.[35] After the Civil War, when a new state constitution was written, the offending provision remained. The Board of Delegates and other Jewish groups issued protests in the newspapers of the state and the new constitution was defeated. In 1868, a new constitution, minus the restrictive clause, was promulgated and adopted.[36]

Jews were equally tenacious in their efforts to eliminate the comparable restrictive clause from the New Hampshire state constitution. The *Asmonean,* in 1850, exhorted the Jews of the United States not to vote for Franklin Pierce for President because he came from New Hampshire.[37] The Board of Delegates drafted a memorial denouncing the New Hampshire law and finally, under the continued pressure of Jews and liberal Christians, the state modified its constitution in 1877, eliminating the disqualifying clause.[38]

There were other minor problems. In 1868, the state of Michigan projected a new constitution which failed to include an explicit reference to religious liberty. Because of this omission, the constitution was defeated, and it was adopted only after it was properly worded.[39]

The constitution of the state of Tennessee contained a provision that the legislature should be opened in prayer by a "Christian" minister. In 1872, the Jews of the state were effective in having the word *Christian* deleted. Immediately thereafter, a rabbi was asked to offer the invocation at the next session of the legislature.[40]

Nevertheless, throughout the country, from time to time, Jews who ran for office were attacked by their opponents for being Jewish, sometimes in an undercover campaign and sometimes even openly. An incident of this sort occurred in Detroit, when, in 1856, a German Jew, Edward Kanter, ran for the state legislature on the Democratic ticket. In the course of the campaign, the city's German Republican press sought to make an issue of Kanter's Jewishness. Despite their attacks, Kanter was elected and received more votes than any of the native-born candidates elected from Detroit. Again, two years later, in 1858, Kanter's candidacy for state treasurer was opposed for the same reason.[41] Sporadic attacks on Jews running for office, because they were Jews, occurred here and there, but in the main were not effective. The success or failure of a Jewish candidate was usually decided by other factors.

Eventually most restrictive state religious laws were eliminated. They were primarily the remaining vestiges of obsolete mores, no longer accepted by the majority, but sometimes difficult to eliminate. Most of them had been honored in the breach, even before they were officially abolished, and when sufficient interest was aroused against them, they disappeared. But local mores and restrictions were more difficult to eliminate.

Sunday Laws

There was no federal law prohibiting business on Sunday, but many states and municipalities enacted such legislation. Many Jews, however, wished to abstain from work on Saturday and to have the right to engage in business on Sunday. There were also a number of non-Jews—Seventh-Day Adventists and the like—who also believed that no one day should be set aside as a religious holiday for the whole community. Therefore, throughout the period the problem of Sunday laws arose in a number of cases in many communities, with varying results.[42]

The Jews of Richmond, in 1845, successfully petitioned the city fathers to abolish Sunday closing laws. The following year, they approached the state legislature with this forthright petition: "Your petitioners wish it to be directly understood that they ask for no special legislation; they desire no favor for themselves which is denied other citizens; they merely desire that they should be upon the same footing, as Jews, with those who are Christians; they ask for no protection of the seventh day which they conscientiously believe and can defend by historical data as being the original Sabbath, but they, as free men, respectfully demand that neither shall the Christian Sunday obtain any legal sanction, at least to the degree of inflicting penalities on those whose conscience does not give it any sacredness. . . ." After a few years, Virginia did amend its law to permit those who abstained from work on Saturday to engage in business on Sunday.[43]

New Orleans was equally liberal. When certain Christian groups asked the City Council to close the coffee-houses, theaters, and other businesses on Sunday, it replied: "We cannot constitutionally favor or recognize the doctrines or customs of any particular sect. The Christian Sabbath has no higher claim upon us for protection and enforcement by law, than the Jewish. It would be quite as proper in our Hebrew citizens to ask that coffee houses should be closed on Saturday, their holy Sabbath." [44] Of course, New Orleans was predominantly Catholic, and its citizenry did not hold as rigid a view about the observance of Sunday. Moreover, many of the owners of the coffee-houses and theaters were Christians.

However, in many other instances the Jews were not so successful.[45] A most peculiar reason for enforcing the Sunday law was offered by a court in Shreveport, Louisiana, in 1874. A Jew of that city was fined for keeping his business open on Sunday. He pointed to a city ordinance permitting him the right to do business on Sunday if he closed on Saturday. The court declared the city ordinance null and void on the ground that Jew and Christian must be equal before the law![46]

Still, as a result of intense pressures from Jews and others, a number of municipalities and states were persuaded to liberalize their Sunday laws. Some permitted work on Sunday if none had been done on Saturday; others had no laws about the matter. All in all, by the end of the period, some twenty-one states had liberal Sunday laws, and in some others the Sunday closing laws were not enforced. In 1877, Jews, Seventh-Day Adventists, and other Saturday observers prevailed upon Senator Horace Gates Jones to introduce a bill in the United States Congress for the protection of seventh-day observers, but the bill died.[47]

Strictly speaking, Sunday closing regulations nullified the spirit of American equality before the law. But many felt that at least one day a week should be set aside as a community day of rest. In addition, many Christian businessmen did not want competition on Sunday, when they were closed. The consensus of legal opinion in this period was that Sunday laws for religious reasons were unconstitutional but, as a civic duty or a police regulation, permissible.[48]

The Bible in the Public Schools

In colonial days, education was usually sponsored by various religious denominations. With the development of the free public school system, the opinion generally prevailed theoretically that the principle of the separation of church and state applied, that religion should not be taught in the schools, but should remain in the province of church or synagogue. President Grant, in 1875, emphatically expressed his opposition to any religious instruction in the public schools.[49] Yet there were many, especially Protestants, who felt that there had to be some religious instruction in the public schools where their children spent so much time, and many teachers throughout the land regularly introduced some kind of religious instruction in their classes. One of the reasons for the organization of Catholic parochial schools was to counteract the Protestant teachings in the public schools.

The principal matters under dispute, especially for Jews, were: Should the Bible be read in the public schools? Should Christian holy days be observed as part of the school curriculum? Jews and many others continued vigorously opposed to the celebration of Christian holy days, but this practice did not diminish, especially around Christmas. At first some Jews raised no objection to Bible reading, assuming that passages would be chosen from the Old Testament. But it soon became apparent that many teachers included sections from the New Testament and even those that were repugnant to Jews. Jews then decided, as a matter of general principle, that they would oppose Bible reading in the schools.

This change of thinking was illustrated in Cincinnati. In 1852, the Cincinnati Board of Education decided to permit Bible reading in the schools. Cincinnati Jewish leaders were assured that only the Old Testament would be used, so they raised no objections. But when it was discovered that sections from the New Testament were frequently read, the Jewish community began to express its opposition. Finally, in 1869, the Board of Education decided to dispense with all Bible reading in the schools. Thereupon, certain Christian groups took the matter to court and the case came before a court of three judges: Hagan, Stohrer, and

Alphonso Taft. Hagan and Stohrer granted the injunction, with Taft dissenting (it is of interest that only the year before, two of these judges, Stohrer and Taft, were among the prominent Christians who helped persuade Rabbi Max Lilienthal to remain in Cincinnati when he was considering leaving).

But Wise, Lilienthal, and the Cincinnati Board of Education carried the case to the Ohio Supreme Court, which overruled the lower court and sustained the Board of Education. This case was widely discussed throughout the country and established an important precedent in other areas.[50] However, many communities continued to permit and encourage Bible reading and the celebration of Christian festivals in the public schools.

Religious Relationships with Christians

On the threshold of a new life, under the new conditions which we discussed earlier, many Jews and Christians were reassessing past patterns and attitudes in interreligious relationships. A few even felt that there need be no different religions in this new land, but that all could combine under one American religion. This attitude helped to produce Ethical Culture and a few other movements. But in the main, Jews and Christians remained faithful to their particular religions, although many thought there could be more understanding and cooperation on joint goals. So the period revealed tentative and exploratory efforts toward interfaith understanding, not common before.

Christians often attended the many banquets and balls given by Jewish congregations and charities, and at such affairs often spoke in laudatory terms about the Jews. Some of these comments were crude and cosmetic, but many were sincere.

Some Christians even sent their children to Jewish day schools, because they were generally known for their high standards of education. And in many communities Christians and Jews used the facilities of each other's houses of worship whenever the temporary need arose.[51]

For the first time in history, as far as is known, a rabbi and minister exchanged pulpits, when in Cincinnati, in 1867, Rabbi Max Lilienthal and a Unitarian minister each occupied the other's pulpit. This soon became a common practice.[52]

Another episode in connection with Lilienthal which may be apocryphal, was reported in 1876. At a public dinner, the archbishop of Cincinnati, noticing that Lilienthal did not eat because the food was not according to Jewish dietary regulations, turned to him and asked: "When will you eat with us?" Lilienthal, it is claimed, replied: "At your wedding." [53] This has become a classic story, with many variations, attributed to a number of clerical duos. Whether it actually happened at this time or not cannot be definitely established, but this is the earliest instance of such an interchange that has come to the attention of this writer.

Naturally, the attitude of liberal Christians was generally more favorable to Jews. More fundamentalist Protestants and some Catholic leaders were not nearly as friendly. [54]

Thus, for instance, when Isaac Mayer Wise, in a lecture before the Theological and Religious Library Association of Cincinnati (many organizations in this period had such involved names), made the point that religious groups should seek each other in friendship, the *Catholic Telegraph* retorted that Wise and the Jews "now extend . . . the right hand of fellowship heedless of the blood of Christ on their own." [55] In 1876, a Baltimore Catholic paper published a series of articles by a priest, denouncing the Jews with the usual stereotypes. The response from Jewish quarters was so vehement that Archbishop Bailey of Baltimore announced that the articles represented the personal opinion of that particular priest and did not reflect the official opinion of the Church. Yet the priest was not reprimanded. [56]

Jews did not hesitate to defend themselves and even to go on the offensive. In a series of Friday evening lectures before his congregation in Cincinnati, Wise demonstrated the superiority of Judaism over Christianity. [57] He even stated: "Wherever the church rules, there is no liberty . . . there is no difference as to what sect predominates; wherever paganism has grown into a system, it is trinitarian; any religion whose votaries are under the delusion that they are better than other people before God and human law, needs a radical reform." [58]

Despite these charges and countercharges, there was discernible in this period, among many Jews and Christians, an effort, a movement, toward mutual understanding and cooperation. In some instances these efforts were largely on the surface, but in others they were more substantive.

Conversions and Intermarriages

During this period, as at all times, there were some Christians who deeply believed it was their religious duty to convert Jews in order to save them from eternal damnation. Numerous individual missionaries and societies developed for this purpose. [59]

Various ingenious techniques were tried, even including the use of

Anglo-Jewish newspapers. The *Asmonean* in 1850 carried a letter from John Neander, a Jewish convert to Christianity, asking all Jews to follow his example. The *Asmonean* must have had great confidence in the loyalties of its Jewish subscribers, for in the same year it printed an advertisement of a book which sought to persuade Jews to accept Christianity.[60]

One missionary group insisted that Christian Jews (Jews who had converted to Christianity) be permitted the right to vote in Jewish congregations and communal organizations.[61]

Perhaps the most unusual argument advanced in behalf of mixed marriages appeared in an article in the *Insurance Monitor* of New York, which cited statistics professing to prove that Jews lived longer than Christians. It concluded that insurance companies should urge Christians and Jews to intermarry, so that their profits would be increased.[62] There is no evidence that anyone was convinced by this argument.

Most of the conversion efforts were basically unavailing. Jews kept advising the missionaries to admit defeat and suggested they would do better to devote themselves to making better Christians of Christians. Even the *Chicago Times* ridiculed the missionary societies in 1869 and observed that the Jews seemed to be happy and contented as they were.[63]

The most revealing commentary on the measure of success of these societies can be found in their own reports. In 1872, the Society for the Conversion of Jews, meeting in Cincinnati, reported that in the thirty-nine years of its activity, it had converted thirty-eight Jews. Finally, realizing its futility, it went out of existence in 1878.[64] In 1873, one missionary, undaunted, determined to convert the whole Jewish community of Philadelphia. He held 334 meetings and distributed 32,000 tracts in one year—and converted one Jew.[65]

There was a case of forcible conversion in New York in 1859, possibly inspired by the Mortara affair of the year before. A Jewish child was secretly baptized by his nurse, and when the Catholic authorities were informed, they forcibly took the child from his parents. But the United States was not Papal Italy, and the court ordered the child returned to his family.[66]

There were some attempts to convert Jews on their deathbeds, especially in Catholic hospitals, primarily when the Jew had no family nearby. Upon his death, the Catholic authorities would claim the corpse as a Catholic. But in every case that became known, Jewish groups or government officials intervened.[67]

Of course there were Jews who converted to Christianity without missionary efforts, usually because of marriage to a Christian or in isolated centers. But this was not a major problem in the period under consideration.[68] Exact statistics on conversions and mixed marriages are not available for the country as a whole. Barnett Elzas did record the Jewish marriage notices found in the newspapers of Charleston, South Carolina, an old, settled community with a Sephardic background. A survey of 190 marriages listed from 1848 to 1881 seems to indicate that about eight of these might have been mixed marriages, approximately 4 percent.[69] This listing did not include marriages of Charleston Jews outside the city, which may not have been recorded in the local papers, or and it is possible that mixed marriages in the city were not announced in the papers, which means that the rate of mixed marriages may have been somewhat higher. Yet it is safe to say that the problem of mixed marriages throughout the country was not a significant one.

On the other hand, a number of instances of Christians becoming Jews, largely because of marriages to Jews, are recorded.[70] In 1863 it was reported that five Swedish families in Wisconsin had decided that Judaism was superior to any other religion, made a thorough study of its history and customs, and become devoted Jews.[71]

The incident that attracted wide attention was that of Warder Cresson, a member of a wealthy and prominent Christian family of Philadelphia. While United States consul at Jerusalem, he became deeply interested in Jews and Judaism. Imbued with the feeling that modern agricultural settlements could succeed in Palestine, he became converted to Judaism. Then he returned to Philadelphia, worked on farms, and studied scientific agriculture for several years, to prepare himself to develop modern agricultural settlements in the Holy Land. His family was shocked by his conversion and his plans, especially since he had decided to devote his whole fortune to the enterprise, and they sought to have him committed. A celebrated law suit ensued, but Warder Cresson proved his sanity. He changed his name to Michael Boaz Israel, returned to Palestine, and in 1850 established a modern agricultural colony at Rephaim. He had won the support of Isaac Leeser, Judah Touro, and other Jewish leaders in this country and abroad, and his colony was a success while he lived.[72]

Summary

Certainly, stereotypes about Jews, traditional patterns of anti-Jewish feeling, and xenophobia persisted in this period and manifested themselves from time to time. They were annoying and distressing to Jews, but did not materially hamper their progress in the new land.

For other compensatory factors were very much in evidence: the liberal attitudes of the founding fathers, the broad spirit of the age, a society which was basically pragmatic rather than theological, and the expanding economy of the country.

Therefore, it can be said that the Jews in this period were able to make significant strides economically; were successful in eliminating many minor legal restrictions in states and local communities; opened up and expanded explorations in interreligious understanding and cooperation; and tended to be comfortable and at ease with their Jewish identity.

In fact, many Jews believed that Judaism, especially as modified by Reform, with its clear and rational beliefs and practices, was more in tune then fundamentalist Christianity with current scientific and industrial ideas and with the spirit of American democracy. It should be remembered that this was the period when Reform Judaism was rapidly expanding throughout the country and seemed to be on the way to be becoming the basic religious expression of Judaism in America. By 1881, 123 congregations (including most of the largest), out of a probable 250 congregations in all the country, were members of the Union of American Hebrew Congregations.[73] The Board of Delegates of American Israelites had merged with the UAHC, and other organizations were considering the same pathway. Isaac Mayer Wise often proclaimed that by the end of the nineteenth century, all of America would accept in principle the superior rational and intellectual qualities of Judaism, and there were many Jews who agreed with him.

Thus, in the main, though they were a small minority in a land predominantly Christian, the Jews of this period tended to feel secure and at home with their fellow citizens.

NOTES

1. I have given this article the subtitle "Some Aspects . . . " because it does not include a number of important items of Jewish-Christian relationships in the period covered that have already been dealt with in great detail in published works. Among these are a number of events connected with the Civil War—e.g., the chaplaincy controversy, General Grant's General Order no. 11, etc.—treated by Bertram Korn in *American Jewry and the Civil War* (Philadelphia, Jewish Publication Society, 1951); the Know Nothing Movement and the Jews, treated in Korn's *Eventful Years and Experiences* (Cincinnati: American Jewish Archives, 1954); the Mortara Case, also treated by Korn in *The American Reaction to the Mortara Case* (Cincinnati, American Jewish Archives, 1957); the many incidents dealt with by the Board of Delegates, summed up in my "The Board of Delegates of American Israelites," *Publications of American Jewish Historical Society* [*PAJHS*], vol. 49, no. 1 September 1959); and other items, "The Jew as a Curio," etc., because of the limitations of space.
2. Allan Tarshish, "The Rise of American Judaism" (doctoral dissertation, Hebrew Union College, JIR, Cincinnati), app. B.
3. Rudolph Glanz, *Studies in Judaica Americana* New York: Ktav, 1970), p. 143.
4. *Ibid., p.* 143.
5. *Israelite,* vol. 9, no. 49 (June 12, 1863), p. 388.
6. *Allgemeine Zeitung,* vol. 19 (1855), p. 287.
7. *Jewish Chronicle,* 1872–73, p. 198.
8. *Asmonean,* vol. 3, no. 9 (December 20, 1850), p. 68, attacks the use of the term *Jew* in law records; *Israelite,* vol. 23, no. 12 (September 18, 1874), p. 6; *Archive Israélite,* vol. 31 (1875–76), p. 190.
9. Booklet, 80th Anniversary, Congregation Bone Brith, Wilkes-Barres, Pa.
10. Felsenthal and Eliassoff, *History of K.A.M.* (Chicago, 1897).
11. *Jewish Chronicle,* vol. 16 (March 2, 1860), p. 2; for a more extended treatment, see Korn, *Eventful Years and Experiences,* pp. 98–118.
12. *Israelite,* vol. 10, no. 29 (January 15, 1864), p. 30.
13. *Allg. Zeit.,* vol. 12 (1848), pp. 419, 519; vol. 21 (1857), p. 28; vol. 34 (1870), p. 272; vol. 41 (1877), p. 734; *Die Neuzeit,* vol. 16 (1876), p. 205; *Der Ungarische Israelite,* vol. 6 (1879), p. 9.
14. *Asmonean,* vol. 1, no. 24 (April 12, 1850), p. 96; *Israelite,* vol. 5, no. 38 (March 25, 1859).
15. Wise, booklet, B'nai Jeshurun, Cincinnati.
16. *Jewish Messenger,* vol. 3, no. 12, p. 92.
17. Minute Book, Baltimore Hebrew Congregation, 1851–66, May 29, 1865.
18. Minutes of B'nai Jeshurun, Cincinnati, 1872–90, September 28, 1873.
19. Morais, *Jews of Philadelphia* Philadelphia: Levytype Co., (1894), chap. 19.
20. *Allg. Zeit.,* vol. 41 (1877), p. 813.
21. *Archive Israélite,* vol. 27 (1866), p. 380.

22. For further details, see Allan Tarshish, "Economic Life of the American Jew in the Middle Nineteenth Century," in *Essays in American Jewish History* (Cincinnati, 1958).
23. Glanz, *op. cit.*, p. 113.
24. *Ibid.*, pp. 113–14.
25. *Ibid.*, p. 345.
26. *Ibid.*
27. Ezekiel and Lichtenstein, *History of the Jews of Richmond, 1769–1917* (Richmond, 1917), pp. 196 ff.; Annual Report of Executive Committee of the Board of Delegates, in *Occident*, vol. 25 (August 1867), pp. 247–54; Letter from Abraham Hart to Myer S. Isaacs, in American Jewish Historical Society Archives material on Board of Delegates, numbered lg; *Israelite*, February 22, 1867, p. 6; March 1, 1867, p. 6; April 5, 1867, pp. 2–3; April 19, 1867, p. 6; May 3, 1867, p. 6.
28. *Israelite*, April 19, 1867, p. 6; April 5, 1867, pp. 2–3; *Archive Israélite*, vol. 28 (1867), p. 444.
29. *Allg. Zeit*, vol. 30 (1866), p. 137; *Archive Israélite*, vol. 27 (1866), p. 241; Glanz, *op. cit.*, pp. 143–46.
30. *Allg. Zeit.*, vol. 44 (1880), p. 456.
31. *Israelite*, vol. 28, no. 26 (June 29, 1877), p. 8; *L'Univers Israélite*, vol. 33 (1877–78), p. 80; *Die Neuzeit*, vol. 17 (1877), pp. 236, 294; *Israelitische Wochenshrift*, vol. 8 (1877), p. 231; Glanz, *op. cit.*, pp. 149–50.
32. *Archive Israélite*, vol. 20 (1859), p. 55.
33. Felsenthal and Eliassoff, *History of K.A.M.; Allg. Zeit.*, vol. 21 (1857), p. 276; *Proceedings of the UAHC*, vol. 1, p. 245.
34. *Occident*, vol. 21, no. 5 (August 1863), p. 219; vol. 22, no. 10 (January 1865), p. 433; *Israelite*, vol. 10, no. 34 (February 19, 1864), p. 268; May, *Isaac Mayer Wise* (New York: Putnam, 1916), pp. 194 ff.; Einhorn, Sermon "War with Amalek"; *Allg. Zeit.*, vol. 28 (1864), pp. 198, 261; *Archive Israélite*, vol. 27 (1866), p. 160; *Allg. Zeit.*, vol. 30 (1866), p. 249; *Proceedings of the Board of Delegates*, 1865.
35. *Occident*, vol. 16, no. 10 (January 1859), p. 503; no. 11 (February 1859), p. 531; *Israelite* vol. 7, no. 9 (August 31, 1860), p. 70; First Annual Report, Exec. Comm., Board of Delegates, June 1860.
36. Memorial to the People of North Carolina by the Bd. of Delegates, July 23, 1866, no. 154; Minutes of Exec. Comm., Bd. of Delegates, July 15, 1866, found in *Jewish Messenger*, vols. 21–22, April 19, 1867; Masserman and Baker, *Jews Come to America* (New York: Bloch, 1932), pp. 136–64.
37. *Asmonean*, vol. 6, no. 13 (July 16, 1852), p. 101.
38. First Annual Report of Executive Committee Comm., Bd. of Delegates, June, 1860; Levinger, *History of the Jews in the U. S.* (New York, 1944), p. 134.
39. *Israelite*, vol. 14, no. 41 (April 17, 1868), p. 4.
40. *Jewish Chronicle*, 1872–73, p. 746.
41. Robert A. Rockaway, "Anti-Semitism in an American City: Detroit, 1850–1914," *PAJHS*, vol. 64, no. 1 (September 1974), pp. 43–44.
42. *Archive Israélite*, vol. 22 (1861), p. 600; *Occident*, vol. 12, no. 2 (May 1854), p. 100; vol. 16, no. 6 (September 1858), p. 265; vol. 17, no. 18 (July 28, 1859), p. 103; vol. 18, no. 39 (December 20, 1860), p. 236; vol. 19, no. 10 (January 1862), p. 451–editorials against Sunday laws; *Israelite*, vol. 4, no. 42 (April 23, 1858), p. 332—editorial against Sunday laws; *Allg. Zeitung*, vol. 19 (1855), p. 337—reports American Jewish agitation against Sunday laws; Annual Report, Ex. Comm., Bd. of Delegates, 1867, in *Occident*, vol. 25 (August 1867), pp. 247–54—discusses restrictive Sunday laws; *Occident*, vol. 26 (July 1868), pp.

145–56—further discussion of Sunday laws, urging other states to follow example of New York, which permits stores to open on Sunday if closed on Saturday; *Proceedings of Bd. of Delegates*—notes that favorable Sunday laws are adopted in Maryland and that the problem is being agitated in Tennessee. In some instances, laws were unchanged, but individual Jews, on presenting clear evidence that they closed on Saturday, were permitted to open on Sunday: *Archive Israélite,* vol. 14 (1853), p. 179—case of a Jew in Boston; *Jewish Chronicle,* vol. 16 (October 21, 1859), p. 8—case of a Jew in Cincinnati; *Allg. Zeit.,* vol. 17 (1853), p. 33—case of a Jew in New York.

43. Ezekiel and Lichtenstein, *Jews of Richmond,* pp. 104–16.
44. Max Heller, "Jubilee Souvenir of Temple Sinai, New Orleans, 1872–1922."
45. Albert M. Friedenberg, "The Jews and Sunday Laws," *PAJHS,* vol. 11. pp. 101–15; Abraham Simon, "Notes of Jewish Interest in the District of Columbia," *PAJHS,* vol. 26, p. 218.
46. Friedenberg, *op. cit.*
47. *L'Univers Israélite,* vol. 33 (1877–78), p. 444.
48. *Ruling Case Law,* vol. 25, ed. McKinney, Rich, Porterfield, and Fisher (Northport, N. Y.: Edw. Thompson Co., 1929), p. 1418.
49. William A. Blakely, *American State Papers Bearing on Religious Education* (New York and Washington: National Religious Liberty Assoc., 1891), p. 202.
50. *Archive Israélite,* vol. 31 (1870), p. 292; May, *I. M. Wise,* p. 246; David Philipson, *Max Lilienthal,* (New York: Bloch, 1915), p. 120.
51. Minutes of Mikve Israel, Savannah, Ga., July 1838—non-Jews gave liberally in 1838 for the synagogue building of this congregation; Glazer, *Jews of Iowa,* pp. 303 ff.—in 1872 Christians helped Jews build the Temple in Keokuk; *Jewish Chronicle,* vol. 9 (1852), p. 387—non-Jews contribute to First Hebrew Benevolent Society of San Francisco; *Archive Israélite,* vol. 31 (1870), p. 349—Christians contribute $400 to building of temple in San Jose, Calif.; Maurice Lebowits, "A History of Jewish Philanthropy in America until the Civil War" (prize essay, Hebrew Union College, 1932), pp. 141 ff.—Jews aid yellow fever sufferers in New Orleans and fire sufferers in Philadelphia, gifts of Judah Touro, etc.; Meyer Stern, *History of Temple Emanu-El of New York* (New York, 1895)— Emanu-El sent $367 in 1863 to the poor of Ireland; *Jewish Chronicle,* vol. 11, (1853–54), pp. 23, 63; vol. 16 (November 30, 1860); *Archive Israélite,* vol. 30 (1869), p. 375; *Jewish Chronicle,* vol. 16 (1859), p. 5; Annual Reports of Mt. Sinai Hospital, New York, 1857–72; Herman Snyder, *History of Brith Sholom, Springfield, Ill., 70th Anniversary*—all list instances of mutual aid.
52. This episode aroused great interest in the American and European Jewish press; *Die Neuzeit,* vol. 7 (1867), p. 157; *Archive Israélite,* vol. 28 (1867), p. 394; *Abendland,* vol. 4 (1867), p. 53; Philipson, *Max Lilienthal,* pp. 93 ff.; Other incidents reported: *Archive Israélite,* vol. 22 (1861), p. 347—Wise speaks at a Christian church in Seymour, Ind.; *Die Neuzeit,* vol. 2 (1862), p. 393; vol. 4 (1864), p. 280—other episodes; *Allg. Zeit.,* vol. 40 (1876), p. 158—Rabbi Wechsler preached in a Methodist church in New Haven; David Marx, *Hebrew Benevolent Cong., Atlanta, Ga.*—many Christian ministers spoke in his temple in this period; Falk, *Temple Beth Zion, Buffalo, N. Y.*—in 1873 Rabbi Samson Falk exchanged pulpits with Frederick Frothingham, minister of the First Unitarian Church; *Allg. Zeit.,* vol. 42 (1878), p. 10—reports the general practice.
53. *Archive Israélite,* vol. 31 (1875–76), p. 606.
54. *Allg. Zeit.,* vol. 39 (1875), p. 401.
55. *Israelite,* vol. 15, no. 30 (January 29, 1869), p. 4.
56. *Allg. Zeit.,* vol. 40 (1876), pp. 158 and 225.

57. Wise, *B'ne Jeshurun, Cincinnati.*
58. May, *I. M. Wise,* pp. 235 ff.; *Israelite,* vol. 15, no. 42 (April 23, 1869), p. 4.
59. *Jewish Chronicle,* pub. by the American Society for Ameliorating the Jews, vol. 4, no. 11, vol. 5, no. 1; May, *Isaac Mayer Wise,* pp. 68 ff.; Wise, *Reminiscences,* pp. 63 ff.; 181; *Occident,* vol. 7, no. 10 (January 1850), p. 41; vol. 16, no. 4 (July 1858), p. 210; *Israelite,* vol. 5, no. 28 (January 14, 1859).
60. *Asmonean,* vol. 1, no. 26 (April 19, 1850), p. 204; vol. 2, no. 9 (June 21, 1850), p. 71.
61. *Israelite,* vol. 6, no. 7 (August 19, 1859), p. 58.
62. *Archive Israélite,* vol. 34 (1873), p. 237.
63. *Ibid.,* vol. 30 (1869), p. 424.
64. *Ibid.,* vol. 33 (1872), p. 662; vol. 33 (1878), p. 252.
65. *Isr. Woch.,* vol. 4 (1873), p. 231.
66. *Jewish Chronicle,* vol. 16 (1859–60), p. 8.
67. *Ibid.,* p. 5.
68. Wise, *Reminiscences,* p. 57; Ezekiel and Lichtenstein, *Jews of Richmond,* p. 57; Isidor Lewi, *Isaac M. Wise and Emanu-El* (New York: Bloch, 1930); Alfred G. Moses, "History of the Jews of Mobile" in *PAJHS,* vol. 12, pp. 113–25.
69. Barnett Elzas, *Jewish Marriage Notices from the Newspapers of Charleston, S. C.,* 1775–1906 (New York: Bloch, 1917).
70. *Israelite,* vol. 7, no. 16 (October 19, 1860), p. 124; Trustees Minutes, Bene Israel, Cincinnati, 1845–69, Nov. 9, 1848; Trustees Minutes, Emanu-El, New York, 1862–76, May 5, 1864, September 6, 1866; Trustees Minutes, Shearith Israel, New York, 1869–94, October 25, 1880; Felsenthal and Eliassoff, *K.A.M.,* Chicago; Simon Glazer, *Jews of Iowa,* Des Moines, 1904, in chap. "Sioux City"; Ezekiel and Lichtenstein, *Jews of Richmond,* pp. 219, 222 ff.; *Allg. Zeit.,* vol. 23 (1859), p. 36; vol. 32 (1868), p. 620—reports conversions in St. Louis and San Francisco; *Die Neuzeit,* vol. 12 (1872), p. 456—conversion in Hartford.
71. *Allg. Zeit.,* vol. 27 (1863), p. 232.
72. Max Kohler, "Early American Zionist Projects," *PAJHS,* vol. 8, pp. 75–118.
73. Tarshish, "Rise of American Judaism," app. A; *Proceedings of the UAHC,* vol. 2, pp. 779–914, 940–1132.

RABBI MAX LILIENTHAL VIEWS
AMERICAN JEWRY IN 1847

By

SEFTON D. TEMKIN

State University of New York, Albany

INTRODUCTION

After the end of the Napoleonic Wars, Germany sent a stream of immigrants across the Atlantic. Departure from the Old World was usually final, and those who stayed at home must have nurtured all kinds of flights of fancy as to conditions in the New World. One immigrant who did pay a visit to the old country has left us an important legacy in literary form. Philip Schaff was appointed to the theological seminary of the German Reformed Church at Mercersburg, Pennsylvania, in 1844. Ten years later he returned to Germany for a short while, and the lectures he delivered at Berlin and Frankfurt, translated into English and published under the title *America*[1] have been recognized as an important description of conditions in this country at the century's mid-point.

No comparable work relating to the development of Judaism in America has come to light. The ambience did not exist for such works to be produced. Schaff's transfer to the United States testified to the existence of a church system organized on a national basis. American Christianity, like American life in general, might have seemed anarchic as compared with the state-regulated systems of the German kingdoms, but it was well organized as compared with American Judaism. Congregational self-sufficiency was the hallmark of the Jewish polity in both Germany and the United States; there was no synod to establish a seminary in

America, no equivalent of the German church diet to interest itself in the situation of brethren who had migrated to the New World.

If there are no full and considered mid-nineteenth-century expositions of the condition of Judaism in the United States on the lines of Schaff's *America,* this does not mean that we are without more limited descriptions of the scene prepared with an eye to satisfying the interest of European readers.[2] Among the earliest such pieces are the letters which Max Lilienthal addressed to the *Allgemeine Zeitung des Judenthums.* Founded in 1837 and edited by Ludwig Philippson, at Leipzig, the *Allgemeine Zeitung* devoted itself to both current events and literary material. It advocated moderate religious reform, with which standpoint the letter here set out appears to be in agreement.[3]

It is unnecessary here to enter into detail as to the career of Max Lilienthal (1815–1882). Born in Munich, he took his doctorate there in 1837. He received his rabbinical diploma from Rabbi Hirsch Aub.[4] In 1839, on the recommendation of Ludwig Philippson, he was appointed director of the modern Jewish school which had been established in Riga. From 1841 to 1844 he was engaged in an attempt to set up a modern system of Jewish education under government auspices for the Jews of Russia. In the latter year he left Russia suddenly and in 1845 landed in New York.[5] Shortly after his arrival the three leading German congregations of the city formed a union, with Lilienthal as their chief rabbi.[6] This office he occupied until 1847, when the union fell apart. Until 1855 he maintained a private school in New York. He then moved to Cincinnati as rabbi of the Bene Israel Congregation (later Rockdale Temple), remaining there till his death. In Cincinnati he introduced far-reaching religious reforms and was associated with the projects of Isaac Mayer Wise,[7] though standing on the sidelines as regards the controversies in which Wise was involved.

In the first part of his article Lilienthal describes the development of Jewish life, particularly in New York City, and also the conditions which immigrants might expect to meet. It cannot be looked upon as a fully worked out review of the scene; rather does the composition bear the marks of lack of revision. Whether as printed it represents the author's intentions with verbal accuracy is uncertain: the circumstances of the age would have precluded the submission to him of the editor's revisions of the ms, if any.

The postscript deals with more specifically religious questions. It is of interest chiefly because it reveals Lilienthal's religious position at that stage of his life. He was for making changes in the external expression of Judaism, provided that these could be justified in the light of the halacha. An analogy can be made with what Isaac Noah Mannheimer had done in Vienna and Nathan Marcus Adler was attempting in England. Lilienthal's emphasis on basing his regulations on the law anticipates the statement made a short time afterwards by his friend and co-worker Isaac Mayer Wise: "I am a reformer, as much as our age requires . . . but I always have the halacha for my basis; I never sanction a reform against the *din* . . ." (*Occident,* VI [March 1849], p. 616). It requires no great flight of the imagination to feel that Wise derived this standpoint from the more educated and more experienced Lilienthal.

No suggestion that the congregational union of which he was ecclesiastical chief was a shaky venture enters into Lilienthal's description. Yet such it proved to be. Had the union of New York synagogues solidified, then Jewish religious life in America might not have developed on the premiss that each congregation is an island unto itself. But the temper of the community was mercurial, and a seemingly trivial dispute, which arose not long after this article was written, caused Lilienthal to withdraw from his office, his plans forgotten, and the union of congregations to fall apart, Lilienthal closes his article with the first half of a sentence from the Roman historian Sallust: "Harmony makes small things grow." Had he written a little later he might have added the second half: *"discordia maximae dilabuntur*—lack of its makes great things decay."

Allgemeine Zeitung des Judenthums

vol. XI (1847), page 20

New York, 30 November (Private Communication

from Chief Rabbi Dr. Lilienthal).

Anyone looking at the development of Judaism in North America's United States can only be filled with heartfelt thanks to God and heartfelt satisfaction with his co-religionists. All over, wherever in the Union one glances, new congregations arise; all over houses of worship are dedicated to the service of the one and only God; and in a few decades Judaism here will have gained as firm a footing as in Europe, or perhaps a yet firmer footing; for here one knows neither conversionism nor a government that is generally anti-Jewish in spirit as is innate with enlightened, "illuminated," and philanthropic Europe.

The leading congregations are to be found in New York,[8] Philadelphia,[9] Baltimore,[10] Charleston,[11] Albany,[12] Richmond,[13] Cincinnati,[14] and New Orleans. Boston, Cleveland, St. Louis, Syracuse, New Haven,[20] and Claiborne[21] are less numerous. These are followed by a number more which have just been organized, such as Chicago,[22] Buffalo,[23] Augusta,[24] etc. Twelve to fifteen years ago one knew only the Portuguese congregations in New York,[25] Philadelphia,[26] and Charleston;[27] for Jews adhering to the Portuguese ritual were the first to emigrate to America; they were well-off folk and maintained the necessary Jewish institutions. Jews adhering to other rituals and coming here from other countries were too isolated and too poverty-stricken to be able to undertake anything on their own responsibility, and accordingly they joined these congregations. One can confidently assert that by far the greatest part of the members of the present Portuguese congregations consists, not of Sephardim, but of descendants of Englishmen, Dutchmen, etc., who in their day joined those congregations. The founders of these congregations were affluent folk who bequeathed important legacies; and in Newport, where today there are no Jews at all, there is a splendid synagogue with an important endowment. In his will the founder laid down the condition that the synagogue should always be maintained in good condition with the interest on the capital, and that the Sephardi minhag only be used in the place of worship. This will of the testator hinders the Jewish immigrants, who possibly would be glad to use this synagogue, from moving there; and thus for decades the place of worship has stood empty and abandoned.[28]

The conflict obtaining in America between natives and immigrants[29] holds true in its own way among the Jews—and as I am more familiar with the story of how the synagogues originated in New York than in other towns I will relate it. But it is also a true image of how the different congregations arose in other large towns.

The Portuguese congregation[30] here is the oldest and best-off in terms of congregational funds. Till approximately twenty-eight years ago[31] it was the only one in this city. Isolated Jewish immigrants arrived and found ample relief at its hands. Since the country was then still very young and those who had immigrated did not shrink from any effort or occupation, they immediately worked themselves up and began to be conscious of their worth. With this consciousness, they meant also to assert their rights and influence at elections. Added to this, the Portuguese ritual was alien to them—hence basis enough for friction. The consequence was that amid bitter hostility a secession took place, and a second congregation, the present Elm Street synagogue,[32] was established. As it rejected the Portuguese tradition[33] and accepted the English ritual, it was, as regards worship, akin to all immigrants, and everyone who arrived in those days joined it, so that even today it is the most mixed of all congregations. Among its members it numbers Englishmen, Dutchmen, Poles, Germans—though up until last year the English tone was predominant. The hazan, the Reverend Samuel Isaacs,[34] preached in English, proceedings in the congregation were conducted in English, since, as the language of country, it was the best means of understanding between men of such varied tongues. However, just this circumstance gave the English further superiority, which led to a fresh division and fresh and violent quarrels. The congregation had bought a fine church in Elm Street and converted it into a synagogue.[35] The English were afraid that they would be ousted from the top management if they were to accept as members and enfranchise, according to state law,[36] everyone who had taken a seat in the synagogue for the duration of a year and paid the customary dues. Accordingly, they denied seatholders the right to vote.[37] This affair led to the most furious charges from both sides, and ended with the Reverend Samuel Isaacs—to whom compensation in the sum of $5,000 was paid—abandoning the English. They are building a new synagogue in Wuster [sic] Street, which should come to more than $20,000.[38]

Another consequence of the same English tradition was that the German Jews who came over here—they did not have mastery over the German language—and likewise were unaccustomed to the differences between the English and the German rituals—separated themselves.[39] Up until ten years ago one saw very few Germans here. Moreover, to begin with the people were poor; also to begin with they received relief; and, unaccustomed to gentlemanly habits, could not hope to be fully accepted immediately. The German, with his perseverance, with his industry, with his love of work, and above all with his thrift, worked his way up very quickly, so that we now see among them folk who came over here as beggars and now have fine businesses and ready means—such Germans intended not to be looked down upon or regarded with indulgence, but to be considered on their own merit. And these circumstances were the occasion for the foundation of the first German congregation, Anshe Chesed, which has a fine synagogue on Henry Street.[40] Its beginning was very small—and so small that to start with services were held in a single room,[41] and on Friday evenings in the winter each person brought a piece of wood with him to warm the room. Five-eighths of the German immigrants were, and for the most part are, from Bavaria, being forced from that country by the Pharaonic Law of 1813, which ordered the increase of the Jews to be prevented.[42] Accordingly, as the first of them succeeded and established their positions, more and more followed, and now year by year the flood of immigration grows mightily, to such a degree that in fact the Anshe Chesed Congregation now already counts about 320 members and seatholders; the second German congregation, Shaarey Hashamayim,[43] is about 220 members and seatholders; and the third congregation about 180.[44] This considerable increase of the Germans required the establishment of the second congregation mentioned, and discontent with the administration brought about its division and the establishment of the third.[45] Though a great deal of money could be saved if these three congregations formed only one in the course of time, another would still have formed since congregations increase quickly beyond measure, and among them one hundred weddings were celebrated in 1846.

The embellishment of the service,[46] which led to so much strife in congregations in Germany as recently as a decade ago, has begun to be desired by several people here also, and the first indirect steps in that direction took place through the establishment of the *Kultus-Verein*.[47] Quarrels similar to those in Germany do not arise in America, since the Church is not under the superintendence of the State, but rather both exist side by side in complete independence of the other. If any kind of idea stirs and it does not meet with general acceptance, those who favor it separate from those who think otherwise and form themselves into a congregation of their own. In this fashion arose the German Emanu-El congregation, which has organized its service according to the arrangement of the Hamburg congregation—though not throughout. The Reverend Dr. Merzbacher[48] was appointed its minister; the choir uses the Viennese and Munich hymnody,[49] and there is preaching in the temple every two weeks. In the course of time a not insignificant number of Jews, partly from Prussian Poland, and partly from Russian Poland, have met together and established a Polish congregation.[50] Since several of them have been in the country a long time and married Christian women who later converted to Judaism, dissension arose in this congregation, which led to its being split, so that we now have nine congregations in New York with approximately 8,000 to 10,000 Jews:[51] the Portuguese with Hazan Lyons;[52] the Elm Street Congregation,[53] Hazan Leo;[54] the Congregation Anshe Chesed, Shaarey Hashamayim and Rodef Shalom: Chief Rabbi Dr. Lilienthal:[55] the Minister of the Temple, Dr. Merzbacher,[56] the two Polish congregations[57] and Shaarey Tefillah: hazan and preacher, S. Isaacs. I enumerate them to you according to the date of their formation; and just as the congregations here have been formed and coordinated, so it has occurred and continues to occur in all the larger communities of North America which I have enumerated.

The feeling for charity in all the communities cannot be praised and acknowledged enough. Apart from the enormous sums which year by year are sent to poor relatives in Europe, no one tires of contributing for the poor and for charitable associations. About twenty of these exist in New York; some are mutual insurance arrangements for their members against the various mishaps of life; some are merely arrangements for apportioning support for the poor. The most important of the latter are the Hebrew Benevolent Society, whose president is the well-known M. N. Noah and which this year celebrated its silver jubilee,[58] and the German Hebrew Benevolent Society,[59] whose president is Mr. Kaiser and which this year gave its third public dinner. One of these I described to you last year. The charity donations on the evening of November 12 realized $3,300 = 5,750 florins this time. One would hardly be exaggerating if one assumed that the income of the nine congregations and the various societies in New York runs to more than $40,000 each year; but this surely very considerable sum is collected only because the greater part of the individuals do far more even than youthful vigor allows. But what does freedom not do?

Things look similar in the larger communities. Let us cast a glance over the wide domain of the Union, where here and there small and isolated congregations develop. Several years ago a Jew moves out to a small town and lives there at a distance and separated from everything relating to Jews and Judaism. It is not known that he is a Jew; he keeps no Jewish commandment, observes no Jewish ceremony. Some time afterwards one more Jew settles, then a second and a third; the holy season of our New Year and Day of Atonement comes, the people think of God and see in their prosperity how much they have to thank Him for, notice their irreligious life and are ashamed of it. The desire stirs in their hearts to return to God. They count themselves and are ten and are in a position to form a minyan. One proposes that they constitute themselves as a congregation, the others gladly agree and are enthusiastic. They deliberate, club up some resources, and then a letter arrives in New York or another large community. The people remit money to send them a *Sefer Torah, Tefilin, Mezuzot,* and *Tsitsit,* give particulars of a hazan and shochet, and if five years later one comes to the kind of place where at one's first visit there had been no trace of a single Jew, one finds an independent, well-organized congregation with a nice synagogue and its own *Beth Hakvorot* [cemetery], and feels amazed at how quickly and how securely Judaism has taken root in the new Fatherland. And this picture is found wherever one turns to look, and in a few decades there are Jewish congregations in every place where civilization sets its beneficent feet and colonists have cleared the virgin forests.

Since the Jew here is not subject to the anti-Jewish discriminatory laws of humane Europe, Jews are found in all positions and branches of trade. In Charleston Jews occupy the leading public offices; equally so in Baltimore, Philadelphia, New York, and other towns; and it is well known that in Congress in Washington several distinguished Jews sit, in the Senate as well as in the House.[60]

That the Jew really loves his America is attested to not only by the individual officers serving at the present time in the Army against Mexico, but also by the Hebrew Volunteer Company formed in Baltimore,[61] which offered its services to the President in the present war. We also count very many Jewish manufacturers, craftsmen in all branches, and if a European friend of the Jews should ask you, "What then, Jews don't go in for trading at all?" You can answer him as ironically as he asks you: "Oh yes, very much, and very profitably, and without it making the Christian population feel injured. The desire for agriculture awakes here and there, and particularly in Wisconsin it is hoped shortly to see Jewish colonies." [62]

Certainly this entire description will not fail to waken in many people the desire to emigrate to America; and, if it is only the right people who are aroused, I will be pleased soon to be able to grip a brother's hand in the new Fatherland. But also allow me the following observations, so as to summon over here only the proper people. America is a young, blessed land, abundant in resources. One who brings with him the desire and capacity for work, who is not discouraged in overcoming the first difficulties which everyone encounters in a strange country, who also leaves in the old country dreams of the old pomposities—he will certainly find his livelihood here and have every opportunity to make of it something very suitable for him. In this country there are no caste divisions, so that a lamp trimmer belongs in his category, a carter in his, a clerk in a third, a merchant in a fourth, etc., and is treated and held in esteem according to this category. Here it is said: One man makes his living through business, another through other means, and in the evening each dons his black dress coat and votes for his candidate for the presidency, just like the wealthy millionaire Astor. Everyone who keeps himself decently and up-rightly is esteemed. But the foreigner coming across here must not believe that New York is plastered with doubloons; must not say, "I did not do that at home, and I cannot lend myself to it." The person thinking thus should remain in Germany, settled down patiently and good-heartedly behind his tankard of beer. Anyone coming here should come with the resolve not to fancy himself too great for any work, ready to put up with many unaccustomed things, and then he will certainly succeed. In this town we have a number of businessmen who do a $100,000–$200,000 business and who did not have a penny in their purses when they arrived six years ago. At first they carried a heavy pack of 100–120 pounds all day long to earn a living. When they had something they began to sell small wares with a horse and wagon, then they established a small busi-ness in the country and now they establish in New York houses which enjoy universal esteem and credit. People will answer me: He who has the desire and capacity for work also produces something in Germany. Of course, that would be true if the Jew did not encounter a thousand re-strictive laws, if we did not have hundreds of people who had not squandered their last possessions in litigation seeking licenses and the right to carry on a trade.

With that money they would have accomplished something here al-ready, and if they had vexed themselves here as much as in Germany—but to no avail—long ago they would have been independent folk whom no gendarme on the highway made anxious. Men of such spirit are suit-able here, and a cheerful and successful future smiles on them in the end.

The second class who are welcome here are artisans. Wages here are high, the opportunity for gain is present, competition in the country is not yet too strong, and in the West abundant profits await all of them. A very trustworthy man from Cincinnati told me that there alone another two hundred shoemakers could make a living. If families would now send on ahead their young unmarried men, whom they know to be capa-ble and to have the spirit to overcome the first drawbacks, they will soon gain a footing, so that their parents and brothers and sisters can come later, and both will be successful.

But now I come to the reverse side. This summer people came over who in the old country had neither the desire nor the capacity to work, people who had to get out of the way of a stepfather or a stepmother, so that thereby someone might be able to get his property for himself and thus were disheartened to begin with; people who were half imbeciles and whom one wanted to be rid of abroad. How were the relatives not afraid to dispatch such persons over here and expose them to boundless misery? By voluntary contributions the communities defrayed the expense of the return journey for many cases. But when people get tired of this, what will be the fate of these unfortunates? Of course, a blockhead—I will be excused the expression—often makes his fortune, and quicker often than the most capable and the most intelligent; but then it is only a matter of luck and not logical enrichment. We need here men with industry, pluck, and patience; that should be the capital that they bring with them. Most assuredly they will then soon establish their own fortune and that of the families whom they get to join them.

A second warning sign I must give the teachers. I have received letters from several who wish to give up their posts and come over here. The rule holds good here that men who have family, position, and livelihood should remain on the other side. For, since for the most part our children understand English only, instruction must be given in English. But these people don't understand it. By the time they learn it they have long eaten up their resources, and what is the family to do in the meantime? The German scholar does not easily give up his diploma-conceit for something else. Thus he becomes unhappy and discontented, and positions cannot always be conjured up with a wishing wand. Then again, it is certainly true that positions for *schochetim* and *hazanim* and teachers are becoming ever more numerous. But it requires some means, however little they may be, to wait for such an opening. Hence I would advise that preferably unmarried people who possess the knowledge required for the position venture over here; they can wait and see more easily; with their smaller worries they can more easily apply themselves to the English language; as they have no families they can more easily undertake journeys into the interior of the country and count on a satisfactory outcome. Because the field of activity here becomes ever bigger, the positions become ever more numerous, and they will be a welcome addition to the laborers in the vineyard of the Lord. May He, the All-benevolent, watch over Judaism in its bloom, now as in the past. Receive good news and heartfelt greetings, for you and all our brothers, from

Your humble servant,

DR. LILIENTHAL, *Chief Rabbi*

Postscript:[63] Permit me now to send you in a postscript a few notes of my activities. At the beginning of the year I informed you that the boards of my congregation, whose zealous cooperation and whose goodwill I cannot acknowledge highly enough, set up, at my instigation, seven committees to lay the groundwork for the various institutions that are needed. For the most part these committees have now completed their work with me.

Confirmation has been introduced into my congregations. Instruction is given by me, always from Hanukkah to Shavuot, and last Shavuot sixteen boys and girls were confirmed. According to the account of all those present—numbering 1,500 persons—the ceremony was one of the most moving they had ever seen, and with God's help this institution has been firmly established here.

The second committee is working for better order in the house of worship. The first steps to this end have in the meantime been taken, and all the regulations are based on the corresponding passages in the codex *Orach Chayim.* The announcement of this runs: (1) Everyone entering the synagogue is to proceed quietly and silently to his place (chap. 93, S-1; chap. 95; chap. 151, S-1).[64] (2) Everyone is to occupy his seat with decorum and remember that he is in a place of worship, in which any indecorous sitting down or moving about is a sin (chap. 9, s-3 Ture Zahav).[65] (3) Conversation with others during the service is strictly forbidden (chap. 51, s-4; chap. 56, s-1; chap. 68, s-1; chap. 124, s-7; chap. 146, s-3; chap. 151, s-1).[66] (4) Noisy prayers particularly crying out and singing ahead, are strictly prohibited. (5) Going out during the service is to be avoided as far as possible. Anyone going out and coming in again is to do so quietly and with decorum (chap. 132, s-2; chap. 146, s-1).[67] (6) The congregation is to stand during the Sabbath morning service for the following prayers—for the first *berachot,*[68] for *baruch she-amar,*[69] for *vayevarech David,* up to *ve-attah,*[70] for *yishtabbach,*[71] for the *shemoneh esray,*[72] for the removal of the scroll and its return,[73] for *hagbahah* and *gelilah*,[74] for the prayer for the country and its government,[75] for the blessing of the new month,[76] for each *kaddish*,[77] for *alenu*,[78] for *anim zemirot*.[79] (7) Children under four may not be brought into the synagogue on acount of the disturbance they occasion (chap. 98, s-1; chap. 124, s-13). The older generation was able easily to accommodate itself to these ordinances, since they are based on the law, and they were bound to satisfy the younger, since they produced orderliness during worship; at the same time they took away from the younger generation the possibility of demanding innovations not based on the law. It is my view that only if he bases all his regulations on the law can the rabbi give satisfaction wholly and completely to all the diverse opinions which prevail in every congregation. With the codex in his hand, he can call out without hesitation to the older generation: Thus far must you go; equally without hesitation can he reply to the younger generation: Thus far may you go. As soon as he relies on his own speculation division is certain and conflict endless. For the most part, my congregations are now used to this arrangement; at the appointed places everyone stands, otherwise everybody is seated. I preach each Sabbath and Festival, but always following the service, so that members of the other synagogues, at which I have not been present at prayers on the Sabbath in question, are able to come to the sermon. After the sermon *Yigdal* is always sung by the cantor and the congregation disperses. Concerning congregational singing, I have the following to remark. We have hit upon the arrangement that the passages which elsewhere are sung by the choir are in my synagogues recited by the whole congregation in a melodious recitative. For I suspect that, owing to the length of the Jewish service, the congregation must become indifferent or bored if it says no word of prayer for two to three hours and is allowed only to listen to the hazan and choir. We are satisfied that everyone waits gladly until an *Omein*, a *yehay shmay reiba*, a *baruch hu*, etc., comes, and that the congregation now responds very well and very devoutly. These are the first steps for the regulation of the service.

With respect to weddings, the committee has laid down that, because here the parties come from different localities, no one knows them and forbidden marriages could easily take place, each engaged couple must first of all see the rabbi and the president of the synagogue in which they wish to be married for a marriage license; that the same be announced on the preceding Sabbath in all synagogues of the rabbinate (this is not *hukat-hagoyim* according to *Yore Dea*, chap. 198)[81]; and that the weddings must, with few exceptions, take place in the synagogue. The weddings themselves take place on the bimah, to which the chupah is fixed, so that the disturbances which the crowds flocking around always used to occasion are avoided. The *shtaray chalitsah* are also introduced and are either signed immediately by the brothers present here or are sent to Germany, etc., for signature, so that, since the brother usually complies, no difficulty arises should the eventuality occur.

Likewise, an organization for *shechita* and the sale of kosher meat has been undertaken by the congregations. It consists of three sections: (1) *shochetim;* (2) Jewish butchers; (3) Christian butchers; and although cases unfortunately still crop up which demonstrate how deeply the evil was implanted, it may nevertheless be hoped that, with the strictness with which the boards supervise this matter, this important item also will in a short time be brought into the desired order.

With regard to cases of death, it is stipulated that no deceased may be buried before twenty-four hours (*Yore Dea,* chap. 368, *Be-er Haytiv,* because of *Maaseh Norah Shevi*),[82] and any person who desires a funeral oration for the deceased can receive it.

Last Shabbat Bereshit I installed a Beth Din of men who offered me their services gratuitously and voluntarily. They are the rabbis of Albany and Syracuse, Herr Wise and D. D. Felsenheld and Kohlmayer. Far from assuming any spiritual authority we have merely proffered our services to all Jewish congregations in the Union who have no rabbi; are prepared to answer all questions submitted; to give a hand by word and deed in the establishment of new congregations; and to be of use as far as possible through drawing up schoolbooks for young people.[83]

Besides, the fundamental principle holds good that we force ourselves on no one, never intervene without being asked, but at all times await inquiries, etc. The Beth Din has started not through the congregations but through the need which we recognized that the congregations must be given an authority to which they can turn for legal decisions when they want to.

But from the outset we turned our special attention to the school, and thank God, in this matter also our effort was not without fruit. It was generally recognized that the congregations are still too young and too lacking in means to be able to cover the cost of good schools. Every congregational school has a teacher who often has pupils of four to five different grades to instruct. Consequently it was necessary to provide better arrangements and separate resources. After several meetings a school association was founded, which is managed by nine directors and one inspector (Dr. Lilienthal). The members pay a yearly contribution of two dollars, each schoolchild, the poor excepted, seven dollars a year. The union school at present numbers three sections, with 120 children, two teachers, and one pupil-teacher, and with God's help will become something sound. Its object is: a commercial and technical school with basic instruction in all Jewish subjects. The commercial and technical school consists of three classes, each with a one-and-a-half-year course of instruction, and two elementary classes. For the time being, since the children are still too young, only the latter are open. For two years already the Anshe Chesed Congregation has had a school with two teachers and eighty to ninety children. As their members also belong to the school association they would readily have given over their school to the school association, but, since it is still too weak in resources to defray the maintenance, the congregation is keeping its school at its own expense for the time being, until the association has gained sufficient strength. While it is very much desired that the association should be universal, it is nevertheless very good that in the meantime the Anshe Chesed Congregation should retain its school, since homes are situated in different parts of the town and therefore the children have the opportunity to attend schools nearer to them.

From last Shabbat Bereshit I also took over the *Shiur* which is learned on Saturday afternoons at a *Chevrah* of Congregation Shaar Hashamayim but have so arranged it that in the first half-hour *Menorat Hameor* —the well-known work on morality—is expounded, and in the second the history of the Jewish people from the Babylonian Exile to our day. Since the latter arrangement was made the *Shiur* has been attended by men of different allegiances. Thereby they come closer, and I believe that by this means I have hit on the right way of mediation and reconciliation. May the Lord give us successes henceforth, and then the united German congregations, with the goodwill which animates them and with the ease of giving here, will progess, and the congregations, synagogues, and schools blossom in every way. *Concordia res parvae crescunt* ["harmony makes small things grow"] is an expression old and true, the more so in such large congregations which grow every day. This year I had in them 100 weddings, one *Chalitzah,* two *Gitin al yeday shaliach*, and *shaalot* without number. God bless my congregations with all the other congregations in Israel, so that His one and only name be glorified over all the world.

Faithfully,

Dr. Lilienthal, *Chief Rabbi*

NOTES

1. "A sketch of its political, social and religious character, New York, 1855." The latest edition is that offered by Harvard University Press, 1961. The German original was published at Berlin in 1855. For the life of Philip Schaff (1819–1893), see *Dictionary of American Biography,* XVI, 417. Curiously, *America,* the only one of Schaff's numerous publications to be widely read today, is not listed in this sketch.

2. The most extensive is *Three Years in America* by I. J. Benjamin, originally published in German in 1863 (English trans., Philadelphia, 1956). It is appropriate to mention also Marcus *Memoirs of American Jews,* 3 vols. (Philadelphia, 1955–56).

3. See *Encyclopaedia Judaica,* II, 647.

4. This appears from the minute book referred to in n. 6 infra.

5. An element of mystery surrounds the exact circumstances of Lilienthal's departure from Russia. In *The "Tzemach Tzedek" and the Haskalah Movement,* trans. Zalman I. Posner (New York, 1962), pp. 87, 90, Rabbi Joseph I. Schneersohn (1880–1850) made statements association Lilienthal's leaving Russia with the misappropriation of government funds, but the account is so obviously suffused with animus against every aspect of Lilienthal's activities that these statements must be treated with reserve. In *The American Hebrew,* LVIII, 668 (April 10, 1896), Marcus Jastrow wrote that about thirty-five years earlier, H. S. Slonimski (editor of *Hatsefirah*) had related to him the circumstances in which Lilienthal had become aware of the conversionist aim of the Russian government's program, and that it had been necessary for him to leave secretly because if he had revealed what had become known to him, he might have been deported to Siberia.

6. See Hyman B. Grinstein, "The Minute Book of Lilienthal's Union of German Synagogues in New York," *Hebrew Union College Annual,* XVIII (1944), p. 321; also the same author's *Rise of the Jewish Community of New York* (Philadelphia, 1945), pp. 90, 91, app. XI.

7. See *Encyclopaedia Judaica,* XI, 243.

8. See Grinstein, *Rise of the Jewish Community of New York,* p. 472, for a list of the New York synagogues established prior to 1860. Up to and including 1847, twelve had come into being.

9. According to tradition, Jewish religious services began to be held in a private house in Philadelphia sometime in the mid-1740s. The first synagogue (Mikveh Israel) was opened in 1771; Edwin Wolf, and Maxwell Whiteman, *The History of the Jews in Philadelphia* (Philadelphia, 1956), pp. 32, 58.

10. By 1847 the following congregations had been established in Baltimore: Nidche Israel (Baltimore Hebrew Congregation) in 1830; Fell's Point Hebrew Friendship Congregation, 1838. See Isaac M. Fein, *The Making of An American Jewish Community* (Philadelphia, 1971), p. 175.

603

11. Kahal Kadosh Beth Elohim dates from 1749. The Reformed Society of Israelites had gone out of existence in 1833, and the schism of 1847 must have been maturing while this article was being written.
12. Congregation Beth El (1838); Beth El Jacob (1841).
13. Beth Shalome (Sefardi) (1789); Beth Ahabah (Ashkenazi) (1841).
14. Bene Israel (1824), of which Lilienthal later became rabbi; B'nai Jeshurun (1841); Adath Israel (1846).
15. Shaarey Chesed (1828); the Portuguese Congregation (1846).
16. Ohabei Shalom (1842).
17. Israelite Society (1839); Anshe Chesed (now Fairmount Temple), (1841).
18. United Hebrew Congregation (1837).
19. Congregation Keneseth Shalom (1839).
20. Congregation Mishkan Israel (ca. 1840).
21. Claiborne, Alabama, is seventy miles northeast of Mobile. *The Jewish Encyclopedia*, I, 314, states that Jews settled there "as early as 1840," but gives 1855 for the organization of a congregation with an officiating rabbi. Sometime thereafter the Jews left Claiborne, and the congregation passed out of existence.
22. Religious services began to be held in Chicago in 1845 (*Jewish Encyclopedia*, IV, 22), and the first congregation, Kehillath Anshe Ma'arab, was established in October, 1846 (*Encyclopaedia Judaica*, V, 411).
23. Congregation Beth El (1847).
24. By 1829 there were a few Jewish families in Augusta; in 1844 a number of German Jewish immigrants arrived and later formed Congregation Children of Israel (1850).
25. B'nai Jeshurun, the first Ashkenazi congregation of New York, had come into being in 1825, twenty-two years earlier.
26. Here Lilienthal's carelessness is more apparent. Philadelphia's first Ashkenazi congregation, Rodeph Shalom, purchased a cemetery as early as 1801: Wolf and Whiteman, *op. cit.,* p. 226.
27. Kahal Kadosh Beth Elohim (1749).
28. Abraham Touro (d. 1822) bequeathed $10,000 to the Rhode Island legislature "for the purpose of supporting the Jewish Synagogue in that State." There is no mention of the ritual to be followed in the synagogue, and the control of the fund was vested in the state legislature and the municipal authority (Morris A. Gutstein, *The Story of the Jews of Newport* [New York: Bloch, 1936], pp. 232, 329). The synagogue was reopened for summer worship in 1850, having been closed for sixty years (Gutstein, *op. cit.,* p. 245). After the synagogue had closed, the "last representatives of the Congregation . . . formally handed over to the active congregation Shearith Israel in New York the title to their closed synagogue, burial ground and other communal property . . ." (David de Sola Pool, *An Old Faith in the New World* [New York: Columbia University Press, 1955] p. 422; see also Grinstein, *Rise of the Jewish Community of New York*, p. 239. A trust deed of 1894 (see Gutstein, *op. cit.,* p. 323) provides that the premises should be used for "religious services according to the Ritual, Rites and Customs of the Orthodox Spanish and Portuguese Jews, as at present practiced and observed in the Synagogue of Congregation Shearith Israel in the City of New York . . . " As may be inferred from the terms of the deed, any earlier "handing over" was not accompanied by a formal vesting of the property in the New York congregation, and the deed appears to have been executed because of a challenge to the rights of the New York congregation made in 1893 (see Pool, *op. cit.,* p. 424). The present writer has not come across any reference to an attempt made

to reestablish the Newport congregation during the period referred to by Lilienthal. See *Encyclopaedia Judaica,* XII, 1043.

29. In 1845 the Native American Party was formed to combat "foreign" influences and uphold "American views." A major plank of the Native American Party—known as the "Know-Nothing Movement"—was the election of native Americans to office and a twenty-five-year requirement for citizenship.

30. Congregation Shearith Israel.

31. Lilienthal apparently mistakes the date of B'nai Jeshurun's founding (1825).

32. Originally located at 533 Pearl Street, B'nai Jeshurun was established at 119 Elm from 1826 to 1850. Grinstein, *Rise of the Jewish Community of New York,* p. 472.

33. The word *"tradition"* is used here to translate the German *Element.*

34. Born in Leeuwarden, Holland, in 1804, Samuel Myer Isaacs (1804–1878) emigrated to the United States from London in 1839 to become the first hazan and preacher of B'nai Jeshurun. He became the rabbi of Shaarey Tefillah in 1847, when that congregation was formed from Bnai Jeshurun. From 1857 till his death in 1878 he edited the *Jewish Messenger.* Isaacs was the first minister to regularly preach in English at an Ashkenazi congregation (*Universal Jewish Encyclopedia,* V, p. 594).

35. For a description of the building, see Grinstein, *Rise of the Jewish Community of New York,* p. 267.

36. A summary of the relevant provisions of the Act of 1784 appears in *New York Jurisprudence* (1966), XLIX, par. 87, n. 19. Its interpretation as affecting the earlier disputes within Shearith Israel is discussed in Grinstein, *Rise of the Jewish Community of New York,* pp. 45–47.

37. An exact parallel of the situation which had led to the English secession from Shearith Israel to form B'nai Jeshurun in 1825. Now, fearing loss of control, the English again secede to form Shaarey Tefillah (1845). Grinstein, *Rise of the Jewish Community of New York,* pp. 52, 53.

38. The reference is to the formation of Congregation Shaarey Tefillah in 1845. As is indicated in Grinstein, *Rise of the Jewish Community of New York,* pp. 49 et seq., 472, this was by no means the first group of Ashkenazim to secede from Bnai Jeshurun. According to Grinstein, it was the English element who seceded from Shaarey Tefillah, and therefore Lilienthal's statement about Isaacs 'quitting the English" must be understood as referring to the English background of B'nai Jeshurun. Shaarey Tefillah worshipped first at 67 Franklin Street and moved to 112 Wooster Street in 1847.

39. Creating Anshe Chesed (1828): Grinstein, *Rise of the Jewish Community of New York,* p. 49. This congregation became part of Temple Beth El, which itself became part of Temple Emanu-el and must not be confused with the New York congregation now bearing the same name. The meaning of the original German is obscure.

40. Anshe Chesed originally held services at 202½ Grand Street, moving, in 1836, to Centre and White Streets. In 1840, the congregation again moved, to 38 Henry Street: Grinstein, *Rise of the JewishCommunity of New York,* p. 472.

41. At 202½ Grand Street: *op. cit.* Grinstein, p. 472.

42. The Bavarian edict of 1813 laid down rules for the restriction of the number of Jews in each district of the country. See Stefan Schwarz, *Die Juden in Bayern* (Munich and Vienna, 1963), p. 187; also *Jewish Encyclopedia,* II, p. 604; *Universal Jewish Encyclopedia,* II, p. 118; Ismar Elbogen, *A Century of Jewish Life* (Philadelphia, 1945), p. xxxii.

43. Shaarey Hashamayim was founded in 1839 as a result of a secession of German Jews from Anshe Chesed. It worshipped at 122 Attorney Street and is now part of Central Synagogue, Lexington Avenue: Grinstein, *Rise of the Jewish Community of New York,* pp. 50, 472.

44. Rodef Shalom, another offshoot of Anshe Chesed, was formed in 1842 and worshipped at 156 Attorney Street.

45. I.e., Shaarey Hashamayim.

46. The reference is to the Reform movement.

47. Established in 1844 to (1) permit Jews "to occupy a position of greater respect among our fellow-citizens," (2) to enable Jews to worship with greater devotion, and (3) to attract the younger generation to Judaism. Grinstein, *Rise of the Jewish Community of New York,* p. 554.

48. In 1843 Leo Merzbacher (1810–1856) was appointed preacher and teacher at Anshe Chesed. In 1845 his opposition to married women covering their hair led to the non-renewal of his contract. In April, 1845, Dr. Merzbacher and his supporters from Anshe Chesed joined with the Kultus Verein and founded Temple Emanu-El. *Encyclopaedia Judaica,* XI. 1396.

49. The Munich hymnody was influenced by Maier Kohn (1802–1875), a German cantor and teacher. In 1825 Kohn was a member of a Munich committee organizing a choir to improve "the standard of the divine service." In 1839 he published the first modern collection of synagogue melodies. The Viennese influence was largely the work of Solomon Sulzer (1804–1890). Sulzer's work was generally accepted in the modern synagogues of Prague (1838), Copenhagen (1838), Breslau (1840), Dresden (1840), and London (1841): *Encyclopaedia Judaica,* X, 1146; XII, 645, 650; XV, 510.

50. Grinstein, *Rise of the Jewish Community of New York,* pp. 472–73, lists three congregations established before 1847 in which a Polish element predominated. The one most nearly preceding the date of Lilienthal's article was Beth Israel (1843).

51. Grinstein, *Rise of the Jewish Community of New York,* p. 469, gives a figure of 10,000 for 1842 and 12,000 for 1846; *Encyclopaedia Judaica,* XII, p. 1070, gives 15,000 for 1847, Grinstein, pp. 472–73, lists twelve congregations as having come into existence by 1847.

52. Jean Jacques Lyons (1813–1877).

53. Bnai Jeshurun, now at West 88th Street.

54. Amsell Leo, having served as a hazan in London, occupied the same office at Bnai Jeshurun from 1847 until he was dismissed in 1855.

55. For an outline of Lilienthal's career see p. 590.

56. See n. 48 supra.

57. Shaarey Zedek (1839) and Beth Israel (1843). Grinstein, *Rise of the Jewish Community of New York,* pp. 472–73.

58. As to the Hebrew Benevolent Society, see Grinstein, *Rise of the Jewish Community of New York,* p. 146; as to Noah, *Encyclopaedia Judaica,* XII, 1198.

59. The Hebrew Benevolent Society was loosely affiliated with B'nai Jeshurun. The German Hebrew Benevolent Society was founded in 1844 and presumably expressed the desire of the growing German community to disburse its own philanthropy: Grinstein, *Rise of the Jewish Community of New York,* p. 147.

60. David Levy Yulee (1810–1866) in the U. S. Senate from 1845 to 1861.

61. Lilienthal is referring to the First Baltimore Hebrew Guards, formed in 1846. See Isaac M. Fein, *The Making of An American Jewish Community* (Philadelphia, 1971), p. 75.

62. The proposal alluded to is not easy to trace. Grinstein, *Rise of the Jewish Community of New York,* chap. 7, deals with "Agricultural Projects." The experiment at Sholem, Ulster County, he concludes, "lasted from 1839 to 1851, and possibly somewhat longer" (p. 122); "no further attempts at Jewish agricultural colonization were made [in New York] until the 1850's" (p. 123). The *Occident,* VI, 213, and VII, 230 (July 1848, and September 1849), refers to the contemporaneous settlement of Jews in agricultural colonies in Wisconsin. Lilienthal was writing in November, 1846, and may possibly have been referring to early discussions of these projects. In *Jews in American Agriculture,* a booklet published in 1954 by the Jewish Agricultural Society, there is a reference to an attempt made in 1843 by a group of New York Jews to start a farm settlement in the Middle West. "Later," the account continues, "this group sent a representative, Henry Mayer, to find suitable land for settlement. He found a tract of land in Cook County, Illinois. . . . Most of the members of the group left immediately for this place and were soon engaging there in farming and in business . . . " Although Lilienthal specifically mentions Wisconsin, he may have had in mind the efforts of this group.

63. Lilienthal describes his activities as chief rabbi of the three federated German congregations: Anshe Chesed, Rodeph Shalom, and Shaarey Hashamayim. See Grinstein, *Rise of the Jewish Community of New York,* pp. 395 ff.

64. In this section of his communication Lilienthal notes the ritual changes he has made justifying them by reference to the provisions of the *Shulhan Arukh.* Sometimes the connection appears tenuous. Thus *Orach Chayim* 93(1) lays down that a person should wait an hour's time before arising to pray and an hour after praying so that it should not appear a burden which he rushes to discharge. *Orach Chayim* 95 deals with posture in prayer, laying down that a person should pray with his feet together and with his head forward and his eyes down, his hand on his heart, standing like a servant before his master. *Orach Chayim* 151(1) deals with the reverence and awe which a person should have in a synagogue and states that he should not conduct himself there in a light-headed fashion by engaging in idle talk, eating, or drinking, and one should not enter merely to escape the heat of the sun or escape the rain, etc.

65. *Ture Zahav (Taz)* is the commentary on the *Orach Chayim* by R. David Ha-Levi (1586–1667).

66. *Orach Chayim* 51(4) cautions against speaking from the beginning of the prayer *Baruch She'amar* until the end of the *Amidah.* 56(1) sets forth the rules as to standing for and responding to the *kaddish.* 68(1) indicates that there are places where it is customary to interrupt the blessings before and after the *Shema* in order to insert the *piyyutim,* but it is correct to prevent this custom because the insertion of the *piyyutim* constitutes an interruption of the prayers in question. (Presumably Lilienthal's point is that if the halachah discourages interruptions for additional prayers, it must forbid interruption through conversation). 124(7) lays down that one is not permitted to talk during the reader's recitation of the *Amidah* and that to do so is an unforgiveable sin. 146(2) (3) prohibits talking during the reading of the Torah and the Haftarah.

67. *Orach Chayim* 132(2) prohibits leaving the synagogue until after the *kedushah desidrah,* for which see Hertz, *Authorized Daily Prayer Book* (New York, 1946), p. 202. 146(1) lays down that one should not leave the synagogue while the Sefer Torah is being read, but that it is possible to do so between *parshiy ot.*

68. These are the early morning blessings set out in Hertz, *Prayer Book,* pp. 18 et seq. The names of passages given in the text have been transliterated. The list is of

interest as indicating where ritual divergences existed among the German Jews of the period.

69. Hertz, *op. cit.*, p. 50.
70. *Ibid.*, p. 99, where the word has no conjunction.
71. *Ibid.*, p. 422.
72. *Ibid.*, pp. 448–67. As it is the universal practice for the members of the congregation first to say this prayer in the standing position, the regulation in the text presumably seeks to enforce the strict rule that they should stand also when it is repeated aloud by the reader.
73. *Ibid.*, pp. 472, 518.
74. *Ibid.*, p. 492.
75. *Ibid.*, p. 506.
76. *Ibid.*
77. *Ibid.*, passim.
78. *Ibid.*, p. 550.
79. *Ibid.*, p. 215.
80. *Orach Chayim* 98(1) says nothing in the text that concerns the bringing of children into the synagogue, and a note by the Ramah implies their presence. However, Lilienthal may have had in mind a note in the Ba'er Heitev, which mentions that the Shelo complains about those who bring children into the synagogue. There is no sec. 13 to chap. 124, but the Ba'er Heitev to sec. 7 does suggest that it is better not to bring into the synagogue children who cannot control themselves.
81. The translator has been unable to establish the passage intended to be referred to by Lilienthal.
82. See preceding note. *Maash Nora ha Shehavi* here presumably refers to premature burial.
83. Lilienthal's Beth Din failed to function, meeting on one occasion only.

ALPHABETICAL LIST OF CONTRIBUTORS

ADLER, Selig: Samuel P. Capen Professor of American History at the State University of New York at Buffalo; author of *The Isolationist Impulse* (1957) and co-author of *From Ararat to Suburbia* (1960).

APPEL, John J.: Professor of American Studies, Michigan State University; editor of *The New Immigration* (1971) and, with his wife Selma, compiler of *The Distorted Image,* an audio-visual unit on ethnic stereotypes.

BARNETT, Richard D.: Former Keeper of the Department of Western Asiatic Antiquities in the British Museum; former President, Jewish Historical Society of England; editor *Sephardi Heritage,* Vol. I (1972); author of many studies in British Jewish History.

CHIEL, Arthur A.: Rabbi, Congregation B'nai Jacob, Woodbridge, Conn.; ordained HUC-JIR, 1946; author of studies of Jews in Manitoba and of Ezra Stiles.

CHYET, Stanley F.: Professor of American Jewish History, HUC-JIR; Associate Director, American Jewish Archives; ordained HUC-JIR, 1957; author of *Lopez of Newport* (1970) and studies of Ludwig Lewisohn.

COHEN, Martin A.: Professor of Jewish History, HUC-JIR; ordained HUC-JIR, 1957; author of many studies on Marranos and other Jews in Latin America; his most recent volume is *The Martyr: The Story of A Secret Jew and the Mexican Inquisition in the Sixteenth Century* (1973).

COHEN, Naomi W.: Professor of History, Hunter College of the City University of New York; author of *A Dual Heritage: The Public Career of Oscar S. Straus* (1969) and *Not Free to Desist: A History of the American Jewish Committee* (1972).

DAWIDOWICZ, Lucy S.: Professor of Social History, Yeshiva University; editor of *The Golden Tradition* (1967) and *The Holocaust Reader* (1975); author of *The War Against the Jews 1933-1945* (1975).

FRIESEL, Evyatar: Professor of Modern Jewish History, Ben Gurion University of the Negev and Hebrew University, Jerusalem; author of *The Zionist Movement in The U.S., 1897-1914* (1970)

GARTNER, Lloyd P.: Professor of Modern Jewish History, Tel-Aviv University; author of *The Jewish Immigrant in England* (2nd ed., 1973); co-author of Jewish communal histories of Milwaukee, Los Angeles and Cleveland; Americana Editor, *Encyclopaedia Judaica.*

609

GOTTSCHALK, Alfred: President, HUC-JIR; Professor of Bible and Jewish Religious Thought; ordained HUC-JIR 1957; distinguished interpreter of Ahad Ha-Am.

JANOWSKY, Oscar I.: Professor Emeritus of History, City University of New York; author of notable surveys of trends and developments in American Jewish centers and of the work of the National Jewish Welfare Board.

KABAKOFF, Jacob: Professor of Hebrew, Herbert H. Lehman College of the City University of New York; author of *Pioneers of American Hebrew Literature* (1966) ; Associate Editor, *Jewish Book Annual*.

KAGANOFF, Nathan M.: Librarian-Editor of the American Jewish Historical Society; editor of the forthcoming anthology *The Jewish Occident*.

KARP, Abraham J.: Professor of History and Religious Studies, University of Rochester; past President, American Jewish Historical Society; former Rabbi, Temple Beth El, Rochester; editor, *The Jewish Experience in America* (1969).

KORN, Bertram Wallace: Senior Rabbi, Reform Congregation Keneseth Israel, Elkins Park, Pa., and Visiting Professor of American Jewish History, HUC-JIR and Dropsie University; ordained HUC-JIR, 1943; author of *American Jewry and the Civil War* (1951) and many other studies.

LEVINSON, Robert E.: Associate Professor of History, coordinator of the Jewish Studies Program, Director, Sourisseau Academy for California State and Local History, San Jose State University, California; author of many reviews and articles on Jewish communities in the West; Executive vice-Chairman of the Commission for the Preservation of Pioneer Jewish Landmarks of the Judah L. Magnes Memorial Museum, Berkeley, Calif.

MAHLER, Raphael: Professor Emeritus of Jewish History, Tel-Aviv University; author of a host of volumes studying the socio-economic and political history of European Jewry in Yiddish and Hebrew, including a five-volume *History of Modern Jewry* (1780-1848) of which an abridgement of the first four has appeared in one English volume (1971).

MEYER, Michael A.: Professor of Jewish History, HUC-JIR; Author of *The Origins of The Modern Jew* (1967) and *Ideas of Jewish History* (1975).

MIRSKY, Norman: Associate Professor of Human Relations and Contemporary Jewish Studies, HUC-JIR; Senior Research Associate (Sociology), Department of Psychiatry, University of Cincinnati; ordained HUC-JIR, 1963; author of forthcoming *Making of a Reform Rabbi*.

PARZEN, Herbert: Special Lecturer in Jewish History and Literature, Theodor Herzl Institute, N.Y.: author of studies of Conservative Judaism and Zionism.

PLAUT, W. Gunther: Senior Rabbi, Holy Blossom Temple, Toronto; ordained HUC-JIR, 1939; editor of source books on the history of Reform Judaism (1963, 1964), and author of new commentary on Genesis (1974).

RAPHAEL, Marc Lee: Associate Professor of History, Ohio State University; ordained HUC-JIR, 1968; co-editor of *Modern Jewish History: A Source Reader* (1975).

RIVKIN, Ellis: Adolph S. Ochs Professor of Jewish History, HUC-JIR; author of *The Dynamics of Jewish History* (1970); *The Shaping of Jewish History: A Radical New Interpretation* (1971).

ROSEMAN, Kenneth D.: Director, Institute for Jewish Life; ordained HUC-JIR, 1966; author of sociological studies of Jewish communal life.

ROSENBLOOM, Joseph R.: Rabbi, Temple Emanuel, St. Louis, and Adjunct Professor, Washington University; ordained HUC-JIR, 1954; author of *A Biographical Dictionary of Early American Jews* (1960).

RUCHAMES, Louis: Professor of History at the University of Mass. in Boston; Chairman of the Academic Council of the American Jewish Historical Society; editor of Volumes II and IV of *The Letters of Wm. Lloyd Garrison* and of numerous volumes on abolitionism and its adherents; ordained HUC-JIR, 1943.

SANDMEL, Samuel: Distinguished Service Professor of Bible and Hellenistic Literature, HUC-JIR; ordained HUC-JIR, 1937; author of many studies of the Jewish Scriptures and of early Christianity.

SELTZER, Robert M.: Assistant Professor of History and Chairman of Jewish Studies Program, Hunter College, City University of New York; ordained HUC-JIR, 1961; author of forthcoming *History of Jewish Thought*.

STERN, Malcolm H.: Director of Rabbinic Placement, Central Conference of American Rabbis, and Genealogist, American Jewish Archives; ordained HUC-JIR 1941; author of *Americans of Jewish Descent* (1960) and many articles based on genealogical research.

STERN, Norton W.: Founder-Editor of *Western States Jewish Historical Quarterly;* editor and author of many studies on modern Western Jewish American historical figures and themes.

TARSHISH, Allan: Rabbi, Temple Jeremiah, Northfield, Ill.; ordained HUC-JIR, 1932; earned first doctorate in American Jewish History at HUC under Professor Marcus; author of studies of the Charleston Organ Case, and of the Board of Delegates of American Israelites.

TEMKIN, Sefton: Professor of Jewish History and Chairman of the Department of Jewish Studies, State University of New York at Albany; author of studies of American Jewish religious history.

INDEX

Note: Individuals and families bearing the same surname have been grouped together, but this does not imply necessarily that they are related.

A

Aaron, Adolph, 439-40
Abne Yehoshua (Falk), 220
Aboab (Curaçao family), 309, 313
Abolitionism, 505-15
Abramowitz, Abraham E., 403
Abramson, Samuel Avigdor, 258
Adams, John, 346, 542; John Quincy, 543
Adath Israel—United Hebrew Community, New York City, 252
Adath Jeshurun Congregation, New York City, 226
Addams, Jane, 129
Adler (Columbus, O., family), 439, 443-44; Cyrus, 11, 136, 143; Nathan Marcus, 591; Selig, 5-21
Agriculture, 227-30, 352-53, 401, 454-55, 460-61, 463, 465-68, 541, 582, 596, 607
Agudas Harabbonim, 238, 240, 246, 250, 255
Ahad Ha'am; *see* Ginzberg (A.)
Ahavai Sholom Congregation, Portland, Ore., 335
Alabama, 371, 592; *see also* Mobile
Albany, N.Y., 404, 592, 601
Albright, William F., 360
Alkalay, Judah, 353
Allgemeine Zeitung des Judenthums (Leipzig), 567, 590-91
Alliance Israélite Universelle, 136
"Allies"; *see* World War II
Amalgamated Clothing Workers Union, 122, 125-27
Amburgh (Columbus, O., family), 436, 439

American Anti-Slavery Society, 510
American Council for Judaism, 10-12, 14-15, 18
American Federation of Labor, 123
American Friends of the Middle East, 15
American Hebrew (New York), 89-90, 131
American Israelite (Cincinnati); *see Israelite*
American Jewish Archives, iv, 1-2, 23, 85, 303, 305, 370
American Jewish Committee, 10-12, 14-18, 108, 110, 127, 132, 135-37, 151
American Jewish Conference, 15-17
American Jewish Congress, 110, 132-35, 139-40, 145-46, 150-52
American Jewish Historical Society, ii, iv, 505
American Jewish Joint Distribution Committee, 111, 116-18, 132, 402, 415
American Society for Ameliorating the Conditions of the Jews, 542
American Sunday School Union, 161
American Zionist Emergency Council, 13
Americanization, 109-10, 122, 126, 128, 133, 136, 143, 147, 149, 151, 171, 173, 181, 196-97, 204, 212, 264, 293, 300, 362-63, 428, 431-32, 483, 488, 539-40, 543
Amerindians, 545, 554-55
Amsterdam, 52, 135, 311, 314, 419, 371, 457
Ancestry, Jewish, 105, 489
Andrade; *see* Da Costa de Andrade

612